THE PAPERS OF

WOODROW WILSON

VOLUME 23

1911-1912

SPONSORED BY THE WOODROW WILSON
FOUNDATION
AND PRINCETON UNIVERSITY

THE PAPERS OF

WOODROW WILSON

ARTHUR S. LINK, *EDITOR*

DAVID W. HIRST AND JOHN E. LITTLE

ASSOCIATE EDITORS

EDITH JAMES BLENDON, *ASSISTANT EDITOR*

JOHN M. MULDER, *ASSISTANT EDITOR*

SYLVIA ELVIN FONTIJN, *CONTRIBUTING EDITOR*

M. HALSEY THOMAS, *CONSULTING EDITOR*

Volume 23 · 1911-1912

PRINCETON, NEW JERSEY

PRINCETON UNIVERSITY PRESS

1977

Note to scholars: Princeton University Press
subscribes to the Resolution on Permissions of
the Association of American University Presses,
defining what we regard as "fair use" of copyrighted works. This Resolution, intended to encourage scholarly use of university press publications and to avoid unnecessary applications
for permission, is obtainable from the Press or
from the A.A.U.P. central office. Note, however,
that the scholarly apparatus, transcripts of
shorthand, and the texts of Wilson documents
as they appear in this volume are copyrighted,
and the usual rules about the use of copyrighted materials apply.

Publication of this book has been aided by a
grant from the National Historical Publications
and Records Commission.

Printed in the United States of America
by Princeton University Press
Princeton, New Jersey

INTRODUCTION

THIS volume opens with Wilson in Kansas City—the first stop
on a speaking tour that will carry him through the Far West,
the Midwest, and then into the South. The tour had been planned
by his friends to test public reaction to a possible Wilson candidacy for the Democratic presidential nomination in 1912. Enthusiastic public reaction encourages Wilson to think seriously about
running and to sanction the establishment of a "publicity bureau"
in New York. However, he refuses to permit his managers to play
preconvention politics in the conventional way, by making alliances with and commitments to state leaders, bosses, and organizations. He must strive for national Democratic leadership, he
insists, his own way—by attempting to rally public opinion to the
principles and cause of progressive democracy. And he wants
that high position only if it comes to him from the people themselves.

After returning to New Jersey in early June 1911, Wilson addresses himself to the affairs of his own state. In a series of
speeches, he leads the movement for adoption of the commission
form of government by New Jersey cities. Next, he undertakes an
intensive campaign to assure the nomination of progressive Democrats for local and state offices. Finally, he stumps the state
again in the general election campaign, appealing for the election
of a Democratic legislature, giving an account of his own stewardship, and, incidentally, revealing how his political thought
and philosophy have grown and matured in the crucible of practical experience.

At the conclusion of this volume in early January 1912, Wilson
seems to be the front runner in the Democratic preconvention
campaign, almost certain to win the presidential nomination.

Most of Wilson's personal correspondence for these months has
survived, and we have included all personal letters of any conceivable significance. However, Wilson saved only a small portion
of his political correspondence. We think that we have been able
to piece together enough of it from what remains in the Wilson
Papers in the Library of Congress, the collection in the Governors'
Files in the New Jersey State Library, and in the papers of Wilson's correspondents to show how he dealt with various state
problems and to document the emergence of a Wilson-for-President movement and the reaction of Democratic leaders and people of all sorts to the rising progressive leader. In addition, we

have used news reports to fill in the gaps and provide a detailed picture of Wilson's career during this period.

An even more difficult problem than reconstructing the Wilson Papers has been coping with the huge volume of Wilson's speeches during these months. The most important ones are printed usually in full; from others we have excised the portions that Wilson repeated many times; and often we have fallen back upon summaries and portions in news reports. A great deal of repetition remains because we wanted to show how Wilson hammered upon certain themes in both state and national campaigns.

All correspondence is reproduced *verbatim et literatim*, with typographical and spelling errors corrected in square brackets *only* when necessary for clarity and ease of reading. Newspaper reports are reproduced *verbatim*, except that we have silently corrected typographical errors when they involved transposed letters or dropped lines. We have reproduced newspaper texts of Wilson's speeches *verbatim*, correcting obvious errors in transcription in square brackets; however, we have silently changed punctuation when we thought the changes promoted clarity and facilitated reading. Finally, we were able to make a few changes on the page proofs employing a method we have devised (after this volume was set in type) for the reconstruction of corrupt texts of speeches in newspapers and manuscript transcripts. Since we have used this new method extensively first in Volume 24, we will explain it in the Introduction to that volume.

Readers are again reminded that *The Papers of Woodrow Wilson* is a continuing series; that persons, events, and institutions that figure prominently in earlier volumes are not ordinarily re-identified in subsequent ones; and that the Index to each volume gives cross references to fullest earlier identifications.

THE EDITORS

Princeton, New Jersey
November 23, 1976

CONTENTS

ILLUSTRATIONS

Following page 332

ABBREVIATIONS

ALS	autograph letter signed
CCL	carbon copy of letter
CLS	Charles Lee Swem
EAW	Ellen Axson Wilson
FPS	Frank Parker Stockbridge
hw	handwriting, handwritten
LPC	letterpress copy
sh	shorthand
T	typed
TCL	typed copy of letter
TLS	typed letter signed
WW	Woodrow Wilson
WWhw	Woodrow Wilson handwriting, handwritten
WWsh	Woodrow Wilson shorthand
WWshLS	Woodrow Wilson shorthand letter signed

ABBREVIATIONS FOR COLLECTIONS AND LIBRARIES

Following the National Union Catalog of the Library of Congress

CtY	Yale University
DLC	Library of Congress
MH	Harvard University
MdHi	Maryland Historical Society, Baltimore
MiU-C	University of Michigan, William L. Clements Library
MoSHi	Missouri Historical Society, Saint Louis
NcD	Duke University
NcU	University of North Carolina
Nj	New Jersey State Library, Trenton
NjP	Princeton University
RSB Coll., DLC	Ray Stannard Baker Collection of Wilsoniana, Library of Congress
Vi	Virginia State Library, Richmond
ViU	University of Virginia
ViW	College of William and Mary
WC, NjP	Woodrow Wilson Collection, Princeton University
WP, DLC	Woodrow Wilson Papers, Library of Congress

SYMBOLS

[May 5, 1911]	publication date of a published writing; also date of document when date is not part of text
[[May 7, 1911]]	delivery date of a speech if publication date differs
[*May 27, 1911*]	composition date when publication date differs

THE PAPERS OF

WOODROW WILSON

VOLUME 23

1911-1912

THE PAPERS OF
WOODROW WILSON

An Interview in Kansas City, Missouri

[May 5, 1911]

WILSON TRUSTS THE PUBLIC

For twenty years Woodrow Wilson, who is in Kansas City today, has been lecturing on government in the classroom. When he became governor of New Jersey he laid off the scholastic cap and gown, but it is worth remarking that he did not put on the statesman's frock coat. For the rest he went on lecturing on government, except that instead of doing it in the classroom he enlarged his forum and is talking to the American people.

That he is a Democrat, the governor of a great pivotal state and that the time is the eve of a Presidential year, does not constitute any good reasons, to his mind, why he should change the habit of twenty years and stop talking now. But Governor Wilson doesn't wear a stateman's coat, and is new to statesmen's ways, language and methods, and that may have something to do with it. Anyway, he still says what is in his mind. Very reprehensible, no doubt, but Governor Wilson does it.

"I do not know why being governor of New Jersey instead of president of Princeton should make any difference," he said this morning at the Coates House. "I suppose the work I am in now would be called practical politics, if that makes a difference. For many years I have s[t]udied our system of government and have written and lectured about it. It has been my habit to speak plainly in the class room. There I was at liberty to express views about men as well as measures. Perhaps I have not that liberty now so fully, but public opinion never makes any mistakes about connecting up the men with the measures they represent."

Trim and upstanding, with a long, lean face, broad shoulders and a well poised head, Governor Wilson might be a prosperous business man. His manner is forceful and direct, and he lays his proposition down to you with an open palm, as if he were quoting a price or naming a day of delivery.

"Why am I a Democrat?" The governor sat forward in his chair and mapped it all out on his palm where it could be read plainly. "The theory of Democracy is that government should be by, as well as for the people. The Republican theory grants that government should be for the people, but doubts the wisdom of letting the people do the governing. The Republican idea of government is that a select board of directors should run things. It may be that they will run things properly, they may intend to run them for the sole benefit of the people—but the theory is wrong. I would have the stockholders, not the directors do the managing, and that is my theory of Democracy—that is why I am a Democrat.

"Now, whether or not the intentions of the Republican board of directors are good the fact remains that it has been under their management that special privilege has grown up in this country. The people and their government have been getting farther and farther apart."

The governor here listened attentively to a suggestion that special privilege had some good friends in the Democratic party, also—perhaps even in the United States Senate, and nodded his agreement.

"But," he said, again tracing it out on his palm, "that is between them and their Democratic consciences. The theory of democracy takes no account of party names. Only those are Democrats who believe in its principles. Public opinion can be trusted to take care of that."

The Knife and Fork Club will see a new type of public man when Woodrow Wilson rises to deliver his address tonight. They will see the "scholar in politics," but not a visionary, a dilettante or a pedagogue. . . . Viewed as a public man one's first impression of Gov. Woodrow Wilson is a strong reminder of the late John A. Johnson of Minnesota.[1] Wilson is a scholar. Johnson was not so fortunate in his equipment of mental training and nobody knew it better than he, but when the subject matter under discussion is the interest of the public the point of view of the two men is essentially the same.

"In my campaign for governor," Mr. Wilson said this morning, "I could go farther and faster with the workingmen than with any other audience. They were in the struggle. The man with the stake, the rich man of the country, has ideas of government that make the stake the essential thing. The man on the street, the man who is in the battle of life, thinks on these subjects and he thinks more correctly than the rich man. That is because he is in the battle and knows conditions at first hand."

"The tariff as it has been in this country in recent years has changed from a system of protection to a system of patronage," he said. "In the new tariff law there were a good many things included that did not belong there. Things were put into it under cover and the people did not know they were there. The bill was full of trickery, but in the revision of that tariff it won't do to upset business conditions throughout the country. An intelligent adjustment correcting the worst schedules first will be necessary."

"What will be the principal issue in the next campaign?"

"That will depend upon what Congress does before the campaign. The next year may settle some things relating principally to the tariff, of course, and the action of Congress may make the issue very different from what it seems just now."

Governor Wilson would not talk about Presidential aspirations. He was not ready to say that he was a candidate and certainly not willing to say that he would refuse what no American who had a chance has ever thought of refusing. . . .

Printed in the *Kansas City Star*, May 5, 1911; some editorial headings omitted.
[1] John Albert Johnson, Democratic Governor of Minnesota from 1904 until his death on September 21, 1909.

A News Report of Two Addresses in Kansas City, Missouri

[May 6, 1911]

WILSON TELLS HOW TO DO IT

GET THE MEN WHO ARE RESPONSIBLE FOR
CORPORATION MISDEEDS.

The new political epoch—a government in which the average man's vote counts as much as the corporation's millions of dollars—was described by Woodrow Wilson, governor of New Jersey, in his address to the members of the Knife and Fork Club at the Coates House last night.[1]

Five hundred and fifty members heard the governor with progressive ideas speak them. They heard him assail the corporations and tell about their methods of controlling our law-making bodies—state legislatures and Congress. He told them how the heads of money interests, who tampered for years with the people's laws in New Jersey, now bow down to the people's laws and keep in the brush when the people's representatives are making laws.

"Less than at any time can it be said that the American people are divided among themselves," Governor Wilson said, "in their

[1] He was introduced by Herbert Spencer Hadley, Republican Governor of Missouri, 1909-13, who, as attorney general of his state from 1905 to 1909, became widely known for his successful prosecution of cases against Standard Oil, railroads, and the International Harvester Co.

ideals and demands through the critical years in what is said and felt and thought. If we had a man of courage, he could set the whole country afire. There were certain cool localities where some persons kept their equilibrium, but in widely separated parts of the country there have been some severe fires raging, which, if they could have burned through the cool areas, would have kindled our country into one great conflagration.

"Quarrels between corporations and the people come up in several states, but the persons in the other states sit idly by because it isn't their fight. But there have been times when it seemed that the whole country would burst out. There is no doubt that we now are face to face with political changes which may have a profound effect on our political life. Those who do not understand the impending change are afraid of it. Those who do understand it know that it is not a process of revolution, but a process of restoration, rather, in which there is as much healing as hurt.

"Many of your corporation lawyers sit off and criticise. If you knew what you should do, if you had any sense, you would change the methods of your companies. There isn't one of you who doesn't know that the methods of corporations are wrong. You know the inside of the machinery and you know what kind of laws would regulate these concerns. But if you sit by and criticise, it won't be long until the people will destroy the corporations.

"I had a conference with corporation lawyers in New Jersey. The conclusion we reached was that well regulated processes are better for the money institutions. Don't you see a new dawn of reform; a new era of excitement? The excitement will give way to enthusiasm, the enthusiasm for reform. The people aren't fearful of reform now. They want it.

"The voters of the United States are divided into two great classes: the progressives and the reactionaries. The progressives look facts in the face and meet them, and the reactionary is a man who has no stomach for facts. The progressive is the man who sees the past as neither here nor there. We generally sum up what we mean by the reactionary forces by speaking of them as embodied in the interests.

"By that we do not mean the legitimate interests but the illegitimate interests, those which have not adjusted themselves to the public interest, those which are clinging to their vested rights as a bulwark against the adjustment which is absolutely necessary if they are to be servants and not masters of the public. The chief political fact is that the Republicans are more closely allied with these interests than the Democrats.

"This circumstance constitutes the opportunity for the Democrats. There are fewer reactionaries in the Democratic party than in the Republican, but those who are in there are as hopeless as those in the Republican party, but they are less numerous.

"The reactionaries are barnacles and must have something ancient to cling to. The ancient policies of the Republicans present a large and most excellent surface for barnacles. But the Republicans have been in office a long time and the surface has grown. The Democrats if they had been in power wouldn't have presented such a large surface as the Republicans, however.

"There are a lot of insurgent Republicans, but I've yet to hear of an insurgent Democrat. Insurgency means a revolt. An insurgent is one who resists and are [is] always in the minority. Those who ought to be resisted are in the majority. The Democrats are not in the majority—Q.E.D.

"Both parties are breaking away from the past whether they will or not because our life has broken away from the past. The life of America is not the life it was twenty years ago. We have changed our economic conditions from top to bottom and with our economic conditions has changed also the organization of our life. The old party formulas do not fit the present problems.

"The new party will have no entangling alliances with certain interests. The voters now are becoming what might be called detachable voters. They don't have to be pried off with a crowbar. They follow their convictions. There was a time, you remember, when a man couldn't have been torn from his party for anything. But times have changed. Voters are detachable by suggestion now. A lot of men are going about the country looking for men of similar mind so they can get together for action. The party that offers that chance first will have the Nation at its back. The old arguments of the parties do not ring [true] any more. The people want new proposals and the party that offers them will win.

"The situation in this country may be summed up about as follows: What we are face to face with today is the control of our politics, therefore our life, by great bodies of accumulated and organized wealth.

"The election machine gets its money now on the understanding that everything political is to be done to safeguard its suppliers. I'm not talking about the dirty, ugly bribery cases, but the whole party."

Then Governor Wilson told about the methods, practiced quite extensively, of the state legislator asking for orders on how to vote when certain measures come up.

"Our state governments often are run automatically by the telephones," he continued. "The official runs to the telephone when a certain measure comes up and calls up the senator at Washington, the party boss, and asks him how he has arranged for him to vote. Or, in many cases, he telephones to a trust official, but in either case the result is the same.

"Our legislative processes are secret. Ninety-nine out of every hundred bills aren't considered on the floor of the house, but by some committee in a secret session, or by some persons other than the committee, who tell the committee how to vote, and the committee tells the members of the house how to vote. Most of the bills are framed in a lawyer's office and sent to the legislature by a lobbyist, who hands it to a representative to introduce.

"There is no partisanship in these deals. It's bipartisanship. The two machines have united for the interests, and there's not much chance for the people when the people's enemies in both parties combine. The machinery of politics is a thing controlled by the interests. And they don't take any chances, but make every move sure. There are no virtuous machine men. The machine men can't be blamed altogether, for that is the game of politics as they learned it. They were reared that way, and they have a sort of piety in doing things as they always have been done.

"The recall is like the gun in the closet—you know you have it if you need it. It is a business principle. When a servant doesn't do his work properly he is discharged, so should a government official [be].

"The thing to do with the corporations is to turn the light on them. They don't like light. Turn it on so strong they can't stand it. Exposure is one of the best ways to whip them into line. Use their names. The laws of libel may interfere, but use their names. Tell who they are.

"We have a Utilities Act in New Jersey that lets a lot of light in on the corporations. They are required by law to register with the department of justice the names of every official connected with the company. Then we know whom to go after when anything out of line is brought to our attention. It's an awful hard matter to find the right man when anything goes wrong in a corporation. When they disobey the law, the guilty person pays the penalty and not the innocent stockholders. The directors who are responsible for the operation of the company may be placed in jail. Fines paid by the stockholders don't punish them, so in New Jersey we put them in jail.

"Indictments are ugly things when drawn against unnamed men. That's why we have their names in New Jersey."[2]

[2] There is an advance printed text of this address in WP, DLC, which Wilson did not deliver but was widely printed by newspapers. Advance text and press releases will not usually be printed in this series.

✧

HIS IMPULSE IS TO ADVANCE.

Things Don't Stand Still—They Go Forward or Backward, Governor Wilson Says

In a brief talk at the Commercial Club rooms yesterday afternoon Governor Woodrow Wilson told an audience of several hundred people what he understands to be the radical or progressive idea in American politics.

After telling a story to illustrate his assertion that he is not a ready speaker, Governor Wilson said:

"I don't know how radical you may be here in Kansas City," ("Pretty radical," someone in the audience said.)

"But," continued Governor Wilson, "all the progressives are getting together in America. Party lines are getting broken. We have to have something to steer by and in both parties men are going in the same direction toward the progressive or radical ideas. Many people have the idea that the progressive wants to go too fast, so fast that he will upset things. We don't want to do that but we can't stand still. We must keep going on if we are to get anywhere.

"When I was in the university men would say: 'Wilson, why in the thunder can't you leave something alone?' My answer was if things left alone would actually stand still I would leave them alone. But they won't stand still. We are going backward if we don't go forward. . . ."

Governor Wilson's short talk was delivered after the reception in the Commercial Club rooms. The reception began at 3:30 o'clock and lasted nearly two hours. It was after Governor Wilson had made a motor car trip visiting the Country Club, Robert Gillham Road, Rockhill Road and the Manual Training High School, where he made a short speech.

In the receiving line Mayor Brown[1] and J. C. Lester,[2] president of the Commercial Club, headed the line. Governor Wilson stood next to Mr. Lester, with George H. Forsee[3] and Governor Hadley on his right. Several hundred people passed along the line, Governor Wilson greeting them cordially and speaking a few words with them.

Printed in the *Kansas City Times*, May 6, 1911; some editorial headings omitted.

[1] Darius Alvin Brown, Republican Mayor of Kansas City, 1910-1912.

[2] John Calvin Lester, vice-president and director of the Ridenour-Baker Grocery Co. of Kansas City.

[3] General manager of Fairbanks, Morse & Co., machine manufacturers, until 1911 when he resigned to become the Commercial Club's industrial commissioner. His job was to collect and disseminate information about industrial development in Kansas City.

From Ellen Axson Wilson

My darling,   Princeton, New Jersey May 6, 1911.

Your telegram from Kansas City has just arrived,[1] to our great satisfaction. I was, at the moment, reading the speech at the breakfast table. I think it was *perfect*! Am very happy to know that it was "a great success." Be sure to tell me in each telegram things like that.

We are about starting to Sea Girt,[2] so I havn't time for a long letter this morning. I am sending this off in a hurry to make perfectly sure of your getting Janie Porter's[3] address, for you know I forgot to give it to you after all. It is—"Mrs. S. C. Candler, 2331 Thompson St., Los Angeles." Tell her I am sending her some lovely pictures of the girls. The photos came day before yesterday and are enchanting.

We have a wonderful day for our trip and are going to have a "real good time." Nothing has happened of course since you left. We are all very well. It is good to have the girls back to relieve the lonliness. I think of you all the time, and love you beyond all words.

Last night I dined with the Fords at Peacock Inn; just the three of us. I had a delightful evening talking politics to Mr. Ford! He has been asked to write an article about you, including both your personality and your politics,—I forget for which magazine.[4] I went to see what the Peacock Inn would charge us by the week and it was *more* than the "Inn"! So that is off my mind. I was afraid that if it was much cheaper we ought to go there. My rock picture is done and is rather stunning, Mr van Laer[5] thinks. I am trying to get courage and send it next winter to the Phila exhibition. With love inexpressible from all of us and above all from me I am, my darling, as ever

Your devoted little wife,   Eileen.

ALS (WC, NjP).

¹ All of Wilson's correspondence with Mrs. Wilson during this trip is missing.
² That is, to go to the governor's summer home in Sea Girt, N. J.
³ Janie Porter (Mrs. Samuel C.) Chandler, a childhood friend in Rome and Savannah, Ga.
⁴ Henry Jones Ford, "Woodrow Wilson, A Character Sketch," *Review of Reviews*, XLVI (Aug. 1912), 177-84.
⁵ Alexander Theobald Van Laer, artist of New York who specialized in water color, whom Mrs. Wilson had met in Old Lyme, Conn. He was lecturing in Princeton at this time.

To Mary Allen Hulbert Peck

Dearest Friend,   The Brown Palace Hotel Denver 7 May, 1911.

This is the first Sunday of my tour, and I steal time for a few lines. I was *so* sorry I got no letter from you before leaving home, —no letter by the boat which must have left Bermuda last week end. It made me uneasy lest something might have happened to you—or you might have 'overdone' again and fallen ill, losing the ground so happily gained. I shall hope with all my heart that it meant nothing untoward.

The 'tour' has begun most auspiciously. We (i.e. Stockbridge, the wide awake newspaper man who is travelling with me as my manager, and McKee Barclay, representing the Baltimore *Sun*, a capital cartoonist¹ and a good fellow, and your humble servant, —such is the party) we [arrived] in Kansas City on Friday. There I was given a lunch and a public reception and a big dinner,— and the diners seemed not in the least to object to my speaking an hour and ten minutes! The day seems to have been a great success, so far as I could judge. What pleases me to the core is that the men I meet, both singly and in the mass, seem to *like* me and accept me as genuine. That's worth the price of the trip. I value that more than all else put together!

10 P.M. I have just come back from a wonderful meeting, where I addressed twelve thousand people. The occasion was the tercentenary of the King James version of the Bible. The meeting was got up by the Bible Society (in view, I believe, of my coming) and was held in the great auditorium in which the last Democratic national convention met. I was delighted to find that my voice carried to every corner of the vast place. I spoke on the Bible and Progress, and the great audience moved me deeply. The Bible (with its individual value of the human soul[)] is undoubtedly the book that has made democracy and been the source of all progress.

This travelling and speaking is strenuous business, but it actually seems to refresh and revive me after the long, anxious, trying grind at Trenton!

I have some relatives here—an aunt[2] who is a perfect dear and beauty and some cousins—with one of whom I was once in love.[3] Another of the cousins is the one-time husband of 'Mrs. Wilson Woodrow.'[4]

Good-bye. Think of me on my wanderings—take care of yourself,—and give my love to all

Your devoted friend   Woodrow Wilson

ALS (WP, DLC).
  [1] Barclay also wrote occasional reports on Wilson's western tour for the Baltimore *Sun*.
  [2] Helen Sill (Mrs. Thomas) Woodrow.
  [3] Harriet Woodrow (Mrs. Edward Freeman) Welles.
  [4] James Wilson Woodrow, former husband of Nancy Mann Waddel Woodrow. She wrote popular literature under the name "Mrs. Wilson Woodrow." Another cousin in Denver was Thomas R. Woodrow.

An Address in Denver on the Bible[1]

[[May 7, 1911]]

The thought that entered my mind first as I came into this great room this evening framed itself in a question—Why should this great body of people have come together upon this solemn night? There is nothing here to be seen. There is nothing delectable here to be heard. Why should you run together in a great host when all that is to be spoken of is the history of a familiar book?

But as I have sat and looked upon this great body of people I have thought of the very suitable circumstance that here upon the platform sat a little group of ministers of the gospel lost in this great throng.

I say the "suitable circumstance," for I come here to-night to speak of the Bible as the book of the people, not the book of the minister of the gospel, not the special book of the priest from which to set forth some occult, unknown doctrine withheld from the common understanding of men, but a great book of revelation—the people's book of revelation. For it seems to me that the Bible has revealed the people to themselves. I wonder how many persons in this great audience realize the significance for English-speaking peoples of the translation of the Bible into the English tongue. Up to the time of the translation of the Bible into English, it was a book for long ages withheld from the perusal of the peoples of other languages and of other tongues, and not a little of the history of liberty lies in the circumstance that the moving sentences of this book were made familiar to the ears

  [1] Delivered in the Denver Auditorium before an audience of some 12,000 persons.

and the understanding of those peoples who have led mankind in exhibiting the forms of government and the impulses of reform which have made for freedom and for self-government among mankind.

For this is a book which reveals men unto themselves, not as creatures in bondage, not as men under human authority, not as those bidden to take counsel and command of any human source. It reveals every man to himself as a distinct moral agent, responsible not to men, not even to those men whom he has put over him in authority, but responsible through his own conscience to his Lord and Maker. Whenever a man sees this vision he stands up a free man, whatever may be the government under which he lives, if he sees beyond the circumstances of his own life.

I heard a very eloquent sermon to-day from an honored gentleman who is with us to-night.[2] He was speaking upon the effect of a knowledge of the future life upon our conduct in this life. And it seemed to me as I listened to him I saw the flames of those fires rekindled at which the martyrs died—died forgetful of their pain, with praise and thanksgiving upon their lips, that they had the opportunity to render their testimony that this was not the life for which they had lived, but that there was a house builded in the heavens not built of men but built of God, to the vision of which they had lifted their eyes as they passed through the world, which gave them courage to fear no man but to serve God. And I thought that all the records of heroism of the great things that had illustrated human life were summed up in the power of men to see that vision.

Our present life, ladies and gentlemen, is a very imperfect and disappointing thing. We do not judge our own conduct in the privacy of our own closets by the standard of expediency by which we are daily and hourly governed. We know that there is a standard set for us in the heavens, a standard revealed to us in this book which is the fixed and eternal standard by which we judge ourselves, and as we read this book it seems to us that the pages of our own hearts are laid open before us for our own perusal. This is the people's book of revelation, revelation of themselves not alone, but revelation of life and of peace. You know that human life is a constant struggle. For a man who has lost the sense of struggle, life has ceased.

I believe that my confidence in the judgment of the people in matters political is based upon my knowledge that the men who

[2] The Rev. Dr. Robert Francis Coyle, pastor of the Central Presbyterian Church of Denver.

are struggling are the men who know; that the men who are in the midst of the great effort to keep themselves steady in the pressure and rush of life are the men who know the significance of the pressure and the rush of life, and that they, the men on the make, are the men to whom to go for your judgments of what life is and what its problems are. And in this book there is peace simply because we read here the object of the struggle. No man is satisfied with himself as the object of the struggle.

There is a very interesting phrase that constantly comes to our lips which we perhaps do not often enough interpret in its true meaning. We see many a young man start out in life with apparently only this object in view—to make name and fame and power for himself, and there comes a time of maturity and reflection when we say of him, "He has come to himself." When may I say that I have come to myself? Only when I have come to recognize my true relations with the rest of the world. We speak of a man losing himself in a desert. If you reflect a moment you will see that is the only thing he has not lost. He himself is there. What he means when he says that he has lost himself is that he has lost all the rest of the world. He has nothing to steer by. He does not know where any human habitation lies. He does not know where any beaten path and highway is. If he could establish his relationship with anything else in the world he would have found himself. Let it serve as a picture.

A man has found himself when he has found his relation to the rest of the universe, and here is the book in which those relations are set forth. And so when you see a man going along the highways of life with his gaze lifted above the road, lifted to the sloping ways in front of him, then be careful of that man and get out of his way. He knows the kingdom for which he is bound. He has seen the revelation of himself and of his relations to mankind. He has seen the revelations of his relation to God and his Maker and therefore he has seen his responsibility in the world. This is the revelation of life and of peace. I do not know that peace lies in constant accommodation. I was once asked if I would take part in a great peace conference, and I said, "Yes, if I may speak in favor of war"—not the war which we seek to avoid, not the senseless and useless and passionate shedding of human blood, but the only war that brings peace, the war with human passions and the war with human wrong— the war which is that untiring and unending process of reform from which no man can refrain and get peace.

No man can sit down and withhold his hands from the warfare against wrong and get peace out of his acquiescence. The most solid and satisfying peace is that which comes from this constant spiritual warfare, and there are times in the history of nations when they must take up the crude instruments of bloodshed in order to vindicate spiritual conceptions. For liberty is a spiritual conception, and when men take up arms to set other men free, there is something sacred and holy in the warfare. I will not cry "Peace" so long as there is sin and wrong in the world. And this great book does not teach any doctrine of peace so long as there is sin to be combated and overcome in one's own heart and in the great moving force of human society.

And so it seems to me that we must look upon the Bible as the great charter of the human soul—as the "Magna Charta" of the human soul. You know the interesting circumstances which gave rise to the Magna Charta. You know the moving scene that was enacted upon the heath at Runnymede. You know how the barons of England, representing the people of England—for they consciously represented the people of England—met upon that historic spot and parleyed with John, the king. They said: "We will come to terms with you here." They said: "There are certain inalienable rights of English-speaking men which you must observe. They are not given by you, they cannot be taken away by you. Sign your name here to this parchment upon which these rights are written and we are your subjects. Refuse to put your name to this document and we are your sworn enemies. Here are our swords to prove it."

The franchise of human liberty made the basis of a bargain with a king! There are kings upon the pages of Scripture, but do you think of any king in Scripture as anything else than a mere man? There was the great king David, of a line blessed because the line from which should spring our Lord and Savior, a man marked in the history of mankind as the chosen instrument of God to do justice and exalt righteousness in the people.

But what does this Bible do for David? Does it utter eulogies upon him? Does it conceal his faults and magnify his virtues? Does it set him up as a great statesman would be set up in a modern biography? No, the book in which his annals are written strips the mask from David, strips every shred of counterfeit and concealment from him and shows him as, indeed, an instrument of God, but a sinful and selfish man, and the verdict of the Bible is that David, like other men, was one day to stand naked before the judgment seat of God and be judged not as a king, but as a man. Isn't this the book of the people? Is there any man in this Holy Scripture who is exempted from the common standard and judgment? How these pages teem with the masses of mankind! Are these the annals of the great? These are the annals of the people—of the common run of men.

The New Testament is the history of the life and the testimony of common men who rallied to the fellowship of Jesus Christ and who by their faith and preaching remade a world that was under the thrall of the Roman army. This is the history of the triumph of the human spirit, in the persons of humble men. And how many sorts of men march across the pages, how infinite is the variety of human circumstance and of human dealings and of human heroism and love! Is this a picture of extraordinary things? This is a picture of the common life of mankind. It is a mirror held up for men's hearts, and it is in this mirror that we marvel to see ourselves portrayed.

How like to the Scripture is all great literature! What is it that entrances us when we read or witness a play of Shakespeare? It is the consciousness that this man, this all-observing mind, saw men of every cast and kind as they were in their habits as they lived. And as passage succeeds passage we seem to see the characters of ourselves and our friends portrayed by this ancient writer, and a play of Shakespeare is just as modern to-day as upon the day it was penned and first enacted. And the Bible is without age or date or time. It is a picture of the human heart displayed for all ages and for all sorts and conditions of men. Moreover, the Bible does what is so invaluable in human life— it classifies moral values. It apprises us that men are not judged according to their wits, but according to their characters, that the test of every man's reputation is his truthfulness, his squaring his conduct with the standards that he knew to be the standards of purity and rectitude.

How many a man we appraise, ladies and gentlemen, as great to-day, whom we do not admire as noble! A man may have great power and small character. And the sweet praise of mankind lies not in their admiration of the smartness with which the thing was accomplished, but in that lingering love which apprises men that one of their fellows has gone out of life to his own reckoning, where he is sure of the blessed verdict, "Well done, good and faithful servant."

Did you ever look about you in any great city, in any great capital, at the statues which have been erected in it? To whom are these statues erected? Are they erected to the men who have piled fortunes about them? I do not know of any such statue anywhere unless after he had accumulated his fortune the man bestowed it in beneficence upon his fellowmen and alongside of him will stand a statue of another meaning, for it is easy to give money away. I heard a friend of mine say that the standard of generosity was not the amount you gave away, but the amount you had left. It is easy to give away of your abundance, but look at the next statue, the next statue and the next in the market-place of great cities and whom will you see? You will see here a soldier who gave his life to serve, not his own ends, but the interests and the purposes of his country.

I would be the last, ladies and gentlemen, to disparage any of the ordinary occupations of life, but I want to ask you this question: Did you ever see anybody who had lost a son hang up his yardstick over the mantel-piece? Have you not seen many families who had lost their sons hang up their muskets and their swords over the mantel-piece? What is the difference between the yardstick and the musket? There is nothing but perfect honor in the use of the yardstick, but the yardstick was used for the man's own interest, for his own self-support. It was used merely to fulfil the necessary exigencies of life, whereas the musket was used to serve no possible purpose of his own. He took every risk without any possibility of profit. The musket is the symbol of self-sacrifice and the yardstick is not. A man will instinctively elevate the one as the symbol of honor and never dream of using the other as a symbol of distinction.

Doesn't that cut pretty deep, and don't you know why the soldier has his monument as against the civilian? The civilian may have served his State—he also—and here and there you may see a statesman's statue, but the civilian has generally served his country—has often served his country, at any rate—with some idea of promoting his own interests, whereas the soldier has everything to lose and nothing but the gratitude of his fellow-men to win.

Let every man pray that he may in some true sense be a soldier of fortune, that he may have the good fortune to spend his energies and his life in the service of his fellowmen in order that he may die to be recorded upon the rolls of those who have not thought of themselves but have thought of those whom they served. Isn't this the lesson of our Lord and Savior Jesus Christ? Am I not reminding you of these common judgments of our life, simply expounding to you this book of revelation, this book which reveals the common man to himself, which strips life of its disguises and its pretences and elevates those standards by which alone true greatness and true strength and true valor are assessed?

Do you wonder, therefore, that when I was asked what my theme this evening would be I said it would be "The Bible *and* Progress"? We do not judge progress by material standards. America is not ahead of the other nations of the world because she is rich. Nothing makes America great except her thoughts, except her ideals, except her acceptance of those standards of judgment which are written large upon these pages of revelation. America has all along claimed the distinction of setting this example to the civilized world—that men were to think of one another, that governments were to be set up for the service of the people, that men were to be judged by these moral standards which pay no regard to rank or birth or conditions, but which assess every man according to his single and individual value. That is the meaning of this charter of the human soul. This is the standard by which men and nations have more and more come to be judged. And so, reform has consisted in nothing more nor less than this—in trying to conform actual conditions, in trying to square actual laws with the right judgments of human conduct and human liberty.

That is the reason that the Bible has stood at the back of progress. That is the reason that reform has come, not from the top but from the bottom. If you are ever tempted to let a government reform itself, I ask you to look back in the pages of history and find me a government that reformed itself. If you are ever tempted to let a party attempt to reform itself I ask you to find a party that ever reformed itself.

A tree is not nourished by its bloom and by its fruit. It is nourished by its roots, which are down deep in the common and hidden soil, and every process of purification and rectification comes from the bottom—not from the top. It comes from the masses of struggling human beings. It comes from the instinctive efforts of millions of human hearts trying to beat their way up into the light and into the hope of the future.

Parties are reformed and governments are corrected by the impulses coming out of the hearts of those who never exercised authority and never organized parties. Those are the sources of strength, and I pray God that these sources may never cease to be spiritualized by the immortal subjections of these words of inspiration of the Bible.

If any statesman sunk in the practices which debase a nation will but read this single book he will go to his prayers abashed. Do you not realize, ladies and gentlemen, that there is a whole literature in the Bible? It is not one book, but a score of books. Do you realize what literature is? I am sometimes sorry to see the great classics of our English literature used in the schools as text-books, because I am afraid that little children may gain the impression that these are formal lessons to be learned. There is no great book in any language, ladies and gentlemen, that is not the spontaneous outpouring of some great mind or the cry of some great heart. And the reason that poetry moves us more than prose does is that it is the rhythmic and passionate voice of some great spirit that has seen more than his fellowmen can see.

I have found more true politics in the poets of the English-speaking race than I have ever found in all the formal treatises on political science. There is more of the spirit of our own institutions in a few lines of Tennyson than in all the text-books on governments put together:

"A nation still, the rulers and the ruled,
　Some sense of duty, something of a faith,
　Some reverence for the laws ourselves have made,
　Some patient force to change them when we will,
　Some civic manhood firm against the crowd."[3]

Can you find summed up the manly self-helping spirit of Saxon liberty anywhere better than in those few lines? Men afraid of nobody, afraid of nothing but their own passions, on guard against being caught unaware by their own sudden impulses and so getting their grapple upon life in firm-set institutions, some reverence for the laws they themselves have made, some patience, not passionate force, to change them when they will, some civic manhood firm against the crowd. Literature, ladies and gentlemen, is a revelation of the human spirit, and within the covers of this one book is a whole lot of literature, prose and poetry, history and rhapsody, the sober narration and the ecstasy of human excitement—things that ring in one's ears like songs never to be forgotten. And so I say, let us never forget that these deep sources, these wells of inspiration, must always be our sources of refreshment and of renewal. Then no man can put unjust power upon us. We shall live in that chartered liberty in which a man sees the things unseen, in which he knows that he is bound for a country in which there are no questions mooted any longer of right or wrong.

Can you imagine a man who did not believe these words, who did not believe in the future life, standing up and doing what has been the heart and center of liberty always—standing up be-

---

[3] "The Princess: Conclusion."

fore the king himself and saying, "Sir, you have sinned and done wrong in the sight of God and I am his messenger of judgment to pronounce upon you the condemnation of Almighty God. You may silence me, you may send me to my reckoning with my Maker, but you cannot silence or reverse the judgment." That is what a man feels whose faith is rooted in the Bible. And the man whose faith is rooted in the Bible knows that reform can not be stayed, that the finger of God that moves upon the face of the nations is against every man that plots the nation's downfall or the people's deceit; that these men are simply groping and staggering in their ignorance to a fearful day of judgment and that whether one generation witnesses it or not, the glad day of revelation and of freedom will come in which men will sing by the host of the coming of the Lord in His glory, and all of those will be forgotten, those little, scheming, contemptible creatures that forgot the image of God and tried to frame men according to the image of the Evil One.

You may remember that allegorical narrative in the Old Testament of those who searched through one cavern after another, cutting the holes in the walls and going into the secret places where all sorts of noisome things were worshipped. Men do not dare to let the sun shine in upon such things and upon such occupations and worships. And so I say there will be no halt to the great movement of the armies of reform until men forget their God, until they forget this charter of their liberty. Let no man suppose that progress can be divorced from religion, or that there is any other platform for the ministers of reform than the platform written in the utterances of our Lord and Savior.

America was born a Christian nation. America was born to exemplify that devotion to the elements of righteousness which are derived from the revelations of Holy Scripture.

Ladies and gentlemen, I have a very simple thing to ask of you. I ask of every man and woman in this audience that from this night on they will realize that part of the destiny of America lies in their daily perusal of this great book of revelations—that if they would see America free and pure they will make their own spirits free and pure by this baptism of the Holy Scripture.[4]

Woodrow Wilson, *The Bible and Progress* (New York, 1912), with corrections from the text in the Trenton *True American*, May 17, 1911.

[4] There is a WWhw outline, with the composition date of May 6, 1911, of this address in WP, DLC.

A News Report of Remarks at a Dinner in Denver

[May 8, 1911]

Bryn Mawr Heckles Wilson On the Presidential Office
At Brilliant Entertainment

A brilliant company was assembled at the home of Mrs. Richard Crawford Campbell,[1] last evening, to take supper with Governor Woodrow Wilson.

Those present besides Mr. and Mrs. Campbell were Governor Wilson, former Senator Thomas M. Patterson, former Governor Alva Adams, Governor John F. Shafroth, Mrs. Sarah Platt Decker,[2] former Governor Charles S. Thomas, Thomas J. O'Donnell,[3] Bishop Henry W. Warren,[4] Dr. William F. Slocum,[5] Miss Anna Wolcott,[6] the Rev. George B. Van Arsdall,[7] W. H. Bryant,[8] former Senator Frank J. Cannon,[9] Miss Fredericka Le Fevre,[10] Miss Sweet,[11] Mr. and Mrs. Henry Swan[12] and Miss Jane Ward.[13]

The table decorations were Bryn Mawr colors, white and gold chrysanthemums and the American flag.

With the supper, began the "heckling" of the probable presidential candidate, and he replied in the midst of a flashing fire of oratory and wit, illuminated by the lanterns of Bryn Mawr and the beacon light of Princeton.

Mrs. Campbell, in expressing the welcome of her home and the Bryn Mawr graduates to Governor Wilson, said:

"It is one of the customs of Bryn Mawr that the sophomores shall welcome the freshmen by presenting to them lanterns to light their way along the path of knowledge—the shaded path—sometimes too shaded; also to bestow upon them advice and to subject them to questions. Following that practice, we offer the lantern and, in particular honor of the guest, the flag as table favors tonight. In honor of old Bryn Mawr, where Governor Wilson was once a revered professor of history and economics, we offer to him the lantern to illuminate his path to the White house; and I shall tender the advice and subject him to the question. For counsel we recommend to him to continue his travels over his country, from time to time, until he shall have attained the exalted office of president; and then we hope he will pretermit the wanderlust which seems to have affected both Mr. Bryan and Mr. Roosevelt so seriously, and remain at home at the capital to govern the country. For the question, which he must answer satisfactorily if he would have our support: Governor Wilson, have you been taught most by your wife? Or by your three daughters?"

Replying, Governor Wilson paid his affectionate compliments to Bryn Mawr. He said that as it aimed to copy Johns Hopkins in his day of professorship there, the fashion was to call Bryn Mawr, "Johanna Hopkins." Governor Wilson accepted the advice and promised to follow it if opportunity should permit, and in answering the question said:

"From Mrs. Wilson, not only have I learned much but have gained something of literary reputation. Whenever I need a poetic quotation she supplies it, and in this way I acquire the fame of possessing a complete anthology of poetry. From my daughters, however, I have learned what every parent knows of himself—that I do not know how to raise children."

Reverting to the work of our universities, Governor Wilson said: "Without disrespect to parents, the best teaching of our schools is to take young men and women away from the methods of preceding generations and to regeneralize their attitude toward the world and its progress. I find that the man of mature years and of achievement who sends his child to college, has implicated and to some extent solidified himself and his views of life within a particular vocation; and if the offspring were to follow rigidly within the lines of parental example in this respect, we would lose much of the breadth and the splendor of human progress. We retain the high standards of the old, while adopting the incentive and the method of the new.". . .

The room was then darkened and Mrs. Campbell, in recognition of the Bryn Mawr spirit, presented to Governor Wilson a tiny jeweled electric light, with the hope that he might find his way to the Presidency of the Republic.

Just as the brilliant assemblage was dispersing, in order to attend the meeting in the Auditorium, Mrs. Sarah Platt Decker gave a sweeping glance around the room at the various former senatorial candidates and asked: "Governor Wilson, take a good look at all these, and answer truthfully, would you not prefer a woman for a senator rather than any one of the men who is present?"

Printed in the Denver *Daily News*, May 8, 1911.

[1] Margaret Patterson (Mrs. Richard Crawford) Campbell, Bryn Mawr 1890, and Richard Crawford Campbell, secretary and general manager of the *Rocky Mountain News*, hosts for the dinner given in Wilson's honor by Bryn Mawr alumnae.

[2] Sarah Chase Harris Platt (Mrs. Westbrook S.) Decker, leader in civil service, conservation, penal, and child welfare reform, former president of the General Federation of Women's Clubs, vice-president of Colorado's first Woodrow Wilson-for-President club.

[3] Thomas Jefferson O'Donnell, attorney and prominent Democrat of Denver.

[4] The Rev. Dr. Henry White Warren, bishop of the Methodist Episcopal Church, 1880-1912.

[5] The Rev. Dr. William Frederick Slocum, Congregationalist minister and professor of philosophy and president, Colorado College, 1888-1917.

[6] Founder of the Wolcott School for Girls of Denver and regent of the University of Colorado, 1910-1916.

[7] Pastor of the Central Christian Church of Denver.

[8] William Henry Bryant of the law firm of Thomas, Bryant and Lee of Denver.

[9] Frank Jenne Cannon, Republican senator from Utah, 1896-99. He switched party affiliation in 1900 and served as state chairman of the Democratic party of Utah, 1902-1904. He moved to Denver in 1909 and was at this time engaged in mining and newspaper work.

[10] Eva Frederica LeFevre, Bryn Mawr 1905.

[11] Emma Sweet, Bryn Mawr 1907.

[12] Henry Swan, Princeton 1905, civil engineer and investment banker of Denver; Carla Denison (Mrs. Henry) Swan, Bryn Mawr 1905.

[13] Jane Shaw Ward, Bryn Mawr 1905.

A News Report of an Address to the Denver Chamber of Commerce

[May 9, 1911]

800 on Feet Cheer Wilson at Banquet

Eight hundred voices sounded a cheer, 800 hands waved 800 napkins and 800 men leaped to their feet as a welcome to Governor Woodrow Wilson in the banqueting hall of El Jebel temple last night.

The demonstration for the New Jersey governor exceeded that other famous demonstration—to President Theodore Roosevelt at the Brown Palace hotel when he returned from his hunting trip near Glenwood Springs and was a banquet guest of the city of Denver.[1]

Never before in the history of Denver has one man been accorded so enthusiastic a reception as that to Governor Wilson last night at the banquet given him by the Denver Chamber of Commerce. From the very beginning enthusiasm reigned and every few minutes some strong-lunged man would shout:

"What's the matter with Wilson?"

"He's all right!" would be stormed back from 800 throats. . . .

The address of S. H. Thompson, Jr., introducing Governor Wilson was particularly complimentary and prophetic of a career for the distinguished New Jersey reformer similar in many respects to that of Washington and Lincoln. He expressed a belief that the country is facing another great crisis similar to those which brought forth Washington and Lincoln and he expressed a belief that Governor Wilson would prove the man to free the

[1] Roosevelt had led a party hunting bear near Glenwood Springs, Col., in May 1905. His returning train was met on May 8 by a large throng in Denver, where he was entertained by the Chamber of Commerce.

country from the oppression of special privilege, as Washington freed it of tyranny and Lincoln of the curse of human slavery.

"My imagination does not keep pace with the great ideas set out in these introductions I have heard tonight," said Governor Wilson in beginning. "The people of the Dencer [Denver] Chamber of Commerce are 'going it some' in the career they have mapped out for me.

"There has been a most radical change in the popular discourse upon public questions in the last ten years. There is not now the popular protest there was ten years ago against the great corporations, the railroads and the trusts. There is not so great a public acclaim against organized wealth.

"Business men have to a large degree ceased to say 'let us alone.' They have come to recognize that nothing that is wrong will be let alone. They understand that nothing is settled unless it is settled right. The plain people and the representatives of large business interests are convinced that they must each understand better the work of the other and that no amount of protest on either side can prevent it.

"A great nation can not always be on the defensive. Its people must be filled with confidence in its future. They must be convinced that everybody will be given a square deal. The period of foreboding is past and the time for concerted action has arrived. Men everywhere are becoming imbued with the spirit of reorganization and reconstruction and are joining each other in asking 'what's the program?'

"We have determined to clear the ambushes away from government. We are going to open the government to the people and make them part of it. The secrecy of government has served its time and the people are demanding to know just how the government is administered, how the laws are made, how they are interpreted and why, and we will have to recognize this demand of the people for their rights.

"The direct primary is one means of opening the avenues of government to the people. It is not a panacea. It is only one step in the right direction. The people of America have grown tired of permitting a few men who have never been elected to any office to name the men for whom they may vote as their public servants. We believe that we can select the men ourselves for whom we want to vote.

"There is no man who can vote for forty or more men in one election and do it intelligently without making a special study of the ticket and the men composing it. There should never be so many men to vote for at one time. The people have not time to make the study necessary to permit them to vote knowingly. But we have no right to denounce the political machines for their dominance under the present system, which makes it impossible for the voters to understand what they are voting for. What we must do is to change the entire system and do away with the conditions which have created the political machine.

"We are going to bring about a new system of economics which will put the people in charge of their own economic life. They are not now in that position. It is necessary to bring about a change in the way corporations are organized, administered and subjected to the regulation of government. The corporations must recognize, when they ask the public to invest in their stocks and securities, that they are public and not private organizations. We must bring about a condition where the officer of a corporation shall be protected in his corporate acts so long as they are within the law, but shall become an outlaw, subject to the same prosecution, conviction and punishment as a private citizen, when he begins to act unlawfully.

"Next we have all made up our minds about conservation. We have agreed that there must be preservation from waste of the great resources of the country. Of course we are in some doubt as to how this conservation policy should be carried out. But at heart we are all, I think, most radical conservationists.

"But there is something more important than the conservation of water power sites, forests and material wealth of the country. We must see to it that the life and energy of our people are preserved. Labor must be so protected that life will not be constantly endangered because of the conditions under which it is employed. The health and vitality of our women and children must be protected and preserved. The principle of conservation should extend to the physique and the morals of a great people.

"Then our system of taxation is, we all agree, in need of a great reformation. Our system of protection should not be maintained as a system of favoritism. There should not be questions in connection with it that the finance committee of the senate will not publicly explain on the floor of the house. We believe in an honest tariff. We have about as jumbled and unscientific a system of taxation as is to be found in any country in the world, and we are going to change it soon and radically.

"Now the commission form of government, of which I wish to speak especially tonight, is one of the means of bringing about some of these reforms. Its first and most important feature is that it presents the voter with a very short ballot, thus making it possible for him to know who he is voting for. In that way it makes it possible for the people to hold their officials directly responsible for their official acts. . . .

"We must get rid of the jungles of city government and through the commission form of government we will be able to do so. When we have rid ourselves of these jungles we will be able to root them out of state and federal government. When we have accomplished this we will begin to realize the original political vision of America. There will then come a time when the courts will make a new interpretation for right and pronounce it not an opportunity to be selfish, but a duty to be just."

Printed in the Denver *Rocky Mountain News*, May 9, 1911; some editorial headings omitted.

An Interview

[May 9, 1911]

WILSON DISCUSSES THE PRESIDENCY

Post a Proud One But Cheeky For Any to Aspire

DENVER, May 9.—Congratulating the country on the recent notable purification of the political atmosphere, Governor Woodrow Wilson, of New Jersey, spoke last night at the banquet of the Chamber of Commerce, where he was the guest of honor. . . .

In an interview before the speech Governor Wilson said:

"Any man who might think himself big enough to seek the office of President of the United States, would be cheeky, but there is no man who would not be proud to be elected to the office of President.

"Really, I have not thought about the Presidency.

"A notion has gone abroad that I whipped the Legislature of New Jersey into performing certain acts," said the Governor, "but that view of the matter is not correct. I did appeal to public opinion, and publ[i]c opinion did the rest. From the reports that have been sent broadcast one would imagine that I disagreed with the Legislature constantly. I wish to correct that impression. My relations with the members of the Legislature were cordial."

Governor Wilson, speaking of the "recall," said that he has not been converted to the belief that it should be extended to embrace the judiciary. He expressed the opinion that the courts had, as a general proposition, behaved in a commendable manner.

Printed in the *Trenton Evening Times*, May 9, 1911; some editorial headings omitted.

A News Report of a Luncheon in Denver

[May 10, 1911]

Gov. Wilson Arouses Denver Ex-Collegians
New Political Bund May Result From Visit

A lot of Denver politicians were born yesterday. At least this is so if the Princeton university men who listened to Governor Wilson's talk to them at the University club yesterday, take his remarks seriously.

Forty Denver men, graduates of Princeton, met with the New Jersey executive at luncheon at noon yesterday. Good fellowship was the keynote of the affair, and the governor entered into the spirit as heartily as did any of those who were once his students at Princeton.

In a short talk, the governor referred in pleasing strain to the college days of the past, and then in more serious tone reminded his hearers that the lessons which they learned in their college days should not be forgotten. He told each of them that those lessons should be turned now to the practical side of life, and that it was the duty of everyone of them to study the political questions of the day, and to take part in the issues which are meant for the betterment of the people.

Governor Wilson's day yesterday was no different from that of Monday. A steady stream of callers visited him at his room at the Brown [Palace Hotel] until 1 o'clock, when he went to the University club. Upon his return to the hotel about 4 o'clock he found callers, and letters from New Jersey which commanded his attention. And here even Uncle Sam broke in on the arrangements of his secretary[1] and the governor had to come down to the hotel desk to sign for a registered letter. "He must sign for himself," said Uncle Sam's mail carrier, and so arrangements were broken long enough to have this done.

Later the governor posed for The News. A picture was taken while he was attending to some of his correspondence. After that more callers, and then the governor prepared to go to the Adams [Hotel] where he spoke to the Mile High club. This was his last speech to a Denver audience. This morning will be spent in rest, and at 12:15 he will leave for the West, going direct to Los Angeles.

Last night Governor Wilson expressed himself as pleased at the reception in Denver. "I always like to come to Denver," he said. His reception, say those accompanying him, has been most cordial here. The audience which greeted Governor Wilson at the Auditorium on Sunday night is the largest he ever addressed.

He spoke at one time to about 10,000 persons in the Stadium at Harvard, but this was an open air meeting. His hearers at the Auditorium Sunday night numbered more than 12,000.

And after it was all over the governor was asked how he liked being governor as compared with the work of college president. "O, I like it," he answered. "It's strenuous, but so was the other work sometimes."

The last hours of Governor Woodrow Wilson in this city are to be spent with relatives. These are Thomas R. Woodrow, special attorney in the city attorney's office, and Mrs. [Harriet] Woodrow Welles, of 1345 Franklin Street. There will be a family gathering at Mrs. Welles' home this morning, and luncheon will be served. Thomas Woodrow and Mrs. Welles are first cousins of the New Jersey executive. Governor Wilson's mother was a sister of the father of Thomas Woodrow and Mrs. Welles.

Printed in the Denver *Rocky Mountain News*, May 10, 1911.
1 Frank Parker Stockbridge.

A News Report of an Address to the Mile High Club of Denver

[May 10, 1911]

GANG POLITICS DENOUNCED BY WILSON

One hundred of the most prominent business and professional men of the city last night heard Governor Woodrow Wilson, of New Jersey, denounce in no uncertain terms the political machines of the day, and more especially the secret methods used by the leaders of the machines of both parties to secure the legislation they desire, or kill that which they do not want.

The speech delivered before the Mile High club at the Adams was the strongest the fighting governor of New Jersey has made since he left the East. He spoke in his usual forceful manner, and did not mince words.

Publicity, and publicity not in parlor language, was the weapon which he urged should be used to fight the conditions of the day. The initiative and referendum he commended in the highest terms as the most effective means to secure relief from these evils.

The subject of his talk was "The Relation of Business to Politics." The analysis of this question, he declared, led to some very ugly circumstances being revealed. He denounced the methods which prevail in legislative halls that allow secret committee meetings. The part banks play in politics also was roundly scored. . . .

At the bottom of the political conditions that have made this state of things possible lies the fact that in our American political system there is no explicit provision for responsible leadership, said the governor. Unlike every other country in the world, he said, there is no man or small body of men, such as the British cabinet, whom the community holds responsible for framing all the measures of the session. The demand for such leadership is the reason, he declared, why the public is coming to look more and more to its governors and presidents to guide legislation.

A governor, he said, is not happily situated to lead a legislature because he cannot sit with it and take part in its debates, and the only way he can legitimately influence legislation is by bringing the pressure of public opinion to bear upon individual members. This method, he said, while usually effective when intelligently applied was not entirely a fair one, for the reason that the members upon whom pressure is exerted have no opportunity for publicly debating the question with the governor.

He pointed out the dramatic effect that would result if the president of the United States could go upon the floor of the senate and there discuss the issues which he raises in his messages to congress. Public attention would be focused upon the debate, and both sides would receive full publicity. Now, he said, every public utterance of the president is published in every newspaper in the country, but those who would answer him can get no such audience, and the president can by mere dictum establish facts because nobody can contradict him before the whole people.

The need of the time, Governor Wilson concluded, is for responsible leadership—someone to drag things out of ambush, explain them to the people, and whom the people can hold responsible. There is no other way, he said, of breaking the stranglehold which money has on politics. He declared that the three rules for insuring popular government are, first, to simplify our institutions; second, to simplify our institutions, and, third, to simplify institutions. They should be made such that the man in the street can see all the processes of government, and understand everything that is done.

Among the implements for the simplification of political institutions the governor advocated the initiative and referendum as a valuable weapon, not to replace representative government, but to insure that representatives really represent. He cited incidents of legislation which had been directly against the interests of the people, and described in some detail the secret processes by which the Payne-Aldrich tariff bill was enacted through the influence of business on politics.

Printed in the Denver *Rocky Mountain News*, May 10, 1911; some editorial headings omitted.

From Ellen Axson Wilson

My own darling,   Princeton, New Jersey May 11, 1911.

You can imagine with what absorbing interest we are following your movements as far as we are able. *How* fine it all is! I am longing for more news though,—more papers,—a few, a very few clippings from Denver are all I have had. The "Times" gives but little, of course, and the other papers I see, the speeches, but few other details. I am hungry for all sorts of particulars. There was one fine article in the "Evening Post" on Sat., I think, telling exactly what I wanted to know.[1] But it seems to me that Stockbridge is not half as good a press agent as Bacon[2] and the "Evening Post" reporter[3] were during the campaign last fall. But the speeches do all that is *necessary*; they are *perfection*;—and I am not the only one who thinks so. How very interesting the story about the telephone from Denver!—the N. Y. reporter asking "what is the news in Denver" and the answer;—"the town is wild over Woodrow Wilson and is booming him for President." Even the "Times" had to put *that* in—as news![4]

By-the-way, *please* don't say again that you "are not thinking about the presidency." All who know you well know that that is *fundamentally* true, but *superficially* it can't be true; and it gives the cynics an opening which they seize with glee. The "Sun" of course had an outrageous little editorial about it.[5]

We are all well; I saw Margaret yesterday in New York. She looked extremely sweet and pretty. On last Saturday, Jessie, Nell and I went to Sea Girt. It was a perfect day and we enjoyed the trip extremely. The house is really most attractive, and the surroundings all that could be desired,—great stretches of well kept grass, and a few good trees. We took a long drive both to the shore and back into the woods in the State carriage with the two fine horses. General Murray[6] telephoned me an hour ago that he wants to come over this afternoon to "talk over Sea Girt" with me.

There is no Princeton news of sufficient importance to be mentioned to so busy a man. Prof Abbott is being talked about a little for President (of Princeton!) Dr. Jacobus was here and interviewed members of the faculty about it. They all like the idea but fear "it would kill him" as Mr. Capps bluntly puts it. Mr. Capps said so many *splendid* things about Mr. Angell,[7] and is so disappointed that his name has been dropped that I can't help being a little disturbed at your having thrown cold water on it. Mr. Capps thinks he would be beyond comparison the best man yet proposed (except of course, Fine.) He says he has grown a great deal in the last few years, and is not so nervous, that he is a man of splendid courage and the highest ideals, &c. &c. Moreover he *is* a good administrative officer; he has been "Dean of Deans" there in Chicago for several years, and two months ago was elected vice-president. Yet Mr. Capps thinks he could be got because he does not believe in the President.[8] Mr. Capps thinks he is not a pragmatist to hurt, and that it is rather foolish for the dept. to make a point of that. He does not *write* or speak about pragmatism; in fact he is not a philosopher at all but a psychologist. Don't you think it would be worth while to write a few lines to Dr. Jacobus modifying what you said before? We are so mortally afraid of this growing movement to stampede the alumni for Hibben. And we don't really believe Abbott will accept it.

But I mustn't write more for you havn't time even to *read* long letters. Ah! how I love, *love, love* you, dearest. I am with you in spirit *every moment.* May God bless you and keep you well and strong to do His work. I am alone, of course, so I can only send my own love.   Your devoted little wife,   Eileen.

ALS (WC, NjP).

[1] The New York *Evening Post*, Saturday, May 6, 1911, carried only a brief story on Wilson's tour, noting that he had spent May 5 in Kansas City as a "guest of civic organizations and the Knife and Fork Club," and that on the following day he had left for Denver, where he would remain for four days. Mrs. Wilson, rather than referring to this item, was thinking of a long news story which appeared in the *Evening Post* on May 8 under the title "Eager to Hear Gov. Wilson, West's Welcome to the Progressive from the East." Describing Wilson's listeners at the Knife and Fork Club as the "largest audience which this famous dinner-giving organization had ever got together," the story quoted Wilson as saying after the dinner: "I never felt such an inspiration from my audience before. I could feel the intense interest of the men to whom I was speaking in a way I have never before experienced."

The reporter also discussed Wilson's possible presidential candidacy, asserting that many Missourians did not think that Champ Clark was seriously considering running or that he should be taken seriously as a candidate, and that the field had really narrowed to Wilson and Judson Harmon. But what undoubtedly told Mrs. Wilson "exactly what she wanted to know" was a paragraph near the end of the story stating that Wilson was getting a "real rest" out of his journey and that he had declared on arriving in Kansas City that he had lost all traces of the fatigue which had beset him at the beginning of the tour and that he "never felt better."

[2] Charles Reade Bacon, who had reported Wilson's campaign speeches in 1910 for the *Philadelphia Record*.

3 Lawrence Perry, special correspondent for New Jersey politics.

4 *New York Times,* May 9, 1911.

5 The New York *Sun,* in an editorial, "Really!", had said:

> Seldom has a sweeter piece of bashful maiden art been offered to a public too unworthy of it than the Hon. WOODROW WILSON'S Denver waving away of the crown:
>
> "Really I have not thought about the Presidency."
>
> How did Governor WILSON discover the miraculous saving grace and merit of the initiative and referendum after warning the Princeton undergraduates against it—or them—for twenty years?
>
> Because he was not thinking about the Presidency.
>
> Why did Governor WILSON, who had long been clothed and starched with all the solemn grandeur of the college don, lament that the dear people had no nickname for him, doesn't yet, in fact, call him "WILSE" or "WOODY"?
>
> Because he was not thinking about the Presidency.
>
> Why is Governor WILSON now performing the duties of the office to which he was elected and for which he is paid by swinging around the circle in the West, pouring to a grateful populace the sincere milk of Bryaniac and Progressive reform?
>
> Because he has not thought about the Presidency.
>
> Really, there is a maxim the Greek and Latin of which it would be pedantic to mention to a wandering tribune, but in plain English it may be commended to this comparatively inexperienced canvasser: "Don't overdo it."

6 Charles Edward Murray, quartermaster general of New Jersey and manufacturer of Trenton.

7 James Rowland Angell, dean of the university faculties at the University of Chicago.

8 Harry Pratt Judson.

An Address to the Jefferson Club of Los Angeles[1]

[May 12, 1911]

Mr. Toastmaster[2] and Fellow Democrats:—Your toastmaster has given me a most generous introduction and you a most courteous reception. I am not sure, however, that with that introduction I fully retain my sense of identity. The introduction soars so much beyond what I have been accustomed to think of myself that I am afraid that I must begin with a running start in order to catch up with the conception. I suppose you thought that, as a radical, I felt very lonely in the East and have come out West for company. But I have this message to bring you, that I have plenty of company in the East. Do not suppose for a moment, gentlemen, that your fellow-citizens of the Eastern states are one whit less ready for the changes which must come upon us than you are. The men who have misled them, the men who have misrepresented them, the men who have held them back, may not be of your thought or your impulse, but the great mass

1 Delivered at a banquet in Hamburger's, a large department store with a restaurant and playhouse. A brief news report of this address is printed at May 13, 1911.

2 George Smith Patton II, prominent lawyer and Democrat of Los Angeles and father of General George Smith Patton, Jr.

of the American citizens, at any rate in the state of New Jersey, and in the state of New York, and I might go on with the catalogue, are as ready as you are for the political regeneration of this country.

Newspaper enterprise is an interesting thing. I met a number of gentlemen of the afternoon newspaper press on the train. They were most engaging fellows and, I am sure, wished to do me entire justice along with the handsome welcome which they extended to me. Apparently they were not satisfied with the expression of my sentiments, but finding that I held one opinion which was likely to be unwelcome in the State of California they were kind enough to promise in their published interviews this afternoon that I was likely to change that opinion.[3] I am sorry to say I shall have to disappoint you in that expectation. What I said to them and what they honestly misunderstood, no doubt, was that, like every man trained to inquiry, I was always open to conviction; but that is a very different thing from saying I expect to be convinced. I do not want you gentlemen to believe that I, the executive of another state, volunteer to thrust my opinions into your local politics. I want it distinctly understood that I understand it is none of my business. And I want you to know that such opinions as I did express were expressed only in answer to questions, which, as usual, I would not dodge. If a man insists upon asking me my opinions, he will certainly get them. I would only prefer, as a matter of taste, on some occasions, that he should not ask them.

Now, gentlemen, as I was coming here this evening and reflected upon the name of this association, my thoughts naturally went back to that great man whose name you have adopted. And I asked myself, what would Jefferson say if a number of men of the Democratic faith were gathered together in the year 1911, if he were present? Jefferson was the author of the Declaration of Independence. But the Declaration of Independence, so far as I recollect, did not mention any of the issues of the year 1911. I am constantly reminding audiences that I have the pleasure of addressing that the rhetorical introduction of the Declaration of Independence is the least part of it. That was the theoretical expression of the views of which the rest of the document was meant to give teeth and substance to. The Declaration of Independence is a long enumeration of the issues of the year 1776, of exactly the things that were then supposed to be radical matters of discontent among the people living in America—the things

---

[3] That is, that he did not favor the recall of judges. See the news report printed as the following document.

which they meant to remedy, to remedy in the spirit of the introductory paragraphs, but which the introductory paragraphs themselves did not contain.

Now, the business of every true Jeffersonian is to translate the terms of those abstract portions of the Declaration of Independence into the language and the problems of his own day. If you want to understand the real Declaration of Independence, do not repeat the preface. Make a new table of contents, make a new set of counts in the indictment, make a new statement of the things you mean to set right, and then call all the civilized world to witness, as that great document does, that you mean to settle these things in the spirit of liberty, but also in the spirit of justice and responsibility. If you remember how that great document calls on all mankind to witness that we are not doing this thing in the spirit of insurgents but in the spirit of free men, men who have the true interests of humanity at heart—now, in a similar spirit, how are we going to realize the conceptions of the author of the Declaration of Independence in our own day? If Jefferson were here I am sure that he would reargue the whole matter from the principles which he held so dear, and the chief principle which Jefferson held dear was this: that whatever was done must be done in the interests of the people as a whole. By this it was meant that every public servant must adjust his conception of public need not to the interests of particular classes, not to the interests of particular circumstances but to the interests of the general body of the nation, without regard to class, without regard in particular to any principles that might have been set up. It is our duty, therefore, to reconceive our politics and our policies in the common interest. Men have talked as if you could get action in politics by a sort of correlation of forces, by putting all the antagonistic forces in such a position as to run at one another, as if by contest you could work out concord, as if by rivalry you should achieve peace. The process is out of the question. Men must revise their thinking and revise their purposes, and alter their standards before you will settle the fundamental questions of our politics.

Let us look at the two things that have been giving us the most trouble. One of them is the political machine. We are not antagonistic to political organizations. We are not so young and inexperienced as to suppose that men can accidentally run together in a concert of action and accomplish political purposes. We know they must take counsel together. We know they must have understandings with one another. We know they must organize such means of co-operation as will make them most effective.

We are not fighting political organizations, but it is not political organizations that we mean, when we speak of the machine. By political organizations we mean that sort of organized co-operation which is intended to accomplish the establishment of principles in practice. That is what we mean by political organization.

Political machines are not organized to accomplish any political purpose. . . .

What we call the machine is the instrumentality by which big business controls politics. That is all that it is. It is inimical to the very spirit of democracy that any group of persons, no matter how important their occupation may be to the community at large, should control the politics of the nation. "Democracy" and "control" are absolutely antagonistic terms—contradictory terms. Anybody less than a majority who organizes control in the democracy is its enemy.

So that whenever you organize control by an interest, even though it may be in some aspects the legitimate interest of a single class, you are cutting at the very root of the whole structure. Some gentlemen have persuaded themselves that they were doing this in self defense. They have said that unless they had some means of controlling legislation under our somewhat confused and disorganized way of accomplishing legislation, that all sorts of law would be put upon them which would be unjust and to their detriment. And it has been necessary for them to stand in with the people who control politics in order to defend themselves. Ah, they have misunderstood the character of the American people. All they had to do if their business were legitimate was to find out exactly what was going on and let everybody else know it. And then nothing would have happened.

The only way to defend yourself against improper legislation in America is to let Americans know it is improper and it will stop. The great antiseptic in America is public information and public opinion. You can clarify and purify the worst things in our life by simply letting the eyes of honest Americans have access to them. So that we are driven to the conclusion that these interests design to accomplish things which they do not care to have exposed to the public view. They want privileges which are exclusive—they want those things which they alone should enjoy—they want protections to which they are not justly entitled.

Look at the other thing that is giving us trouble—it is simply another side of the same picture. Look at the corporations.

We are not hostile to corporations if corporations will prove that they are as much interested in the general welfare and the general development as we are. We are not opposed to anybody who is serving the public—who is honestly serving the public by giving them honest service and at a reasonable rate, not with the primary idea of squeezing and exploiting the public, but with the primary idea of serving the public. America is not jealous of wealth, but it is jealous of ill-gotten wealth. America is willing to give largess of infinite fortune to anybody who will serve her, but she is very chary, if she could have her own way, of giving fortunes to anybody who will impose upon her. . . . The alliance of these men with politics is the most demoralizing thing that could possibly descend upon any country. And it has descended upon us. Those are the things that need correction, in our politics, and these are the things to which a man who acted in the Jeffersonian spirit would have to address himself.

The question is not whether all men are born free and equal or not. Suppose they were born so, you know they are not. They may have been born free and equal, but they are neither free nor equal if things of this sort can go on and continue to go on so that the problem of [the] Jeffersonian is to discredit and break up the machine. How to dissolve the partnership between the machine and the corporations—that is the problem of modern democracy. If that is the problem, why are we going far afield? Why, instead of passing laws with regard to corporate action and the use of corporate money in politics, are we going abroad and saying, "We want the Initiative and Referendum and Recall," as if we skirted the outskirts of the whole business?

Why, it is because we do not feel that as things are at present organized we have really got access to our own government. In order to prevent these things from being done we have first got to force ourselves into the citadel. So long as machines can control nominations they can maintain these secret partnerships and understandings, in spite of us. So long as [the] legislature originates with the nominations of machines and take their orders from machines, public opinions play a small part in legislation, and the orders of the machine will always be the orders of the partnership and will be carried out. That is the reason we have made up our minds to take nominations into our own hands and dispense with the nominating machine. . . .

Another thing we have made up our minds to in most parts of America, and I do not think anyone in the East is so much behind you in matters of this sort—if we cannot get legislation from our legislature, then we will make it for ourselves. We are in the attitude of those who should say: "We elected you to do this, but for some reason we are too polite to inquire into your inability to do it. Therefore we relieve you of the necessity. We will do it ourselves. We don't need you. We know exactly what we want, we know how to formulate it and we know how to put it into effect." Some gentlemen talk as if that were destroying republican government. To my mind it is restoring republican government. It is reminding these gentlemen that in order to be representatives they must represent. In other words, it is recalling with a voice that is sufficiently audible, it is recalling these men to the conscience [a consciousness] of their real function.

Take the matter of recalling all elected officers. That is business. Nobody in his senses would continue to employ a person who refused to do what he had been employed to do. It is not yet the experience of America, and I venture to say it never will be, that men are recalled because they acted upon an honest difference of opinion and judgment from that which has been uttered by their constituents. The recall is going to be used, I feel safe in the prediction, against those who wilfully and dishonestly do the things which are contrary to the interests of their communities. One of the most interesting things I have been told since coming to this city is that Los Angeles, that stand[s] for the rest of the country as a place that has been more ready than the rest to try these recalled radical experiments, has, in the use of her new machinery, proved herself one of the most self-possessed and conservative communities in the United States. Of course, she has. You are representative Americans. You are not unlike the rest of America, and when people are running their own business they are always conservative. The trouble is that the machine is not conservative, because it is not running its own business—it is running your business and it does not care what it costs you—it does not care how many mistakes it makes, provided it keeps control and has the profits without the responsibility. But when you are running your own affairs you pay the bills. You suffer the consequences of your own mistakes. You are conscious at every turn of the matter that you are handling your own affairs and keeping your own fortunes in your own grasp. Nothing steadies a community like that. Nothing steadies a state or a nation like the consciousness that they really have their own choice. . . . That seems to me to be the moral of our present-day politics. In the first place, not to be abashed, not to say, apologetically, "Yes, I am a radical," but to say: "Yes, I am a radical, aren't you?"

Isn't everybody a radical in the sense in which I have just now described radicalism? The people are radical—that is to say, the people are ready for any reasonable programme that will get them the goods. The goods not being anybody's ruin, not any damage to the honest business of the country, but the modest control of their own affairs.

I will not permit without challenge the men who are holding back, the men who are afraid of the people, to use the handsome word "conservative" and appropriate that to themselves. I maintain that those of us who believe in the so-called radical programme are intelligent conservatives, and they are the unintelligent conservatives. The distinction which I make is that timeold distinction between liberals and Tories—between men who can move and men who are such Bourbons that they cannot forget anything and cannot learn anything, because the so-called standpatter is a man who is himself to the top of his bent. I suppose a man on an ice floe in the Arctic region thinks he is standing still, but he is not. There is a great drift of the universe under time. I suppose the so-called conservatives suppose they are standing where their fathers were. They are doing nothing of the kind, because the country is not where their fathers were.

There is a great drift, historically a glacial movement, that they are not aware of. That is the movement of inevitable and compulsive circumstances. I have said again and again that I am willing to let things alone if things will let me alone. If you will guarantee that things will stay at a tolerable pass I won't claim I am wise enough to change them. But when I see they are changing, when I see great tendencies are setting which are inimical to the happiness and prosperity of the whole country, I cannot stay still. I must bend with other men who see those same things to change those tendencies, to see the country is not debauched and ruined by them. And I challenge any man who sees the superficial signs of our times to state that things can stand still in America. They cannot stand still. You know that the thing works in the night while you are asleep. You know, while you are walking around with your hands in your pockets, whistling, thinking the world is going on as usual, there is a little group of gentlemen in some room, somewhere, putting up a job on you. If you will turn all the private rooms in the United States wrong side out, so everyone can see what is going on, I too will put my hands in my pocket and whistle. But as long as there are doors behind whose curtains gentlemen whom I could name are concocting schemes, I am going to keep hustling around looking through keyholes and knocking at doors, and finding out what is going on, and raising a hue and cry. It makes life more interesting, for one thing. . . .

And so it seems to me that the refreshing circumstances of our time is that the American nation is sitting up and taking notice. The old lethargy is gone. The new impulse of public duty, a new aspect of eagerness is coming into the veins of Americans again. I cannot be mi[s]taken about this. I have been addressing public audiences in this country for twenty years, and there is a look in men's eyes now when public affairs are discussed that I never saw there before, not a look of excitement, that forebodes danger or disturbance, but a look of keen intelligence and a sort of confident mental expectation that things are going to happen, that things are feasible, that ways have been discovered in which to make them happen, that a new atmosphere of confidence and of enlightenment has begun to spread abroad from one part of the country to another. So that, for the first time, we are able to handle things, not as partisans but as patriots, not as men who are trying to remember how they voted yesterday but as men who are confident how they mean to vote tomorrow. Not as those who are counting the cost to themselves but as those who are calculating the interests of the community with keen consciousness that they are part and parcel of the common fortunes of the men about them. I have never known a time when it was safer to discuss things and safer to attack things.

Without any intention of arguing, but to revert to the question of the recall of the judges, I will venture to say this: that if you believe in it, as I am told you do, the best thing a stranger can do is to tell you he does not believe in it and put you on your mettle to say why you believe in it. We are not children, we are grown up, and if we do believe in a thing we shall give our reasons therefor. And if we do not believe in it we should be able to give our reasons for it. And the result ought to depend upon the reasons, not upon the impulse. It is a case of "put up or shut up." It is a case of justifying your course or abandoning your course. It seems to me the most wholesome circumstance that can arise in America is when we are not deciding things by passion but by cool determination of what is just and reasonable and advantageous to do in the long run—not to satisfy present impulses, but to establish things that we want to stand by generation after generation. That is the only standard to set up here. I am not going to argue [it] here, because it is a pending issue in this state, and as I have said with perfect frankness, it is none of my business. But I do want to say that it is very refreshing to a man who has opinions to go out among people who want to know what his real thoughts are. They do not want to know what he hopes—they are not interested in his "weather eye." They are not interested in his surmise as to what may happen to him, but they are genuinely interested if he will pay them the compliment of being frank with them, to know what he really thinks without fear of favor, and they are particularly pleased when they find that the things he is afraid of are the things every man ought to be afraid of, because we ought to be afraid of ourselves, we ought to be afraid of the selfishness that is in the hearts of all of us; we ought to be afraid of that spirit of self-interest to which it is so easy to yield. We should be afraid of this brand of politics, regarding it as game, when we ought to regard the whole thing as pregnant with the vital issues of life.

We ought to be afraid of thinking of our own generation only, when we ought to think of the long future of America. Because I, for one, feel, as I am sure you do, that I would have reason to be ashamed of having sprung from a great race of Americans if I do not do everything in my power to make the future of America greater than her past. Born of a free people, we, above all other men, are under bonds to prove ourselves worthy of freedom. And not only that, but to hand the freedom on, enhanced, glorified, purified, in order that America may not look back for her credit upon the days of her making and of her birth, but look forward for her credit to the things that she will do in the advancement of the rights of mankind.

FPS T transcript with additions and corrections from the partial texts in the Baltimore *Sun*, May 14, 1911, and the *Los Angeles Examiner*, May 13, 1911.

A News Report About Wilson's Arrival in California

[May 13, 1911]

CROSSING STATE LINE DOESN'T CHANGE HIM.

Gov. Wilson of New Jersey, a Democratic Presidential Possibility, Comes to Los Angeles Firmly Opposed to Applying the Recall to Judges, Unlike a Political Tourist Who Preceded Him.

Hon. Woodrow Wilson, New Jersey's Governor, Princeton University's former president, and the White House hope of Democracy, crossed the State line between Arizona and California yesterday on his way to Los Angeles without changing his mind. Wherein he differed from an illustrious political tourist who came to California two months ago on the same route.[1] It shows a difference between radicals, at least.

For Gov. Wilson is a radical. He has admitted it repeatedly, and subscribes to all the Oregon, Arizona and California fads except the judicial recall. He is an advocate of municipal com-

[1] Theodore Roosevelt.

mission government and of Canadian reciprocity,[2] and as such entertains the idea that Democracy's hope may not be in vain. But he will not discuss whether he is a Presidential candidate or not.

But a Governor doesn't always travel with a skilled publicity man across the whole country at a time when politicians are making up their minds and make political speeches unless he has some faith in the promise of the future. So he entered California divested of practically all his present and past honors, and established in the public mind as a Presidential possibility.

The purpose of Wilson's visit is to speak before the City Club,[3] but his coming has inspired activity by the Princeton Club,[4] the Democrats, and the New Jersey Society,[5] and each will entertain him. After tonight's speech he will remain until tomorrow afternoon, when he will board the Yale[6] for San Francisco. There he is to speak Tuesday night. Later in the week he will speak in Portland and Seattle.

Wilson is simple, warm natured, frank. He has the pedagogic way of making his points. Earnestness more than eloquence impresses. He seems to believe absolutely all he says and what he says is radical though he brands it pure conservatism.

Now 55 years from date of his birth in Virginia, he retains abundant vigor of youth, is hardy and in splendid health, although his furrowed cheeks and slender physique suggest doubt as to the health. He is an omnivorous reader, a writer, a lecturer, and now a spellbinder. An author of many works on the politics and history of the American people, a lawyer and a doctor by degrees conferred by many schools and universities, he is to some extent a replica of the characteristics of his illustrious predecessor-tourist who changed his mind. Likewise Gov. Wilson is no friend of race suicide, as his three grown daughters testify. He loves the out-of-door life and nature study.

But he is against the recall of the judiciary.

Talking about the State line, Gov. Wilson was asked:

"Didn't you feel at once a new atmosphere and an altered state of mind on the important question of recalling judges."

[2] For a discussion of the reciprocity agreement and the controversy about it, see WW to Mary A. H. Peck, March 5, 1911, n. 3, Vol. 22.

[3] A news report of this address is printed at May 14, 1911.

[4] He dined with the Princeton Club at the Alexandria Hotel before speaking to the Jefferson Club of Los Angeles.

[5] The New Jersey Society gave him a reception at 9 A.M. on May 13 in the Alexandria Hotel.

[6] A steamer of the Pacific Navigation Co., which made the trip from Los Angeles to San Francisco in eighteen hours. However, Wilson changed his plans and made the trip on the "Owl," a Southern Pacific night train.

"I must confess that I didn't," said the Governor of New Jersey.
"In fact my mind has not changed at all on this question.
While I believe in restoring popular government, I fear the very
means which would produce immediate benefit in the case of
unfaithful administrative public servants might bring mischief
to the bench. We want judges who will decide the law, whether
we like the law or not. If we do not like the law there are political processes to change it. The initiative, referendum and the
recall are such processes. Our judiciary, in my judgment should
stand outside the pale of politics and that is where I would put
it long before I would turn to the [r]ecall."

This declaration is a contrast with the contrary statements
of Col. Roosevelt on the same question two months ago. On the
Arizona side Roosevelt was for the Arizona constitution, judges
recall and all.[7] On the California side he was met and converted
to the other end—for California at least. Then he hurried to San
Francisco and praised the passage of three laws that the Legislature had defeated the day before he praised 'em. Next he told
Berkeley how to vote against a Socialist, and the Socialist was
elected.[8]

With a meteoric splash of adversity like that preceding him,
Gov. Wilson has landed in the puddle of California radicalism
with more grace than Roosevelt did. If he does not fall down at
San Francisco and Berkeley, as the African hunter did, he will
get by all right, and Democracy's hope will remain effervescent.

Gov. Wilson deplores the presence of the judicial recall in
the Arizona constitution, as Roosevelt did not.

"But I would not refuse the State admission to the Union because of it," said he. "Opinions differ. I expect respect for my
own, and I respect those of others, even though I differ radically,
as I do on this one question."

After a pause he continued: "I would make the process of selection of judges such that only fit men could gain such a position. That is the true way. The trouble comes when concrete
cases are presented to the people. Unfaithful judges are discovered and there is no way to remove them except by impeachment.
Immediate rather than ultimate redress is sought, and the recall
is urged. Now it is true that we may have unfaithful judges,
but are they not so few that we can better afford to suffer them
until political processes eliminate them than to inspire an effort
to render popular rather than judicial decisions? To my mind

[7] See G. W. P. Hunt to WW, Jan. 2, 1911, n. 2, Vol. 22.

[8] Jackson Stitt Wilson, former Methodist minister and prolific author, had
been elected Mayor of Berkeley in 1910.

it is far better to reform the method of choosing judges than to endanger their independence, as the recall, I fear, will do."

As to all other offices Gov. Wilson favors the recall.

He points out that the system of appointing all judges, in use in many States, is better than electing them. Since his incumbency in New Jersey he has appointed seven or eight judges and at no time has either a bar association or any other influence sought to direct the appointments, he says. The judges are appointed for a term and are removable only by impeachment and the Governor declares that "Jersey justice" is synonymous with the truest administration of justice.

"I deem appointment far better than election," he declared, "unless the process of nomination and election is made so that the best men may be chosen. If they are not chosen it will be the fault of the people."

He is also an advocate of the commission form of government, and was instrumental in having this system extended by statute to thirty-two middle-class cities of his State. In his dealings with the Legislature he was radical and dominant much after the manner of [Hiram Warren] Johnson in California, and by similar methods drove through radical legislation.[9]

Gov. Wilson's first trip to California, although preceded by the hurrah of President-making, was as modest almost, as that of a commercial traveler. His retinue consisted of one impressed secretary, Frank Porter Stockbridge, of New York, magazine writer and Wilson enthusiast, and McKee Barclay, of the Baltimore Sun, which has found a Democratic Moses and intends to specialize on his promise.

Each of the trio possessed one suit of clothing and necessary other articles of apparel to be well dressed. One of them had two extra clean shirts—possibly the Governor. The remainder of their luggage is back toward the Colorado line somewhere.

"I don't know what I'll do for a dress suit," said the Governor.

"Every function is informal," said a Princeton man, who went to Barstow to met his old "prexy."

"Bless us," said the Governor, looking down at his plain gray suit.

They traveled not in compartments or staterooms, but in ordinary berths. The possible-President and his Warwicks looked like the usual eastern tourists. And so they acted. At every stop the Governor, with the enthusiasm of a Kid, jumped off the

---

[9] For a discussion of Governor Johnson and the work of the session of the California legislature just ended, see George E. Mowry, *The California Progressives* (Berkeley and Los Angeles, Cal., 1951), pp. 135-48.

train to have a view. When he got off at Barstow he found the advance guard of the Princeton grads in Southern California. Two were recognized by Wilson before they saw him. He was on the step of the moving train, so he jumped and seized their arms.

On the remainder of the trip other sections of reception committees from the City Club, Princeton Club and the New Jersey Society boarded the train. At San Bernardino Lynn Helm, who was a classmate of Wilson at Princeton, found the Governor just preparing to shave himself, but he postponed it for a chat with Helm at lunch. At Pasadena Jeff Chandler[10] headed a combined Princeton-Democratic group and another bunch represented the Jerseyites. When La Grande station was entered the Governor disembarked with Helm, and witnessed a furious rush from the waiting plaza, where 300 men stood. Many of them were singing songs of old Nassau and others were City Clubbers, hopeful Democrats and Mayor [George] Alexander.

The Governor was officially greeted by the Mayor, President E. C. Bellows of the City Club,[11] Lorin A. Handley of the Princeton committee,[12] and a hundred singing grads wearing the orange and black, and a hundred more of the City Club Reception Committee.

The Governor was taken at once to the Alexandria Hotel with his companions. As each took a room with a bath, and retired to it promptly, and reappearance close to the dinner hour indicated a change in appearance, it is assumed that another lie about Democrats has been nailed.

Printed in the *Los Angeles Daily Times*, May 13, 1911.

[10] Jefferson Paul Chandler, Princeton 1893, lawyer of Los Angeles.

[11] Edward Clark Bellows, consul general in Japan, 1900-1905; Los Angeles businessman and independent Republican.

[12] Lorin Andrew Handley, A.B., Hanover College, 1902, A.M., Princeton 1904; sometime educator, at this time city clerk of Los Angeles.

A News Report of an Interview and a Speech to the Jefferson Club of Los Angeles

[May 13, 1911]

250 DEMOCRATS AT BANQUET HAIL WOODROW WILSON

GOVERNOR REITERATES OPPOSITION TO JUDGES' RECALL

Princeton Alumni Shout Famous "Tiger Yell" as Toastmaster Introduces Distingushed Speaker

Governor Woodrow Wilson of New Jersey, traveling through the West on a "tour without political significance," was, last night, at the banquet given in his honor by the Jefferson Club, nominated for the Presidency by the toastmaster, George Patton. Several hundred Democrats stood up, waved napkins and beat their hands together in a frenzy of enthusiasm.

"I am not bothering my head about the Presidency," said Governor Wilson yesterday, in an interview given to an "Examiner" reporter. "I find plenty to keep me busy in my present job. I consider it the duty of a man in my position to be ready at any time to ruin his chances; that is to say, to act without regard to the effect it will have on his chances. If he cultivates the weather eye he proves himself unfit for the office he holds. For that reason I have endeavored studiously to exclude the thought of the Presidency from my mind altogether."

Governor Wilson believes that President Taft will be the candidate of the Republicans, the reactionaries controlling the convention, and that a progressive will be the Democratic nominee. He asserted to the "Examiner" reporter that he found both Democrats and Republicans all the way across the country predicting Democratic victory in the next election. . . .

Printed in the *Los Angeles Examiner*, May 13, 1911; one editorial heading omitted.

A News Report of a Luncheon Speech in Pasadena, California

[May 13, 1911]

GOVERNOR WILSON IS GUEST OF PASADENA

Greeted by More Than 300 at Luncheon at Hotel Maryland

Governor Woodrow Wilson of New Jersey, found that all Pasadenans are for the day, at least, democrats, or better, non-partisan enough to see a big man and know him when they see him.

No citizen of the United States has ever been given a heartier or more sincere greeting than that accorded the great reformer of the east, the historian of international reputation and the model college man and university president this afternoon, by the leading men of Pasadena.

Met in Los Angeles by a small committee, taken to Annandale Country Club where he was greeted by Mayor Thum[1] and the larger reception committee, Woodrow Wilson, the man, found several hundred interested men of the Crown City to greet him when he reached the Hotel Maryland.

[1] William Thum, author of *A Forward Step for the Democracy of Tomorrow* (Boston, 1910); Mayor of Pasadena, 1911-13.

Then followed an informal reception, in which Mr. Wilson met most of those present, personally. When asked how he liked Pasadena and the southland, Mr. Wilson said: "Splendidly. It is magnificent and the progress of your people is delightful and extraordinary. I have enjoyed my short stay here to the utmost.["]

It was nearly 12:30 o'clock when President Geohegan[2] of the board of trade escorted Governor Wilson to the table in the annex dining room. The governor had brought with him a little party of Princeton men and when the repast had been served it was a splendid welcome which Judge Belmont Perry, formerly of New Jersey[3] and president of the New Jersey society [delivered]. Judge Perry eloquently told why Woodrow Wilson is an honored guest of Pasadena, and then Rev. T. M. McNair, of Pasadena, a classmate of Governor Wilson at Princeton and a famous football star in his time,[4] paid a pretty tribute to the guest of honor in a brief address of welcome.

Governor Wilson was tendered an ovation when he started to speak and his address was liberally punctured by applause. His speech, which was in part as follows, was easily one of the strongest addresses ever heard in Pasadena:

"It is very delightful to find myself here among friends," began Governor Wilson, "for I instinctively realize that I am with friends. Not alone the little group of Princeton men, but men whom I know I can be friendly with.

"One very interesting thing I realize about you and that is that you are a sort of cross-section of American society. You are bred here, there and everywhere—detached pieces of old America, and you show the stratification more clearly than the people living in the older settled sections. You have been blasted from the rocks and old hill-sides of the east and show the true vein of ore. In fact, you are sample Americans.

"You are fortunate in having escaped in some degree from provincialism and do you know that New York is the most provincial place in the world? It views everything, all news, every endeavor, from the stand-point of its effect on New York. It looks at the happenings of Europe from that stand-point and when it hears that rich Americans are abroad it takes an interest because

[2] Harry Geohegan, president of Crown Hardware Co. of Pasadena.

[3] Former lawyer and Democratic politician of Woodbury, N. J., who had practiced law and engaged in journalistic work after moving to California in 1898.

[4] The Rev. Dr. Theodore Monroe MacNair, Princeton 1879, Presbyterian missionary in Japan and professor of history, economics, English, and anthropology at Meiji Gakuin, the Union College of the Presbyterian and Reformed Churches in Tokyo. He was in California on convalescent leave.

it knows that some day it will have to witness their return and handle their goods.

"Some time ago, I was the guest of the St. Nicholas club,[5] an organization made up of men who have resided in New York for some impossible length of time, and when they asked me to talk I told them frankly that I looked upon them with a great deal of curiosity, for all the rest of the country had been moving forward while they were simply standing still. They were really sitting at the seat of custom and taking toll.

"Many of the people of the east look upon the west as simply a development out of the east, which the west is not. I met one New Englander and told him that it seemed to me that many New Englanders looked upon the growth of all outside of New England simply as the expansion of New England.

" 'Well, isn't it true?' responded he.

"It is not true. Each portion is colored by its own life and is not merely the expansion of some old settled section. It is not the simple expansion of a pattern. The stuff is new. The color is new. We are in the west, a mixture out of all nations, a movement out of the south, a movement out of New England, all met and crystallized in a multiform life not merely localized prepossession. . . .

"We are here to retranslate the principles of this nation, not to reminisce about them. This is but the forecast of things which must come, and it is to meet these things that we should be prepared. The task is not an easy one.

"If you but knew of the inside tendencies of some of your universities you would know something of the problems, and they are problems in politics. Who are the trustees of most of these universities? They are usually men of large wealth and corporate connection. Be they ever so honest—and those I have met are honest in their views for higher education—their point of view is wrong. Their point of view is not the point of view for young men to be brought up under. I tell you that the college politician makes the real article look like an amateur.

"Those trustees are inclined to yield to those who command the greatest resources. That is a polite way to put it, is it not? Everybody implicated must change his point of view before the problem can be solved.

"How I wish that I could convince a large body of the men representing the big interests that there is no business which is

[5] About this affair, see the notes for an after-dinner speech printed at April 8, 1901, Vol. 12.

strictly a private interest. I wish that I could convince them of the wrong of that classic expression, 'The public be damned!' . . .

"What we want is men who will play the game fairly; men who will lay all the cards upon the table so that we can see whether the pack is stacked or not. . . .

"What the people want to know is a man's tendencies. They cannot expect to agree with him on all things but they want to know what he is about. Today the real business of politics is non-partisan. You, here in Pasadena, have taken the offices into you[r] own hands and do not elect officers on national party lines. This is a step in the right direction.

"No man should allow his stomach to become so squeamish that he does not allow himself to know the facts. The standpatter does not want to know the facts and when the dish is passed to him he says he does not like it. 'I know it's good though I have not tasted it,' says he.

"I tell you it is time to eat the food of truth because something is going to happen. The world is running away with you and the world is a pretty poor broncho to bust. Read the signs of the times for I tell you there is an extraordinary turn in the tide coming.

"I do not mean by this that everything is going to be upset, for it is not but if the gentleman insists upon being upset and the wave comes along, he probably will be. If you see an avalanche coming and you refuse to move you will probably be struck and you will never be missed.

"But I am counting on ordinary discretion. There are thousands of men in this country who have no consciences, but they do have a weather eye. The conscience of America is going to start the change and the weather eye is going to do the rest."

At the conclusion of the luncheon, Governor Wilson held another informal reception in the hotel lobby, after which he was taken back to Los Angeles in an automobile. As he left the dining room the Princeton men met, formed a circle and sang the songs of old Nassau. Governor Wilson joined in the singing and the cheers for old Princeton. The final[e] come [came] when the Princeton men gave three ringing cheers for the governor, who, to them, will always be the former president of Princeton.

Printed in the *Pasadena*, Cal., *Star*, May 13, 1911; some editorial headings omitted.

To Mary Allen Hulbert Peck

Dearest Friend,   Hotel Alexandria Los Angeles 13 May, 1911.

It may be impossible to-morrow (Sunday) to write more than a line or two, so I am seizing a spare moment to-day to begin my weekly message to the dear friend of whom I think so constantly, and whose thoughts, I am happy to know, follow me so generously wherever I go.

The journey has really been most interesting and delightful, so far. Here I am on the far coast, in California, with long days of travel back of me, and yet I am refreshed and rested, rather than fatigued. Here is proof enough of the strain I have been under for the past six months! A journey of three thousand miles, with a rush of engagements and speeches at every stop, is a rest and vacation!

To my great surprise and delight a letter from you[1] has followed me here,—dear Ellen was sweet enough to forward it. How happy I was to see it! But it makes me wonder where I am to send this hurried epistle, for it says that you may sail from Bermuda to-day! I shall send it to Miss Learned's[2] at a venture. Why do you go there,—where you will certainly have to work,—to determine the daily menu and manage the servants? Have you forgotten your experience the last time you were there? I have not—and you *ought* to go where you can really rest *and get well*.

May 15—The[re] was, as I feared, not a moment to write yesterday—and there is *only* a moment to-day. I am now in San Francisco and am scribbling this line to express my delight at finding another letter and note from you here![3] Bless you! How fortunate I am to have such a sweet and thoughtful friend! And the *tone* of these letters—the note of keen enjoyment in them—of returning health and spirits,—the delicious atmosphere of Bermuda and of thoughts in tune with the dear place of rest and beauty. My heart leaps up with joy at every sentence into which you put a passing rhapsody about the sea, the kids on the hillside, the sail flashing in the enchanted air. I know what these rhapsodies *mean*—I follow your thought and your mood with such ease and a pleasure so deep and comprehending that they mean returning health and joy in living, as distinctly as if I were with you and could see the light leap into your eye, the sunny smile flash out at me, as it always does when you are happy and your thoughts spring spontaneously out. How well I know and comprehend. I'd rather have those letters of inconsequential flashes than any other sort.

I do not know how to tell you of my journey. I have been

astonished to find out how much everybody knew about me beforehand and how cordial, how eagerly cordial, they are. They
seem really to think me one of the leaders of the country, to
whom the people, and men of all sorts, must look for successful
and enlightened and determined leadership. It daunts me to see
their admiration and trust. I shall have to be a much better man
than I really am now to deserve even a part of the confidence
they now have of me. My present "national prominence" will
probably not last till next year in its present proportions, but it
is extraordinary while it lasts. How great a matter a little fire
(i.e. a little honest performance) kindleth!

They will not let me write. They rush me forward from one
thing to another. I can only send my love to you all, speak my
delight that you are back where[4] (or *near* where) I shall be by
the 4th of June, tell you that I am well, and ask you always to
think of me as

Your devoted friend,   Woodrow Wilson

ALS (WP, DLC).
  [1] It is missing.
  [2] Florence J. Learned, proprietress of Elmwood Court in Pittsfield, Mass.,
where Mrs. Peck frequently stayed.
  [3] These are also missing.
  [4] At the home of the Washington Augustus Roeblings, 191 West State St.,
Trenton, N. J., where Wilson sent this letter.

A News Report of an Address to the City Club of Los Angeles

[May 14, 1911]

'PEOPLE OF U. S. SHOULD NAME SENATORS'
—WOODROW WILSON

Progressive Democrat's Speech Is Cheered
by Great Throng at the Auditorium

With an address before an audience that filled Temple Auditorium to the topmost gallery,[1] Governor Woodrow Wilson closed
his speech-making in Los Angeles last night. Today he goes to
San Francisco, and then to cities along the coast, preaching the
doctrine of Progressive Government and the principle of restoring the government to the people.

Governor Wilson likes to call himself a Progressive rather than
an Insurgent, and points out a distinction between the terms,
defining an Insurgent as one who has rebelled against the authority of the majority of his party, whereas a Progressive is one who
is taking the lead in the councils of his party. "But," he main-

tains, "if the Democratic party had been in power for the past fifteen years, I should most likely be now an Insurgent Democrat instead of a Progressive Democrat."

It was a busy day for the Governor, beginning with a reception by the New Jersey Society at the Alexandria in the morning, an automobile ride to the Annandale Club, where he met members of the Pasadena Board of Trade, then to the Maryland for luncheon, dinner at the California Club as the guest of Lynn Helm, and concluding with the address at the Auditorium. He did not confess to any feeling of ennui, however, and was at his best when he appeared before the immense audience. His entire discourse was delivered with a smile that betokened good humor, yet did not detract from the sincerity of his utterance. He told many droll anecdotes and started many a laugh, but through it all he rapped the power of corporate influence in politics and described in serious manner the steps that are being taken by the people to get control of the government for themselves.

Governor Wilson's delivery was of a character that compelled attention, and his address was of the kind that prompted frequent interruptions of applause. Seated on the platform were nearly four hundred men—city officials, county officials, members of the City Club and their guests. Mayor Alexander occupied a seat alongside of Governor Wilson, and General E. C. Bellows, vice president of the City Club, who acted as chairman, sat on the other side. At the left of the stage was a jolly party of Princeton alumni, and they let loose the Princeton yell when Governor Wilson made his entrance and when he was introduced. . . .

Governor Wilson spoke entirely without notes or manuscript and did not once hesitate in his discourse. At the close of his address he was compelled to remain on the platform for a few moments to accept the felicitations of hundreds in the audience. . . .[2]

Printed in the *Los Angeles Examiner*, May 14, 1911; two editorial headings omitted.
[1] To an audience, according to the *Los Angeles Daily Times*, of 2,500.
[2] Here follows Wilson's advance text.

From Ellen Axson Wilson

My own darling,   Princeton, New Jersey May 15, 1911

I wanted to write a real letter tonight but a visit and some necessary business interferred and now it is nearly half past ten; and I have had a very tiresome day and can scarcely keep my eyes open. So it must be only a little note after all;—still I do not really believe that you have time to *read* more during this wild Western tour!

My amazement at your powers of endurance is more profound than usual tonight because of the exhausting effect upon me of the awful club "breakfast" which came off today here at the Inn.[1] It lasted four hours, there were a dozen speeches, most of them very poor;—and I was bored almost to extinction. So I am perfectly sure that I would rather die than go to as many public dinners as you do. All the other women at the table with me had to make speeches later and of course had no conversation in the mean time. I had to do all of that. It was deadly.

Thank you very much, dear, for the clippings. They were most welcome; and the telegrams still more so. The one from Los Angeles was especially satisfactory and reassuring. I am inexpressibly thankful that you are standing it so well and *enjoying* it indeed. And what a wonderful triumph you are having! And no one is in the least surprised for all *knew* beforehand that it would be so. As the "Press" said they are "so worn to a frazzle praising" you,—that they take every sort of demonstration as a mere matter of course.[2] News comes from Washington that Bryan has now conceded your nomination.[3] Whether true or not I do not know. I enclose todays editorial from the "True American." I think it handles that remark of yours which has caused so much comment very well.[4] Another paper defended you well too. It said that your mind was occupied not with an *office* but with *principles*, and that you were equally ready to work for them as a leader or in the ranks.

The children have, I dare say, had a great day;—they went all the way to Phila. in an automobile, with the Huntingtons,[5] leaving at half past seven. They were in the highest spirits over it, and as it has been a perfect day I am sure they have had a good time. I am not leaving until Friday and they will come back on Thursday early to help me pack for the summer. But I shall have Titus[6] and do all the heavy part tomorrow.

Your dear birthday telegram came a little while ago. It was *lovely* in you, dear, to remember to send it amid all your distractions, and I *love* you for it,—as well as for everything else that you say and do. Ah, dearest, how happy you make me,—and how passionately I love you! I am in every heart throb—in every thought,   Your own   Eileen.

ALS (WC, NjP).
  [1] She referred to the first subscription breakfast of the Present Day Club of Princeton, a women's organization founded in 1898, held at the Princeton Inn.

2 She probably referred to a recent news story in the New York *Press*.

3 At the end of a news story, "Governor Wilson in the West," *Princeton Press*, May 13, 1911, the reporter commented on the creation of Wilson-for-President clubs and added: "In Washington a campaign button inscribed 'For President Woodrow Wilson,' under the Governor's portrait, is being worn by his advocates, and it is reported that Mr. Bryan has become convinced that Governor Wilson will be the Democratic candidate for President."

4 The enclosed editorial, "Woodrow Wilson's Leadership," Trenton *True American*, May 15, 1911, sought to explain Wilson's comment in Denver to the effect that he was not thinking of the presidency. After noting manifestations of incredulity, including those of the New York *Sun*, it said: "Yet every man and woman who knows Woodrow Wilson well knows that he told the truth. WOODROW WILSON'S MIND IS NOT DISTURBED BY THE BUZZING OF ANY PRESIDENTIAL BEE." Wilson, the editorial continued, had always thought first of his duty to the people who had entrusted to him the administration of the affairs of a great state. He had performed that duty with "a fidelity and completeness that as compared with the average public man's record is nothing short of marvelous."

5 The Editors have been unable to identify them.

6 Columbus A. Titus, janitor, of 58 Wiggins St., Princeton.

A News Report of a Busy Day in San Francisco

[May 16, 1911]

Presidential "Bee" Fails to Buzz Fast Enough to Keep Pace With Jerseyite.

SILENT ON HIS CANDIDACY.

Woodrow Wilson, Governor of New Jersey, arch apostle of progressive Democracy, nemesis of ring politicians and prominent candidate for the Democratic nomination for President in 1912, spent a Rooseveltian day in this city yesterday, despite the fact that he does not happen to be on the same side of "progress" as the redoubtable Colonel.[1]

Governor Wilson arrived here from Los Angeles at 8:30 in the morning; at 9 he was housed at the Fairmont; within ten minutes thereafter a stream of callers kept the Governor and his two secretaries busy until lunch time, when he was rushed off to the University Club, where he was the guest at a luncheon given by Charles N. Black and A. S. Lilley.[2]

The University Club luncheon hardly over, he was rushed off to the Argonaut Hotel, where local members of the Democratic State Committee were awaiting his arrival. He remained with the committee until a few minutes past 4, then returned to the Fairmont Hotel, where a group of newspaper representatives and a corps of camera men were in waiting to secure views of his person and his opinion on every conceivable question, public and private.

The Governor good-naturedly received those in waiting, and replied to their many questions with the best of humor, despite the fact that he appeared rather fatigued from the activities of the day and needed a respite to prepare for the speech which he made at the banquet tendered him at the Fairmont last night by the members of the Princeton, Yale and Harvard clubs of this city.

Informed of the decision of the United States Supreme Court dissolving the Standard Oil Company of New Jersey, the parent corporation of the Standard interests throughout the world,[3] he quickly replied:

"That is just what I have been expecting. The decision is in line with others that have been laid down by the courts throughout the country. Just as the people are progressing, so is that sentiment to be noticed in the courts of this country. Other decisions of a similar nature, I am certain, will surely follow. In New Jersey there is no doubt whatever that we will now begin to reform the laws of the State regarding the incorporation of companies."

Asked for his opinion concerning the Progressive movement here and in the East, Governor Wilson stated that the result of breaking away from party lines was more apparent on the Coast and in the states adjoining the Coast States than in the East. He said:

"The sentiment is general everywhere. But the general protest against the way in which the machines of both parties have been bunkoing the people seems to have had a more practical outlet here than in the Eastern States. California takes its place among the foremost of the progressive sections of the country. I say this with reference to both parties. The party division line is being eliminated all over the country, but nowhere to the extext [extent] that it is here."

Reference to the recent socialistic victory in Berkeley brought from the Governor the remark that in his opinion it would be found that the vote for socialist candidates throughout the country in the recent spring elections was a 20 per cent socialist vote and an 80 per cent protest vote.

Despite the many interviews hurled at the head of the visitor and the volley of questions asked throughout the day, he refused absolutely to make any statement regarding his candidacy for the Democratic nomination for President of the United States other than to say that he had never heard of the nomination being refused.

Governor Wilson will be entertained at luncheon today by the president of the University in Berkeley,[4] after which he will deliver an address at the Greek Theater. The lecture is scheduled for 2 o'clock, which will be open to the public in general. He leaves for Portland at 9:40 o'clock tonight.

Printed in the *San Francisco Chronicle*, May 16, 1911; some editorial headings omitted.

[1] Theodore Roosevelt.

[2] Charles Newbold Black, Princeton 1888, vice-president and general manager of the United Railroads of San Francisco, and Alexander Spinning Lilley, Princeton 1892, building contractor of San Francisco.

[3] Rendered by Chief Justice Edward Douglass White on the previous day, it held the Standard Oil Company to be a combination in restraint of trade and ordered this holding company to divest itself of its thirty-three subsidiaries by transferring back to the stockholders of the original companies the shares which they had exchanged for shares in Standard Oil. In his decision, White declared that the Sherman Act did not prohibit all contracts and combinations which on their face seemed to be in restraint of trade, but only those which the courts might deem to be unreasonable, that is, those entered into or formed for the direct purpose of restraining interstate or foreign commerce. Heretofore, the Supreme Court had ruled that the Sherman law proscribed all restraints, reasonable (that is, those ancillary to an otherwise legal contract) and unreasonable. Since 1897, White had argued that the framers of the act had intended to outlaw only unreasonable restraints. White's view finally prevailed in the Standard Oil decision, and the so-called rule of reason was established in American judicial doctrine. For Wilson's later assessment of the effect of the decision on Standard Oil, see n. 4 to the address printed at June 2, 1911.

[4] Benjamin Ide Wheeler.

A News Report of an Address in San Francisco

[May 16, 1911]

WILSON HAILED AS POLITICAL PROPHET

Governor of New Jersey Given True Collegiate Welcome at Banquet Here.

Governor Woodrow Wilson of New Jersey made 400 members of the Harvard, Yale and Princeton Clubs, gathered at a banquet in his honor at the Fairmont Hotel last night, squirm with mingled emotions.[1] Some of them laughed, others blushed.

The former president of Princeton University and the possible candidate of the Democratic party in 1912 for President of the United States, is a very candid man. Also he hits straight from the shoulder. . . .

[1] Governor Johnson had been scheduled to introduce Wilson but refused to attend the banquet when he learned that it had been arranged for and was to be attended by a number of the representatives of San Francisco's largest corporations, including many of his bitterest political enemies. Ray S. Baker, *Woodrow Wilson: Life and Letters* (8 vols., Garden City, N. Y., 1927-39), III, 222. The reasons for the discomfiture of many of the banqueters will soon become apparent.

Getting away from an academic discussion of what is wrong with politics in America, he came down to the word "you."

"I find hope," he said, "in the fact that a man such as I is able to talk to and come into contact with the very men who do such things."

"Such things" referred to getting representation in State bodies for special interests, not the people as a whole. In this connection he had spoken of modern methods of bribery—such as teaching representatives that they could not get accommodations at banks or be successful in their business unless they did as the "big interests" wanted them to do.

Then he went on to tell these well-groomed men of affairs that they were honorable men, but that they had not realized what they were doing in a political way.

"You thought you were acting in self-defense," he said, "that you were defending property. As a matter of fact, you were debauching business and injuring property."

These direct sentiments were received with great cheering.

The Governor came to San Francisco with a nicely prepared analysis of political conditions that he thought would fit out here. But his few days on the coast taught him new things. He threw away his old speech[2] and talked the latest thing that came into his mind.

Applying the microscope to political things, he found what he was pleased to call "fragments." He found California peculiar. It was part of, and yet separated from, the rest of the country. He found here a virile body of individualists. And here was the danger.

"We have been too busy chasing after wealth and material things for our individual comfort to pay much attention to things for the common good," he said.

"Why cannot California," he asked, "a State of extraordinary variety, set the United States an example of voluntary concerted action in matters of the public welfare?"

Governor Wilson had gained the impression in the South that most of the people in the State came from the East. He formed a fine theory on this basis, but Garret W. McEnerney, toastmaster at the banquet,[3] told him a few things about the Native Sons, and that theory went up in the air.

The country is certainly in need of a physician, according to the Governor. He was referred to by all the speakers as a rare doctor in things political, but no mention was made of things

---

[2] A printed press release is in WP, DLC.

[3] Garret William McEnerney, prominent lawyer and Democrat of San Francisco.

presidential. Not even Theodore Bell[4] in his swing of oratory about the eternal snow on the mountains and the ever living roses in the valleys, went so far as this.

The country was compared to a man who has "lost himself" in a desert. The man has not "lost himself," the Governor explained, but only his bearings. We have been walking with downward gaze and have awaked to see a strange landscape.

"I stand for progressive principles," he said, "but I do not stand for destruction. I have studied the past and I know that these progressive policies mean a renewal, a freshening, a recreation of the principle of self-government.

"You must let the people into the game or they will break in."

The Governor was received with marked enthusiasm and his speech was interrupted several times by cheering. College yelling lent a familiar flavor to the scene from the Princeton professor's point of view. . . .

"The reform processes of our present programme," he said, "are processes of restoration, they are processes of recreation. In representing these reform programmes I am representing their renewal and not their destruction.

"Moreover, gentlemen, I have seen the inside of politics. I have seen it before I stood on the inside of politics. In other words, I knew what some of these gentlemen were up to before I made the rash attempt to stop some of them.

"Money is at the bottom of it all, but not money that you can put your hands on—not bribes. That is all old-fashioned and crude. The present plan is, if they find men who do not do what they are told to do in politics, they cannot get accommodation at the banks—that is the long and short of it.

"Now, when are you going to take charge of this matter? Do you approve of it? You don't for a moment excuse that; and yet you know that those things are going on.

"I do not know that it is going on in California. I do know it is going on in New Jersey. I know it is going on in many other places, and that is why I form a shrewd conjecture of California.[5] Now, believing you to be what I have analyzed you to be, representative Americans, taken from all parts of the country, being men alert to your own interests—is it not possible for you to assert your own judgments and see that they do not take place?

[4] Theodore Arlington Bell, congressman from California, 1903-1905; unsuccessful Democratic candidate for governor in 1906 and 1910; at this time practicing law in San Francisco and Napa, Cal.

[5] William Henry Crocker, president of the Crocker National Bank of San Francisco, speaking for Yale after Wilson, evoked great laughter by saying: "I am not guilty. We do not carry on banking in San Francisco the way they do in New Jersey." San Francisco Examiner, May 16, 1911.

"The man who didn't take orders couldn't get accommodation at the bank or couldn't get invited into polite circles. Your real, genuine insurgent didn't get invitations. He is not only a political but a social outlaw. So by one process or another—of cold water and hot water—we suppress them.

"Now the thing that makes me hopeful and not pessimistic is that I can say such things in companies that do such things, and not only not be put out of the room, but meet with most generous applause, because, gentlemen, the whole thing is that you are perfectly honest—I give you the credit of belonging to that large class of men who did these things and didn't realize what they were doing.

"They thought they were acting in self-defense—they thought they were defending property, their independence in business, whereas all along they were making property less secure than it ever was before and debauching business; making property less secure, because if you keep the average rank and file of the people of the United States out of the game they will break into the game some way or other and upset property and everything else.

"Men are asking themselves now not 'Which party do I belong to?' but 'What lines of cooperation do I want to change; what programmes are the wisest programmes?' That is what men are asking themselves.

"The general question of debate is that things are wrong. Every man who respects himself and who loves his country must address all of his energies to remedying those wrongs.

"How are we going to get together in order to solve these problems? I haven't got a potent remedy. I have no pill against earthquakes. I have no small corrective for a complicated situation. My mind thinks in one measure at a time, but I want them to follow in sequence. So with politics.

"What we want now to do is to determine our direction just as much as to determine our speed. Let's start even and agree upon the direction, and then afterwards, since the progressives outnumber the conservatives, we will set the pace.

"We are now about to find out whether America is entitled to her prerogative. Her prerogative is to exercise constructive genius. We have now to show whether we can point the road once more towards those table lands of achievement and principle to which mankind may follow for all time."

Printed in the *San Francisco Examiner*, May 16, 1911; some editorial headings omitted.

A News Report of an Address on Corporations at Berkeley, California

[May 17, 1911]

PRINCETONIAN IS WARMLY GREETED

Scholarly Arraignment of Wild Finance Evokes Auditors' Prolonged Cheers.

FLAYS BIG CORPORATIONS.

BERKELEY, May 16.—"Certain notorious financiers have been taking joy rides in our corporations, and now instead of punishing the lawless chauffeurs we are trying to wreak vengeance by destroying the machines. Dissolution is possible, but it is unnecessary. Save what might be a useful social agency and punish the men who have been maladministering it."

In an address delivered before 5000 men and women in the Greek Theater yesterday afternoon, Governor Woodrow Wilson of New Jersey thus epigrammatically summarized his opinion of the United States Supreme Court decision dissolving the Standard Oil Company. This utterance was part of an address on corporations, which was replete with epigrams and commonplace homilies used with good effect by the speaker to illustrate the various phases of what he called "the most absorbing topic now before the American people."

Governor Wilson's address was interrupted by numerous outbursts of applause, and it was noticeable from the start that the audience was heartily in accord with the sentiments he voiced. His remark that "the progressives were engaged in a process of preserving business by moralizing it," evoked three minutes of uninterrupted cheering. His statement that the people were "engaged in a justifiable burglary in that they are trying to break into their own institutions," brought cries of "Yes, yes," from different parts of the amphitheater.

Governor Wilson was introduced by the President of the University of California, who reviewed the conditions that have brought about the present political upheaval. He referred to Governor Wilson as one of those who had been largely instrumental in opening the eyes of the masses, and declared that he was a citizen of whom every college man might well be proud. . . .

As the commencement-week guest of the State University authorities, Governor Wilson was entertained by the president of the University at luncheon here today.

Mayor Beverly Hodgehead of Berkeley,[1] Warren Olney Jr.,[2] Professor Adolph C[aspar]. Miller of the department of economics, Professor Charles Mills Gayley, head of the English department; Secretary Stockbridge and R. Barclay were also guests at the luncheon.

Following the luncheon, a short trip of inspection of the University campus, including the new Doe Library building and California Hall, preceded the address in the Greek Theater.

Members of the Princeton clubs of Los Angeles and San Francisco attended the exercises. Students of the Berkeley High School were dismissed during the afternoon to enable them to attend the lecture.

Governor Wilson left last night at 9:40 o'clock for Portland, where he will remain a day before proceeding to Seattle.

Printed in the *San Francisco Chronicle*, May 17, 1911; some editorial headings omitted.

¹ The current and first Mayor of Berkeley. He was about to be succeeded by Jackson Stitt Wilson.

² Member of Page, McCutcheon, Knight and Olney of San Francisco; attorney for the regents of the University of California and general counsel for the Western Pacific Railway Co.

A News Report and Interview

[May 18, 1911]

U'REN FIRST GAINS GOV. WILSON'S EAR
VISITOR IS IMPRESSED

MEDFORD, Or., May 17.—(Special.)—W. S. U'Ren has stolen a march on the Democrats of Oregon. Woodrow Wilson, possible Presidential candidate for President next year on the Democratic ticket, has been roped and tied by the man from Oregon City, who quietly slipped down over the California line today and is now personally conducting the visitor into "our midst."

When Governor Wilson's train rolls into the depot at Portland, Mr. U'Ren will not be in evidence. His plan fulfilled, he will quietly drop off the train at Oregon City and have nothing to say for publication. But Governor Wilson will have been informed on the political situation in the state and will know how to greet and what to say to certain of the prominent ones in political circles.

Quietly, with no word to any of his friends, Mr. U'Ren left Oregon City last night and journeyed south. He traveled to Hornbrook, Cal., and there swung aboard Mr. Wilson's train and made himself very much at home in the Governor's drawing-room.

"Just for a friendly chat," explained Mr. U'Ren this afternoon, but those who have followed his career are wondering just what he told Governor Wilson and what effect it will have when the

Democrats of the state find out about it. The result of his "friendly visit" may be manifest before the Governor leaves the state.

"So this is Oregon," commented Governor Wilson this afternoon at [as] his train rolled over the Oregon line and for the first time he found himself within the boundaries of the state, the laws of which he took occasion to laud in his inaugural address last Fall in New Jersey.

"I am very glad to be here, and shall enjoy my stay with you very much indeed. For years I have watched this state and I am very glad that I am to meet your representative men and become acquainted first-hand.

"You may tell the people of Oregon," Mr. Wilson added to the representative of The Oregonian, who met the train at the state line, "that I feel they have done a great deal in developing the movement of popular government throughout the country. The state enjoys an enviable reputation for progressive laws and politicians the country over have their eyes turned this way. We of New Jersey have adopted many of your laws and hope later to secure the initiative and referendum.

"The laws of recent years adopted in this state seems [seem] to me to point the direction which the Nation must also take before we have completed our regeneration of a Government which has suffered so seriously and so long from private management and selfish organization. Primary laws should be extended to every elective office and to the selection of every committee or official in order that the people may once for all take charge of their own affairs.

"To nullify bad legislation the referendum must be adopted and it is only a question of time until it will be extended to the Nation. The better education of the people, through the various states, of which Oregon was the first, will enable them to pass intelligently upon National measures. In such manner will popular government be lifted from the ranks of theory to actuality and a democracy which represents the will of the people be established."

Governor Wilson evaded a direct question as to his candidacy for the Presidency on the Democratic ticket next year, saying that many things could happen between that time and this that might throw an entirely new light on the situation. However, he said that it was his belief that the Democratic forces would be victorious in November, 1912.

He declined to discuss the merits of Champ Clark, Judson Harmon or Joseph Folk in connection with the nomination.

"The Presidency of the United States," he said, "is not an office for which a man can start out and declare he is fitted. On the other hand no man can refuse such a nomination for the office if it be offered him.

"No," he said in reply to a question, "I have not yet made up my mind on the subject of the recall of the judiciary. I am open to conviction but I as yet fail to see where it would be a wise law in many respects, as fear of the people's displeasure might lead some judges to cater more to popular expression than to an interpretation of the law. It is a great problem, and must be approached cautiously."

Mr. Wilson declined to discuss the recent decision of the Supreme Court in the Standard Oil case, as he had not seen a copy of the decision. "I have noticed much newspaper comment on the subject," he said, "especially in regard to the use of the word 'unreasonable,' and from this it appears that the Supreme Court was legislating and not interpreting. However, this is not my view, as until I have read the text of the decision I must decline to express myself."

Mr. Wilson was asked regarding the appointment of Henry L[ewis]. Stimson, of New York, to the Cabinet of President Taft[1] and whether this was an effort on the part of the President to bring the warring factions of New York into harmony.

"On the face of it," he replied, "it looks as if such were the case, but as I have been in the West the past two weeks I am not fully in touch with the subject. I know nothing of Mr. Stimson's qualification for the place.

"While I am in Oregon," continued Mr. Wilson, "I intend to study at first hand the workings of the initiative and referendum. I believe that this law is really a solution of popular government, as the lawmakers know that the people who elected them can at any moment take the lawmaking back into their own hands. Representatives working in the shadow of such a law are persuaded to keep in line.

"New Jersey will also hold a primary election in the Spring to express a preference for Presidential candidates and will instruct the state delegation how to vote at the convention. This is one of the provisions of our primary law and I feel that it is good."

"Will you carry your state at this election?" he was asked.

"I would not be at all surprised," he answered.

Governor Wilson while passing through the Rogue River Valley constantly commented upon the beauties of the valley, which

---

[1] As Secretary of War.

at this season of the year is perhaps more beautiful than at any other season. He expressed a great desire to reach Portland and get into immediate touch with conditions in the state.

At Medford Governor Wilson was met by a large number of business men, who greeted him as "Our next President." The Rogue River University Club had a large delegation to meet him. He was asked to deliver a five-minute address, but asked to be excused, as he has a severe cold and his voice is strained from speaking.

Printed in the Portland *Morning Oregonian*, May 18, 1911.

A News Report About Wilson's Arrival in Portland, Oregon

[May 19, 1911]

"PLACE TOO BIG TO DECLINE"—WILSON

New Jersey Governor Has One Answer to Question Always Asked Him.

Governor Wilson, of New Jersey, who arrived in Portland yesterday and will remain through today, has grown accustomed on one trip across the United States to hearing one question asked —and to returning the same answer.

"Are you a candidate for President of the United States?" is the question every interviewer, in big city and small town and in village and hamlet, asks.

"The position is too big to be a candidate for, and too big to refuse," is the answer, invariably. It is not many words for a university president to have learned by rote. The question never varies. The answer is always the same.

"My ideas of reform," he said yesterday, "are not negative, but rather reconstructive. The editorial in the Oregonian this morning expressed my views better than I can say now, and you may quote what was said as being my real sentiments."[1]

"If I have observed any difference between the East and the West, it has not been in political sentiment, but in temperament. There is more freedom of action here in the West; you are younger and there exists a sort of brotherhood of pioneering. This is manifest in a desire to get out and move quickly in public matters that is more apparent with you than with us."

Mr. Wilson said that he understood the "Oregon system" to mean a system that took to the primary all of the elective offices, from President down, and eliminated party conventions.

"In New Jersey we differ somewhat with you," he said. "We have party affiliations still. Our voters declare their preference for United States Senator and the candidates for the Legislature sign a statement that they will vote for the person receiving the largest number of votes in the party.[2] Republicans vote for their own candidates and Democrats for theirs. Of course, I favor the Oregon method, without regard to party affiliations."

From the hour of his arrival at the Portland Hotel Mr. Wilson received a steady stream of callers. He remained in his rooms, the suite occupied by Colonel Roosevelt on the occasion of his recent visit, all day, except for a trip to the home of his cousin, Captain A. M. Wilson,[3] at 686 Hoyt street, where he took luncheon with Captain and Mrs. Wilson[4] and their daughter, Elizabeth. He afterward visited friends of Governor Wilson's wife on Portland Heights. The automobile in which he began the journey was mired near Twentieth street and he went the rest of the way by streetcar.

On his return to his rooms Mr. Wilson declined an invitation to address the Oregon chapter of the American Mining Congress and received a delegation from the Democratic State Central Committee, headed by Bert Haney[5] and M. A. Miller, of Lebanon.[6] Samuel J. Rich, Democratic National committeeman from Idaho,[7] joined the conference later and with them all the visitor for an hour informally discussed the political situation.

Harvey Beckwith, president of the Portland Commercial Club,[8] greeted Mr. Wilson on his arrival from the south and introduced his associates, Ben Selling, W. A. Montgomery, W. J. Hofmann, Arthur L. Fisk, B. O. Souffer[9] and M. A. Miller. The reception committee escorted him in an automobile to his hotel, viewing him with interest all the while. They found him to be a man of medium stature and slight frame, with the appearance and manner of a student. Mr. Wilson has a soft voice. Though Mr. Wilson is a Virginian, he has no peculiarities traceable to his Southern ancestry. He wears glas[s]es and has large eyes and the high brow that goes with a poetic temperament. He speaks with distinct endeavor to be precise. Often he concludes with: "That is not just as clear as I wish to put it. Let us try it another way." His greeting of his visitors is warm, his handshake hearty. His manner of dress is neat. He wears a watch chain that crosses his vest from pocket to pocket. He looks his auditors straight in the eyes.

There is to be no change in the programme for today. The address at the Armory will be delivered at 7:30 instead of 8 o'clock. There will be a formal dinner in his honor at the University Club at 6 P.M., preceded by an informal reception beginning at 5:30 P.M. There will be a luncheon in his honor at the Y.M.C.A. by the "Oregon Advocates of Better Government." He will leave at 10 P.M. for Seattle.

Printed in the Portland *Morning Oregonian*, May 19, 1911; some editorial headings omitted.

[1] He referred to an editorial entitled "Plain Words and True," Portland *Morning Oregonian*, May 18, 1911. It quoted approvingly Wilson's statement in Kansas City that the initiative and referendum were restorative measures necessary only when genuine representative government did not exist on the state level; deplored the excessive use to which they had been put in Oregon ("The Legislature is being set aside. It has been degraded and humiliated."); and expressed the hope that Wilson would suggest a means of restoring representative government in Oregon.

[2] The New Jersey procedure was not precisely as Wilson stated. See n. 1 to the news report printed at April 14, 1911, Vol. 22.

[3] Alfred McCalmont Wilson, Princeton 1895, son of John Adams Wilson, Woodrow Wilson's first cousin.

[4] Edythe Pardee Wilson.

[5] Bert Emory Haney, member of the law firm of Joseph and Haney of Portland and chairman of the Democratic State Central Committee.

[6] Milton Armington Miller, merchant of Lebanon, Ore.

[7] Samuel Joseph Rich, lawyer, large-scale farmer, active in Democratic politics; recently appointed state commissioner of immigration, labor, and statistics.

[8] He was also general agent of the Wells Fargo Co. in Portland.

[9] Benjamin Selling, local clothing merchant; William Andrew Montgomery, vice-president of J. K. Gill Co., stationers and booksellers; William J. Hofmann, advertising manager of the Portland *Morning Oregonian*; and Arthur L. Fisk, business manager of the Portland *Oregon Daily Journal*. The Editors have been unable to identify Souffer.

A News Report of an Address to the Commercial Club of Portland

[May 19, 1911]

WILSON PRAISES 'OREGON SYSTEM'

Woodrow Wilson, Governor of New Jersey, in the presence of 200 of Oregon's prominent and influential citizens at a banquet given in his honor by the Portland Commercial Club last night, expounded, praised and indorsed the "Oregon system," although admitting that it needed "practical testing" to make it operative to the complete satisfaction of the masses. Governor Wilson took up his theme after Colonel C. E. S. Wood[1] and McCready Sykes, of Boise,[2] had spoken on the subject. . . .

The large dining-room in the Portland Commercial Club was beautifully decorated. On all of the tables were large bouquets of Scotch broom, representing the colors of Princeton University.

[1] Charles Erskine Scott Wood, lawyer of Portland, graduate of the United States Military Academy, 1874; veteran of several Indian campaigns, author.

[2] Benjamin William M'Cready Sykes, Princeton 1894, a fruit grower of Boise, Idaho.

On the walls and from the rafters flags were draped, while candelabra with electric bulbs of varied colors added luster to the scene.

There were many Princeton men at the speaker's table and during the progress of the dinner they gave evidence of their ability to give the Princeton yell vigorously. Another college delegation was composed of former students of Wesleyan University, of Connecticut. When Mr. Wilson arose to speak napkins were waved, cheers resounded and the Princeton yell was heard over all.

President Beckwith, of the Commercial Club, acted as toastmaster. At his left sat Governor Wilson and on his right was Governor West.[3] Mr. Beckwith said, when calling the assemblage to order, that for the first time he found himself sitting between two Democratic Governors. Governor Wilson said in part:

"I came to Oregon not to instruct you in anything, but to be myself instructed more intimately in the things you are doing. This trip is as much for my own education as anything else. It has never been my privilege before to have been upon this Coast, but I have followed as far as one can from a distance and have been very interested in the extraordinary things that you have been doing.

"I did not suppose even before I got here that there was unanimous agreement regarding the advisability of some of the things you have put into your constitution. There is not anywhere any such unanimity, and I for my part think it well that there should not be. I am very glad that I am not a standpatter, but I am glad that there are standpatters. I am glad because we need a lot of ballasting.

"I read in the paper[4] this morning just as I was approaching this city, that there were two Legislatures in Oregon, one was at Salem and the other was under Mr. U'Ren's hat, and the implication of the statement was that it was very undesirable to have a Legislature like that under Mr. U'Ren's hat and that it would be very much more desirable to have one of your own choosing sitting in Salem, where you can visit it occasionally.

"You at least have this advantage in respect to Mr. U'Ren: You know where to find him, and if you don't find him, you know what to do with him. You can say that your Legislature

---

[3] Oswald West, Democratic Governor of Oregon, 1911-15.

[4] Wilson later referred to this editorial as having appeared in the Portland *Morning Oregonian*, May 18, 1911. No copy of the issue containing this editorial is extant.

is at Salem. Can you find it? Do you know who runs it? Do you know its purposes? If Mr. U'Ren has proposed anything, has he proposed it to you? If the Legislature wants to propose anything all it has to do is to get somebody to propose it, whom it does not know half as well as you know Mr. U'Ren. The bill may then be privately considered in committee, along with a hundred bills that are not even read. I am supposing these things to be true in your Legislature at Salem. I know they are true in various Legislatures with which I am more familiar.

"I have never been interested in theories, gentlemen. All my life long I have been interested in facts, and if you want to discuss one system as against the other you have got to contrast the facts on the one side with the facts on the other. Now before you ever installed your initiative and referendum, what did you do? You limited your Legislature to 40 days in two years. What does that mean? That means that you were afraid of it—suspicious of it—didn't dare trust it—wanted to minimize it, and you regard it as dangerous.

"All over the United States you will find Legislatures limited in their jurisdiction. You are doing the same thing yourselves. Why are you suspicious of your Legislatures? Why don't you trust them? We have a legislative session in New Jersey every year, and the Legislature can sit as long as it pleases, and generally does sit three months every year, and yet we haven't found that New Jersey has been turned upside down by our Legislature.

"We haven't been suspicious of our Legislature—but that is another story. Our Legislature has often done things that have brought about a condition of almost pessimistic despair. But we didn't curtail it. After all, we are not bought and are able to encounter all the difficulties of the system.

"Why are you suspicious of your Legislature? Why, the average American citizen suspects the Legislatures and yet he doesn't know where the measures originate. Where do the measures originate? I dare say some of the gentlemen in this room know where some of them originate.

"I knew where a great many of the measures of the New Jersey Legislature originated until the last session. They have been drawn up in the offices of certain corporation lawyers. That is where they were drawn up, almost invariably; and those gentlemen, if you please, objected to anybody else drawing them up. They object to having an ordinary citizen not connected with a big corporation assume to suggest a bill.

"You have a legislative session of 40 days and at the last session introduced some 700 measures. How can you adopt 700 measures in 40 days? And I suppose you count Sundays in your 40 days?

"The fact that in our constitution-making in this country we have everywhere gone more and more into detail is undoubtedly an evidence of the fact that the people are not willing to leave the things about which they are most concerned to the discretion and action of the Legislatures," continued Mr. Wilson. . . .[5]

Printed in the Portland *Morning Oregonian*, May 19, 1911.
[5] Here begins the advance text, a printed copy of which is in WP, DLC.

A News Report of an Address to the Press Club of Portland

[May 19, 1911]

PRESS CLUB IS HOST

New Jersey Executive Tells How People Appreciate and Reward Those Officials Who Do Not Betray Them in Office.

"All that is necessary to success in politics is to be honest. The American people will lionize you. They will carry you about on their shoulders and ascribe to you merits which you really do not possess, and all the time you have simply been an honest man," said Governor Wilson speaking before an audience of more than 150 at the Press Club, following his address at the Commercial Club last evening.

Introduced by John L. Travis,[1] vice-president of the club, Mr. Wilson was greeted with round after round of applause when he arose to speak. His appearance in the clubrooms had previously been greeted with resounding cheers. In the course of his talk he said:

"There is a general impression among newspaper men that I dragooned the Legislature of New Jersey into passing a great deal of reform legislation. I did nothing of the sort. The people of New Jersey simply started in by showing a certain number of gentlemen, known as the Democratic machine, and another lot known as the Republican machine, that they had nothing to do with the election of a United States Senator. Later on the people showed these same gentlemen that they had nothing to do with legislation.

"Why, there were men in that Legislature who hadn't voted their own minds for years and, if I know anything about human nature, they took a positive delight in feeling that they had no longer to bow to dictatorship and delight in putting through the legislation desired by the people. Newspaper men who covered the sessions at Trenton for years came to me day after day with expressions of amazement.

"To illustrate to you what honest public discussion will do, I could name one man in the Legislature of New Jersey[2] who could defeat any bill he spoke against, and simply because the people of New Jersey knew he was honest. Members of the Legislature would come to him and say 'For God's sake, Joe, don't speak against that bill. I've got the money,' or something to that effect, knowing that if he did speak against it they would have to vote against it and give the money back.

"Theodore Roosevelt's success in the political world, aside, of course, from his ability, was his constant habit of telling the people everything, of telling what he knew at the opportune moment. He was possessed of means and went into the political game. He attended caucuses and conferences and expressed his opinions and told them to the public. Finally they said 'all right, we'll put you in office and see you make a fool of yourself.' They did, but he did not make a fool of himself. Finally they conceived the idea of shelving him by means of the Vice-Presidency. Providence intervened and he became President. He had knowledge of all the ins and outs of the political game, he courted publicity and every time he made a speech, politicians shivered in the corner. They did not know what he might 'blab.' He 'blabbed' with a fine disregard for their feelings.

"Roosevelt played politics whether he was in office or not. The trouble with the majority of people is that they have become possessed of the idea that to be in politics they must be in office."

Governor Wilson devoted a part of his speech to cautioning newspapermen to be careful in their writing. He urged them to always try and give an accurate idea of every side of a public man or a public discussion, not a caricature. . . .

Printed in the Portland *Morning Oregonian*, May 19, 1911.
[1] John Linn Travis, city editor of the Portland *Oregon Daily Journal*.
[2] Joseph P. Tumulty.

An Address in the Portland Armory[1]

[[May 19, 1911]]

Your greeting is very cordial and gracious. It gives me a touch of the tonic spirit in your air. It has seemed to me that this Ore-

[1] Delivered on the night of May 19. "The distinctive feature of last night's meeting," reported the Portland *Oregon Daily Journal*, May 20, 1911, "was the

gon atmosphere is charged with electricity. Since I came I
haven't been able to make an assertion that has not been chal-
lenged. I had to use my quickest wits to hold my own. In Oregon
men think.

At the same time, though you may not think it, the people of
the East are wide awake. I was introduced by Mr. Selling as from
the Far East. I am from the Far East, all right enough, but not
from the Orient. The Far East of America has none of the quietude
of thought [for] which the Orient is noted. But the people of the
East to whom I refer are the people of New Jersey and New
York and Pennsylvania.

I am not familiar with the extraordinarily beautiful scenery
I have found in Oregon, but I am familiar with the kind of people
I have found here, and you are the true American brand.

There is a stubborn body of men in the East who resisted the
movement forward that is so well known in the West, but they
are yielding now. It is the men who came out of [the] East who
made the West. Some out there in the East who didn't move don't
want to move yet.

In the East there is now an entirely different temper. Not long
ago there was uneasiness and fear of the forward movement.
Even in Oregon the gentlemen who sit here on the platform a
few years ago were considered dangerous.[2]

You at first condemned the things these men proposed, but
you have since accepted most of it. You have thus made yourselves their partners.

So in the East are men who have thawed out under the processes of argument, and they are thinking and approving the
forward movement. Yet as I came west I did not travel through
zones of opinion. The East is as fertile with thought and the
coming processes of change as is the West. There is, I say, a
different temper throughout the nation. We are recovering the
true structure of American political society. Our problem is to
establish sympathies as broad as American society, so that the
body of the people, and not special interests, may govern. . . .

---

reception given Wilson by the people. When he stood before them the applause
was a storm. Men and women alike in the great crowded room stood on their
feet. The fluttering handkerchiefs made the scene all white. He smiled upon
the tense, upturned faces. He raised his hand for silence. The people would
not be still. The applause became deafening."

[2] Seated on the platform with Wilson were representatives of the University
Club, the Commercial Club, the local and state Democratic committees, the
Business Men's Club, and reform leaders such as William S. U'Ren and Thomas
Nelson Strong, chairman of the Committee of 100 of Portland and vice-presi-
dent of the National Municipal League and of the National Civil Service
Reform League.

Now the excluded partners are breaking into public business. We are actually taking the liberty of assuming a part of our own affairs. It has taken the initiative and referendum to show that all the people can get in. The object of the initiative and referendum, as I take it, gentlemen, is not to conduct the affairs of your government. It is not to supplant your Legislature, as I view it. In adopting the initiative and referendum you did nothing new. It may be that I am trampling upon cherished ideas out here in Oregon, yet it is a fact that it is one of our oldest forms of government and was used by the early Kings of England in their contact with the people. I expect that you will still use the legislature as your system of legislation. The reason you adopted the initiative was because you lost contact with your Legislature. The initiative and referendum is the extraordinary means to secure the contact. You do not intend to make the initiative and referendum your legislative body. I have heard since I have come to Oregon that some of your citizens have "held up" the initiative and referendum and others have "loaded it down."

And while you have adopted this new method of legislation, do not console yourselves with the idea that you have corrected your evils. If I am rightly informed, your Legislature has not improved to any marked degree in its contact with the people. You have made no progress, for to make this movement a success you must purify your legislative assembly, and make it responsive. The initiative and referendum may have made the members of the Legislature nervous, but it has not changed their character. To get results you must continue in your work by making the Legislature a truly representative legislative body.

Then, I am not familiar with your initiative measures, submitted on the ballot at your last election, but I am familiar with the physical form of the ballot, and I must say it was a very formidable document. It contained more names on it than I could possibly think a man could manage to look up if he had a year at his disposal. Now, in Princeton, the ballot had some 25 names on it. I did not know them all, and did not have the time to find out, for I was working and could not stop; and then I doubt, if I did, whether I would have had the time to find out between primary day and election. If you want a representative condition, you must apply reason to your method and seek to give the voter an opportunity to vote intelligently. . . .

You need to adopt what is known as the short ballot, to have the least possible number of officeholders, and be in a position to hold them responsible. It is unimaginable to me that the people of Oregon should adopt the initiative, referendum and recall and then continue their government in so unintelligent a manner that they do not know whom to recall.

There are too many in the Legislature. To fix responsibility you would first have to find to what committee a bill was referred, who was the chairman of that committee, what happened when the bill was up for consideration before the committee and who worked the process by which it was smothered. The right way is to have the system so simple that you know immediately who is responsible. The problem is to make the Legislature more responsible, to reduce the number of elective officers and control those you do elect.

You must establish some form of responsible leadership. Some leaders are admirable, but systems are such that they cannot be held responsible. Suppose you have a leader who goes on invoking the initiative and referendum. He can easily get a sufficiently large fraction of your people to put their names on his petitions. I will admit that this system develops more leaders than any other process, but they are not leaders you choose and therefore you cannot hold them responsible.

The people are clamoring for their executive officers to act as their leaders. . . . The people of the whole country are discontented unless the President and their Governors assume the role of leadership. . . . It is the bounden duty of an executive to act as spokesman and painstaking and conscientious representative of the people and the people's bounden duty to simplify their form of government. The people do not understand the ins and outs of legislation. An executive's duty is to find out what they want done and do it.

You don't want the Legislature bossed by the Governor; of course not. I have not the time to go into details and catch my train, but it can be arranged to give them a chance to answer on the same platform with him. You will then begin, when matters are debated freely and openly, to get things into such shape as to make the initiative and referendum unnecessary. I predict that if you find means of doing that you will do something else. You will not limit your legislative sessions to 40 days every two years. You will not want your legislators to stop at 40 days unless they have finished threshing out every vital question—unless they get through with the processess and arrive at the correct and honest conclusions. . . .

Printed in the Portland *Morning Oregonian*, May 20, 1911, with additions from the partial text in the Portland *Oregon Daily Journal*, May 20, 1911.

A Report of an Address in Portland
on Problems of Government

[May 20, 1911]

WILSON OPPOSES JUDGES' RECALL

With capitalists, labor leaders, single taxers, founders of the
Oregon System, business and professional men composing his
audience at the Y.M.C.A. yesterday at noon, Woodrow Wilson,
Governor of New Jersey, opposed fully and completely, the application of the recall to the judicial system of the state. He told
the audience that he was still "obstinate and obdurate" and felt
that the adoption of the law meant in substance that "if the
decision does not suit then the judge can be changed instead of
the law, because it is easier.

"That is poor logic, gentlemen, and while I am a poor logician, even I can see it," he added. . . .

The luncheon was under the direction of the "Oregon Advocates of Better Government." Fully 200 were present and listened
for more than an hour as Dr. Wilson discoursed on some of the
issues. When introduced by W. S. U'Ren, who briefly told of the
work of the advocates of the "Oregon System" in 20 years, the
Governor arose, but the banqueters would not permit him to
speak from the floor. Replying to calls, he mounted the platform, in the center of which was a pulpit. Placing his hand on
its top he looked cautiously over the assemblage and said:

"I do not like this. It makes me feel like a preacher, but it is
natural, for I find it is not the first time that I have stood with
both feet upon one platform."

Mr. U'Ren introduced Governor Wilson as "the greatest constructive statesman of the century," and added: "If he is that,
he is the greatest constructive statesman in the world." Dr. Wilson replied that he felt that the characterization was rather too
large. He said in beginning his address that the presence of the
founders of the "Oregon System" was admirable, because it
showed that there were men who were willing to give attention
to governmental questions and settle them if possible.

Dr. Wilson was interrupted only once, and then he gave a
quick answer. He had been telling why he was opposed to the
recall of the judges and said that it was not advisable to change
existing conditions by the "simple waving of the hand."

"That is not the best way to secure results or to place in effect
a reform," he said. "Patience and deliberation are essential." At
this point, a man at the foot of one of the banquet tables called
loudly: "That is not logic."

"Quite true, my friend, but I am not a logician," was the reply. "I am not a dealer in logic. I do not believe in logic. But it is good sense, and that is quite essential in the treatment of a governmental subject."

Dr. Wilson spoke of the temptations that beset legislators. He said that Oregon's allowance of only $3 a day he regarded as inadequate, insufficient and harmful, and calculated in its last analysis to have an effect the opposite of that expected.

"Now, in New Jersey," the speaker continued, "we pay $500 a year to members of the Legislature, and they meet yearly as well as serve a greater length of time. It is not enough. It is my belief that a competent sum should be paid for public service, so that the public servant shall be beyond temptation for the bare necessities of life. I remember a member of the New Jersey Legislature who was honest and who desired to do the right thing. He had a small business. The long session of the Legislature drew so heavily upon his business that it languished, and when the session neared its end he was near bankruptcy. This man had notes in the bank and we found that certain interests were forcing payment and would not let up unless he voted for a certain man for United States Senator. Had it not been for the 'indiscreet' acts of men like myself, that man would have become a bankrupt or have voted for the big interests. Happily, we made it public and he was cared for. I cite this to illustrate the fact that a man must receive sufficient salary to avoid temptations if you expect good government, and do you not see that it is the very thing which puts at naught all of your efforts to resist the encroachments of big business? You proceed to elect a man whose financial condition will permit temptation, and then, to make the temptation doubly effective, you give him only $3 a day—not enough for his living expense. It is working at cross purposes."

Dr. Wilson said he did not regard it as surprising that the founders of the "Oregon system" had held together so many years. "This group of men," he continued, "is not surprising. I find such groups all over the country with similar objects—better government. During the past 20 years it has been my province to address many audiences having for their object the improvement of our governmental condition, and I find this to be true that there is a constant growing movement for the betterment and amelioration of governmental conditions.

"It may be strange to hear it, but you know I am in favor of celibacy among legislators as I am among Christian ministers. If you want men to be independent let them become bachelors.

Did you ever think of it that most of our temptations come as a result of our desire to help others dependent upon us? A man with family ties will fall into temptation quicker than one who has no one dependent upon him, strange as it may seem, and therefore it might be well to choose celibates as legislators."

Dr. Wilson indulged in a fleeting, quiet smile.

"A man came to me recently," he continued, "and asked me this question: 'Do you not believe that the present broadcast spread of corruption is a sign of decadence?' Now that man got little sympathy from me. I told him, 'Why, my dear sir, it is quite the contrary. I see in this breaking out of the scandal in Pennsylvania with regard to the capitol,[1] and in Adams County, Illinois,[2] nothing more nor less than the treatment of the disease. It is simply the evidences of the awakening of the public conscience. We must smell things out. It is right to have a vigilant nose. The world for years suffered from inflammation of the bowels, but one day a doctor discovered that it was due to appendicitis. Now hundreds of lives are saved yearly and when you are cautiously opened and the difficulty is removed there is no trouble thereafter. It is the same with us; these outbreaks are only the evidence of the recrudescence of the public conscience.'

"If the initiative and referendum fails, it is not because of the law but is due to the fact you do not rise equal to the emergency. No government is better than we make it. We are past the age of hysteria. We have become a part of a sane and sensible treatment of subjects before us. It is an enlightened age

[1] At this very time the final criminal and civil suits in the scandal surrounding the building of the capitol in Harrisburg were drawing to a close. The scandal had "broken out" during the spring and summer of 1906 just before completion of the new building, when William H. Berry, elected state treasurer in 1905 as a Democratic reform candidate, had discovered that the state had been grossly overcharged and swindled in the construction and furnishing of the capitol. In January 1907, the legislature appointed a Capitol Investigating Commission, the report of which during the following August tended to confirm Berry's charges. Criminal and civil suits settled by the time of Wilson's remarks had resulted in the return to the state treasury of $1,300,000—about one third of the total amount stolen from the state—and the indictment and conviction of several contractors and the former state treasurer, auditor general, architect, and superintendent of public grounds and buildings. See Sylvester K. Stevens, *Pennsylvania: The Heritage of a Commonwealth* (4 vols., West Palm Beach, Fla., 1968), II, 812-13.

[2] He referred to a vote-selling scandal in Adams County, *Ohio*, which at this time was being investigated by a grand jury. Vote selling had been flagrant and widespread in the county for many years, but it was not until after a close election in November 1910 that a serious investigation was launched by the county judge, Albion Zelophehad Blair. A grand jury, empaneled on December 13, 1910, completed its work late in the summer of 1911, by which time nearly 1,700 voters, or 26 per cent of the county's electorate, had confessed to selling votes, been fined or sentenced, and disfranchised for a certain period. See A. Z. Blair, "Seventeen Hundred Rural Vote-Sellers," *McClure's Magazine*, XXXVIII (Nov. 1911), 28-40.

and if I could invent a perfect government I would not do it, for the sole reason that the effort to get it is one of the greatest charms of the victory and is the principal incentive to our human activity that permits of enjoyable rest.

"It may be that I am very stubborn or stupid and while I heartily favor the use of the recall for all administrative offices, I do not approve of it for the judiciary, on the theory that one of the great dangers with which we are beset in our effort to secure better government is impatience. We are prone to use too much haste, to take too many short cuts, I admit that logically it is unanswerable that if we elect judges we have the right to recall them, but I don't care a peppercorn for logic. We choose our judges to interpret the laws as they are, not as we would like to have them be. If the laws are not what we want them to be, we have every chance in the world to change them, yet under the recall we would take vengeance on the judges instead of remedying the law which we do not like. It seems to me that this is poor logic. It is said that our courts have fallen into the habit of assuming legislative powers, and we have a good opinion in the recent United States Supreme Court decision, but I really believe that that great tribunal has been slowly adjusting itself to the changing conditions in our life. It has been the history in the long series of decisions handed down by that tribunal that it has adapted itself to meet new conditions by slow and solid advancement."

An informal reception was held at the University Club at 5:30 P.M. and dinner was served in the club dining-room at 6 o'clock. Dr. Wilson spoke briefly and was escorted from the table to the Armory.

Printed in the Portland *Morning Oregonian*, May 20, 1911.

An Interview in Seattle

[May 20, 1911]

WOODROW WILSON WELCOMED ON HIS VISIT TO SEATTLE

Gov. Woodrow Wilson, of New Jersey, former president of Princeton, at present the most logical successor to William Jennings Bryan as the leader of the advanced wing in the Democratic party, and a strong presidential possibility, came to Seattle this morning. . . .

In a conference with C. G. Heifner,[1] chairman of the Democratic state committee, the governor inquired about Alaska conditions. Heifner is chairman of a conference committee of Seattle political and commercial organizations which is making a hard fight for Alaska self-government and the opening of parts of Alaska to development.

Mr. Heifner started a movement among the Far Western states to demand that a home rule bill pass the present Congress and he has allied with him all the Democratic leaders of the Coast. Governor Wilson frankly admits that he is uninformed on Alaska matters and added today:

"I do not believe the East knows very much about Alaska; in fact my experience has been that men from Alaska were divided in their opinions. In a general way I have been led to believe that if the grip of those interests which seek to gobble Alaska could be broken that country's development would be hastened."

Later Governor Wilson recalled that he had heard some one of the members of his reception committee declare that he hoped the New Jersey executive had not brought with him the "Oregon system." It was explained to Governor Wilson that practically all of Oregon's so-called "system" had been adopted in this state and he said:

"The initiative, referendum and recall are measures whose adoption are matters of local concern. I am not prepared to state that they should be adopted throughout the country; in fact, they might be dangerous in some localities. They are questions that must come to the people when they are ready for them.

"Without studying the question closer and its application to the specific locality, I am somewhat in doubt whether or not these measures could be safely applied in a state where, for instance, there was a large preponderance of prejudiced vote. Conditions might be such elsewhere that they would be unnesessary.

"I do not believe it was ever the intention of the framers of the initiative, referendum or recall movements to make common use of them. It would be too cumbersome to do all our legislation by the initiative and referendum. But they are a most efficient club to hold over our lawmakers. At all times the Legislatures know that if they are not responsive to public will, the people have the power to put their own views into operation.

"While it is true that one of the first uses Oregon made of the referendum was to demand a vote on university and school appropriations, I do not believe the Oregon university suffered by that action. It gave the university an opportunity to go before the people and to bring the school to the attention of thousands who had barely known of its existence. I believe that experience was a healthy one.

"Naturally there will be abuses of such a system, but the advantages far outweigh any of the disadvantages. The effect, however, is more important in the manner in which it tends to make the governments more responsive.

"In New Jersey we have enacted several laws that, I believe, will result in sending an entirely different class of men to our Legislatures and will result in much beneficial legislation in the future.

"We have done away entirely with conventions, nominating all officials by direct primary; even to delegations to national conventions. In our delegate primary we provide a method for the voter indicating his choice for President.

"We have a very stringent corrupt practices act; we have created a public utilities commission and compel every public utility corporation to file with the attorney general a statement of the manner in which it does business so that the official who offends against the act can be punished individually as well as holding his corporation responsible.

"We have reorganized our school system and a bill was passed authorizing the cities of New Jersey to adopt the commission form of government.

"Representatives from thirty-two New Jersey cities asked for the commission form of government and I believe as soon as the law becomes effective they will take advantage of it. The system apparently is popular in New Jersey and I believe it is coming into general practice."

Governor Wilson would not discuss the Standard Oil decision, saying that he had heard little comment of importance, except a feeling that the court had written a word into the law that he regretted had been introduced.

Printed in the *Seattle Daily Times*, May 20, 1911; some editorial headings omitted.
    1 Charles G. Heifner (he never divulged his middle name), chairman of the Democratic State Central Committee and investment banker of Seattle.

A News Report of Remarks to Democratic Leaders of the State of Washington

[May 21, 1911]

DEMOCRATS GIVE WARM RECEPTION TO GOVERNOR WILSON AT BIG BANQUET

When Gov. Wilson descended from his room to the main floor of the Hotel Washington and entered the large dining room on the arm of Chairman Charles G. Heifner, of the Democratic state central committee, there was not a vacant table or chair in the room, except the two awaiting his and Mr. Heifner's arrival.

As sight was caught of him the company arose, and he was loudly cheered as he was escorted to his seat at the head table.

He kept up a running chat with all those about him, and seemed to enjoy his warm reception. Upon being introduced he announced that he hardly believed so many Democrats could be gathered in Seattle, that he had been informed that Washington was not very fertile Democratic ground.

"The signs of the times," said Gov. Wilson smilingly, "indicate an awakening. It is already upon us. It is for us to rise to the opportunity, not simply declare that the outlook for the Democratic party is promising, but to join hands in making it successful by the adoption of what I like to call conservative radicalism."

Gov. Wilson said that we were often reminded of the Declaration of Independence, that its most attractive portion was its fine rhetorical introduction, that the remainder of it was good concerning the time for which it was intended, but that to be of service now it should provide for the needs of 1911.

His speech was well received throughout its delivery, and when he finished he was again loudly cheered.

Printed in the *Seattle Post-Intelligencer*, May 21, 1911.

A News Report of a Speech in Seattle on Commission Government

[May 21, 1911]

Speaks at Dreamland.

After the Democratic dinner, Gov. Wilson addressed a crowded house at Dreamland Pavilion, making a short address on the commission form of government in American municipalities. At Governor Wilson's suggestion, the New Jersey legislature, which adjourned three weeks ago, passed an act authorizing cities of that state to adopt a commission form of government by charter amendment. Representatives of thirty-two cities and towns appeared before the legislature and urged the change.

Mayor George W. Dilling[1] presided over the Dreamland Pavilion meeting and partisan politics carefully was avoided by either the presiding officer or the speaker. Governor Wilson's discussion of the commission form of municipal government, though academic, was liberally applauded.[2] . . .

Immediately after the Dreamland Pavilion meeting, Governor Wilson was escorted to the Press Club where for more than an hour he mingled with the newspaper fraternity in Seattle. In [a] speech to the working newspapermen, an opportunity to greet the New Jersey executive, introductions were made as the men employed on Sunday newspapers came in, a program of speech-making being carried out at the same time. Governor Wilson made an intimate speech to the working newspapermen discussing their work and responsibilities in the light of his experience as an educator and statesman.

Though worn out by the exactions of his trip and a strenuous day of speech-making and visits in Seattle, Governor Wilson remained at the Press Club until nearly midnight.

Printed in the *Seattle Times*, May 21, 1911.
  [1] Republican Mayor of Seattle.
  [2] Here follows the text of Wilson's news release, a copy of which is in WP, DLC.

To Mary Allen Hulbert Peck

The New Washington Hotel
Dearest Friend,   Seattle, 21 May 1911

I feel as if I were firing into the air, writing to you now. In one letter you said you were to sail on the 13th, and now, in the delightful note forwarded to me here[1] (the delicious little epistle full of the ecstasy with which you respond to nature, as she enchants you in Bermuda) you say either the 20th (yesterday) or the 27th. Of course I stopped directing my letters to Bermuda on the first intimation of a definite date, and, equally of course, I dare not despatch one thither now. If you went without letters the last two or three weeks you were in Bermuda, it is, Madam, no fault of mine. And yet that does not comfort me. I hate to write *in vacuo*. And where shall I send this? To Mrs. Roebling's, at a venture!

I am having a sort of a triumph out here. Wherever I go they seem to like me—men of all kinds and classes. My big meetings, where miscelaneous audiences gather, by the hundreds and by the thousands—as at San Francisco and at Seattle—remind me of my campaign meetings in New Jersey—those which gathered toward the close of the campaign,—they are so friendly, so intent, so easily held and moved. It is almost amusing to have scores of persons (who do not know real political facts as well as they might) speak of me, in a sort of matter of course way, as the next President of the United States. Even the politicians out here seem to assume that I will be the Democratic nominee next year! *I* assume nothing. I will not allow myself to be duped or made a fool of; but it is astounding to find how they have watched me here and how well they know me. They receive me as they would a familiar leader.

I get very tired, but I keep well. Indeed I have cured a stubborn cold by the way. To-night I turn Eastward (Gott sei dank!). I go directly from my engagement at Lincoln on the 27th to North and South Carolina and shall not be in Trenton until about the 4th of June. How I hope I shall find you there! It is inexpressibly delightful to think of seeing you.

Your devoted friend   Woodrow Wilson

ALS (WP, DLC).
1 Both letters are missing.

From Ellen Axson Wilson

My own darling,   Old Lyme [Conn.], May 22 1911

I am reduced to despair by the discovery—this moment made—that I have not your Minneapolis address! The girls took the telegram giving hotels to send off the message to Portland, and with their usual carelessness did not return it! So I can only send this to "The Publicity Club"—and hope for the best! Somehow that does not sound like an established Club with a house of its own, but only an "organization."

The dear "lettergram" from Portland was handed me on my arrival at the station here. It was *lovely* in you to send it! And the other one, equally delightful, came this morning. I am inexpressibly thankful that you can still report yourself "well." There also came today letters from Janie and Burney Porter,[1] and of course they are mad over you and in love with you too. They also sent an interesting and *long* clipping from a Los Angeles paper. So I feel very much in touch with my darling just now. Some of the cousins, I suppose, in Denver sent quite a packet of clippings from there which reached me here Saturday night, and were very much enjoyed. Otherwise I have not seen many from the West. I hope you will come back *loaded!* Is'nt it all perfectly splendid and wonderful? It is like a royal progress. Surely you must be a man of destiny.

The weather is beautiful here today, and I made a beginning at the painting but did not accomplish much,—better luck to-morrow. Everybody was trying apple-blossom subjects, and everybody swearing over them and declaring them impossible. The Robinsons[2] are here[3] and he is *much* better and in good spirits. Mr. Cohen[4] came today, Everett Warner[5] has been here most of the winter. And there are also in the house Mr. Griecken, the impressionist,[6] his wife[7] and two pretty little children. (One of whom, called "Tihte,"[8] is at this moment bawling at the top of her voice!) They were both born in France. Mr. Ramsdell[9] came on the same train with me and is staying in the house until Mr. Bicknell[10] comes, when they will both go up to the house on the lake. That is all except a Mr. Knapp[11] who has nervous prostration and is here with a nurse—a young woman. His wife[12] is a sister of Tom Perkins.[13] He played on the Yale football team for years (is an '82 man) and was afterwards a very successful lawyer. But he broke down from overwork five years ago and has never been able to use his mind since, though he is always trying. I have never seen such an image of despair. It makes one's heart bleed to look at him.

It is rather hard luck to find such a case in the house, for I have been having a peculiarly sad time with Stockton—since you went away,—and in fact reached here almost used up over it. That is why I did not write you on Saturday or Sunday. I staid in bed Saturday morning and Sunday afternoon, and am now as well as ever. (I would not mention poor Stockton to you at all while you have so much else on your mind but for a special reason which will appear in a moment.) The doctor, the nurse and I have been trying desperately for many weeks to rouse him to do some sort of work especially preparing his Chatauqua lectures. He said he could not work away from Princeton and his books and yet he declined to go to Princeton. But finally a week ago he went; and I was very hopeful,—for a few hours only. It was all an utter, dreadful failure. It seems quite certain now that he will never take up his work in Princeton again;—and he himself has "decided" never to take it up anywhere. His latest idea is to "go into a monastery." He insists upon having a priest sent for with whom he can confer on the subject.

But Dr. Dercum[14] says that if he gives up his profession he is lost,—it will be only a question of time when he will have to be committed to a hospital for the insane. In this strait I have thought that his old friend Dr. Vincent the new President of Minnesota[15] might help by offering him some small place there, —some little lectureship or instructor-ship for a year. Of course he knows—none better—how extremely valuable Stockton will be to him there if he *does* get well, for he knows his brilliant Chatauqua career. Stockton says his moral collapse has been so complete that it would be a farce for him to talk to boys about literature and life. In view of that notion (out of which he can't be argued) it might be better if he could do a little teaching in American history instead, while he was "finding himself" again.

He is perfectly competent to do it. Even you have scarcely read and studied it more. Of course I am writing this hoping you may have an opportunity to speak to Dr. Vincent about it while there. If you see him he will be almost sure to ask you about Stockton. But you must not go *out* of your way to do it, dear—because of course it can be done after your return,—though time is rather precious as things stand. It is that at least which has decided me to write of it,—most unwillingly. He and Rogers the nurse went back to Phila. on the ten o'clock train;[16] I leaving on the twelve. The day before Helen Bainbridge[17] came at one o'clock and staid until six, and Stockton spent the evening. Of course he did not know that she was in Princeton. I had to rise almost at day-break to do my neglected packing,—then Helen met me in New York and came all the way to New Haven just to go on talking it over. It was pretty bad; but she *is* a splendid girl.

But I must stop if this is to reach you in Minneapolis. We are all perfectly well. I saw dear little Margaret in N. Y.

Ah darling, how I wish I could tell you how I love you and adore you and long for you. Oh for "the great heart word"—Always and altogether   Your own   Eileen.

ALS (WC, NjP).
  [1] Presumably a brother or nephew of Janie Porter Chandler. The Los Angeles city directory listed Burney Porter as a teacher.
  [2] William S. Robinson, water colorist of New York, and Lois Ball Robinson.
  [3] That is, at Miss Florence Griswold's in Old Lyme.
  [4] Lewis Cohen, landscape painter of New York.
  [5] Everett Longley Warner, water colorist and etcher of New York.
  [6] Edmund William Greacen of New York.
  [7] Ethol Booth Greacen.
  [8] Nanette, who later became an artist.
  [9] Fred Winthrop Ramsdell, landscape and portrait painter of Lyme, Conn.
  [10] Frank Alfred Bicknell, landscape painter of Lyme.
  [11] Howard Hoyt Knapp, former lawyer of Bridgeport, Conn., at this time convalescing in Hartford.
  [12] Emily Hale Perkins Knapp.
  [13] Thomas Jefferson Perkins, Princeton 1894, who practiced law in New York and lived in Englewood, N. J.
  [14] Francis Xavier Dercum, M.D., Philadelphia neurologist and pioneer in the treatment of mental disease.
  [15] George Edgar Vincent, educator and sociologist and for many years an official of the Chautauqua Institution.
  [16] Stockton Axson had returned to a mental hospital in Philadelphia.
  [17] Presumably a woman friend of Stockton Axson; she is unknown to the Editors.

To Henry Smith Pritchett

Minneapolis Club
My dear President Pritchett: Minneapolis, Minn. May 25, 1911.

I sincerely hope that you are quite well again. I was distressed to hear of your illness though I am sure that you must have enjoyed Bermuda.[1] It is a very happy form of punishment for physical bad behavior to be sent to that delightful place.

As usual, I am resorting to you for advice. You may have noticed we have just passed several statutes in New Jersey which will involve a rather radical reorganization of our school system. Among other things involved is the appointment of a State Commissioner of Education who will have very wide powers in association with a small board of public education. The salary of the place has been fixed at Ten Thousand Dollars and I am left at liberty in making the appointment to choose anywhere in the United States. If you had such a man to choose and the object was to reorganize the State Supervision of Schools and exercise unusual powers of regulation and supervision, whom would you turn to? It is absolutely necessary that he should be a man of tact as well as firmness and resource because this reorganization is a good deal resented by the High School principals and other men who have been prominent in the loose go-as-you-please administration which has criticized [characterized] the State for a long time past. A man who did not know how to exercise his powers with tactfulness and consideration would be in hot water all the time and probably would not accomplish what he set out to do.

I feel rather heavily the responsibility of the choice and would like to be guided as frankly as possible.

With warm regard

      Cordially and faithfully yours,   Woodrow Wilson

TLS (Carnegie Foundation for the Advancement of Teaching).
[1] See H. S. Pritchett to WW, April 9, 1911, Vol. 22.

A News Report About Wilson in St. Paul
and Minneapolis

[May 25, 1911]

WILSON AT CAPITOL

The governor's salute of seventeen guns welcomed Governor Wilson to the state capitol at 4 P.M. yesterday. Colonels, majors and captains, waiting in the Governor's reception room, jumped uncomfortably as the first shot boomed forth; then everybody laughed and the rest of the salute went on without even making the stenographers nervous.

At 3 P.M. Governor Wilson was met at the Minneapolis club, Minneapolis, by two automobile loads of representatives of the Association of Commerce.

In the automobile with Governor Wilson were Ralph W. Wheelock, secretary to Governor Eberhart;[1] C. L. Kluckhohn,[2] Fred B. Lynch[3] and Governor Wilson's secretary, Frank P. Stockbridge. In the automobile following were Pierce Butler, T. D. O'Brien, Timothy Foley, Judge J. W. Lusk, Paul Doty and Senator James D. Denegre.[4]

Senator Denegre was a student at Princeton when Governor Wilson was professor there. He has met him at class reunions since and once entertained the then President Wilson at his home in St. Paul,[5] and the two had several personal chats during the interims in the program.

Governor Wilson first met personally in the Governor's reception room the heads of the state departments, the Governor's staff and St. Paul newspaper men. A firm hand grasp and a smile were meted out to each man. In a trip through the capitol he asked few questions, made few comments, but his smile was in evidence a great deal.

"Billy" Williams,[6] member of Governor Eberhart's staff, guided the party through the capitol. He showed him the historic paintings and the mementoes of the Civil war, the House and Senate and supreme court chambers, and even the broken clock in the House chamber.

Governor Wilson asked how the clock happened to be broken. Senator Denegre explained how, the last night of the last session, the clock had been broken in an endeavor to make it honest. An indication was given him of the bills that were defeated by the refusal of a few members to allow the clock to be turned back. Governor Wilson, at the conclusion of the recital, just smiled.

At the conclusion of his tour of inspection Governor Wilson told "Billy" Williams that he considered the capitol one of the finest public buildings in the country.

Then he descended to the rotunda to address the public gathered in the balconies. He looked around and remarked whimsically: "I see I shall have to break my rule and play to the galleries." The crowd appreciated the witticism.

His speech was short, but was well received by the audience. "I am sorry that my good friend Governor Eberhart could not be here," he said. "I had counted on seeing him on my trip.

"In walking through this building I was irresistibly reminded of your former Governor John A. Johnson. I little thought when last I saw him that he would be no more when I should visit here.

"In my travels through the country I have seen no fairer spot

that [than] Minnesota. It is one of the typical states of the great
Northwest that has produced so many great and good men. You
have a wonderful state and a wonderful people."

After shaking hands all around again he was whirled away
to The Saint Paul. There was a mere handful of people present
when he arrival [arrived] at the hotel. He retired immediately
to his room. . . .

Printed in the *St. Paul Pioneer-Press*, May 25, 1911; some editorial headings
omitted.
    [1] Adolph Olson Eberhart, lieutenant governor, 1907-1909; he succeeded to the
governorship on Governor Johnson's death on September 21, 1909.
    [2] Charles Louis Kluckhohn, businessman and philanthropist of St. Paul;
founder of the St. Paul Commercial Club and president of its successor, the
St. Paul Association of Commerce.
    [3] Frederick Bicknell Lynch, lumberman of St. Paul and member of the
Democratic National Committee since 1908.
    [4] Pierce Butler, member of the law firm of Butler, Mitchell and Doherty
of St. Paul and a regent of the University of Minnesota; Thomas Dillon O'Brien,
associate justice of the Minnesota Supreme Court since 1909; Timothy Foley,
one of four brothers who organized Foley Brothers, Inc., general contractors
of St. Paul; James W. Lusk, lawyer and president of the National German
American Bank of St. Paul; Paul Doty, manager of the St. Paul Gaslight Co.; and
James Denis Denègre, Princeton 1889, lawyer of St. Paul and state senator.
    [5] When Wilson spoke to the Princeton Alumni Association of the Northwest
in St. Paul on April 24, 1903. See the news report printed at May 2, 1903, Vol.
14.
    [6] Billy (such seems to have been his name) Williams was the governor's
executive aide. Appointed by Governor Johnson in November 1904, he served
fourteen governors and retired in 1957. He died on November 13, 1963.

A News Report of a Luncheon Address
to the Publicity Club of Minneapolis

[May 25, 1911]

Secret Alliances With Politicians to Frame Laws Being Broken
by Awakened Conscience, Speaker Tells Minneapolis.

Addressing one of the largest gatherings that ever attended
a Minneapolis Publicity club dinner, Governor Woodrow Wilson
of New Jersey yesterday spoke on the relationship of business
and politics.

The assemblage was a notable one and listened with the utmost attentiveness to the address. G[eorge]. Roy Clark, president
of the club, presided and the speaker was introduced by President
Vincent of the University of Minnesota. . . . Over 624 guests
sat down to the dinner and many were unable to attend on
account of the lack of room. It was given in the dining room
of the West hotel.

In his introduction, President Vincent drew a parallel between
the old grove of Academus in Athens, where scholars were wont
to congregate. He said that men scoffed at them as visionaries,

but later a leader among men arose among them. That in the present day, a scholar had become a leader of men.

A standing reception was given Governor Wilson, who spoke for an hour, without notes and without hesitation.[1] . . .

Printed in the *Minneapolis Morning Tribune*, May 25, 1911.

[1] Here follows most of Wilson's advance text, a copy of which is in WP, DLC.

A News Report of an Address to the Association of Commerce of St. Paul

[May 25, 1911]

ST. PAUL MEETS GOV. WILSON

Two Hundred Prominent Citizens at Banquet in His Honor
at The Saint Paul.

Minnesota yesterday had its first acquaintance with Woodrow Wilson, governor of New Jersey and possible Democratic presidential candidate. Its citizens met the man and heard his views on public questions. . . .

The banquet at The Saint Paul last night, ending the first day of Governor Wilson's visit to the Twin City, brought together a distinguished group of scholars, professional men, business men and statesmen. It was held in the palm room, which was elaborately decorated. . . .

About two hundred guests attended the banquet. President Kluckhohn briefly introduced President Vincent, who introduced Governor Wilson.

The governor spoke fully an hour and a half without notes, yet gave a clear, analytical and finished address. . . .

Governor Wilson began by telling a little incident of an address in New York while he was president of Princeton university. In that speech he said there was no such thing as public opinion in New York, for the man who plunged his head into a newspaper in the morning and formed an opinion was not making public opinion, but when a gathering at the store in a crossroads town had discussed a subject their verdict was public opinion, whether it was right or wrong.

Incidentally he said tobacco chewing, whatever else may be said of it, had at least this virtue: It gave a man time to think while he chewed. The next day he was quoted as an advocate of tobacco chewing. The thing grew as it went, and soon he was quoted as saying that tobacco chewing bred statesmen. Before it ended he received the advertisement of a tobacco company quoting him as advocating tobacco chewing.

"I am not attempting on this trip to form public opinion, but to educate myself in what is public opinion," said Governor Wilson.

"Nothing is more instructive to me than interviews with men I have met and the impressions I am gathering from these meetings.

"Every time I am told 'this is a representative gathering.' But what are you representative of? You are representative of the success of men in various lines in St. Paul, representative of leadership. You are men who have arrived or are arriving. But where did you come from? Where are all the men who have been left behind in this race in life? There is a great deal more in life than a little company of well-fed men like this.

"I used to ask myself while at Princeton, 'What is the duty of a university to a young man?' I answered by saying that its duty was to make him as much unlike his father as possible. Not that there was anything wrong with the father, but usually by the time a man is old enough and rich enough to send a son to a university he has become so engrossed in his business that he has forgotten the broad view of the public good. Our duty is to take men and reintroduce them to the country as it is; to make them forget the interests of their fathers and to see how the interests of all the people are linked together. We must resaturate each generation in the general views of life.

"What we so easily lose is our sense of relation. I have remarked before that the fatigue of a journey across the continent is not so much the trip as the conversation one hears. Men get together and talk about their business, their experiences and their success as if there were no other thing in the world. We never get so much as an intimation that there is such a thing as the general good.

"Men get a fixed point of view from which they can't stir. They make themselves the center of the universe. The good of an association like yours is that it makes you see there is such a thing as the general good.

"The United States is at present engaged in the occupation of trying to realize itself as one great nation instead of a body of warring communities. We have just passed through a period of alarms and agitation, when people said certain interests were trying to exploit the country and they did not know where it would stop. We have heard rumors of wars to come, of sullen men who were going to take things into their own hands and not put up with these special privileges that were enjoyed by some.

"That period of excitement has passed. You don't find men afraid of the future, but thoughtful. They are sure something is going to happen, but sure it will be manageable, that it will be based on justice and not on rioting.

"Let us see what the elements are in the situation and take stock of these national movements. What impresses me is that the whole country says the Democrats are on trial. If so, what is the standard you use or what is the trial going to be if you have no standard? In other words, what do you expect?

"You hear of Republican insurgents. Insurgents against what? They must be insurgents against something and must be in the minority or else they would not be insurgents. George Washington would have been a rebel if the revolution had failed. He was the Father of His Country because he won. Let us see what they are insurging against.

"You of the West realize what has passed and what will take place. The pioneers were men who did not lack character or initiative. But they could not develop the country alone. They were calling eastward for capital. They were so anxious for capital they would give it any terms. They would give unlimited franchises and their rights for years to come. The result was a most marvelous development of the country.

"Then they discovered these gentlemen came near owning us, and found they were the master of communities. That was perfectly natural. These initial processes are necessary if we want to develop so fast, and Americans won't develop slowly. You are impatient to see your visions realized in your own time.

"The problem now is to control wealth, to see that it is your instrument and not your master. I am not uttering a tirade against wealth. If I see a jungle grow up where I scattered all kinds of seeds, I'm not going to be angry at what I might have foreseen."

Then after a pause he continued:

"But I am going to get the ax and clear the jungle."

There was some applause, and he continued to explain that he would leave the large and useful trees, but would clear out the underbrush and weeds and have everything open so it could be seen.

"Take this conservation question," he continued. "We have seen so much scooped that we don't want to see any more. I have been through a country lately where there is much discontent with conservation. But the discontent is not with the policy, but because no policy is stuck to—because there is nothing settled.

"As to the great storehouse in Alaska, all are agreed that no small combination shall get hold of it. It is only a question of the method.

"We must see to it the men who control our wealth do not control us. But no one man can become so strong that he can control our wealth; it must be done through combination.

"There was a time when we were overawed by this thing we had made which we called a corporation. Then we said to ourselves, the corporation consists of individuals and if the corporation violates the law we can arrest the individuals who are responsible. The minute you take that common sense view, the problem is solved. The back is open—go around and look in. Treat them as groups of individuals and then they will be controlled by you.

"Fining a corporation will do no good. At best you are fining the stockholders, who very often do not know what is going on. At the most you are fining the corporation. If you make the fine so heavy you break up the corporation you are disturbing modern business.

"Don't disturb modern business—disturb the men who are abusing the opportunities of modern business. Here is the answer to the insurgent movement. They are saying that the party has been in league with this big business and they want no more of it.

"Now you are saying to the Democrats, 'You have been standing and laughing at the Republicans. Now we will give you a chance to see if you can do better.['] The country is turning to them now. There are not enough insurgent Republicans to do anything, and if the Democrats won't serve you, where in the name of heaven are you going to turn? But purified politics and rectified business are not going to come if you simply sit and wait.

"There is this thing we call the tariff. Some big men built it and many little men have tinkered with it. Some thought they were doing a big, patriotic thing, some knew they were only feathering their own nests. Now this tariff may be a desirable thing on the whole, but there are so many rotten pieces in it that we must overhaul it. It may be necessary to tear the whole thing apart and then perhaps we can't put it together. But rather that than have all the sneaking schemes and rotten jobs we now have in the tariff.

"There is another thing we are going to hold up to the Democrats and insurgent Republicans. Some of the insurgents have shied and looked in a very cautious way at this reciprocity question. The insurgents look very much askance at this job they have cut out for themselves. They have said they are for it, but now they want to wait and consult with certain interests and factions at home. In the next month we will have a list of the genuine insurgents.[1]

"And the Democrats? There is nothing to complain of in the House, but there is a variety in the Senate. But we are going to judge the Democrats in the Senate as we judge the insurgents, and they are going to rise or fall as they come up to the test.

"The only comfortable ones are the standpat Republicans; but they don't have to think anyhow.

"We want to revise the tariff and all federal taxation. It is going to be for the benefit of everybody. We want the colossal corporations to be our instruments and cease to be our masters. Public opinion will be educated so it will be solidified and clarified.

"And the best way to start is to get our stomachs ready for the facts, including the facts about yourselves. Ask yourself, 'Am I building solid enterprises or flying kites?' I am certain if the business men of any one city would lay aside the personal view and work for the common good that city would assume the lead in American business, and every other city would be bound to follow. Infinite prosperity would ensue, because you always get better business from unsuspicious customers.

"We must make our governments accessible to public opinion. Suppose you think the last Legislature did not act as you wanted; all you can do is to vote for another man from your district. But was the man from your district responsible? You don't know, under our complicated system, whether he was one of the few who really controlled things or not. And the chances are that if you send another set of men, they wouldn't do much better.

"Our American communities are groping a good deal in the dark about their Legislatures. They feel they can't control them —that they are controlled by other masters. The whole thing is so complicated they cannot understand how or why things are done as they are.

"Why is there such a rapid spread of the commission form of government? Because it is comprehensible by anybody. Some one suggested to us our present system of checks and balances, and we thought it was a fine thing," said Governor Wilson, and then he went into a satirical explanation of how the mayor of a city cannot do anything without the consent of the council, how the council can't do anything without the consent of the

[1] See n. 1 to the second news report printed at June 5, 1911.

board of finance, how that board must have the approval of the board of audit, how the thing ordered by the council must be done by the board of public works and so on.

"What body of American men would set up any other business than the business of government under such a system?" he asked. "The commission form of government provides a government of a few men and lets them run it. There are so few we can watch them. They can't hide behind any one else. By this simplification the American people get control of their business. You get a government you can understand without leaving your business."

Another essential in American government, according to the speaker, was to establish responsible leadership. Under the present system a candidate for governor or President can go about and tell the people what ought to be done and when he is elected on that platform he is unable to do it because he has no control over Congress or the Legislature, whose members were elected on different platforms and in a different manner. We must simplify and concentrate authority, he said. He suggested the general principles of the commission form of government could well apply to the state.

"Some men turn pale at this thing we call the initiative and referendum," he continued. "What does it mean? Simply that we have made things so complicated we have to try something to get what we want. It is a clumsy and possibly a dangerous thing, but it is our means of getting what we want. In other words, 'a poor thing, but our own.' When we are in despair about our legislatures we can get something done if we have the initiative, and we can stop the things they do if we have the referendum. We can't all go to the Legislature and lobby and have hearings before the committee, so we will have a hearing all over the state."

In closing, Governor Wilson reiterated his belief there was nothing alarming in the future; that when the American people have made up their minds what they want they will soberly go about it and get it. They must not leave it to the different sections to determine what they want, but must make up their minds in common council what is good for the whole country.

Printed in the *St. Paul Pioneer-Press*, May 25, 1911; some editorial headings omitted.

A News Report of an Address at the University of Minnesota

[May 25, 1911]

WILSON GLAD TO BE A "RADICAL"

This was another busy day for Governor Woodrow Wilson of New Jersey. He went to his room at the Minneapolis Commercial club last midnight after what he called "a mighty neat" affair in St. Paul, and immediately retired. Despite the fact that he had ahead of him a tiresome trip between tomorrow night and next Monday at noon, he awoke at 8 o'clock this morning cheerful and feeling fit. Then he bathed, shaved, had his injured thumb dressed by his secretary, Frank P. Stockbridge, and had breakfast. For about an hour he dictated to a stenographer, having a bundle of mail and telegrams from New Jersey. Then he went to the university where he addressed the student body.

Governor Wilson urged the students to enter politics whenever they felt there was a call for it, saying it would lift politics to a higher plane. When Governor Wilson, in the absence of President Vincent, was introduced by Prof. W. M. West, head of the history department,[1] as "the hope of American Democracy," there was barely standing room in the chapel, and prolonged applause greeted the introduction of the visitor.

Governor Wilson spoke, in part, as follows:

"In coming to the university this morning I felt a certain reluctance, because in my long association with the administrative life of Princeton it makes it a very difficult matter to avoid those regrets which naturally come from disassociation with that life. The hardest thing that I ever did was to turn aside from that occupation in which I spent the most active years of my life.

"But I was teaching politics and had long instructed my students to go into active politics when a call came to them. The call came to me and I had nothing to do but to take my own medicine or prove my life teaching contradictory. I don't know that there is any sharp demarkation from the leader in the class room and the leader in a political forum. I am not aware of any sharp break in my life in leaving the university to enter politics.

"There was one thing, however, that I was not prepared to find. After dealing with college politicians I find that the men with whom I am dealing with now seem like amateurs. The college politicians have a subtle gift of making the worse appear the better cause. Another thing which I have noticed is that there are too few college men going into politics. If college bred men give their attention to public affairs politics would be put on a higher plane of thought, a more impartial scale of judgment, and would be more purely conducted.

"This is the time for disinterested thinking. It is easy for men to think with passion, but the problems of state should be dealt with as dispassionately as are your experiments in the laboratory where the object is to find facts and truth and not to find what you were searching for or to verify some preconceived idea.

"I don't think that the men who made the Constitution or fought in the Revolution were uncommon men. They were made of the same stuff that we are. They were great because they lifted themselves from the small circle of self-interest to see the greater need of the country as a whole. There are many standards of greatness. We call a man great who has built a great building or written a great book, but we say a man has noble character if he has a margin of moral energy which he is willing to spend for the benefit of society. The nobility of America is made up of those of moral energy who so express themselves in service, usefulness and betterment.

"The nation does not consist of its leading men. It consists of the whole body of the people. You never heard of a tree deriving its energy from its buds or its flowers, but from its roots. The settlement of the great problems of America likewise finds root in the great American masses.

"There is one thing I wish to say to those who keep a partial view of religion. The only thing that kept civilization alive in the mediaeval age was the democratic character of the Roman Catholic church. There was not a chancellory in Europe it [but] did not depend for its administrative ability on the ecclesiasts of the church. It depended on the poorer classes for these leaders. There was not a peasant so poor that he could not become a priest, and there was not a priest so humble that he could not become a pope of all Christendom. From bottom to top the Roman church supplied the middle ages with their administrative ability.

"So it all comes back to the people. It is to the people that we must look to work out the problems of democracy. When some call us radical we accept that term with gladness. Do you know what a radical is? He is a man who goes to the root of things, and when you go to the root of things you get to the body of the people. It is the problem of Democracy to recover power and the opportunity for the average man of the people.

"If you don't subscribe to radicalism, you don't subscribe to Americanism. There is no need of being afraid of this radicalism. If there is anything sound it is the mind and character of the average American. The whole nation remains cool when parts of it are hot. Don't let the people chiefly interested settle your political problems. See that they are settled by the greatest number of people, for the larger the jury, the better the verdict.

"The American people have the gift of reorganization or readjustment. They are now in a period of recrudescence and the political entity will be conducted in the same manner that has marked the nation from the beginning and will mark it until its death."

It was after 12 o'clock when he returned to the club, where he was the guest of honor at a luncheon given by the Twin City Princeton society. Here he talked along educational lines.

Printed in the *St. Paul Dispatch,* May 25, 1911; some editorial headings omitted.
[1] Willis Mason West, professor of history, University of Minnesota, 1892-1912.

A News Item

[*May 27, 1911*]

WILSON AT BRYAN'S HOME

Commoner Telegraphs Greetings From New York.

LINCOLN CHEERS GOVERNOR

Chicago, May 27.—A missed connection caused Gov. Woodrow Wilson several hours delay at Omaha yesterday, and a delegation, led by Harry S. Byrne, a former Baltimorean, who knew the Governor at Johns Hopkins University,[1] rushed him to the Omaha Club, where the visitor met a number of prominent business men at luncheon. Some of the Wilsonites insisted on having the Governor set a distant date for a more extended visit to the city, but no engagement was made.

After leaving Omaha, Governor Wilson was met by a delegation from the Lincoln Commercial Club, headed by George J. Woods, its president.[2] They boarded the train at a little Nebraska town west of Omaha and traveled with him to Lincoln where he was scheduled to deliver the last speech of his Western trip. With them was Charles W. Bryan, William J. Bryan's brother and business manager.[3] He invited the Governor to visit Fairview, the Bryan home, and turned over to Governor Wilson a telegram which had been sent in his care. It was dated New York and read:

"I regret very much that engagements in New Jersey prevent my welcoming you to Lincoln. I hope you will enjoy your visit and carry away pleasant recollections of our city and State.
W. J. BRYAN."

The visit to the Bryan home was one of the pleasantest incidents of the trip. Mrs. Bryan,[4] who met the Governor and the party of Lincoln men who accompanied him, proved a winning and gracious hostess. She expressed regret at Mr. Bryan's absence, entertained the party pleasantly in the cool rooms of the big mansion and then sat down for a half hour's talk with Governor Wilson, in which matters that concerned Fairview and the Wilson home in New Jersey figured more than politics.

Printed in the Baltimore *Sun*, May 28, 1911; two editorial headings omitted.
[1] Harry Stephenson Byrne, Johns Hopkins 1901, lawyer of Omaha.
[2] George Jedediah Woods, president of Woods Bros. and Boggs, a real estate firm; secretary of the Woods Investment Co.
[3] Charles Wayland Bryan, publisher and associate editor of Bryan's weekly, *The Commoner*.
[4] Mary Elizabeth Baird Bryan.

A News Report of a Day in Lincoln, Nebraska

[May 27, 1911]

OUTLINES HIS VIEWS
NEW JERSEY GOVERNOR WARMLY WELCOMED IN LINCOLN.

Dr. Woodrow Wilson, the scholar-governor of New Jersey and potential candidate for the presidency of the United States, received an especially enthusiastic welcome from the people of Lincoln yesterday. He came as the guest of a non-political organization, the Lincoln Commercial club. He received marked attention from all classes of citizens regardless of politics. He visited the university and was greeted by a great crowd of students as one who speaks the language of their tribe. In the afternoon a public reception was held in his honor at the Lincoln hotel and in the evening he addressed the largest gathering ever assembled for the annual banquet of the Commercial club. From the time he arrived from the north at 3:15 in the afternoon until he left for the east at 11 o'clock last night he was the recipient of every possible attention without the least political bias. At the same time everybody looked upon him as a presidential possibility, and that fact crept out continually in the conversation of those who greeted him and in the speeches of introduction at the formal dinner in the evening.

Because of the delay east of Omaha which prevented the distinguished guest from making connections with the train that arrives in Lincoln before noon, Governor Wilson was unable to reach the city until 3:15 in the afternoon. A committee of the Commercial Club consisting of W. A. Selleck,[1] C. W. Bryan, and President George J. Woods met him at Ashland and escorted him to the city. At the Burlington depot the party was met by the

[1] William Alson Selleck, a Republican lawyer and partner in the Western Supply Co. of Lincoln, wholesalers of plumbing and heating supplies.

reception committee of the club with several automobiles and taken directly to the Lincoln hotel.

Among those who acted on this informal reception committee were: J. E. Miller, P. L. Hall, Judge Lincoln Frost, R. M. Joyce, John Dorgan, Chancellor Samuel Avery and F. M. Hall.[2]

Governor Wilson went at once to his room but soon reappeared and held an informal reception in the lobby of the hotel. Perhaps a hundred men were there to shake hands with him. The reception committee saw to it that he was kept busy responding to introductions. W. H. Thompson,[3] democratic candidate for the United States senate at the same time that it is rumored Governor Wilson will be the democratic candidate for president and A. E. Cady,[4] formerly republican candidate for governor in this state, were in the city on other business. Both chatted with the executive of New Jersey. The talk was kept pretty well away from the discussion now going on concerning democratic presidential timber.

"I have been in the west many times," said the governor while shaking hands right and left, "but have never been in Lincoln before. Nice city this. I have been in Omaha several times, and do not count the west at all a stranger to me. Tomorrow I go direct to North Carolina to fill a long-standing engagement for a commencement address."

Governor Wilson smilingly refused to discuss the political situation as regarding the presidential possibilities. To members of the reception committee who met him part way to Omaha he talked freely of political conditions. He declared himself surprised and delighted with the manifestations everywhere of the progressive sentiment in the west, and presaged that it means much in the future policy of the nation. . . .

[2] John Eschelman Miller, president of Miller and Paine, Inc., a general merchandise store in Lincoln, Democratic state senator, 1909-10, and Mayor of Lincoln, 1917-20; Philip Louis Hall, until 1885 a practicing physician, at this time president of the Central National Bank of Lincoln and of the Bank of Mead, Neb., since 1908 vice-chairman of the Democratic National Committee; Lincoln Frost of Lincoln, one of Nebraska's first juvenile court judges; Robert Michael Joyce, vice-president and secretary of Henkle & Joyce Hardware Co. of Lincoln, a Republican; John Thomas Dorgan, president of the Whitebreast Coal & Lumber Co. of Lincoln; Samuel Avery, Chancellor of the University of Nebraska since 1909; and Frank M. Hall, a Republican and an attorney in the Lincoln firm of Hall, Woods, and Bishop.

[3] William Henry Thompson, lawyer and banker of Grand Island, Neb., Democratic nominee for the United States Senate in 1900 and for governor in 1902. He was not the Democratic senatorial candidate in 1912 and did not go to the Senate until 1933, when he was appointed to an unexpired term and served until 1934.

[4] Addison Edgerton Cady, president of the Nebraska Mercantile Co. of St. Paul, Neb., member of the Nebraska House in 1889 and of the state Senate in 1905; unsuccessful candidate for the Republican gubernatorial nomination in 1910.

Shortly after 4 o'clock Governor Wilson was again taken in tow by Commercial club members and taken first to the university campus where he viewed the annual competitive drill exercises then in progress. From there after a very short stop he was whirled to the state house. Governor Aldrich[5] was not in the city, he having gone away to make a commencement address, but several state officers had lingered in the governor's reception room in hope of seeing the distinguished guest. A call was made on ex-Chancellor E. Benjamin Andrews,[6] now ill in a local hospital. The chancellor and the governor were old friends, both being college professors at the same time, the one as president of Brown university,[7] the other as professor of history at Princeton from which position he stepped to the presidency of the institution and from that to the governorship of his state. Mr. Andrews telephoned to C. W. Bryan that he would be delighted to meet his friend but considered it something of a hardship on the latter. Governor Wilson considered this the most important stop on his brief trip around the city. Fairview and the aviation grounds at the state fair grounds, were also on the trip. W. J. Bryan was not in the city.

At the state university Governor Wilson's automobile was driven into the center of a hollow square, the various cadet companies and 500 spectators ranging themselves on the four sides. The crowd then surged in about the automobile, the students cheering lustily for the former Princeton president. As Governor Wilson rose after an introduction by Chancellor Avery, the familiar college yell, "What's the matter with Woodrow Wilson?—he's all right," delayed his opening remarks.

"You are very kind," remarked the recipient of the attention. "But you are taking a great deal for granted when you say that I am all right. In viewing you it occurs to me that I am not accustomed to seeing my students in uniform. I know, however, that you are a uniform lot and I know something of what is beneath the uniforms at any rate.

"I realize that you are interested in me because of my position in politics. The college man who has the temerity to break into politics is naturally a curiosity. However, I did not go into politics; I was pulled in. For twenty years I had been preaching the

---

[5] Chester Hardy Aldrich, Republican Governor of Nebraska, 1911-13.

[6] The Rev. Dr. Elisha Benjamin Andrews, Chancellor of the University of Nebraska, 1900-1908.

[7] He was president of Brown University from 1889 to 1898, when he resigned because his views favoring bimetallism had brought down upon him the ire of the trustees and alumni. Wilson had strongly supported Andrews in this, one of the greatest educational *causes célèbres* of the nineteenth century. See WW to F. W. Taussig, Aug. 21, 1897, n. 2, Vol. 10.

doctrine that every man owed it to his country to take part, to his full ability, in affairs of government. Consequently, when they came to me I had to take my medicine. It was a case of put up or shut up. Being naturally a talkative individual, I shut up.

"I know that you are not here to hear a speech, but rather merely to see a human curiosity. Therefore, I thank you."

The third annual banquet of the Commercial club was held at half past six o'clock at the Lincoln hotel. An effort to make it a formal affair was defeated by the extreme heat which caused more than one half of the members to appear in the coolest neglige costumes they could find. Three hundred and twenty-five men gathered in the foyer of the hotel, and after a brief period of presentation to the guest of honor filed into the banquet hall and took possession of five tables stretched along the length of the room. To facilitate serving so great a crowd the food was placed on the tables as far as possible and the waiters had nothing to do but replenish dishes and serve two or three courses.

During the dinner the orchestra added to the jollity by furnishing special music and singing a song in which Governor Wilson figured in a way not at all to his disadvantage. The boosters who had gathered some songs on their recent trade trip also rose now and then to help matters along, and were encored until their repertory gave out.

George Woods, president of the club, who with Governor Wilson, Chancellor Avery, Mayor Armstrong,[8] Victor Rosewater[9] and members of the local reception committee, occupied the table of honor on the stage, began the formal proceedings by welcoming Governor Wilson and referring to him as one of the half dozen men from whom the people of the United States will choose their next president. Three of these men, he said, were either visiting in Lincoln, or lived here permanently. Governor Wilson, was one of these and Mr. Bryan was the other two. After a short story, a few more brief remarks and a telegram from W. J. Bryan, Mr. Woods introduced Mayor Armstrong, who was received with rounds of rousing and prolonged cheers.

Mayor Armstrong's voice was not strong enough to fill the large banquet chamber easily. He complimented the guest of honor as a progressive politician come out of the so-called conservative east to talk to the progressive west. The Commercial club, said he, had been delighted ever since it became known that the scholarly believer in progressive thought had agreed to speak at the annual

[8] Alvin H. Armstrong, elected Mayor of Lincoln on May 2, 1911, for a two-year term. He was also president and treasurer of the Armstrong Clothing Co.

[9] Editor of the *Omaha Bee*, member of the Republican National Committee since 1908 and chairman in 1912.

meeting. The mayor gave way to Chancellor Avery, introducing him to the audience.

The chancellor remarked that as he had followed the tall figure of the mayor into the banqueting hall he had wondered if he should address him as "your highness." Whether or not he should be called "your serene highness" would depend on the outcome of the next few days in the city of Lincoln.[10] This jocular remark brought instant response from the audience. Chancellor Avery paid a tribute to the speaker. In eastern college circles in which the Nebraska educator had moved the president of Princeton had been considered the greatest of them all, and since he had become the governor of New Jersey he had been known as one of the greatest governors of them all.

Governor Wilson, introduced by Chancellor Avery in lieu of both the ex-chancellor friend of the speaker and the absent governor of Nebraska, was received with rounds of applause, the audience rising to its feet to cheer.

After some pleasant introductory remarks and a tribute to "the great Nebraskan, W. J. Bryan," in which the speaker stated the "sage of Fairview" stands in a peculiar relation to democracy in that he had been a leader of thought in the days now past and gone when it took the utmost courage in any man to keep the attention of the people directed at the things that required a remedy. He had played a distinguished and valuable part, and now at last the nation had passed the period of awakening and was not [now] awake.

Governor Wilson dwelt on the value of states' rights as a method by which the reforms now well under way can be carried through without wide national disturbance. He pointed out that each state represents within itself a peculiar condition and a peculiar problem set to be solved. Each state is grappling with its own paramount issue, and when taken together as a whole, the reform spreading gradually from state to state and intermingling, the whole nation is leavened. The governor declared himself a defender and a believer in states' rights, but not the kind that had disrupted the nation before the civil war. The states' rights he advocated was a doctrine without passion and without prejudice.

As an illustration of what he meant by the necessity of the states taking up reform each by itself, he cited Nebraska and Kansas "that brace of states in the middle west, the pacemakers for the nation," who had led in reform experiments that have now

10 Armstrong had been elected as a "wet" candidate. Prospective saloonkeepers were flocking to the city hall to secure petition blanks for their new licenses, which were to be issued on June 1.

become settled policies in many parts of the nation. In the east people had shuddered at the mention of the "referendum" and "recall." They declared that the doctrine struck at the fundamental theories on which our government is constructed, that it changed representative or delegated government into direct government, and no precedent of a long life for such doctrines could be pointed to. The governor himself, in his eastern college, was won to the doctrines slowly. He used to prove to his classes that the referendum and the initiative would not work. The mischief of it was, said he, that he could still prove it. But the principle does work. It has been tried. Theory had been overthrown by practice.

In Nebraska the reforms had begun by commissions to correct the evils of corporate control of power which the people had recklessly given away years ago in order to tempt capital away from the east and into western development. That was why, said he, that the central west became a pioneer in reform. Its early policy had made the evils to be corrected more glaring than those existing in the east.

In California the people had grappled with the Southern Pacific and taken back the control unto themselves. In Massachusetts the mistakes of easy political life had been gradually corrected until on the statute books of that state are now many of the best laws to be found. A machine still exists there clothed with the odor of respectability, but the people are awakening and the delicate process of retirement is being practiced. In New Hampshire the people have taken back the control which years ago they filtered away. In New Jersey the troubles were too many to be told, but the people have awakened. This is the state by state system of reform which the governor advocated, and through which he expects to see the nation soon on a different basis, and the system which he now calls "states rights."

Governor Wilson discussed legislative reform. "Don't blame your legislators for what they have been doing. You are yourselves to blame. You have built up a system of enacting legislation that is too complex for any average mind to follow. There is no leader created by law. Diverse committees and diverse methods so cover up the progress of bills that no one can tell why they go to certain committees, what is done with them there, why they linger in those committees, and what power brings them forth or bids them stay. If there is no power within a legislature which can hold the body together you may be sure some power will arise without the lawmaking body.

"Under the system you have developed you do not have time to nominate your own candidates for office and at the same time make a living. You let others do that for you. It thus becomes easy for a coterie of persons to control nominations, and what is easier than that these same influences shall say afterwards what these delegated representatives shall do and say. The initiative and referendum, or the taking back by the people of the power to control to themselves is a step in the right direction but it will not cure the evils. The people must simplify the processes of legislation and must then take charge themselves. This must be done state at a time, each state taking its own way about it."

Dr. Wilson admitted that he had said many unkind things about the republican party, but he did not mean the large class of respectable republicans but rather the leaders of the party who have fooled this large and respectable class. He had heard insurgent republicans dubbed by the standpatters as "boxer" republicans. He considered it a good name, and wanted to say that the "boxer" bands were raising the dickens all over the country and would in his opinion continue in a rising degree to do so. . . .[11]

Printed in the Lincoln *Nebraska State Journal*, May 27, 1911; some editorial headings omitted.
[11] Here follows Wilson's advance text, a copy of which is in WP, DLC.

From Henry Smith Pritchett

My dear Governor Wilson: [New York] May 29, 1911.

I have your letter of May 25 from Minneapolis and it is not necessary for me to say that I take great interest in the appointment of your State Commissioner of Education. These places ought to be amongst the most important educational posts in the country and it will mean much to education if a man of the best type can be brought to the position of Commissioner. With the authority which he will have under the recently revised statutes it will be possible, it seems to me, for the right man to effect a reorganization of the school system which will contribute greatly not only to its efficiency, but to the relations of one school to another—for example, of the elementary and secondary schools to each other, of the secondary school to the college, and of the whole school system to the industrial schools. I am, therefore, greatly interested in seeing you find the right man.

I suppose I know as many men who would be thought fit for this post as anyone, but when I take into account the varied qualifications which are needed—educational knowledge, courage, organizing power, and with it all infinite tact, I find it very difficult to point you to a man who can be had who has all these qualities.

There is one man who I feel sure could do the job and he, I think, might be had, and this is Chancellor James H[ampton]. Kirkland of Vanderbilt University. Kirkland has the educational knowledge and the organizing power. He is one of the most clear and convincing speakers of whom I know and has shown his ability to get along amicably and well with the most uncomfortable and warring elements. The great development of standards in the South in the last ten years is due to him more than to any one man. I would like very much to see him undertake this task, but I do not know whether he could be induced to give up the university at this time. He might be tempted somewhat on the ground which I have set forth in several of my reports—that these places at the head of the educational system of a state ought to call out the service of the best men in education. I am sure Kirkland could do the work; whether he can be had or not I do not know.

Another good man is David Snedden, now State Commissioner of Education of Massachusetts, although he has been in his present post only for a few years and might not like to leave it. He is a younger man—about forty-two or three, not the equal of Kirkland in clear and logical statement or in administrative experience, but nevertheless of great ability.

Professor Ernest Carroll Moore, at the head of the Department of Education at Yale, is a good man and made a good record as Superintendent of Schools of Los Angeles, from which place he went to the Yale professorship. He is a man of about forty. My only question about him would be whether his organizing power is equal to the demands that would be made upon it in such a place, but I should consider him a very promising man. I am inclined to think you could get him, although he only went to Yale a year and a half ago, for the reason that the Department of Education at Yale is a pretty thin decoction and is not likely to be anything else for some time to come.

There are several men connected with the Teachers Colleges of the larger institutions—for example, Professor Henry Suzzallo at Columbia and Professor C[harles]. H[ubbard]. Judd of the School of Education at the University of Chicago, who are extremely able men with good ideals of education, but who, in my judgment, would be likely to fail from the standpoint of tact and sound judgment of men. Outside of this possible limitation, both of these men are well worth considering.

This is probably a longer list than you care to have me send you at this moment. I add simply a line to say that if I can be of the slightest service in this matter or any other, you know how gladly I will render it. If you think I can be of any service by coming over and chatting with you, I shall be glad to do so, or if I can be of any service in dealing with any of these men, please do not hesitate to call upon me. I am sure you know without my repeating it that it will be a pleasure to me always if I can be of the slightest assistance to you in the work which you are doing.[1]

Faithfully yours,   [Henry S. Pritchett]

CCL (Carnegie Foundation for the Advancement of Teaching).
[1] About Wilson's action in this matter, see WW to C. N. Kendall, July 7, 1911.

A Commencement Address at the University of North Carolina

[[May 30, 1911]]

I have presided over many a commencement, but I have made few commencement addresses. I have frequently given advice, but it has been principally to young men that I have talked. I got up this morning feeling a little gloominess on account of my separation from young gentlemen about to graduate. I wish to address myself to young men today, not because, as is usually stated, they will some day be mature men, but because this is with them a veritable starting point in life, and a starting point in the nation itself—when a man comes to himself.

This nation is coming to itself, and we must ask, "For what port are we bound, by what chart do we sail?" Man comes to himself when he has found his place in the general order of things around him, and has found his relation to his place. He must learn to play the role of co-operation, to lend his power to the general powers of the team. Kipling's "Ship That Found Herself" is an illustration of my point. Man must find his place in the game of life, where he does not make the rules; but must win his individual place by learning that the individual is related to the race. A man goes out in the world with bolts riveted with stiff notions that require adjustment. He goes from the college class room without knowing the law of actualities. He has learned that a body falls in a vacuum at a given rate, unpulled by other bodies. But outside a vacuum other forces must be reckoned with and adjusted. Do not take yourselves as abstract propositions, for you need to be adjusted. You'll soon have to bear up and take the consequences. It is all right to go out with a certain consequential air, for it will be so brief that I would not deprive you of its enjoyment. The world is going to digest you.

Are you digestible? Will you sit well on the stomach of the world? Will you be palatable or disagreeable? Men will test you and will either absorb you or dispel you. We need to study to adapt ourselves to things. Adjustments are painful things, but they are the things that really test character. I hear a good deal of nonsense about practical studies. It doesn't do to ask such questions. Dr. [Charles] Hodge was once asked by a young collegian if he could smoke and be a christian, with the implication that he could not. By way of reply Dr. Hodge asked the young man if he had seen anything in the Scriptures to the contrary, to which a negative answer was given. Dr. Hodge paused a moment and then said to him: "Don't put a private interpretation on the Scriptures, or you may smoke hereafter yourself." Nor must you put your private interpretation on the principles of life, or you'll smoke with heat from the friction of adjustment.

Affairs need now to be adjusted politically. There is a growing cynicism on the part of young men especially with regard to politics. "What self-respecting young man will plunge into the game and defile himself?" seems to be their sentiment. They think the talk of ideals and of high standards of action are all reserved for the hustings, and are affairs with which practical politics could not deal. There is a movement towards socialism which rests not upon the hope that their program may be carried out, but upon disgust with the existing conduct of affairs. I know a socialist mayor, a pleasant young man,[1] who met me in overalls and jumper and told me that the vote that elected him was twenty per cent socialist and eighty per cent protest. There is a growing number, a great volume of protesting votes. Men hope nothing from parties, seeing that they play the game of tweedle-dum and tweedle-dee.

I will give a short sketch of what has happened in this country. Not long ago the President of the United States offered the South a partnership with the Republican party, making a statement to this effect, "If you will vote with the Republican party you may participate in prosperity which this party enjoys by virtue of its materially prosperous citizens and combinations of the country."[2] The historical explanation of this situation is that we started not with capital and equipment but only muscle and brains; men were face to face with a great crude continent, a store house of infinite wealth that they had to get at with their hands. They fought this task of getting a material hold for one hundred years. They did not know of the existence or location of the splendid infinite wealth of the country. This little band of people strung around through a string of small settlements called

[1] See n. 3 to the address printed at June 2, 1911.
[2] See n. 2 to the notes for an address printed at Jan. 25, 1909, Vol. 19.

in vain to the people of the old world. But only a thin stream of men came with no wealth. They had only men to work with. With nothing but the power of unassisted brains they threw off the yoke of the greatest kingdom on earth and by sheer manhood convinced other nations that it was not safe to lay a heavy hand upon them.

I was in the great West the other day, and the thing I found them talking about was the history of their enslavement. In their wild desire for development, they had called on the East for money and had given too much bond. They gave kingdoms and empires to capital to tempt it from the East. They gave franchises for railroads and water-power rights and the power of eminent domain to condemn the right-of-way and finally the very powers of government. The East came and has answered the expectation of development, but the price demanded was high. The West can today show you the perfection of their development and tell of the wonderful speed with which things have been done, but the people of the West are now coming to count the cost. They have been employees of the East. Their forests are gone, for in the wasteful days of haste a forest was burned down to make a right-of-way and men are looking around to find out how the country can save what she has left. The old states said we are not working for the long reckoning but the present. They have given away their powers until it is true today that the powerful hands are private hands instead of those of the states. Fortified by private rights these "interests" exceed the power of government. Common law could have checked these combinations, but it was not used and now the national government, which has no common law, has undertaken by the statute law to call these combinations to account for their use of power; and it has found that these men have been exploiting the nation.

The country has now reached its maturity and is coming to itself. It is now going to take charge of its own affairs with sober repentance and serious care. An Easterner once said to a man from the West, in discussing President Roosevelt, "It is all right for him to be right, but he needn't go around with a brass band about it"; and the Westerner was just about right when he said, "That is just what you Easterners do need. You damn fools have been asleep so long that you have got to have something like that to wake you up." Now we have no right to call another man a damn fool, but we can apply it to ourselves; we know the facts. For several generations we have been doing this; we have been asleep. The development of America is not the unique thing about our national history. England and Germany have developed the same trade and have attained the same material prosperity. The unique thing is the powers we have given away.

The fundamental question to be asked is "What in every relation of life is the relation toward other people?" Every right has a correlative duty; but in our history the interests have forgotten the duties in development and increase of the rights. I have the right to use my property for my own advancement, but with possession also comes the duty to use it so that it shall not harm my neighbors.

If I disregarded this duty there is no remedy but the force of public opinion. Now this remedy is being applied and is coming out and saying that we must recover the control of what we once owned and have now lost. The tendency of every modern progressive program is one of readjustment and recovery and not of destruction. The strength of the socialist party in the country is not founded on the hope that the program of that party shall ever be realized, but rather grows out of rebellion against existing conditions.

Ordinarily when we think of conservation we think of the saving of our forests and water power, but there is a deeper meaning behind the term, the people have to be conserved and restored to their former condition of high ideals and virile initiative. We have been making our people employees when they should instinctively have been masters.

At a dinner at the house of the junior Senator from New Jersey[3] recently, I professed myself two kinds of a Democrat—first, because I was brought up to be one; and second, because by study and maturing of my judgment, I have become convinced that the Democratic party is in the right. At that time somebody asked, what is a Republican? I answered that a doctrine of the Republican—that is the standpat kind which is the only kind that can be classified, for the others have gone out to graze and can not be placed at any one time—is a man who believes that the government should be conducted by the men who are the material successes and have established the material prosperity of the country and themselves. This is the only way to explain the partnership that has existed between the Republican party and the corporate interests. By this partnership, I do not mean anything dishonest, but rather the result of that sort of consciousness on which the theory of the Republican

[3] James E. Martine. Wilson's memory about this incident was inaccurate. He referred to a dinner given him by the members of the New Jersey Senate on March 3, 1911, when he explained the difference, as he saw it, between a Republican and a Democrat. See the news report printed at March 4, 1911, Vol. 22.

party is based. I am a Democrat because I dissent from the Hamiltonian theory. The judgment of other men than those specialized in the service or control of one interest is more valuable in the conduct of the business of the government of a country than of these men to whom the Republican party has given and still gives the readiest ear. You must absolutely bury yourself in a business to make a great success of it. The very trend of the business of the country is to make a man absolutely immerse himself in one special thing and become forgetful of the general things and interests of the country. I go to men on the make and not to men ready made to draw inspiration in the affairs of government.

The lawyers who have made the great combinations of corporations burglar proof know of the right and the wrong in the system. The Democratic party has no blood in its eye, but it asks for readjustment. Great corporation lawyers and great captains of industry are now coming around to the so-called academic belief that that which opposes special privilege is close to the right.

The great sign of hope in the country today is this. Business men not long ago were continually saying let us alone, don't bother and advise us in this delicate operation of the world of business. They don't say that now and for two main reasons; first, because they know it would be of no use; and second, because those men who look on things just as they are, are not wanting to be let alone. The good business man is sick of his partnership with those who have proven pirates and he now turns about to see a regeneration.

Are you, the young men of the graduating class, going out knowing that things are afoot worth your while and knowing where to strike? There are no laws of fair play in politics. You can strike below the belt, if below the belt lies the vulnerable spot. Today there has grown up a partnership not only between the corporations and the machine of one party, but there exists in some places to-day a bi-partisan machine which controls the policy and votes of the men from both parties. The use of money to-day is not the old fashioned crude use in the direct purchase of a vote, but in getting the control over the vital parts of a people. Not long ago a man said to me, "Governor, I wish to God that I could stand by you, but they have my notes." At that time in New Jersey he knew that his employer wanted him to do what the people did not want him to do. There was a chain of banks all over the State that had notes against men who were trying to expand their businesses and these banks would tighten up on the signer of the note when word came that he was not obeying the orders of the big interests that controlled the line of banks. One young man employed in some highly specialized technical work of one corporation had his wages docked when he voted against James Smith, Jr., for the United States Senate and was discharged when he voted for an employers liability law.[4] But, thank God, a new time has come now when the public is coming to know about these things and will no longer allow them to be done.

We have got to learn that it is not a matter of knowing what to do, but of telling others what is right. When I first got into politics I was called a schoolmaster, but I did not object to the term. A schoolmaster as I understand the word is one who makes a specialty of knowing things and of telling them to other people. This is my mission for New Jersey. If you tell the people of the United States the truth and they believe you, you can neither be given nor deprived of power. Your influence will not depend on the rank of the office you hold, for you connect directly with the people themselves.

The American people are trying to get at facts and to apply the old tests of honesty and integrity of purpose. The distinction of American polity is that its builders sought to construct every part of it in the interests of mankind. The care which our government takes for immigration proves this true and the second generation of the immigrants who have come to this country furnishes the vindication of this American policy.

The atmosphere we must strive for is one of individual worth and integrity. Young men, do not go out of this University without taking with you all the strength of the traditions that glorify the place left here by the men who were here before. The propelling power of the present toward greatness in the future is the tradition of the past. No man is remembered except for the good he did mankind.

Gathered here today is a company of gentlemen who did something that could by no conceivable chance benefit their private fortunes.[5] They performed an act of self-abnegation and absolutely unselfish service and now their presence makes glad

4 Allan Bartholomew Walsh of Trenton, former superintendent of the electrical testing department of John A. Roebling's Sons Co., Democratic member of the Assembly in 1910 and 1911. He was secretary of the Mercer County Board of Taxation, 1912-13, and served in Congress, 1913-15.

5 He referred to a group of Confederate veterans who were being awarded degrees. Of the 308 students from the classes of 1861-68 who left the university to fight, 106 received degrees in 1911. Thirty-one men in this group were living at the time, but news reports do not indicate how many actually attended the commencement exercises.

this commencement day. Some like self-sacrifice, some like devotion to a public sentiment so high, is what I ask from the university man of today. Let love be the motive of life, but not self-love. A man finds himself when he begins to find another better than himself and he finds himself more fully when he begins to love a cause better than the object of his love. These lines from an old ballad illustrate the highest ideal of love:

> "I could not love thee, dear, so well,
> Loved I not honor more."[6]

Printed in the Chapel Hill, N. C., *University Record*, No. 93 (June 1911), pp. 39-46.

[6] Richard Lovelace, "To Lucasta: Going to the Wars."

A Portion of an Address in Raleigh, North Carolina[1]

[[May 31, 1911]]

Mr. Chairman[2] and Fellow Countrymen:

It is very delightful to return to the Old North State and to feel that having been one of you I do not need any formal presentation or introduction to you. You know that it is only true of the region in which a man is born, that nothing there needs to be explained to him. Everywhere else in the United States you find some little strangeness which needs to be interpreted to you, but I do not find anything in the South which does not seem native to my own habit and thought. (Applause.)

Whenever I am introduced in the complimentary terms which your chairman has used, I look around with some trepidation to see how many Princeton men may be present who have known me in the past, and if I see many of them, I feel an uneasiness not unlike that of the old lady who went into a sideshow at a circus and saw, or thought she saw, a man reading a newspaper through a two inch board and quickly getting up, she said: "Let me out of here, this is no place for me to be with these thin things on." When there are too many who have known me in the past, I feel that in the pose of greatness my disguise is much too transparent. And yet it is one of the delightful things of the present moment, ladies and gentlemen, that public speech seems to have returned to something of its old power and significance. I have just been from one side of this great continent to the other, and everywhere I have felt the same thing that I felt in New Jersey last autumn during my political campaign. The audiences in New Jersey did not gather their millions to make a great hurrah for this party or the other; their speakers did not feel at liberty to attack parties nor to attack persons. There was a certain compulsion growing out of the audience itself to discuss the serious questions of the day, as if the discussion itself were a piece of public business. Never before in my observation and views, have audiences in America addressed themselves more seriously than now to the consideration of public questions, demanding to hear the truth and to be led towards those solutions of problems which will lift them to higher levels of endeavor and achievement.

There is no pleasure that I can find in public speech merely as a piece of self-indulgence; there are some speakers of whom one suspects that. I once overheard Mr. Joseph Choate say of Mr. Chauncey Depew: "When I speak, and when most men speak, our object is to discuss something, and we think we have something to say, but with Chauncey it is a form of sensual indulgence." (Laughter.)

There are speakers whom I could name, of whom you could say the same thing, but they would be rebuked in the atmosphere of the present-day discussion. A friend of mine[3] said to me: "If you wish to consider me witty I must trouble you to have me make a jest." And I say of our public speakers, if you wish us to believe you have thoughts worthy of belief on public affairs, we must trouble you to produce them; you must say something and substantiate it by thoughts and arguments which will bear the examination of serious and critical men, for we have come to a serious and critical age in which it is necessary to do something in particular. . . .[4]

Printed in the Raleigh, N. C., *News and Observer*, June 2, 1911.

[1] Delivered in Capitol Square at 5 P.M. before, as the Raleigh *News and Observer*, June 1, 1911, put it, "a great assemblage." Wilson came from Chapel Hill to Raleigh with his nephew, George Howe III, in the morning of May 31 and was the guest of honor at a luncheon at the Josephus Daniels'. After his speech, he was entertained at dinner by Colonel Benehan Cameron, scientific farmer and president of the North Carolina Railroad, and Sallie Mayo Cameron. From 8 to 10 P.M. Wilson was given a reception by the Capital Club of Raleigh.

[2] Albert Lyman Cox, chairman of the committee on arrangements for the Wilson-in-Raleigh day, at this time practicing law in Raleigh and later (1933-61) a prominent Washington attorney.

[3] Augustine Birrell.

[4] The balance of this address repeated much of what Wilson had said in his western speeches.

From Ellen Axson Wilson

My own darling,   Lyme [Conn.] June 1st [1911]

Your telegram from North Carolina was most welcome, and made me feel a little nearer to you. But oh dear, how long it is yet before I am to really see you! Not until the last of next week I suppose. *You* didn't tell about the broken thumb!—but the papers did! How very distressing! I am anxious to know all about it;— if it was very painful, &c. One paper said it was "almost well"— which I sincerely hope is the case. I also hope these cheerful "night letters" have not been concealing anything else. Oh how glad I am that that trip is over!—and how inexpressibly proud of you I am!

Jessie is coming on the next train, Nell not until tomorrow. She is visiting in New Castle, Del. The Smiths[1] also come to-morrow; and you and Margaret about the same time. I hope you will arrange to come together. She goes to Phila. the first of next week to see her throat doctor.

I have been getting on rather well with my work, though we have had so much rain that I have been able to sketch out of doors only six days out of the thirteen. We have gorgeous clearing weather today,—superb violets and blues like "the lake country" after a rain, and I have just got a sketch that is full of pure colour and rather free,—though very rough.

The news from Stockton is *much* better. They have actually succeeded at last in persuading him to work at his lectures. Dr. Dercum says he has written two,—nearly three—and they are extremely interesting and well written. Nothing could be more encouraging, and surprising too;—in view of the way things have been going for the last two or three months. He also says now that he *will* come back and take up his work in Princeton after all. God grant that this better mood may last! I am sorry now that I wrote you as I did in my letter to Minneapolis (Did you get it by the way?) I had to send it to the "Publicity Club" for want of any other address. I saw in the paper that Pres. Vincent was away, so I trust my letter did not give you any trouble.

I wonder how long you will be in Washington;—and if exciting things will happen there.

Did you see the account of the informal poll of the Democratic representatives in which four-fifths (of those voting) voted for you for nominee?[2] It is interesting about Senator Gore too.[3] I am very curious to know how Bryan behaved when you were in Lincoln,—if he invited you to his house, &c.

But I must stop and dress to go and meet Jessie. Sterling[4] is coming for me. Am delighted that you had such a nice restful *family* time at Chapel Hill. I am afraid that, judging from her "fool" letters, you had a bad half hour with Margaret Flinn[5] in Columbia.

Good-bye and God bless you, my darling. I love you inexpressibly. As ever,   Your devoted little wife   Eileen.

ALS (WC, NjP).

[1] Lucy Marshall Smith and her sister, Mary Randolph Smith, old friends of New Orleans.

[2] According to a news article in the *Newark Evening News*, May 17, 1911, an incomplete poll indicated that about four out of five Democratic congressmen supported Wilson for the presidential nomination in 1912. It further revealed that Northerners regarded Wilson as a Northerner or Easterner, while Southerners looked to him as a representative of their region. The poll also suggested that Wilson appealed to former supporters of William J. Bryan.

[3] In a letter to Henry S. Breckinridge of May 25, 1911, published in the *New York Times*, May 27, 1911, Senator Thomas Pryor Gore of Oklahoma had announced his support for Wilson as the Democratic presidential nominee. Gore praised Wilson for his high-minded political philosophy and achievements as governor and concluded: "It is easier to nominate a Democrat who deserves to win than to nominate one who is able to win. We must seek a leader in whom these two qualities are united. I believe that Mr. Wilson answers both requirements."

[4] Unidentified.

[5] Margaret Smyth Flinn Howe, estranged wife of George Howe III.

A News Report of Remarks in Columbia, South Carolina

[June 2, 1911]

WILSON SPEAKS ON LOVED SPOT

Y.M.C.A. Cornerstone Laid on Old Playground.

Woodrow Wilson, governor of New Jersey and one of the few men in the United States who is being seriously considered as the standard bearer of the Democratic party in 1912, came back home yesterday.

It was a pleasant moment in his life and he said that he would have been disappointed had he not been given the privilege of addressing the people of Columbia at the cornerstone laying of the Y.M.C.A. building. He delivered the principal address in the First Baptist church, rain forcing an abandonment of the exercises on the site of the new building on Sumter street. There were several hundred Columbians present to hear his address and he was given a most cordial welcome back home, as a former Columbian.

It was most appropriate for Gov. Wilson to deliver the address at the exercises. The lot on which the new building is being erected was presented to the association by Mrs. James Woodrow[1] of Columbia, an aunt of Gov. Wilson. It was on the lot next to the Woodrow home where Gov. Wilson played when a boy. The occasion was sacred for it brought sweet memories to him. He said that it was easy to speak without personal feeling. He paid a high tribute to the work of the Y.M.C.A.

"I congratulate all on taking a new start in the old enterprise of the salvation of the world," said Gov. Wilson in speaking of the aims of the Y.M.C.A. . . .

The address of Gov. Wilson was short and impressive. He was greeted with applause and was referred to as the next Democratic president by T. S. Bryan.[2] Mr. Bryan said that it was most appropriate to have Gov. Wilson as the speaker of the afternoon. He said he would ask Capt. W. E. Gonzales[3] of The State to introduce Gov. Wilson. The introduction by Capt. Gonzales was very appropriate.

Gov. Wilson engaged in a few pleasantries as to introduction and said that he thought that he had been most fortunate on the present occasion. He was glad to come to Columbia and he was glad to speak on the occasion of the laying of the cornerstone of the new Y.M.C.A. He spoke touchingly of his uncle, the late Dr. James Woodrow, and said that his life had been an inspiring example to him. He said that such occasions must have a touch of the spirit. He pointed out that the people do not attend the exercises incident to the laying of a cornerstone of a great commercial establishment.

The Y.M.C.A. as a great world movement was praised by Gov. Wilson.

"The Y.M.C.A. is transforming the face of great kingdoms," said Gov. Wilson. This statement was made with reference to the work of the association in China.

Printed in the Columbia, S. C., *State*, June 2, 1911; some editorial headings omitted.
  [1] Felexiana Shepherd Baker (Mrs. James) Woodrow.
  [2] Thomas Smith Bryan, general secretary of the Columbia Y.M.C.A., banker, and owner of a book store and printing firm.
  [3] William Elliott Gonzales, editor of the Columbia *State* and captain of the 2nd South Carolina Volunteers in the Spanish-American War.

An Address in Columbia to the South Carolina Press Association[1]

[[June 2, 1911]]

Mr. Chairman[2] and Gentlemen of the South Carolina Press Association, Ladies and Gentlemen:

I am very much indebted to Mr. Kohn for the generous terms in which he has introduced me, but I must warn you not to take them too seriously, and I am very much obliged to you for

  [1] Delivered in the Columbia Theatre.
  [2] August Kohn, retiring president of the South Carolina Press Association, head of the Columbia bureau of the Charleston *News and Courier*.

the very gracious receptions you have given me. I have looked about me with much apprehension lest I see too many persons in the audience who, having known me when a boy in Columbia, for it is very inconvenient when one is too indulgent of the voice of boyhood to know how then to disguise himself. . . . But it is a great privilege to come back to a place which a man has known and loved, and receive such a reception as you have given me, and it is an added privilege to be able to talk to people who know and discuss questions of our national life, because we are very much preoccupied with these questions, ladies and gentlemen, and it is worth while to discuss them very seriously indeed.

During the campaign which was recently waged in New Jersey, I felt when I met the audiences which I met from time to time as though a very singular and significant change had come over the politics of my friends and neighbors in New Jersey. I have been to a great many political meetings in my time, but I have never before seen such political meetings as came together in New Jersey last autumn. I do not mean that they were bigger than usual, though they were big—but that a new atmosphere prevailed. Those people had not come together in order to hear the platitudes that were ordinarily uttered in praise of one party and in dispraise of the other. They were not interested in the repetition and discussion of old party formulas. They knew there were things that should be done in New Jersey. They knew that both the parties in New Jersey had for many campaigns been promising to do them. They knew that they had not been done, and they wanted to know what was going to happen. They wanted to hear a very serious discussion of the actual situation of affairs, and of the actual state of facts, not only in New Jersey, but throughout this country. They wanted to learn what it was that was standing between the people of that State and of other States, and their declared purposes in public affairs.

In brief, in every one of those meetings, one felt the electric touch of serious interest and knew that he was in the midst of something that was like the transaction of business. It was not oratory, it was not display, that those people had come together for: It was for the consideration of the things that touched them intimately in their every-day life. For we must not conceal from ourselves, ladies and gentlemen, that there has been a formula of cynicism, of political cynicism, in this country of recent years. I have lived through a great many years with young men, and I have seen the change of attitude that is coming from them with regard to public affairs. They had to come to think that neither party was ever going to fulfil its promises. They came to think that the game of politics was a mere game, that the promises of politics were meant to deceive voters out of votes and nothing else. And they [there] had come from them that concern which had seemed to raise the threat of revolution in this country. For you have not failed to observe the very rapid spread of socialistic sentiment in America. I was crossing the plains of New Mexico [Nebraska] the other day, and I stopped in a little town where the train stopped long enough for me to get out and stretch my legs, and while I was on the platform a very prepossessing young man in overalls[3] came up to me and introduced himself as the mayor of the town, and told me he was elected as a Socialist, but I said, what did that mean? "Why, sir," he said, "I am not deceived by the vote; it was 20 per cent. Socialist and 80 per cent. protest," and what this country was in danger of, and is in danger of, is an enormous vote cast in blind protest against the way in which public business has been conducted. Men are tired of the hypocrisy, and they are going to see a change wrought, no matter what party it is necessary to support in order to see it. So that when I came [come] before a thoughtful audience like this I feel, as I felt in New Jersey, that this is part of the transaction of the nation's business. We are here for very serious purposes, to consider an actual situation, and it is necessary that we should discuss the facts and prepare our stomachs for the facts. There ought not to be any rose water in this business. There ought to be the best of feeling.

We ought to be very careful that we do not indict men whose purposes have been correct, whatever may have been their performance. We ought to see to it that we do not promote publicity, but we ought to see to it also that we speak the truth very plainly and without reserve. And I want you to remember throughout what I have to say, that I am addressing primarily the little company of gentlemen who have recently been assembled in this State to discuss the interest of the periodical press of South Carolina, for it seems to me that there is something very meet that ought to be discussed by the men who are conducting the newspapers of a great State.

I do not understand that the editing of a newspaper is merely to display a state of mind. I must say very frankly that in a great many of the editorials I read, I see a great many things referred to, I see a great many things taken for granted that are nowhere explained in the other parts of the newspapers. I see editorials about what the big interests of the country are trying to do, what

---

[3] Edward E. Mauck, Mayor of Wymore City, Neb., population 2,613. He worked on the Chicago, Burlington & Quincy Railroad.

the passions of politics are known to be. But the news columns do not supply me with the items by which I can put the picture together and understand it for myself. A newspaper is not intended merely to express the opinions which the editor holds. It is also intended to supply the reader with sufficient information to determine for himself whether the editor knows what he is talking about or not. (Applause.)

And that information is not merely the sundry and casual news of the day, and the editorship of a newspaper is a minor kind of statesmanship. You want to assemble your news in such a way and emphasize it in such a way that you will present to your readers a picture of the life of the State and of the life of the Union, so that the reader will have a means of knowing exactly what the important transactions of our local and national life are. Then with how much keener interest will he read the editorials? How much more interesting it will be, as well as how much more easy to form an opinion, and how much more worth while it will be. So that I say a newspaper is not merely intended to show the editor's state of mind. It is intended to show what the present state of mind arises from, what it is based upon. So that I want to ask your consideration of these two things—of two things.

In the first place, what are the economic facts to which we are constantly going back in our thoughts as the starting place for the arguments which we make upon public affairs? We have gone through a great many years of discussion or rather of statements about predatory wealth, by which we are led to understand that certain gentlemen are going about and seeking to make a prey of us because of the power they are able to exercise through their money. But we lack details. We lack, in first place, the lists of the men who are referred to, for it can not be meant that all of our men of means are seeking to make a prey of us. We want to know who the gentlemen are that are referred to, and in the second place we want to know how they are seeking to make a prey of us. For I can not lock my doors against unseen and unknown dangers. I can not defend myself against thieves in the night. I can not see things that are stalking in the dark. If you want to help me defend myself tell me exactly what it is I have to fear, and then perhaps I can discover the means to make my defense against it.

What is [it] that we are afraid of? In the first place we thought some years ago that what we were principally afraid of was the deliberate violation of restraint of trade and restraint of everything that was inconsistent with everything against the men who made the combinations, and so we passed the anti-trust act, and we have ever since then been trying to interpret the meaning of the anti-trust law, and the trusts are just as much in power now as they were when the supreme court of the United States began to interpret that statute. You dissolved the Standard Oil company, but its power is not dissolved.[4] You dissolved the American Tobacco company but somehow its grip continues to be felt in its constituent parts in our several communities.[5] Are we so young, are you so infirm, are you so innocent as to suppose that that is the only way in which it is done? That is the conspicuous way, but men are getting too wise to do it in that way, and you must go very much into particulars.

I would that every newspaper in the country would publish the circumstances of its own locality as it knows it in order that we may see what exactly it is that we have to fear, and [t]here is a great deal to be feared—not fear as those who fear when they think themselves defenseless, but as those fear who fear only ignorance and who are sure when they know they can take care of themselves. For I am not afraid that the American people will not know of remedies for the evils so soon as it distinguishes what those evils are. I am therefore eager that the American people should be minutely informed—surely that is the duty of the press—and gentlemen of the press, there are opportunities in your own community. For example, a farsighted member of congress proposed that the United States should put into its postal laws that no newspaper should be allowed to use the United States mails that did not publish a list of the stockholders or owners of the papers, in order that every reader should be able to know whose opinion it was that was expressed in the newspaper, and whose opinion it was that was excluded from the newspaper, and it was pointed out that that would not go to the root of the matter because gentlemen who own and control the

[4] For a discussion of the Supreme Court's Standard Oil decision, see n. 3 to the news report printed at May 16, 1911. Wilson's assessment of the effects of the decision was substantially correct, for, despite the dissolution decree, complete power over the constituent companies was still retained by John D. Rockefeller and his associates. See Allan Nevins, *John D. Rockefeller: The Heroic Age of American Enterprise* (2 vols., New York, 1940), II, 602-608.

[5] On May 29, 1911, the Supreme Court, following the "rule of reason" set forth in the Standard Oil case, decreed that the American Tobacco Company and its co-defendants constituted a combination in unreasonable restraint of trade and an attempt at monopoly as defined by the Sherman Antitrust Act. However, rather than ordering an outright dissolution of the combination, the court remanded the case to the next lower court (the Circuit Court of the United States for the Southern District of New York) with instructions that it determine upon "some plan or method of dissolving the combination and of recreating, out of the elements now composing it, a new condition which shall be honestly in harmony with and not repugnant to the law." U. S. *v.* American Tobacco Co., 221 U.S. 106 (1911).

press and the influences which the press was exercising upon the public were not so innocent themselves as to hold the stock and let it be known; they would put the stock in the names of uninfluential and unimportant persons, and they would immediately make a private arrangement with that person by which that stock should be hypothecated and controlled by others who were not the nominal owners. So that in some bank lay the nerve centre of that newspaper, and the opinions or influences of that newspaper were controlled by the men who controlled the uses of money made by that banking institption [institution]. See how the thing is made of quicksilver; when you put your finger on it all the constituent parts scatter. See how far you have to go in order to know what is going on in this country.

Suppose you want to develop some undeveloped coal mine, or some undeveloped power or resources of your own community. You go to New York and seek the large man of capital. It may be his money is necessary to develop your coal mine; and suppose you invite the persons whose money you seek to borrow to send down a man, an expert, to look at the property, and suppose he goes back and reports that the property is absolutely good and that the investment will be thoroughly worth while, and then suppose that just as you are about to conclude the contract somebody intimates to the bank that they are very much interested in companies that are exploiting coal mines elsewhere, and that they do not want any competition in your neighborhood, and that they will make it hard for that bank to get any further business from them if it seeks to develop something that comes in competition with them; and suppose that when all the papers were about to be signed and ready to be signed, and the next morning you find they won't sign them, and you go home and your coal mine lies undeveloped.

And suppose there is a water power near your city, plenty of water power to supply you cheaply with motor power and force for your mills, and with lights for your city, and you seek capital to develop that water power and strike the same snag. Suppose there is a great combination in your region of the country that controls some of the chief water powers of the region, and they let these gentlemen know that they are involved also in this enterprise and that it will be made very inconvenient and difficult for them if they allow any competition in water power to enter their region which they have set apart—then you will begin to understand something of the modern situation, something of the system, spelled with a capital S—then you will begin to see that certain great financiers controlling the great business of capital have divided this country up and they have said: "We do not intend to develop water power in that particular community except for ourselves, and we do not intend to let anybody develop coal mines in that part of the country except ourselves, and inasmuch as we do more business than anybody else it will be thoroughly worth the while of the bankers not to make enemies of us, and we have got that part of the country under our control."

A man invents a new piece of machinery, of agricultural machinery, that he knows will be a valuable labor saving machine, and he goes to the banks of Chicago, St. Louis or New York—I want to say parenthetically that I am not giving you hypothetical cases. I know what I am talking about—as the man said, I am not arguing, I am telling you. Suppose he goes to the banks of these great cities and says, "I want a million dollars to build my plant and advertise my product and get it on the market," and suppose everyone says to him that it is an admirable thing and that he is very welcome to the money if he allies himself with the American Harvester company.[6] At one time the American Harvester company was all financed from one office.[7] The American Harvester company is a perfectly honest corporation, and I am very glad to say that it is not now financed from that one office; but suppose that from that office, constituting the whole nerve center of the money seat of the company, you find that you cannot manufacture your article unless you go into financial arrangements controllable by the American Harvester company. What are you going to do about it? There is no doubt about your inventive genius. There is no doubt about your opportunity to make a legitimate fortune. But you can not get your start. You have got to commend yourself to the combinations of money in a particular part of the country, or you are not allowed to make your beginning. What I ask you is, what does that mean, ladies and gentlemen, with regard to the development of American genius? What do we mean, after such things, when we say that the doors of opportunity are wide open to every man in America? They are not? Some of them are shut and double bolted, and we know who has locked them and bolted them, but they cannot be reached by the Sherman anti-trust law. They have not formed any combination. They have not got into any tangible trust. They have not got any power of incorporation. The supreme court of the United States can not touch them under existing circumstances.

6 He meant the International Harvester Co.
7 J. P. Morgan & Co.

What I want to expound to you tonight is this, that there is a huge system of control which we are firing wide of when we utter our diatribes against corporations and trusts. The real trust in this country is a tacit combination of interest without any illegal agreement of any kind, or anything that any lawyer can put his hands on. It is the concentration of the money power. Part of it is due to our banking system, and that is a long story and would tire you, but this circumstance will interest you, that almost all the surplus moneys of this part of the country go to the city of New York, and in some other parts of the country they go to Chicago, and if you are not known in Chicago, and if you are not known in New York, and are not authenticated there in the way these gentlemen or combinations of gentlemen approve, you can not start your enterprise. What does that mean? A man can start along with the competence and knowledge of his enterprise—if a man has got to start in Columbia on the knowledge that they have of him in New York, it may be that he can not start at all. The resources of this country are by the banking system so concentrated in a place where it is difficult to be known, and where you must hope to be before you can start, that a man who is not known there perhaps can not hope to make one.[8]

So it is like the Irishman and the dictionary—he has to go to the dictionary to find how to spell a word and when he doesn't know how to spell it there is no use to go to the dictionary. A friend of mine asked me the other day how to spell "gnat" and he said, "I looked under the n and I looked under the k and I could not find it in the distionary [dictionary]." I told him to try g. He said he had never thought of g. In the financial world you have to know how to spell things and to know securities. You offer them one kind of securities and they say, "I never heard of those securities." You have to offer them something that has already attracted their attention in order to negotiate a loan, and so you are dependent upon the approval of the concentrated body of wealth over which you have no means of control. That is one part of the system, and that is the political part of the system. The real thing that we are interested in in public life, ladies and gentlemen, is not in this system standing along [alone] and unaided, for if it stood alone and was unaided it would break down. We are interested in that system, as it is a system by itself, a partnership with political organization. There never would have

[8] This was Wilson's first discussion of the so-called money trust, but it had no national repercussions, as the wire services did not report this speech. The headline of the news report preceding this text read: "WOODROW WILSON WARNS AGAINST MONEY POWER."

been some of the colossal political organizations that now exist if it were not that gentlemen controlling those organizations had formed a partnership and alliance with the business which is seeking thus to control the enterprises of the country. How does it control the enterprises of the country? You know that legislation has a great deal to do with the enterprises of the country. You can get favorable legislation and unfavorable legislation if you control the legislature.

It is told of a governor of a certain State, which contains parts of a great many of the important railway systems of the country, that at the suggestion of the gentlemen who were at the head of one of those railway systems, he drew up a bill and promoted its passage through the legislature in their favor. As a matter of courtesy he accepted for his services the sum of $50,-000, and then after the bill drawn by himself had passed the legislature in the interest of this railroad corporation he coolly demanded of this railroad corporation [$50,000] to sign it.

They objected to it, whereupon he accepted $50,000 from another corporation to veto it. Do you see no connection, have you heard of no connection between the politics of this country and this kind of business? Have you not heard it suggested that a man was a fool who went to Washington and did not know how to make $50,000 a year? Have you heard no intimation of this sort? Why should there be any money in politics for anybody, if there are no people who pay the money for the politics? Men do not give money unless they get something for it. There must be a quid pro con [quo]. There are various ways in which you expect to get your money back.

I heard this illustration from a Kentucky gentleman. He was speaking of a great campaign fund and said it was not used for direct vote buying. He said: "Down in Kentucky, where I come from, we get most of our water from pumps, and of course you know that the plunger of a pump will sometimes go dry and it will not bring the water up, and the prudent housewife draws a bucket of water before she goes to bed and then in the morning she pours the water in and that lets the water come out.["]

But you will observe that that first water which comes out is that which she poured in, and all I mean to intimate is that this water is poured in to make the pump suck.

And these gentlemen who make the campaign contributions know the law of nature, by which that water is to come out first and they expected to see that same water again and to promote their enterprises.

If you were taking up campaign contributions and would receive a very large contribution from a business concern and then some political question were to come up that affected the interest of that company, wouldn't you feel that possibly you were under a sort of tacit obligation to go slowly in endangering the interests of that company after you had taken their money? I do not know whether you would or not, but a great many politicians do and they do step very gingerly where they are dealing with the interests of that company. For example, there are franchises to sell or obtain, there is restrictive legislation to prevent, there is favorable legislation to obtain, there are transactions which may be promoted or called for, there are preliminary tips which may be given out so that a man may know what is going to happen so that he may make his investments accordingly.

Surely you are not so unobservant as not to know the ins and outs of politics. There was a time when all that it was necessary to do in order to control politics was to make campaign contributions, and the reason the Republican party could get greater campaign contributions than the Democrats was that it had more to give, not only because it was already under the control of the national organization, but because the central organization was the tariff organization, and that it was by the efforts of the tariff that half of the big businesses of this country was being conducted, and it was behind that great pillar of defense they were formed. They could stand any amount of money to support the party that was going to continue the effect and force of the tariff.

A member of the New Jersey legislature came to me during the last session and said this: "Governor, I would to God I could stand with you, but they have got my notes." What did he mean? What did he mean? Why, in New Jersey, as everywhere else, there is a telepathic or telegraphic or some other kind of connection between the banks of the State. They wanted that man to vote in certain ways which would serve their interests. I do not know that I want to criticise them for it, for that is neither here nor there. I am not trying their characters before the bar of judgment. They probably thought that the interests they wanted safeguarded were interests coincident with the company itself; but that is neither here nor there. They wanted them safeguarded. They were afraid that if this man voted the way he wanted to vote, those interests would be jeoparded, and he knew that if he did not vote the way they wanted him to vote he could not renew his notes and that he would be put out of business.

We pay our legislators in New Jersey $500 per year—that munificent sum. He can not support a family on that, he can not support himself on [in] New Jersey on that. And this man was engaged in business for himself and those he loved, and he knew that he would be upon the streets if he could not have credit at the banks. What man can conduct his business without some credit at the banks? And if the banks won't extend you credit you are absolutely at their disposal, and the instance I have cited was not an isolated instance.

I have been interested to tell the story of what has happened in New Jersey: Don't you see the subtle ingenuity; don't you see the close analogy to your individual genius and your property? You can not make any money in politics if you do anything in politics that will bring you into collision with their interests and the alliances, these subtle, hidden alliances. For if you inquire into the motives of those things, men can give you probably many excuses for what they have done. Only what you can not explain is the coincidence that these things happen chiefly to those men who are in the way of those who are exercising these great powers.

Now, I do not know whether these things happen in South Carolina or not, and I do not care. I do know that they do happen in other parts of the country. I have heard anyway, that there were troubles of this kind in South Carolina.

But it is not for me to judge, and it is not for me to denounce them, but I think it is only fair to observe that we have put ourselves into the system which is now controlling us.

The American people are, as you know, impatient to get at their resources. They do not want to use two generations when they can do it in one. They say "You would not have known this place four years ago." They want to tell you, "See this beautiful valley with all the abundant growths. Why, two years ago there was not a blade of grass in this valley, and irrigation and reclamation did it." That is what they are proud of. How did they get it? They could not have got it by their own efforts and muscle.

As we march across this continent, we have heard it said to the men in the East who have accumulated their money, "I need your assistance, your money, and we will give you anything you want, we will not ask you any questions. Do you want franchises and railroads? Well, we will give them to you. Moreover, we will do you every courtesy, and give you every alternate section of the land, and if you will cross the continent with rails, we will make you a present of an empire in the richest lands of the continent, where the cities will be, because of the confluence of the waters and the lay of the land, and we will let you own the places where the people must come and abide, in order to borrow your money into our coffers." They came and brought their capital and developed the country.

They did just exactly what the South is doing today in calling on capital outside its own borders, to come on its own terms. Keep it up and they will possess the lands, and then you will turn around and say, "What have we got for this?" There were we with our own genius, our own knowledge of our affairs, and we have brought it about that we are not our own masters. And then we [you] will have to look about you, and you will find that your constitutions are a barrier over which you can not climb because of the sanctity of the obligation of contracts—the contracts that your legislatures, as well as your individuals, have entered into. And then what are you going to do about it? Are you going to cry out against the consequences of your own folly? Just because you have had a spendthrift youth, are you going to have a sour manhood?

These are the things that it seems to me the newspapers of South Carolina and of every other State should lay before their readers in detail, not in order that you should wreak vengeance on anybody; [not] that the spirit of revolution should come into our hearts because of this wrong we have done to ourselves. But before we can start in the direction of hopeful remedy, we must know the facts and all of us, knowing them, realize that we are all partners to the folly, and know that we must apprehend every in and out of the complicated position before we can start, because we are dealing with the texture of a complicated social structure.

We do not want to dissolve our communities. We want to discover our common interests, not fight one another. But they are to come together in a generous, frank, open understanding, so that we shall see the remedies at the same time that we see the circumstances, and who shall bring this about more readily than the editors of the newspapers? What are you doing with the news of the day? Are you analyzing it? Are you penetrating it? Are you displaying it so you can see its index finger? Are you elucidating it? Are you filling it with reasonable suggestions and, above all things, are you bringing the moral from modern life to your professional classes?

There is a professional class, to which I myself was trained. I mean the legal profession, whose assistance you require at every turn of this complicated business. But we have first got to use them, we need their aid, and we first have got to show them that they can give it to us.

I remember some years ago addressing the chamber of commerce of Cleveland, Ohio,[9] when I was attempting to discuss some very intricate corporate properties [problems]. I said, "I know there must be many corporation lawyers here whose business it is to advise corporations, and I know without consulting you, because I have heard it said in other parts of the country that you are very sharp criticisers of our recent legislation, and that you are afraid that they will cause the ruin of your client's business." "Very well," I said, "suppose that the criticism is just. Who is qualified to point out where the mistakes have been made and what ought to be done but yourselves? You know what the corporations are doing. You know how close they are sailing to the wind. You know the things they are doing that they ought not to do. So if you want to save your corporations from the day of judgment which is waiting for them, come out in all frankness and disclose your full knowledge to our legislators and assist them to a remedy." But I said this, and having been a lawyer myself, I said, "I have not the least hope you will have sense enough to do it." That was said a good many years ago, and I want to say as quickly as possible that I have changed my mind. I think they are going to do it.

There are good lawyers all over this country who know they must come forth and tell what they know in order to save our country from some of the critical mistakes that have been made. For our supreme court in the future, ladies and gentlemen, has before it two colossal endeavors. One is to get our economical development into our own hands and the other is to get our political institutions into our own hands.

I would rather, after an experience of 54 years, consult the ordinary man of business in a small way who is in the great struggle for existence with regard to the real situation in America than to discuss it with any captain of industry, because our captains of industry that I know of have charge of so great affairs he has lost his vision of the course of American affairs, and the man who knows the strength of the current is the man who is trying to swim against it.

Have we lost the vision of America? Have we forgotten that America was intended for the service of mankind? Have we so lost that vision that we suppose that America was intended for the creation of wealth only? We shall cease to be America when we prefer our material resources to our spiritual impulses, and I tell you that what is to be recovered in the immediate future of America is that original spirit of her affairs shown in those

[9] His address, "Ideals of Public Life," is printed at Nov. 16, 1907, Vol. 17.

days of the Revolution, when men turned their back upon their interests and set their feet in the path of duty.

Do you remember what the great Washington said in those discouraging days when they were without a quorum in Philadelphia, before the convention could get together to form the constitution of the United States? They had waited week after week for so much as a quorum of the States to get together, and in a hopeless mood one day they were talking of compromising, of trying something in the stead of the big thing they had hoped for to accomplish, and Washington said: "Gentlemen, we must set up a standard to which the wise and prudent will resort." That was the spirit which courage marked. It was not the spirit of accommodation, but the spirit of standardized duty, of the full vision of what was necessary to do.

Do you remember that beautiful position of Utopia, in which he agrees how in that critical time America, with perfect self-poise, will set up a new occasion without having wept a single tear or drained a single drop of blood from mankind.[10] We shall accommodate interest with interest. We shall readjust our institutions to the common standards of power, and then we shall erect a new politics for a new age, without having drained a single tear or a single drop of blood from mankind.

Printed in the Columbia, S. C., *State*, June 3, 1911.

10 What Wilson undoubtedly said was something like the following: "Do you remember that beautiful passage from de Tocqueville, in which he told how in that critical time America, with perfect self-poise, set up a new government without causing a single tear to be shed or draining a single drop of blood from mankind?" Wilson paraphrased this famous passage from Alexis de Tocqueville, *Democracy in America*, Vol. 1 Chap. 8, many times.

Two Letters from Ellen Axson Wilson

My own darling,   June 2 [1911] Lyme [Conn.]

Just a line to catch the morning mail. There is a persistent rumour that is worrying some of your friends, that another "tour" is being arranged for you,—the inference being that you are *consenting*. Of course I know that you are not;—that there is no truth in it, beyond the fact that much pressure is doubtless being brought to bear on you to fall in with such plans. But it is said to be making a bad impression,—in New Jersey particularly, but also in New York,—and I was wondering if it could not be publicly contradicted in some way. I enclose an editorial that alludes to it.[1]

Such an absurd thing happened to me yesterday! I went down

to meet Jessie and she did not come. Immediately on my return I looked at the letter to see if I had made a mistake, and lo! it said she was coming on Thursday *June 16th.* Just two weeks later! I was so sure she was coming *this* week, that I did not notice the date. And there was not a word to explain the delay,— much less ask permission! She sure is emancipated! I remember now that she did speak, long ago, of the possibility of staying at the settlement[2] for a while in June. Very disappointing for me! It is a lovely morning, and I am as well as can be. What a tremendous ovation you had in Raleigh!

I love you, *love you, love you!*

Your devoted little wife,   Eileen.

ALS (WC, NjP).
  [1] It is missing.
  [2] The University of Pennsylvania Settlement, 2601 Lombard St., Philadelphia, where she was then working.

My own darling,   Lyme [Conn.], June 2 [1911]

I forgot in my haste to mention one little matter of importance, and that is Julia Dodge's wedding.[1] You will want to write to Cleve—possibly you may be able to go to Riverdale on the 8th. I have sent a present; it is a little picture by Van Laer, a *beauty*! It seemed silly to get silver for those millionaires. This was framed already in a *very* handsome rich, gold frame with a shadow-box, so that it makes quite a handsome present. The frame alone was $20.00! It was $75.00 framed. I knew of course that under all the circumstances we *had* to do it well. I had it sent up here and made a lovely copy of it for myself!! It has just gone off today. It is a beautiful little bit of autumn gold—Keats "universal tinge of sober gold."[2] I enclose the wedding-card.

With devoted love, I am always and altogether—

Your own   Eileen

ALS (WP, DLC).
  [1] Julia Dodge, daughter of Cleveland Hoadley Dodge and Grace Parish Dodge, married James Childs Rea, Princeton 1904, employed by the Oliver Iron and Steel Company of Pittsburgh, in Riverdale-on-Hudson, N. Y., on June 8, 1911.
  [2] *Endymion: A Poetic Romance*, Book I, line 56.

Two News Reports

[June 5, 1911]

WASHINGTON GLAD TO GREET WILSON

Jersey Governor Lion of the Hour Yesterday Among Democrats

WASHINGTON, June 5.—That Democratic members of Congress recognize in Governor Woodrow Wilson of New Jersey a strong possibility for the Democratic nomination for President a year hence, was evidenced in the most emphatic manner yesterday when practically every Senator and member of the House who was in Washington over Sunday visited him in the New Willard Hotel. Among them was Speaker Champ Clark, who himself figures largely in the calculations of those who have an eye to the future occupant of the White House.

On the last lap of a 9,000-mile journey which carried him to and from the Pacific Coast with a side trip into the state of South Carolina and North Carolina to spread the gospel of Democracy and civic duty as he views it, Governor Wilson came unheralded into Washington late Saturday night and spent a day in the very shadow of the White House. The Governor had not planned to visit the national capital while Congress is in extra session and the fact of his being here was a circumstance growing out of the vicissitudes of a month's almost steady railroad travel. He left Columbia, S. C., Saturday morning at 5 o'clock and his train connections were such that he could not reach his home in Princeton without a wait of several hours at Trenton in the middle of the night. To avoid this prospective discomfort the Governor determined to stop in Washington over night and proceed to New Jersey at a more convenient time of day. He arrived in Washington Saturday evening at 9 o'clock and went directly to the New Willard Hotel. Senator Martine and Representatives [William Edgar] Tuttle [Jr.] and [Edward Waterman] Townsend of New Jersey happened to be in the hotel at that time and, of course, discovered the presence of the distinguished Jerseyman in the city. A local newspaper man also recognized the Governor on his arrival at the hotel and it was not long before the arrival of Mr. Wilson became noised about among the Washington correspondents. He was soon besieged by reporters and all of the local papers yesterday carried big stories about his being in town.

As a result of the announcement of his arrival in Washington, the Governor early yesterday morning found himself the chief political attraction of the day. His rooms in the New Willard immediately became the mecca towards which Democratic statesmen gravitated throughout the day. Although no list of the visitors was kept, at least 100 members of Congress called upon him before he left here in the evening. On coming into the city he had calculated that he would start for New Jersey during the afternoon, but his time was so occupied in receiving distinguished callers that it was 7 p.m. before he was able to leave without being discourteous to those anxious to shake his hand and have a few words with him.

So frequently was the Governor interrupted by the introductions to members of Congress who called to pay their respects, that he could scarcely catch a minute to talk at length about his views of the political situation as a result of his trip across the continent.

On [a]ccount of the tense situation in Democratic ranks as a result of William J. Bryan's criticism of the House Democratic leaders in connection with the proposed revision of the wool schedule,[1] Washington correspondents were especially anxious to obtain an expression of opinion from the Governor on this subject. At first the Governor was disinclined to make any comment but later in the afternoon he gave out the following statement:

"The resolution passed by the Democratic caucus is a very frank statement and justifies itself by showing that the Democratic party is trying to do the best that is possible and practicable under the circumstances. I mean that when we are revising a system, such as the tariff as a whole, we can make compensations of revenue along the whole line, but in revising schedule by schedule we cannot make these compensations except in individual schedules. That is one of the penalties of the step by step process. It does not seem to me there is any abandonment of principle in the action taken. It looks to me as though the Democratic principles had been reasserted. While I am in favor of free wool every Democratic platform has declared for a gradual tariff reduction."

It was obvious to those who were about the Governor during the day that nearly every caller approached him holding the view

[1] The special session of the sixty-second Congress adopted a number of special tariff bills, including one revising the wool schedule of the Payne-Aldrich Act. Oscar W. Underwood, chairman of the House Ways and Means Committee, proposed reducing the tariff on wool from 44 to 20 per cent; Bryan demanded free wool. The Nebraskan issued a statement on May 29 designed to influence the House Democratic caucus, which was to meet on June 1 to consider the wool bill. "The republicans want protection on wool because they believe in the principle of protection," he declared. "Let no democratic advocate of a tax on wool masquerade behind the pretense that he is voting for a revenue tariff; let him not add hypocrisy to the sin which he commits against his party." In a thinly veiled attack on Underwood, Bryan added that Democrats in Congress should not endanger their party's chances in 1912 "by a cowardly surrender to the relatively insignificant number of democratic protectionists who clamor for a tariff on wool in order to win the support of those wool growers who go into politics as a matter of business." *The Commoner*, XI (June 2, 1911), 1. The Democratic caucus approved Underwood's wool bill on June 1, but also adopted a resolution declaring that a more drastic reduction in the wool schedule was impossible because of previous Republican extravagance. New York *Evening Post*, June 2, 1911. Bryan continued his attacks on Underwood during the summer of 1911, indeed, through all the Democratic preconvention campaign after the Alabamian became a presidential candidate. Meanwhile, Taft had successfully vetoed the wool bill.

that he is formidably eligible to become the Democratic standard bearer in the next Presidential campaign. Many of those
who complimented him on the splendid work that he had done
as Governor of New Jersey, while at the same time expressing
admiration for his view of public affairs in general, expressed
the hope that he would be called to higher duties. The Governor
was easily accessible to all who called and under these circumstances it was impossible for him to hold any confidential talks
with national leaders.

"I suppose my political views are pretty well known by this
time," said the Governor during a brief respite from handshaking.
"I may say, however, that one thing struck me particularly during my journey through the West. That is, the political trend
everywhere now seems to be an abandonment of the old party
lines."

Printed in the *Trenton Evening Times*, June 5, 1911.

✧

GOV. WILSON TAKES ISSUE WITH BRYAN ON WOOL QUESTION

Stops in Washington on Way Home and Commends House Caucus for Refusing to Put Wool on Free List.

WASHINGTON, June 4.–Gov. Woodrow Wilson of New Jersey
to-day threw down the gauntlet to William Jennings Bryan on
the wool question. Gov. Wilson stopped off here on his way home
from a tour of the far Western States and all through the day
his suite in the Willard was crowded with Senators and Representatives who discussed with him the political outlook. He declared Democratic prospects were never brighter. . . .

"I was delighted with the reception I received in the West," he
said. "At Lincoln, Neb., I was received royally. Party lines have
been demolished completely in the West so far as the desires
of the progressive people are concerned. I found that there was
virtually no difference between a Democrat and a progressive Republican except on the tariff question."

Asked if he included in this class the insurgent Senators who
have been fighting reciprocity with Canada,[1] Gov. Wilson smiled
and said:

"They are not exactly the class of progressives to whom I
referred. I am heartily in favor of reciprocity, and I think most
real progressives are likewise.

"I was not able to find any difference between the progress
for which the people of the West are fighting and the progress

for which we are fighting in the East. The people of some of the Western States have actually put the progressive measures on the statute books. While we in the East have not had as much success we are fighting for virtually the same things.

"There is little difference in what the Eastern American wants and what the Western man has gotten. They have gotten their desires a little faster than we have, and they have used means which we may not use in the East. There is no doubt in my mind that we will continue fighting in the East until we get virtually all they have accomplished in the West.

"The initiative and referendum they have gotten in the West is the same that we want in the East and the same that we will eventually get. I am and always have been in favor of the initiative, referendum and the recall—except in the cases of Judges—simply as a safeguard, to be used only when it is necessary for the purpose of putting the will of the people above the will of the men who happen to be in office.

"I do not think the Western people expect to use any of these safeguards often. They merely want them to protect themselves when they feel that their desires are being trodden under foot. I believe that they will work the greatest benefits when applied, but I do not think they need in any way overturn the electorate except in segregated instances. Oregon used them often when they were first put into effect, but only to standardize their form of government.

"My trip through the West has convinced me that the prospects of the Democratic party for success were never brighter. The present House has redeemed its promises, and the people of the West realize it. They feel that they are not being hoodwinked, but that they are being given the legislation that they expected.

"The party is stronger than it was last November when it carried the election. It is advancing by leaps and bounds. The growth of Democratic sentiment is more than normal; it seems to be at high tide. No man can tell what the next year will bring, but I believe that a continuance of the present policies of the party will mean success in 1912."

Gov. Wilson will go to Trenton tomorrow.

Printed in the New York *World*, June 5, 1911; some editorial headings omitted.

1 Insurgent Republican senators who were fighting the reciprocity bill included William Edgar Borah of Idaho, Jonathan Bourne, Jr., of Oregon, Joseph Little Bristow of Kansas, Moses Edwin Clapp and Knute Nelson of Minnesota, Coe Isaac Crawford of South Dakota, Albert Baird Cummins and William Squire Kenyon of Iowa, Asle Jorgenson Gronna of North Dakota, and Robert Marion La Follette of Wisconsin. They opposed reciprocity because the agreement provided for virtually free trade between Canada and the United States in agricultural products, lumber, and minerals, which their states produced.

From Andrew Jackson Montague[1]

My dear Governor Wilson: [Richmond, Va.] June 5, 1911.

Since reading your Congressional Government I have taken great interest in your suggestions as to the inefficiency of the American Cabinet. I am very eager to know if you have made a complete reply to President Lowell's reply to your writing on this subject.[2] If so, I will be very happy if you will advise we [me] where I can obtain your literature on this subject. My desire for this information is quickened by the fact that I expect to address the Pennsylvania Bar Association on the 24th instant, and have taken for my subject "A More Effective Cabinet." I have about worked out my address, but in revising it I am anxious to have some literature upon the subject as I know your contributions usually contain. If this does not trouble you I will be happy to have an immediate reply.

The State Bankers Association of this State are eager to have you at their Banquet on June 17th at the Hot Springs. And I believe the representative of this Association has written you extending this invitation. I have been approached to insist upon your acceptance. I know your time is much occupied, and I do not know that you will find it convenient to come, but if you can I trust you will do so. You have many friends in this State who would be only too eager to see you in Virginia, and who would give you an enthusiastic delegation in the next National Convention. The State is, however, now quite well controlled by the machine or reactionary element; and while I think they could be beaten in your behalf, yet your visit and cooperation would conclude the matter in your favor, in my judgment.

Perhaps you would like to visit the State under more influential auspices, or in rather a more disseminating and distributing medium than the Bankers Association. This you can think over and if you desire I will be pleased to have your views at any time with such confidence as you may impose.

Sincerely yours,   [A. J. Montague]

CCL (A. J. Montague Papers, Vi).

[1] A progressive Democrat, in 1901 he fought Virginia's Democratic machine controlled by Senator Thomas Staples Martin and won the gubernatorial nomination, serving as governor from 1902 to 1906. In 1905 he was defeated by Martin in Virginia's first senatorial primary. From 1906 to 1909 he was dean of the Law School of Richmond College (now the University of Richmond). He resumed the practice of law in Richmond in 1909, was elected to Congress in 1913, and served in that body until his death in 1937.

[2] Abbott Lawrence Lowell, "Ministerial Responsibility and the Constitution," Atlantic Monthly, LVII (Feb. 1886), 180-193.

To Andrew Jackson Montague

My dear Governor Montague: [Trenton, N. J.] June 6, 1911.

Allow me to acknowledge your letter of June fifth and to say that I am very sorry indeed to say that I never had time to make a formal reply to President Lovell, except in an essay which appeared in the Atlantic Monthly about the latter part of 1885 or early part of 1886.[1] The subject you have chosen for your address before the Pennsylvania Bar Association is in my mind a very fundamental one and I wish most sincerely that I had something serviceable that I could send you.

It is very kind of you to second the invitation of the State Bankers Association[2] and I wish most sincerely that I could accept it, but the truth is I have already been too much away from home and feel that I ought to stick by my desk now for a good while to come. One or two engagements already made will take me away but they are near at home.

With warmest regards and particular appreciation of what you so kindly say about the feeling in Virginia concerning myself,   Cordially and faithfully yours,   Woodrow Wilson

TLS (A. J. Montague Papers, Vi).
    [1] "Responsible Government under the Constitution," *Atlantic Monthly*, LVII (April 1886), 542-53. It is published in this series at Feb. 10, 1886, Vol. 5.
    [2] The invitation itself is missing.

To George Brinton McClellan Harvey

My dear Colonel Harvey: [Trenton, N. J.] June 6, 1911.

Thank you for your letter of June fifth.[1] It is clear in my mind that it would be a very great mistake for me to accept any more invitations away from the State than are already on my calendar, and I am sorry to say it seems to me impossible for me to come to Vermont.

It would be very delightful to have a talk with you a little later in the season; as soon as I really have seen my family who are now in Connecticut I shall hope to make an opportunity to see you.

The trip was indeed a most delightful and refreshing and enlightening one. I shall have many things to tell you about it.

In haste,   Cordially yours,   Woodrow Wilson

TLS (WP, DLC).
    [1] It is missing.

To Walter Hines Page

My dear Page: [Trenton, N. J.] June 7, 1911.

Thank you sincerely for your letter of yesterday.[1] I hated to rush away from Washington without seeing you again, but it was due to the generous way in which you treated me and left me to the rush of visitors of every kind who had to be seen, but who inevitable [inevitably] kept us apart.

It increases my confidence vastly to be trusted and believed in my [by] men like yourself and the others who are so generously advising and working with me.

I have been thinking a good deal about the matter we discussed the other day with regard to a manager. I find in so many quarters the feeling that in some sense the movement in my favor ought to be allowed to "take care of itself"; that my present judgment, at any rate provisionally, is, the further we keep away from the usual methods, the better. Of course I am far too well acquainted with practical considerstions [considerations] to think that the matter can be allowed to take care of itself. But if we were to secure the services of a man of large caliber who would direct attention to himself inevitably and who would stand in the same category as in the case of the one who is managing for Harmon,[2] I think we would seem to have descended into the arena and would create some very unfavorable impressions.

I would like soon to get hold of you and talk along this line: Would it not be well for the present at any rate to maintain merely a bureau of information and co-operation which a man like Stockbridge could, at any rate, manage until he obviously came to the end of his capacity, at which time we could alter the organization. My idea is that we could refer everybody who wanted such information as co-operation must depend upon, to Stockbridge. He could constitute the necessary clearing house and by mere diligence in keeping track of everything, prevent matters from getting into confusion, or persons in different parts of the country working at cross purposes. He could be supplied with the necessary judgment in important matters by counsel with ourselves.

This is all too complicated a matter. I am going to see McCombs to-morrow and I shall try to arrange, through him, for a little conference.[3]

What you tell me about the conservation group excites my interest greatly.

In haste, with warmest appreciation,

Cordially yours,   Woodrow Wilson

TLS (W. H. Page Papers, MH).

¹ It is missing.

² In February 1911, Governor Harmon had named as his preconvention campaign manager Hugh Llewellyn Nichols, a lawyer of Batavia, Ohio, who had been the Governor's state manager when Harmon was re-elected in 1910. On March 1, 1911, Harmon appointed Nichols lieutenant governor to succeed Senator-elect Atlee Pomerene, Princeton 1884, lawyer of Canton. Nichols continued to serve as Harmon's manager until the end of the preconvention campaign.

³ Wilson and his friends decided that Stockbridge should set up an information office which would confine its activities to sending out biographical data on Wilson, literature and editorials relating to him as governor, and extracts from his speeches. McCombs was to be responsible for collecting funds. The office, temporarily located at 225 West 39th Street in New York, moved to 42 Broadway about July 1. William Gibbs McAdoo joined Stockbridge and McCombs in the summer of 1911. The Wilson nation-wide campaign effort grew from this small beginning.

To John Sanburn Phillips¹

My dear Mr. Phillips: [Trenton, N. J.] June 7, 1911.

I am very sorry to say that it has proved impossible for me to see Mr. Baker² to-day or to-morrow. I am so pressed for time in my work here that the best I can see ahead of me is this: If Mr. Baker would be kind enough to look me up at the Hotel Sterling in Trenton on Wednesday evening next the fourteenth, I would be very glad indeed to see him.

In haste,   Cordially yours,   Woodrow Wilson

TCL (RSB Coll., DLC).

¹ President of the Phillips Publishing Co. of New York and editor-in-chief of the *American Magazine*.

² Ray Stannard Baker, a leading muckraker and one of the editors of the *American Magazine*. Baker hoped to persuade Wilson to write a series of articles for his journal. For the outcome, see WW to R. S. Baker, July 18 and 24, 1911.

A News Report

[June 8, 1911]

FOR GOVERNING BY COMMISSION

Governor Wilson Cheered as He Urges Bayonne Voters to Change Rule.

BAYONNE, June 8.—Governor Woodrow Wilson was cheered last night in the auditorium of the High School here by fifteen hundred men and women when he declared that government by commission is going to be adopted throughout the country and that he believed Bayonne will be the first city in the State to decide for the new order of things.

The meeting was under the auspices of the Government by Commission Association, and all political parties and factions were represented. The Governor was accompanied by his secretary, Joseph P. Tumulty, and Senator James F. Fielder. He said:

"I have come here to-night because I believe in government by the people. For fifteen years I have been interested in this question which you are to vote on next Tuesday. Many cities have adopted it, and I have not heard that the people were sorry.

"Commission government was discovered by force of necessity.[1] I have no patience with political machines and believe they were invented to torment us. We alone are responsible for such machines. Ninety-nine out of every hundred men vote with ignorance as to the ability and character of nine-tenths of the candidates.

"While we have been electing we have not been selecting, and now we are going to start to select. The intelligent electorate has permitted itself to be fooled. While at Princeton I did not know half the men I voted for, and I regularly made a fool and dupe of myself.

"I have learned there is nothing in that to feel chesty about. Both machines are about the same. You are going to get commission government, and then you will not have one official board working against another.

"While we are a religious people, we have depended altogether too much on Providence. The devil sat up all night to devise the present plan of government for cities, and so arranged it that the people could not tell what was going on or whom to hold responsible. It was made as complicated as possible. Neither you nor I can make a machine run the way it was not intended to be run. I want it to be up to somebody in particular to give us good government. The men you elect to office are going to be as straight as a gun barrel, and the people will be looking down into the barrel."

The Governor denied that the police or firemen would suffer by commission government, and said they will be free from being made the spoils of office, as they are at present. He said when people are followed about by a spot light they are going to behave. In referring to those opposing commission government he said:

"I am sorry for those who are side-stepping. I pity cowards and despise liars. I am sorry for the men who are fooling themselves. The people are going to recover their own. I think you in Bayonne are going to have the pleasure of doing this thing first.[2]

"The American people are sitting up and nobody is going to fool them again. They know the game, and have their guns ready. What dignity is there in holding offices and going around like a squirrel in a cage? Under commission government there will be dignity for every man in office, and they will be compelled to give good, clean and honest government.

"I am for commission government from one end of the gamut to the other. We have not been voting beyond the surface and merely pricked the bubble, but did not draw blood. You are going to vote for a board of governors and call time on them, if they do not do right. You will then be in charge of your own business.

"I have been teaching that the referendum and recall would not work, but the deuce of it is they do work. Objections to commission government are very important, only they are not true. We have enough men to man the deck of our ship and we will win."

Printed in the *Newark Evening News*, June 8, 1911; one editorial heading omitted.

1 About the origins of the commission plan of city government, see n. 2 to the address printed at June 13, 1911, and the accompanying text.

2 As it turned out, Bayonne rejected the commission plan by the suspicious majority of two votes on June 13, 1911.

From John Garland Pollard[1]

Dear Sir: [Richmond, Va.] June 8th, 1911.

Your recent patriotic speeches appeal very strongly to me, and I am especially pleased at the success which attended your efforts to place upon the statute books of your state statutes embodying reforms which were needed, and which will serve as an example to other Commonwealths.

I am anxious to see the principles for which you stand presented in this city, and I write to know whether you would be willing to speak here under favorable auspices.

If you do not think it premature, I would be glad to begin the organization of a "Wilson Club" for the purpose of calling upon you to become a candidate for the presidency, and have you come and address the organization at some public meeting. If, in your opinion, now is not the time for the organization of such a club, I would be glad to arrange for your coming under other auspices.

I had the pleasure of meeting you some years ago at the Virginia State Bar Association,[2] and since that time I have followed your public utterances with great interest. You have a great many friends in Richmond.

                 Very truly yours,   [John Garland Pollard]

CCL (J. G. Pollard Papers, ViW).
    [1] Richmond attorney and legal scholar, active in the anti-machine Democratic faction.
    [2] When it met at Hot Springs, Va., in August 1897. Wilson's address on that occasion, "Leaderless Government," is printed at Aug. 5, 1897, Vol. 10.

To Cleveland Hoadley Dodge

My dear Cleve,   Lyme [Conn.], 9 June, '11

As I passed through Princeton the other day I heard something that gave me the greatest concern,—that forces were at work which might succeed in making Hibben President. That ought to be prevented at all hazards. No one would so lay the dear old place at the mercy of the reactionary forces. I know Hibben thoroughly and know him (alas!) to be hopelessly weak and utterly in love with what would ruin the place—viz. the Pyne-West standards and ideals. I know, too, that Fine and Elliott (and I dare say everybody of that calibre) would resign at once. It would be fatal.

No doubt you know all this but I thought it my duty to take no risks and to tell you so.

I hope everything went happily yesterday.

In great haste to catch the post.

Aff'y yours   Woodrow Wilson

ALS (WC, NjP).

From Josephus Daniels

Dear Sir: Raleigh, N. C. June 9th, 1911

I am sending you today a bundle of News and Observers of our issue of the week in which you spoke in North Carolina. I have marked all of the articles that I thought might interest you. Of course, I do not think that you will have time to look over half of them but thought you might wish to glance at some of the articles.

Our people were greatly pleased with your visit and with your speeches and the majority of the papers of the State have spoken of you in the kindest terms. I have heard many of our leading people say that your nomination for the Presidency would insure a Democratic success and a Government that will mean better things.

My wife and boys,[1] who with me, greatly enjoyed your visit to our home, join me in sincere regards and hope that we may have the pleasure of a visit from you again.

With sentiments of esteem and high regars [regard],

Sincerely,   Josephus Daniels

TLS (Governors' Files, Nj).
[1] Addie Worth Bagley (Mrs. Josephus) Daniels and Josephus, Jr., Worth Bagley, Jonathan Worth, and Frank Arthur.

To Josephus Daniels

My dear Mr. Daniels: [Trenton, N. J.] June 13, 1911.

Thank you heartily for your letter of June nineth and for your courtesy in sending me the marked papers. I shall greatly enjoy looking them over.

I was greatly refreshed and delighted by my visit to Raleigh and Chapel Hill and the memory of your personal kindness has lingered with me as the pleasantest part of the trip. Mrs. Daniels and you were certainly most generous hosts.

I sincerely hope that the boy[1] is coming along famously as he promised when I saw him and that all goes well and happily with you.

With the most cordial regards,

Faithfully yours,   Woodrow Wilson

TLS (J. Daniels Papers, DLC).
[1] Worth Bagley Daniels was recovering from an appendectomy.

An Address in Trenton on Behalf of Commission Government

[[June 13, 1911]]

I do not feel that I deserve any thanks for being here tonight. It is my business to be here tonight; it is my business to go wherever my fellow-citizens wish to hear me discuss the fundamental questions of our public life. That is what I am for.

Mr. Campbell[1] has been very kind in his reference to my trip into the West. Campbell and I were fellow-students in Princeton, and Princeton men are always kind to one another, but I must say that I am quite confident that I got a great deal more out of that western trip than anyone else who had anything to do with it, because it was one of the most instructive experiences of my life. I had supposed, for one thing, that we had a special gift of political thought in New Jersey. I knew how absolutely wide

[1] John Alexander Campbell, Princeton 1877, who introduced him.

awake the people of New Jersey were concerning their own political affairs. I found, to my surprise and gratification, that the
people of this country, from one ocean to the other, are just as
wide awake, and that there is going through this whole great
nation a process of thought which, when it comes to the fullness
of time, will be absolutely irresistible, and that runs along a single line, namely, the resolution of the people of the country to
have control of their own affairs. There are differences of opinion as to how this is to be accomplished, but there is no difference
of opinion as to what it is that is to be accomplished, and there
is no difference in the prediction that you will hear upon the lips
of all thoughtful men from one side of the continent to the
other, that by some means or another it will be accomplished,
and that nothing can withstand it.

I have been deeply interested in the matter of commission
government for a great many years. I have waited, sometimes
with waning hope, for the people of this country to wake up to
the real interests and the real facts of the situation, for it is a
mortifying circumstance for an American to reflect upon that
until very recent years, all the best governed cities in the world
were outside of America; and amongst those people who claimed
political enlightenment and political advancement, the worst
governed cities were in America, which we love, of which we
were proud, where we claimed we had a special gift for politics,
where we maintained we had been the first to light a lamp to
show the way to political freedom and political emancipation;
that in America, the most enlightened country in the world, there
was the worst city government in the world. Nobody pretended
to deny the fact who knew anything about what he was talking
of. We used to speak with a great deal of condescension about
the old countries of Europe where there was not the same
protection for the individual voter that there is in America; where
there was the hard hand of a controlling despotism, and yet
we have to admit that in the midst of this apparently despotic
situation there were admirably governed cities, the like of which
we could not show in free America. But there was a glaring
anomaly in the matter. But we ought to be fair, fellow-citizens,
fair to ourselves, fair to the very men whose administration of
our affairs we are likely to condemn in the midst of the present
agitation.

There is nothing to be gained by vituperation, there is nothing to be gained by being unfair; we may as well face the facts.
It is we who built this unsatisfactory system. The men we put
into office did not make it; they did not create the conditions

which are so unsatisfactory; it is we ourselves who created them, and we created them with a sort of pleasurable ingenuity, as if we knew how to do what we wished to do in building up what we conceived would turn out to be the responsibilities of government, and in our Yankee ingenuity we made a machine so complicated that we could not run it ourselves, because the peculiarity of our present city government is that it is so complicated that nobody except the professional politician knows the ins and outs of it. It is a perfect labyrinth, where you can play hide and seek with the men you elect from one year's end to another, and never find them. I admit it shows a certain degree of political originality to make a labyrinth in which you cannot find your own man.

I daresay this was to be a garden of pleasure for us. Away back in the time when they had leisure to spend their ingenuity upon gardens, they loved to make labyrinths. They would build alleys of evergreens that interlaced so that even in broad daylight you could not find your best friend in the garden; you could whistle for him, and you could not tell by his answering whistle where he was, because there was such a subtle return of the echo from this group of nodding and noble trees to the other, and it was like a game of the wits not only to find your friend, but, after you had sought for him for an hour or two, to find yourself and get back to the place where you had started.

I am not inventing anything. I am describing a garden in which I played when I was a youngster. I have lost myself there a hundred times when I thought I knew the garden. The gardener was very proud of that; that was what the garden was for; it was to afford youth his concealment, which was very pleasant, very advantageous when we were young on a moonlight night; very good when we wished seclusion and did not want to be found. And I remember very delectable evenings in such gardens as that. But that is not the model upon which to construct government, not the principle upon which to construct something upon which you wish the light of publicity constantly to be thrown. The fact of the matter is that you cannot find out what is going on amidst such a labyrinth.

Now, the interesting thing that has happened is that when anyone wants to control that government in their own interest, they do not have to control all of it. They have to make up their minds only which part of it they want to control. You have heard of bargains in politics, I dare say; you have heard of deals; you have heard it said that professional politicians will trade offices for one another, and you have afforded them the most abundant and glorious opportunity to do so. All that they have to do in order to accomplish these trades and exchanges is to concentrate public attention upon the top of the ticket, the mayor and the council, and then while you are fighting about who is to be elected to this or that elective board, they are planning as to who shall go on this or that appointive board. Some gentlemen who are opposed to commission government are opposed to it because they control certain boards of the city and know that the game will be up when it is open.

Have you noticed any vociferous and loud opposition to commission government? Not a bit of it. It is all conducted in whispers; it is all conducted in private conferences; it is a gum shoe opposition, and for the very good reason that they dare not come out in the open and say why they oppose it. There are no arguments for us to answer except those we have heard whispered, intimated, conjectured, and repeated from private conversations. Why do newspapers that really want to oppose this thing do it covertly, on the sly, by intimation, by indirection; why do they sow the seed of opposition by intimating that so and so has been the objection and then not answering the objection? Why are they afraid? Why is any man afraid to come out with an honest opinion? Upon my word, gentlemen, the thing I think is lowest in human life is cowardice.

There are objections which honorable men can urge to the commission form of government; there are things which can be said against it, but I do not hear men saying them. Why are the things that are urged against it not those things which can be honestly urged against it in public? Why? Because the opposition is based upon their interest. When you have learned a complicated game and know how to play it and nobody else does, you do not want the game interfered with, and another game substituted which everybody understands and which everybody can play. Of course, you do not want it. If you have gained the skill and intricacy and secretness of the thing you don't want to be interfered with, because you will be put out of business. Now, who will be put out of business?

It is a little bit pitiful to my mind that certain classes of office holders in our cities have grown restless and fearful in the presence of this agitation. It amazes me that the members of a great police force should, as has happened in some cities (I do not know whether this happened in Trenton or not), set themselves out to oppose a change like this on the ground that it renders their hold upon their appointments precarious and doubtful. Do these gentlemen mean to tell us their hold upon office is now definite and certain? Does not everybody in the state know that jobs of this sort, where they are not protected by Civil Service or Tenure of Office acts, are the mere football of politics, and that upon every change from one faction to another in the same party these men are at once the victims of the change? Does not everybody know that the members of our police forces and our firefighting forces, in most of the cities, those men who are the defenders of order, our lives and property, ought never to be subjected to these changes at all? Do not they have to do the secret and dirty work of politics, and do they not know that if they do not do this work they will be rejected and put out of place? Does any man dare stand up and deny that such is the fact? Is not it notorious from one end of the United States to the other that the particular seat of the spoils system is in offices of that kind, and that the machinery of political control is built up out of the personnel of these manly fellows who would like to do their duty without let or hindrance. When I see these handsome fellows, manly and self-respecting, handling our traffic with the ease of men who know how to, commanding their fellows; when I know the stability of our order depends upon their fidelity to duty; when I know that kind of man, upon a sudden summons, will face any mob and dare any danger in order to defend us, and then know that they must yield their manliness, keep their ear open to secret political intrigue, I am mortified—mortified for their sake, doubly mortified for my own. Now does any man mean to maintain to me that a responsible commission, saddled with the responsibilities of government from which they cannot escape, will treat these men in that way? If any man does maintain that, I pity his ignorance. He does not know anything about it, the way this thing is actually operated. If you want security, if you want tenure of office, put trustworthy and responsible men at the head of your government.

You have often heard recited the circumstances which gave rise to this experiment in government in the United States. It originated in Galveston, Texas, after that dreadful catastrophe where the sea rolled in and almost washed the city out of existence.[2] In the wreckage of the city they could not put this intricate form of government in operation at once, and so there had to be some form of government substituted, and in order to get on their feet again they contrived this method of selecting five of their fellow-citizens. And whom did they select? Did they stop and pick out ministers of the gospel? (Laughter.) Did they

[2] See n. 2 to the address printed at March 9, 1909, Vol. 19.

stop and pick out a less reputable, but still eminently respectable class called college professors? Did they go around the business houses and ask the most respectable and distinguished men of business to serve them? All that was impossible and was not thought of. They had to take the men already in the business, so they selected the politicians, the men who had been running the political machine, and, as I have been told, they picked out five machine politicians. They did not have time to choose anybody else, and everybody else was too busy.

It was exactly as it was out in Chicago after the fire, only they were not far enough advanced then to choose a different form of government. But I remember old Dr. Collier[3] telling how his church was blotted out, and the most of his congregation homeless, they met on the ashes of the church the Sunday following the fire and said: "We cannot keep a church together until we have roofs over our heads; we will adjourn our congregation until we have built houses," and Dr. Collier said, "If necessary, I will go back to my original trade of blacksmithing and shoeing horses. You need not bother about me or my salary until a year from now. Then we will get together again and see what we can do. I will take care of myself." Society was reduced to its elements. You could not ask men who had houses to build and businesses to reconstruct to take charge of this end. Then what happened? Five of the old-time politicians were chosen, and it was as if a miracle had happened; they were as straight as strings. All the alleys were down; everything was open; everybody was watching; everything had to be done and they had to do it. Men mind their Ps and Qs in such circumstances.

If you saddle an officer with something that he shares with other officers, then he can have an understanding with them that when he is blamed for anything he will pass it on, and that man will pass it to the next, he to the next, and by the time it gets to him again the whole thing will have lost its venom and impetus. The people will say: "We do not know who did this; it was outrageous, but we cannot catch the man." If every line, no matter how complicated or indirect, leads right to your own blessed self, then, for once in your life, you are going to be a very reputable and respectable citizen. You will take no chances, you do not want to lose your reputation. The whole thing will

---

[3] Robert Collyer, at this time pastor emeritus of the Church of the Messiah (Unitarian), New York. He was a blacksmith in England from 1837 to 1850 and continued this trade for several years after he immigrated to Pennsylvania. From 1859 to 1879 he was pastor of Unity Church in Chicago. It was destroyed in the great fire of 1871 but was soon rebuilt on a larger scale.

brand you as a knave or a fool and you do not like the choice. You would rather prove that you can do it and that you will do it.

Now that is what happened in Galveston, and they have never gone back to the old form of government. They kept it. Not only that, but they so attracted the attention of the whole United States, that it has spread and spread and spread, until something like 150 cities have adopted it, and rejoiced when they found themselves liberated from the influences that oppressed them up to that time.

You have no idea how old the story which Judge Murphy[4] has just told you became at the State House this winter. Why, I had the Board of Water Works (I think it is called that) almost in tears in my office because they said: "We want to pave the streets of Jersey City; we want to make them clean, but that confounded Finance Board won't give us the money." So they introduced a bill providing that the Finance Board be authorized to give them such and such a proportion of the money yielded from liquor licenses. Then they introduced another bill saying that the Finance Board must act within thirty days upon their request, because it was a favorite trick of the Finance Board not to act at all. And we at the State House are expected to spend our time in adjusting the quarrels and amending the government of the great city of Jersey City which is chuck full of intelligent men who can take care of themselves. We do not know how to take care of Jersey City at the State House, but Jersey City is full of men ready to act, who do know how to take care of Jersey City.

There is one thing that I am unalterably against—I am against the government of localities from the capitol of the state, and every chance I get I shall do anything that lies in my power to concentrate the responsibility and to widen freedom of self-government in our localities.

I do not know whether it was just or not to assign to the Board of Water Works such and such a percentage of the excise tax, but because I did not know whether it was wise or not, I vetoed the bill, because I said: "If the citizens of Jersey City choose to tie themselves up in a hard knot, I am not a citizen of Jersey City, and I am not going to undertake to untie the knot." "If I had my choice," I said, "I will give it an additional jerk and tie it tighter so they will find out once for all they have got an impossible form of government." Then I said, "Perhaps they will take things in their own hands and co-ordinate things and manage their own government." I asked these gentlemen why public opinion in Jersey City put up with this state of affairs, where

4 James Murphy, corporation counsel of Jersey City.

one board was fighting another board, or defeating its purpose, if that was the case. And one of them said, "You know, Governor, you can't get the people's attention concentrated on that."

Now, that's just the point, you cannot. But if there is one board responsible for the government of the city, the attention of the people is concentrated all the time. It does not wander.

I once heard that very charming person and very admirable actor, Joseph Jefferson, discoursing to a group of men on the art of acting. He said: "One of the indispensable rules of the stage was this: when the person is supposed to be speaking, saying his lines, nobody else on the stage ought to do anything to distract attention from him. What by-play there was on the stage should be of such a quiet, unobtrusive sort that the eyes and attention of the audience would not be withdrawn from the speaker." That is the rule and secret of attention; that the concentration of attention is at the base of every act of comprehension. Now here is a stage in Jersey City, and in nearly every other city in the state, where all the actors are talking all the time, and where the by-play is so active that nobody knows what the plot is. The thing is against all laws of dramatic art.

I was in the great state of Oregon not long ago, and it happened one of the biggest newspapers, when I arrived in Portland, uttered this complaint—and I wish to say, by way of preface, the state of Oregon is celebrated for its rather advanced and radical legislation in recent years, and the man known to have originated most of the machinery is a very quiet, efficient matter-of-fact man by the name of Yurens [U'Ren]. Almost all of the measures that have been submitted to the people by way of initiative have originated from a group of gentlemen of whom Mr. Yurens is the centre, so most of the changes of recent years have come from him. This paper did not like the situation, and it said, rather ironically: "There are two legislatures in Oregon—one in Salem, the capitol of the state, and the other goes around under Mr. Yurens's hat.["] I had occasion to make an address that night, and I commented upon this. I said: "If I had my choice, I would rather have a legislature running around under Mr. Yurens's hat than a legislature under God-knows-who's hat, because you at least know the man's name and can bag him, whereas, if you do not know under whose hat the thing is going you may go out with a general hunting commission and shoot the wrong man. You generally blame the wrong man.["]

I have very little sympathy with the criticisms against our Legislature and city councils. We have almost come to the place that we feel there has to be intrigue in order to accomplish anything in which, if there is no central force, there has been some lateral force. Suppose you invented a machine, which, instead of working straight at the piston, had all sorts of little circuitous pipes and lines that got daintily at the piston rod and gave it a little shove here and another there. Then you said "confound this machine, it's nothing but a system of intrigue." That would not be just. You invented the machine. Nobody is a fool but you. You invented the machine. Why don't you make another that works according to the principles of simplicity, direction and concentration of force? It can be done at the cost of a vote, and it can be easily done, provided you are just and fair.

I do not know whether the gentlemen who constitute the present city government of Trenton are opposed to the commission form of government or not. I asked and could not find out. I know a number of those gentlemen, and I believe them to be just and public-spirited and honest, as a [I] claim to be. I am not here to utter any indictment against them, or to suggest suspicion of the methods they have adopted if they are opposing this change.

I do not think it is fair to make this a contest against anybody. That is not the way you accomplish anything, except injustice. There is no blood in anybody's eye who is concerned in this campaign for commission government. It is a means of rectifying our own mistakes and putting, it may be, some of these very gentlemen in a position where they can accomplish something that probably they have struggled in vain to accomplish for their fellow-citizens in Trenton. I believe that it will lead to a degree of stability in the government, a degree of non-partisan integrity which has never been known and never can be known under the existing system. You almost obliged men to conduct government under the present system by indirection.

One of the things about the year 1911 is that men in America are not acting by impulse any more. They are acting by thoughtful design; they are not excited; there is not the slightest of the spirit of the mob; they are not out to wreak vengeance upon anybody, but are concentrating their thought upon this question: What are the measures by means of which we can change the existing situation? The existing situation is that your vote generally results in nothing. I have dealt for a great many years, as many of you know, with young men. I have noticed with young men of recent years a growing spirit of cynicism and almost of despair. They have said again and again, "You have said a great many things about the duty of citizens. Men ought to go to the polls and vote; you say the government is no better than the citizens, and if it is not good it is the fault of citizens."

How many times have I not said that and have you not read it from your newspapers and heard it from the platform. They say "We do go to the polls, we do everything that is in our power to do and nothing results. We turn out one set of men and put in another and they do exactly what the other set does. We change parties and come home with a sigh of relief and say 'that will settle something,'" and at first it goes very well. Then that party settles into the old rut, just as if there were a toboggan and you put the officeholder at the top and let him slide. That has not been because of the inferiority or depravity of human nature, because I come back to the proposition with which I started. Human nature is better instructed, guided and supported in America than anywhere else in the world, and they have good government in foreign cities, but they are less intelligent than we are. When I look into it I find a very interesting circumstance. In English or Scottish cities no voter ever votes for more than one person. He never has a chance to vote for more than one person. He votes for the member of the City Council from his own division of the city. In the city of Glasgow, which is one of the best governed cities in the world, there are thirty-two voting divisions and thirty-two members of Council, and no voter votes for more than his man in his district. These thirty-two men, after they assemble, divide themselves into as many committees as there are departments in the city government, and the whole responsibility of all acts rests upon them jointly and severally. Do you think it would require a great deal of intelligence or many meetings to find out how your man was voting in the council or committee, or a very difficult process to substitute someone else for him if he was not doing what you expected him to do.

You know the reason we cannot yet adopt that system in America. We have formed the trading habit. We know by painful experience that if you selected five commissioners from five divisions of the city, every time anything came up that old American habit on the part of the individual commissioner, supposing he represented in the whole city the one-fifth of it, would lead him to say, "No, I am not going to vote for it unless my district gets as much as the other."

I know a city that lies alongside a great river. The greatest artery of the city, where the great movement of people naturally takes place, lay, of course, through one ward of the city. That was the place to build a great broad bridge, broad as a great street, and let the people have free exit over it to the opposite bank of the stream. They spent twenty years getting that bridge, because there were other wards on the river, and the men who represented the other wards would not vote for the bridge in that ward unless they got bridges in their wards. You laugh, but if you laugh at that, why don't you laugh every day. That's what takes place every day. If you do not know it, it is because you cannot know it, you are not taking notice, the thing is too complicated for you to understand. That is going on all the time, this system of trading, and, therefore, in this bill which you are contemplating adopting in Trenton there is a provision for electing the five commissioners at large so that not a mother's son of them will get the idea that he represents anything but the whole of the city of Trenton. I dare say we will outgrow that trading habit some of these blessed days, and then we can concentrate our attention on one man at a time; we can understand one man at a time, and it complicates matters to understand five men at a time.

Foreign cities are, almost without exception, governed by the process of the selection by the voter of one man to represent him, and that makes all the difference between the system abroad of selecting men and the system in America of electing men. I wish every voter could see the world of difference between those two processes. We elect men galore, but the nominating machine selects them. If you want the privilege of selecting your men as well as electing them you will simplify your form of government until you have the whole thing in the palm of your hand and have only to flip a little finger to make them think it is an earthquake. These are not accidents. All the best governed cities in the world are governed according to that plan. The principle is the principle which Judge Murphy properly selected as the centre of the whole proposition—the principle of responsibility. Nothing moralizes like responsibility; nothing sobers like responsibility. I have a suggestion to make to you. If you have a very able friend who is very radical, put him in office and see him tame down. Say, "All right, my friend, you are such a smart Alec; you know how this thing ought to be done. You stand on the street corners and rant. You know so much about it, suppose you try it." You make out of him the sober and responsible wheel horse.

The gentleman in the front row asks who will furnish the information which will enable us to criticise intelligently the things the government is doing, and who will do the criticising? You will notice that this bill provides there can be no secret sessions. It provides that every session shall be so open that anybody that can get in the room and behave himself and keep order can come in. Therefore the newspaper and citizen who has nothing to do with it, can, by personal inquiry, find out what is going on from day to day. There are all sorts of private committee meetings; private sessions of the council itself under the present system. There is an insistence upon privacy and secrecy in certain departments of affairs. This bill absolutely wipes that out. You will have to depend upon your newspapers if you do not depend upon yourself, to tell you what is going on, if you do not wish to inquire about it for yourselves, or do not wish to fight for yourselves. But the access is yours. You do not have to have a ticket of admission; you do not have to have anything except citizenship to entitle you to admission.

Now for the rest you ought to make a point of electing somebody who will have the indiscretion of being exceedingly talkative. An indiscreetly talkative official is a great public asset; he will let things out. There have been gentlemen who have risen high in the public life in America who might be mentioned, who have exercised the greatest power and exerted the greatest influence because they would talk, and would upon occasion tell anything they happened to know, and so inquisitive they were generally on the inside and knew a great many things.

You cannot invent a system of government that will be public in the sense that those who constitute it will get up on the steps of City Hall and harangue the passer-by as to what is going on. If you do not look on you do not see anything, but you can see anything for the pains of looking on. There will be no screens, no shades to the windows; the bar will be open and everybody who transacts business there will be in the public gaze. Every transaction will be publicly recorded and open for public criticism. There is no concealing things that are done by a single body. That is the point I wish to come back to again and again. There is every possibility of concealing things divided among numerous parties.

One of the most annoying things in the world is to go to a five-ring circus. For my part I want to see what is going on in all the rings, but my mind is so interested and my eye so lagging, that I cannot see more than one at a time, and with my inquisitive nature I generally miss them all by trying to see them all.

Now, I propose that you make out of your city government a one-ring circus, where particularly noticeable it will be if anyone attempts an unusually acrobatic feature.

Do you not realize, gentlemen, the significance of the meeting of this evening? We are here to discuss a matter, which in our thoughts particularly concerns the city of Trenton, but we really discuss a matter which concerns mankind. If America fails in the great undertaking of city government; if she does not know how to make 52 per cent of her population happy and free and comfortable, then where will the world look for guidance along the road of liberty. If we fail mankind to whom shall the men of the nations look? When I see an earnest body of men gathered together to discuss a serious, businesslike proposition, simple as it is important, such as you have before you tonight, I think I feel some of that great spirit of mankind which is abroad, where we note the beat of its wing, of that spirit which is always beating upward, upward, in the heavens, always calling out to men what the prospects are right ahead; always calling cheer to them that the road, though it be outside, it not a road which leads to nowhere, but is a road which leads to the accomplishment of the destiny of the human race. Whether Trenton do this thing now or another day is one of the items in the great combined struggle of mankind towards the light, towards the political light. America is finding voice; America is taking on again the armor of her indomitable perseverance and hope, and she will again say to her enemies, "We hold you in laughter; we hold you in contempt; the night is ours and day is ours to possess."

Printed in the *Trenton Evening Times*, June 14, 1911; with corrections from the partial text in the Trenton *True American*, June 14, 1911.

To John Garland Pollard

My dear Mr. Pollard: [Trenton, N. J.] June 14, 1911.

You are very generous and I appreciate your letter of June eighth very deeply. I do not know what advice to give or opinion to express about the formation of a Wilson Club. I am entirely inexperienced in matters of this sort and have not felt that I could myself take any part directly or indirectly in promoting the sentiment which seems to have gathered in favor of my nomination.

My own amateur judgment in the matter would ne [be] that the formation of clubs before, at any rate, the Autumn, would be premature, but I should feel that that depended almost entirely upon local conditions and that men experienced in Virginian politics should determine a question of that kind.

It moves me very deeply that men like yourself should feel such confidence in me. I wish that I felt free to come to Richmond to speak, but I am bound by an extraordinary network of engagements and obligations here and have very little freedom. I exhausted my leave of absence in my recent tour to the West.

Cordially and faithfully yours,   Woodrow Wilson

TLS (J. G. Pollard Papers, ViW).

To Cleveland Hoadley Dodge

My dear Cleve: [Trenton, N. J.] June 15, 1911.

Your letter sent to me at Lyme[1] relieved my enxieties entirely and pleased me more than I can say. It was so straight out and so like you and so full of sterling good sense that it swept my brain of all cobwebs about the anxious Princeton business.

Mrs. Wilson was delighted, as I am, with your suggestion about joining Mrs. Dodge and you on the yacht for a day or two. I am sure it would be possible almost any week end that you might suggest. I can generally get free here by Thursday morning, and if you are planning to be free at some week end before the fourteenth of July for an outing of the sort you suggest, I am sure we could arrange it. It is certainly generous and delightful of you to suggest it. I do not know anything that would do me more good than a long leisurely talk with you on all the subjects that are buzzing in my head.

I have been delighted to hear from many quarters how happily the wedding went off and I hope that when you get a chance you will send our love to the young people.

Always affectionately yours,   Woodrow Wilson

TLS (WC, NjP).
[1] It is missing.

To Henry Watterson

My dear Colonel Watterson: [Trenton, N. J.] June 15, 1911.

It seems as if I never had real leisure to settle down and talk to my friends by letter as I should wish to, and now that I have a moment in which I can give myself the indulgence of turning to you, I find that I am uncertain where to send the letter. I am sending it to Louisville at a venture.

I knew of your return by the glowing accounts of some friends met here and there who told me that they had been on the same steamer with you and had enjoyed Mrs. Watterson[1] and you so much. Your letter of May first from Chateau Des Grotteaux[2] gave me a great deal of pleasure. It is heartening to be remembered by you thus constantly and I hope that in the near future I may have the pleasure of seeing you and having a long talk over the many matters which now fill my head, and in some degree perplex my thought.

Pray let me know the next time you are accessible to this part of the country so that if I may snap my tether I may get at you.

I hope that the winter abroad netted Mrs. Watterson and you a genuine access of health.

With warmest regard,

Faithfully yours,   Woodrow Wilson

TLS (H. Watterson Papers, DLC).
  [1] Rebecca Ewing Watterson.
  [2] It is missing.

News Reports of Two Addresses to Reform Democrats in Harrisburg, Pennsylvania

[June 16, 1911]

CLUB LEAGUE FORMED BY REAL DEMOCRATS

HARRISBURG, Pa., June 15.

With Dr. Woodrow Wilson, governor of New Jersey, a political practitioner who has been awarded a master's degree, in attendance, the State Federation of Democratic Clubs was born here this afternoon.[1] The new organization, after the manner of Democratic meetings, adopted resolutions and elected officers. Then Doctor Wilson, having in mind the matter of the traditional "be it resolved" of similar occasions, proceeded to give the organization some advice that, notwithstanding its youth, made it sit up and take notice. . . .

The Democrats who met here today represented the anti-Guffey element in the party,[2] which has already ousted Arthur G. Dewalt as state chairman and elected George W. Guthrie as his successor, and which has made Congressman A. Mitchell Palmer national committeeman in place of Colonel Guffey, whose place was declared vacant at a meeting of the Democratic state central committee here in the early spring.[3]

The organization formed today is an attempt to give substance to the reorganization movement, of which Vance McCormick, of this city, has been the most conspicuous figure. . . .

Aside from the election, the resolutions and the adoption of a constitution, the only real business was Governor Wilson's speech. The New Jersey executive was introduced while the resolutions committee, appointed by the gathering, was deliberating. It was fully five minutes after Governor Wilson was introduced by Congressman Wilson, who was chairman of the gathering,[4] before the visitor could make himself heard, as the delegates stood up and cheered until out of breath.

"I am," said Governor Wilson, "one, who, during the greater portion of my life have been living in the presence of the future, I mean that it was the 'coming man' with whom I had most to do as a teacher. What I have seen in my work you have seen in yours. I see before me those who are upon the front of the tide in a great movement.

"The tides of mankind are always rolling in and humanity is always making on the shore. I have, during the last few years, gained a powerful impression of the irresistible forward movement of the race. And so have you, or you would not be here.

"I am not one of those who believe that the young man is always a radical. The hold of the past is strong upon him. He clings to the opinions of his fathers, and it is not always good for us to cling to the traditions of the fathers.

"I for one, have wearied of general utterances. We have long said that we desire to destroy special privilege. Who would disp[u]te that program? We would open the gates to opportunity, but we must also open the gates so wide that no man can ever again close them upon us.

"For years we, as a people, squabbled about the tariff. We argued free trade versus protection. That was the old way. Never was there a balloon that was blown into more fantastic shapes by the wind of rhetoric than this tariff. We found out that the tariff may mean work. But we have learned that it may mean a lot of other things besides. We have learned that for one thing it means the grafting of our own incapacities upon the federal government. We have learned that the tariff not only means being protected, but that it sometimes means being carried. We have learned that it is a system of patronage, a great plum tree.

"This tariff that once strutted as a hero is now seen as the villain of the great monopoly play, and its every ugly feature stands revealed. And so the tariff play is over. The facts have rung down the curtain upon it.

"In these times we hear much of Republican insurgency. There is but one definite thing that Republican insurgency so far teaches us—that there are so many things to be dissatisfied with that every man, no matter what his taste, can be suited. The Republican party is so insurgent that it finds every time it tries to get together that it is widely seperated.

"The result is that there has come to the Democratic party a wonderful accretion of power. What are we going to do with it? That's the question. We must know not vaguely, but definitely. My friends the steam is all ready, the power is at hand, things are possible, but we must know what to do with the steam and how to apply the power. The length of our day depends not upon our fund of indignation; not upon our private characters, because a good man may likewise be a fool; but upon our knowledge. We will get no further than the definite exact and scientifically correct program that knowledge frames for us."

[1] In the Board of Trade Auditorium.
[2] About the division in the Democratic party in Pennsylvania at this time, see V. C. McCormick to WW, Feb. 6, 1911, ns. 1 and 2, Vol. 22.
[3] On March 14, 1911. See Stanley Coben, *A. Mitchell Palmer: Politician* (New York, 1963), pp. 34-38.
[4] Representative William Bauchop Wilson. Previously a miner, he helped to organize the United Mine Workers of America and was the secretary-treasurer of the union from 1900 to 1908. In 1911 he was chairman of the House Committee on Labor. He was Secretary of Labor, 1913-21.

❖

MONEY MONOPOLY IS THE MOST MENACING, WILSON'S WARNING

Credit Is Dangerously Concentrated, Says Governor

LIBERTY IN PERIL

HARRISBURG, Pa., June 15.

Two thousand persons sized up the governor of New Jersey and the speaker of the national house of representatives as they sat and talked tonight upon the platform of the Casino Theater at a mass meeting held under the auspices of the State Federation of Democratic Clubs. This federation was organized today by the progressives of the party in this state.

Incidentally, Champ Clark and Woodrow Wilson sized each other up. That they were both Democrats who were regarded as presidential timber was the assurance given to the audience by Congressman A. Mitchell Palmer, who introduced them.

Governor Wilson made a remarkable address, in which he declared that the great problem that confronts his party is banking reform. "The great monopoly of this country," he said, "is the money monopoly." The control of credit is dangerously concentrated, he declared, and the growth of the nation is in the hands of a few men.

"Did you notice," said Governor Wilson, "what E. H. Gary, steel trust chairman, said when he was testifying at Washington? Have you realized that he laid bare the facts of the great money monopoly that exists in this country? If you did not notice what Gary said, you have not been working at your jobs as citizens. He, a master of big business, revealed the fact that a few men control the business of this country.[1]

"Now a money monopoly exists. It must be destroyed. It must be destroyed in the interests of those who now direct the affairs of the money monopoly. For if it is not destroyed the whole fabric will sooner or later fall, and in that fall the innocent and the guilty will suffer alike.[2]

"Big business is beginning to realize the dangers that exist. I have heard, you have heard, how we are oppressed. I have little sympathy with these wails. We know what is wrong. I know what is wrong, not because I am smart, but because the facts are plain.

"The corporations are not to blame because you have no public utilities bill in the state. You, the people, can obtain the passage of such a law if you decree it. Those who don't know how to put teeth into a public service commission bill can find out. We passed a pretty good bill in New Jersey." . . .[3]

Printed in the Philadelphia *North American*, June 16, 1911; some editorial headings omitted.

[1] Elbert Henry Gary, chairman of the board of directors and of the finance committee of the United States Steel Corp., testified before the House Committee to Investigate the United States Steel Corporation on June 1, 2, 7, and 8, 1911. This special committee, popularly known as the Stanley Committee after its chairman, Augustus Owsley Stanley of Kentucky, was established to determine whether United States Steel and other companies had violated the Sherman Act and most particularly whether the formation of United States Steel in 1901 had constituted a violation. Gary's testimony on June 1 and 2 largely concerned the administrative structure and organization of that corporation and the interrelationships of its subsidiaries. The effect of Gary's testimony on June 7 and 8 was to confirm the oft-repeated allegation that capital and credit were largely concentrated in New York and that a few investment companies, of which J. P. Morgan & Co. was the leader, dominated credit and controlled the distribution of securities. House of Representatives, *United States Steel Corporation, Hearings before the Committee on Investigation of United States Steel Corporation* (8 vols., Washington, 1911-12), I, 61-300.

[2] Concerning this subject, the text of Wilson's press release (a printed copy is in WP, DLC) read:

"Beyond all these, waiting to be solved, lying as yet in the hinterland of party policy, lurks the great question of banking reform. The plain fact is that control of credit—at any rate of credit upon any large scale—is dangerously concentrated in this country. The large money resources of the country are not at the command of those who do not submit to the direction and domination of small groups of capitalists, who wish to keep the economic development of the country under their own eye and guidance. The great monopoly in this country is the money monopoly. So long as that exists our old variety and freedom and individual energy of development are out of the question. A great industrial nation is controlled by its system of credit. Our system of credit is concentrated. The growth of the nation, therefore, and all our activities are in the hands of a few men who, even if their action be honest and intended for the public interest, are necessarily concentrated upon the great undertakings in which their own money is involved and who necessarily, by very reason of their own limitations, chill and check and destroy genuine economic freedom. This is the greatest question of all, and to this statesmen must address themselves with an earnest determination to serve the long future and the true liberties of men." This text, sent out by the wire services, was widely reprinted in the newspapers.

A News Report of an Address to the New Jersey State Bar Association

[June 17, 1911]

WILSON WARNS BAR MEMBERS

ATLANTIC CITY, June 17.—Governor Wilson's address following the banquet last night was the topic of comment at the opening of the final session of the New Jersey State Bar Association here this morning. The Governor had arraigned the lawyers and criticized the making of decisions upon technicalities. . . The Governor had taken the lawyers by surprise by his departure from the usual after-dinner talk in his plain words about the legal profession. Among other things, he said that what was regarded as a profession had become a business. No other subject was as freely discussed by the delegates. . . .

Governor Woodrow Wilson's speech in part follows:

"The people of the United States are in a very critical mood as to the courts," said Governor Wilson, "and while the respect for the courts is inherent in us all, it certainly has been strained. As for myself, I have a deep-seated, I might say an incorrigible, reverence for the courts.

"I don't want them touched by profane hands; and I agree with what Judge Carrow[1] said, that as far as the courts in our State of New Jersey are concerned I have never even suspected them of being venal. But I must say that our courts, even our courts in New Jersey, have not satisfied the State in regard to its social and its legal development. If we are still to be reverent to the court we must be very sure it is deserving of our continued reverence."

There was no applause when the Governor said this, but instead absolute silence. Every one of the prominent New Jersey attorneys who listened seemed almost dumbstruck.

In beginning the speaker turned the flash of fire upon the lawyer, particularly the corporation lawyer.

"When I look around me," said the Governor, "it astonishes me to think to what I might have come if I had continued to practise law. Still, I have been teaching law all my life, and have been in touch with the currents of lawyers' thinking. This profession has not undergone the same liberalizing in this country of ours that has attended it in other countries. In America alone has it remained a truly technical profession.

"It used to be that the lawyer occupied a position analogous to that of the family physician. He was the special counselor of the citizen, the family and of communities. He is that no longer. He deserved the confidence that was given to him then.

"There are a few men who still bear that relation, but they are very few. You here before me are specialists in technical advice along very narrow lines. Most of you are advisers of the corporations. I know many lawyers who, when a general law question comes up, are obliged to go out and try to find a lawyer.

"The task that is on my shoulders, to find a man suitable for judge, is a very hard one. The field, I may say to you, is getting mighty small. If you have to get a judge you must find a man that knows the general law. It is getting so that you have to catch 'em young and make them judges.

"The community does not any longer regard you lawyers as a body of guides in its affairs. The trouble is that you have abandoned statesmanship to climb to technicality. I am not saying this by way of criticism, but you are now in the business of giving expert advice in technical matters. This I may say to you is not a profession any longer; it is a business.

"We have intensified our technicalities. We have constructed so impregnable a tangle of technicality, an ambush of technicality that surrounds the law and the courts, that we must tear the veil away in order to see the face of the facts.

"We must tear away the shell to get to the kernel, and it seems to the people as if it were all shell, and as if there wasn't going to be any core. Now, you may restore your profession to the confidence of the people, if you will. You may do it in a single year, if you want it done. Why do you not do it? You say you are acting for the community. If you are, why do you not get rid of the technicalities instead of setting up the difficulties anew?

"Let me say that these difficulties and technicalities will be torn away. If this change is wrought without your assistance, it will be wrought to your discredit. There is no mistaking the spirit of the times. If that spirit is hostile to institutions those institutions will fall."

At this point one lawyer cried out loudly, "You just bet they will," this with fervency of feeling.

Printed in the *Newark Evening News*, June 17, 1911; some editorial headings omitted.
¹ Former Judge Howard Carrow of Camden, at this time president of the New Jersey Bar Association. A prominent Democrat, he served from 1898 to 1912 as member-at-large of the Democratic State Committee, in 1904 and 1908 as a delegate to the national Democratic conventions, and in 1908 as a member of the National Democratic Committee. Wilson appointed him judge of the Court of Common Pleas of Camden County in 1912.

To Witter Bynner¹

My dear Mr. Bynner: [Trenton, N. J.] June 20, 1911.

I am sorry that you should not have had an earlier reply to your inquiry² about my position on equal suffrage. I must say very frankly that my personal judgment is strongly against it. I believe that the social changes it would involve would not justify the gains that would be accomplished by it. In the midst of my busy days it is impossible for me to argue the matter as I should like to in a casual letter, but I owe it to you to give to you this very frank statement of my views.

I am warmly obliged to you for the kindly judgment you express of my work in your letter.

Cordially and sincerely yours,   Woodrow Wilson

TLS (W. Bynner Papers, MH).
¹ Poet and editor of Windsor, Vt.
² It is missing.

To Cleveland Hoadley Dodge

My dear Cleve: [Trenton, N. J.] June 20, 1911.

Thank you with all my heart for your affectionate letter of June nineteenth.¹ It has warmed the cockles of my heart.

I admire very greatly what you and Mr. Perkins have done with regard to my newspaper friend and I cannot believe that it can turn out otherwise than fortunately.² He is a fine dellow [fellow] and the paper ought to be a good investment, so far as I an outsider can judge.

Thank you for what you suggest about the yacht. I am sure Mrs. Wilson and I would be only too glad if it should turn out to be possible.   Affectionately yours,   Woodrow Wilson

TLS (WC, NjP).

1 It is missing.
2 Dodge and George Walbridge Perkins had lent about $35,000 to Henry Eckert Alexander, publisher and editor of the Trenton *True American*, to bolster the newspaper's sagging finances. *Campaign Contributions: Testimony before a Subcommittee of the Committee on Privileges and Elections*, United States, 62nd Cong., 3rd sess. (2 vols., Washington, 1913), II, 948-50, 957-60.

A Statement on Trenton's Adoption of Commission Government

[June 21, 1911]

It may be that this is only the beginning of this part of the fight for the people's right to control their own government, but certainly the result in Trenton is most auspicious and encouraging.[1] It represents what will happen everywhere just so soon as the people really understand the full significance of the issue they are voting upon.

Whether the fight goes rapidly or slowly toward success, it is sure in the end to result in the firm establishment of popular control, and as yet no better instrument of popular control in city government has been found than the commission form.

The men who have worked for this object in Trenton are certainly to be warmly congratulated on the success of their work and on the intelligence with which their efforts were pushed forward.

Printed in the *Newark Evening News*, June 21, 1911.

1 The voters of Trenton had just adopted the commission plan by a vote of 6,792 to 4,890.

An Address in Hoboken, New Jersey, on Behalf of Commission Government[1]

[[June 21, 1911]]

Mr. Chairman[2] and Fellow Citizens: I am very much complimented by the generous reception you have given me. That reception, perhaps, creates a sufficient excuse for my beginning what I have to say with a word about myself. I read in this afternoon's paper an advertisement concerning the commission form of government from the friends of the measure which I must say attributed to me a role in this matter which I do not deserve to have attributed. I am very anxious indeed to serve in this

1 Delivered in St. Mary's Hall under the auspices of the Commission Government League of Hoboken.
2 Willy Gottfried Keuffel, president of the Keuffel and Esser Co. of Hoboken, manufacturers of surveying and nautical instruments.

matter as a private in the ranks. This is not a matter in which I consider myself commissioned by anybody to speak for anybody. I want to speak my own deepest convictions as a citizen of this great State and of the United States, concerning what I regard to be one of the fundamental questions of self-government. I do not want any man to vote for commission government because he believes in me. I want him to vote for it because he believes in it. (A voice: "You are it.")

I want everything that I say upon the subject to bear the closest and most impartial scrutiny of those who will address themselves fairly to the question. This thing may not be adopted in Hoboken now; but it will be sooner or later. We are not in this thing as amateurs, for amusement; we are in this fight to stay, and we are going to win.

I want to serve a notice on every man who opposes what I conceive to be the interests of the people and their self-government, that I am enlisted for life against them.

I do not say that by way of passional feeling or defiance, but in order that you may realize at the outset that I come here because I felt that I must come; that where my assistance was in the least degree useful in a great cause, it was my duty to render it. In order also that you may realize that I am not speaking casual opinions, opinions formed since the production of the Walsh act, I will say I am speaking opinions rooted twenty-five or thirty years deep and based upon a study of municipal government which has lasted during the greater part of my mature life. This is not a casual matter—not a matter of to-day, not a matter of only New Jersey, and the gentlemen who suppose that because the cities of New Jersey have not yet had the privilege of trying this experiment it is problematical how it will work, are proving nothing else except their personal ignorance.

I want to speak the words of moderation and the words of kindness. Many of the gentlemen who have arrayed themselves against this measure[3] are my friends, as they are Senator Fielder's[4] friends. They are men of ability, they are men of intelligence, and my feeling towards them is not one of hostility, but one of amazement. That men experienced in politics, men who know the great game of human affairs as they know it, should be so absolutely blind to the signs of the times and the great forces of the nation as to withstand this thing—I am amazed that they did

[3] The Democratic City Committee of Hoboken had just adopted a resolution opposing commission government for Hoboken on the ground that the Walsh Act had been in effect for such a short time that the people did not understand all its provisions.

[4] James Fairman Fielder had spoken before Wilson.

not see this great opportunity that was offered to put themselves at the head of this movement to take advantage of the opportunity to prove their devotion to the interests of the people. Instead of arguing merely to retain friends of theirs in office, they should argue to put the people of Hoboken in power.

I know the reputation of some of these gentlemen whom they wish to see retained in office, and I can frankly say that, as far as I am personally concerned, I also wish to see them retained in office; and I believe that every righteously judging man who knows an efficient official from an inefficient official will wish to see those who are efficient retained. For we are now about to begin, by the adoption of this kind of government, the operation of public judgment upon city affairs. And no commission will dare face public opinion after deliberately removing efficient officers from their places of service.

It does not make very much difference from this point of view whom you elect to be your commissioners—why, there are instances by the half dozen in the United States where men were chosen commissioners under acts similar to this who had no special sagacity or independence in politics. Take the conspicuous instance where five old-line politicians were made commissioners.[5] These men had not enjoyed a very high reputation in their community and when they were put in this position of responsibility from which they could not escape they were as straight as strings.

Do you suppose that gentlemen are going to commit questionable acts with the spot light following them wherever they move? Do you suppose that when they are responsible for everything, they are going to be silly enough to try to dodge? When they are lashed to the mast do you think they are going to try to go ashore?

It is sink or swim with the things they are themselves doing; there is no escaping the responsibility and there is no device like this for registering the operation of public opinion.

Therefore, it seems to me that what we have to address ourselves to in this matter is a very simple proposition indeed. It is not a political question in the sense of being a party question. It is not a question, as some gentlemen seem to assume, of the theoretical structure of a government. I am very much amused when I see how much in love gentlemen fall with the division of the powers of government into the executive, the legislative and judicial—when they don't want anything disturbed.

[5] That is, in Galveston.

And how absolutely indifferent they are to it when they want things done in their own interest.

Do these gentlemen suppose we are children and amateurs and have not seen government worked? Why, one of the amazing propositions in the advertisement to which Senator Fielder has referred is this, that they point out the beauty of the present arrangement that if you want anything done in Hoboken you haven't the power or the sense to do it yourselves, and that you have to come down to Trenton to get it done. Now, how many representatives have you in the Legislature at Trenton? (A voice: "None.") I mean how many has Hoboken or Hudson County? You have to ask the legislators of the State of New Jersey, who constitute the majority of the Legislature, and have outsiders sit as a jury upon your needs—and you know how they sit as a jury.

They say, "of course, my dear fellow, if you give something we want down our way, you can have everything you want."

Now, I have had a great deal of experience in these matters. I have had men come from the various municipalities of this great county with actual tears in their eyes beseeching me to sign certain bills, by which the Legislature at Trenton thrust its hand into your government, and without saying so much as "By your leave," undertake to set up boards or change salaries and other things that are your business and not theirs—and I have consistently vetoed the bills.

And they have said to me, "Aren't you going to come to the assistance of the people of Hoboken,["] and I have said the people of Hoboken have not asked me to come to their assistance.

But when I know by some regularly constituted method what the people of Hoboken want I will do my best to help them get it. But I am a partisan of local self-government, and I am not going to undertake to govern the City of Hoboken by my judgment in Trenton.

Senator Fielder did not speak with as much feeling as he might have when he spoke of the government of Jersey City.

It is perhaps in its structure, with the notable exception of one in the State of New York, one of the most unhappily and impossibly constructed governments in the world.

It is made up on the principle that nobody can do anything in particular without consulting everybody else under a system which makes it highly probable that everybody else will wish to head it off and prevent them doing it. Why, they can't even pave a street in Jersey City without getting into a row about it. A row, mind you, that is guaranteed under the charter! Because an elective board asks an appointive board to do so and so, and the appointive board in the same boat of cross currents of politics won't give them the money to do it, and they come to Trenton and say: "Can't we get a law through that will oblige these men to act upon our request within thirty days?" My reply was: "No; I want the people of Jersey City to realize just what a hole they are in."

If they want a good government, a simplified government, they can have it for the asking—and you can have it for the asking.

What we are considering here to-night is, down at the bottom, simply—do you want to run your own affairs, or do you not? Do you want to have an arrangement by which every ambuscade possible can be worked on your [you], or do you want to know what is going on?

These gentlemen opposing this matter are deceiving themselves. They are fighting for power in a way that is absolutely sure to forfeit it. We just had an election in the city of Trenton.

Preparations for this election made singular combinations. I saw men around the State House putting their heads together that had never put them together before. I saw two old machines, Democrat and Republican, drawing together in an amicable co-operation that was most interesting; and I saw after the results were announced last night 3,000 men suddenly organize themselves into a parade—some of the best and most thoughtful and independent men of all classes in the city—and gather in a mass, which you could not penetrate, around the headquarters of the City Commission League, with what in their hands—an American flag! A symbol of their emancipation from privately concerted control, and their introduction into the liberty of self government.

What is commission form of government? It is a form of government similar to that of all the best-governed cities in the world. I wonder if the people of Hoboken and the people of America realize until this movement began in America all the best governed cities in the world were on the other side of the Atlantic. I wonder if the people of America realize that in respect to the improvements in government they are the most belated people in the world. We think of ourselves as a lot of free, untram[m]elled radicals who will do what we blame please. As a matter of fact we are in most respects, city government in particular, behind all the rest of the world. I am not now speaking of the Hottentots, or of those parts of the world not in our class, but of all the parts of the world that are in our class. And in every instance the best city governments are upon the model suggested in the Walsh act. I do not mean that they are exactly similar, but are based upon the same principle, namely that you elect a single body which is responsible for the whole of your administration from top to bottom. There is not a single exception so far as I have been able to discover. Isn't [it] an interesting circumstance that Scottish cities and English, and French cities and German cities and Italian cities—wherever they are well governed are governed upon the same principle? If these differences of race, of national government don't make any difference, there must be something in the principle. Don't you see?

If the same principle everywhere works the same result you have got to take off your hat to the principle, and say there must be something worth looking into in this matter.

We are under a singular disability in the United States. We have to elect more people than anybody else undertakes to elect. For example, compare Glasgow or any other foreign city. No voter ever votes for more than one person. He votes for the councilman from his ward, and that is absolutely the only official which any citizen of Glasgow ever votes for, and Glasgow is celebrated from one end of the world to the other as one of the best governed and most enlightened cities in the world. It manages and owns all its street railways; it has a system of street railways that is not excelled anywhere in the world; and there never has been the slightest intimation of graft of any kind. It owns its own water works, its own gas and electric works, it owns anything it chooses to own and runs it honestly and economically; all upon a system so simple that no man votes for more than one person.

Now, why can't we divide the city of Hoboken into five districts and in each elect one commissioner? Why? For a reason I don't like to give, because it is not very flattering to our vanity. But the reason is that we have gotten into the habit of trading, and we have found out that when we elect members of a council by wards they are going to do the very thing that is sometimes done in the city of Trenton—trade favors ward for ward. And if the members from one ward ask for something, the members from the other wards have got to have something in order to vote for it.

Take the well known instance of a city that lay on the banks of a great river. It was necessary at one particular point to build a great bridge wide enough to accommodate the coming and going of from four to six vehicles abreast in order to relieve the congestion. In order to get that bridge, six other bridges had to be built that the city did not need at all. In order that there might be something for the councilmen and contractors and all the rest of the crowd in all the other wards, the thing was divided up ward by ward, even the purchase of the material. I am sorry to say that has become a habit of American government. And it is to break up that habit that this act requires that the choice shall be at large, and that no one of the five shall represent less than the whole city.

There won't be any basis for trade—nobody to trade with—they will all represent the same people, all be exempt therefore from the time-dishonored American temptation.

But in every other country in the world with whose arrangements I am familiar, you elect your own representative, and you have him on the hip. You can watch him, know his disposition from top to bottom and at any time you can substitute some one for him—and he knows it—and the result is he represents you and does not represent himself.

Senator Fielder was saying that he had been converted from the old American theory that the people should elect to every office. It does not take you a long time, if you think that over, to follow him in his conversion, because the point is not that the people haven't intelligence enough, but that they haven't time enough. If you were going to make your living you can't pick out fifty or sixty officers every two or three years for your city. You can't pick out fifty or sixty officers for your own business —and you don't try to. Every business I know of is organized so that the head of the business appoints a few superintendents. Each one of these appoints his subordinates, or rather, a group of gang bosses, who appoint and choose their subordinates, and the man who owns and controls the business does not attempt to appoint his own employees. If he did he would not have time to conduct the business. If he was going to pick out everybody, from the superintendent to the boy that sweeps the office, he would have to do as the professional politician does—make a business of choosing men for office. That would have to be his job.

Now if you want to control any part of the modern city government you know perfectly well how to control it. Don't bother about the head of the ticket—the Governor or Mayor, the Board of Aldermen or the Council. If it is the Board of Works you want to control, concentrate your attention on that. The voters are not going to pay any particular attention to who is nominated for the boards. Therefore you go and make your private arrangements with those who do the nominating. In nine cases out of ten nobody is watching, and you can work it to a "T." And the head of the ticket, if sufficiently well known, is going to carry the whole gang in.

You have seen a lot of politics in Hoboken, and you don't need to have me come here and tell you how it is worked.

I am not here to indict the men who have worked it. You have made it necessary by this stupid complexity that men should be professional politicians—by which you mean professional choosers of officeholders. We have substituted what was intended to be a process of select for a mere process of going through the forms of elect.

I ask every man here to carry home with him the idea that to select the man is to know what you are about and to pick him out for "try." To elect is to let somebody else select and merely go through the process of voting for him.

Now, how many men have you time to select in the busy lives you lead? How many men have you time to find out about after the other fellows have selected?? And if you don't like the selections on one side what do you know about the selections on the other side? You have got to go it blind whichever ticket you vote. I know it because I have gone it blind myself.

I have time and again committed the profound immorality of voting for scores of men I never heard of, and didn't know anything about. I must say that I have tried to find out something about the multitude of comparatively unknown men for whom I was supposed to vote, and I could not discover anything. Therefore I had to do the "suffering act" of exercising a suffrage law—an ignorant fool led to the polls by the nose! Now I am tired of that for my part. I want to know whom I am voting for.

Let me call your attention to some very interesting things. You have heard, I dare say, many things about the Judiciary of the State of New Jersey, but among the things that you have not heard, whether you considered them corrupt. You know, as the whole country knows, that the State of New Jersey has an incorruptible judiciary.

You have had all sorts of governors in New Jersey—good, bad and indifferent. Very good, very bad and very indifferent. And if you will look back over the judiciary appointments you will find for the most part they all made just the same kind of appointments to the bench. Why? Because they alone were responsible for those appointments. They could not get behind anybody else; they knew that the whole responsibility lay with them, and thus did not dare monkey with it. They knew that the people of New Jersey would not stand for it; that men might play this trick in the game of politics, but they must not take advantage of their office to gain personal advantage in the appointment to the Supreme and Appellate courts of this State.

Don't you see the moral? Make it a single responsibility and you moralize the man who exercises the responsibility. He may exercise a bad judgment and appoint Mr. A when Mr. B would have been better, but he dare not appoint a man on the ground that he will be serviceable to him, or serviceable to a party, instead of serviceable to the people. The same principle is operated all along the line.

Is Mr. McGovern[6] really a diligent and great Recorder. Then there is not any commissioner that you would elect that would dare to remove Mr. McGovern from office. It all depends upon your known and settled opinion concerning Mr. McGovern. It does not depend upon the commissioner. It depends upon opinion, the whole atmosphere "Opinion" sustains or destroys responsible officials. So that when Senator Fielder and I became partisans of the so-called short ballot we are partisans of the people's control. I can use this image. Suppose you had a great machine, in order to run which you had simultaneously to move a hundred levers. You know you can't simultaneously move more than two. If you were an acrobat, you could move two with your feet, but you can't move a hundred. Everybody would regard that machine as a clumsy and impossible invention and say, "Who can run a machine like that?" You can appoint half a hundred men to run the machine. They can co-operate with that simultaneous co-operation which is necessary for the efficiency of the machine. Concentrate the power in one lever! Then put one man at the lever.

In the one instance you had something you could not control; in the other instance you have something you can control. And under the infinite beauty of a unified system, exemplified in so many machines, originated by American ingenuity, a single touch of one man can control an instrument so powerful as to do the work of a thousand. We glory in it. We think it the very flower and illustration of our genius. And yet in government we do exactly the opposite and go about with our chests stuck out and say we are a self-governing people.

When you make these indirect arrangements, which make it necessary that somebody else should arrange your business for you, then they are going to become partisans of that kind of government.

But the kind that you ought to be partisans of is the governing you can do for yourselves. I have tried to illustrate in every political transaction in which I have taken part, ladies and gentle-

6 John Joseph McGovern, Recorder (police magistrate) of the City of Hoboken.

men, the spirit of generosity and of fairness. I would not have you believe that I have spoken with the least qualification when I have spoken of some of the gentlemen of whose views I have even made fun, as my friends. At any rate I can speak of myself as their friend. And I would have you understand that I am not attacking them because they are running a system which they did not make. They are running a system which you made, or have allowed to exist.

The whole blame, if there is any, is upon ourselves and not upon them; but we would be very blameworthy if we did not exercise our own judgment as to the way in which these things are to be changed and improved. And I want every man in this audience to realize that this is a part of something wonderfully great that is only beginning in the United States.

We are going to witness (even those of us who have reached or passed middle life), we are going to witness in this country a slow, thoughtful, patient, majestic, irresistible change by which the people are going to take charge of their own affairs.

I am interested in this question for Hoboken. But Hoboken is a very small item in the progress of human affairs. Here are several thousand people, living together in a community which is not sufficient a community, for you have not yet consulted enough together as to your common interests. You illustrate in a single part of this great commonwealth in which we live, the impulse and the purpose, the vision and the hope of a great people, and the people of this State illustrate the impulses of a nation.

Do you know what I found in traveling from one side of this continent to the other and back again? I found, to my great mortification, that the people in distant States were surprised that the people of New Jersey had awakened to their own powers and to their own interests. And I told them that the people of New Jersey had been awake for a long time, but that they were awake and were discouraged by the fact that they had been fooled for a long time; that they had elected men to do things and the things had not been done. They knew what they wanted just as well as any people in the nation; that they were just in the situation of that commonwealth of Pennsylvania. The people of Pennsylvania know what they want, are wide awake and abound in intelligence; but they have not yet found the people to do the things they wanted done. They are looking for them, and when they find them there is going to be an earthquake in Pennsylvania.

There is a slow-making volcanic force, not of revolution, but of resolution, in the people of that great commonwealth, as in this, that some day adds to the great voice of humanity where deep cries unto deep in the struggle of the human spirit for liberty!

We are not going to trample the men under foot who have misled us. We are going to take them into the party—elect them commissioners, I hope—some of them—and show that, by happy Christian revenge, that we know what we are talking about—and that even they can be converted to commission government—when it is put into their own hands.

But there is this rising tide which creates in men feelings like this. I was talking to an old gentleman the other day about the signs of the times, and he said:

"I tell you, sir, I feel exactly as I did in ante-slavery days. I feel there is a great cause of human freedom involved in the things happening now, and I have the feeling I had before I enl[i]sted in the army.["]

There isn't going to be any bloodshed, no internecine strife between brothers of the same blood, no turmoil nor tumult, nor upsetting of institutions; but there's going to be a great drawing together of generous human spirits in the first great cause of liberation, which we have been forgetting in our struggle for more material supremacy and wealth. And America is once more going to strip the veil from her eyes and, with a new and virgin beauty, is going to see again the image of her liberty.

Printed in the Jersey City *Jersey Journal*, June 22, 1911.

To James Alfred Hoyt, Jr.

My dear Mr. Hoyt: [Trenton, N. J.] June 22, 1911.

Only a great pressure of public business has prevented my replying sooner to your letter of June third,[1] which I warmly appreciated not less than the very generous extracts which you were kind enough to enclose.

I do not feel that I shall ever care to undertake an active campaign for the Presidential nomination. I should feel that a nomination obtained in that way was hardly worth having, but the spontaneous efforts made by my friends in various qyarters [quarters] have been to me the most delightful proof that I have been able to accomplish at least something, and I want to say that one of my greatest gratifications is your own generous attitude.   Cordially and sincerely yours,   Woodrow Wilson

TLS (WP, DLC).
[1] It is missing.

To Cleveland Hoadley Dodge

Dear Cleve,   Lyme [Conn.], 23 June, 1911

Pardon pencil; I have no pen at hand with which I can make out to write.

It will be delightful to join Mrs. Dodge and you on the yacht on the morning of the first of July (Saturday). Unhappily I must be down in Cape May County for an early afternoon function on Monday, the third,—and that means that I must get down to New York Sunday night, so as to be off early the next morning. This cuts an outing which it gives me joy to look forward to cruelly short, but I am a free man no longer, and must take what I can get—if you are generous enough to consent to such a pro-gramme and can do so without inconvenience to yourselves.

Mrs. W. joins me in warmest regards and warmest thanks to you both.   Affectionately Yours,   Woodrow Wilson

ALS (WC, NjP).

From Newton Cloud Gillham[1]

Dear Sir: Kansas City, Mo. June 23, 1911

I write you for the sole purpose of urging you to acceed to the demands of the people, to-wit, that you accept the leader-ship of the Democratic Party and become its nominee for the Presidency in 1912. The people of this great Central West in their search for a man whose leadership, and progressiveness befits him to fill the office of Chief-Executive of America have turned toward you and exclaim in single accord "Ecce Homo!"

There are evils claiming great power—termed in biblical lore, "Spiritual wickedness in high places"—they are running ram-pant, almost unrestrained. But I do not believe, Mr. Wilson, that there are any evils so great or so ingrown that the people cannot correct when they have seen where the evils lie and the reme-dies to be applied. It is not, however, the purpose of this letter to point out these evils or even to prescribe a remedy, but rather to express to you a confidence in you to both ferret out and apply an effective remedy.

As a further argument and an inducement to you to make this race, I beg lief to report that I am now actively engaged in the organization of a "Woodrow Wilson for President" club. It is already a most promising and healthy child, one that would turn even a Melen's[2] food baby green with envy because of its very fatness. The obstetrics concerning the which produces some most interesting facts—facts that appeal to reason and lead me to believe that it is Principal operating and that you are the man to succeed Mr. Taft.

This is the way I view the situation; of all the Favorite Sons of all the States, our own Mr. Clarke[3] is your most dangerous opponent. The substance of Mr. Clarke's strength, however, lies in his having a solid Missouri delegation, without the which he is even weaker than his rival for State honors, Mr. [Joseph Wingate] Folk. The love existing between the forces of these gentlemen, is so infinitesimal that to even an interested observer, it would in all probabilities go unmarked and unobserved as such— the chances for them to get together and send an instructed delegation is very remote. It looks like they would defeat themselves. I do not think Missouri can send an instructed delegation.

Very truly yours,   Newton C. Gillham.

TLS (Governors' Files, Nj).
  [1] Attorney of Kansas City, Mo.
  [2] A popular brand of baby food.
  [3] That is, Champ Clark.

From A. S. Colyar[1]

Personal.

My dear Sir: Charleston, S. C. June 23rd, 1911.

If you could make one more town [tour] of the Southern States and arouse the ire of such contemptible asses as the contemptible Governor of South Carolina, and get such cattle as this to oppose your candidacy would be the biggest advertisement you could get to secure a nomination.[2] Blease and Bleaseism denunciation of you has made you 20,000 friends in South Carolina.

I am very frank to say to you, that on account of personal friendship I have promised Gov. Harmon of Ohio, but, if you receive the nomination, it will give me great pleasure to cast my vote for you at the polls, as I am sick and tired of Taft and graft, which is only a big bag of bran in the White House.

Yours truly,   A. S. Colyar.

TLS (Governors' Files, Nj).
  [1] The Editors have been unable to find any information about him.
  [2] Governor Coleman Livingston Blease, notorious racist and demagogue, announced his opposition to Wilson for President immediately after Wilson's visit to Columbia. While espousing Harmon's candidacy, Blease frankly admitted that he opposed Wilson because he had accepted the hospitality of William E. Gonzales, Blease's mortal enemy, and because Gonzales was the leader of the Wilson movement in South Carolina. Charleston *News and Courier*, June 4, 1911.

To Mary Allen Hulbert Peck

Dearest Friend,   Lyme [Conn.] Sunday 25 June, 1911

It always gives me a heavy heart not to know when and where I am going to see you again. Just now, though I *think* that you are in Pittsfield, I *feel* as if you had disappeared into space, and I am at a loss where to turn to get the consciousness of you again. It was *such* a delight to see you in Trenton. It did for me *there* what your visit to Princeton did for that dear old place of my labours and my disappointments. It made that office which I call "mine" for the time being,—and which seems to me just one of a score of public rooms,—a place where I can be conscious all the while of what so seldom fills and beautifies the tiresome, formal place,—of friendship, of those deepest human relationships of sympathy and mutual generous understanding that make life possible and full of strength and joy. The imagination cannot do everything. There must have been actual *presences* in rooms like that to make it possible to regard them with a *personal* feeling,—to feel joy and quiet happiness (drunk at invisible sources) in them. I shall call on the Roeblings now, too, with a changed attitude. It will not be merely a call on *them*! Ellen was *delighted* with the beautiful lace collar. She sends you her love,—and will write at once. I have seldom seen her so pleased. It was "exactly what she wanted—and wanted so *much*"! How delightful to have such things happen!

This is just a message. I am plodding along as usual: there is nothing to tell—and writing seems so specially tedious after having seen you and talked again as of old. All send love

Your devoted friend   Woodrow Wilson

ALS (WP, DLC).

A News Report About a Statement Concerning Alaska

[June 28, 1911]

WILSON TELLS ALASKA NEEDS

TRENTON, June 28.—The recent decision of the Department of the Interior against some of the principal claims to coal lands in Alaska[1] has been received with much interest by Governor Wilson, who has been making a close study of the entire subject. Speaking of the decision to-day the Governor said:

"My recent visit to the State of Washington has greatly enhanced my interest in this particular question. I know how deeply important it is to the people both of Alaska and of the Northwest in general that the question of the use of the coal lands of Alaska should be settled and settled very definitely. The many legitimate interests have suffered in the Northwest from the long delay, however necessary that may have been, in the settlement of this question.

"The whole country realizes the significance of this particular matter, but perhaps the country does not realize the very great injustice that is being done the people of Alaska by withholding from them a territorial form of government.[2] This matter need not involve in any way the question of conservation of the resources of Alaska for the national government. It is a question of general self-government. The people of Alaska are clearly entitled to enjoy territorial self-government, and it is of the utmost importance to their welfare and to the whole progress and temper of life in the Northwest that it should be granted to them.

"It is greatly to be desired that public opinion should concentrate itself upon this matter with energy and intelligence, and that Congress should act in the liberal spirit of those who would promote the liberty of American citizens, wherever they are, particularly when they are living under circumstances of strained difficulty."

Printed in the *Newark Evening News*, June 28, 1911; some editorial headings omitted.

[1] The Department of the Interior, on June 26, 1911, made public the decision of Fred Dennett, Commissioner of the General Land Office, to cancel the so-called Cunningham claims to coal lands in Alaska, together with a note of Secretary of the Interior Walter L. Fisher concerning Dennett's decision. New *York Times*, June 27, 1911. The Cunningham claims had been the basis of the Ballinger-Pinchot controversy, about which see n. 3 to the address printed at Nov. 4, 1910, Vol. 21.

[2] The perennial question of self-government for Alaska acquired a new impetus with the election of a Democratic House of Representatives in 1910. Bills providing for a popularly elected territorial legislature were introduced in both houses of Congress in April 1911 and were at this time under consideration in their committees on territories. It was generally conceded in both chambers that passage of a home-rule bill was only a matter of time. President Taft, who had earlier opposed the measure, on August 24, 1912, signed a bill providing for a popularly elected legislature for Alaska. See Jeannette P. Nichols, *Alaska: A History of its Administration, Exploitation, and Industrial Development During its First Half Century Under the Rule of the United States* (Cleveland, 1924), pp. 368-69, 383-405, and Ernest Gruening, *The State of Alaska*, rev. edn. (New York, 1968), pp. 142-57.

To Hardin Mallard[1]

My Dear Mr. Mallard: [Trenton, N. J.] June 28, 1911.

In reply to your important letter of June 17th,[2] I will say that I have never expressed myself as opposed to State-wide prohibition. I think the question wears its different aspects in different

States and the policy that is wise to persue in one may not be the policy that is wise to persue in the other. I do not feel that I have a right to a judgment with regard to what would be the most effective thing to work for in Texas. It is hard enough to form my judgment as to what is right in New Jersey. I hope you will feel at liberty to absolutely deny the statement that I have made a declaration against State-wide prohibition.

Woodrow Wilson

Printed in the Dallas *Home and State*, XIII (July 8, 1911), 8.
1 Of Mineral Wells, Palo Pinto County, Tex.
2 It is missing.

Remarks on the Defeat of Commission Government in Hoboken and New Brunswick

[June 28, 1911]

"COMMISSION WILL WIN AT LAST," SAYS WILSON

TRENTON, June 28.—The defeat of the commission plan of government in Hoboken and New Brunswick yesterday,¹ although somewhat of a disappointment, was not at all surprising to Governor Wilson. In speaking of the situation today he pointed out that the campaign in the two cities was a very brief one and no doubt presented new questions to a large proportion of the voters. It is not to be wondered at, the Governor remarked, that fundamental changes of this sort should require time to accomplish.

Notwithstanding the temporary setback to the movement, the Governor believed that the lesson taught would be instructive and serviceable, since it shows exactly what forces are opposed to the commission government and what work must be done to offset their influence.

Commenting further upon the situation the Governor said:

"Friends of the commission form of government now know exactly what they have to contend with and who they have to contend with. I cannot but regard it as very unfortunate that the men responsible for the official organization of the two great parties should have shown themselves opposed to this great measure, undoubtedly intended to place in the hands of the people the power to control their own government. I am afraid that in the long run this opposition on their part will be very hurtful to their influence and reputation. They will find that as opinion grows clear and strong on this subject, it will begin to be felt that they acted in their own interest and not in the interest of the people.

"This line-up is extremely instructive and also very service-able. It shows just what work remains to be done and just how to do it. There is only one instrument of effective self-government, and that is the instrument of public opinion, and when that once declares itself everything will be simplified. The friends of commission government have no need to be anxious about the ultimate verdict of the voters of our cities."

Printed in the *Newark Evening News*, June 28, 1911.

[1] Commission government was defeated in Hoboken by a vote of 4,922 to 2,969; in New Brunswick, by a vote of 2,500 to 1,135. Trenton *True American*, June 28, 1911.

Two News Reports of an Address in Newark

[June 29, 1911]

NEWARK DEMOCRATS HAIL WILSON AS LEADER AND AS THE NEXT PRESIDENT

Newark, New Jersey, June 28—Governor Wilson, of New Jersey, was given a great reception at the dollar dinner in the Krueger Auditorium, in Newark, tonight, held under the auspices of the Woodrow Wilson Democratic League of Essex County. He was cheered by more than a thousand men and women, who took part in the affair and was hailed as the next President of the United States.

The dinner marked the opening of the 1911 election campaign of the reform element of the Democratic party which has accepted the leadership of Governor Wilson and repudiated the regular party organization and its leader, State Chairman James R. Nugent.

John J. Gifford,[1] president of the league, introduced Thomas L. Masson, of Life,[2] as toastmaster. The Governor was one of the speakers, being preceded by Mr. Gifford, Mr. Mas[s]on, State Senator Osborne, Speaker Kenny of the Legislature and Assistant District Attorney Dudley Field [Malone], of New York.

Letters were read from Senator Owens, of Oklahoma,[3] and Congressman Robert Buchanan.[4] All the speakers and both the letter writers made optimistic reference to Governor Wilson as a presidential possibility next year, and every time his name was mentioned in that connection the diners became enthusiastic at times to the point of hysteria. . . .[5]

Printed in the Trenton *True American*, June 29, 1911; some editorial headings omitted.

[1] John James Gifford, coal and ice dealer of Newark.

2 Thomas Lansing Masson, managing and literary editor of *Life*, the humor magazine.
3 Robert Latham Owen.
4 Frank Buchanan, Democratic congressman from Illinois.
5 Here follows Wilson's advance text.

✧

[June 29, 1911]

WILSON TWITS THE OLD GUARD ON ITS FIGHT

Commission Rule Bound to Be and Politicians Stand in Own Way.

SPEECH AT DOLLAR DINNER

Old-line politicians encountered heavy going at the dollar dinner of the Wilson Democratic League of Essex County in Krueger Auditorium last night. Governor Wilson, in the course of a stirring speech on commission government, classed the old guard crowd with that portion of the populace of which it has been remarked, "They are more to be pitied than scorned." . . .

Governor Wilson took up the subject of commission government during the latter half of his speech. His remarks were as follows:

"You have heard of a reform known as the commission form of government for cities. I have no more interest in that reform than any other public-spirited citizen, but I want to express my gratification that the gentlemen who have opposed it[1] in some quarters have done us a service by showing their real spirit and their real methods.

"We have been talking about bipartisan machines, and they have given us a public illustration, an example. We have been talking about men who have been fighting for the organization and not fighting for the public, and they have given us an open illustration and example.

"We have been talking about the need of electoral reform, and they have given us an open illustration of the necessity of it.

"We have seen a case—if my information is correct—of two repeaters from the City of New York appearing in one of the courts of this Commonwealth, and represented in that court by the official legal representative of the city and of the machine.

"How kind it is for those gentlemen to identify themselves. How kind it is of them to show us that they believe in that way of carrying elections.

1 In Hoboken and New Brunswick most particularly. Newark did not vote on commission government until 1917, when it adopted it.

"The matter of city government and its life, gentlemen, is a matter of public opinion. You cannot force public opinion too fast. You must convince the people of our cities that this change is necessary before it will take place.

"I am not deceived into supposing that so large a process of manipulation was carried on as to determine the elections in Hoboken and New Brunswick. The majority was much too large to make any such supposition as that just or reasonable.

"The people of those cities have not yet been convinced of the necessity for the change, and I am not impatient to wait upon their conversion to that opinion.

"I feel only the very serene confidence that so soon as they make up their minds what they want they will calmly take it because we have now furnished them with the means by which they can take it and not be cheated of the result.

"One or two elections don't count in a lifetime, and those of us who believe in things have enlisted for the rest of our lives. Do the gentlemen who, for the sake of maintaining their own power, resist these changes suppose that we are going to sit in the game for any shorter time than they are?

"Whatever may be the limitations of individual human life, there are men so moved by conviction, so confident in the hope of reform, so certain of the legitimate and just demands of the people, that they can fight these battles with the debonnair air of those who see the future, of those who know there is nothing that can stop the heroic progress of the American people in the movement toward the control of their own affairs.

"They may use this method or that, but the men who stand against them will not stand as dust in the balance when the final reckoning is made. I may not live to see these things, but I have always believed in the immortality of the soul, and I hope it will be possible for my ghost to revisit this world to see the changes which I confidently expect to take place. But I don't think I will have to wait for my ghost.

"Things are happening in this country every day. You can hear something drop every day. The only thing is—and the thing I sincerely deplore is—that some men won't see it.

"I tell you frankly, gentlemen, that I do not feel the least personal hostility to the men of whom I have been speaking, perhaps very harshly. I believe that some of these men are just as honest as any one of us, but that they don't see it, they don't believe it.

"It is incredible to them that the times have changed. It is incredible to them that everything but political organization is going to count in the future. It is incredible to them that time has been called on the methods to which they have become accustomed.

"Some of them are amazingly good fellows, are among the most attractive men I know. If I did not think that I understood things a little bit better than they do I would be very much tempted to follow them, because I like them so much. They are good company. They are the kind of men you instinctively feel an affection for.

"They couldn't have any power if they were not. You don't get icicles into such places as they occupy. You don't get men without a lot of animal magnetism about them into such places as they occupy, you don't get men without a lot of wits into such places.

"But they are like athletes trained in a game after the rules of the game have been changed. They have such extraordinary political gifts, they are such good athletes, that the deepest pity of it is that you cannot make them forget and begin all over again and play the game according to the new rulings of the people.

"I would a great deal rather work with these men than against them, and when I am with them I cannot get very mad, but when I am not with them I know I ought to be mad through and through.

"I think there is a spirit in every man who feels as I do—a feeling of deep pity that it should be so, that men should not see that in order to retain a little temporary power which renders them open to suspicion that they are fighting what is infinitely greater, the power that carries them to honor and trust.

"When I see the leaders of the two machines in a great city[2] fighting the change to commission government and know that if they only realized the real conditions and the real principles of public life in this country they could enter into the fight and have the very distinguished honor of being the commissioners and renovating the government, then I say what a pity it is that men with the best gifts for these things should turn away from them and decline immortal distinction. That is what they are doing.

"I would to God that they could see what they are about, for after their little day of power is past they are going to be forgotten, or, if remembered, will be remembered with condemnation and perhaps contempt. It would be to their advantage to enjoy an unenviable oblivion.

2 Here he probably referred to Hoboken.

"What a pity it is, what a tragedy it is, when men do not see the moral truth with regard to great public situations, for the American people has now awakened to the truth of the situation." . . . Later on the Executive said:

"I would love some day to retire to the quiet of a studious place and write the real opinion of the American people of some of the gentlemen whose names need not be mentioned. There is a sweet revenge left to those who write history. They can indulge themselves in a modest way; and if they have the art of literary composition, what they tell you to think about the leading characters in national history will be your opinion and not what these gentlemen have thought about themselves. But whether any one person has the liberty and the occasion to indulge in this happy revenge or not, the revenge is certain to come.

"How sad it is, gentlemen, that men engaged in public life cannot be conscious always of that great summing-up that comes at the end of the trial. The jury is not this generation; the jury is the next generation which will not be deceived by the glamor of the personality of these men, which will not be under the influence of fear or of admiration. They will sit without ever hearing the thrilling tones of voice; without having seen the moving expression upon their countenances; they will sit in cold judgment and say, 'These men served America,' or 'These men forgot the service of America and served themselves.' And the verdict will be written for all eternity. The verdict cannot be reversed. There is no court of appeal.

"How solemn a thing it is then to dedicate yourselves—as you of this league have dedicated yourselves—to the permanent things as contrasted with the transitory things, the permanent things of good government as distinguished from individual fame and fortune.

"I can tell you—without the least affectation, gentlemen—that I am sorry that this league bears the name of an individual. No man can be sure that that individual will always live up to the principles by which he tries to square his conduct. There may be a day of disappointment, but there can be no day of disappointment with regard to principles.

"No man can be disappointed who devotes himself, his energy and his conscientious endeavor to the cause of good government."

In the earlier part of the speech the Governor took a cue from the remark of Mr. Gifford about political organizations, and said:

"Mr. Gifford said—and my thought cried amen to what he said —that we are not fighting political organizations whose intention is to serve the public interest. We are fighting organizations only whose intention is not to serve the public interest—and we are finding out which is which. They are offering to stand up and identify themselves. They are going out in the open and declaring their methods and their purposes and their processes as much as to say: 'Here are we; we are not the servants of the public; we are the servants of the organization for its own sake and our own sake. We defy you to enter our entrenchments and dislodge us.' Very well, their defiance is their identification. We know whom we have to fight. We have their names on a list, and when we get through with them they won't be missed."

In another part of his address the Governor remarked that he had been classed as a radical, and in regard to this, said:

"There is many a grave finger pointed at me, and at the men who think as I do, which is meant to be a finger of warning: Look to that fellow, look to him because he will upset the arrangement of our present society and those arrangements are the foundations of our present prosperity. Look to him or he will disturb the very foundation of your life. And there is nothing that so quickly frightens him as the idea of a certain person whom they trusted going so fast and so far that the conditions of his life may be materially altered, and all his calculations of interest and support upset. There is no mistaking the fact that there is a great deal of uneasiness abroad because the country listens and listens so raptly and acquiescingly to the radical speakers of our time. But don't deceive yourselves as to the number of persons who are uneasy. The real uneasiness of this country during the last two or three decades has been due to the fact that there were so few persons who spoke for change, who spoke for a somewhat radical change in our political and economical ar-[r]angements, and they are the persons who are now uneasy that the number of speakers has multiplied, the persons whose arrangements will not bear looking into. I have had a good deal of intercourse with radicals. I have talked with radicals from one side of this country to another, and I have not found a single radical in the United States who wants to disturb anything honest."

Printed in the *Newark Evening News*, June 29, 1911.

To Henry Watterson

My dear Colonel Watterson: [Trenton, N. J.] June 29, 1911.

Your letter of June twenty fourth[1] makes me regret even the delightful thing I have promised to do. I have promised to stay while in Lexington[2] with Desha Breckinridge.[3] Moreover, the meeting is to occur just before I shall be obliged to be back in New Jersey at the annual encampment of our State Troops, and just after speaking engagements here which I find it impossible to escape.

You make me very sorry that I am so tied hand and foot. Nothing could be more delightful than to come and see you. I have never yet had the pleasure of meeting Mrs. Watterson and it is a pleasure too long delayed.

May I not express again the access, self confidence and courage that it gives me to think of your friendship and support, and to thank you for the counsel which has guided and sustained me.
Cordially and faithfully yours,   Woodrow Wilson

TLS (H. Watterson Papers, DLC).
    [1] It is missing.
    [2] He was to speak to the Kentucky Bar Association in Lexington on July 12, 1911; his address is printed at that date.
    [3] Desha Breckinridge, Princeton 1889, publisher and editor of the Lexington, Ky., *Herald*, and a leader of the progressive faction of the Democratic party in Kentucky.

To William Gray Schauffler[1]

My dear Doctor Schauffler: [Trenton, N. J.] June 29, 1911.

I am to-day making the appointments to the new State Board of Education and I take the liberty of begging that you will accept an appointment on the Board. I am sure that it will be of the greatest service to the State.

The statute directs me to assign terms to the several members appointed and I beg that you will accept the term of four years.
Very sincerely yours,   Woodrow Wilson

N.B. It is reported at the State House that the work in the Department here is practically stopped, and I suggest that since you are the only member of the old Board I am reappointing, that it might be advisable for you to take the initiative in getting a meeting of the new Board as promptly as possible for organization and action. I hope to have the name of the Commissioner ready for announcement next week or within the next ten days. The others members of the Board are as follows: John P. Murray, Joseph S. Frelinghuysen, Henry Jones Ford, D. Stewart Craven, Edmund B. Osborne, Melvin Rice, John C. Van Dyke.

TLS (WC, NjP).
    [1] Physician of Lakewood, N. J., a member of the old State Board of Education.

To James Alfred Hoyt, Jr.

My dear Mr. Hoyt: [Trenton, N. J.] June 30, 1911.

I am your debtor for your letter of June twenty-sixth.[1] I ought to have told you in my last letter that a personal friend of mine— a young lawyer in New York, who was my pupil at Princeton, Mr. William F. McCombs, 96 Broadway—has generously undertaken to make his office a sort of clearing house of information for those who wish to co-operate in the matter of pressing my name for the nomination for the Presidency. I am sure that he would be very glad to co-operate with you in any matter and I am going to take the liberty of sending your letter to him.

I am sorry to say that Professor Axson has been dreadfully ill all winter with nervous prostration. The reports from the Doctor are at last very encouraging and they believe he will recover his tone and strength again. We have been very anxious about him. I know he would send his warm regards if he knew he had the opportunity.

                    Cordially and sincerely yours,   Woodrow Wilson

TLS (WP, DLC).
    [1] It is missing.

To Mary Allen Hulbert Peck

                    The Bellevue-Stratford Philadelphia 2 July, 1911.

How delightful it would be to get a letter from my dear friend Mrs. Peck, of whom I think so often and upon whom I depend to keep me in spirits by evidences (such as she so perfectly understands how to give) that she is thinking of me and keeping pace, with all her insight and sympathy, with what I am doing! I wrote to her last Sunday, before leaving Lyme for Trenton, but when I got back from Trenton on Friday there was no line from her. The Thursday she left Trenton I went to the Hotel Manhattan and inquired for her, but she was not there,—at any rate by twelve o'clock, the latest hour I could be there. And so I have missed her at every point and have felt forlorn. I have heard from her only through Mrs. Roebling, who told me on Thursday last, when I called on *her*, that she had heard from her from Pittsfield—and that made me wish that I could have put Mrs. P. under obligations to *me* for a letter, by entertaining her! Mrs. R. and I deplored the fact that Mrs. Peck had chosen to go back to Pittsfield, where she had suffered so much and where she ought *never* to have lived. Such a flower cannot grow in New England air. A life of suppression, of *self*-suppression, is deadly to it. She ought to live in the South or in the free West, where people are spontaneous and genuine and free from everything that is morbid, as she is: where people give themselves out, without reserve, in warm, simple-hearted friendships. I marvel that, now she is free to choose, she should return there, to be wounded again both by memory and by present circumstance! How can she ever be, fully and freely, her own light-hearted self there,— full of the joy and the power of life, enjoying and being enjoyed? How do you explain it—by habit, merely? Can't you change her plans? It distresses me to think of her *never* being released from the restraints and stiflings that have marred her splendid vitality. They have deepened her life, but she need not endure them any longer.

I am here to start early in the morning to fulfill a duty speaking engagement at noon to-morrow at Cape May in my exacting State—on the fourth at Ocean Grove. I am, tired

Your devoted friend   Woodrow Wilson

ALS (WP, DLC).

A News Report of an Address at Stone Harbor, New Jersey

[July 5, 1911]

WILSON SWAYS HEARERS AT STONE HARBOR FETE

STONE HARBOR, July 5.—By clipping the golden cord that held suspended the great lift bridge over Great Channel, Governor Woodrow Wilson Monday formally opened the new Ocean parkway from Cape May Courthouse to this newest of South Jersey resorts and welcomed to Stone Harbor the first automobiles that ever set wheel upon the island. . . .

The Governor's address was a message of optimism, progress, individual responsibility in the management of American government and in the correction of the abuses that have fastened themselves upon American society. He pleaded not for "unreasoning radicalism," but for that true radicalism that goes to the root of things and opens the gate of opportunity and progress.

He appealed for a program based upon knowledge of the facts, and warned against revolutions undertaken for revenge or selfishness. Special privilege he denounced with fervor, but he reminded his hearers that not all the special privileges enjoyed in America were stolen or corruptly obtained. Rather, he declared, many were the result of the improvidence and impatience so characteristic of Americans, and it was the people themselves who were responsible for half their present problems and misfortunes.

The problem, he said, of restoring equality of opportunity, would never be solved by a blind attack upon those who enjoyed the bounty we have bestowed upon them, but only by a just, considerate readjustment of conditions, based upon knowledge of the exact facts. . . .

Printed in the *Newark Evening News*, July 5, 1911.

A News Report of a Fourth of July Address

[July 5, 1911]

WILSON SPEAKS IN OCEAN GROVE

OCEAN GROVE, July 5.—Speaking before an audience of 6,000 persons in the Auditorium yesterday afternoon, Governor Wilson, in a patriotic address, said that his favorite motto was "Put up or shut up." He was talking about pessimists who decry the condition of certain things and who are continually declaring that the world is growing worse. The Governor said that such people ought to hire a hall and preach their beliefs.

Dr. Wilson received an enthusiastic welcome when he arose to speak and he was also given the Chautauqua salute. In opening his address he said that this was his second Fourth of July oration. He said that America was so patriotic that there should always be an abundance of Fourth of July addresses, and no community was so poor that it could not afford at least one.

Talking about laws, Governor Wilson said that "we have worried along under some bad statutes and some bad city governments, but America is so healthy that we can stand it." He went on to say that there was [were] no demagogues in the United States, whereat a man in the audience called out the name of Roosevelt. The Governor did not appear to notice the intrusion.

Speaking of seeing the American flag on the high seas, the Governor said that the reason that most ships were British was "because of our stupid navigation laws."

"The bitterness of the struggle is long past," the Governor said in part. "We look back to it without resentment and deal with the great nation from which we separated not only without hostile feeling, but with genuine cordiality and affection sprung out of memories of common origins and common institutions."

The Governor was drawing lessons from the revolution, out of which grew the new America, and he pointed with simple but telling force to the need for new declarations of independence upon the part of the people if the nation so built shall endure. Just as the colonists rejected a government unsuitable to them, so the people must now see to it that their own government, then constructed, shall be to them what was intended by its founders.

"It is an interesting and delightful circumstance," the governor continued, "that the celebration of the Fourth of July never grows stale with us. The birth of the nation will always be for us a memory of thrilling and transcendent interest. We can never cease to rejoice that a free government came into existence in such memorable circumstances on this continent, which was destined to be devoted to free institutions. The greater the nation grows the more vital will her early history seem to us, the more truly significant of the important and memorable things that were to follow.

"It is not the memories of the struggle that made us free, not the definate [definite] recollection of the causes and provocations of the War of Independence that excite us. These things grow dim with us. We have lost the feeling of a small and struggling nation. We have taken our place in the great family of nations, alongside the great power whose rule we then flung off.

"The very men who led the Revolution reverenced the constitution of the mother country, knew the long and handsome history of the struggle for liberty by which it had been built up; knew that, even in that day of blunders and of mistaken policies that alienated her colonies, her government was the freest in the world, the model of all peoples who then looked to see representative government supplant the tyranny that held other lands in its grip.

"Their motive was the permanent motive in the history of all liberty. What gives the American Revolution its character and distinction is not that the colonies in America rejected a government unsuited for England, but that they rejected a government unsuitable for themselves. The whole point of the struggle was that the English government could not understand them and their affairs, could not adjust its authority to their interest, would not give them the latitude and freedom necessary for their own development, was too narrow in its conception of authority to allow colonies anywhere to grow to the full stature of vigorous States.

"It was a case of maladjustment and of authority exercised in a way that was not suitable to the real circumstances and interests of those upon whom it was exerted. Our connection with England cut off, the struggle, the incessant, implacable struggle, was transferred to this side the water. Having cast off the authority of England as unsuitable, we set about putting together institutions for ourselves which would be suitable, and the history of our politics since that great transaction has been the history of readjustment. At each stage there has been disclosed a new necessity for some fresh declaration of independence, independence of this, that or the other wrong adjustment of law or unfortunate development of economic relationship.

"The thing to be proud of and to base our hope upon is that these declarations of independence have one by one been made effectual as the first declaration was. It is my wish to-day to dwell upon the things that have so far kept us from error and misfortune.

"In the first place, we have at each stage of this struggle for development and constant readjustment looked at the facts with clear, unclouded eyes. We have had the sagacity at each stage to see things as they were, to handle them as we handled the original matters of revolution, not as fancies, but as definite, indisputable facts. This is our title to self-government.

"In the second place, at the same time that we saw clearly, we have acted in a spirit of self-possession; like men, not like children; like men schooled to the orderly developments of law, unlike impatient novices, who think that law can be thrust aside and every process hastened beyond the pace with which law can be kept up.

"We have been blessed, moreover, with calm leadership. Our development has been guided by men who not only had a full comprehension of what it was we desired and needed to have, but also of the means, the reasonable and prudent means, by which it could be obtained. Statesmanship naturally flourishes among a people habitually self-possessed and masterful, habitually able to see things as they are.

"We have accordingly acted upon constructive, not destructive, programs; by process of common counsel and not by process of impatient revolt. We have been masters of our own life and of our own fortunes because we have been masters of ourselves.

"It is for such reasons as these that we take leave to be proud of the history of American freedom. It has not been the pursuit of phantoms. We have made slow conqu[e]sts of opportunity. We have reverenced law and yet have made it serve our purpose. We have treated constitutions like vehicles of life and not like mere lawyers' documents, and this because we have always known what it was we would be at.

"We do not interest ourselves in our politics because it is a diverting game, but because it is the means of our life. Our object is that every man should have his free opportunity; that no man should enjoy privileges not open to his neighbor; that no man should rule us without our consent; that the instruments employed, whether political or economic, should be our own, to be used as we deemed best. Our programs have thus been always broad, hard-headed, definitely aimed and contrived, and we shall remain free and powerful so long as we retain this spirit and this method.

"I dwell upon these things because so many men in recent months have seemed to fear that we were about to experience a change of plan and a loss of the practical genius which has so far safeguarded us. They seem to fear this because there is now so much plain speaking about the things that need to be remedied. But this is the ground of our safety, not of our danger.

"We shall endanger our lives only when we cease to be outspoken and candid and fearless of the truth. It is the spirit of America that we should know her people, her conditions, her prospects, as they are. If we speak plainly it does not mean that we shall act hastily or unjustly. On the contrary, it means that when we do act we shall know what we are about and shall reproduce the spirit of American liberty in our thoughtfulness as well as in our audacity. Every step of American development has safeguarded everything that deserved to be permanent and cut off only what was an excrescence and unsuited to the deeper process of our life.

"The future will be like the past and will reveal an ever-increasing genius for that which builds up, purifies, strengthens, illuminates and conserves for the prudent uses of posterity."

Printed in the *Newark Evening News*, July 5, 1911; some editorial headings omitted.

To Mary Allen Hulbert Peck

Dearest Friend,   [Trenton, N. J.] 5 July, 1911.

I wonder if you have been getting my letters? I have been using the wrong address,—at least I did Sunday when I wrote from Philadelphia; I stupidly put *Fern*wood Court on the envelope instead of *Elm*wood! But surely they know you well enough in Pittsfield by this time, even at the Post Office to find you *without* an address!

I hope with all my heart that you have not had in Pittsfield the *dreadful* heat we have been obliged to endure here. My "work" goes inexorably on, no matter what happens. Monday I had to go down to the very point, almost, of Cape May, for a speech; and yesterday, the 4th, I went to Ocean Grove to deliver *an oration*. I went down and back in "Sads"[1] automobile,—which made the journey at least tolerable. I have to sleep at the hotel here[2] in a room into which not a breath of air finds its way these stifling nights,—so here I am, writing to you! It's bed-time and I have had a long day of hard work (spending this evening dictating an address to be delivered to the Kentucky Bar Association next week), but the office is the only place I have found where there is air enough to breathe. A little, demure breeze steals in at the window that overlooks the river (how delightful it is to have you *know* the office!) and, since I must sit here to avoid stifling in this (for the time being) City of Dreadful Night, I might as well give my thoughts of you the form of these scribbled lines. I still feel as I did when I wrote on Sunday,—so sorry to think of you *in Pittsfield*, in your wrong setting, where people do not understand you, and where your free, gay spirit,—so generous, so rich in quick and catholic sympathies, is cabined and suppressed—where you seem an outlaw when you in reality square your thoughts instinctively with all the noblest and truest laws of the human spirit—and love God even when you think yourself most in rebellion against him. Nowhere but in that morbid atmosphere would you have misinterpreted *yourself* as I have heard you do—*speaking* New England judgments of yourself until I was like to burst with hot, indignant dissent. *Can't* you—*wont you* live in the South or in the West—or even in normal New Jersey? Why perversely go back to the place that nearly starved the life out of you? But I *must* go to bed! I feel better for having had this little word with you. I can now sleep refreshed.

                    Your devoted friend,   Woodrow Wilson

ALS (WP, DLC).
    [1] Wilbur Fisk Sadler, Jr., Adjutant General of New Jersey.
    [2] The Hotel Sterling.

From J. Silas Harris[1]

My dear Gov.:   Kansas City, Mo., July 5th-11

I thank you for your kind letter of the 29th ult., and replying thereto will say that delegates appointed to the National Negro Educational Congress are men and women, who are willing to defray their own expenses. The honor of appointment at the hands of the Governor is all that they ask. I hope that you have a number of Negroes in your state who have enough interest in their race to attend this Congress. Hoping that you will appoint a delegation of your ablest and best men and women,[2] and assuring you of my high regard for you personally I am,

Yours truly,   J Silas Harris.

TLS (Governors' Files, Nj).
[1] Principal of the Summer School, a public school in Kansas City, Mo., and president of the Negro National Educational Congress, an organization founded in 1910, with headquarters in Kansas City.
[2] See T. A. Spraggins to WW, July 26, 1911.

To Edward W. Grogan[1]

My dear Mr. Grogan: [Trenton, N. J.] July 6, 1911.

You mistook me if you thought that I was treating your first letter[2] as a communication of a politician, or if you supposed that I was trying in any way to avoid the important question you put to me. The reply I made was made in all sincerity. I believe that for some states Statewide Prohibition is possible and desirable, because of their relative homogeneity, while for others I think that Statewide Prohibition is not practicable. I have no reason to doubt from what I know of the circumstances that Statewide Prohibition is both practicable and desirable in Texas. In my reply to you I was only trying to state what I think must always be kept in mind,—the wide divergence of conditions which make it impossible to reply to any single question like those of prohibition in terms which would fit the whole country.

With much respect,
Cordially and sincerely yours,   Woodrow Wilson.

TCL (WP, DLC).
[1] Owner and operator of a farm and cattle ranch near the town of Byers in Clay County, Tex. His middle name was probably Wesley.
[2] It is missing.

To Herman Bernstein[1]

[Dear Mr. Bernstein: Trenton, N. J., c. July 6, 1911]

I do not see how there can be any divergence of feeling among patriotic Americans concerning the situation in Russia with regard to the religious discriminations made by the Russian Government.[2] I haven't had time to give the matter any detailed consideration. The principle involved admits of no argument.

Cordially and sincerely yours,   Woodrow Wilson.

Printed in the Trenton Evening Times, July 13, 1911.

[1] German-born, Russian-reared author, journalist, and translator of Russian literature, at this time living in New York City. Since 1908 he had made three investigative trips to Russia as a correspondent of the *New York Times*.

[2] There was at this time increasing agitation, particularly among Jewish-American organizations and humanitarian groups, to persuade the American government to abrogate the Russian-American commercial treaty of 1832 on the ground that the czarist regime discriminated against Jewish Americans by denying them visas. The movement culminated in the passage with only one dissenting vote of a resolution by the House of Representatives on December 13, 1911, stating that Russia had violated the treaty, declared it terminated, and called on the President to give formal notice of its abrogation. President Taft gave diplomatic notice of the termination to the Imperial government on December 17, 1911, to take effect December 31, 1912.

To Calvin Noyes Kendall [1]

My dear Mr. Kendall: [Trenton, N. J., c. July 7, 1911]

I was away when your letter of the 30th[2] came, and have only just now returned to my desk.

Your letter gratifies me very much. My own judgment is clear that you are the man I am looking for.[3] If you feel as your letter indicates, that you would like to speed the appointment, a conference upon that point is not necessary. We can wait until your engagement at Hampton is finished and meet as soon as possible in New York.

I suggest this because [I find] myself entangled with many things which make my movements uncertain.

May I suggest also that you write the school authorities in Indianapolis ascertaining whether they would be willing to release you at this time? I take it for granted that they would, but realize what you, of course, owe them in the circumstances.

Your letter put my mind very much at ease. I shall look forward with genuine pleasure to our work together.

I am sending you a summary of our recent school legislation under another cover.

With much regard,

Sincerely yours,   Woodrow Wilson

Transcript of WWsh (WC, NjP).

[1] Superintendent of schools, Jackson, Mich., 1886-90; Saginaw, Mich., 1890-1892; New Haven, Conn., 1895-1900, and Indianapolis, Ind., 1900-1911. While in the latter city he was also a member of the Indiana State Board of Education.

[2] It is missing.

[3] To be New Jersey Commissioner of Education. James Kerney, *The Political Education of Woodrow Wilson* (New York and London, 1926), pp. 121-22, describes the background of Kendall's appointment as follows: "Wilson made a personal matter of the selection of a new commissioner of education. . . . For this place he picked a friend, Calvin N. Kendall, who was superintendent of schools at Indianapolis. They had lectured together and had known each other in educational work. . . . Kendall was on a lecture tour in New York State when Wilson hit upon him for the job. Wilson sat down and wrote a telegram in his own firm hand offering the commissionership to Kendall. In the telegram

he set forth the salary and the fact that the commissioner had the widest powers for the purpose of creating a new and efficient educational organization in the State. 'You could count on my most cordial support, and I wish to urge it upon you with the utmost cordiality,' wired Wilson. Kendall sent word back that he would be at the Hampton Institute giving a series of lectures the following week and requested Wilson to write him there and name a day when it would be convenient for Kendall to come to New Jersey for a conference."

To Cleveland Hoadley Dodge

Personal.

My dear Cleve: [Trenton, N. J.] July 7, 1911.

I have been thinking about the conjunction of friends you proposed the other day and it is my strong judgment that much the wisest course is for me to come up to Riverdale to spend the night with you some time. I think the yachting trip would be unsatisfactory and perhaps open to misconstruction.

It was a perfectly delightful experience to be on the yacht with you. It has refreshed me and made the work even of this hot week very much easier.

Always affectionately yours,   Woodrow Wilson

TLS (WC, NjP).

A Fragment of a Letter from Henry Beach Needham[1]

[Wyncote, Pa., c. July 8, 1911]

attracts far more attention.

As usual, the publisher is calling loudly for copy,[2] and I beg to ask that you get it back to me, with your changes, at the earliest possible moment.

If this letter is not altogether clear, please remember it is written at the end of a twelve hour day, and my "think tank" is about run dry.

Faithfully yours,   Henry Beach Needham

TLS (MiU-C).
  [1] Free-lance journalist.
  [2] Wilson and Needham had recently completed the interview printed at Aug. 26, 1911.

To Mary Allen Hulbert Peck

Dearest Friend,   Pa. Station [New York, July 10, 1911]

I misread the time table and have five minutes more than I thought.

I did not answer your qu. about address. I shall be back from Ky by Friday. Address me thereafter at Sea Girt (Governor's Cottage), N. J. We establish ourselves there this week.

Would you mind writing what was on your mind about 'Sad'? I am careful, now that I am in politics, of *every*body.

God bless you. Take care in this dreadful heat.

Your devoted friend   W.W.

ALS (WP, DLC).

Fragment of a Letter to Henry Beach Needham

[New York, July 10, 1911]

Thank you sincerely. I am *en route* to Ky and send this to you with genuine appreciation[.] I beg that you will accept my corrections.   W.W.

ALS (MiU-C) written on fragment of H. B. Needham to WW, July 8, 1911.

An Address to the Kentucky Bar Association[1]

[[July 12, 1911]]

THE LAWYER IN POLITICS

The lawyer is, by very definition, an expert in the law; and society lives by law. Without it its life is vague, inchoate, disordered, vexed with a hopeless instability. At every turn of its experience society tries to express its life, therefore, in law: to make the rules of its action universal and imperative. This is the whole process of politics. Politics is the struggle for law, for an institutional expression of the changing life of society.

Of course, this is the deeper view of politics. It is not the view of the mere party man or of the professional politician. He thinks chiefly, no doubt, of the offices and their emoluments; of the tenure of power; of the choice of policy from day to day in the administration of the various departments of government; of the hundred advantages, both personal and partisan, which can be obtained in a successful contest for the control of the instruments of politics; but even he cannot escape the deeper view at last. He must express the policy of his party or the advantage gained by his occupation of office in statutes, in rules of law, imposed in the interest of some class or group, if not in the interest of society at large. He is really, in the last analysis, struggling to control law and the development and use of institutions. He

[1] Delivered in the Opera House, Lexington, Ky.

needs as much as the statesman does the assistance of the legal expert, the skill of the technical guide; the lawyer must be at his elbow to see that he plays the game according to the nominal rules.

The lawyer, therefore, has always been indispensable, whether he merely guided the leaders or was himself the leader, and nowhere has the lawyer played a more prominent part in politics than in England and America, where the rules of law have always been the chief instruments of contest and regulation, of liberty and efficient organization, and the chief means of lifting society from one stage to the next of its slow development.

The lawyer's ideal part in this unending struggle is easy to conceive. There is long experience stored up in the history of law. He, above all other men, should have a quick perception of what is feasible, of the new things that will fit into the old, of the experiences which should be heeded, the wrongs that should be remedied, and the rights that should be more completely realized. He knows out of his own practice how pitiful, oftentimes, against how many obstacles, amidst how many impediments, often interposed by the law itself, sometimes interposed by the ignorance of society or by the malevolence of designing men, the men about him make their daily effort to live free from the unnecessary interference or the selfish stupidity or the organized opposition of their neighbors and rivals. He knows what forces gather and work their will in the field of industry, of commerce, of all enterprise. He, if any man, knows where justice breaks down, where law needs amplification or amendment or radical change, what the alterations are that must be effected before the right will come into action easily and certainly and with genuine energy. He should at every turn be the mediator between groups of men, between all contending and contesting interests. He should show how differences are to be moderated and antagonisms adjusted and society given peace and ease of movement.

He can play this ideal part, however, only if he has the right insight and sympathy. If he regards his practice as a mere means of livelihood, if he is satisfied to put his expert advice at the service of any interest or enterprise, if he does not regard himself as an officer of the State, but only as an agent of private interest, if, above all, he does not really see the wrongs that are accumulating, the mischief that is being wrought, the hearts that are being broken and the lives that are being wrecked, the hopes that are being snuffed out and the energies that are being sapped, he cannot play the part of guide or moderator or adviser in the large sense that will make him a statesman and a benefactor.

It is a hard thing to exact of him, no doubt, that he should have a non-professional attitude toward law, that he should be more constantly conscious of his duties as a citizen than of his interests as a practitioner, but nothing less than that will fit him to play the really great role intended for his profession in the great plot of affairs. He must breed himself in the true philosophy of his calling. It is his duty to see from the point of view of all sorts and conditions of men, of the men whom he is not directly serving as well as of those who he is directly serving.

This is a matter of character, of disposition and of training outside the schools of law, in the broader schools of duty and of citizenship and of patriotism. It is a great conception when once a lawyer has filled himself with it. It lifts him oftentimes to a very high place of vision and of inspiration. It makes of him the custodian of the honor and integrity of a great social order, an instrument of humanity, because an instrument of justice and fair dealing and of all those right adjustments of life that make the world fit to live in.

If I contrast with this ideal conception of the function of the lawyer in society what I may be excused for calling his actual role in the struggle for law and progress and the renovation of affairs, I hope that I will not be interpreted as suggesting a view of our great profession which is in any wise touched with cynicism or even with the spirit of harsh criticism. The facts do not justify a cynical view of the profession or even a fear that it may be permanently losing the spirit which has ruled the action of the greater members of the bar and of the immortal judges who have presided at the birth and given strength and fibre to the growth and [of] liberty and human right. I wish to submit what I have to say in all fairness and without color even of discouragement.

The truth is that the technical training of the modern American lawyer, his professional prepossessions and his business involvements, impose limitations upon him and subject him to temptations which seriously stand in the way of his rendering the ideal service to society which is demanded by the true standards and canons of his profession. Modern business, in particular, with its huge and complicated processes, has tended to subordinate him, to make of him a servant, an instrument instead of a free adviser and a master of justice. My professional life has afforded me a rather close view of the training of the modern lawyer in schools, and I must say that it seems to me an intensely technical training. Even the greater and broader principles of which the elder lawyers used to discourse with a touch of broad philosophy, those principles which used to afford writers like Blackstone occasion for incidental disquisitions on the character and history of society, now wear in our teaching so technical an aspect, are seen through the medium of so many wiredrawn decisions, are covered with so thick a gloss of explanation and ingenious interpretation, that they do not wear an open and genial and human aspect, but seem to belong to some recondite and private science.

Moreover, the prepossessions of the modern lawyer are all in favor of his close identification with his clients. The lawyer deems himself in conscience bound to be contentious, to manoeuvre for every advantage, to contribute to his clients' benefit his skill in a difficult and hazardous game. He seldom thinks of himself as the advocate of society. His very feeling that he is the advocate now of this, now of that, and again of another special individual interest separates him from broader conceptions. He moves in the atmosphere of private rather than public service. Moreover, he is absorbed now more than ever before into the great industrial organism. His business becomes more and more complicated and specialized. His studies and his services are apt to become more and more confined to some special field of law. He grows more and more a mere expert in the legal side of a certain class of great industrial or financial undertakings. The newspapers and the public in general speak of "corporation lawyers," and of course the most lucrative business of our time is derived from the need that the great business combinations we call corporations have at every turn of their affairs of an expert legal adviser. It is apt to happen with the most successful, and by that test the most eminent, lawyers of our American communities that by the time they reach middle life, their thoughts have become fixed in very hard and definite molds. Though they have thought honestly, they are apt to have thought narrowly; they have not made themselves men of wide sympathies or discernment.

It is evident what must happen in such circumstances. The bench must be filled from the bar, and it is growing increasingly difficult to supply the bench with disinterested, unspoiled lawyers, capable of being the free instruments of society, the friends and guides of statesmen, the interpreters of the common life of the people, the mediators of the great process by which justice is led from one enlightenment and liberalization to another.

For the notable, I had almost said fundamental, circumstance of our political life is that our courts are, under our constitutional system, the means of our political development. Every change in our law, every modification of political practice, must sooner or later pass under their scrutiny. We can go only as fast as the legal habit of mind of our lawyers will permit. Our politics are bound up in the mental character and attitude and in the intellectual vigor and vision of our lawyers. Ours is so intensely and characteristically a legal polity that our politics depend upon our lawyers. They are the ultimate instruments of our life.

There are two present and immediate tests of the serviceability of the legal profession to the Nation, which I think will at once be recognized as tests which it is fair to apply. In the first place, there is the critical matter of reform of legal procedure—the almost invariable theme, if I am not mistaken, of all speakers upon this question from the President of the United States down. America lags far behind other countries in the essential matter of putting the whole emphasis in our courts upon the substance of right and justice. If the bar associations of this country were to devote themselves, with the great knowledge and ability at their command, to the utter simplification of judicial procedure, to the abolition of technical difficulties and pitfalls, to the removal of every unnecessary form, to the absolute subordination of method to the object sought, they would do a great patriotic service, which, if they will not address themselves to it, must be undertaken by laymen and novices. The actual miscarriages of justice, because of nothing more than a mere slip in a phrase or a mere error in an immaterial form, are nothing less than shocking. Their number is incalculable, but much more incalculable than their number is the damage they do to the reputation of the profession and to the majesty and integrity of the law. Any one bar association which would show the way to radical reform in these matters would insure a universal reconsideration of the matter from one end of the country to the other and would by that means redeem the reputation of a great profession and set American society forward a whole generation in its struggle for an equitable adjustment of its difficulties.

The second and more fundamental immediate test of the profession is its attitude toward the regulation of modern business, particularly of the powers and action of modern corporations. It is absolutely necessary that society should command its instruments and not be dominated by them. The lawyer, not the layman, has the best access to the means by which the reforms of our economic life can be best and most fairly accomplished. Never before in our history did those who guide affairs more seriously need the assistance of those who can claim an expert familiarity with the legal processes by which reforms may be effectually accomplished. It is in this matter more than in any other that our profession may now be said to be on trial. It will gain or lose the confidence of the country as it proves equal to the test or unequal.

As one looks about him at the infinite complexities of the modern problems of life, at the great tasks to be accomplished by law, at the issues of life and happiness and prosperity involved, one cannot but realize how much depends upon the part the lawyer is to play in the future politics of the country. If he will not assume the role of patriot and of statesman, if he will not lend all his learning to the service of the common life of the country, if he will not open his sympathies to common men and enlist his enthusiasm in those policies which will bring regeneration to the business of the country, less expert hands than his must attempt the difficult and perilous business. It will be clumsily done. It will be done at the risk of reaction against the law itself. It will be done perhaps with brutal disregard of the niceties of justice, with clumsiness instead of with skill.

The tendencies of the profession, therefore, its sympathies, its inclinations, its prepossessions, its training, its point of view, its motives, are part of the stuff and substance of the destiny of the country. It is these matters rather than any others that bar associations should consider; for an association is greater than the individual lawyer. It should embody, not the individual ambition of the practitioner, but the point of view of society with regard to the profession. It should hold the corporate conscience and consciousness of the profession. It is inspiring to think what might happen if but one great State bar association were to make up its mind and move toward these great objects with intelligence, determination, and indomitable perseverance!

Woodrow Wilson, *The Lawyer in Politics* (New York, 1912).

To Henry Watterson

PERSONAL

My dear Colonel Watterson: [Trenton, N. J.] July 14, 1911.

It went mighty hard to have to run down to Kentucky and back again and deny myself the pleasure of seeing Mrs. Watterson and you. I felt like taking the law in my own hands and playing truant and going down to Louisville in spite of my greater obligation to be back and attend to business. I write now merely to send my most affectionate regards and to say how much it delighted and encouraged me to read the generous editorial in yesterday morning's Courier-Journal.[1]

Cordially and sincerely yours,   Woodrow Wilson

TLS (H. Watterson Papers, DLC).

¹ The editorial, "A Possible President," Louisville *Courier-Journal*, July 13, 1911, consisted largely of lengthy quotations from Wilson's speeches on political and corporation reform, a brief review of his meteoric rise to political prominence, and a quotation from William Bayard Hale ("Woodrow Wilson: Possible President," *World's Work*, XXII [May 1911], 14339-53) enthusiastically praising Wilson's personality and gifts of leadership. The statements in the editorial which represented Watterson's own sentiments appeared at the beginning, middle, and end:

"Woodrow Wilson stands before the public today as that rarest of phenomena, a public man who, elevated to office, faithfully keeps his pre-election promises."

"The Courier-Journal cannot think of Woodrow Wilson without recalling Samuel J. Tilden. How much alike they seem, as doctrinaire Democrats; as faithful and courageous party leaders; as practical and pre-eminent officials; how much they think alike, and talk alike, and write alike."

"Assuredly that is the kind of man for the times and the kind of man militant Democracy has long been looking for."

To William C. Liller

My Dear Col. Liller: [Trenton, N. J., July 14, 1911]

Thank you sincerely for your frank and important letter of July 6,¹ which an absence from home has delayed my replying to before. I think that if any Democrat will candidly examine my record, both before and since I became Governor, he will have no doubt that I am of the genuine brand. My secretary is ready at any time to supply any one who wishes to know about such things with a list of the appointments I have made. They will show anybody at once that I have acted in the strict interests of the party as well as in the interest of the public.

In haste, with warmest appreciation,

Sincerely yours, Woodrow Wilson.

Printed in the *New York Times*, Aug. 7, 1911.
¹ It is missing.

To Newton Cloud Gillham

My dear Mr. Gillham: [Trenton, N. J.] July 14, 1911.

Your letter of July sixth¹ is certainly most generous and I want to thank you for it very cordially. I have not felt at any time that I was at liberty to press any claims I might have for the Democratic nomination for the Presidency, but the interest in the matter which has been displayed in all parts of the country has given me the deepest gratification and I particularly appreciate the disposition of men like yourself in desiring to render any assistance that may be possible. A generous friend and one time pupil of mine in New York, has offered to make his office a sort of clearing house of information in this matter and I am going to take the liberty of sending your letter to him.

Cordially and sincerely yours, Woodrow Wilson

TLS (photostat in RSB Coll., DLC).
¹ It is missing.

An Address in Jersey City on Behalf of Commission Government¹

[July 14, 1911]

It is a privilege to be here tonight and I am obliged to you for the great reception you have given me. I thought as I was sitting here, how appropriate it was that this meeting should occur in this place, this place where things that are permanently true are discussed, where partisanship is excluded, the place where men seek to learn the facts, the place to which men send their children that they may be schooled in the knowledge of the truth; it is certainly an appropriate place for a meeting of this sort.

I deem it an honor to stand beside the distinguished Mayor of your city² in the advocacy of the change we are discussing in the form of government. Certainly he is giving you an example of very fine citizenship. He referred to the Commission Government as the Governor's cause. I accept that characterization of it because I believe it to be the people's cause, and I am proud to have my name identified with anything that is their cause. This is no personal fad of mine. This is something that has been tried all over the world and wherever it has been tried it has succeeded. Gentlemen spoke of it as an experiment and they spoke in ignorance, spoke of it as a new thing which had to be explained, when it is an old thing, long ago tried and proven by the men of many races and many governments.

All the best governed cities in the world are governed upon a plan which is practically the commission plan of government. I challenge any man who knows the facts to contradict or controvert that statement. The Governor is for it, and the only reason the Governor is for it is because he happens to know how good government is conducted elsewhere. (Applause.)

The commission form of government is the form under which the people can manage their own affairs if they choose. Of course, if they don't choose that is none of my business. If the people of Jersey City do not want to assume the control and direction of

¹ Delivered in the High School auditorium. Joseph A. Dear, Jr., president of the Commission Government League of Jersey City, presided.
² Henry Otto Wittpenn, who had delivered the opening speech.

their affairs it doesn't concern me; it is none of my business. I can't help it if they do not want to assume control, that is their work.

I have been down to the State of Kentucky, the hospitable State of Kentucky. I am not quite as fresh as I would be if they had not been so hospitable. As I was coming home I stopped at the city of Huntington, and a man who did not know that I was interested in commission government told me that the population of that town had increased in a greater ratio than any other town in the State or in the United States with one or two exceptions. He told me he attributed it to the fact that it has had a commission form of government for five years.

Taxpayers in that town get what they pay for, and they get something (laughter), and manufacturers from every part of the State go there for the reason that it is the place to bring their industries and their men in order that the health of the men and their own wealth might be saved and secured against the misgovernment and mismanagement of some other places. He, as I have stated, did not know that I was coming to Jersey City to make a speech and that he was supplying me with an illustration. He said that the people of this town had discovered how to govern themselves.

Commission form of government is the very one to take up because it is so easy to understand. You elect five men to run the government and you hold them responsible for running it right. You can watch five men where you could not watch twenty-five. (Laughter.) If you have read the Walsh Act you will find that it forbids that anything the five men do should be done in private with closed doors. It makes it absolutely obligatory upon them to publish everything that they do, with the vote included. You can get at the votes and see who votes aye and who votes no. Then you can see how they are running the government.

You have had mayors who were industrious in the performance of their duty and have done everything in their power to give you good government. But it was not in their power to do everything. You have an elected Street and Water Board, and you have an appointed Finance Board. The streets of Jersey City are not in an ideal condition. For my own part I don't blame the Street and Water Board, neither do I blame the Finance Board, but I blame the circumstances that two independent boards have to come to an agreement on a thing on which they disagree.

You cannot conduct a responsible government unless you arrange matters so that there won't have to be antagonism between boards and that someone with authority will give you what you

know they have the power to give. There will be no more disagree-
ing and crossfire of criticism as to the responsibility from one
board to another. You will have your men, and if you don't like
the way they are conducting your affairs you have the recall.
You can step up and with your watch in hand and call time. The
thing need not work more than one year before you call time on
any or all if it does not work right.

After I reached the city this afternoon, I had a paper put in
my hand which caused me a good deal of distress. I know all the
members of the City Committee, most of them I believe to be
my friends. I know that I am their friend. It distressed me that
they should put forth such a set of representations against commission government as are in the resolution they passed last
night,[3] because there is one very serious error in that statement.
I want to draw attention to one part of the statement.

They said that Jersey City once tried the commission form of
government and it nearly put the city into bankruptcy. They referred to the Bumsted Commission.[4] Do you know what the facts
are? I want to lay them before you and explain them, for it is
very important that you should know.

They referred to an act of the Legislature of the State in 1871,
which reorganized the government of the City of Jersey City. So
far from concentrated power in the hands of a single board,
that act leaves the city with a Mayor with his usual powers, the
Councilmen and Aldermen with the usual powers of Councilmen
and Aldermen, and at least three commissions—the Fire Commissioners, Police Commissioners and a Board of Public Works,
and what did each do? The Boards were named in the act, which
named all three of those boards.

Each of the names of the members was determined in Trenton, not in Jersey City. No man in Jersey City had a vote for any
one of them and it was reserved for the Legislature itself to determine their successors, and the Board of Public Works named
in Trenton by certain private managers who knew what they
were about, had the power of determining and holding every con-

[3] The Democratic City Committee adopted a resolution on July 13, 1911,
urging the voters of the city to reject the commission form at the special election to be held on July 18. The resolution was preceded by a lengthy preamble
listing numerous arguments against commission government. It would not work
in a city as large as Jersey City, would result in autocratic and unconstitutional
centralization of power, lead to a skyrocketing of the tax rate, etc. The chief
argument, however, was that corporations and special interests favored commission government because it would increase their control over the common people.
Jersey City *Jersey Journal*, July 14 and 15, 1911.

[4] William H. Bumsted was a prominent Republican politician in Jersey City
in the latter half of the nineteenth century and a leader in the movement for
the reorganization of his city's government. The "Bumsted Act" of 1871 is
described by Wilson in the following paragraph.

tract made by the city of Jersey City for every kind of public work. Every job that could be given to anybody that was worth money, was determined by those in Trenton, or rather, by a little coterie of individuals in Jersey City. I call upon those gentlemen to retract the statement, the statement that Jersey City ever had an opportunity to live under the commission form of government. (Prolonged applause.) There is nothing in that Act that resembles it, except the arbitrary government from the city of Trenton, and there is not a piece of self-government in it.

These boards whose members were named at Trenton had all the real powers of the city and voters of the City of Jersey City voted for nobody that had real power to control and serve them and their affairs. I have just half an hour ago read the act, and I hope that these gentlemen who authorized that statement will read it themselves, before they go to sleep tonight. It is a sad job, I say it not in condemnation, but in real pity. It is a sad job when men attempt to deceive the voters of a great city in that way.

Now the government by commission cause is going to gain by every act of that sort. Governments, ladies and gentlemen, do not depend upon individuals, they do not depend upon organizations, they go their way without either. I thank God, I am in pretty good health, and I am going to stay in this till I am finished, and I need only the faith and confidence of my fellow citizens. There is one thing that interests me more than anything else, and that is the privilege of the defense of the poor man. You know the circumstances, it must be plain to everybody, that poor men are in the vast majority and that rich men are in the small minority. If, therefore, we can, by any means, put the government in the control of the majority you have it in the control of the poor man. Now, I am going to do that at every turn of my political endeavors, not because I have blood in my eye against the rich. I know a good many rich men who have permitted me to associate with them, who are perfectly honest and public-spirited men, but who have private interests in many cases as distinguished from general interests, and because they are so absorbed that they cannot comprehend the point of view of the ordinary man, who are absorbed by the circumstances which govern their lives. You must standardize the lives of all men by the standards of the ordinary lives of men and experiences.

My object in advocating Commission Government is to give to the poor man the controlling voice in the government itself.

Don't you realize that the rich man with plenty of money to

hire his own private lawyers can take care of himself in any conditions, and the ordinary man has not this, unless his right is maintained without cost to himself, I mean outside of the cost of common taxes, unless there are men in public office who are in sympathy with his point in view? Unless he has such men in public office, he goes to his work in the morning unhappy, he goes to his home in the evening discouraged.

Under the present form of government in Jersey City, and most all places in New Jersey, the great majority have nothing to do with the conduct of the government. How do I prove this? In this way: You cannot control a government unless you select the persons that conduct it. There is a distinction that I want every man to carry home with him, and that is the distinction between the word "select" and the word "elect." It doesn't do you a particle of good to elect men unless you first select them. So long as political organizations have the right to select the men who are to go on your ticket, you might as well stay at home and not vote. I say that although I am a militant party man. I am a Democrat from the top of my head to the soles of my feet, and I mean that word with a big D as well as a little d, and I believe in organization, not for the sake of getting office, but for the sake of the promotion of principles that I believe in, of giving men what is due them; I believe in organizations for these reasons.

It is the curse of politics, the understanding between machines of different parties. It is dividing up the offices on the private understanding and the influences upon which those who are selected are put on the ticket. Who pays for this? They pay for it who expect to benefit by it. Who expects to benefit by it? The men with special privileges, who have favors to seek from the government, which they hope to obtain, and which are given to those who most liberally contribute to the expenses of the campaign. If you could only have the subscription list published, it would be like a list of those who expect to derive a private advantage from those whom they have helped to elect. And the consequence is that the only names with regard to which the nominating machine is at all careful are the one or two names at the top of the ticket. The man for Mayor must be one to whom they cannot object. How many of the men on the ticket do you know? You may know ten and another man may know ten, but they are not the same ten and you cannot find out any more. The average ignorance as to the ticket is so complete that even if the newspapers should publish the records there will be so many you won't take the time to read it. It must be printed in such small type that it hurts your eyes. At every election in New

York the New York Evening Post takes the trouble to publish the record of every man on the ticket. It takes so much space that it must be printed in the smallest type that can be read without the use of a magnifying glass. Yet I don't believe among the conscientious and painstaking men more than one out of a hundred or even thousand read these records. They vote the ticket without knowing who is on it. They delegate the business of government to the men who select these persons. If you select you can realize who are going on the ticket. I say, therefore, that of the people that vote for the ticket as now nominated in Jersey City, the great majority does not exercise the right of self-government, because it does not select the men.

I do not care how honest a committee is, I would not trust the most honest committee in the United States to supplant the people of the United States in the selection of the government. They may be the noblest gentlemen in the land, we are not deputing the government to them, and you may say what you please, but the selection of the men to govern you is the only kind of self-government. You cannot criticize their measures, you must depend upon their character and their sympathy and their understanding of you. Suppose the body of people in this room should determine to do something. They could not all do it. They must deputize somebody to do it. You would prefer to take the people you know best, who understand the matters, and would do them with constant reference to your opinion. That is the commission government—the selection of the men to conduct the affairs of the community. This same statement I have just referred to has intimated this would not be constitutional. I congratulate the committee upon having lawyers more astute than any Supreme Court in the United States. It has never been suspected by any Supreme Court in the United States that commission government is unconstitutional.

I have heard something that I am going to take leave to disbelieve. I have heard that the policemen and firemen are working against Commission Government. I have met a good many of these men and I think they are manly and intelligent, and I do not believe that they would work against Commission Government. Committees from these gentlemen have come to Trenton this winter with almost tears in their eyes, asking me to protect them against the injustice in politics. I mean from Jersey City, not from some other place, and they came to me and asked me to sign the tenure of office act, to make their tenure secure against the politicians, and I signed it.[5] And now that Jersey City has

5 Wilson referred to Chapter 378 of the *Laws of New Jersey*, *1911*, pp. 781-

at last an opportunity to secure a responsible form of government, in which the citizens of Jersey City could make the politicians accountable for making them the pawns of the game and their tools, they turn against it. If this is true, they either deceived me when they went to Trenton or are deceiving themselves now. Don't you know, ladies and gentlemen, if you don't know, that these men are not being paid more than a reasonable wage now, and if you have a responsible form of government, they are not going to lower the efficiency by decreasing the wages. I dare say they are going to economize, but not in these essential departments of the city government.

I have heard it said that a vote for commission government is a vote for local option. That is a most amazing piece of ignorance. The commission form of government cannot change the law of the state with regard to local option or anything else, and the commissioners of Jersey City would not be able to do anything which the law does not permit them to do. If there is something the law permits them to do that the community wants, they can do it, but they cannot do anything that the community wants that the law does not permit, nor can they do anything that the law permits that the community does not want. It must be something that the community wants and the law permits. There is no reason that leads me to believe that is the desire of Jersey City. It would seem that their argument is to prevent the opinion of Jersey City from prevailing in Jersey City. If that is their position I am absolutely against them.

I am an advocate of self government by each self governing community. I am not going to insist that the result agrees with my opinion. There are a great many things that I would like to see Jersey City do, which they are not going to do. That does not change my advocacy of the principle that Jersey City can do anything it pleases. The only way to learn how to live is to live as you please and then take the consequences, because the advantage of a form of government like this is that if, after you have gone in, the water is too cold, you can come out again. You know that (I forget how many, I'm very poor at figures), I believe, 159 cities in the United States have adopted this form of government and not one of them has regretted it. There is not a single case that can be shown where there is any regret that has been expressed except by those who were hurt. Of course, if I

83, which, in cities and counties of the first class (that is, Newark and Jersey City and Essex and Hudson counties), abolished fixed terms of office for all persons except elected officials and a few other specified groups and declared that henceforth such persons could be removed from office only for just cause and after a public hearing as specified in the act.

am run over I am sore at the people in the band wagon. This is an arrangement where the great majority can get on the band wagon. My only embarrassment in speaking for commission government is that I don't know what to say. It is like trying to teach a group of grown men their a, b, c's. I would insult your intelligence if I explained it to you in detail, because the detail is the one thing that you don't have to take care of if you have a reasonable form of government.

One of the things that embarrasses me in Trenton every day is this (I have a case of this sort only too frequently): My attention is called to some very serious miscarriage of justice in some part of the State. I have had the pitiful figure of a woman in my office, according to whose story all her property has been taken away by the machinations of designing men, and she, unable to employ counsel, unable, apparently, to obtain the ear of the court, or to obtain the ear of the commonwealth's attorney, the Prosecutor of the Pleas, unable to do anything except make her way to the Capitol of the State and ask the Governor if he was not powerful enough to help her. My heart has bled as I had to tell her: "My dear woman, I have no power at all. All I could do would be to come down, if I find what you state was true, to tell the people who elected those gentlemen what miscarriage of justice occurred, and could do nothing more." It is a good while before next election, and by that time it would be forgotten, and the same thing would go on. I cannot remove the Prosecutor.

I cannot remove the Sheriff. (Loud and continued applause.)[6] If the Sheriff in some county won't impannel an honest jury, I cannot remove him. I cannot remove any Sheriff in the State; there is nothing I can do if I knew the community was absolutely upset by disorder of any kind, unless the local authorities of the community ask me to do something to enforce the law by the authority of the State.

What I have illustrated before from my experience happens every day of my life. Suppose that by some kind of concentration of authority in the affairs of the State every officer of the State was responsible to some central body, and therefore in the selection of that central body you maintain the processes of justice throughout the State, what zest you would take in electing that body and what kind of vigilance you would bring upon the body.

I want to predict here and now that the processes of politicians not thus accountable in every sphere of government are going

[6] He referred to James J. Kelly, sheriff of Hudson County, who was present. According to the Jersey City *Jersey Journal*, July 15, 1911, Kelly's eyes did not fall when the remark was made, but his face turned red.

more and more to the bad in view of this concentration of authority which will give to the people absolute control over their own government.

Then there won't be any graft. Graft is one of those plants which grows in the dark, which grows in cellars, otherwise known as committee rooms and conferences. It grows where no pure air can penetrate, and the moment the sun strikes it, not only does it shrivel up, but everybody connected with it shrivels up.

The reason I have always been the advocate of publicity is because I have seen it work. Don't you know the considerable work that publicity did in connection with those outrageous scandals connected with the erection of the State Capitol in Harrisburg, Pa. Every man who did not go to the penitentiary dies of sudden diseases or committed suicide, or wastes physically under the eyes of his comrades, to find life intolerable under their honest gaze. And many would have sought the cover of the penitentiary to hide from that honest gaze.

No one of us is honest enough to boast about it. It is a mighty good thing for the honesty of most of us that we are watched. The man ought to be thankful because he is conspicuous, because it keeps him straight, and he cannot do any shady business in public unless it is known by everybody, and therefore, he should take such care to stay in public so that if he wants something, and somebody dangles it before him and shows it to him, he will say: "For God's sake, take that away and stop dangling it in front of me, don't let anybody see it," because he is afraid of publicity, because he knows that the eyes of his fellow men are upon him. And so he will not do it, even if it is all right, because it is something he wanted to do. But that is cowardice. Everyone should have the courage of his convictions.

Gentlemen have managed government so long that they imagine that they own it, and that they might pocket the money of the public without fear, but the people of Jersey City, ladies and gentlemen, have the chance of their lives to show they understand government, to show that they are not children, to show that they cannot be fooled, that though men may fool themselves and place as many obstacles in the path of Commission Government, they cannot take it away.

I know conservatism. I had to be turned out of it myself. I was born a conservative. If only to save existing civilization, if only to regulate, it is not conservatism to go slowly. You must get a move on, and if those of us who are called radicals get a move on it is because we are going to preserve the institutions of America and not because we are going to destroy them. Nevertheless, I know the point of view of the conservative. There are some to whom a new idea is painful. I sometimes fancy they are like a sensitive mass which has received a deep impression from circumstances. If you take an iron, heat it and then try to make another impression, it is exquisitely painful.

I have that experience going through a picture gallery. There is nothing finer in the world than going through the long galleries where there are good pictures. The bad pictures I except, they make no impression. You receive so rapid a succession of impressions—a landscape, a figure, a battle scene, then something else—that your mind is worn out and it won't work. A conservative is prejudiced against anything that changes. You must adjust yourself. It takes wits to adjust yourself. You do not want to play a new game. You say, "No doubt the other game would be interesting and quite worth while, but we don't know it and won't play it. We are going to stick to the present game because we know the rules." I tell you, gentlemen, there is a zest in commission government not found in any private arrangement ever conceived by the mind of man. That wine, the wine of absolute confidence, of your fellow man, quickens every drop of blood in your body.

Is it not worth while to learn the easily acquired rules of that game, the attention to the interest of the community? A man is big only when he goes outside of the narrow circle of his self interest. He acquires the only kind of self greatness. There is the greatness of individuals, the painter, the poet, who in some small den, if they have the light and the materials, can produce immortal work. But it is not this kind of greatness I mean, it is the greatness of society, in which he serves, serves the public in truth, the greatness consisting in perceiving the point of view, the energy, the service to the interest of the community. Is there nothing in that; is there nothing of the idea that America goes from one state of greatness to another, by such greatness?

I heard read on the last Fourth of July the great Declaration of Independence. How many people know the principles of the Declaration of Independence, and really know what it contains. The fundamental principle of the Declaration is that when a set of institutions do not suit the people living under them, it is their fundamental right to change them. I have actually heard a man interpret the Declaration of Independence as if it was an act of impiety to change any part of the form of American government. A man who believes that does not know what the Declaration of Independence means. It means that if you choose you can make a new America from it. If you have made up your mind to do it, you owe it to a decent respect for the opinion of mankind to tell people why you do it, and that is what I am contributing to do to-night. I owe it to the decent respect to the opinions of the people opposed to commission government to tell them why we are going to adopt it. (Applause.)

We are going to adopt it. It doesn't make any difference whether we adopt it next Tuesday or not. Some gentlemen may be astute enough to stop it next Tuesday. That will be a mere incident; we are going to keep on, marching onward until this is accomplished, and accomplished it will be. When men understand it, they are going to place faith in it, and then the result will be irresistible.

The progress of the Walsh act is rapid. Once it is started you cannot stop it. If you want to stop it somebody else will start it. Everything is perfectly fair in the game. Sooner or later Jersey City, together with the other cities of the State, is going to adopt it. Now, I have a great many friends in Jersey City. All I ask you to do is not to come in at the tail end of the procession. I have told you where we are going—will you join? (Cries of "Yes! Yes!") Now, mind you, this is not a three months' enlistment; this is no war that is going to end in a single campaign. Having joined, you join for life. Get busy. Go to the polls with the firm determination to get five voters besides yourself for commission government; and in that ratio, until the polls cannot hold the people voting for commission government. And then the great spirits of those immortal men who made our history will march in fancy at the head of the procession. They said nothing about commission government. They did not conceive such a thing. I can imagine the spirit of Washington welcoming the indomitable spirit of Andrew Jackson, and the fine visionary spirit and great conceiving mind of Thomas Jefferson, marching regnant, yet invisible, at the head of the great army that is going to make known the mind of the majority of the people in America.[7]

CLS T transcript (C. L. Swem Coll., NjP), with corrections from the complete text in the Jersey City *Jersey Journal*, July 15, 1911.

[7] For the result of the vote, see n. 1 to the news item printed at July 19, 1911.

From Lee Douglas[1]

Dear Governor Wilson:　　　　　Nashville [Tenn.] July 15, 1911.

Dr. Allen G[arland]. Hall, Dean of the Vanderbilt University Law School, who is also Superintendent of the Monteagle Assembly at Monteagle, Tenn., has asked me to extend to you through him an official invitation to deliver an address on August 19th (Saturday) before the Sunday School and Bible Institute which will be in session at Monteagle at that time. I am enclosing to you under separate cover a catalogue of the Monteagle Sunday School Assembly, also a program of the Bible Institute, etc.

Of course you are familiar with Monteagle, and the fact that it is the leading Summer Chautauqua in the South. When I had the privilege of seeing you at Trenton last June, you will recall that I mentioned the desire of all of us here to have you take a southern trip, or at least to make an address or two at Nashville this Summer. I believe that if you could arrange to be present even for a day, the opportunity afforded would justify the tediousness of the trip. There is a very large regular attendance at the Assembly and of course the number would be greatly augmented by your coming, so that Dr. Hall feels sure that there would be a representative audience from a dozen southern states numbering from three to four thousand people to hear you. The expenses of your trip would be paid by the Assembly.

I trust that you may not think me officious in saying also that it might be of the greatest benefit in another way. As you know there is a very strong sentiment here for you and our idea is to organize at the proper time non-partisan clubs in the interest of your candidacy, with the Princeton Alumni as a nucleus.[2] The sentiment and enthusiasm is gaining strength every day and of course your presence would mean a great deal to your friends who desire, with your permission, to do what they can, and as early as the situation will justify.

I am sorry that on account of Senator Lea's[3] indisposition, and the very serious illness of his wife,[4] the meeting that Mr. Howe[5] and myself discussed with you has not yet been consummated, although I am sure that but for this, Senator Lea would have come to Princeton to see you last month.

It is very probably [probable] that he will be in Nashville on August 19th and if so of course he would, I know, be very glad to see you, either going to or coming from Monteagle.

Dr. Hall has asked me to assure you that he would be very glad to have you address the Assembly at any time that you could come; but suggested August 19th as the most suitable date in every respect.

Sincerely trusting that you may be able to come to Monteagle[6] and assuring you of my most earnest desire to serve you in any way that I can in Nashville, I am,

Most respectfully,   Lee Douglas

TLS (Governors' Files, Nj).

1 Princeton 1906, lawyer of Nashville and one of the early Wilson men in Tennessee.

2 For the background and development of the Wilson movement in Tennessee, see Arthur S. Link, "Democratic Politics and the Presidential Campaign of 1912 in Tennessee," *The East Tennessee Historical Society's Publications*, No. 18 (1946), pp. 107-30.

3 Luke Lea, Democratic senator from Tennessee, later the most prominent Wilson supporter in that state.

4 Mary Louise Warner Lea.

5 The Editors have been unable to identify him.

6 See L. Douglas to WW, July 31, 1911, for Wilson's reply to the invitation.

To Mary Allen Hulbert Peck

Dearest Friend,   Sea Girt, N. J., 16 July, 1911.

Here we are, at Sea Girt. Ellen and the girls came down on Friday, and I got here on Saturday (yesterday), riding all the way down from New York, *via* pretty Staten Island, in my campaign manager's car. (Of course I have no campaign manager in fact; but Wm. F. McCombs, of New York, a very generous friend and a one-time pupil of mine at Princeton, has insisted upon making his office a sort of clearing house of the big correspondence that is going on from one end of the country to the other about my possible nomination for the presidency,—and a splendid fellow he is. He tells me that he dictates some fifty letters a day on the subject!) The house is really delightful and already we are beginning to feel familiar with it. After the camp[1] is over (24 July to 12 Aug.) we shall, I hope, have some free and quiet days here,—and then you can come down—can't you?—sometime before autumn—and make the pleasure of the place perfect for us! There is a little room in which, I think, you can be quite cool and comfortable.

My trip to Ky. was quite delightful, in spite of the truly terrible heat in which it was made. Lexington is certainly the place for free and gay and perfect hospitality! The men were cordial and altogether interesting, and the women were bewitching. I got, one day, into a bunch of beauties that made my head swim. They were as sweet to me as they were delightful to look upon, —partly, I hope, because they liked me and not *altogether* because they thought me 'distinguished.' The men thought that it was the mint juleps that made me talk so at my best, but—it was not! Besides, they did not know that by nature I am "a very talkative gentleman." I have been told so by a lady altogether more charming and delightful than all the Kentucky beauties put together. In the little church to which we went this morning I saw a lady across the church with a beautiful profile, the line of whose nose and the sweet turn of whose eyebrow and temple were

so like those that mark the beauty of the frank lady aforesaid
that I had a thrill of deep pleasure and a sort of sense of comradeship!

To pass through New York without seeing you—to speak over
the telephone with you *in the same town* and then take a train—
was as much as one ought to be called on to do. Of such stuff
are moral heroes made,—if it is meself that says it. All join me
in affectionate messages.

Your devoted friend,   Woodrow Wilson

ALS (WP, DLC).
  ¹ The annual encampment of the New Jersey National Guard. In addition to
military training, it involved numerous ceremonial and social functions requiring
the governor's participation.

To Cleveland Hoadley Dodge

My dear Cleve.,   [Sea Girt, N. J.] 16 July, 1911.

Thank you for your note. I drop you a line, in haste, to say
that it looks as if the visit to Riverdale were going to be rendered
impossible. I will see you as soon as possible and explain why,—
a letter long enough to explain can't be written in these hours of
our first settling down at Sea Girt. I am greatly disappointed. A
visit with you is always such a refreshment and delight to me!
That day on the yacht was a perfect delight! But I am no longer
free to choose what I shall do.

All join me in warmest regards to you all, and I am, as always
Affectionately and Gratefully Yours,   Woodrow Wilson

ALS (WC, NjP).

From Walter Hines Page

My dear Wilson: Garden City, L. I. 16 July 1911

Of course you don't want a drum-major nor a brass band. (You
see, I come back to the old subject.) You don't want any artificial
force at work at all. The things you stand for and the force of
your personality—these must win: a prize won otherwise would
not profit you or the nation.

Yet everything in this world that looks towards the massing
of men or the direction of forces must have organization. Organization is necessary in our dark world for men of the same
mind to find one another. Else they will march at cross-purposes
and straggle out of the highway. Organization is necessary to

prevent waste and duplication of effort; and, most of all, it is necessary to save your time & strength.

I hope, therefore, that some man has come within sight who will be looked to in political circles as a man for your friends to confer with and who will be looked to for instructions, in a sense.

I see that Senator Watson, of W. Va.,[1] is playing with his thoroughbreds & entertaining his friends at his race-track. *He needs something better to run than horses!* That's mere play.

This thought keeps coming to me & I keep passing it on to you.
Yours sincerely,   Walter H. Page

ALS (Governors' Files, Nj).
[1] Clarence Wayland Watson, Democratic senator from West Virginia, 1911-13.

To Lawrence Gilman[1]

My dear Mr. Gilman: [Sea Girt, N. J.] July 17, 1911

Mr. Charles Johnston[2] kindly sent me the enclosed article of his for my comment and revision.[3] I have taken the liberty of making a few alterations, which he gave me permission to do, and am now sending it to you as he requested before his departure for Europe.   Sincerely yours,   Woodrow Wilson

TLS (CtY).
[1] Music critic and author, at this time managing editor of *Harper's Weekly.*
[2] Author, translator, and free-lance journalist of New York.
[3] Johnston's interview is printed at Aug. 19, 1911.

From William Frank McCombs

My dear Governor: New York July 17, 1911.

I have the letter of Mr. [Henry E.] Alexander which you were kind enough to send. I do not think he quite appreciated the situation when he wrote you. So far as Mr. Measday[1] is concerned the situation is this: Mr. Measday in fact represents the New York World and the "North American" of Philadelphia and is to be paid by them for such matter as they use. The plan is that he shall represent as a staff correspondent the Trenton True American, The Philadelphia Record and the Standard News Association of New York, and that other newspapers will be added to his list from time to time, which he will represent as a correspondent, actually furnishing news to them. He will not be cast in any wise in the roll of a publicity agent for you. He will merely give to the other correspondents, as a matter of courtesy, such news as he gets, and they will in no wise be led to believe that he is a publicity agent for you. It is the usual custom among newspaper correspondents to exchange news and to assist each other in the collection of news; so that Mr. Measday's position will not be at all anomalous. I quite agree that if he were with you as a publicity agent it would be bad judgment, but I am sure the situation is sufficiently guarded so that no risk is taken. Mr. Measday will see Mr. Alexander tomorrow and I think after they have talked the matter over, Mr. Alexander, as a newspaper man, will change his position. I feel sure that Mr. Measday can be of assistance and can change the situation in respect of promulgating the correct facts of what you are doing and having the news sent out in its true perspective. Mr. Measday has his instructions and you may trust him not to do any "hippodroming or faking." In my view it would be advantageous to have him around.

Yours sincerely,   Wm. F. McCombs.

P.S. I am having ten thousand copies of the "Philadelphia North American" editorial printed[2] and will have it sent out under the auspices of one of the Woodrow Wilson clubs so as to give it a "local habitation."   W F McC.

TLS (Governors' Files, Nj).
    [1] Walter Measday, reporter for the New Work *World*. He became Wilson's private secretary and personal press agent in early 1912.
    [2] "True Americanism," Philadelphia *North American*, July 6, 1911. The editorial quoted excerpts from fifteen Wilson speeches with the comment: "Entirely apart from politics, present and future, we count it no exaggeration to declare our opinion that no other American has approached more nearly to Jefferson and Lincoln in wonderful facility and felicity of stating the problems and their solutions which touch real Americanism from every angle."

From Calvin Noyes Kendall

My dear Governor Wilson: [Indianapolis, Ind.] July 17, 1911.

    I wish to again express to you my appreciation of the honor which you have given me in tendering me the appointment as Commissioner of Education of New Jersey. It is my earnest hope that my work in the state may justify your confidence.

    I have sent you some of our local newspapers giving editorial comment relative to the appointment.

    The Board of School Commissioners here, as I anticipated, expect me to make things ready for my successor, whoever he may be. I do not see how it will be possible for me to close affairs here before September, as I stated to you in Trenton.

    While I am in New Jersey I will have a conference with Dr. Schauffler with reference to the affairs at the office at Trenton, and endeavor to make some arrangement so that the routine work of the office may go on until I can personally take charge.

I hope that I may be able to see you, too, while I am in Trenton. It will be necessary for me to be in Indianapolis again on Monday, the twenty-fourth.

Again thanking you, and with kind regards, I am

Yours sincerely,   C. N. Kendall

TLS (Governors' Files, Nj).

To Ray Stannard Baker

My dear Mr. Baker: [Sea Girt, N. J.] July 18, 1911.

Thank you for your letter of the seventh.[1] I have given the matter of the articles you propose my very careful consideration and it has been with the utmost reluctance that I have come to the conclusion that it is impossible for me to write them. I use the word impossible with deliberation, because I know now just what is ahead of me; at the same time, I also know the conditions it has always been necessary for me to establish before I could really write anything that was worth reading.

I need not tell you how warmly I appreciate not only the suggestion but the cordial manner in which it was made and urged. I can only beg that you will assure the editors of the American Magazine [of] my warm appreciation and my genuine regret that it is out of my choice to do what they so graciously requested.

With warm regards,

Cordially yours,   Woodrow Wilson

TCL (RSB Coll., DLC).
  [1] It is missing.

To Henry Beach Needham

My dear Mr. Needham: [Sea Girt, N. J.] July 18, 1911.

I want to thank you very warmly for your letter of the fifteenth.[1] It has given me a great deal of genuine pleasure. That I should have won your confidence and support puts me in heart. I do not know how these things happen, but I do know that I am that I am [sic] very deeply appreciative.

Cordially and sincerely yours,   Woodrow Wilson

TLS (U.S. Presidents' Papers, MiU-C).
  [1] It is missing.

From William Lawrence Wilson[1]

My dear Governor: Baltimore, July 18, 1911.

I have just received your letter of July 17th and hasten to reply.

I notice you do not agree with me in urging Fentress[2] to go ahead and I am writing him today that he can disregard my suggestions. The only thing that I urged him to do was to get in practically the same shape as we are in Maryland. That is to get his first few members and have a President and Secretary elected so that when the time comes a campaign for members could be made by authorized persons. This was all I wanted him to do but I left it entirely to his own judgment.

I am glad to read what you say about Mr. McCombs for although I have only seen him a few times I have grown extremely fond of him and consider him a most able man. I really think that you are nearly as fortunate in having him as a supporter as he is in having you to work for.

In your letter you did not say anything about being able to see me and I suppose my request which was contained in the last paragraph of my letter was overlooked. I am plan[n]ing to be in New York the latter part of this week and will try to see you if you are in Trenton at the time.

With kindest regards, I remain,

Faithfully yours,   William L Wilson

TLS (Governors' Files, Nj).

[1] Princeton 1903, president of the Wilson Maltman Electric Co. of Baltimore and secretary and treasurer of the Woodrow Wilson Democratic Association of Maryland.

[2] David Fentress, Princeton 1896, lawyer of Memphis, Tenn., later one of the leaders of the Wilson movement in Tennessee.

A News Item

[July 19, 1911]

Sea Girt, July 19—Gov. Wilson, upon his arrival here this morning, said that he was highly pleased with the result of the Commission Government election in Jersey City.[1]

"I am very much gratified," said the Governor, "that the Commission Government advocates are so pleased with the situation resulting from yesterday's election. If they had another week to campaign, Commission Government would have won out. The next time it is put to a vote in Jersey City I am confident Commission Government will be overwhelmingly adopted."

Printed in the Jersey City *Jersey Journal*, July 19, 1911.

[1] The voters rejected commission government, 11,585 to 13,068, in the special election on July 18.

A News Report of a Speech to Monmouth County Democrats

[July 19, 1911]

LAWS' CRITICS HEAR WILSON

Governor Arrives After Katzenbach Hits Referendum and Nugent Smites Geran Law.

DEMOCRATS ARE ROUSED

ASBURY PARK, July 19.—Arriving at the big dinner of the Monmouth County Democratic committee here last night after Frank S. Katzenbach Jr. had attacked the initiative and referendum and other "new-fangled" ideas, and after James R. Nugent had taken a fall out of the new election law, Governor Woodrow Wilson trained his guns on the machine politician. In a speech that lasted an hour, he poured shot after shot into politicians who, he said, cared little or nothing for the principles of the Democratic party, but whose sole aim was selfish gain. . . .

The Governor said at one point in his speech that he believed in harmony of the kind that would make the man who lost a fight continue to be a good sport.

"I have no challenge but this," he said. "If you agree with me, stand by me. That's all I ask. If you don't agree with me, and your opinions are honestly formed, I'll grasp your hand. But if you cut under, and try to stab me in the back, I'm your enemy, and I'll tell the world that you are a scoundrel."

At another point he said:

"It is no part of my privilege to say anything to pull down the reputation of any individual man. It is my right to fight against all odds. I owe it to knighthood and to the law of chivalry to give every man fair play, and by the same law it is mine to claim that every man who comes into the lists shall be fair spoken. I do not bear ill-feeling. I am willing to clasp hands with any man who believes what I believe and will work with me to win it. Harmony is born of the spirit of the man who drives hate from his heart and tries to give every other man just what he wants for himself—fair play." . . .

Printed in the *Newark Evening News*, July 19, 1911.

From Francis Fisher Kane

My dear Dr. Wilson: Drifton, Pa. July 19th [1911].

I have just got back from Harrisburg. The telegraph office is not open & I have to write.

In our endorsement of you[1] we only recognized an obligation long since due. We could not have made our fight here in Pennsylvania against the "bi-partisan machine" without the inspiration which came from your defeat of Smith in New Jersey. Therefore you have been, and will be, our political saviour.

This has been so much on my mind that I have to write it out.

It has been a hard battle, and Palmer, Guthrie & McCormick are deserving of infinite praise. Thanks to them and to their uncompromising attitude, we have once and for all time put away from us the unclean thing.

Do not take the trouble to acknowledge this letter.

Yours sincerely, & ever gratefully,

Francis Fisher Kane.

I am not unmindful of course of your direct aid—your two great speeches, at the Philadelphia dinner[2] and the Clubs Convention[3]—but back of them was what you had done and what you were doing. The Pennsylvania Democracy could endorse no one else. I can almost say it would not exist without you.

ALS (WP, DLC).
[1] The Democratic State Committee had just adopted a resolution endorsing Wilson for the presidency. The old guard rump state committee had already taken similar action.
[2] The Philadelphia speech is printed at Feb. 21, 1911, Vol. 22.
[3] That is, in Harrisburg.

To Mary Allen Hulbert Peck

Dearest Friend,   Sea Girt [N. J.], 20 July, 1911.

I am distressed and alarmed at not hearing from you! I am so afraid that you are ill, or that Mrs. Allen is ill, or—that something has happened! When I was in Trenton on Tuesday ("Governor's Day"), Mrs. Roebling called me up on the telephone to ask me if *I* had heard anything from you recently. She said that she had written to you several times but could get no reply and that she was really anxious. She said she was going to write to Mrs. Crane[1] and ask her to find out. Not a word have I heard since I heard your voice over the telephone as I was passing through New York on my way to Kentucky. Nellie and Jessie were making a visit in Richmond, nearby Pittsfield, last week, and went over to call on you, but said that you were still away,—and that was after the time when you expected to be back when we talked over the telephone. Altogether, I do not know what to think. I have been very much depressed, by all sorts of painful conjectures, and can only beg that, if you cannot write yourself, you

will get Allen or Mrs. Allen to send me some word of you. Please
do that, and do it as soon as you can!

There is nothing to tell of myself, even if I felt like talking
about myself—as I do not, when my thoughts are full of what
concerns those whose friendship and companionship constitute
so much of my happiness and strength. The days go with me as
usual,—not in a calculable routine, to be sure,—with an incalculable variety, on the contrary; but with a round of duties and
interruptions and engagements to which I have become accustomed and to which I have at last adjusted myself reasonably
well. I am well and do what I have to do with energy enough and
satisfaction enough. Sea Girt is good to live in for a little while,
&c. &c., but some of my friends are very far away and it is an
anxious business waiting for news from them!

With affectionate messages from all,

Your devoted friend   Woodrow Wilson

ALS (WP, DLC).
[1] Josephine Boardman (Mrs. Winthrop Murray) Crane.

To Alexander Mitchell Palmer

My dear Mr. Palmer: [Sea Girt, N. J.] July 20, 1911.

It was certainly an act of most thoughtful kindness on your
part to send me the telegram[1] I received last night about the
action of the Pennsylvania Democratic State Committee. I need
not tell you how deeply I have been gratified by it. The support
of the Pennsylvania delegation at the National Convention will
mean a vast deal; but what will mean more will be the character
of the men from whom I am receiving this generous endorsement in Pennsylvania.

Let me congratulate you also on the prospects of effective
party action in Pennsylvania under the stimulation of such leadership.

Cordially and sincerely yours,   Woodrow Wilson

TLS (WP, DLC).
[1] It is missing.

From Henry Watterson

My dear Governor: Louisville, Ky., July 20, 1911.

Mrs. Watterson and I were disappointed that you were not
able to give us a day and a night. I daresay that you are as busy
a man as I am and have scarcely a moment you can call your

own. I had hoped to be with George Harvey some time during the Summer; but the exigencies of our state campaign will keep me at home. I am flattered by my friends into the belief that old as I may be I am still good for something. It will be early enough in the Fall to begin to talk seriously about next year.

I enclose you two or three clippings which may amuse an idle moment.

Remember me to Mrs. Wilson and the young ladies, and believe me,   Your Friend   Henry Watterson

TLS (Governors' File, Nj).

A News Report of an Address in Passaic, New Jersey, on Behalf of Commission Government

[July 21, 1911]

PASSAIC HEARS THE GOVERNOR

PASSAIC, July 21.—Democrats and Republicans alike were enthusiastic in their greeting to Governor Wilson in the High School auditorium here last night when the Executive spoke in support of commission government. The Governor's address was punctuated several times with applause as he made the telling points in his argument.

The voters of this city will go to the polls next Tuesday to decide whether the new form of government as provided under the Walsh act will be adopted. The special election is being looked forward to with much interest and it was agreed that the Governor made many friends for the new form of rule last night.

Picturing the present system of municipal government as an impenetrable cloak behind which the responsibility for the government is hidden, Governor Wilson stirred his auditors to cheers when he referred to commission government as the modern means of placing the control of the government in the hands of the people.[1] . . .

Printed in the *Newark Evening News*, July 21, 1911; some editorial headings omitted.

[1] For the outcome in Passaic, see n. 1 to the news report printed at July 27, 1911.

From Mary Allen Hulbert Peck

Dearest Friend: [Pittsfield, Mass.] July 22nd [1911]

How sweet you were to telephone! Your good letter came in the morning but I was too busy with my duties as nurse to write

then and hoped to have a free moment in the evening. Mother
has been quite ill. Summer grippe was the diagnosis, but with
a woman of her age any number of complications may arise and
the constant use of the stethescope alarmed me. She is better
however, and hopes to get up tomorrow.

This is a heaven sent morning. I can smell the woods in the
cool breeze that comes from the Western hills, and have all the
old longing to run abroad in them. I'm horribly afraid that when
the longed for opportunity comes, I will be too rheumatic and
stiff to frisk much, but my fancy is still nimble and I hope it will
ever be, and that counts for something. I seem to be always mark-
ing time, and surely there must be some great enjoyment in
store for so long a training.

I am just beginning to realize to the full my blessed freedom.
It is *wonderful.* I think of you, and all life is meaning to you
now, and all *you* mean to life. You are the larger part of my life,
even to the part you play in directing me when I fill ice or hot
water bags. A case where "blow hot—blow cold" means stead-
fastly. I am sure Murray Crane[1] has some great scheme afoot,
and I hope to know what it is. Isn't Mr. Roosevelt getting ready
to run for the Presidency again? Mr. H. Dawes[2] thinks you have
talked too much, and are the worst demegogue of this or any day
for decades. I fairly *hiss* when anyone doubts your sincerity, calls
you a "clever politician," or insinuates you are other than you
are—the best, the finest, the noblest gentleman and statesman
the world has seen. So now—*there*! There is really nothing definite to tell of the gentleman[3] referred to several times, save that
I distrust him, perhaps unjustly. I think him quite capable of
being in the confidence and benefiting thereby, of F. Roebling,[4]
but if you prove the strongest man of yr. party he will side faithfully with you, because he may achieve further greatness by *that*
road. His enthusiasm for you expressed in no mild terms at the
C. C. dinner[5] was good to hear, but a year before I had heard
his opinion of you and your ability, and it stuck stubbornly in
my memory. He knows you better now, as the world does, & may
be quite honest. Of that you are a better judge than I. If he has
enough money already, he will play straight. Miss Anna Dawes,[6]
who has ceased to talk recipes to me, and tries to bring the conversation around to you, thinks you have been "too previous,"
that if the Convention were to be held *now*, you would be nominated but any one or thing may swing popular favor away from
you in the intervening time. I insist upon the recipes and gossip,
saying I know nothing of politics, having a mind too feeble to
grasp the subject, for it's hopeless to make the world, unless it

be on the same plane—realize that you are honest, that you must be *yourself*, acting according to your conscience and convictions, even though it means defeat, failure in the eyes of that world. That you would like the people to give you the greatest office of the country, it would be absurd to deny, but I need not tell *you* that you are judged by *their*—the politicians'—standards, not your own.

Bless you! This must bore you. I know so little, I can only feel. You are and will be the leader of the many who have been dumb and helpless, because there was no one to honestly voice their sentiments, or lead them to victory.

You are a great and good man, my dear friend, and I am the proudest woman in the world to feel that you find me worthy of calling me yours. I devote much of my spare time to beautifying my "figger" rolling industriously 50 times every night, my great ambition being to roll under the bed, an ambition *almost* achieved.

I wish I could see you to talk over *my* plans. We are still thinking of Hot Springs in August, and I am looking forward to a few days with you all at Sea Girt, whenever Mrs. Wilson finds it most convenient. She is dear & sweet to want me, and if I can arrange it en route from or to *somewhere*, it will be delightful. I have not been out at all, I mean socially, and have many visits to return. Pittsfield however is just as objectionable as of old, but the country is exquisite—I love it!

Katherine[7] has a little boy, born Thursday and is doing well, so both the children[8] now have a boy & girl & I'm a grandmother indeed. I have two new pairs of glasses!

And I am your devoted   M.A.P.

How shall I address yr. letter? Are you Hon or Gov? *Answer*

ALS (WP, DLC).

[1] Winthrop Murray Crane of Dalton, Berkshire County, Republican senator from Massachusetts, 1904-13.

[2] Henry Laurens Dawes, Jr., member of the law firm of Pingree, Dawes & Burke of Pittsfield. His father was Republican senator from Massachusetts, 1875-93.

[3] General Sadler.

[4] Ferdinand William Roebling, Sr., secretary and treasurer of John A. Roebling's Sons Co. of Trenton, active in Republican politics.

[5] Wilson's speech to the Trenton Chamber of Commerce on March 7, 1911, a news report of which is printed at March 8, 1911, Vol. 22. Sadler, president of the Broad Street National Bank of Trenton, was the toastmaster on that occasion and introduced Wilson.

[6] She is identified in WW to Mary A. H. Peck, July 11, 1909, n. 2, Vol. 19. She was a sister of Henry Laurens Dawes, Jr.

[7] Her stepdaughter, Katherine Peck (Mrs. Mahlon) Bradley.

[8] Her other stepdaughter was Harriet Peck Snitcher.

To Mary Allen Hulbert Peck

Dearest Friend,   [Sea Girt, N. J.] 24 July, 1911.

The camp has opened ("Camp Wilson") and I am more subject to interruption than ever. Even my Sundays are gone,—till this military business is over. I literally did not have fifteen minutes to myself yesterday. Even Monday is better. I can at least *steal* a few minutes to-day and write a sentence or two at a time. If the poor screed sounds disconnected, remember that is was punctuated with every kind of public business!

Your letter came yesterday. Our little talk over the telephone had relieved my anxiety (what a comfort the telephone is, and how tantalizing!), but I needed the letter to reassure me entirely and feel that I had a real knowledge of what you were doing and thinking about,—and *what* a pleasure it was to see it! And what a delightful letter it was. What chiefly delighted me about it was its tone of strength and vital enjoyment once more,—as if you were again in sight, at least, of the joy and sweetness of being alive—and free—and of realizing the love and loyalty of your friends. *Of course* Pittsfield is the same old hateful place, *to you,*—but when your spirits rise up and feel the charm and power of Nature about you I know that you are breathing freely again and that your heart is really at ease. The mood is communicated to me. I feel as I used to when we took those delectable walks to the South Shore,[1]—when you were like a gay child of Nature, released into its native element, and I felt every quickened impulse of the blood communicated to me. It was seeing (or, rather, experiencing) Nature with a new directness and freshness and poignancy to receive all its suggestions through you,—interpreted by you. And so, when the same note comes to me in your letters I get the same quickened happiness from it—except, alas! that I have only your written words, not you! Your generous praise of *me* (which I could not accept as a critical judgment) so evidently comes from your heart—and not from your head—that I accept it with joy, as an evidence of the same intoxication of high spirits and of consciousness of your friends' devotion to you. Let us know *all* your movements, as long in advance as possible, and you may be sure we *will* catch you as you come or go—or know the reason why! Delightful letters are all very well, but the lady herself is none the less indispensable—and that at short intervals. I am well and fit. All join in the most affectionate messages with

Your devoted friend   Woodrow Wilson

ALS (WP, DLC).
[1] Of Bermuda.

To Henry Watterson

PERSONAL.

My dear Colonel Watterson: [Sea Girt, N. J.] July 24, 1911.

Thank you for your letter of July twentieth and its enclosures. It is always a genuine pleasure to read your editorials. They are so straight-forward and have such extraordinary vigor that they always quicken the blood and put tonic into a man.

I hope that I shall not have the ill-luck again to be near Mrs. Watterson and you and not see you.

Cordially yours,   Woodrow Wilson

TLS (H. Watterson Papers, DLC).

To Ray Stannard Baker

My dear Mr. Baker: [Sea Girt, N. J.] July 24, 1911.

You may be sure that I did not come to my decision about the articles without the greatest reluctance.[1] I know that I am turning away from an opportunity of unusual importance and interest but I really have no choice in the matter and it would be quite as impossible for me to supervise and cooperate in the preparation of articles embodying my views as to write them myself. Indeed, my experience is that it is easier to write them myself than to cooperate with others or to revise what others have written.

I never dreamed in former years that I should get into a position where my time and energy were so absolutely absorbed and where it was so literally impossible for me to write.

With warm appreciation of your kindness,

Sincerely yours,   Woodrow Wilson

TCL (RSB Coll., DLC).
[1] Baker's letter to which this was a reply is missing.

To Henry Smith Pritchett

My dear President Prickett: [Sea Girt, N. J.] July 24, 1911.

Thank you sincerely for your letter of July twentieth.[1] It reassures me about my choice for Commissioner of Education. I have known Mr. Kendall for a long time and was fortunately able to judge personally of his qualities and character.

It is very kind of you to think of my need for rest but apparently that is something which governors who try to do their duty are not allowed to get. Fortunately I am keeping very well and feeling very fine.

    With warm regards,

Faithfully yours,   Woodrow Wilson

TLS (Carnegie Foundation for the Advancement of Teaching).
  [1] It is missing.

To Edwin Bird Wilson[1]

My dear Mr. Wilson: [Trenton, N. J.] July 24, 1911.

    Allow me to acknowledge your very kind letter of the twentieth and to say that it will give me real pleasure to sign your diploma if you desire. If you will be kind enough to send the diploma to me, I will sign it and return it at once.

    You are very generous in what you say of your desire to help in any way that you can help politically. In spite of the reports of the newspapers to the contrary, I am not making any attempt to capture the nomination but you may be sure that I warmly appreciate your suggestion and will keep it in mind against a possible occasion.

Cordially and sincerely yours,   Woodrow Wilson

TLS (received from Ethel Wilson Fruland).
  [1] Princeton 1901, head of the advertising department of the Bankers Trust Co. of New York.

From Daniel Moreau Barringer

Personal

My dear Woodrow,   Philadelphia, Pa. July 25, 1911.

    I am glad to tell you that I am back again in Philadelphia and greatly benefitted by my two months' trip to Europe. I was seriously ill last December and January and was in great need of the trip. Mrs. Barringer[1] also derived much benefit from it. It was the first time she has ever left the children,[2] except for a few days, and she was naturally very anxious concerning them, but as good luck would have it not one of them was ill for a day during our absence.

    I send you a clipping from the New York Times of May 10th, 1911.[3] My eye happened to fall upon these most interesting statistics the day we sailed from New York and having plenty of leisure I read the article very carefully several times on the way over and became more and more impressed with the startling facts to which it calls our attention. When one remembers how this same group has added to its power since May tenth one almost shudders at the possibilities of this growing power. In a short time this group, or some similar group, will, unless prevented by proper legislation, control in a large measure at least the credits of the country. When that time arrives it can easily ruin any man or group of men in business it may wish to ruin and thus stifle legitimate competition. This money trust is to my mind by far the most insidious and dangerous of all the trusts, and, as in the case of cancer for which no cure is known at present, it is better to cut in [it] out bodily with a knife as soon as possible rather than to have it spread and eat into the vitals of our form of government. There are so many people in America now who, I thank God, place patriotism above avarice and who are more or less awake to the rapidly growing power of this and similar groups of financiers, who are in reality working together although they may appear to be rivals, that I cannot help believing when the Democrats get into power with you, as we all hope, as their standard-bearer two years hence something radical will be done. Far better a number of small panics than to have the revolution which this sort of thing will eventually bring about if it is not corrected and regulated within the next few years. I know you feel as deeply as I do about these matters and understand them far better, so I will not weary you with further discourse. It has occurred to me to send you these statistics because they seem to be authentic and are not taken from some muckraking magazine article.

If you have time to run down and spend a night with us we will have Davis[4] do the same and we three can have an old time chat together. Try to do this if you can.

With best regards in which all of us join to you and yours, I am,   Affectionately,   D. M. Barringer

TLS (Governors' Files, Nj).

[1] Margaret Bennett Barringer.

[2] Brandon, Daniel Moreau, Jr., Sarah Drew, John Paul, Elizabeth Wethered, Lewin Bennett, and Richard Wethered Barringer, all born between 1899 and 1909.

[3] The article discussed a chart submitted by the Alpha Portland Cement Co. in hearings before an examiner of the Interstate Commerce Commission in New York. The chart, which was printed with the article, attempted to reveal the widespread influence of the United States Steel Corp. and J. P. Morgan & Co. in the railroad and industrial affairs of the country. The chart named the members on the boards of directors of these two companies, and after each name listed the other business concerns on the boards of which he also sat. It then gave an estimate of the total capitalization and the combined gross annual income of the concerns with which each director was associated and then added up these figures to produce a grand total capitalization of $14,388,975,728 and a gross annual income of $3,936,547,078. When the capitalization and income of U. S. Steel itself was added, the figures became $15,857,629,339 and $4,640,-508,502, respectively.

[4] Edward Parker Davis, classmate and physician of Philadelphia.

From Francis Fisher Kane

My dear Governor Wilson: Drifton, Pa. July 25th [1911].

Thank you for your note. I was ashamed afterwards of my clumsily expressed letter, but what I tried to say was true.

"Are they going to submit?"[1] I should say, Yes, in the end, but the victory—the complete victory—may be long in coming. It cannot come until the primary election next April when we vote for party committee-men and delegates to the State and National Conventions. This coming September we have primaries in Pennsylvania for the nomination of county and municipal officers—the mayoralty and a host of county and city officials in Philadelphia. But the Republican organization put through an Act of the Legislature which postpones the nomination of party officers until the primary in April. So that Donnelly & Ryan[2] will be in control of our City Committee until then. It is going to be hard to dislodge them. When young Cadwalader[3] was recently turned out of the Registration Board Donnelly's man was put in by our Republican Governor,[4] and it is altogether likely that until Donnelly & Ryan are defeated at the primaries, the Republican organization will throw its crumbs to them. They will have the minority offices—at least the places subject to appointment—until next spring. And the local press is helping them and calling our battle a mere factional fight!

Still, the State is with us solidly. Leave out Philadephia & Pittsburgh and the party is with the reorganizers almost unanimously. So far as the State at large is concerned we shall "stay on top," and if we can organize an effective reform organization in the two cities—it has been done before—that organization will be recognized by the State Convention. Of course Donnelly sees this, but we see it too.

I have great confidence in the staying power of both Guthrie and Palmer. Palmer, as you have doubtless divined, is a hard fighter. His blood is roused and he has a personal reputation at stake. His position on the Ways & Means Committee makes him the best National Committee-man we could have had, and he in turn could not go back on the movement without great loss of prestige. I believe him too to be absolutely sincere in his abhorrence of the old bi-partisan machine. Guthrie is "downright good,"—one of the best men I know. His position in our State independent of politics, as Grand Master of the Masons, for instance, and his independence in politics, having been the one real reform mayor that Pittsburgh has had within a generation, make him an ideal State Chairman. He will not compromise with the Hall-

Dewalt crowd,[5] they don't attract him and he knows them well.

I get great comfort from considering the character of these men—Palmer, Guthrie, and McCormick. They will not back down no matter how much cold water the [Philadelphia] Record pours upon our movement. Johnny Dwyer (the managing editor) will see this in the end.

By degrees, I hope, he and the crowd back of him will see that the men up the State are in earnest & will not go back.

Much depends upon the coming mayoralty election in Philadelphia. We must do our part in saving the city. If we put up Norris (the Democrat who spoke at our dinner)[6] Donnelly will probably take him and the Keystoners[7] wont. Thus we shall have the opposition divided—a Keystone ticket and a regular Democratic ticket—just as it was last summer when with Berry and Grim in the field we lost the governorship.[8]

I am going to Philadelphia on Friday to a conference out of which I hope will spring a committee that will represent the decent Democrats of the town and that can treat honestly and effectively with the Keystoners, and prevent them "doing business" with Donnelly. We are trying to keep our plans absolutely quiet until the committee is formed.

These are the difficulties ahead of us. Without doubt the voters are with us; I have proofs of this on every side. But as you would say, we must have a programme and *that* should interest us.

You will excuse me for the length at which I have written you. I could not otherwise answer your question.

The National Convention is not being forgotten by us. May-be the line of cleavage between ourselves at the old crowd will be maintained until then. I believe it will, and I hope and pray that at Baltimore we may still be found anti-Donnelly as well as pro-Wilson men. The latter we joyfully pledge ourselves to be.

Yrs. faithfully,   Francis Fisher Kane

ALS (Governors' Files, Nj).

[1] That is, would the minority conservative Democratic faction led by James M. Guffey submit to the reform Democrats, the "reorganizers," who now controlled the Pennsylvania State Democratic Committee?

[2] Charles Donnelly and Thomas J. Ryan, who controlled the Democratic party machinery in Philadelphia.

[3] John Cadwalader, Jr., lawyer of Philadelphia and member of the Board of Registration Commissioners of Philadelphia County, 1906-11. Both he and his father had long been active in the Democratic party in Pennsylvania.

[4] John Kinley Tener, Governor of Pennsylvania, 1911-15.

[5] The conservative Democratic faction led by Arthur Granville Dewalt of Allentown, recently-deposed state chairman, and State Senator James Knox Polk Hall of Ridgway, Pa.

[6] George Washington Norris, Philadelphia banker active in Democratic politics, who spoke with Wilson to the Democratic Club of Philadelphia on February 21, 1911.

⁷ An independent party of reform Democrats and Republicans which ran William H. Berry for governor in 1910.
⁸ See V. C. McCormick to WW, Feb. 6, 1911, n. 2, Vol. 22.

From Thomas Bell Love

My dear Governor Wilson: Dallas, Texas July 26th, 1911.

I have intended writing you since my return from Atlantic City to express my great regret that business engagements in the East and the necessity of getting home as early as possible rendered it impossible for me to call on you at Trenton, in view of your absence in Kentucky at the time I had planned to call. I have been very much engrossed with the prohibition campaign which has just ended and in which I stood for Statewide Prohibition. While at least 50,000 majority of the white men of Texas voted for prohibition, we were defeated by a majority of about 5,000 in a total of 460,000 votes cast. My chief motive for espousing the prohibition side of the contest was to eliminate the influence of the liquor oligarchy in Texas politics and Government, it being the only dangerous special interest left with any potency in the State. While the Amendment was defeated the liquor machine is destroyed. Another such victory as it has just gained is wholly unnecessary for its undoing, for all thoughtful men concede that it is already undone, and I am very confident that its undoing makes certain the sending of a Wilson delegation to the next National Convention.

I have just had a long talk with Mr. Armistead, of San Antonio,¹ and with his concurrence and at the suggestion of other friends, I am issuing a request for a conference of Texas Democrats favorable to your nomination to be held in Austin on Saturday, August 5th. At this meeting a State organization will be formed and an invitation extended you to visit Texas this fall, and deliver an address, preferably during the State Fair at Dallas some time in October. It is of prime importance that you should visit Texas at that time. We will now proceed to form an organization throughout the State and personally I am supremely confident as to the result.

I am anxious to obtain a copy of your Kentucky address, which I have been unable to see. We will have a number of prominent men with us in the contest who were against Statewide prohibition. All the good men were not on my side on this issue, but practically all of the bad ones were on the other side.

With best wishes, I am,

Very truly yours,   Thos. B Love

TLS (Governors' Files, Nj).
¹ George Daniel Armistead, staff correspondent for the San Antonio *Express*. Wilson appointed him postmaster of San Antonio in 1914.

From Traverse Alexander Spraggins[1]

My dear Sir: Jersey City, N. J., July 26th, 1911.

Your communication of July 19th, just came to hand, and in reply thereto permit me to thank you for the honor you have done me in selecting me to represent the Negro Citizens of this State, as a delegate to the Negro Educational Convention to be held at Denver, Colo.,—August 12th to 15th of this year.

It is a pleasure at any time for me to help at any time in any cause that will advance the interests of the Colored people of this State, and you may be assured that at any time that you may call upon me to render such service, I will be glad to do it. At no time should the expense in any [way] be taken into consideration.

I have the honor to be,

Your obedient servant,   Traverse A. Spraggins.

TLS (Governors' Files, Nj).
¹ Lawyer of Jersey City.

To Daniel Moreau Barringer

My dear Moreau: [Sea Girt, N. J.] July 27, 1911.

Thank you heartily for your letter of July twenty-fifth. It is delightful to know that you and Mrs. Barringer benefited so much by your European trip. I shall now feel easy about you until you overdo it again.

The matter treated of in the New York Times of May tenth, of which you send me a copy, is indeed the gravest matter of all. I agree with every word you say. I have spoken of this matter once or twice in my public addresses and you may be sure that if ever I have the opportunity, I will tackle this thing with all the force and sagacity at my command. It is the root of the whole evil.

I wish I could look forward with some freedom to coming down and spending the night with you but, alas, I am tied by the leg. I have not had a half day's leisure since the fifteenth of September, last.

With most thoughtful greetings to you both,

Most cordially yours,   Woodrow Wilson

TLS (D. M. Barringer Papers, NjP).

A News Report of a Statement About the Adoption
of Commission Government by Passaic, New Jersey

[June 27, 1911]

GOVERNOR PLEASED BY OUTCOME IN PASSAIC

SEA GIRT, July 27.—Governor Wilson, in commenting upon the result of the commission government election in Passaic,[1] had the following to say yesterday afternoon:

"The result of the election in Passaic shows, as the result of the election in Trenton did, what a thorough and systematic canvass of the voters will accomplish. But what renders the election in Passaic particularly interesting is that it afforded an opportunity to make a first test of the operation of the new system of voting under the Geran law.

"All reports agree that the test was eminently satisfactory, that fraud and manipulation were practically impossible and that no watchers were needed at the polls. The voters of Passaic had an opportunity to express their preference freely and without obstruction or embarrassment of any kind."

Printed in the *Newark Evening News*, July 27, 1911.
    [1] Passaic adopted commission government on July 25 by a vote of 1,789 to 859.

From Rees P. Horrocks[1]

Dear Sir: Little Rock, Ark. July 27, 1911.

At your suggestion I called on Hon. Wm. F. McCombs in New York City and found him, as you stated, intensely interested in you. We discussed the status of the affairs in this state and he asked me quite a number of questions and asked for suggestions, all of which I most willing gave.

On the evening of the 25th inst. Woodrow Wilson Club No. 1 was organized in this city, and the membership is composed of the best and most influential of this city, all of whom are most enthusiastic friends of yours, and I know will do all in their power to cause other clubs to be organized over the state. Among the members of this club, the Governor of this State is represented, also the Secretary of State and State Treasurer, both of which are members.[2] I enclose herewith newspaper clipping which gives a brief account of this meeting.[3] Mr. McCombs referred to an appointment you had in Texas and inasmuch as Arkansas was his home[4] it would give him the greatest pleasure to have his folks meet the next President of the United States without having to go to Washington City to do so. He promised to use his best offices to that end. I thus warn you so that you may be prepared for his assault.

After and before leaving you I conversed with a large number of people, all of whom were enthusiastic for you, and strange as it may seem, every one of them were of the opposite party, republicans I mean not socialists. I so informed my friends at our meeting the other night which pleased them very much, and my remarks as to the fact were heartily applauded.

I notice in the August Number of the World's Work a statement which was certainly most gratifying. It showed the poll taken by this magazine and it certainly was a fine campaign document.[5]

Again thanking you for your courtesy, I am

Your sincere friend,   Rees P. Horrocks

TLS (Governors' Files, Nj).

[1] Clerk of the board of directors of the Little Rock, Ark., public schools.

[2] Governor George Washington Donaghey; Secretary of State Earle William Hodges; and Treasurer John Wesley Crockett.

[3] This clipping is missing.

[4] McCombs was from Hamburg, Ark.

[5] The article was "A Little Presidential Primary," *World's Work*, XXII (Aug. 1911), 14716-20. The magazine had mailed 2,415 sample ballots to randomly selected names on its subscription list, sending to each state five times as many ballots as the state had electoral votes. The ballots included the names of four Democrats and four Republicans but permitted write-in votes as well. Fifteen hundred and five ballots were returned. The tally gave Wilson 519 votes; President Taft, 402; Theodore Roosevelt, 274; Judson Harmon, 96; Robert M. La Follette, 91; Champ Clark, 45; and William J. Bryan, 34. The remaining forty-four votes were scattered among thirteen write-ins. Another significant result of the poll was that, among the 80 per cent of the respondents who chose to indicate their usual party preference, Wilson received the votes of 145 Republicans and 22 independents while Roosevelt, the next highest, received twelve Democratic votes and two independent. The article also included a chart breaking down the vote by state.

From James Edgar Martine

My dear Governor: Washington, D. C. July 28th 1911

The outrageous remark, reported to have been made by James Nugent,[1] is most shocking; every Senator in this body have expressed their condemnation and disgust, at the expression. I feel this must eliminate him from the Councils of the Democratic party of New Jersey, and the association of decent men. With highest regard I am   Sincerely—   James E Martine

ALS (Governors' Files, Nj).

[1] James R. Nugent and several friends had dinner at Scotty's Cafe in Neptune Heights, N. J., on July 25, 1911. Several officers of the New Jersey National Guard, then on duty at Sea Girt, were also present. They reported later that Nugent sent a bottle of wine to their table and then addressed all the diners

present: "I propose a toast to the Governor of New Jersey, the commander-in-chief of the militia. He is an ingrate and he is a liar. I mean Woodrow Wilson. I repeat he is an ingrate and a liar. Do I drink alone?" According to the reports of the incident, he did drink alone amidst "a most pronounced silence." The national guard officers left the restaurant immediately.

Two days later, Nugent issued a statement in which he admitted that he had proposed the toast. He explained that he and his friends were celebrating his birthday (July 26) and that his remarks came after dinner when they "were indulging in champagne" and were intended only for the ears of his party. He further claimed that his cronies had goaded him into proposing the toast by jibes about his poor relationship with Wilson.

The incident led to immediate demands that Nugent either resign or be ousted as chairman of the State Democratic Committee. Ten members of that committee conferred among themselves and with Wilson at Sea Girt on July 27, and nine of them that same day sent a letter to Nugent demanding that he either resign or call a special meeting of the full state committee at once. *Newark Evening News*, July 26, 27, and 28, 1911. For the dénouement, see H. E. Alexander to WW, Aug. 10, 1911, n. 3.

From William Frank McCombs

My dear Governor: New York July 28, 1911.

I have just returned from a six days' trip through New England and had a number of conferences with the local leaders. I have an understanding with Ex-Governor Higgins of Rhode Island that he is to call an informal meeting of the committeemen from the various New England states, for the purpose of discussing your name with a view to a coalition.[1] I think this is important in this aspect: That if we can get the New England people to come out for you it will have a strong effect upon the sentiment of the rest of the country. Among others I was in conference with the Chairmen of the State and City Committees in Massachusetts and am sure that progress was made. Yesterday I had luncheon with Mr. Gaston, who you will remember ran twice for Governor in Massachusetts.[2] He would be a very strong influence for us because of the respect in which he is held in New England. You will recall no doubt that he is President of the National Shawmut Bank. He expressed a desire to meet you in the near future and suggested that he would be in New York some time during the coming week, and I told him that if you and he should be here on the same day I would be very glad if you both would dine with me. He is to let me know two days in advance of his coming. I believe a meeting with Mr. Gaston would be of advantage in the situation. If you agree with me and can be here, won't you be good enough to let me know your convenience.

With reference to the questions which Mr. Bryan has asked the various Presidential possibilities to answer,[3] may I offer the suggestion that it would be best either to take no notice of them or, if any notice is to be taken, to answer them after the rest of the gentlemen mentioned in connection with the office have replied. My instinct is that it is good policy not to answer them at all.[4] I expect to be in the neighborhood of Seagirt tomorrow and Sunday and will come in and see you if you are not otherwise occupied.   Yours sincerely,   Wm. F. McCombs

TLS (Governors' Files, Nj).

[1] James Henry Higgins of Pawtucket, Democratic Governor of Rhode Island, 1907-1909, at this time practicing law in Providence. B. R. Newton to WW, Aug. 7, 1911, seems to imply either that this proposed meeting did not take place or, if it did, that the participants decided that the time for action had not yet come.

[2] William Alexander Gaston, corporation lawyer and president of the National Shawmut Bank of Boston; Democratic candidate for governor in 1902 and 1903; member of the Democratic state and national committees.

[3] William J. Bryan published in his weekly, *The Commoner*, on July 21, 1911, a list of nineteen questions which he recommended that his readers should put to all those spoken of as candidates for the Democratic presidential nomination in 1912. The subjects covered included tariff reform, separation of governmental powers, the "rule of reason," the antitrust laws, direct election of senators, the federal income tax, independence for the Philippines, publicity of campaign contributions and expenditures, state rights, the labor planks of the Democratic platform of 1908, regulation of railroads, and currency and banking reform. Only Governor Thomas R. Marshall of Indiana and ex-Governor Joseph W. Folk of Missouri answered them in full. Their responses are printed in *The Commoner*, July 28 and Aug. 4, 1911, respectively.

[4] Soon afterward Wilson wrote to Charles W. Bryan: "The more I think over the questions published in the Commoner, the more clear it comes to me that a formal reply to the questions would put me in the position of seeming to try to *qualify*. A majority of the questions indeed of those that are vital and pending I have more than once spoken out plainly about in my public addresses, which I find have been very widely read and understood. I think that the best plan I can follow is to touch upon these matters with perfect frankness at every opportunity that offers, and I am sure that in the long run nobody will doubt my frankness." Quoted in C. W. Bryan to W. J. Bryan, Aug. 26, 1911, TCL (received from Paolo E. Coletta).

From Alexander Jeffrey McKelway

Dear Governor Wilson,   Atlanta, Georgia. July 28, 1911.

I wired you this afternoon[1] advising you to accept the invitation of the Georgia Legislature[2] to address them while in session this summer. I think your presence here will clinch the nail, so far as Georgia is concerned. I enclose a clipping from today's Atlanta Georgia[n].[3] Hooper Alexander,[4] by the way, is the unquestioned leader of the House this session, and one of the purest, bravest and most unselfish spirits I have ever met in public life. He has become intensely interested in the campaign for your nomination. You two think alike on a great many questions and I want you to know him.

Cordially Yours,   [A. J. McKelway]

CCL (A. J. McKelway Papers, DLC).

¹ His telegram is missing.

² The invitation is also missing.

³ The enclosure is missing, but it was a clipping of a news story in the *Atlanta Georgian*, July 28, 1911, reporting the adoption of a joint resolution by the Georgia legislature inviting Wilson to speak and Governor Hoke Smith's hearty endorsement of the action. It quoted the remarks of Hooper Alexander in support of the resolution.

⁴ Born in Rome, Ga., in 1858, he was a lawyer of Atlanta and member of the Georgia House of Representatives, 1904-12.

From Charles Wayland Bryan

Dear Mr. Wilson: Lincoln, Neb., July 29, 1911

By direction of my brother, W. J., I sent you under separate mail this week a copy of the little two-volume set of his speeches.¹ He thought perhaps you might be interested in reading his speeches on the subjects of "Bank Guarantee" and the "Trust" question. In this week's Commoner we publish Governor Marshall's reply to the questions that we submitted in a previous issue of The Commoner to presidential possibilities. In next week's issue, we publish Governor Folk's reply, and I take the liberty of enclosing herewith a copy of same which may be of interest to you.

You probably observed by the press reports that we blocked the efforts of the Harmon boosters in the recent Democratic state convention in this state. His supporters in the convention consisted chiefly of the delegation from Omaha together with a few men of the same character from different parts of the state. They, however, were not numerous enough to cause any serious trouble and we had no trouble in carrying out our plan of preventing an effort to endorse anyone for the nomination. The people of this state will be left untrammelled to decide the question of candidate at the primary next April when they vote direct on the subject, and there is no doubt but that Nebraska will be found in the progressive column, supporting a candidate who is in sympathy with the progressive Democracy of the country. We had sufficient friends in the convention to have given Mr. Bryan a personal endorsement, but as we were working for principle rather than personal compliments and as a personal endorsement of him would have caused considerable friction from the Omaha corporation, brewery contingent, and would have kept the local strife in this state stirred up so that it would not have been possible to have gotten the progressive forces together in the state election this fall or next year, we suggested the harmony plan which was adopted in the convention and we wrote the platform so that the principles that Mr. Bryan has fought for not only in this state, but throughout the country, were specifically endorsed. As no principles were endorsed but what he had led the fight for and no other principles mentioned, it was a happy harmony basis, viewing it from our standpoint.

I also enclose an interview[2] which I had given out following the convention, which clearly shows that Mr. Bryan's desires were carried out. I believe that the joint effort of the friends of all the progressive candidates in identifying their respective leaders with the progressive movement will make it so apparent to the Democrats throughout the entire country that Mr. Harmon is the choice of the old reactionary corporation crowd that a quietus will be pretty effectually put on his candidacy before spring. We also believe that the plan of questioning candidates, which we have inaugurated, will do much to clarify the political atmosphere, as Mr. Harmon cannot answer the questions satisfactorily to the Democrats throughout the country, whose only desire is to secure legislation satisfactory to the masses without alienating the support of the corporations and corporation newspapers, whose efforts are directed towards having a candidate's friends talk to the public for him rather than do it himself, and thus they try to make the real Democrats believe that the candidate is on the square and at the same time assure the business interests that they will not be molested in their efforts to take advantage of the people under the guise of law. This was the plan carried out by Mr. Taft, Mr. Roosevelt convincing one element of the people that Mr. Taft was progressive, and by Mr. Taft's brother[3] pledging the interests of the East that they would not be molested in case his brother was elected.

Your visit through the west made a pleasant impression and the seeds sown then are still developing. If you will permit a suggestion, however, it is that if you will take occasion to make another speech or two and take the people's side on two or three other questions in as emphatic a manner as you have on other questions which you discussed on your western trip, or if you will feel it advisable to make public statements, either through The Commoner or in public interviews, on some of the subjects mentioned in The Commoner's list of questions, such as the "Standard Oil Decision," "Bank Guarantee," "Free Raw Material," etc., it would be an inspiration to your friends throughout the country who have been praising your position on the subjects that you discussed during your western trip, but who are now confronted with the question of your attitude on the subjects on which they have not yet learned your views.

I hope you will pardon the length of this letter. My only excuse is that, as we devote our entire time in an effort to secure remedial legislation for the masses, we are inclined to take too much of some one else' time when we have an occasion to talk to him through a letter where he has no opportunity to suppress us.

With kind personal regards, I am,

Very truly yours,   Chas. W. Bryan

TLS (Governors' Files, Nj).

1 William J. Bryan, *Speeches of William Jennings Bryan*, revised and arranged by himself, with a biographical introduction by Mary Baird Bryan (2 vols., New York and London, 1909).

2 It is missing.

3 Henry Waters Taft, lawyer in the New York firm of Strong & Cadwalader.

From Pleasant Alexander Stovall

My dear Governor: Savannah, Ga. July 29th, 1911.

I have seen a great many comments in the papers, some in the Georgia Press, about your position on the initiative, referendum and recall. I do not remember to have read what you said in your books, but they say you have become a convert to this system in your recent speeches in the West.

Now this is confidential. You need not be afraid to write to me. At present advised I do not think much of the initiative, referendum and recall. However I would like to know something about it so I can be prepared to meet this criticism without in any way involving you in the discussion; that is without quoting from you directly.

Yours very truly,   Pleasant A Stovall

TLS (Governors' Files, Nj).

To Mary Allen Hulbert Peck

Dearest Friend,   Sea Girt [N. J.]. 30 July, 1911.

Truly, I know what 'public life' is now! I have no private life at all. It is entertaining to see the whole world surge about you, —particularly the whole summer world,—but when a fellow is like me,—when, i.e., he *loves* his own privacy, loves the liberty to think of his friends (live with them in his *thought*, if he can have them no other way) and to dream his own dreams—to conceive a life which he cannot share with the crowd, can share, indeed, with only one or two, who seem part of him, rebellion comes into his heart and he flings about like a wild bird in a cage,—denied his sweet haunts and his freedom. Sometimes (as I must have told you more than once) my whole life seems to me rooted in dreams,—and I do not want the roots of it to dry up. I lived a dream life (almost too exclusively, perhaps) when I was a lad and even now my thought goes back for refreshment to those days when all the world seemed to me a place of heroic adventure, in which one's heart must keep its own counsel while one's hands worked at big things. And *now* this is that dreaming boy's *Sunday*: he must sit at the edge of his front piazza flanked by a row of militia officers and be gazed at, while a chaplain conducts service on his lawn, with a full brass band to play the tunes for the hymns; then he must have the chaplains of the two regiments in camp, plus the Catholic priest, and everybody else that happens along, in for lunch. In the afternoon he must receive and pay military calls and attend a review. The evening brings callers galore from all along the Coast! Where and when does one's own heart get a chance to breathe and to call up the sweet memories and dreams upon wh. it lives?

The first review has come off—the occasion on wh. it was obligatory that I should wear a frock coat and silk hat on horseback, and ride, with a mounted staff of seven officers, around the lines, in the presence (this time) of five or six thousand people. I tried to beg off from the costume and get leave to appear in riding togs, but my staff advisers were very firm with me, and I had to do "the usual thing." Evidently, though 'commander-in-chief,' I am under discipline. I was very much amused at the universal surprise & delight that I could sit a horse. It was the general verdict that, as I rode, even the plug hat did not look ridiculous. After all, it is the conventional head gear in riding to the hounds, and so has *some* equestrian associations. One of my staff went so far as to say that the troops moved admirably in the review because of the psychological effect of a commander-in-chief who looked and acted the part in a way to satisfy the imagination. It would be silly for me to repeat that big compliment to you—or *any*one—if I did not know how perfectly you would understand. I repeat it because of the delightful circumstance that I know it will give you pleasure. What could a man ask more of his friend?

The days grow barren because I do not hear from you. One delightful letter, like the last, goes a long way; but I am selfish and want more—that I may constantly know what is passing in your thoughts. All send love.

Your devoted friend   W.W.

ALS (WP, DLC).

From Mary Allen Hulbert Peck

Dearest Friend: [Pittsfield, Mass.] July 30th [1911]

This has been an uneventful, uninteresting week. Mother is better but so weak and feeble that I can not leave her alone at all. We may leave for Hot Springs Tuesday, possibly not until the 8th, our departure depending upon whether or not we can get rooms in a cottage near our friends. This summer here has decided us in one thing, that of knowing the climate does not agree with us, and we will all be glad to get away. It is a beautiful country, and I am loth to leave it on that account. The town and the small circle I once called mine is unchanged save that its characteristics are now displayed by another generation. My immediate circle is depleted by death and being retired by the "young set," and I long to get away among those by whom I am not identified with Mr. *Pecks* hateful name—I loathe it! If Mrs. Roebling is ready for us, we shall go to her (if we do *not* go to the Hot before the 15th) about the 9th, staying there the intervening time, when I shall hope to see you. We will stay in Virginia until late September, then go to the apartment at 39 E. 27.[1] So much for our *plans*. What we will do, I do not know. Do you think I would like a home in England? Would *you*?

August 3rd

I have waited before sending this to be able to write definitely of our plans. We leave here Monday, and go to Mrs. R. on Wednesday, to stay until the 15th. I am writing Mrs. Wilson to say that if she wants & can have me for a day or two during that time, I'll be delighted to come, if not then the first of the second week in September. Will you still be at Sea Girt? I feel very dull and hate being shut up in these two 3rd story rooms. This is a hateful letter, no answer to yr. delightful one, but this is a blue period for me, fight it as I may. Of course your troops would be inspired by you, "you're sure the foine gintleman." I wish I had been there. A young officer in the Engineers is to be in N. Y. the first of the week. Can you arrange that he come with us for a day to get something of our militia and *you*? I must hear from Mrs. Roebling again before I leave, as the Col. is not very well and something may happen to change our plans.

Always yr. devoted friend   Mary Allen P.

ALS (WP, DLC).
[1] Her apartment in New York.

To Thomas Bell Love

My dear Mr. Love: [Sea Girt, N. J.] July 31, 1911.

It was a matter of very keen regret to me that I missed you when you were in New Jersey. I was particularly anxious to have a talk with you and to cement our acquaintance.

Your letter of July twenty-sixth has interested and gratified me very much. I have been planning all Spring to hold a week open for a visit to Texas in October and you may be sure that I will be pleased to meet your wishes in that matter. I am particularly anxious to fix the exact date of my visit to the State Fair because I have promised to fulfill an engagement in Wisconsin[1] in connection with it and the gentlemen in Wisconsin are impatient for a decision as to the date.

If you could suggest, after the meeting of the fifth, the particular date at which it would be best for me to be there, I would greatly appreciate it.

With warmest regard,
                    Sincerely yours,   Woodrow Wilson

TLS (photostat in the T. B. Love Papers, Dallas Hist. Soc.).
    [1] Actually, Wilson gave two major addresses in Madison, Wisc. The first is printed at Oct. 25, the second at Oct. 26, 1911.

From William Frank McCombs

CONFIDENTIAL:

My dear Governor: New York July 31st, 1911.

I have received a letter from Professor Droppers of Williams College,[1] in which he informs me that he is friendly, and has quoted from a conversation that was recently had with Mr. George Fred Williams concerning you, in which Mr. Williams expresses unequivocal approval.[2] Professor Droppers and Mr. Williams want to arrange a time to come and see you, and I have suggested that you will be in Sea Girt until the autumn and that they write you concerning the meeting. You will recall that Williams was a great Bryan enthusiast, and I was told up there that he still had a strong influence among the radical element of the party.

I am sending you herewith an editorial which appeared in the "World" this morning.[3] I am informed that its purpose is not as bad as it looks. It is just another signal. Of course, if we spent our time looking at the signals that are hung out in all quarters, we would never move, and this, in my judgment, accounts for the fact that most men are termed "average." However, it occurs to me that if you would write me a letter in answer to my inquiry of today, setting out the meaning (although I think it is clear enough) of your Harrisburg address, I can use it in a certain quarter, without its being given the atmosphere of an explanation or any publicity. I have read the speech and of course you did not say that the twenty thousand banks in this country were controlled by trusts. I know that what you were aiming at was the concentration of banking in the hands of a few men in New York, and were pointing out the stifling effect upon the industry of the rest of the country.

May I suggest that you send me a list of the names that we talked about yesterday, at your earliest convenience, as I want to make use of it in the very near future.

Yours sincerely,   Wm. F. McCombs

TLS (Governors' Files, Nj).

¹ Garrett Droppers, Professor of Economics at Williams College. Wilson appointed him Minister to Greece in 1914.

² Lawyer of Boston; congressman from Massachusetts, 1891-93; active in the Democratic party in Massachusetts since 1884; a strong supporter of William J. Bryan since 1896. Actually, Williams supported Clark in the preconvention campaign in 1912. He later served as Minister to Greece, 1913-14.

³ The editorial, "Is Woodrow Wilson Bryanizing?", New York World, July 31, 1911, excoriated Wilson for his remarks on the alleged money monopoly in his Harrisburg, Pa., speech of June 15, 1911. "The World," it began, "yields to none in admiration of Gov. Wilson's political genius. Intellectually he is, perhaps, the best-equipped Democratic leader since Tilden. He is the greatest living American artist in the use of words. . . . He has courage. We hope to be able to support him for the Presidency." The World held no brief for the money magnates, the editorial continued, "but proved financial abuses do not justify so gross an exaggeration as to call 20,000—yes, over 20,000, National and State —independent banks and trust companies a money trust." Wilson had "painted a vivid picture of misused concentrated power not warranted by facts." This was especially regrettable "because unquestionably there is a general tendency toward exaggeration of any public wrong—a tendency to yield or appeal to public clamor instead of to public intelligence." Bryan and Roosevelt were frequent offenders in this regard.

Why had Wilson made this "baseless and preposterous claim"? The World suggested by a series of rhetorical questions that Wilson's political ambition was running away with him: "Does Gov. Wilson think that playing to the gallery will promote his Presidential candidacy? Does he believe that efforts to win Mr. Bryan's approval and to capture his following will increase his political strength? Is he Bryanizing himself? Is he preparing with his initiative, referendum and recall programme and his money-trust bugaboo to swallow Mr. Bryan's entire Confession of Faith?"

The editorial concluded with the assertion that it asked these questions "in a distinctly friendly spirit, because it feels sure that Gov. Wilson's best friends and admirers wish he would examine his conscience and, in his own interest, ask himself these questions."

Actually, the editorial misconstrued Wilson's remarks at Harrisburg. He had said nothing at all about 20,000 banks and trust companies. In its misconstruction, the World was following the lead of an editorial in the Springfield, Mass., Republican, which it reprinted on the same page with its own editorial. "Is Woodrow Wilson Bryanizing?" was reprinted and widely commented upon throughout the country.

From Lee Douglas

Dear Governor Wilson: Nashville [Tenn.] July 31, 1911.

I have your letter of July 26th and all of us regret very much that you find it impossible to come to Nashville and Monteagle next month.

May I ask that you bear in mind our invitation to speak at the Tennessee State Fair September 18th to 23rd,[1] so that if by any chance there should be a break in your obligations and engagements, you might find it possible to come to Nashville at that time. You see we are exceedingly anxious to take advantage of the sligh[t]est opportunity which would provide a way for your coming.

I wish to thank you very much for the concise statement of your position on the initiative and referendum, and feel sure that what you have written will be of great service in clearing up the misunderstanding.

Senator Lea will leave Nashville this week for Washington, if Mrs. Lea's health continues to improve. He wishes me to thank you for the very kind expressions as to the health of Mrs. Lea and himself.

Assuring you of my best wishes, I am,

Most respectfully,   Lee Douglas

TLS (Governors' Files, Nj).
[1] Wilson was unable to accept this invitation.

To Alexander Jeffrey McKelway

My dear Mr. McKelway: [Sea Girt, N. J.] August 1, 1911.

It was with a pang of genuine regret that I felt obliged to declined the invitation to address the Georgia Legislature, but it is a case where I am obliged to prefer my duties at home to my inclination and to my personal interest. I should be ashamed of myself if I were to do these things in a way that would involve in a way a neglect of what I ought to do here. I know you will agree with this judgment.

I am very much interested in what you say about Mr. Hooper Alexander. I sincerely hope that some opportunity may be afforded me of meeting him. I am sure from his name that I know of his family and antecedents.

Cordially and sincerely yours,   Woodrow Wilson

TLS (A. J. McKelway Papers, DLC).

From William C. Liller

Confidential

My dear Governor Wilson: Indianapolis [Ind.] August 2, 1911

The enclosed is sent you in the strictest confidence for your *personal* information.[1] Kindly return same to me after you have noted same. I would suggest that the nature of this communication or the fact that you have seen it be withheld from Mr. Tumulty for reasons probably well known to you.

As soon as the laws of New Jersey, enacted by the recent legislature, are compiled and printed, I shall be glad to have a copy for my library.

I would also be glad to have one of the photographs made by Prince in Seattle,[2] if you can spare one with your autograph thereon.

With kindest regards and best wishes,
Faithfully your friend,   Wm C. Liller

TLS (Governors' Files, Nj).

[1] It is missing but was a letter from Robert S. Hudspeth to Liller (no date given), most of which was printed in the *New York Times*, Aug. 7, 1911, as follows:

"Regarding the effort of friends of Gov. Wilson to make him a Presidential candidate; and your kind suggestion that I co-operate, I would say that I appear to be persona non grata so far as this movement is concerned in New Jersey. For some reason best known to the Governor and his friends, all those who appear to have been identified with active politics heretofore in this State have been relegated to the rear and are not invited to participate in any movement or action affecting the governor or his political future.

"I was very active in helping to secure the Governor's nomination, attended the original conference with him when it was suggested that he become a candidate, took an active interest in the campaign, spoke at various times throughout the State, spent a great deal of money, and when the result was assured received very flattering assurances from the Governor of his appreciation &c., and then I was dropped.

"This has all been very disappointing to me, as I have devoted many years of my life in the attempt to co-operate in restoring New Jersey to the Democratic column.

"Under such circumstances it is hardly necessary for me to say to you that it would be rather humiliating for me to knock at the door which has been so discourteously, to say the least, closed against me."

[2] George Prince, photographer, 1925 2nd Ave., Seattle.

From Daniel Moreau Barringer

Personal

My dear Woodrow: Philadelphia, Pa. August 2, 1911.

I was very glad to receive your letter but disappointed that you are so "tied by the leg" that you do not see your way clear to even spending a night with us. Remember that whenever the opportunity offers the latch-string of Poplar Grove reaches to Trenton, so all you have to do is to pull it.

Apropos of the matter mentioned in your letters (I shall regard yours of course as confidential) I send you an editorial from the Philadelphia North American on which my eye happened to fall this morning.[1] I did not know until your letter arrived that you had referred to this subject in your recent public addresses. You will, of course, know just how and when to talk about it. There is perhaps some danger in dwelling upon it too much for fear that so doing may prevent you from ever having an opportunity to play a notable part in cutting out by its roots this dreadful growth upon our body politic. It is going to be removed, in my opinion, as certainly as we are living men, else the Republic will fall. I only wish the vast majority of voters could see the danger as you and I see it and grapple with it before the combination of the great money interests becomes so powerful that it can defy correction except at the cost of a revolution, which these blinded, ignorant plutocrats seem to consider impossible. I wonder if you ever saw a book called "Caesar's Column" written by Boisgilbert ("Ignatius Donnelly") in 1888.[2] If not I want to show it to you some day. It is a wonderful prophecy.[3]

Since the statistics published in the New York Times of May 10th were apparently so carefully gathered and were used as evidence in some suit at Washington, the particular group named[4] (there are others) has added to its power, as you of course know, by absorbing the Mercantile Trust Company through its ownership of the Banker's Trust Company and also the Baldwin Locomotive Works, and probably by other deals. There can be no doubt that it is this reaching out in a number of directions at the present time and will further add to its power. Where this will end no man can foresee. I feel as deeply about this matter as I can feel about any public matter, largely because I have five little boys who will shortly be men, and I assure you I do not relish the prospect of these boys becoming the slaves of some such group of the controllers of capital and being obliged to do their bidding, whether it be right or wrong, or face ruin as an alternative if those in control so decree. In short I am very anxious to do what I can to insure them the same liberty of thought and speech and of action as their ancestors have had in uninterrupted succession since the first one came to this country in 1742. Will it be so?

Pardon my writing at such length. I merely wish you to know how deeply I feel in regard to the matter. Meanwhile we will

regard all that has passed between us as confidential. It is better
so.   Affectionately yours,   D. M. Barringer

TLS (Governors' Files, Nj).
    1 "What Happened to the World?", Philadelphia *North American*, Aug. 2,
1911. It printed an editorial from the New York *World* of July 17, 1911, and
the "Is Woodrow Wilson Bryanizing?" editorial of July 31 in parallel columns.
The former defended Wilson's Harrisburg speech against a severe criticism
of it by the *New York Times*; said that it was perfectly obvious where the
"money monopoly" was—in Wall Street; and asserted that the "money monopoly" (primarily J. P. Morgan & Co. and its allies) controlled not only credit
but railroads and other corporations as well. In fact, the editorial concluded,
there had been created in Wall Street practically a central bank, one more
powerful than the old Bank of the United States. "Something," the *North
American* editorialized, "has happened to the World. It has seen a light, daz-
zling—indeed, blinding."
    2 Edmund Boisgilbert [Ignatius Loyola Donnelly], *Caesar's Column: A Story
of the Twentieth Century* (Chicago, 1890).
    3 Combining elements of the utopian romance and the novel of social protest,
Caesar's Column portrayed an American society of 1988 which was hopelessly
divided between a small, all-powerful plutocracy and the extremely degraded
and downtrodden masses. The result was a cataclysmic revolution which destroyed all western civilization. Only the hero and a few others survived to
establish a utopia.
    4 The members of the board of directors of the United States Steel Corp. and
of J. P. Morgan & Co. See D. M. Barringer to WW, July 25, 1911, n. 3.

From William Frank McCombs

My dear Governor: New York Aug. 2, 1911.

I am enclosing herewith a letter from General Clarkson,
whom you will no doubt remember as long in Republican politics and a Federal officeholder under several Republican administrations.[1] Also a letter from Mr. McAdoo, and from Jerry B.
Sullivan.[2]

General Clarkson is very friendly to you; he is willing to work
quietly in your behalf and is an old hand at the game. He could
be of assistance.

I think if you could arrange to make a speech at Des Moines
in November, as suggested, it would be an excellent idea. The
fact that the speech would be made before the State Teachers
Associations would be a good auspice, and I think a speech in
Iowa at that time would serve a very good purpose. I hope you
will see your way clear to do it. Your reply to the invitation
should, of course, be sent to General Clarkson.[3]

I am receiving repeated and urgent requests for you to speak
in Michigan during the fall. From the letters I get they come
from all quarters of the United States. Here is another point of
practical advantage for a speech. I am making a strong effort
to get them to declare for you out there and have a very good

chance of success. It seems that one or two of the Detroit leaders declared for Harmon and this made the country leaders angry. I think, if you could go out, that a speech would have the effect of pushing the proposition over the line. Furthermore, I have heard some rumors about the possibility of Governor Johnson[4] for the nomination, and I want to head that off by crystalizing the sentiment early for you.

If you think well of this and will suggest some time that might be available, I will take it up.

Yours sincerely,   Wm. F. McCombs

TLS (Governors' Files, Nj).

[1] James Sullivan Clarkson, co-proprietor and editor-in-chief of the Des Moines *Iowa State Register*, 1868-89, also active in railroad construction in Iowa. He was chairman of the Iowa State Republican Committee, 1869-71; member, Republican National Committee, 1880-1896; postmaster, Des Moines, 1871-77, and first assistant postmaster general, 1889-90. He declined offers of two cabinet posts under President Benjamin Harrison; moved to New York in the late 1880's and served for a time as president of the New York and New Jersey Bridge Co.; surveyor of the customs, New York, 1902-10. His letter is missing.

[2] Jerry Bartholomew Sullivan, lawyer and prominent Democrat of Des Moines.

[3] Wilson was not able to speak in Des Moines in November.

[4] McCombs had not heard about the death of Governor Johnson of Minnesota!

From Solomon Bulkley Griffin

My Dear Gov Wilson: Springfield, Mass. August 2, 1911

I am the managing editor of the *Springfield Republican*, & have been asked to discuss in the *Atlantic Monthly* the question, what do the qualities which Governor Wilson possesses portend to the Republic? You know my brother, Dr Edward H. Griffin of Johns Hopkins, & I am sure that Col George Harvey or President Garfield of Williams, where I am a trustee, will vouch for me as a discreet person. So much by way of introduction.

You can best say what your ambition is for the country—& I wish you would do it, as confidentially as you may care to do it, but frankly. I am to be for four weeks at The Balsams, Dixville Notch, N. H., there to lie fallow mentally—but I'd like to be mulling over the main body of my ultimate discourse, the body of whose doctrines it is for you to supply. I should like anything vital in print your secretary can lay his hands on & send to me, but should hope you would dictate that which will go beyond all that. Biography is to play slight part—purpose, thought, definite aim more. You have digested, matured & shaped an ideal & a method—it is no doubt defined on many lines. Can you not draft something like a program which I can weigh & set forth? You are the best interpreter of the Woodrow Wilson of today. I hope to get many sidelights on you. Long ago I told Dr Garfield you were the most essentially democratic figure in the college world. Now you have been called to aid in the larger national readjustment—& I want to gain a sympathetic hold on your thought & intent.[1] Hence this request & appeal.

I am sincerely yrs   Solomon Bulkley Griffin

ALS (Governors' Files, Nj).

[1] Solomon B. Griffin, "The Political Evolution of a College President," *Atlantic Monthly*, CIX (Jan. 1912), 43-51. This article was more concerned with Wilson's evolution as a practical politician than with his political thought. It described briefly his career as President of Princeton University and Governor of New Jersey. Griffin's only real contribution to the dissemination of Wilson's political ideas was to quote verbatim the fourth, fifth, and sixth paragraphs of WW to S. B. Griffin, Aug. 21, 1911. Griffin concluded his article by making the increasingly common comparison of Wilson to the late Governor Samuel J. Tilden of New York and suggesting that the Democratic party would do well to choose such a progressive but prudent leader as its presidential standard-bearer in 1912.

From Rudolph Isaac Coffee[1]

My dear Governor,   Pittsburg, Pa. 3 August 1911.

On my return to Pittsburg from a brief outing, I found your splendid lines of July 24th. It was a great pleasure to feel that you had been using your influence with fellow Democrats to blot out the shame of the Westmoreland coal district.[2]

Though the strike is officially over, the moral aspect of the matter must not be dropped. Since the men returned to work, at the Jamison mines alone, Mrs. Fox[3] informs me that a miner a day is being killed.[4]

We are still hoping that the House will order some investigation,[5] and I trust you will keep this matter well in mind. The Democratic party can do no greater service to the nation than to sieze [seize] hold of ethical issues. There never was a more flagrant abuse of power than in this coal district, and we need the aid of the Democratic party, and your help to re-assert the rule of justice.

Very sincerely yours,   Rudolph I. Coffee.

TLS (Governors' Files, Nj).

[1] Rabbi of the Tree of Life Synagogue of Pittsburgh. Coffee had been active in attempts to have the strike (discussed in the next note) submitted to arbitration.

[2] Coffee referred to a strike in the extensive bituminous coal fields of Westmoreland County just east of Pittsburgh, which began on March 10, 1910, and ended on July 3, 1911. The most important issue was unionization, which the operators hitherto had successfully resisted. The United Mine Workers of America organized thirty-two locals in the county during the first months of the strike. In addition, the workers demanded wages and working conditions comparable to those of the previously organized miners of adjacent Allegheny County, which included Pittsburgh. The strike eventually involved thirty sep-

arate coal companies and more than 10,000 men. The companies discharged all workers known to be involved in the strike, hired numerous strikebreakers, many from outside Pennsylvania, and paid the salaries of many deputy sheriffs and deputy constables hired to protect men and property. There was much destruction of property during the course of the strike, and the report cited below directly attributed ten violent deaths to it. The executive board of the UMW was ready by late June 1911 to surrender and recommended that the strikers end the struggle. They did so at a convention in Greensburg, the county seat, on July 3. See *Report on the Miners' Strike in Bituminous Coal Field in Westmoreland County, Pa. in 1910-1911, Prepared under the Direction of Chas. P. Neill, Commissioner of Labor,* 62nd Cong., 2nd sess., House of Representatives, Doc. No. 847 (Washington, 1912).

3 Mrs. John T. Fox of Pittsburgh, who was investigating conditions in the mining areas of Westmoreland County on behalf, as the *New York Times,* June 1, 1911, put it, of "a committee of Pittsburgh women."

4 Mrs. Fox referred to accidental deaths in the mines, and she considerably exaggerated their number. The report cited above makes it clear that the number of accidental deaths in the mines had risen considerably during the course of the strike due to the inexperience of the strikebreakers, many of whom remained on the job after the strike.

5 That is, the United States House of Representatives. Representative William B. Wilson of Pennsylvania had proposed on May 26, 1911, that the House Labor Committee conduct an investigation of the Westmoreland strike, but his resolution never emerged from the House Rules Committee. However, on June 8, 1912, the House accepted a resolution introducted by Curtis Hussey Gregg (whose district included Westmoreland County) requesting the Secretary of Commerce and Labor to transmit to the House of Representatives any information in his possession concerning the strike. The report, sent in response to this request on June 20, 1912, is cited in n. 2 above.

From Isabella Hammond Demarest[1]

Dear Sir: Closter, N. J., August 3, 1911.

The Woman's Christian Temperance Union of New Jersey, (10,314 members,) marks with keen interest the public acts of its state officials and especially those of its Governor.

It has had much to commend and honor you for during your past year of official service, and it thanks you that the punch at your Sea Girt function on "Governor's Day,"[2] (as chronicled by a reporter,) did not even carry the color of things harmful. It desires through you to especially thank Mrs. Wilson through whose direction this was said to have been.

It also thanks you for the public recognition at the opening of the luncheon of the presence of the Divine Master at the feast. We thank God and take courage.

Respectfully,   Isabella Hammond Demarest

TLS (Governors' Files, Nj).

1 Mrs. John Z. Demarest of Closter, N. J., corresponding secretary of the Women's Christian Temperance Union of New Jersey.

2 Thursday was traditionally "Governor's Day" at Sea Girt. There were three such days in 1911—July 27, August 3, and August 10. The governor invited many New Jersey politicians and state and local officials to luncheon and they, together with a great number of tourists, watched military maneuvers and a review of the troops by the governor.

From Lorin Andrew Handley[1]

Dear Governor Wilson: Los Angeles, Cal. Aug. 3, 1911

Knowing that you would be very busy upon your return I have not written you concerning the progress of our work out here. We followed you on the remainder of your journey and were encouraged and pleased with the reports we received from the various cities. The trip was a most fortunate one, both in advancing progressive principles and in acquainting the people with your words and work.

The Wilson Club has been planning all this time for the various work it must do. We are keeping in mind the peculiar primary law that was passed by our last legislature, which starting with the delegates elected at the last August Primary to the County Convention, reorganizes the party throughout the State.[2] The delegates to those conventions are the most important gentlemen in the State of California at the present time, but our club is encouraged to believe that this State will instruct its delegation properly when they meet, according to law, not before next March.

We are preparing to send out a letter, similar to the one enclosed,[3] to each Democrat in the County. We are going to enclose the North American Editorial with excerpts from your various addresses.[4] Then we propose to carry the campaign beyond the ranks of the party, many Republicans indicating their desire to join the Club. One of the members of the Board of Directors was a Republican, but has changed his registration in order that he might serve upon the Board and take an active part in the Club's work.

We have been very pleased with the trend of events during the past few months. We believe that the party is making good on the whole at Washington and that the feeling throughout the Country is growing that next year a Democratic President will be elected, provided the Democratic party has the good sense to choose a man of the people.

We believe also that your position is growing stronger every day and that if you can be nominated, there is no question of your election over Mr. Taft. Anyhow, this is our earnest hope and we are going to do everything we can out here to help the matter along.

We would be glad to receive any suggestions you care to make and to do anything we can to further the Wilson movement throughout the country.

I am in communication with Mr. Stockbridge and expect to continue to be advised and get information from him.

Yours very sincerely,   Lorin A. Handley

TLS (Governors' Files, Nj).

¹ President of the recently organized Woodrow Wilson Club of Los Angeles. Handley had been a student at Princeton Theological Seminary, 1902-1905, and had received the A.M. from Princeton University in 1904. At this time he was a lecturer at the Bible Institute of Los Angeles.

² The law regulating primary elections passed by the California legislature in 1909 provided that the delegates to the county party conventions should be the same delegates elected at the last preceding primary. This meant that the delegates elected at the primary of 1910 would at the county conventions elect delegates to the state party conventions, which would in turn elect the delegates to the national party conventions of 1912. However, a special session of the legislature in early 1912 adopted a new presidential primary law providing for the election of all delegates on a statewide ticket.

³ It is missing.

⁴ See W. F. McCombs to WW, July 17, 1911, n. 2.

From William Frank McCombs

My dear Governor: New York August 4th, 1911.

I have your letters of August 2nd and 3rd. I understand your situation thoroughly as to the proposed Iowa engagement. I suppose you have written General Clarkson about it. At your convenience I shall come down shortly and take up some other matters with you.

I have your letter with reference to the "World" editorial. I think it may be of value, but I do not want even to seem to put you in the position of seeking the support of a paper. I notice in some of the clippings which Mr. Tumulty has sent me that the "American" article[1] has been quoted in some of the papers and is attributed as an interview to me. I am thinking in some way of getting the matter in its true light to these papers. The interview which I gave the "Times"[2] later turned the edge of the "American's" statement, but, of course, the papers generally did not get that. I will take care of the matter. However, my view is that it is not at all serious. We may expect all sorts of newspaper comment, inasmuch as we have non-friends as well as friends. The knowledge of the bureau is having its good effect too. The volume of enquiry is enormous. We can easily overcome the anti-organization idea.   Yours sincerely,   Wm. F. McCombs

TLS (Governors' Files, Nj).

¹ "Gov. Wilson's Headquarters Opened Here," *New York American*, July 20, 1911. It discussed the opening of the information office, alleged that an effort was under way to organize Princeton alumni throughout the country as Wilson "boomers," described Wilson's western tour, and noted plans to publish Wilson's speeches during the gubernatorial campaign in book form. All these, the article said, were part of a systematic campaign to win the presidential nomination

for Wilson. Wilson was sufficiently disturbed by this article to tell a reporter for the *American* that he had "no campaign." The New York office, he explained, had been opened simply because the volume of his mail about the presidency had become so great that he could no longer handle it. The *American* printed Wilson's comments on July 21, 1911, but added a description of the activities of the Wilson headquarters intended to belie his words.

2 "Country is Eager to Hear of Wilson," *New York Times*, Aug. 1, 1911. Mc-Combs described briefly the work of the office at 42 Broadway, insisting that it was confined largely to sending out information about Wilson in response to inquiries. He asserted that there was no systematic effort to secure convention delegates and portrayed the Wilson movement as an entirely spontaneous phenomenon.

From John Arthur Aylward[1]

My dear Governor: Madison, Wis., August 4, 1911.

As I am interested in the success of the Democratic party and its presidential nominee, I make free to address you. I am not a Governor nor a near Governor, although I was the Democratic nominee and candidate for Governor in this state in 1906 and again in 1908.

In response to a letter of inquiry to my partner, the Democratic State Chairman, Joseph E. Davies,[2] I have just written Wm. F. McCombs something of the political situation in this state. You know the desperate struggle that has been waged in the Republican ranks in Wisconsin between the Progressives and the Stalwarts. We have had the same battle to wage in the Democratic ranks. But for the past eight years our party platform and our candidates and the great body of the Democrats of Wisconsin have been thoroughly progressive. For the reason largely that we have been making the fight for progressive principles we turn to you when we consider our next presidential nominee.

Wisconsin, by reason of the contest the progressive Republicans and progressive Democrats have been waging, should be a fertile field for you, but like other fields it needs cultivation. The evidence gathers that as the prospects for Democratic success brighten the same forces,—the special interests—which have brought the Republican party to almost certain defeat, are now active in seeking to control the Democratic organization, state and national.

Mr. Davies and I have long talked the situation over between ourselves and among our friends and have decided to give such assistance here and elsewhere as we can give. This not with any expectation or hope of reward but solely because we believe you the best candidate mentioned and because you best represent the progressive thought of the country and are best qualified to fill the exalted office of President, if elected.

Mr. Davies, as state chairman may not feel free to let you use his mailing lists for your committee, if you have one, but I have a private mailing list quite as full, which I have used in my campaigns which is at the service of your committee. By the way, if you will pardon a suggestion, if you have not a committee you should have one and an active one at once.

Now while we are anxious to assist you in your nomination we want you to help us to that end by addressing a Democratic gathering or rather by delivering a public, semi-political address while you are in our city in October. What form the meeting will take would depend upon your wishes; it may be a dollar banquet at which we will invite the Democrats from all over the state to attend or an open address at the University Gymnasium. We believe that the Wisconsin Democrats who never get anything but the glory of fighting are entitled to some such recognition from you when you come into the state and in addition it will help us put Wisconsin in the Wilson column.[3]

Mr. Albert G. Schmedeman,[4] Democratic candidate for Congress at the last election, as president of the Madison Club will invite you to be the guest of the Club at a dinner or luncheon during your stay. The Club is composed of the business men of the city and we hope your engagements will permit that you will accept such invitation.[5] Mr. Davies and I will each claim the honor of entertaining you at our homes during your stay but will determine such question amicably between ourselves on his return. He is now in England and he plans to return by way of New York and to call upon you on his return trip.

Trusting I do not intrude and that you will be able to favor us in the way suggested, I remain,

Very truly,   John A. Aylward

TLS (Governors' Files, Nj).

[1] Member of the law firm of Aylward, Davies, Olbrich & Hill of Madison, progressive Democratic leader in Wisconsin.

[2] Joseph Edward Davies, lawyer of the aforementioned law firm and also member of the Democratic National Committee.

[3] Wilson's address to the Democratic League of Wisconsin is printed at Oct. 26, 1911.

[4] Albert George Schmedeman, clothing merchant of Madison, active in Democratic politics.

[5] Wilson was the guest of honor at a reception at the Madison Club on October 26, 1911.

To William C. Liller

My dear Colonel Liller: [Sea Girt, N. J.] August 5 [1911].

Thank you for your letters of July thirty-first[1] and August second with their interesting enclosures.

The letter from Judge Hudspeth really distresses me. I had no idea that he felt as he does and wish very much that he understood better than he appears to understand my real feeling which has always been one of genuine cordiality and friendship.

I, of course, knew of and deeply appreciated the great service he rendered in the campaign last autumn, but I distinctly remember getting the impression, I would have said from conversations with Judge Hudspeth himself, that he had had enough of active participation in politics after his long service as chairman of the State Committee, which he rendered at a great sacrifice of personal profit and convenience. When the question of the election of a senator arose, Judge Hudspeth was perfectly frank and I honored the position he took very much. He frankly said that he would like to be left out of the matter entirely because of his lifelong friendship with Ex-Senator Smith, although his personal judgment was that Mr. Martine ought to be returned to the Senate. I interpreted this to mean that he would rather not appear, at any rate during that season, as a supporter of my administration. Certainly, he was never by any act I was conscious of "dropped" or slighted. It distresses me that he should have received that impression.

As to your kind urgency that I should attend the rally of the Democratic Clubs at Columbus, I must say frankly that that is out of the question. I think it would be a great mistake[2] even if I were free from engagements at home. My heart will be with the convention and I wish with all my heart that we lived in a simpler world in which I could frankly take part in such meetings.

With kind regards,

Sincerely yours,   [Woodrow Wilson]

TCL (Governors' Files, Nj).
1 W. C. Liller to WW, July 31, 1912, TLS (Governors' Files, Nj).
2 Because he would be going into Governor Harmon's own state.

From Thomas Bell Love

My dear Governor Wilson: [Dallas, Tex.] August 5, 1911.

I received your letter of July 31st in due course. While at Austin Monday I received a telegram from Mr. Ed J. Ward, of Madison, Wisconsin, inquiring if October 28th would be a satisfactory date for your address here. After conferring with the State Fair management and with friends, I wired him that that date would be satisfactory, so that it is generally understood now that that is to be your date here. In taking this action I assumed that you had suggested to Mr. Ward to send the telegram and that the date he named would be satisfactory to you.

I am leaving for Austin tonight where we will begin the organization of the Woodrow Wilson movement in Texas on Monday, and I am confident we will extend an invitation to you to deliver an address at the State Fair on October 28th.

Very truly yours,   Thomas B. Love.

TCL (T. B. Love Papers, Dallas Hist. Soc.).

To Mary Allen Hulbert Peck

Dearest Friend,   Sea Girt, New Jersey 6 August, 1911.

The politicians of the State and of the country have conspired against you. They have chosen Sunday as the particular day when I will be 'at leisure' (alack a'day! I do not so much as know that there *is* such a thing as leisure any more!) and can listen to endless expositions of "the situation"—for scores of them (would have one think that they) are engaged in electing me President of the United States. I get *very* weary of it all—especially when I am eager to turn to the dear friend from whom I get—all that these fellows cannot give me—and much more than the presidency can ever yield me of delight and release from care. What is more refreshing and rewarding than to turn to the friend with whom you never have to consider a phrase or a thought,—with whom you can *let yourself go*! It is as if you breathed another air than that of the work-a-day world in which you toil and plan and struggle—the air of the world in which your spirit is free and native and full of the play and gayety of an untrammeled life!

Alas that your letters should be sad and dispirited and plaintive with fatigue and disappointment! and hurrah that you are getting away from Pittsfield, where the pain and disappointment centre! How I have longed to have you get away from there to some air you could expand your lungs in! You can only starve and suffocate, at once, there. Alas for your plans, and ours! They do not fit. The camp lasts until the 12th; I go away for the 14th, 15th, 16th, and 17th; and, meanwhile the children have the house *packed* with their young friends,—and the *second* is just the wrong week in Sept,—the week of the Conference of Governors. *Some*thing must be done. *Could* you, if we can find a bed for you, come for the 11th to the 14th,—as just better than nothing? Surely we can twist things about a bit! How jolly that you are going back to the apartment in N. Y. I can at least catch an occasional glimpse of you there, even if everything should miscarry between now and then. If you are to be in Trenton this week I shall make a desperate effort to see you there.

11 Aug., 1911

This is dreadful! I was interrupted—*absolutely* prevented from finishing the letter—and here it is the 11th—the very day I suggested! Forgive me! I literally could not help it. And now, assuming of course that by this time you were in Trenton, I have just come from the 'phone, where I understood the maid who answered at Mrs. Roebling's to say that you were ill in bed and were not expected just now. She was vague and confused in what she said and I am trying to believe that I did not get it right. But I am none the less deeply distressed and anxious. You *must* come with Mrs. Allen, too, of course to us here on the 18th and stay through the 23rd. These are our *only* free dates between now and the middle of Sept. We *cannot* take No. I *must* see you. I shall not be fit for the autumn campaign otherwise. It would be heartbreaking if *any*thing should prevent,—particularly illness. I am writing this in a distracting rush, but with all my heart, and Ellen's too

Your devoted friend   W.W.

ALS (WP, DLC).

To Warren Worth Bailey

My dear Mr. Bailey: [Sea Girt, N. J.] August 7, 1911

Your letter of August fourth[1] has given me a great deal of pleasure and I want to thank you for it very warmly. It goes exceedingly hard to be obliged to say that I cannot come to the meeting you are planning for September fourteenth but you will understand the reason when I tell you that our Legislature is annually elected here and we go into the primaries in September so that September is the heart of our campaign. I have promised to be constantly on hand to lend my assistance in the counsels and action of the party and should feel that I was distinctly derelict in duty if I were to leave the State at that time. I know that you will recognize how imperative these reasons are and will accept my assurances of great regret.

I particularly value your generous letter. It made me exceedingly proud that the great, old State of Pennsylvania should back

me up as it did in your Committee. I have since then felt as if I
were a real candidate.

Cordially and faithfully yours,   Woodrow Wilson

TLS (W. W. Bailey Papers, NjP).
  [1] W. W. Bailey to WW, Aug. 4, 1911, TLS (Governors' Files, Nj).

From Byron Rufus Newton[1]

My dear Governor Wilson: Boston Aug. 7, 1911

We had the great pleasure yesterday of meeting here Mr
[John F.] McDonald, chairman of the democratic State Committee, Judge Corbett[2] and several other prominent democrats, all
of whom declared that there is a very pronounced Wilson sentiment throughout this part of New England, which they propose
to bring to the surface at the proper time. They do not, however,
think it expedient to do very much in the way of stirring up
things locally, just now.

When Mayor Fitzgerald[3] returns from Europe in a few weeks,
they would like to meet you, possibly in New York, if convenient.

They expect Gov. Harmon here to address them at an outing,
September 9.   Very truly yours   Byron R Newton

ALS (Governors' Files, Nj).
  [1] On the staff of the *New York Herald*, 1902-10, at this time press agent for
McAdoo's Hudson & Manhattan Railroad Co. By now he was also working at
least part time in the Wilson headquarters at 42 Broadway.
  [2] Joseph J. Corbett, lawyer of Boston and "special justice" of the Municipal
Court of Charlestown, Mass.
  [3] John Francis ("Honey Fitz") Fitzgerald, Democratic congressman from
Massachusetts, 1895-1901, Mayor of Boston 1906-1907, 1910-1914.

To Thomas Bell Love

My dear Mr. Love: [Sea Girt, N. J.] August 8, 1911.

As a matter of fact, I did not suggest the date, October twenty-
eighth, to Mr. Ward, but it will suit me perfectly well and I shall
take pleasure in making my arrangements accordingly. I am
sincerely obliged to you for your interest in the matter.

I feel that the work you are doing in Texas is in every way
most generous. I sometimes wonder what I have done to deserve
such confidence and support. It stimulates me immensely.

You may be sure that I shall look forward to the date in
October with the keenest interest.

Cordially and faithfully yours,   Woodrow Wilson

TLS (photostat in the T. B. Love Papers, Dallas Hist. Soc.).

From William Frank McCombs

My dear Governor: New York Aug. 8, 1911.

I have no doubt that you will be pleased at the result in Texas yesterday.[1] In the event that you have not already seen it, I am sending you a clipping from one of the papers of this morning.[2] I had been in correspondence with all of the gentlemen mentioned in the clipping for several weeks, and advised them to take this action. I am very glad indeed that they were able to carry it through. You will observe that the article refers to several converts to your cause. I believe we may safely expect a large addition of converts from all over the country very shortly.

I am also enclosing an editorial which gives the Liller matter the interpretation which I feared.[3] I am in receipt of a number of letters asking about Liller; also some warnings against him, which would seem to confirm our view that his position in this matter should be made very clear immediately. My own mind works to the idea of a capital operation and many others with whom I have talked feel the same way about it.[4]

Rabbi Stephen S. Wise has just written me a letter in which he asks for literature and information about you, for the purpose of a magazine article which he is preparing. You no doubt recall that he is a very prominent Hebrew. He is for you. Can't you suggest some things that we should send him in addition to the stock that we have. I think his article[5] will carry great weight.

I have had a talk with Mr. Lochran,[6] the Tammany man who recently brought some leaders to see you. He said they went away with a favorable impression. He asked my judgment as to others going to see you and of course I have approved. The effect of seeing the future President in the flesh and of talking to him is always excellent.

I have a letter from Mr. John A. Alyward [Aylward], who is a law partner of Mr. Joseph E. Davies, Chairman of the Democratic State Committee of Wisconsin, who answers a previous letter of mine to Mr. Davies in the latter's absence. He tells me that the friends of Folk, Harmon, and Clark are at work for them in Wisconsin and suggests organized effort for you there. I am writing him a letter approving of the suggestion and am telling him that I think your friends there should get together there early, for the purpose of pushing your name at the primaries. He also suggests that while you are in Wisconsin that the party be allowed to tender you a Democratic banquet and that you consent to make a public political address, and that they will notify the Democrats all over the state and give them an opportunity to meet you. He believes that such a meeting would be the means of practically committing the state to you. Inasmuch as you are going there, I think this would be an excellent idea. I have suggested that he write you. Wouldn't it be a good idea to let Mr. Tumulty put this on your diary for consideration?

I have a tremendous mass of political information that I am getting every day, and each mail seems to be better in tone for you than the previous one. Of course, I cannot hope to put all of the developments before you, although I wish I might. I have decided to get along with week-end vacations for the rest of the summer and will be available at any time that you think it advantageous.

The Mayor[7] has appointed me Trustee of the College of the City of New York. Yours sincerely, Wm. F. McCombs

TLS (Governors' Files, Nj).
[1] See T. B. Love to WW, Aug. 9, 1911, two letters, and T. B. Love to WW, Aug. 16, 1911.
[2] An unidentified clipping entitled "Texans Booming Wilson," describing the organization of the Woodrow Wilson State Democratic League of Texas.
[3] An unidentified clipping of an editorial entitled "An Alignment of Progressive Forces," which described in sardonic terms Liller's efforts to establish a National Progressive Democratic League at Trenton in support of Wilson's presidential candidacy.
[4] He apparently succeeded in aborting Liller's plans, for the league was never organized.
[5] Insofar as the Editors have been able to determine, Wise did not write the article.
[6] Frank E. Loughran, lawyer of New York.
[7] William Jay Gaynor, Mayor of New York since January 1, 1910.

Two Letters from Thomas Bell Love

My dear Governor Wilson: [Dallas, Tex.] August 9, 1911.

As you have doubtless learned ere this, we formed a State organization at Austin on Monday. There was a great deal of enthusiasm manifested and a widespread interest developed. The general consensus of opinion about Austin at this time, the Legislature being now in session, is that the Texas delegation will be a Wilson delegation. Under separate cover I am sending you an invitation to visit us and deliver an address during the State Fair. The date formerly suggested, October 28th, will be entirely satisfactory.

I sincerely hope that you will see your way clear to accept the invitation and to advise us of your acceptance as early as possible.

With kind regards, I am

Very truly yours,   Thomas B. Love

My dear Sir: [Dallas, Tex.] August 9, 1911.

I am instructed by the Woodrow Wilson State Democratic League of Texas, which was organized at Austin, Texas, on Monday to extend to you an invitation provided for by a Resolution which was duly adopted by the League at its meeting, which reads as follows:

"BE IT RESOLVED By the Woodrow Wilson State Democratic League of Texas, That we cordially and most earnestly extend an invitation to Governor Woodrow Wilson to honor Texas and her Democracy by visiting the State and delivering an address during the State Fair of 1911 at Dallas, on some date which will suit his convenience."

We sincerely trust that you will be able to accept our invitation and that you can advise us in the near future of a date that will suit your convenience. The State Fair opens on October 14th and closes October 29th. I am

Very truly yours,   Thomas B. Love
President Woodrow
Wilson State Demo-
cratic League of Texas.

TCL (T. B. Love Papers, Dallas Hist. Soc.).

From William Frank McCombs

My dear Governor: New York August 10, 1911.

I have received a letter to-day from Mrs. Borden Harriman,[1] in which she says she is going to enlist herself for you and has asked me to come and have a talk with her. Mrs. Harriman is a very strong character and may be of assistance.

Having gotten the approval of a majority of the voting population of the United States, I send you this as an indication that the ladies are falling in line for you as well.

In a talk with Mrs. Harriman on the suffrage question not long ago, I told her that women are queens and reminded her that royalty never votes. I am informed to-day that the "squall" in the World office is about over and that we may now expect some gentle and soothing zephyrs.

Yours sincerely,   Wm. F. McCombs

TLS (Governors' Files, Nj).
[1] Florence Jaffray Hurst (Mrs. Jefferson Borden) Harriman, active in the woman suffrage movement as well as in New York charitable and civic activities, member of the board of managers of the New York reformatory for women at Bedford.

From Henry Eckert Alexander

Dear Mr. Wilson: Trenton, N. J. Aug. 10, 1911

I enclose proof of article meant for the reading of "organization" men.[1] I disapprove of it from beginning to end, and hope that you will not permit it to be used. I, like you, have called it "a two-edged sword"—but it isn't that. It cuts one way—it doesn't cut at all the other way. The man who asks *documentary proof* that you will do the decent thing by organization is an ass, an ignoramus or a faker pure and simple. Why the very theory of "organization" is that the so-called leaders have to be dealt with and "satisfied." The little people just "go along." I tell you that from the standpoint of the most practical politics the most impressive thing that the organization little fellows have to tell those higher up is that they hear both Democrats and Republicans say that they want to vote for Wilson for President, that he is a big, broad-gauge man and that they believe in him. All that means that he will be a big winner with fine prospects of carrying through county and other local tickets besides state tickets in doubtful states. Besides there will be a re-alignment of forces in 1912. The reactionaries will fight you in spots to the last and the progressives will go to you ten to one to help you build up a great progressive party—where will the "organization" come in? It will not be the old organization. It will be new organization that must count.

Hastily yours,   H. E. Alexander

I don't want to bore you, but when Colonel Nelson's[2] Kansas City Star orders story tonight on "Nugent deposed"[3] you can guess that the tremendous Wilson sentiment that is compelling organizations to get into line is based on something subtler than *a guaranteed list of party workers* whom Gov. Wilson has rewarded! You start with Pennsylvania's 76 delegates—and no peanut politics in it, either. Don't you think that the methods that produced the immediate Pennsylvania action will show as satisfactory results elsewhere?   H.E.A.

ALS (Governors' Files, Nj).

[1] The Editors have been unable to find this article; it was undoubtedly suppressed.

[2] William Rockhill Nelson, founder, owner, and editor of the *Kansas City Star*.

[3] Nugent had just been ousted from the chairmanship of the New Jersey State Democratic Committee as the result of his insulting toast to Wilson on July 25, 1911, about which see J. E. Martine to WW, July 28, 1911, n. 1. Nugent had refused either to resign or to call a special meeting of the state committee. However, a majority of the committee met at the Hotel Coleman in Asbury Park on August 10. Much to their discomfiture, Nugent himself attended, together with a group of strong-arm friends. The scene that ensued was, according to all reports, riotous. In order to prevent a quorum, Nugent's cronies

threw out of the meeting a man representing one of the committeemen by proxy. Nugent made a short speech defending himself and then left the room accompanied by another committeeman, Charles H. Gallagher of Mercer County. Gallagher's withdrawal meant the absence of a quorum. Just as the meeting was about to adjourn for lack of a quorum, another committeeman arrived, and the office of state chairman was declared vacant. Nugent next day declared the meeting illegal. However, the decision stood, and the state committee, meeting in Trenton on August 24, elected Edward E. Grosscup of Gloucester County as chairman. *Newark Evening News*, Aug. 10, 1911; Trenton *True American*, Aug. 11, 1911; and Link, *Road to the White House*, pp. 281-82.

From William Frank McCombs

My dear Governor: New York August 11th, 1911.

I quote you an extract from a letter of one of your supporters in Michigan. "I am surprised and very much pleased at the Republican support that I find Governor Wilson has and unless some untoward circumstances arise see no reason why he should not sweep the board in the coming campaign. It is not necessary for a candidate to have an opinion upon every conceivable subject; indeed, very often, except outside of the prominent issues in the campaign, it is not advisable to express opinions. Conditions often change and that which seems simple before an effort is made to accomplish it, very often becomes most difficult." This expresses the tenor of a number of letters which I have received. I merely submit it for your consideration. Of course, timidity may be a positive vice in addition to being an indication of weakness. But there is a great force in the above suggestion.

It has often occurred to me that the great fertility of mind and wide knowledge reflected in your speeches has been one of the reasons why you are considered very radical in some quarters. For if we are given an idea which has never occurred to us or which we do not understand it is human to call it radical. I recall in one of your lectures at Princeton the statement that if people say "I never heard of such a thing" it is a powerful argument in the influencing of public opinion against it.

I am leaving for the White Mountains tomorrow in my car and am taking Judge Gavegan[1] with me. You perhaps recall that he is an adviser of Mr. Hearst and is an influential factor with the labor organizations. I am always available to you and my office will know where I am at all times.

Yours sincerely,   Wm. F. McCombs

TLS (Governors' Files, Nj).
[1] Edward James Gavegan, judge of the New York Supreme Court.

From McKee Barclay

Dear Governor,   Baltimore, Md. Aug. 11, 1911.

You are to be invited to speak on The Commission Form of Government at the Convention of The State Board of Trade at Braddock Heights[,] Md. The date is somewhere about November 15. I hope you will find that you can accept. . . .

Blair Lee, Progressive and Wilson man, is campaigning against Gorman for the gubernatorial nomination.[1] There is danger of having the presidential campaign drawn into the matter and things are in a decidedly critical condition. Delicate handling is needed and to speak plainly, I think that your presence in the state is needed. In my opinion if you can find the opportunity to make about three speeches here we will have such a strong public demand for you that the politicians will find it absolutely impossible to get away from you. Of course it is up to us to create that situation first—meaning, to see that you are insistently invited.

I will let you hear from me soon on this matter.

With best wishes,   Yours Sincerely,   McKee Barclay.

ALS (Governors' Files, Nj).

[1] Blair Lee, Princeton 1880, lawyer of Silver Spring, Md., and Arthur Pue Gorman, Jr., lawyer of Baltimore and member of the Maryland state Senate, 1904-10. Gorman defeated Lee for the gubernatorial nomination by a vote of sixty-five to sixty-four in the Maryland state Democratic convention of 1911. Gorman in turn was defeated in the general election by the Republican candidate, Phillips Lee Goldsborough.

From Mary Allen Hulbert Peck

Dearest Friend: Pittsfield, Massachusetts August 12 [1911]

Let us throw politics to the dogs! We'll talk of important things like the weather, which is intoxicatingly beautiful, and more heaven sent than usual today, of the robin chirping outside my window, the sound of the cool breezes in the leaves and the faint touch of autumn in the air, and about my nurse, who has just left me in tears, and thinks I am "wonderful." Of course it flatters me although I pretend it doesn't. I had such an amusing time with her, and as soon as I could have a time free from gargling and biting a thermometer I began to give give [sic] instruction. She is a shy, narrow, timid helpless soul, in a body of the same sort. So *stiff* she worried me every moment using *tons of* strength and nervous force to do the least of things, and on the way to a breakdown from over-conscientiousness (mercy! what a long word). She left, as I said, in tears, protesting that she had no right to take any pay, it was a liberal education to be with me, a paper with written directions for all kinds of exercises, and— I think—a little crack through which she will dare to peep sometimes. I like to teach, and if I knew anything worth while I think I could, but I fancy it's chiefly because I like to hold the "centre plank." I am vain. You notice this is not "some little both of thee and me," but just *me*.

I know all about you for the papers tell me you are a demagogue & a boss, and Mr Nugent says you are an ingrate and a liar, and I have private information that you are a "gentleman & a scholar" with a private opinion that you are perfect and a *man*.

My room has been a bower of flowers, and I am spoiled by the entire household, but I want to get away. I shall be strong enough to travel by Wednesday, I hope, and will go to you & Mrs. Wilson for a day or two anyway. Will you thank your dear lady for wanting us. Mother will not be with me as she doesn't want to travel in the warm weather. So Allen will take me down to Hot Springs where the Dr. thinks I should go for a while.

Please be careful, and never, *never* expose yourself to the chance of any crank injuring you in some way. Don't be too democratic—let them guard you. Of course you will be President. I can see you receding from me now, only in the opportunities for seeing you often however, and I always *understand*. I must stop. I am tired but I am every day and hour

More devotedly your friend   M. A.

ALS (WP, DLC).

From August C. Streitwolf

My dear Governor: New Brunswick, N. J., August 12th, 1911.

While I thoroughly realize that it is distasteful to you to even acknowledge receipt of any communication on the Nugent subject, I cannot refrain from giving vent to my unbounded joy in having him decapitated from the state committee. Middlesex County is in bad shape politically and the enclosed article[1] correctly expresses the two representatives of the State Committee who are known to be against you and me. I have every reason to know that Mr. M. F. Ross controls the County Committee and I have anticipated their action of refusing to endorse me. I have several petitions for my renomination circulated throughout the county and at the date of this letter have secured over one hundred signatures in less than three days effort. The County Committee meet on Thursday to take action on "candidates" at which time I expect to be most graciously "turned down." Should this be so I have determined to give them the hardest fight that they have ever witnessed.[2] I did intend to get to Sea Girt before this that I might have the benefit of your good judgment. I realized that the Thursday I was present was the not the proper time for such discussion.

Sincerely yours,   A. C. Streitwolf

TLS (WP, DLC).
 [1] It is missing.
 [2] He won the fight for renomination and was re-elected to the Assembly in November 1911.

From McKee Barclay

Dear Governor,   Baltimore, Md. August 14, 1911.

Since writing you of the prospective invitation to speak at Braddock Heights I find that there is a plan on foot to invite you to deliver an address in Baltimore in the month of December —during "Maryland Week." From your point of view this is better than the other engagement unless the date is too far distant, —for the reason that the state leaders will be in Baltimore while many of them will probably miss the State Board of Trade affair.[1] Mr. [Oliver Perry] Baldwin, managing editor of *The Sun*, is one of the moving spirits of the Maryland Week celebration and he asked me to say that he hoped you would hold up your acceptance of any invitations that would conflict with his affair as I will either run over to see you or write you fully just how matters stand.

I am enclosing an interview that shows how o[u]r present governor feels toward you.[2] In passing I will say that every progressive vote in the state is for you—not a single exception. Our only anxiety is as to how the hardshells and grafters will go.

I also enclose some portraits—proofs from a cut made from a drawing by one of our men. The original pen drawing goes in a frame on the wall of my library.

Yours Sincerely,   McKee Barclay

ALS (Governors' Files, Nj).
 [1] Wilson spoke twice during a visit to Baltimore on December 5, 1911. See the three news reports printed at Dec. 6, 1911.
 [2] The interview with Governor Austin Lane Crothers, which appeared in the Baltimore *Sun*, Aug. 15, 1911, is missing. In the course of his remarks supporting Blair Lee for the Democratic gubernatorial nomination, Crothers praised Wilson, as follows:
 "We don't want to back off the road of progress we have been traveling. We must go on. As an example, from all over the nation arise plaudits for the great Governor of New Jersey in his work, showing that the people everywhere are progressive. Shall Maryland, once entered upon the same course, turn her back now?"

To Mary Allen Hulbert Peck

Trenton, N. J. Aug. 15, 1911

Ellen joins me in begging that you and Allen come to us Friday morning   best train leaves New York at nine four morning.   Woodrow Wilson.

T telegram (WC, NjP).

To an Unknown Person

My dear Sir: [Sea Girt, N. J.] August 15, 1911.

I do not believe that the inhabitants of the Philippine Islands are prepared for independence. I believe that they should be prepared for independence by a steadily increasing measure of self government.   Very truly yours,   Woodrow Wilson.

TCL (WC, NjP).

To Thomas Bell Love

My dear Mr. Love: [Sea Girt, N. J.] August 15, 1911.

Allow me to acknowledge with appreciation the receipt of your two letters of August ninth, one conveying the kind invitation of the Woodrow Wilson State Democratic League of Texas, and the other suggesting that October twenty-eighth would be an acceptable date for me to come to the State.

That date suits me as well as any other date in that crowded month and I shall look forward with genuine pleasure to being there.

Will you not convey to the Woodrow Wilson State Democratic League an expression of my warm appreciation of their generous action and my pleasure that they should desire my presence in the State. It makes me proud to have such friends.

Cordially and sincerely yours,   Woodrow Wilson

TLS (photostat in the T. B. Love Papers, Dallas Hist. Soc.).

From Thomas Bell Love

My dear Governor Wilson: Dallas, Texas, August 16, 1911.

I am enclosing you herewith clipping of an address issued by the Executive Committee of the Woodrow Wilson State Democratic League of Texas, which appeared in all of the leading dailies of the State on last Sunday,[1] which address was prepared by Hon. T. W. Gregory of Austin,[2] one of the leading lawyers in the State and one of the oldest and most influential of the alumni of the University of Texas.

In order that you may understand something of the personnel of this, the working committee of our organization, I want to give you some information as to the men who make up the committee.

Mr. Gregory, of whom I have spoken, is vice-president; the other vice-president is Col. O. T. Holt of Houston,[3] a very eminent lawyer and of high reputation throughout the State. Although he was a Confederate soldier, he is hale and hearty and very active. He was National Democratic Committeeman from Texas for twelve years prior to 1896. He is an Anti-Statewide Prohibitionist, while Mr. Gregory is a Statewide Prohibitionist.

Mr. Armistead I am sure you know all about.

Mr. R. C. Roberdeau, the Treasurer, is a leading banker of Austin,[4] and was for years prominently connected with the Texas National Guard. He is an anti-prohibitionist.

Col. R. M. Wynne of Fort Worth[5] is an old-time lawyer and Confederate soldier, who is now superintendent of the Confederate Home at Austin and is very popular with the Confederate voters throughout the State. He is a State-wide Prohibitionist.

Mr. W[illiam] T. Bartholomew is a very able and capable young lawyer of San Angelo and is a Statewide Prohibitionist.

Mr. C. E. Gilmore of Wills Point,[6] is a prominent member of the Legislature and has just retired from the presidency of the State Press Association. He is the editor of a very influential country weekly and is a Statewide Prohibitionist.

Col. A. R. McCollum of Waco[7] is a prominent Anti-Statewide Prohibitionist and is the editor and publisher of the most influential and best known weekly newspaper in the State. He is a man of great influence and standing.

Mr. A. D. Rogers of Decatur[8] is a prominent and influential member of the Legislature and a State-wide Prohibitionist.

Hon. Cato Sells of Cleburne, the Chairman of the Committee, is a prominent banker, scientific farmer and Statewide Prohibitionist. He was formerly for many years National Committeeman from Iowa and was United States District Attorney there while Governor Harmon was Attorney General. He is a very intelligent and influential man among all classes.

I have burdened you with these data thinking they might prove worth while, and also to show that we have given both sides of our recent legal controversy representation which is entirely satisfactory.

I am receiving information daily from influential men throughout the State, as well as from newspapers, advising me that they will assist in the movement. As I have advised you from the beginning, I think there is but little doubt of the issue, although we are going to leave nothing undone.

If any of your speeches have included a statement of your views on the tariff question, or any phase of it, I would be glad to have you procure a copy to be sent me. I do not remember having seen published such a speech and I have some inquiries as to this matter.

I also have a letter from Mr. T. M. Scott of Paris, Texas,[9] and from others, wanting to know, if possible, something as to the length of time you will be in Texas on the occasion of your visit, when you will arrive in Dallas and leave Dallas. I know this is sometime ahead, but would be glad if you could give me some definite advice on this point.

I have received your letter of August 8th and am glad to know that October 28th is satisfactory for your address here.

The work I am doing in this matter is not generous, as you suggest, but selfish. I am so constituted that I derive more self-satisfaction from the consciousness that I am endeavoring to contribute in some way to the general welfare than from most things else, and it is so gratifying to know that our efforts stimulate you in your great mission, that we are many times repaid for the efforts we are putting forth.

With kind regards, I am

Very truly yours,   Thomas B. Love.

TCL (T. B. Love Papers, Dallas Hist. Soc.).

1 "To the Democrats of Texas," published on August 13, 1911. After reviewing Wilson's political career, it declared that the South had long awaited the opportunity to offer once again one of her own sons to the nation. Wilson was that man, and Texas should take the lead in making him President. Finally, it urged Texans to organize Wilson clubs in their own communities and support the worthy cause. See Arthur S. Link, "The Wilson Movement in Texas," *Southwestern Historical Quarterly*, XLVIII (Oct. 1944), 172.

2 Thomas Watt Gregory, lawyer of the firm of Gregory, Batts & Brooks. Best known for his role in the prosecution of the antitrust case of State of Texas v. Waters Pierce Oil Co., he later served as Attorney General of the United States in the Wilson administration.

3 Orren T. Holt, lawyer, also vice-president of the South Texas National Bank.

4 Roger Courtland Roberdeau, vice-president of the American National Bank and treasurer of Travis County.

5 Richard Moore Wynne.

6 Clarence Edgar Gilmore, editor of the *Wills Point Chronicle* and member of the Texas House of Representatives, 1907-11.

7 Augustus R. McCollum, editor of the Waco *Tribune*.

8 Armoth D. Rogers, in the real estate business and also a traveling salesman, member of the Texas House of Representatives, 1911-14.

9 Thomas McGee Scott, Princeton 1904, member of the firm of Scott & Baldwin, investment bankers dealing in farm and city mortgages.

A News Report of a Speech to the Warren County,
New Jersey, Farmers' Picnic

[Aug. 17, 1911]

WILSON READY TO FIGHT HARD
WARREN FARMERS STIRRED

BELVIDERE, Aug. 17.—Governor Woodrow Wilson made announcement to 15,000 persons at the Warren County farmers' picnic here yesterday afternoon that he intended to make a hard fight in the approaching campaign[1] for the success of those legislators who have stood by him. The Governor made it plain that to secure his support the candidates must be men of high principles.

"I serve notice on all the constituencies of the State that I intend to stand by the men who stood by me," he said. "If there is to be a fight I want to help do the fighting. But I expect that guaranteed, copper-riveted candidates will be put up for election. By 'guaranteed,' I mean people who do things above board and have no private understandings."

The Governor then paid a tribute to Senator Johnston Cornish, of Warren County, who has been a stanch supporter of the Governor both in the Senate and as a member of the State Democratic committee. Senator Cornish was one of the State committeemen who signed the letter demanding James R. Nugent's resignation as chairman, and also voted against Nugent at the Asbury Park meeting.

"I want to say a word for Senator Cornish," said Governor Wilson to the great gathering of the Senator's constituents. "From the first time that I attempted anything at Trenton until now Senator Cornish has stood by me. The Senator is a very frank man and he has told me several times why he stood by me. He has said again and again: 'Governor, I know the people of Warren County and I know what they want me to do.' Senator Cornish was one of the hardest workers in the Senate for the success of the Democratic program."

There was a note of warning in an additional word uttered by the Governor, on the subject of candidates.

"I want any man who is your candidate," he said, "to be out in the open where we can look at him. I dont want any underbrush where he can lie down and hide himself. If he goes into private conferences with men he ought not to talk to we want to know what the conference was about. Has some one come into the county to put up a game? We want to know all about it.

"I'm going to tell all I know and I tell you, privately, I know a good deal. I am on to their curves. I am not so innocent as I look."

Governor Wilson made no direct reference to the ousting of State Chairman Nugent, but some pointed remarks on State leadership were interpreted by his hearers as bearing on the Nugent situation.

"We have come upon a time," declared the Governor, "when the leadership of the State does not belong to men who rule only through private understandings. A man has got to be a leader now because he does lead, because he does what he says he will do. No other kind of leadership is possible. Everywhere in the country the people believe the same thing—a leader must deliver the goods. Leaders who haven't principles worth while and that they will live up to have been asked to take a back seat and they will never be asked to give it up.

"I sometimes look with amazement at certain men who call themselves politicians and yet who decline to stand for what the people want. There are men whom I could name in the various counties who have had the chance of their lives and have refused it. I myself have asked them whom they served—the people or the organization. I serve notice on them now that the game is up for them. They have preferred burial with dishonor to life with honor.

"I have talked with these men and reasoned with them and I believed, as they left me, that they had seen the light. But straightway they have returned to their practises as a hog to his wallow.

"These antagonists are not to be worried about; I pity them. I pity the man who at midday things [thinks] it is still night. I never met more confirmed stupidity in my life. I have no more feeling against them than I have against the blind fish that digs his nose in the mud because he cannot see.

"There are some men who you think, perhaps, have gone into politics for glory. They have not; but for duty. They intend to make those on the other side sorry they are in politics. We are in the fight for life, and, thank God, we are in good health."

Governor Wilson commented on the commission government election in Trenton. He said that it was an illustration of the rule of the people. There had been a combination, he declared, to fool the people, but the people were not fooled.

No one had a better time at the picnic, apparently, than did the Governor. After luncheon at one of the hotels he sauntered through the picnic grounds with his secretary, Joseph P. Tumulty, and Senator Cornish. At first he got along without much interruption and had a lot of fun watching the throng enjoy itself, but when it became noised about that the Governor was close at hand he found it hard work progressing through the crowds eager to shake his hand.

Warren County is looked upon as one of the stanchest Wilson counties of the State, and one of its greatest desires is to see Governor Wilson President of the United States. At least that was the way it looked yesterday. About every third man who grasped the Governor's hand assured him he would be glad to vote for him for President. To one and all the Governor returned a gracious smile as he thanked them for their good wishes.

One elderly lady said enthusiastically:

"I've shaken hands with Governor Wilson. I hope before I die to shake hands with President Wilson."

While the Governor was speaking the crush on the speaker's stand became so great that the frail structure began to sag. For a minute it appeared that it would crash to the ground. Unmindful of the danger, Governor Wilson continued to speak. The danger was overcome by partly clearing the stand.

Printed in the *Newark Evening News*, Aug. 17, 1911; some editorial headings omitted.
1 That is, the Democratic primary campaign.

A News Report of a Visit to Cape May County

[Aug. 18, 1911]

GOVERNOR WOODROW WILSON PAYS A VISIT TO CAPE MAY COUNTY

Governor Woodrow Wilson made a flying trip to Cape May County last Monday[1] and in his short visit covered a large section of the county and was received very enthusiastically everywhere. The governor was met at Broad Street Station, Philadelphia, on Monday morning by a special escorte in charge of Evans G. Slaughter, chairman of the Democratic County Committee.[2] The party consisted of M. H. Kearns, of Cape May; J. Thompson Baker, O. I. Blackwell, Wildwood; William Oakes, chairman of the reception committee from the Holly Beach Yacht Club; George N. Smith and Charles A. Norton, Holly Beach.[3] From

1 August 14.
2 Evans Griffith Slaughter, proprietor of the Hotel Aldine Apartments in Wildwood.
3 Michael H. Kearns ran a cigar store in Cape May and was a Democratic state committeeman; Jacob Thompson Baker was a lawyer and Mayor of Wildwood, 1911-12; O. I. Blackwell was a lawyer and real estate agent; George N. Smith was a commissioner of Holly Beach (now a part of Wildwood); Charles A. Norton, was a commissioner of Holly Beach and ran a livery stable. The Editors have been unable further to identify Oakes.

Broad Street the party went in taxicabs to the Chestnut Street wharf and there took the Reading ferry to Kaighn's Point, Camden, the terminal of the Atlantic City railroad. There they were met by C. H. Ewing,[4] superintendent of the road and his first assistant. A special sight-seeing train was in readiness and they left at 10.10, arriving at [Cape May] Court House at 11.40. The trip was made on a sight-seeing engine. This engine is arranged for sight-seeing purposes and has a special cab arranged in the front on top of the boiler for passengers. At Court House the party was met by a committee from the Dias Creek Fishermen's Association, composed of Joseph Camp, president; Ralph Schellenger and B. L. Howell.[5] In their charge the party proceeded in autos through Court House and Dias Creek to Norbury's landing at Green Creek, where the governor was shown maps of the bay and with glasses was shown the outline of the cove affected by the law passed last winter which caused the arrest of seven of the fishermen who were innocent of their violating the law. This law prohibited net fishing in Delaware Bay. As no protests were offered the governor signed the bill. The fishermen on the bay shore have been fishing this way for years and had not been informed by our county representatives in the legislature of an impending law nor of its passage, so they kept on fishing in their usual way. As a consequence about two months ago someone made a complaint and seven of them were arrested and brought before Justice of the Peace Henry Coombs and about 40 more were in line for prosecution. Representatives immediately went to the governor and stated the facts of the case, who with the assistance of the State Fish and Game Commission, conferred with the United States Attorney General and had the prosecutions withdrawn and the men were let off by only paying the costs of the trial before the justice.

From the landing the governor was taken to the cross roads at Green Creek and there under the large oak tree was introduced to a crowd of about 1,000 people from that section of the county by Joseph Camp. He explained to his hearers that the bill had been passed by both houses of the legislature and as no protests were offered he signed the bill, though he would not have done so if he had known it affected them. He said they should have been informed by their representative of the bill's presence and if they failed to do so they were not properly represented. He advised them to have a bill prepared to put before the legisla-

---

[4] Charles H. Ewing, superintendent of the Atlantic City Railroad, 1910-1912.
[5] Camp was a clammer and crab trapper; Ralph Schellinger was a farmer, part-time fisherman, and a member of the Democratic committee of Middle Township; Burt L. Howell was a clammer and crab trapper.

ture next winter covering their case and put it before the legislative committee and if they did not get satisfaction, then come
to him again. He was applauded enthusiastically by the great
audience and after a general hand shake, he was taken in the
auto again and proceeded to Rio Grande and then to Cape May
to the Hotel Lafayette, where he was met by a reception committee from that city. He then rested about half an hour in his
room, after which he came down stairs to a luncheon prepared
by the Cape May committee. As he was descending the stairway,
the band which was in attendance struck up "All Hail the Chief"
and he was given a great ovation by a crowd numbering near
2,000. He was then tendered an elaborate luncheon at the hotel
by the committee with about 20 representative business men
present. After the luncheon the crowd clamored for a speech
and though he was not booked for one there, he was introduced
to the audience by Mr. Slaughter and spoke about ten minutes
from one of the small balconies on the second floor of the hotel.
Taken in autos again the party was shown over Cape May, going
up to the new hotel and back and then to Schellenger's Landing,
where they were met by members of the Holly Beach Yacht Club.
The governor was taken in the handsome speed boat of Com-
modore W. L. Dickel,[6] the Gibson Girl, and in other boats the
party were shown the new inland waterway to the club house at
Wildwood Crest. There he rested about twenty minutes and was
then taken on an auto tour of the island, going to Anglesea and
back over various avenues to Wildwood Manor where accom[m]o-
dations had been engaged for him. He rested here about an
hour and then at seven o'clock in company with his escorte and
the Yacht Club committee was taken in autos to the residence
of J. Thompson Baker on Atlantic avenue where he was received
by the Poor Richard Club, of Philadelphia, and a number of local
citizens. A luncheon was served here and the party was again
taken in autos to the ocean pier and there the governor was put
in a rolling chair and taken down the boardwalk preceded by
an escorte of members of the local police forces and followed by
members of the Holly Beach Yacht Club. The walk was lined
with sight-seers eager to get a glimpse of this great man who
has become quite well-known since his election as governor of
New Jersey last fall. Continuous cheering marked the movement of the party the entire length of the walk to the Crest Pier
where they witnessed an excellent display of fireworks provided
by the Wildwood Crest Borough Council. After the display

---

6 William L. Dickel of Philadelphia, treasurer and director of the Gibson Dis-
tilling Co. of that city.

they were again taken in autos to the Holly Beach Yacht Club house on the shore of Sunset Lake where the governor was given a grand reception by the members and a large number of their friends. A banquet was served in the dining room which was one of the most elaborate ever given at the club. Frank G. English, president of the club,[7] introduced Judge Curtis T. Baker[8] as toastmaster for the evening and he responded and called first on Justice of the Supreme Court Charles [Grant] Garrison, of Camden, who responded in a very interesting talk and combined humorous remarks which kept the audience in a jolly mood. Governor Wilson was then called on and he made a very interesting speech. He said that he had combined duty with pleasure and by joining two or three appointments had been able to get to [the] county on that day and fulfill some of his promises.

He said it seemed strange that we had grown so close together here, and yet some of the boroughs wanted the public to know where the entrance to their town was and had marked it with an arch. And to make this more emphatic, he said the arches were illuminated at night. He said we were foolish to have four single governments here and should consolidate and adopt a commission government. After the banquet he was escorted to the Manor by Messrs. Slaughter and Kearns where he spent the night. Tuesday morning he took the 7.08 Broad street station train to North Philadelphia, where he took the New York express for Trenton. His excellency seemed very well impressed with our county and Five Mile Beach.

Printed in the Wildwood, N. J., *Beach Weekly Journal*, Aug. 18, 1911; two editorial headings omitted.
[7] He was probably the Frank G. English of Philadelphia, who was listed as a "builder" in the city directories of that period.
[8] Curtis Thompson Baker, judge of the Court of Common Pleas of Cape May County.

A News Report of an Address in Camden County, New Jersey[1]

[Aug. 18, 1911]

GOVERNOR TELLS FARMERS TO BREAK UP MACHINES IN STATE

CAMDEN, Aug. 18.—Standing again in the presence of 5,000 or more farmers of South Jersey, from whom, ten months ago, he asked support in his gubernatorial campaign, Governor Woodrow Wilson yesterday rendered an account of his stewardship, again scored corruption in present-day politics, exposed the real protection by which "big business" manipulates and controls and, as a further step in the right direction, urged the farmers of five counties to organize their own cooperative warehousing and transportation association, with a bureau to collect and disseminate information on conditions all over the country.

With his favorite weapon, publicity, the Governor took another whack at the machine bosses who, defeated and shorn of power, are still attempting to discredit him. He branded them as "neither Democrats nor Republicans, who speak untruths and know it, and who, delegating to themselves the title of party organization, are neither part nor parcel of any party."

Governor Wilson declared in his speech that one of the best habits a man could form is that of non-partisan voting. He added that he wanted men to vote the Democratic ticket so long as they believed it represented their best interests, and that he wanted no man to support the Democratic party who does not think that.

Proving again that he is capable of meeting the most subtle machinations against his administration and the welfare of the people, he announced that many men now seeking the support of voters for the coming campaign are pledging their support to the Governor, knowing they have no intention of redeeming their pledges if elected.

"I have a pretty good idea who they are," he said, "and if you are in doubt of a man's sincerity, because of his past conduct, I shall be glad to tell you whether, in my opinion, he would or would not support me if elected.

"I believe you will credit the statement that what I am most interested in is the party devoted to the interests of the whole people, and that only. I am not interested in running for office. It is an occupation not at all times pleasant. But I am enlisted for the rest of my life to make it just as hot as I know how for those men who do not represent the people.

"And I want you to fully understand by that what I mean. They have said that I am trying to break up the party organization in New Jersey; that I have disrupted organizations and am ruling the Democratic party. I am not; and they know I am not. They know, too, that what they have said is not the truth. I hope my words convey the retort they can understand.

"Let me tell you, too, that they are getting very nervous. Not because I am fighting them. No, that's not it. But because they know that you, the people, are on to them.

"Don't forget that the great commercial, industrial and financial privileges and combinations that we are now attacking so bitterly all over this country would be perfectly harmless if they were not served, and served in the most subtle way, continually, by the very men I speak of. Run them out into the open, and when you get them out where all men can see them, be sure that you have your gun ready.

"Some persons are disposed to criticize all politics, all politicians and everyone actively interested or identified with government. Let me say to you that we could not live peaceably together if we weren't interested in politics and our political institutions.

"And politics, therefore, should be one of the big, important central parts of our lives. And there are a great many things like politics that we must be active and interested in, or we will be of little value to ourselves or our country in politics. . . .

"The whole of the United States is now wide awake. A new day has dawned in our politics, and the sun will not go down upon that day until human liberties are abundantly vindicated. If men die in the cause, their blood will be the seed of multitudes more. We now know what it is we desire. We are s[e]eking to purge our hearts and clarify our understanding, and if God pleases and lets us live, we shall look upon the day when America was regenerated."

Printed in the *Trenton Evening Times*, Aug. 18, 1911; some editorial headings omitted.
[1] Wilson spoke about mid-day at Washington Park, a picnic and amusement area located some three miles south of Gloucester City, Camden County. *Camden Daily Courier*, Aug. 17, 1911.

An Interview

[Aug. 19, 1911]
A Talk with Governor Wilson
By Charles Johnston

I came from a talk with Governor Wilson convinced that I had met not only an administrator but a leader and inspirer; one who, holding high ideals, is able to inspire high ideals in others, touching them with some of his own fire.

I met Governor Wilson in the evening, in a cozy little hotel a hundred yards from the Trenton State House.[1] Very cordially and simply he invited me to go with him to his office in the State House, where quiet talk might be more easily compassed. The Governor's room has more the air of a study than an office, its high windows looking out on tree-shadowed lawns that stretch toward the Delaware River.

When the lights had been turned on, for it was already dusk, I began to explain the purpose of my coming, greatly impressed

[1] Hotel Sterling.

and touched the while by the Governor's engaging frankness, his direct and cordial simplicity. Saying that it had seemed to me that, in a Democratic period, the rights and duties of the separate States ought to be of most vital interest, I told Governor Wilson that I had asked three of his distinguished colleagues to tell me which side of State government appealed to them as most interesting and vital. And I outlined their replies.

Governor Wilson answered that, for his part, he found not one side, but all sides, of State administration most interesting. He was interested not so much in a special problem as in the general problem.

"To my mind," said the Governor of New Jersey, "the great question is one of adjustment. We have the economic problems of the day. We have public opinion. We have our systems of legislation. The problem is, to adjust these three factors. We have first to instruct public opinion on the great economic problems. Then we have to bring public opinion to bear on legislative action. At present there are too many barriers between. Public opinion is checked and thwarted, and cannot make itself immediately effective.

"Here is an illustration of what I mean. If you made a complicated machine, say an automobile, and so constructed it that in order to exercise control over it you had to control each part separately, to get your hand on each part in order to start it, and once more to get your hand on each part in order to stop it, you could do nothing with it, simply because you have only two hands. What you need is a single lever to control the whole complicated machine, so that you can start it by a single motion or stop it by a single motion. Then you have it under your control.

"We have done something very like this with our government. We have made a great, complicated machine, and each part separately answers to our hands. But there is no one lever to control the whole machine, therefore it is not controlled at all. We fancy that when we have elected a whole series of officials each one of whom is answerable, each one of whom may be rejected when he stands for re-election, we have a government machine which is answerable and under our control; but it is not so; we are mistaken. For no one really knows who all the different officials are who are responsible for the running of the parts of the governmental machine; nor can we bring them all to book at once, since their terms are not concurrent. So we cannot even control them all at the same time when they stand for re-election.

"We need the single lever to control the several parts of the complicated machine. It is for that reason that the country is demanding the leader in the eye of all, chosen by all, answerable to all, as it does in the case of the President. The call of the day is for leadership; the people demand, and will support, the men who rightly interpret public opinion and who, interpreting public opinion, are ready to make that opinion operative.

"When I was running for Governor I said very frankly that, if elected, I should take my election as a mandate to lead; a declaration by the people of New Jersey that I was required to be the leader of the State, the single lever, effective for the control of its government. My opponent[2] said that, if elected, he intended to be a 'constitutional' Governor; that he would make recommendations to the Legislature, and then leave the Legislature alone to decide whether his recommendations should be carried into effect. I said that, if that was what was meant by a 'constitutional' Governor, I intended, if elected, to be an 'unconstitutional' Governor; for I should hold that I had a mandate from the people of the State not only to recommend reforms, but to use every honorable means in my power to have them made into laws.[3] I offered myself as a leader, and I hold that the people of New Jersey accepted my offer."

This declaration is noteworthy; the principle of the single lever to control the machine not only defines Woodrow Wilson's ideal of leadership, but further explains his policy in detail, showing, among other things, why he advocates the commission government of cities, as securing real control in a few immediately responsible hands, as against the "many-headed multitude" of office-holders, practically responsible to no one, or responsible only to the boss of the local "machine."

Even more noteworthy, it seems to me, is the fact that Governor Wilson was speaking not especially of boss-ridden or corrupt government—though there the need of true leadership is most conspicuous and imperative—but rather of the normal working of the State or national governmental machine. It is so constructed, so complicated, that, in Governor Wilson's view, the machine of government cries for leadership, not at one time only, but at all times. Naturally, perhaps, this suggested to me a question whether the structure of the machine of government should not itself be altered, to make possible the one lever with its direct

2 Vivian Murchison Lewis.
3 For Lewis's pledge, see H. E. Alexander to WW, Oct. 1, 1910, n. 1, Vol. 21; for Wilson's first public response, see the address printed at Oct. 3, 1910, *ibid.*

control. Would Governor Wilson advocate constitutional amendments making such a change?

Governor Wilson replied:

"I have always been an evolutionist. Therefore I believe that constitutional amendments should be the result of evolution; they should not precede and force, but should record and embody growth which has been already gained. Therefore I do not think that the difficulty would be effectively solved by constitutional amendment.

"There are two parts of the matter: first, the fuller control of the executive forces by the Governor; and, second, the guidance of legislation by the Governor. As to the first, the fuller control by the Governor of the executive powers. This is very difficult where the State officers, like the Secretary of State, the Treasurer, the Auditor, and the Attorney-General are all separately elected. Here, in New Jersey, only the Governor is chosen by a State-wide election. The Secretary of State is appointed by the Governor, but for five years, so that each Governor inherits his predecessor's Secretary of State, who may be of the opposite party. The State Treasurer and Comptroller are appointed by the Legislature, not by the Governor. This shows how difficult it is for the Governor really to exercise full executive power and influence.

"Then there is the quite different question of the guidance by the Governor of legislation. It is not enough for the Governor to recommend such legislation as is demanded by awakened and enlightened public opinion. The Governor should, further, bring strong pressure to bear on the Legislature to bring about legislation which is needed to give effect to the will of the people. I do not mean that he may follow the old way, and use the club of patronage to bring about what he wants. That, I hold, is wholly inadmissible. But I think that the Governor should bring pressure to bear on the Legislature through public opinion; first, by making clear to the public what the issues are, and then by directing the force of public opinion thus aroused upon the Legislature."

We then spoke of the sharp separations created by the American Constitution, under which the President has no place on the floor of the Legislature, has no direct representative in either House, as compared with the position of the Prime Minister of England, who not only has his dominant place in one or other House of Parliament, but, even more, is always the effective leader of the majority party in the popular House. I asked Governor Wilson whether he would like to see, or like to have, some such position; so that, as Chief Executive, he could meet his

Legislature and talk things over face to face. Governor Wilson said that, for some reasons, he would like this very much. "But," he added, very characteristically, "I would not approve of any plan which merely set the President or the Governor up before the Legislature to answer the questions of legislators. I would not like to see him badgered unless he also had the right to badger!"

Then came a reflection, prompted by a fine sense of justice:

"One thing," said Governor Wilson, "has always struck me as unfair. When any vital question is being debated in Congress, for example, whatever the President says will be reported everywhere, and will become known throughout the length and breadth of the land. But what is said in reply by those who oppose the President will not be universally reported nor become generally known. I felt the same thing during the last session of the State Legislature here. I felt that whatever I said about the measures under discussion would be heard and believed, but that what was said in reply would not be equally widely known or credited. This was fundamentally unfair. Therefore I abstained from making statements that would be affected by this tendency. What I did, instead, was this: I told the men who opposed me that I was ready to go down with them to their counties and debate the matter at issue with them before their own constituents. But the trouble was that they were not willing to go. In ways like this, by arousing, instructing, and directing public opinion, the Governor may bring the right and worthy kind of pressure to bear on legislation.

"Take the case of Governor Hughes. Mr. Hughes began with the theory that his duty as Governor was simply to recommend legislation, leaving it to the Legislature to carry it out. But later on, when he saw that things were at a deadlock, he went out to the public, aroused public opinion by an aggressive campaign, and directed such a force of opinion upon the legislators that they were compelled to create the Public Service Commission to carry out the will of the public."

I asked Governor Wilson whether he would advocate a change giving the Governor, or the President, the power to initiate legislation; to give him some such status in the Legislature as the English Premier has. To this Governor Wilson replied:

"There is not the slightest practical difficulty in getting legislation introduced. What you suggest would simply introduce the British Constitution. But I think it is better to go on doing things in our own way until we hit upon a distinctively American way of accomplishing what is needed."

The practical solution is, therefore, once more, leadership. I asked the Governor how his ideal could be harmonized with the new methods, such as the "Oregon plan," which tended to throw all responsibility back on the individual voter. To this the Governor replied with a smile and an anecdote:

"When I was in Oregon on my Western trip," he said, "and was studying the initiative, referendum, and recall, they told me that if I wished to study them all at once I should look under Mr. U'ren's hat. I replied that I had much rather find responsibility under one man's hat than under no man's!"

We came back, therefore, to leadership. Governor Wilson made it clear that the real leader is not the man who impresses his own wishes and views on others, but rather he who rightly hears and rightly interprets the finest and best public opinion. He gathers the general inspiration and brings it to a focus.

"It is something like what Bagehot says of Sir Robert Peel: 'It was not that he did extraordinary things, but that he did ordinary things extraordinarily well.[']⁴ He is the true leader who interprets the general conscience rightly, and rightly makes it operative."

In conclusion, I asked Governor Wilson whether there might not be some conflict between his view of leadership, inspiring as it is, and the accepted theory of American government, that the executive and legislative powers should be isolated and kept apart. To this the Governor replied, and I find his reply profoundly suggestive:

"Is that really the American theory? Was it not rather a departure from the first ideal, a departure belonging to the day of lesser men? Did not Jefferson and Adams, and, most of all, Washington himself, exert, and intentionally exert, an immense influence on legislation? Is not that the true American ideal?"

A stirring and potent appeal. Then I asked the Governor whether, if his ideal was leadership, and if the true leader is he who rightly interprets and makes effective the general conscience, he did not bring everything back, in the last analysis, to the general conscience. And was not this a tremendous expression of faith in the honesty and righteousness of the general mind?

Governor Wilson replied:

"Yes, necessarily so. How could it be otherwise?"

Printed in *Harper's Weekly*, LV (Aug. 19, 1911), 11-12.

⁴ Wilson was paraphrasing the sentence in Walter Bagehot's essay, "The Character of Sir Robert Peel," describing Peel as the perfect type of a "constitutional statesman,–the powers of a first-rate man and the creed of a second-rate man."

To Mary Allen Hulbert Peck

Dearest Friend,   Sea Girt, New Jersey, 19 Aug., 1911.

It would be hard to express our disappointment that you are not here,—or our concern at the cause! These days, Friday to Tuesday, we had been carefully hoarding, as the *only* days in all this month when I could be at home and enjoy a little freedom,—and that you could not come was like the dashing to pieces of a long cherished plan, which *can't* be put together again. Worse still was the cause, your illness—your relapse, when you *should* have taken care of yourself and got well and come to those who love you! It goes hard to give it all up, and go on from task to task with none of the coveted pleasure to make the way seem fair and easy. Ellen has just sent you a night letter begging you to let us know your movements—for if you are to be in New York on Tuesday evening, for example, it is possible I may get in to see you,—if I know the hour and the place. Otherwise, alas! we shall have to wait to catch you on your return from the Hot Springs next month. There will be the mischief to pay if we do not get hold of you then! On Thursday we set out, in an automobile, to make a tour of the public institutions of the State,—the various Homes, Reformatories, Asylums, &c. &c,—which will take us a full week,—and the day before we start, Wednesday, the 23rd., I have been obliged to fill with other public engagements. So, you see how literally the 18th to the 23rd. was the only time I could count on that might be blessed with your presence. I have not written recently because I was looking forward so constantly, from day to day, to seeing you *soon*, and writing, in such circumstances seemed so poor a thing. I am running these few lines off to-night (Saturday) both because I hope they may catch you before you get off, and because there is, apparently, no longer and [any] hope of having free Sundays. The politicians of the whole country choose that day on which to look me up and gosip about national politics. I keep perfectly well, but get *very* weary of all the talk,—much of it so futile,—and wish again and again that hard, honest work by which things were accomplished might be substituted. But this is not the best time to speak of such things: I am tired and cross and anxious,—tired by the week's goings on; cross to have missed the deep pleasure of having my dear friend here, whose presence is a great reward; and anxious, *very* anxious that she is ill and does not take care of herself! I had best go to bed and forget everything except that I am   Her devoted friend   Woodrow Wilson

ALS (WP, DLC).

From William Jennings Bryan

My Dear Gov,   [Lincoln, Neb., c. Aug. 20, 1911]

I wish you would read the Dem platforms of 1900 1904 & 1908 & my speech on Imperialism in 2nd vol of my speeches.[1] I think you will on reconsideration be willing to endorse our platform.

Yours truly   W. J. Bryan

I am anxious for you to speak out against the "rule of reason" decisions. They repeal the criminal clause of the anti trust law & Pres Taft has taken the trust side. I think Congress will take the other side.

ALS (WC, NjP) written on WW to an unknown person, Aug. 15, 1911.
    [1] "Imperialism" was originally delivered in Indianapolis on August 8, 1900, on the occasion of his acceptance of the Democratic presidential nomination. It was reprinted in W. J. Bryan, *Speeches of William Jennings Bryan*, II, 17-49.

To Solomon Bulkley Griffin

My dear Mr. Griffin: [Sea Girt, N. J.] August 21, 1911.

I owe you a very earnest apology for my long delay in replying to your kind letter of the second of August. It has not been due to neglect but merely to the fact that so many things of apparent public importance pressed upon me that I had no time and, for that matter, no right to think and write about myself as you had so generously invited me to do.

I knew, besides, that what I might write would be of little value to you. I have tried hard all my life *not* to analyze myself, not to think what I might "portend" in the life about me.

My duty is a very simple one, as I see it. We have come to a point of crisis in our affairs, both economic and political; I have studied affairs all my life and must do what I can to assist in the solution of the problems that face us. Else, of what use have my studies been or the training I have taken such pains to give myself in understanding and expounding matters of this very sort?

Our representative institutions have lost their purity and their reality because of the intervention of political machines between the people and those who should be their representatives, an intervention which began to have its full sinister effect when great business interests began to make use of those machines to control legislation in their own behoof. Such an alliance was not particularly formidable until the business interests which made up one side of the partnership became themselves colossal and began to throw the control of industry and commerce into a comparatively few hands. Formidable enough because of their mere size and resources, those interests became the most formidable power in modern society when they consummated that alliance.

The long dominance of these interests in our economic life and in the control of our politics has, of course, produced results in our law and in out [our] economic organization, in the development and control of our national resources and in many other ways, many of which are highly inimical to economic freedom and individual privilege. These results must be studied and what is wrong about them must be rectified.

My function is to put what brains I have at the service of the people, whose life these things dominate: to find out what is going on; to speak of what I find, clearly and without fear,—if possible, without passion or prejudice; and to cooperate in carrying out such remedies as may prove practicable.

That is all I can say. I cannot analyze or interpret my powers or my character. They must appear in what I say and do. It would be affectation to attempt to interpret my motives. I try to purge them of selfish elements,—it can be known only when I am dead whether I have succeeded or not.

You have been very generous to write me as you did. I remember with pleasure that I have met you; I know and honor your brother; everything I have heard about you has excited my admiration and confidence. I am sincerely obliged to you.

Again apologizing for my apparent neglect of your gracious letter,   Sincerely yours,   Woodrow Wilson[1]

TLS (Connecticut Valley Historical Museum).
[1] There is a WWsh draft of this letter in the Governors' Files, Nj.

To Walter Hines Page

My dear Page: [Sea Girt, N. J.] August 21, 1911

Your letter of the sixteenth of July has been lying a month unanswered, chiefly because I found my mind quite at sea about the matter it discusses. I now reply, not only because there is a momentary lull in my engagements, but because I am ashamed to keep you waiting any longer not, I am sorry to say, because my thoughts have put in from sea and effected a landing. I wonder if you would be generous enough to have a talk about the matter of the general concentration of effort with Mr. McAdoo. I have found him very sagacious and very wide-awake, and I should think that you two could get together in your thinking very quickly.

My instinct, of course, is against having a real political campaign manager but by mind is always to let.

I need not tell you how it warms my heart to have you constantly thinking of me as you do.

Cordially and faithfully yours,   Woodrow Wilson

TLS (W. H. Page Papers, MH).

To Thomas Bell Love

My dear Mr. Love: [Sea Girt, N. J.] August 21, 1911.

Allow me to acknowledge the receipt of your letter of August sixteenth and to thank you for the detailed information given with regard to the gentlemen who have accepted leading places in the organization of the Woodrow Wilson State Democratic League of Texas. This information not only encourages me but will be of the greatest use to me. It is most gratifying that men of such calibre should take part in this movement.

I shall take pleasure in asking Mr. Stockbridge, in New York, to send you such extracts from my speeches as bear on the tariff.

I have received many cordial letters from Paris urging me to visit the City on the occasion of my coming to Texas; but, unhappily, I have been obliged to say the same thing in reply to all of them. I am, as a matter of fact, doing a somewhat questionable thing in coming to Texas at all in October because that is the heart of our annual campaign to elect members of the Legislature. I feel in conscience bound, therefore, to make the trip as brief as possible. I shall be obliged to be there only long enough to fill the engagements I have already made in Dallas, hurrying back at the earliest possible hour. I wish sincerely that it were otherwise.

I read with the greatest interest the last paragraph of your interesting letter. From all I have known of you, it is certainly characteristic that you should feel as you do about the endeavors you are making to promote my candidacy. The delightful thing about it is that you should consider that particular effort a service of the country.

If you think that it would be best for me to write short letters of appreciation to the gentlemen you have named in your letter, I hope that you will say so. I do not like to volunteer such letters unless they will be acceptable.

Cordially yours,   Woodrow Wilson

TLS (photostat in the T. B. Love Papers, Dallas Hist. Soc.).

From William Frank McCombs

My dear Governor: Jefferson, New Hampshire Aug 21st 1911

I think Mr. Wiley[1] has accepted the "faith" and from his assurances I believe the "Times" will be all right. He asked me to suggest to you a meeting in the latter part of September at a luncheon or dinner, of the Times editorial staff with you. He will arrange it at your convenience.

I think the suggestion is very valuable; if you agree, won't you let me know what time will suit you & I will communicate with him. We will both be in New York early next week.

I enclose an editorial from last Sundays "Times."[2]

Perhaps you have seen it, but I forward it, in the event you have not.

I have an appointment to see Mayor Fitzgerald on the way down.   Yours sincerely   Wm. F. McCombs

ALS (Governors' Files, Nj).

[1] Louis Wiley, business manager of the *New York Times*.

[2] "Some Talks with Mr. Roosevelt," *New York Times*, Aug. 20, 1911. It consisted largely of quotations and paraphrases of portions of an article of the same title by the English journalist, Sydney Brooks, in the London *Fortnightly Review*, xcvi (Aug. 1911), 247-57.

The portions of Brooks' article which the *New York Times* included were sensational in view of the fact that the quarrel between Roosevelt and Taft was not yet out in the open. Roosevelt said that he was deeply disappointed in Taft. He had chosen Taft for the presidency, not because he was the best man, but because he was the best man available. Taft had abandoned both the Roosevelt cabinet and policies, and his conduct in office had forced Roosevelt "to confess to a decided error of judgment in selecting him as his successor." He regarded Taft as a perplexing failure. However, he, Roosevelt, was still not to be reckoned an anti-Taft man.

Concerning Roosevelt's own future, Brooks asserted that the ex-President was not and did not expect to be a candidate for the presidency "in the ordinary sense of the word"; however, he might accept another nomination should popular opinion point "unmistakably and overwhelmingly" to him.

Brooks predicted that Wilson would be the Democratic candidate in 1912 and that Taft would again be the Republican nominee in spite of strong opposition from the progressive wing of the G.O.P. Then came the following comments: "It is typical of the complex upheaval that is going on in American politics that a Republican of Mr. Roosevelt's views, confronted with the alternative of supporting Mr. Taft or Mr. Wilson, would probably have great difficulty in deciding how to vote. On pretty nearly every important issue Mr. Roosevelt, I should judge, is in closer sympathy with Mr. Wilson than with Mr. Taft, and a comparison of the two men's records might, not unnaturally, induce him to think that, as an instrument for carrying out Progressive policies, Mr. Wilson would be far more effective and dependable than Mr. Taft. It does not necessarily follow that . . . Mr. Roosevelt will support the former rather than the latter. Party loyalty is a strong factor in his composition. . . . For an ex-President to break with his party would involve a tremendous wrench, and one that Mr. Roosevelt as yet hardly contemplates. Mr. Roosevelt's friends, however, being less committed by past responsibilities, are freer to do as they think best; and, in the event of Mr. Wilson being brought forward as the Democratic nominee, I am convinced that many thousands of Republicans, and among them those who were, and are, and will remain, Mr. Roosevelt's most ardent followers, would vote for him in preference to Mr. Taft, even though the ex-President himself were to sacrifice his personal predilections to his sense of party loyalty."

From Joseph R. Wilson, Jr.

My dear Brother: Nashville, Tenn August Twenty-second 1911.

Yesterday afternoon I was invited to a conference of gentlemen held in the office of Lee Douglass, a Princeton alumnus and a young attorney here, for the purpose of advancing the interests of Woodrow Wilson for the Presidential nominee. There were present Lee Douglass and his law partners, Messrs Norvell and Thruston, W. L. Granberry, Judge Ewing, Mr. Smith, managing editor of the Tennessean and American, a Mr. Scott, Mr. Elliott, Judge Matthews of one of the local courts, and myself.[1] We discussed ways and means for advancing your interests, much enthusiasm being shown, and the result was the election of Judge Matthews as chairman, Douglass as secretary and the appointment of an executive committee composed of Judge Matthews, Judge Ewing, Granberry and myself to meet subject to the call of the chairman the main purpose being the launching of a Woodrow Wilson Club when the proper time seems at hand. I urged the necessity for eliminating state factional politics, the issues here having nothing to do with the National campaign. I have found that this is a very delicate matter owing to the intense factional antagonism prevailing in this state.[2] I have taken the position that the people of the state, the Democrats, will get together if they are let alone and will give their hearty support to the party Presidential ticket, but that this cannot be accomplished if left to the self constituted leaders of either faction. The other gentlemen seem of like mind. I found a disposition on the part of one or two to stress the strength of the "Regular" Democracy, they taking the position that those in sympathy with this faction are in the majority. I hope you will not be too greatly influenced by any such contentions if they are made to you. The strength of the "Regular" faction certainly cannot be discounted, but certain it is that the Independent Democrats of the state are to be considered, to say the least of it, and should not be antagonized in the campaign by official and exclusive recognition of the "Regular" faction, so called. Both factions have state committees. Both factions have affilitated [affiliated] with elements in the Republican party. The leaders of both are contending continually for supremacy in the control of the state election machinery. Their fight is based *solely* on state issues, and should not be permitted to enter into the National campaign at all. Neither faction should be antagonized by any endorsement of the other. I hope such complications may be avoided in your interests.

It was decided yesterday afternoon to keep in close touch with Mr. McComb in New York securing such literature as he thinks suitable for distribution in Tennessee. It is hoped and proposed to ultimately form a state organization.

I understand the Harmon people have sent a man here and have opened head-quarters. What is being done there I do not yet know. They have been working quietly. I believe from talks with Democrats of both state factions from throughout the state, that Tennessee instructions can be secured for you if the campaign is carefully handled, but it will require much tact to prevent factionalism from creeping in when it comes to forming organizations in this state.

We agreed that the meeting yesterday was to be entirely confidential for the present.

Kate and Alice join me in great love.

Your aff. brother,   Joseph.

TLS (Governors' Files, Nj).

[1] Persons mentioned in this sentence who have not been identified heretofore were Gates Phillips Thruston, Jr.; Charles Stephenson Smith; and Thomas E. Matthews, judge of the First Circuit Court of Davidson County. The Editors have been unable to find any information about Scott and Elliott.

[2] This factionalism was a continuation of the bitter struggle between the prohibitionist and anti-prohibitionist wings of the Democratic party in Tennessee, which had culminated in the murder of Edward Ward Carmack on November 9, 1908, and the adoption of a statewide prohibition law in January 1909 (about these events, see J. R. Wilson, Jr., to WW, Nov. 5, 1908, n. 2, Vol. 18).

In 1909 and 1910, the factional struggle centered on the words and acts of Governor Malcolm Rice Patterson, an outspoken opponent of state-wide prohibition, who pardoned one of the men convicted of Carmack's murder, allegedly tampered with the judiciary in the Carmack case, and was generally believed to be less than vigorous in his enforcement of prohibition. The prohibition Democrats held their own state convention in May 1910, took the name Independent Democrats, and endorsed candidates for the state supreme court opposed to Patterson and the regular party organization. The Independent candidates won an impressive victory in the election in August. In an effort to unite the party, Patterson withdrew from the gubernatorial contest on September 11, 1910. However, the Independents, in their own convention on September 14, voted to support the Republican candidate, Ben Walter Hooper. The Regulars countered by nominating Robert Love Taylor, United States senator and a popular ex-governor. Hooper easily defeated Taylor in the November election, and the Independent Democrats won enough seats in the lower house of the legislature to hold the balance of power between the Republicans and the Regulars. As a result, the legislature was deadlocked by various obstructionist tactics of one faction or the other through much of a long session from January to June 1911. The only notable result of the session was the compromise choice of Luke Lea, an Independent, prohibitionist, and strong Wilson supporter, as United States senator. Despite repeated efforts to end the party split in late 1911 and in 1912, the factions remained irreconcilable on the prohibition issue, and in November 1912 Governor Hooper again defeated the Regular Democratic candidate with the aid of the Independents. See Eric Russell Lacy, "Tennessee Teetotalism: Social Forces and the Politics of Progressivism," *Tennessee Historical Quarterly*, xxiv (Fall 1965), 219-40; Arthur S. Link, "Democratic Politics and the Presidential Campaign of 1912 in Tennessee," pp. 107-30; and Paul E. Isaac, *Prohibition and Politics: Turbulent Decades in Tennessee, 1885-1920* (Knoxville, Tenn., 1965), pp. 170-205.

An Announcement

[Aug. 23, 1911]

GOVERNOR'S WIFE TO ACCOMPANY HIM

They Will Leave Sea Girt Tomorrow to Inspect State Institutions

Governor Wilson will start from Sea Girt tomorrow on his first inspection trip of some of the state institutions. The tour will consume an entire week, and Mrs. Wilson is to accompany her husband. The itinerary, which has been prepared by Mrs. C. B. Alexander, of Hoboken, who is a member of the executive committee of the New Jersey State Charities Aid Society, is as follows:

August 24—Leave Sea Girt and proceed to Vineland, where the Soldiers' Home, the Home for Feeble Minded Children and the Home for Feeble Minded Women will be inspected. The inspection will be continued on August 25.

August 26—To Jamesburg, to inspect the State Home for Delinquent Boys.

August 27—To the Tuberculosis Sanitarium at Glen Gardner, to be followed by an inspection of the proposed site for the State Reformatory for Women, and of roads which are under construction in the neighborhood under the supervision of Road Commissioner Colonel Edwin A. Stevens.

August 28—Inspection of the State Village for Epileptics at Skillman.

August 29—Inspection of the State Hospital for the Insane at Morris Plains.

August 30—Inspection of the State Reformatory at Rahway.

The trip will be made in Mrs. Alexander's auto, Mrs. Alexander herself being of the party.

Printed in the *Trenton Evening Times*, Aug. 23, 1911.

From John Garland Pollard

Dear Mr. Wilson: [Richmond, Va.] August 24th, 1911.

Resuming our correspondence concerning your nomination for the presidency, will say that since I last wrote, I have made a half dozen speeches in different parts of the State in the pending senatorial campaign.[1]

It may be gratifying to you to know that whenever your name is mentioned in public speech it brings forth great applause. The people have evidently been studying your course, and it meets with their hearty approval. I am greatly interested in the principles for which you stand and when you, or your friends, think

that the time has arrived for active work in your behalf, I stand
ready to render you service.

Very truly yours,   [John Garland Pollard]

CCL (J. G. Pollard Papers, ViW).
¹ About this campaign, see H. St. G. Tucker to WW, Dec. 29, 1910, Vol. 22.

From Burt. E. Brown¹

Dear Sir: Lawrence, Kansas, 8/24/11

The Kansas Democratic Club, the only organization of Democrats in the state of Kansas, closes it final meeting of the year
with a banquet. This last meeting night falls annually on Washington's birthday.

The Democrats of Kansas for a number of years have made
this occasion the big political event of the year. The constitution
of the club provides that the guest of honor shall be a speaker
from outside of the state. Wm. J. Bryan, Champ Clark, Gov.
Taylor, Joseph W. Folk, Senator James A. Reed² and others of
note at different times have been the principal speaker and honor
guest.

As President of the Kansas Democratic Club, I recently sent
out one hundred letters of inquiry to the prominent Democrats
in the state presenting the names of various prominent Democrats for our guest of honor at the banquet ne[x]t year.

The result was quite surprising and interesting from the fact
that every one of the one hundred returned an answer to my
inquiry, and every one expressed a preference. I will give you
the result of the hundred votes for principal speaker at our banquet next year: Wilson (yourself) 70, Harmon 24, Bryan 2,
Champ Clark 2, Gaynor 1, and Folk 1.

The Democracy of Kansas were never better organized, their
fighting strength has never been as effective as at present, and
with the proper kind of a start such as we propose to begin with
at the banquet next February, we are sure to put Kansas in the
Democratic column next year. The Republican party in this
state are split in twain, and the indications are that the factions
will get farther apart as the time for the next election draws
nearer.

I am a commercial traveler, and cover the entire state and
I am glad to say that you have many warm friends among the
Progressive Republicans of Kansas as well as among the Demo-
crats.

On behalf of the Democrats of the greatest state in the Union,

I extend to you a genuine democratic invitation to be our guest of honor at our banquet to be held on the evening of February 22nd, 1912, at Topeka Kansas.[3]

Choose your own subject, and let me know at your very earliest convenience whether you can be with us. With kindest regards, I am,   Very Truly Yours,   Burt. E. Brown

TLS (Governors' Files, Nj).
  [1] Kansas representative of the Robeson Cutlery Co. and the Rochester Stamping Co., both of Rochester, N. Y.
  [2] James Alexander Reed, Democratic senator from Missouri, 1911-29.
  [3] Wilson accepted; a news report of his speech is printed at Feb. 23, 1912, Vol. 24.

An Interview

                                              [Aug. 26, 1911]
WOODROW WILSON'S VIEWS

An Interview by
Henry Beach Needham

Lord Rosebery confessed that he wrote his monograph on Napoleon in order "to lay a literary ghost."[1] So with the reporter. When the opportunity offered to interview Woodrow Wilson, my first desire was to lay the ghost of a prejudice.

"Governor, I became prejudiced against you the first time I heard you speak."

Mr. Wilson, sitting in the chair-car on his return from Harrisburg, where he had arraigned the bi-partisan machine of Pennsylvania, looked the reporter in the eye, sizing him up, as it were, and waited unconcerned for what was to come.

"You were speaking at the University Club banquet in Washington, several years ago. It was Washington's Birthday."[2]

Mr. Wilson nodded. "I remember the occasion very well," he said.

"In your speech you referred to Washington's Farewell Address, and interposed this parenthetical remark: 'Which *he* did not *write*.' You did not explain who did write Washington's Farewell Address, nor did you indicate what authority you had for your statement. And it struck me at the time," I continued, "that the remark was pedantic, a gratuitous slap at the Father of our Country—and on his birthday, too."

  [1] Archibald Philip Primrose, 5th Earl of Rosebery, *Napoleon: The Last Phase* (London and New York, 1900). The quotation appears on page 222 of the English edition and on page 244 of the American edition.
  [2] See the news report printed at Feb. 23, 1906, Vol. 16. The remark quoted by Needham is not mentioned in this report.

The Governor of New Jersey smiled. "I remember how I kicked myself after I had made that statement," he said. "I can only account for it in this way—that most men, on some occasion or other, cannot resist the temptation to play the Smart Aleck."

Mr. Wilson might have resented what a type of public man would have called my "reportorial nerve." Or he might have lugged in Alexander Hamilton, ascribing to him the genius of Washington's great address. But it is worth our while, in seeking an estimate of the man, to consider that Mr. Wilson did neither. He was not resentful; he did not try to square himself. He made fun at his own expense, which mighty few statesmen have the good sense to do. From this it is fair to assume that, while he takes his work seriously, he does not take himself in deadly seriousness. And he meets every question, every issue, fairly and frankly—as this interview will show.

"Of all men in public life," he said, "the people hate worst the side-stepper." . . .

Governor Wilson is the public man with a programme. He believes that a party should have a programme, and he holds that the programme must be carried out. In his speech at Harrisburg he insisted that the National Democratic party have a definite programme. . . . To the surprise of some folk, Governor Wilson attacked the "money power." . . . I referred to this part of the Governor's speech, and asked him if he would go more into detail regarding this reform. "I have not given sufficient study to the question," he replied. "As it is the greatest question before the country to-day, it requires a great deal of consideration and involves wise and sound economic planning."

"But Mr. Aldrich and the lame ducks of the Monetary Commission have presented a brand of currency reform—"[3]

[3] For the origin and work of the National Monetary Commission, see n. 3 to the address printed at March 9, 1909, Vol. 19. With the investigations and research of the commission behind him, its chairman, Senator Nelson W. Aldrich of Rhode Island, was ready by January 1911 to submit for public comment and criticism a preliminary draft of what soon became known as the Aldrich Plan. On January 16, 1911, he released a pamphlet, *Suggested Plan for Monetary Legislation, Submitted to the National Monetary Commission by Hon. Nelson W. Aldrich* (Washington, 1911). It provided for the creation of one central bank for the United States called the Reserve Association of America (in later versions it was called the National Reserve Association of the United States) with a capital of approximately $300,000,000 and with fifteen branches, controlled by member banks, in various sections of the country. The Reserve Association would carry a portion of member banks' reserves, receive all deposits of the federal government, and issue currency based upon gold and commercial paper, currency which would be the liability of the Reserve Association and not of the government. The Reserve Association would be overseen by a governing board consisting of public officials and private members; however, it would be managed by a board of directors consisting mainly of bankers and businessmen.

This and the later versions of the Aldrich Plan were the result of the collec-

"I am afraid that any measure of that character bearing Mr. Aldrich's name," replied Mr. Wilson, "must have been drawn in the offices of the few men who, through the present system of concentrated capital, control the banking and industrial activities of the country."

In Washington I was talking with a Progressive Republican. He told me that, in certain events, he believed he would have to support Woodrow Wilson for President in 1912–"provided," he said, "I can be sure just where Wilson stands in regard to Federal regulation." This I repeated to Mr. Wilson in the course of our interview, with the idea–I confess it–that it might draw him out on the subject of Federal power. It didn't. If he was pleased at the thought that certain Progressive Republicans were casting eyes in his direction, he did not show it. He nodded in a polite but somewhat perfunctory manner, and said nothing. Then this cross-questioning:

"Before you entered public life, rightly or wrongly, you were regarded as a steadfast adherent of the antiquated doctrine of States' rights."

"I do not like the expression States' rights now," said the Governor. (He did not emphasize the "now," but he did not slur it.) "It implies a feeling of jealousy between State and Federal administration. I prefer the expression States' *functions*.

"The State and Federal Governments are in the same case, but not in the same boat. They must seek the same course under different captains and with different crews. They should act together, in harmony, to safeguard the people's rights. But it is inevitable that co-operation is more difficult than action under a common authority. Let me illustrate.

"There is a public utility corporation in New Jersey which has

tive work of Aldrich; Abram Piatt Andrew, Jr., Princeton 1893, Assistant Secretary of the Treasury; Henry Pomeroy Davison, a partner in J. P. Morgan & Co.; Frank Arthur Vanderlip, president of the National City Bank of New York; Paul Moritz Warburg, the leading American authority on central banking and a partner in Kuhn, Loeb & Co., an investment house of New York. The plan occasioned widespread discussion and criticism in both banking and political circles.

On October 14, 1911, Aldrich released a second version of his plan: *Suggested Plan for Monetary Legislation, Submitted to the National Monetary Commission by Hon. Nelson W. Aldrich*, 61st Cong., 3rd sess., Senate Doc. No. 784 (Washington, 1911). The most important additions in the new version were provisions for the admission of state bank and trust companies to membership in the Reserve Association and specific requirements for reserves to be held against deposits of various classes, both for member banks and for the association itself. Finally, on January 8, 1912, the National Monetary Commission submitted its *Report* (62nd Cong., 2nd sess., Senate Doc. No. 243 [Washington, 1912]), which included a final version of the plan recast in the form of a bill for congressional consideration. See also Nathaniel W. Stephenson, *Nelson W. Aldrich: A Leader in American Politics* (New York, 1930), pp. 373-410 *passim*.

a monopoly of the water in the northern part of the State.[4] This company determined to extend its mains to Staten Island and supply water to the residents of another State. Now it is necessary for us to conserve our water supply; some day the northern part of the State will be even more thickly populated, and the question of pure drinking-water may come to be serious. On the other hand, from the Government reports we know that there is an adequate supply of water on Staten Island itself. Therefore we are opposed to the plan of a private corporation to take the water out of New Jersey and divert it to the use of the people of New York State. And so we stepped in and forbade the water company to extend its mains to Staten Island.[5]

"Certain men—I can only conjecture who they were—brought influence to bear on the War Department to have the Federal Government insist that the mains be laid in order to provide water for the Government's forts on Staten Island, and the activity of the War Department in that matter will bear looking into. This was only a ruse, for it was expected that the Jersey corporation was to have the War Department's permission to sell water to private individuals throughout Staten Island.[6] We have fought, and we will continue to fight, what I may call Federal interference with State functions. There is no jealousy involved between New Jersey and the authorities at Washington. Of course the

[4] The Hudson County Water Co., with general offices in New York and a New Jersey office in Jersey City.

[5] In late 1904, it became known that the Hudson County Water Co. was extending its pipes from Bayonne, N. J., under the Kill Van Kull for the purpose of providing fresh water to residents of Staten Island, N. Y. Alerted to this fact by Governor Franklin Murphy just before the end of his term of office, the New Jersey legislature on May 11, 1905, enacted a law forbidding any individual or corporation to divert fresh water from any surface source in New Jersey to any other state (*Laws of New Jersey, 1905,* Chapter 238, pp. 461-62). Attorney General Robert Harris McCarter then applied to the New Jersey Court of Chancery for an injunction against the water company. The injunction was granted on August 22, 1905, and the case was carried to the New Jersey Court of Errors and Appeals and thence to the United States Supreme Court. The latter body upheld the constitutionality of the New Jersey statute, declaring that a state had the "power to insist that its natural advantages be unimpaired by its citizens" and that, in the exercise of this power, it could prohibit the diversion of its waters to points outside its boundaries (Hudson County Water Co. *v.* McCarter, Attorney General of the State of New Jersey, 209 U.S., 349).

The water company later sank wells to tap the underground flow of the watershed streams. At the urging of Governor John Franklin Fort, the legislature adopted a law expressly forbidding this form of the interstate diversion of water (*Laws of New Jersey, 1910,* Chapter 98, p. 148).

There is a brief, and dateless, account of this affair in William E. Sackett, *Modern Battles of Trenton* (2 vols., Trenton and New York, 1895-1914), II, 233-39.

[6] As Wilson suggested, another ploy of the Hudson County Water Co. was its attempt to convince the War Department that Jersey water was necessary to insure an adequate supply for the troops stationed on Staten Island. Ultimately, Secretary of War Henry L. Stimson decided that additional water was unnecessary. *Ibid.,* pp. 235, 237.

Federal Government may have all of our water it needs and desires *for its own purposes*, but we contend that its authority shall not be invoked merely for the purpose of aiding and abetting a private corporation to circumvent the law of the State, and thereby place in jeopardy the interests of a large number of the people of New Jersey."

"And the corollary of that proposition, Governor—suppose the rights of the people are not safeguarded by the State, suppose corporate regulation can be secured only by the Federal Government—what then?"

"I have no quarrel with that. Federal regulation is all right, indeed it is essential, in regard to those matters which belong within the Federal jurisdiction. But I object to anything that weakens the essential Government units. The States have their jurisdiction, and it is not going to further representative government to weaken State functions by loading on the Federal Government powers which do not properly belong to it. Nor is that necessary, in my opinion.

"Think how far we have progressed in a very short time. Think of the awakening in a State like California, where the Government, it was said, was completely dominated by the Southern Pacific Railway. Think of the awakening in New Jersey—the State known as 'the mother of trusts.' And, while it may seem like absurd optimism, I am willing to stake my reputation that Pennsylvania will soon follow the example of New Jersey and California, and take back its Government from boss domination and from the control of big business. One State after another will restore popular government and will resume its State functions. The people, who have been the excluded partner, are taking part in the business of running the Government. We are actually taking the liberty of assuming the direction of our own business."

The way Mr. Wilson said this, the enthusiasm with which he allied himself in the fight against what he calls "government of, by, and for the trusts," clearly indicated that he was in the fight to stay. Yet it seemed that something more might be said on the subject of State and Federal regulation, and so the point was pressed.

"When we discuss the powers of the States in our day," continued the Governor, "we are not reviving the old academic question of States' rights. We are beginning to look upon the rights of the States as we look upon the rights of individuals—not so much emphasizing the selfish and independent powers involved as the duties which are correlative to the rights. We now think of the right of the individual as an obligation to be just rather than as an opportunity to be selfish. Likewise, we now think of the rights of the States, not as their prerogative to serve their own interests without regard to the interests of the country as a whole, but rather as their opportunity to render service in the general development—in the readjustment of those relations, already unsatisfactory, which threaten to become dangerous both in the field of industry and in the field of politics.

"The Federal Government can go no further than the broad outlines of regulation. It can only sketch in broad outline the economic and political regulation which is necessary for the life of the country. The States must fill in the detail, providing the regulation which adjusts commercial enterprise to the daily life of the community. It is for the States to see to it that there is no essential antagonism between the use of wealth and the development of a wholesome life, that the gates of opportunity are not closed, that men are everywhere free to work, that communities are protected against disease, particular classes against the crushing burdens of certain kinds of labor, that the streams are utilized as the sources of power and refreshment, that the forests are conserved within their borders—"

"By 'their borders' you mean the borders of the State?"

The Governor nodded—"that the forests are conserved within their borders, that the resources which ought to be common are not monopolized and used exclusively for private benefit and profit.

"Of necessity, the States are the chief battle-ground of economic reform. It is the States which incorporate the great business undertakings that threaten to bulk larger than the States themselves in the power which they exercise. The whole problem of the regulation of public service corporations, for example, is a State problem except in so far as the arteries of inter-State commerce are directly concerned. For the daily convenience and freedom of our people, the control of trolley lines, gas companies, electric light and power companies is even more important than the control of great railways. And as the States act wisely or unwisely, courageously or hesitatingly, in this control, so will the life of the people of the States be clogged or cleared, assisted or impeded, and so will political and economic conditions be improved or rendered worse."

It was the Governor of New Jersey who was speaking, and it was natural that he should emphasize the governmental problems which are essentially the problems of the States. And perhaps Mr. Wilson is right in asserting that the proper regulation of the public utilities of a State mean more to the "daily convenience and freedom" of its people than does Federal regulation in the fields which are inter-State. But many people throughout the country seem inclined to draft Woodrow Wilson from the public service of his State and set him to work solving our pressing National problems. So it may be rather important to form some idea as to how he would advise Congress were he President of the United States. A few things about President Van Buren are still remembered, notably that a State cannot be "coerced."[7] Again the point of Federal regulation was pressed, with a specific question:

"Take the question of Conservation, Governor—is that a State or a National question?"

"It is both," answered Governor Wilson, promptly. "But it is more a question for the State than for the Federal Government. The Federal Government can act in the matter only in so far as it still controls lands and forests and mines and watercourses. The great bulk of the land of the continent and of America's resources passed out of Federal control long ago. It is the States which must determine by their policy whether the natural resources of the country are to be exhausted or renewed, wasted or conserved, and the matter will require all the more careful statesmanship and planning because it will touch life very intimately at many points."

Still Mr. Wilson was not specific enough to satisfy the inquisitive reporter; so more questions:

"Suppose a river had its source in New Jersey, flowed into New York, and double-tracked into Pennsylvania, how about the regulation of its water powers?"

"Assuming that it is a navigable stream," replied the Governor, "regulation rests with the Federal Government; is within the authority of the War Department. But if it is not navigable, New Jersey would have to conserve the water powers within its own borders, likewise New York and Pennsylvania."

Mr. Wilson practiced law before he became a college professor. He is an excellent lawyer to-day.

"Take the Government forests; they lie within the borders of different States. Do you favor turning these forests over to State administration—practically to State control?"

"As the land lies within the borders of the State, I favor co-operation between State and Federal authority. The details of the regulation of our National forests I have not sufficiently studied to determine the problem of practical administration."

"You referred to the 'great business undertakings that threaten

[7] Needham obviously should have said President James Buchanan.

to bulk larger than the States themselves.' What then? Mr. Gary, of the Steel Trust, says that he favors Federal regulation, and would have the Government fix prices."[8]

"Federal license, or Federal incorporation"—said Governor Wilson in a disparaging tone, and then he shook his head. "The big corporations owe their existence to the laws of the States."

"And their license?"

"To the inadequacy of State laws or their non-enforcement," replied the Governor; "and the States ought to provide regulation and control."

"But if the States fail?"

"The States, many of them, are doing so much now that I don't believe they will fail. I could not believe that and believe so intensely as I do in the restoration of popular government. I am opposed to the addition of greater scope to the Central Government at the expense of the atrophy of the parts of the body politic.

"This is one of the reasons, the main reason, why I have so heartily advocated the so-called commission form of municipal government—another of our New Jersey reforms. What the people demand is a businesslike, non-partisan, economical, efficient government. Government is, of necessity, in many of its parts, a technical and complicated thing. We shall not be safe merely by having experts. We shall be safe only when we have experts who are also capable of being leaders."

A Federalist or a States' rights man? Woodrow Wilson is neither. He does not fear Federal regulation, but he believes that Federal control and regulation of great corporations other than railways is "not sufficient." The States must lend a hand. However, this does not mean that he may not come to believe in National incorporation or Federal licensing of industrial corporations. He is not afraid of changing his mind, and the fact that his position regarding a governmental policy to-day is diametrically

---

[8] Gary made this widely quoted statement in his testimony before the Stanley Committee on June 2, 1911. Gary began by remarking, "I believe we must come to enforce publicity and governmental control." When asked if he meant governmental control of prices, he replied: "I do; even as to prices, and, so far as I am concerned, speaking for our Company, so far as I have the right, I would be very glad if we knew exactly where we stand, if we could be freed from danger, trouble, and criticism by the public, and if we had some place where we could go, to a responsible governmental authority, and say to them, 'Here are our facts and figures, here is our property, here our cost of production; now you tell us what we have the right to do and what prices we have the right to charge.' I know that is a very extreme view . . . but . . . I believe it is the necessary thing, and it seems to me corporations have no right to disregard these public questions and these public interests." In response to further questions, Gary made it clear that he believed that the national government had the power to fix prices in interstate commerce. *Hearings before the Committee on Investigation of United States Steel Corporation*, I, 79-80.

opposed to his position when he was merely a political writer does not cause him a particle of uneasiness. He smiles, and meets the charge of inconsistency squarely.

"You have certainly shown that you are not afraid to change your mind, Governor."

"I hope I have grown," he replied. . . .

"The correspondents are saying in Washington, 'Wilson could be elected—but he can't be nominated.'"

"That is pretty near right," said the Governor, unwittingly. "I refer, of course, to the difficulty of nominating Wilson," he hastened to reply by way of correction. And he was thinking only of that.

"I certainly have not the audacity to seek the nomination," he continued, "but no man is big enough to refuse it. And to seek the nomination would be a waste of energy. The machine organizations of both parties are opposed to Progressive candidates. Public opinion alone can force the selection of a Progressive. If the organizations are determined to nominate a man of their own kidney, why, one is dished. And, if public opinion doesn't grow and develop, one is dished, anyway."

Governor Wilson aspires to the Presidency. Whether or not he is seeking the nomination in the practical way—forming alliances in this State and that, and scheming through his friends and supporters to corral delegates to the National Democratic Convention—I do not know. I didn't ask him. But he is surely seeking the nomination in the right way—in the twentieth-century, "back to the people" method. Wilson is the "1911 model" candidate. . . .

Printed in the New York *Outlook*, xcviii (Aug. 26, 1911), 939-51.

A News Report

[Aug. 26, 1911]

WILSON PARTY AT JAMESBURG TODAY

Main Object of Tour of Institutions is to Plan Better Way to Spend Money

VINELAND, N. J., Aug. 26.—With Mrs. Woodrow Wilson accompanying him and his daughter, Miss Jessie Woodrow Wilson, much interested in settlement work, as one of the inspecting party, Governor Wilson yesterday completed his survey of Vineland's three great institutions. The Governor's party were at the State Home for Women on Thursday, when they witnessed an opera rendered by the feeble-minded inmates. Yesterday morning a visit was paid to the State Home for Soldiers, Sailors or Marines and Their Wives, and in the afternoon inspected the famous Training School for Feeble-Minded Children.

Governor Wilson's present inspection of the state institutions also has no precedent, but Mrs. Wilson's presence on the trip is altogether such an exceptional thing that she was asked about it.

"I am getting interested, that is all," was her quiet reply.

Mrs. Wilson wanted to see about these things. They say that in Princeton, when Woodrow Wilson was president of the university, she was a mother to every college boy, and it seems that her motherliness is extending, as her husband's life has broadened, to these bigger things. For assuredly no one will spend even one-half an hour in the Vineland Training School for Feebleminded Children without realizing what a big problem is there presented, and, what is more, without thinking that sooner or later the institution is going to solve the problem.

"My husband's life has changed from that of a quiet university president to that of the head of a great commonwealth," says Mrs. Wilson, "and why should not mine change along the same lines? No one knows what good I might be able to do or what help I could give him by having broad enough knowledge of the big questions of charities and correction with which he will have to deal, especially where they relate to women and children. My family cares have diminished, and there is a bigger family awaiting me."

It is said that a primary purpose of Governor Wilson's tour of the charitable and correctional institutions of the state just begun, is to find some way to plan the use of the state's money in this direction better than has hitherto been done. Mrs. Wilson's determination to go along grew out of what she had heard through Mrs. C. B. Alexander, and her desire to help as other women are helping.

"It is not only just an experience, it is seeing things that I ought to see," she commented, after the inspections yesterday. "Thus far I have seen things that have been wonderful, and have seen that such good is being done that I cannot help but be delighted."

One soon comes to think, after watching Mrs. Wilson in her role of "inspector," that she is being guided in what she is doing by strong common sense and her characteristic broad motherhood for every one, especially unfortunates. She did not care to know about trifles, but the essentials interested her exceedingly.

Today the Governor and Mrs. Wilson, Miss Wilson, Mrs. Alexander and the rest left by automobile for the Jamesburg State Home for Boys, and the tour will be continued through the state until the middle of next week.

Printed in the *Trenton Evening Times*, Aug. 26, 1911.

To Thomas Bell Love

My dear Mr. Love: [Sea Girt, N. J.] September 1, 1911.

Thank you for your letter of August twenty-eighth. I shall try at once to have the data sent to you that you wish, along with copies of the laws passed by our Legislature in obedience to our p[l]atform demands.

It is certainly most gratifying to learn of the surprising progress that sentiment for me is making in Texas.

Cordially and faithfully yours,   Woodrow Wilson

TLS (photostat in the T. B. Love Papers, Dallas Hist. Soc.).

To Robert Garrett

My dear Mr. Garrett: [Sea Girt, N. J.] September 5, 1911.

I thank you for your letter of August thirtieth.[1]

I have heard from several quarters of the existence of such a letter as you describe, from Mr. Cleveland.[2] It of course must have grown out of the feeling established in Mr. Cleveland's mind by Andrew West in the later months of Mr. Cleveland's life. I have no doubt that my Princeton enemies will use it at some time, but I think they will be very slow to do so, because it will necessarily bring out from me a statement of facts which will leave them in a sorry plight. I shall not hesitate to state the case very explicitly, if they provoke the statement. I hope that your judgment jumps with mine that that would be justifiable.

I think that the question of the initiative and referendum is a special question, so far as the South is concerned. The mixed character of the electorate in respect of the races stand there as a very serious bar to their adoption. I have never regarded them as of universal application.

But I have been convinced by the experience of Oregon that they can be effectively used and that their use brings out every discriminating vote on the part of the people. I am inclined to think that our present impression that the people would not exercise that sort of right in a way that would be fortunate, rests upon the fact that they have never been tested. They have been given a very subordinate part in affairs, because they have been ruled in recent years wholly under the guidance of machines.

I am going to ask some friends in New York, who have made a collection of my speeches, to send you such passages as they have on this subject.

Please never think that any letter from you will be bothersome. I value your friendship very deeply indeed.

Cordially and faithfully yours,   Woodrow Wilson

TLS (Selected Corr. of R. Garrett, NjP).
[1] It is missing.
[2] He referred to a letter, allegedly written in the heat of the graduate college controversy, by Grover Cleveland to Henry van Dyke, saying that Wilson was a man of "ungovernable temper" and accusing him of a "lack of intellectual integrity." See H. B. Thompson to C. H. Dodge, April 15, 1910, n. 4, Vol. 20. There will be many references to and documents about the alleged Cleveland letter in this volume and the next.

From Henry Watterson

My dear Governor Wilson: Louisville, Ky., Sept. 5, 1911

I enclose two clippings which will show you the line that I am taking. My aim is to identify you with the Tilden personality and situation of 35 years ago.[1] If we succeed in this the battle is won.

I am of course making love to Champ Clark, who is not only an old and close friend, but a Kentuckian, who will be useful in the last equation.

Robert and Hattie[2] spent two days with us on their way home, and of course we had lots of talk.   Your Friend   H.W.

TLS (Governors' Files, Nj).
[1] The enclosures are missing, but they were editorials in the Louisville *Courier-Journal* of July 13 and Sept. 5, 1911. The former is described in WW to H. Watterson, July 14, 1911, n. 1. In the latter, " 'Old Times Come Again,' " Watterson said that, as it had been in 1876, the primary issue of the day was reform, particularly tariff reform, and he quoted extensively from the Democratic platform of 1876 to prove his point. Predicting that the rallying cry of the Democratic party in 1912 would be, as it had been in 1876, "A Tariff for Revenue Only," he added: "Taft stands where Hayes stood thirty-five years ago. Shall it be Woodrow Wilson who stands where Tilden stood?"
[2] That is, Robert Ewing and Harriet Hoyt Ewing of Nashville, Tenn. Mrs. Watterson, Rebecca, was Ewing's sister.

From Burton Jesse Hendrick[1]

My dear sir: New York. September fifth 1911.

I enclose a letter from my friend, Mr. McAdoo, which explains itself.[2] I hope that you will be able to arrange for me to see you at an early day. McClure's Magazine would like very much to go into your career in great detail, and in this we should be happy to have your co-operation.[3]

Could you kindly drop me a line letting me know whether you will be able to talk matters over with me, and if so, when and where I could most conveniently see you?

Very sincerely yours,   Burton J. Hendrick.

TLS (Governors' Files, Nj).
  [1] Editor of the New Haven *Morning News*, 1896-98; staff writer for the New York *Evening Post*, 1899-1905; staff writer for *McClure's Magazine* since 1905.
  [2] It is missing.
  [3] Wilson did cooperate. The result was Burton J. Hendrick, "Woodrow Wilson: Political Leader," *McClure's Magazine*, xxxviii (Dec. 1911), 217-31.

A News Report

[Sept. 7, 1911]

GOVERNOR'S VIEWS ON STATE WARDS

The overcrowded condition of many of the penal and charitable institutions of the State was the fact that most impressed itself upon Governor Wilson during his recent tour of inspection, he says. Another thing that impressed him was that there is no law providing for a general redistribution of inmates when such a course becomes desirable.

In speaking of his trip through the State the Governor said that he was generally pleased with the manner in which the asylums, prisons and homes in which the wards of the State are housed, are managed. As the result of his observations he will have some suggestions to make, he said, but his ideas will not be made known until he has gone deeper into the situation.

Speaking of the conditions at the State Hospital at Morris Plains, the Go[v]ernor said he thought prompt action should be taken to eliminate the overcrowding. He found that the attic is being used to house patients and that cots are placed in all of the halls, thus greatly interfering with the work at the hospital.

To a somewhat lesser extent similar overcrowding exists in a number of the institutions visited by the Governor. These conditions have been pointed out from time to time in the annual reports of the institutions, but as yet no effective remedy has been provided by the succeeding Legislatures to whose attention they have been brought.

The Governor's study of the personnel of the inmates of some of the institutions convinced him that there was much sound reason in the views recently expressed by Commissioner George B. Wight,[1] of the Department of Charities and Corrections, that many transfers would be desirable. For example, the Governor said, at the Rahway Reformatory he found a number of boys who should, without doubt, be in the home for the feeble-minded.

In other penal institutions the Governor found many insane convicts who should be housed in an asylum if proper provisions were made for that purpose. It is probable that questions of this character will be considered by the Governor in his next message to the Legislature.[2]

Printed in the Trenton *True American*, Sept. 7, 1911; two editorial headings omitted.

[1] The Rev. Dr. George Wight, Methodist minister, former superintendent of the public schools of Atlantic County, and Commissioner of Charities and Corrections, 1905-12.

[2] In his second Annual Message to the New Jersey legislature (printed at Jan. 9, 1912, Vol. 24), Wilson called for a coordinated and comprehensive system of charities and correction and recommended the granting of greater authority to the commissioner and a small advisory board.

To Bruce Barton[1]

My dear Mr. Barton: [Sea Girt, N. J.] September 7, 1911.

I greatly regret that absence from home has prevented my having the pleasure of seeing and talking with you. Now that I am back, engagements fill every hour, as you may easily imagine.

I have always had an almost unconquerable inclincation [disinclination] to talk about the deep things that underly motives and conduct. So far as I am concerned, I would be a very unsatisfactory man to interview. I am sure you or no one else would know on which side I am.

Cordially yours,   Woodrow Wilson

TLS (de Coppet Coll., NjP).

[1] Amherst College 1907; managing editor, the Chicago *Home Herald*, 1907-1909; at this time editor of the New York *Housekeeper*.

An Address at the Dedication of a Synagogue[1] in Newark, New Jersey

[Sept. 7, 1911]

I am very glad to find myself in this place. I have derived both pleasure and instruction from the solemn exercises this evening. I count myself fortunate that some instinct suggested to me the appropriate subject. Those who invited me here were generous enough not to suggest what I should speak about, and yet, as if by some intimation of what was to be said here by others, I chose to speak of this as of a House of Peace.

[1] Of the Congregation Oheb Shalom.

I do not wish to speak of peace in the ordinary sense—as if I were to discuss peace as referring to the disarmament of the nations, the accom[m]odation of morals among men, among people, but I wish, if possible, to lay before you a suggestive analysis of what is involved in the conception of peace.

I suppose that every place dedicated to the worship of God should be a place of light, and comfort, and healing, and I suppose that the essential conception of peace is that it should involve perfect accommodation—the accommodation of the spirit, the accommodation of the purpose, the accommodation of the light to the circumstances that surround us and the forces which govern the world, particularly those forces which proceed from the law and providence of God.

I do not see how any ignorant person can achieve peace. I do not mean that learning is necessary to peace, but that a conception of life is necessary to peace—a perception of its significance, a perception of the relation of the individual to the interests of his own soul and to the interests of the persons about him.

The first condition precedent to peace is enlightenment. How shall a man find his way in the dark? How shall a nation know righteousness unless it have a standard? How shall any man find peace if he search like one who does not know what he seeks? You do not find peace in the mere pursuit of pleasure or in the mere pursuit of wealth, or in the mere pursuit of notoriety, for those things are not standardized.

What constitutes pleasure? There is no satisfaction in pleasure for its own sake. Pleasure is a realization that no man knows the value and delight of who does not know the strain of work and the constant burden of anxiety. Pleasure is simply a release of the spirit to play after the day's work, and business is very much more interesting than pleasure. The things you organize are very much more interesting than the things you do in a debonair spirit of a holiday. You know that you are alive—that all the pulses of life beat joyously in you when you know you are accomplishing something. You never accomplish anything by pleasure. You make yourself fit for accomplishment by the right sort of pleasure, but that is not what you are after. You refresh yourself by a swim in the sea, but it is not your object of life to swim at sea. You wish to come out of the waves with increasing vigor, for something in particular. And so you do not know and cannot know what peace is until you know what you have purposed to accommodate your life to. You are seeking about without purpose if you are seeking peace without a knowledge of the right road.

Now, the first guide to the right road is the conception of justice. It is in vain to seek peace so long as justice is not done. No man can be at peace with himself who does not do justice to his neighbor; no man can be at peace with society, if society does not do him justice. The whole progress of liberty has been a revolt against injustice; it has been an effort to see that the scales of fairness and equity were duly impartial as between man and man; it has been a revolt of the human spirit against oppression and suppression.

Man says, "I was born in the image of God and I insist upon the dignities and regal privileges which come from such an image. I will have no man put shackles upon my spirit," and so the fundamental conception of all peace is justice. You cannot come to an agreement about any undertaking unless you can show of it that the terms constitute a square deal, and just so long as men purpose in, politics or anything else, to take advantage of their fellow-men instead of to serve them, there can be no peace, and for my part I am ready to say this: that as against injustice, I consider myself the servant of peace by declaring war. Let no man say that the man who works for justice works to upset anything when he works to establish anything. In order that there may be a workable basis to a conceivable purpose in life, there cannot be any traceable pattern unless the hand of God is the hand of justice.

And then in the next place one of the bases of peace is Good Will. By good will I do not mean mere sentiment. I have never found any mere impulsive sentiment a good working instrument of life. I have to admit I like some men who don't deserve to have anybody like them. I cannot control the instinctive impulses which draw me to this man and make this other repulsive. My mere likes and dislikes are no bases for my life or action. No matter how taking such the man is I ought not to be his companion. I may find his companionship ever so enjoyable and diverting, but that cannot be the law of life. By good will, as I conceive it, is meant a voluntary, a cheerful, a sympathetic accommodation of your life to the life of the people about you. It does not mean you are to be fair to the man you like and ignore the principle of fairness to the man you don't like. That is not good will. That is not the good will which can bring peace into the world, because good will that brings peace into the world must be universal, must be impartial, it must ignore that most incalculable of all things, namely, personal tastes and preferences. It is an opening of the heart to look into the eyes of every man and recognize in him a kindred spirit. It is the instinct by which we accommodate ourselves by generous impulse to the assistance of those who need us—to the defense of those who need defense.

And there is another element in peace and that is truth. Some men and some nations try to organize their life upon a basis of peace when they are not willing to digest the facts of life. If you want to have peace, you must, first of all, have a stomach for the [f]acts. You cannot go about supposing life is all rose color and you cannot go about supposing life is all solemn[n]ess. You must not go about supposing men will injure you if you let them follow their best instincts. You must not go about supposing that if you let them have their way they will follow their worst in-stincts. You must take men as they are and work in the common clay just as you know a potter works in the physical clay. You must try to make the thing do what it won't do. You must not become a pessimist if it does not do what you want it to do and you must not be a foolish optimist. You must expand your course upon the expectation that ideals cannot be reached in a single generation and yet you must not believe that those ideals can never be reached.

Look at the splendid progress of mankind. Look at the gra-cious providence of God which has brought more and more light unto the world, more and more judgment, more and more recog-nition of the rights of all races of people. The greatest brother-hood of mankind has made great strides within the short reaches of recorded history and there is approaching upon our modern times a sort of expectation of still greater days to come, when every man may lift his eyes with hope to the horizon, when there has come a day of peace and righteousness—when the nations shall be glad in the presence of God. This, it seems to me, is the message of the meaning of peace.

How shall people live unless a man love his fellow-men, un-less there is justice, unless a man sees that the road before him is a certainty, and how shall a people be lifted from one love to another in that world-over struggle for righteousness?

I pray with you that this house may indeed be a House of God, and as a House of God a place and a foundation of Peace.

FPS T transcript (WP, DLC), with corrections from the partial text in the *Newark Evening News*, Sept. 8, 1911.

From Thomas Bell Love, with Enclosure

Dear Governor Wilson: Dallas, Texas, September 7th, 1911.

I enclose you letter which I have just received from Mr. W. F. Kelly, Secretary of the Woodrow Wilson Club at Galveston.

I am sending you this because I want to know if there is any possible foundation in fact for the matter referred to in the letter which I have underscored, in order that I may know how to best handle it if I should hear very much of it.

I have advised Mr. Kelly with reference to the other matters referred to in the letter. Things are moving along nicely, and I am sure our prospects are constantly improving.

With kind regards, I am

Very truly yours,   Thomas B. Love.

TCL (T. B. Love Papers, Dallas Hist. Soc.).

E N C L O S U R E

W. Frank Kelly to Thomas Bell Love

Dear Sir: Galveston, Texas. Sept/6/11.

We have organized a Woodrow Wilson Club, in this community with several hundred members, and are preparing to make an active campaign in his behalf. Yesterday however, I solicited an old confederate soldier, and a Viriginian, and one who claims to be a relative of George Washington, to become a member, and he declined upon the ground that Mr. Wilson had at some time in the past stated something rather uncomplimentary about George Washington, and for a further reason that Mr. Wilson had advacated and was in favor of negroes and whites attending the same schools. This may give us a clew as to some of the propositions we will have to meet.

Will you at as early a date as possible let me know what foundation in truth there is for this statement, especially the latter. At the same time you might advise me with respect to his position in regard to the demand of Union Labor, this being quite a Labor stronghold.

We are also going to try and get him to visit Galveston while he is in Texas, this fall. Would like to have your assistance along this line.   Yours truly,   W. F. Kelly

TLS (Governors' Files, Nj).

From William Frank McCombs

My dear Governor: New York September 7, 1911.

I have your letter of yesterday.[1] I am very glad indeed to have the suggestions which you make. They will serve as a guide to me in dealing with him. I think it will be very easy to arrange an understanding such as you suggest. I tried to arrange a conference this afternoon, but was unable to do so.

I had the clippings of all the papers followed very carefully to see if any mention was made of the statement. No paper has adverted to it and I don't believe any one will, for it was given by Mr. Kinkead to the Newark Evening News exclusively.[2] I did my best after the fact was given to this paper to turn the edge of it by talking to the reporter about something else, so as to diminish its importance.[3]

In the very large mail that I have received during the past few days I have a perfectly splendid letter from Judge Ben Lindsey of Denver, in which he says that he wishes very much to come out for you strongly and to bend every effort in your behalf. He says that several months ago he committed himself in a way to Folk, but that he is going to write Folk and ask him to release him, so as to be free to work for you. Judge Lindsey would be a very valuable accession because of the great respect in which he is held in this country. I am going to suggest to him that he issue a public statement in your behalf, and that he undertake to write a number of articles, setting forth the reasons why he supports you.[4]

Mr. [Winthrop M.] Daniels and the counsel for the Utilities Commission came in to see me yesterday and we discussed the matters previously adverted to at considerable length. I will take the liberty tomorrow of sending to you certain suggestions along this line. Of course I do not wish to seem to be pushing myself into the Commission's business, but I have some suggestions which I will throw out for what they are worth.

Jerry Sullivan, who is said to be the strongest Democrat in Iowa, is to be in New York in a few days. He is the gentleman, you will recall, whom General Clarkson thought it of the highest importance that you should see, and it is at General Clarkson's instance that he has come on to see you. The General communicated with me this afternoon with reference to the matter and I told him I would immediately write you and find out at what times it would be convenient for you to see Mr. Sullivan. If you will let me know I will arrange it.

Yours sincerely,   Wm. F. McCombs

TLS (Governors' Files, Nj).

¹ It is missing.

² Eugene F. Kinkead who, in a statement published in the *Newark Evening News*, Sept. 4, 1911, said that he and William Hughes would soon begin a tour of Illinois, Minnesota, Michigan, and other states in the Middle West for the purpose of organizing Wilson supporters in that region.

³ In the same news story, McCombs was quoted as saying that the tour was

being undertaken in response to requests from every state in the Union; that he had no doubt that Wilson had enough strength to be nominated on the first ballot at the Democratic national convention in 1912; that standpat Republicans were calling Wilson a radical because he would be the strongest Democratic candidate; and that the Governor was working to establish truly representative government.

4 Lindsey never wrote the articles. He supported Theodore Roosevelt in 1912.

From Burton Jesse Hendrick

Dear Governor Wilson: New York. September seventh 1911.

I thank you for your kind letter. I shall be at your house at half-past eight next Wednesday evening unless I hear from you before that date.

> Very sincerely yours,   Burton J. Hendrick.

TLS (Governors' Files, Nj).

From William Edward Dodd[1]

Dear Sir,   [Chicago] Sept. 9. 1911

It may be impossible under existing conditions in the United States to elect such a man as you are to the presidency but I certainly hope that it is not and that you may be the one to lead us out of the wilderness. If I only had any influence I should be glad to do anything that I could to bring about that result. This is a rock-ribbed Republican ward in the city of Chicago; but Merriam carried it by overwhelming majorities twice recently[2] and he told me not long ago that if the Democrats put up Wilson the Republican progressives have "no kick" and that they will seek only to get hold of the machinery of the regular organization in order to be ready for a future contingency (when the Democrats, as they must if in office, become stand pat). He is the strongest man in Chicago on his own footing, i.e. without the aid of any "interest" and I think he represents a widespread opinion.

But can we secure control of the Democratic convention next time when there is so much intrigue, so much political strength in favor of a man whose convictions on great questions are unknown or hostile to those you entertain. I was in Virginia in July and saw something of the campaign against Martin & Swanson, counterparts of James Smith & Co in New Jersey; you have many strong friends in Virginia, but the regulars must be whipped into line else they will go bag and baggage for Harmon. Ex-Governor Montague, the elder Meredith,[3] Jones and Glass are for you in outspoken way. The problem of your friends is to win some of the machine men. If [Edwin A.] Alderman can not do this, no one can; but he is not a real progressive. Pardon such a letter; my excuse is my interest and my admiration for the Governor of New Jersey   Yours   Wm. E. Dodd

ALS (Governors' Files, Nj).

[1] Professor of American History at the University of Chicago since 1908.

[2] Charles Edward Merriam, Professor of Political Science, University of Chicago, alderman from the seventh ward, 1909-11.

[3] Charles Vivian Meredith, Richmond lawyer; city attorney, 1885-98; frequently a delegate to state and national Democratic conventions. He was also a member of the Virginia constitutional convention, 1901-1902.

An Interview

[Sept. 11, 1911]

Wilson on America's Money Trust

Sea Girt, N. J., Sept. 10.—"If the present trend of events by which the money power of the country is rapidly falling into the hands of a few is not changed, the economic health of the Nation is doomed."

With this forceful statement, Governor Woodrow Wilson, of New Jersey, reiterated the assertion that a money trust exists in the United States more pernicious in effect than any other monopoly.

"It is not an easy task to deal with this concentration of money and industrial capital. It must be undertaken with the greatest conservation and carried out with a courage that will brook no interference from politics.

"The men who can be of most value in changing the conditions of which complaint is made are those who have the most intimate knowledge of the country. Unfortunately, the majority of these men are themselves a part of the so-called money trust.

"It must be conceded that the small banker, the small merchant and the small manufacturer have as much right to transact business and receive a fair profit therefrom as the big financial institutions and industrial trusts.

"I am told that now it is next to impossible for the small banks to get a share in the big deals necessarily controlled by the big banks, simply because the big fellows have so much money they do not need outside assistance and save all the profits for themselves.

"I am now seeking expert advice on the Aldrich bill, which I understand contains a provision allowing National banks to establish and maintain branches.

"At a glance this seems to be a move to further concentrate the money power, as it will stifle the small banks which have no wealthy parent institution to carry them through hard times. If this bill is only what it appears to be, I will certainly oppose it in my public utterances." . . .

Printed in the Trenton *True American*, Sept. 11, 1911; some editorial headings omitted.

To John Garland Pollard

My dear Mr. Pollard: [Sea Girt, N. J.] September 11, 1911.

I would have long ago acknowledged your kind letter of August twenty-fourth had I not been absent from home on a tour of the public institutions of the State. Its contents fill me with pleasure and pride. There is no place I should like to be approved of more than in Virginia.

Cordially yours,   Woodrow Wilson

TLS (J. G. Pollard Papers, ViW).

From Nelson Burr Gaskill[1]

Dear Governor Wilson: Atlantic City, N. J. Sept 11. 1911.

You stirred my pulses so thoroughly tonight that before I go to sleep, I must give vent. It was a splendid act to talk to that particular audience in that particular strain.[2] They need some idealism and most of all, some moral courage. You coined a phrase there that should echo and re echo in the being of every man, dogs excepted, in that room. "Put your thinking on a war footing." That is fine.

The men in that room have made Atlantic City what it is because they did nothing to prevent it, and with a few exceptions, are but "setting" even now. "The conscience of a coward," I think they will want to forget that!

And the encouragement of it to me. You have made easy what was assuming a rather awe inspiring aspect. So you have thanks as well as cheers. The thanks could not come out till now but the cheers could hardly be kept in decorous bounds at the time.

You have given me a pleasant and a helpful memory.

Sincerely yours,   Nelson B. Gaskill.

ALS (Governors' Files, Nj).
  [1] Princeton 1896, assistant attorney general of New Jersey, 1906-14.
  [2] A news report of Wilson's address is printed at Sept. 12, 1911.

From Daniel Moreau Barringer

Personal

My dear Woodrow,   Philadelphia, Pa. September 11, 1911.

No doubt your eye fell upon the enclosed.[1] If not I think that it may be interesting reading for you. I know Untermyer and know him to be an exceedingly astute, shrewd lawyer. How sincere he is or whether his so-called statement is made as a trap for you I do not know. What he has to say sounds fine and the remedies which he has to propose seem all right to a "layman" like me. By the way I see that Cyrus [McCormick], as the head of the Harvester Company, comes in for his implied condemnation[2] and in my judgment rightfully so. No matter how honestly these combinations of capital are run they contain a great element of danger, as you and I so thoroughly appreciate, and in the long run, as Mr. Untermyer points out, and for the reasons which he gives they are likely to be destructive of general prosperity. No one can deny the accuracy of the statement that such combinations are "under the control and protection of the interests that dominate our great banks and trust companies and have a grip on their distribution of credits." You know much better than I can possibly know just how far it is wise at this time to call attention to the deadly disease which is attacking the vitals of our form of government. I earnestly wish that you were already in the position to point out and apply the remedy without having to get the nomination first.

With heartfelt regards from us all and knowing that you wont mind my writing you in this personal way when I see something that I think it is to your interest to also see, I am,

Affectionately yours,   D. M. Barringer

TLS (Governors' Files, NJ).
  [1] A clipping, which is missing, from the Philadelphia *North American*, Sept. 8, 1911, of an interview in Paris with Samuel Untermyer, senior member of the New York firm of Guggenheimer, Untermyer and Marshall, counsel for many corporations. "Governor Woodrow Wilson, of New Jersey," Untermyer said, "did not mistake or overstate either the facts or the immediate, overshadowing peril from the growing concentration of the money power in America. The situation is unlike anything to be found in any other part of the world. Every man with an intimate acquaintance with the conditions knows that the dangers are little understood as yet and are vastly underestimated."
  [2] "What earthly chance would any body of men have today of successfully competing with the United States Steel Corporation, or with the Harvester company, or any of the other combinations that are under the control and protection of the interests that dominate our great banks and trust companies and have a grip on their distribution of credits?"

From Fred J. Cross[1]

Honorable Sir: Monticello, Iowa. Sept. 11th. 1911.

Our mutal friend, and your namesake Wm. L Wilson of Baltimore, has enlisted my services in your behalf, to the end that you receive the Democratic nomination for President.

I have interviewed some of the leaders of the different Democratic committees of this district, (5th. Congressional) and they assure me they will do all in their power to boost your cause, and as soon as I am able to be out they are all willing to be organized into "Wilson clubs."

Your prospects in this State are excellent, your cause only requiring diplomatic presenting from now on. Champ Clark is at present the only other person mentioned as a possibility.

I have written your publicity man, Stockbridge, giving him the names of a few publishers, whom I think it would be wise to put on his mailing list for literature etc.

I am aware that you are a very busy man, consequently will not encroach on your time with numerous nor voluminus communications, although I think best interests will be conserved by an occasional exchange of Greetings.

Hoping for your success, I am

Yours truly   F. J. Cross

TLS (Governors' Files, Nj).
  [1] Engineer and owner and manager of Cross Hardware and of the Overland Automobile Agency, Monticello, Ia.

A News Report of an After-Dinner Speech in Atlantic City, New Jersey

[Sept. 12, 1911]

GOVERNOR SORRY FOR COWARD IN OFFICE

ATLANTIC CITY, Sept. 12.—Expressing pity for the coward in office, Governor Wilson, speaking here last night at a dinner of the Hotel Men's Association, declared that the privilege of public office is a privilege of self-development.

"I am not speaking," he said, "of the man who has no conception of the public welfare but of the man with red blood in his veins and a conscience. Such a man cannot absorb this spirit without desiring to promote the welfare of the common people. This feeling should pervade our courts as well as public office. I am sorry for the judge who cannot get the zeal of public righteousness into his blood with absolute intolerance of the man who cannot rise to higher things. A man cannot come to appreciate the wrong that stalks abroad with little concealment without wanting to expand and do something for the public good.

"A man is what he thinks. If you could get the thoughts in a man's heart you would get the measure of the man. I am sorry for any man in public office who is afraid of anybody, because I cannot imagine anything more terrible than the conscience of a coward.

"Because of a petty fear of what may occur to him he dares not do his duty. What a dog he must be. I wouldn't want to spend my waking hours or my sleeping hours as a dog. There is no use thinking if you do not put your thoughts upon a war footing. There is no nobility in knowing the truth and not daring to fight for it."

The Governor said he had never been interested in thinking in and for itself. "Learning is attempting to understand life," he continued. "Man is trying to understand his environment and spiritual impulses. Learning is useless unless it interprets life. It is the business of the courts to deal with life out of joint."

The dinner was in honor of John J. White, a member of the association,[1] and recently appointed to the Court of Errors and Appeals.

Other speakers were Supreme Court Justice Charles G. Garrison, Judge White and Albert T. Bell,[2] former president of the association. Governor Wilson, who was accompanied here by Edward Grosscup, chairman of the Democratic State committee, left after the banquet by auto for Spring Lake.

Printed in the *Newark Evening News*, Sept. 12, 1911.

[1] John Josiah White, owner of the Marlborough-Blenheim Hotel of Atlantic City, who had played a conspicuous part in the reform movement in his city in 1910 and 1911.

[2] Albert Thomas Bell, treasurer of Chalfonte-Haddon Hall of Atlantic City, president of the Hotelmen's Association, 1905-1906.

To Thomas Bell Love

My dear Mr. Love: [Sea Girt, N. J.] September 12, 1911.

Thank you sincerely for letting me see Mr. Kelly's letter. There is no possible foundation in fact for the statement repeated in his letter about my advocating common schools for negroes and whites. I cannot imagine where this statement can have originated.

Thank you for the assurances of your letter. Your support and approval are deeply gratifying to me.

Cordially yours,   Woodrow Wilson

TLS (photostat in the T. B. Love Papers, Dallas Hist. Soc.).

To William Edward Dodd

My dear Mr. Dodd: [Sea Girt, N. J.] September 12, 1911.

I have read with interest your kind letter of September ninth and appreciate very much the sentiment contained therein. It always puts me in heart for the further performance of my official duties to be reminded of the sentiment which men like yourself have.

Yours very sincerely,   Woodrow Wilson

TLS (W. E. Dodd Papers, DLC).

Three News Reports about the Governors' Conference at Spring Lake, New Jersey

[Sept. 12, 1911]

GOVERNORS OF THE UNION IN SHORE PARLEY

Jersey's Executive Welcomes Visitors, Who Form Temporary Organization.

SPRING LAKE, Sept. 12.—Opening with an address of welcome by Governor Woodrow Wilson, the fourth annual conference of Governors of the States of the Union got under way here to-day. The first session was given up entirely to discussion of subjects which are dear to the hearts of the Executives themselves and concerning their own interests only. . . .

In welcoming the visitors, Governor Wilson said: "It is my very simple but very pleasant function, gentlemen of the Conference, to welcome you to New Jersey. You are indeed most welcome, and we are very happy indeed that New Jersey should have been chosen as the place of the meeting of this second independent conference, if we may so call it.

"We are very happy to have anything vital happen in New Jersey, and it is because we believe that this conference has a vital meaning that we are particularly glad to have it meet here. I suppose every one will agree that there never was a time in America when large questions of State were being more seriously or more universally debated than now, or more searchingly looked into, in order to sustain their real foundations of prudent and wise action. There was never a time, either, it seems to me, when there was more pleasing and profitable candor in public affairs than now.

"I find myself deeply interested in this conference because of the personal experiences of last autumn. As Governor-elect at that time I had the privilege of accompanying Governor Fort to the conference in Kentucky,[1] and I was aware of it then, as I am aware of it now, that it was an important part of my education. What I learned at that conference from the candid expression of opinion by the governors who constituted the conference has been exceedingly and permanently profitable to me.

"I believe that the country in general has a mistaken view of this conference, if I may judge from my correspondence, which has certainly been voluminous. Everybody writes to say that this subject or that should have a permanent place in the conference and that the conference should go into detail upon every subject, with the idea that the conference does what it never undertakes to do, and I dare say never will—that is, passes resolutions and makes, as it were, manifestos to the country upon matters which it discusses. That is not, in my judgment ought not to be, the function of this conference. We are here for our own benefit chiefly, to make this sort of a clearing house of experience and of thought, for the purpose of bringing about a very vital unity in this country. Within the sphere of the Federal powers, of course, the Federal Government provides us with a vital union, but there is so wide a sphere outside of the Federal power, and in that sphere we view it. Then there is another very interesting thing about it. The states of this Union expect their governors to exercise leadership, leadership of the most careful and frankest sort, and therefore it is of the utmost consequence to the country that men who attempt to exercise leadership should come together in common council to consider the affairs that the whole country is concerned in, but that you individually have to deal with. It is of very much importance to draw the country together in thought; it is of very much importance to draw the country together in a united purpose, in a common motive, which constitutes patriotic action. So it seems to me that in so far as we act with a union of minds in this conference we have rendered America a deep service, because there are many subjects of legislation, many subjects that are non-partisan in character, in which it is possible to have common council, to agree upon a course that has no color of partisan advantage, that is merely a discussion of fundamental conditions, merely a discussion of fundamental difficulties, merely a discussion of the social complexities which constitute the difficulties with which we have to contend in America today. Upon these things we act and we confer; and the vitality of this conference consists in the fact that it has, I will not say emancipated itself, but released itself from Federal guidance. We are now an independent body, acting on our initiative and under our own guidance, and one of the most important things to consider is what sort of an organization we desire to maintain; and therefore this vital and voluntary way of seeking a common path is a very happy thing to look upon; and I am particularly glad, as I began by saying, that this should happen once, at least, in New Jersey.

"Gentlemen, you are very welcome here. Colonel Cowan,[2] who had charge of the conference in Kentucky, tells me that he has come here to study how we follow the simple life. Our simple life confronts you. I welcome you here with all my heart."

Printed in the *Newark Evening News*, Sept. 12, 1911; Wilson's text from the *Proceedings of the Fourth Meeting of the Governors . . . at Spring Lake, New Jersey September 12-16, 1911* (Lakewood, N. J., n.d.), with minor corrections from the text in the *Newark Evening News*, Sept. 12, 1911.

[1] The third meeting of the Governors' Conference held at Frankfort and Louisville, November 29 and 30 and December 1, 1910.

[2] Andrew Cowan of Louisville, commander of the artillery brigade, VI Corps, Army of the Potomac, in the campaign ending at Appomattox; at this time president of Andrew Cowan & Co., wholesalers of hardware, leather, and mill supplies, and of the National Oak Leather Co.

❖

[Sept. 13, 1911]

REFERENDUM DEBATE OF WILSON AND O'NEAL

SPRING LAKE, Sept. 13.—Not only did the paper on "Strengthening the Power of Executives," which Governor Emmett O'Neal, of Alabama, read before the House of Governors here yesterday afternoon, stir up a lively discussion, but it brought Governor Wilson, of New Jersey, to the forefront in the defense of the principle of the initiative and referendum.

Many of the Governors told about experiences in their own States with regard to the subject, but what Governor Wilson had to say following the remarks of Governor O'Neal was so strongly in defense of the initiative and referendum that Governor O'Neal, after replying to Governor Wilson, walked out of a low window near where he was sitting, and, turning to a newspaper man, said that he thought Governor Wilson had treated him most unfairly. The Alabama Executive plainly showed that he was angry.

There had been no provision made in the program for discussion of the initiative, referendum and recall, but after the Alabama Executive had read his paper the real subject was entirely forgotten. . . . Governor O'Neal said that it was pleasing to know that this "insidious popular vagary" will meet with the almost unanimous opposition of the American bar. He said that the recall would destroy independence of character and loyalty to principle, and "would convert the public officer into a spineless and servile hireling, stirred by every passing breeze of public opinion, obeying every popular impulse and yielding to every wave of popular passion and prejudice."

Governor [Albert Waller] Gilchrist, of Florida, told of the situation in his State and in a way opposed the principle of initiative and referendum, although his stand seemed to be one of "on the fence." Others who spoke, telling of how the matter was considered in their home States, were Governors [Francis Edward] McGovern, of Wisconsin; [Herbert Spencer] Hadley, of Missouri; Kitchen, of North Carolina,[1] and [John] Burke, of North Dakota.

After Governor Kitchen get [got] through Governor Wilson rose, and his remarks were listened to with silence by the throng. He said:

"Mr. Chairman and fellow-Governors. There is an apparent difference of opinion among us, which I venture to think is not a real difference of opinion. I would not like to see Governor O'Neal even temporarily put in the position of being jealous of the power and authority of the Executive.

"It seems to me, in the first place, that there is no danger of public opinion in this country being jealous of this discussion, because every evidence of the time is that the people of the United States desire their executives to exercise a great power. It has just been disclosed here, in the remarks of the various speakers that have preceded me, that nine persons out of every ten take it for granted that governors possess the very powers that we are claiming they ought to possess; that we are doing things that they have naturally assumed we have the power to do. The effect of the papers that have been read here today is that the governors have actual power without which they cannot successfully fulfill the obligations of their offices. At the same time it seems to me that on the question of the initiative and referendum it is necessary that we carry the analysis a little further than it has been carried. Governor O'Neal was discussing the giving of the power to the Governor to see that the laws are really put into effect. But the administration of the laws is not the whole matter. A very important thing—a fundamentally important thing—is the source of the law. Some of the laws that we have had are bad laws, and they are bad for a reason which connects itself with this discussion. The people of the United States want their governors to be leaders in matters of legislation, and they are more interested in that power of the

---

1 William Walton Kitchin.

governor than they are in the extension of the Executive's power. They want him to be a leader in legislation, because they have serious suspicion as to the source of the legislation; and they have a serious distrust of their legislator.

"It may be—it may very likely be—that such distrust has not disclosed itself, for example, in Alabama; it may be that in Alabama the people trust their representatives fully, and it may be that their representatives really speak their will in the legislation of that state. If that is true, the initiative and referendum have nothing to do with the discussion, for the initiative and referendum in our day are not proposed in order to change our system of government, but, if I may use the expression, to revivify it, to reconnect it wherever necessary, but only where necessary, with the real movement of public opinion; and therefore the Governor is strengthened by direct possession of authority from the people.

"One of the most interesting governments in the world, and a government that is the most free government except our own, is based upon this very principle. The Executive of Great Britain undertakes to formulate practically all of the legislation of the Kingdom; when the legislature refuses to follow it, it dissolves the legislature and goes back to the people and says 'Will you send us men who will follow us, or will you not?' The consequence is that that is the strongest government in the world, not only, but the most direct democracy in the world. Therefore what I would urge as against the views of Governor O'Neal is that there is not anything inconsistent between the strengthening of the Executive and the direct power of the people. On the contrary, I think all the strength in our government comes from direct contact with the people themselves.

"There was only one feature in Governor's O'Neal's address to which I have serious objection. He spoke of the caprice of the majority. I have known of instances of the caprice of the mob, but I have never known of any instance, in any large voting population, where the result of the vote was spoken of as a caprice. I have heard gentlemen, in recent speeches, or, rather, I have read of gentlemen speaking recently in distrust of the people and using that old erroneous phrase 'mob rule.'

"What is a mob? A mob is a body of people immediately associated with each other, acting under the impulse of some passion. But that does not apply to a thousand men in a community, in scattered sections, casting their ballots. Has anybody yet known of an instance which could be called an instance of caprice under such circumstances? There may be impulse, and there may be caprice under the impulse of some local circumstance, but I have yet to hear of an authentic instance of the caprice of a population acting at the polls. Therefore if there be no caprice, if there be a means of ascertaining the real moment of public opinion, isn't that a dignified, strengthened and clarified extension of the Executive power?

"I do not believe that there is any essential difference; if I may use the word with a small d, we are all democrats; I wish, for the salvation of your souls, that I could say with a big D also. But we all believe in democratic government, and I would be very uneasy if I thought for a moment that there was any distrust of the fundamental principles of democracy, but I do not believe it. I believe that Governor O'Neal feels as Governor McGovern feels, and that we are merely at odds as to the best method of giving expression with reference to that great public opinion upon which we all depend."

Governor O'Neal was on his feet in an instant. Sawing the air, raising his voice to a shout and eyeing Governor Wilson, he orated:

"I would rather stand with Hamilton and Madison than with some of the prophets our States are turning out. Let us not forget that the purpose of government is to limit the power of the majority and of Constitutions to protect the minority from the tyranny of the majority. Leaving aside the initiative and referendum, the recall of judges would surely institute mob rule."

"Don't you all forget that the 'caprice of a majority' gave you all your jobs," broke in Governor Gilchrist of Florida, in a soft Southern drawl, and for the moment there was peace that followed the laugh from the 200 men and women in the audience at the expense of the Governors.

After the gathering Governors Wilson and O'Neal shook hands and decided that they had not fully understood each other on the floor.

Printed in the *Newark Evening News*, Sept. 13, 1911; Wilson's text from the *Proceedings of the Fourth Meeting of the Governors*, with corrections from the text in the Philadelphia *North American*, Sept. 13, 1911.

✧

WORKINGMEN'S COMPENSATION IS DISCUSSED
WILSON TALKS ON SUBJECT

SPRING LAKE, Sept. 13.—Discussion of a topic which is of paramount interest in New Jersey, "Employers' Liability and

Workingmen's Compensation," held the attention of the Governors in conference here this morning, when the entire time was given up to two papers, one by Governor Marion E. Hay, of Washington, and the other by Governor Eugene N. Foss, of Massachusetts, followed by remarks by many of the other visiting Executives. . . .

In discussing workingmen's compensation, Governor Wilson, of New Jersey, said, "I started a scrap yesterday; I don't know that I want to start another one. New Jersey has passed a law, very much along lines already described by Governor Foss, of Massachusetts. I will not go into that, therefore, but speak, rather, to this point: the real difficulty in the whole matter is that we haven't, under our constitutional limitations,[1] the right to pass compulsory legislation of this character. That is the crux of the whole matter.

"I think the whole country is disposed toward legislation of this sort; therefore the thing for me to discuss is the difficulty with our own act. We only fairly display the weapon. The act provides for compensation very similar, in sums to be paid injured employes, and in other details, to those described. We haven't got to the point of a permanent commission. I hope we shall get to that point. We have continued the commission on whose report the act was founded, with instructions that it shall collect information on the act and make suggestions for its improvement and, perhaps, its extension, and report at future sessions of the Legislature. But, after all, sir, the trouble is with the indemnity companies; they haven't only raised the rates, but they have raised them to the extent of a thousand per cent. in some instances, in this state. These gentlemen, it seems to me, are singularly unwise; they are acting without any forecast of the future. It must be evident to them that action without forecast will absolutely make it necessary to have a state system of insurance for labor. My idea is to have everything left, that can be so left, to private initiative and undertaking, but these gentlemen are making it impossible.

"Then there is another interesting aspect, that has not yet been alluded to. It is all well enough for the State of New Jersey to adopt a general law for the employers of large numbers of employes. But what is to become of the small corporations, which, under the strain of such a cost, might go bankrupt if they cannot pay these rates to their workingmen? They should be secured by law. We therefore have not protected employes until we have seen to it that their claims are paid. That is another circumstance pointing toward state insurance.

"I cannot say that all employers in this state have been in-clined to meet us half way. There are some lawyers in New Jersey who are absolutely ingenious in inventing devices to evade the law, and one or two very large employers of labor have been extremely illy advised in this matter, and are going to take the law to the Court of Errors and Appeals of the state to have determined whether the club contained in the first part of the act is an constitutional club or not.[2] Our Legislature had the right to abolish the defenses so often alluded to, and alluded to with such disapprobation, by the gentlemen who have already spoken.

"New Jersey, in other words, is catching up with the pro-cession very fast and I think she is alive to the signs, which are now becoming obvious to everyone."

Printed in the *Newark Evening News*, Sept. 13, 1911; Wilson's text from the *Proceedings of the Fourth Meeting of the Governors*.

[1] Earlier in the year, the New York Court of Appeals had declared that state's workmen's compensation law in violation of state and federal constitutional guarantees of due process because of the law's compulsory features. About this matter, see n. 7 to the speech printed at April 13, 1911, Vol. 22. The New Jersey legislature had tried to avoid contravening the due process limitation by making its act technically elective. See WW to Mary A. H. Peck, April 9, 1911, n. 5, *ibid.*

[2] He referred to the Newark District Telegraph Co., for one. Sexton *v.* the Newark District Telegraph Co. (86 *Atlantic Reporter* 451) was the case that tested the New Jersey legislation of 1911. On February 26, 1913, the New Jer-sey Supreme Court upheld the act, denying the employer's contentions that it violated the Fourteenth Amendment and the state constitution because it did not provide for jury trial in all cases.

Two Letters from William Frank McCombs

My dear Governor: New York September 13, 1911.

I communicated with the Chairman of the City Committee of Boston[1] with reference to the invitation.[2] He thoroughly under-stands the situation. When I was there a few days ago the lead-ers discussed with me the matter of getting up a large dinner after [the] election in your honor, to which the Democratic lead-ers of New England would be invited. I told them that when their ideas had been crystallized on the subject it might be a good thing to take it up with you. Personally, I think it would be a good idea, as your appearance in New England at an early date would be advantageous. The affair could be conducted along very dignified lines.

I answered Judge Ben Lindsey's letter to me yesterday in which he asked me what he could do to serve your cause. I sug-gested that he write an article for one of the prominent peri-odicals entitled "Why I Am for Woodrow Wilson," and offered to supply him with whatever data he required for the purpose. His reputation in the country is very high and such an article would be of great advantage.

Along this line—I have for months been receiving letters from the very strongest men in all sections of the country, expressing approval of the idea of your nomination. These men have asked me how they can help you. I have conceived the idea of asking them to write short statements which will be entitled "Why I Am for Woodrow Wilson." I would then put these statements in our daily sheets for distribution throughout the country and give them proper publicity through the newspapers. These statements could be given out in installments, so as to spread them over the time up to the Convention. I put the idea before my staff this morning and they were quite enthusiastic about it. What do you think of it? What I want to get into the minds of the people is that you are approved by the very solidest men in the various communities from the Atlantic to the Pacific, and that the level headed business men, as well as the level headed men in public life are taking a live interest in you. I have a large number of splendid names that can be used. They would be quite willing to aid the cause in this way. I should pay more attention to the Eastern States in this regard than to other sections.

Sam Untermyer has just arrived from Europe. It occurs to me that it might be a good idea if you and he met some time in the near future. I know it would please him tremendously. He is strong in New York in every way and could be very useful. Furthermore, he is so thoroughly posted on the money power question that I think it might be of interest to talk it out with him. I should be pleased to arrange the meeting if you agree with me.

I had a talk with the Managing Editor of the Times[3] and Mr. Wiley a few nights ago. I think I know at least a part of the reason why the Times has been cool about you. The Managing Editor told me that several months ago you had written to him complaining of their correspondent in New Jersey; that they had immediately written to you and asked for some particulars and that the letter was never answered.[4] I can straighten that feature out if you will let me have the facts and I think it important to do so.

While I was in the mountains Lynn Helm called at the office and in my absence talked to Mr. Newton. He came to discuss what he considered was a real grievance, and I give it to you just as Newton reported it to me, so that you may take it for what it is worth. He said that a number of people in California, including himself, Alexander S. Lilley, Charles Black, Jeff.

Chandler, Harrington Brown,[5] and others had spent a great deal of time and money in the matter of your entertainment and arranging for speeches in California, that you had been entertained at various houses, and that you had never made any acknowledgment of the courtesies extended. He put it this way: "The Governor never sent us so much as a postal card." He said that he had spent $4000 or $5000 himself in the matter. He further said that he made the statement genuinely in your interest and that something should be done to correct this feeling. I have written Mr. Helm today, suggesting that if he does not feel like writing to you in the matter, he send me a letter, which I shall treat as strictly confidential if he so desires, and that if he wished I would take the matter up with you. I suppose I will hear from him and when I do I will see you.

I sent Mr. Newton to Chicago a few days ago to make a quiet inquiry as to your strength there. He saw representatives of all factions and has reported to me today that at the present time you are considered there far in the lead, and that it is merely a question of maintaining your position. This I have from other sources as well.

The idea of your nomination is spreading amazingly. I know you would be surprised at the favorable newspaper comments you are receiving all over the country and the fine tone of the letters from strong people, coming to me in scores. Of course elections are decided by people in business, the dry goods merchant, the artisan, the banker, and so on. My feeling is that the conviction is spreading that you wish to foster legitimate business and not destroy it and that, while you are working in the interest of progress, you desire nothing other than conservative progress. I am genuinely delighted at the advance your cause is making every day.

Yours sincerely,　Wm. F. McCombs

[1] Joseph Adolphus Maynard, salesman for a plumbing supply company, president of the Democratic City Committee of Boston, 1910-1913.

[2] An invitation to a Democratic rally on September 23, 1911, which Wilson was unable to accept. Dudley Field Malone spoke in his place.

[3] Carr Vattel Van Anda.

[4] This exchange is missing.

[5] Princeton 1876; president of the Southern Refining Co. of Los Angeles, producers of oil and related products, a member of the Good Government Club, the Municipal League, and the City Club. Wilson appointed him postmaster of Los Angeles in 1914.

My dear Governor:　　　　　　　　New York Sept. 13, 1911.

Mr. J. W. Binder of New York,[1] who is taking a very active interest in you and who is travelling in the West on business—

but at the same time spreading the Wilson gospel, encloses the attached card.[2] Mr. Baker[3] has been nominated for Mayor of Cleveland. While Ohio will be committed to Harmon, Mr. Baker takes this means of expressing his friendship and has said to Mr. Binder: "I think there is no man in the country more able or better fitted to be President of the United States." He has also said to Mr. Binder that so far as he is concerned if Harmon is "out" at the convention you will be "next." Mr. Baker wishes this to be conveyed to you through me.

Yours sincerely,   Wm. F. McCombs

TLS (Governors' Files, Nj).

[1] Jacob W. Binder, former editor of the *Pottstown*, Pa., *Daily News* and of the *Philadelphia Press*. Wilson appointed him postmaster of Hackensack, N. J., in 1916.
[2] It is missing.
[3] Newton Diehl Baker, city solicitor of Cleveland, 1902-12; mayor, 1912-16. Wilson appointed him Secretary of War in the latter year.

To Daniel Moreau Barringer

My dear Moreau: [Sea Girt, N. J.] September 14, 1911.

Thank you warmly for your letter of September eleventh. It is delightful to be assisted in my thinking by such suggestions. You are always thoughtful and generous. I wish I had time for a real letter and a real talk.

Affectionately yours,   Woodrow Wilson

TLS (D. M. Barringer Papers, NjP).

From Andrew Jackson Montague

(CONFIDENTIAL)

My dear Governor: [Richmond, Va.] September 14, 1911.

Doubtless copies of the enclosed paper have been sent to you, but should you not have seen them I venture to place one under your eye.

The Ohio Press Bureau[1] is quite active in sending literature to the papers here, but so far I have seen no publication.

The initiative and referendum are much feared by the liquor interests of Virginia who are quite closely allied with the Machine and which will fight you unless you cannot be beaten, and in the latter event they will be your original friends.

The Interest will also oppose you. [George Hutcheson] Denny, the President of Washington and Lee, has been put forward to criticise you, and especially your views on the progressive policies of a growing democracy. He addressed the Virginia Press Association some weeks since, which served him an occasion for this purpose. He appealed "from Philip drunk to Philip sober" and such other tawdry stuff.[2] I had imagined Denny would have been eager to support you, but he hopes to be Governor, so I am told; and his ambition had been thus appealed to.[3]

If Alderman is sincerely your friend you may counteract Denny. The former is, however, very diplomatic, and you should look clearly at any limitations or qualifications attached to his assurances or observations.

Of course you should not be embarrassed by the factional divisions in Virginia, and it would be well to secure cooperation among your friends in each division.

I do not mean to intrude or advise, but have thus ventured to suggest that you may be upon your guard.

Sincerely,   [A. J. Montague]

CCL (A. J. Montague Papers, Vi).

[1] Harmon's publicity organization.

[2] Denny spoke to the Virginia Press Association in Natural Bridge, Va., on July 11, 1911. The lengthy excerpts of his speech printed in the *Lexington, Va., Gazette*, July 12, 1911, and the Richmond *Times-Dispatch*, July 12, 1911, do not include any criticism of Wilson. The discussion of the conference in the *Lexington Gazette*, July 19, 1911, would seem to indicate that "Philip drunk to Philip sober" was a reference to the criticism of the Virginia press by the Anti-Saloon League of the state.

[3] Actually, Denny soon became President of the University of Alabama, a position he held until 1937.

From Fred Loring Seely[1]

Dear Sir: Atlanta [Ga.] September 14, 1911.

I am enclosing herewith a copy of a little note[2] that is going out to the eight hundred Managing Editors of Democratic dailies now receiving The Georgian daily, covering all the Democratic dailies in the United States. The paper has been going to them now for nearly two weeks and this letter is going to them to remind them of it and get them interested in this daily feature. I thought possibly you would be interested in seeing how it is being handled.

I had planned to write you a very long letter about the unfinished matters left over from my visit. The visit, while most delightful, was terribly unsatisfactory to me, in that I was able to bring up but a fraction of the things I had hoped to talk over with you. Furthermore, I fear that, with my thoughts crowding me as they were, what I said must have been very poorly handled.

I drew the conclusion that one of the most important steps lacking was a proper relation with Mr. Hearst, who, as I explained to you, was signifying his choice of Mr. Clark. I thought over this thing very seriously and set about the next morning to use my offices in this connection, the result of which I presume Mr. Stockbridge has outlined to you. This is so important a matter, however, that I fear very much to leave it hanging in the condition it is in. I fear, too, that Mr. Stockbridge, in his hurry, may not have been able to convey the whole thing to you, and if I can possibly do so I am going to run up to New York, in the course of a week or ten days, and endeavor to finish what I started. I am sure a great deal was accomplished.

I wish you would write me at Asheville, N. C., where I go tonight, something of your engagements and what day, in the course of the next ten days, you could spend some little time with me, preferably in New York, at which time this thing can be properly attended to.

Very respectfully yours,   F. L. Seely

TLS (Governors' Files, Nj).
¹ Founder (in 1905) and publisher of the *Atlanta Georgian*; crusader for prohibition, abolition of the convict-lease system, and governmental reform.
² It is missing.

To Solomon Solis Cohen¹

My Dear Dr. Cohen: [Trenton, N. J.] September 16, 1911

I hope you knew when you wrote me your letter of September 14th² what my reply would be. There could be only one answer from any thoughtful or patriotic man. I entirely sympathize with the agitation in the Russian matter, and am sincerely obliged to you for having called my attention to the papers which you inclosed.   Sincerely yours,   Woodrow Wilson

Printed in the Philadelphia *Jewish Exponent*, LIV (Nov. 17, 1911), 2.
¹ Affiliated with the Philadelphia General, Jewish, Jefferson, and Rush hospitals, a specialist in the treatment of tuberculosis; also a leading anti-imperialist.
² It is missing.

To Mary Allen Hulbert Peck

Dearest Friend,   Sea Girt, New Jersey 17 Sept., 1911

Pardon pencil. I am writing from bed. I've been bad and am bilious and the doctor has made me lie up all day. But it's practically over, and to-morrow I shall be "up and at 'em" again. For this is to be a strenuous week. I am to get into the primary fight with both feet!

This scribble is to inform you that when you leave Hot Springs on Saturday you are to come straight to Sea Girt. By that time an opportune pause will have come in my rush and I can give you something more than a casual glance. That's a bargain, isn't it? We shall count on you!

Not writing to you these long weeks past has been a trial to me,—much greater than the disappointment, I venture to think, which you are sweet enough to say it has been to you not to hear from me. Writing to you makes thoughts of you so direct and vivid—and that is so refreshing and delightful. It has been *impossible* for me to write or do *any*thing I wanted to do. Absolutely every waking minute of every day has been exacted of me as a Governor and a "Possibility," and no amount of longing for an absent friend could effect a rescue. This past week, besides, we have had the Conference of Governors on our hands.

There is a young lady here, a Miss Finch,[1] who remembers you with gratitude and enthusiasm in Bermuda, as her fairy godmother and sponsor, and as one of the most delightful ladies that any land could contain,—as who does not who has known your sweetness and your charm there? It was there I became

Your devoted friend   Woodrow Wilson

All join in the invitation and in affectionate messages. There is so much to talk about.

ALS (WC, NjP).
[1] The Editors have been unable to identify her.

A News Report of Two Addresses in Newark, New Jersey, Opening the Democratic Primary Campaign

[Sept. 19, 1911]

WILSON MAKES REPORT OF HIS STEWARDSHIP
TALKS TO TWO THRONGS

Governor Wilson came to Newark last night to report to the people what the progressive Democrats of the State have done since assuming power. He also put labels on the Democratic candidates for nomination to the Legislature. . . .

The people who heard the Governor numbered between 5,000 and 7,000, according to the individual estimater. He spoke at two ends of the city—Harburger's hall, in the Ironbound District,[1] and the First Troop Armory, in Roseville avenue. . . . At both

[1] A working class district.

places the Governor was greeted with hearty applause, his talks were punctuated with it, and when he concluded each he was enthusiastically cheered.

After the Roseville address the Governor was almost mobbed, so much so that the police had to form a cordon about him and fight their way through the throng. . . .

Governor Wilson's speech at the First Troop Armory was as follows:

"Mr. Chairman and fellow citizens. I suppose you know what it is all about. I realize that this is a very unusual feature of a campaign; it is, so far as I know, unprecedented that the Governor of your own State should come and advise you as members of his own party how you should pick and choose among the candidates of the Democratic party. It is nothing less than that audacious and un[u]sual thing that I have undertaken.

"I want to say that I speak with a deep sense of solemnity because it is no light matter to discriminate between men in a public way. It is a very responsible thing, even in private, to utter a personal judgment, but it is much more serious and responsible thing to utter the thing in public.

"But I feel myself bound by a solemn promise. This is the first time I have had the opportunity of redeeming that promise. When I offered myself as a candidate for Governor last autumn, I said that we had a definite program to which, as a party, we were solemnly pledged; that I would consider an election as a choice on your part to be your spokesman and the leader of my party, and that I promised to report back to you the men who had done what they promised to do and the men who had not.

"Very well, I am here to report. I did not make that promise lightly; I know what it involved. I hoped that it would not be necessary to fulfil it and I regret that it is necessary to fulfil it and that some of the men who deserved to be marked, noted and remembered as those who were not faithful to the promises of the Democratic party, should have come from the great county of Essex.

"There is a contest on, is there not? Who are the parties to the contest? You will hear it said that the contest is—I mean said in some quarters—that the contest is between the regular Democrats of the county and the Wilson Democrats of the county. The Wilson Democrats are the only regular Democrats. How are you going to prove regularity? Was there anything irregular in my nomination and election? Where does the irregularity come in? It comes in when men fail to fulfil the pledges they made as Democrats.

"Now, the only men who are trying to discredit the present Democratic administration of the State—I mean the only men in Democratic ranks—are the men who were unfaithful to their pledges last autumn, and they thereby, in my opinion, read themselves out of the Democratic party.[2]

"Fighting the regular organization! We are the regular organization, and these gentlemen who kicked over the traces are the insurgents; insurgents against the solemn promises of the Democratic party; insurgents against the regular methods by which the opinion and choice of the people are to be declared; they are insurgents against the very essence of Democracy; they are a very small, I will not say contemptible, minority; they are a very small and negligible minority.

"Why do I make these confident statements? Why, simply because I have the documents; I know the inside of everything that happened at Trenton last winter; I took pains to know the inside, because I had promised to report and I did not want to come and report what I did not understand.

"Some people have said that I have changed some of my opinions about some of the politicians. If you had seen some of the things I saw you would change your opinions, too. If you can't do the things that are necessary to be done with kid gloves, as you would prefer to do them, in order not to soil your hands, why then you must get a club, and you must not resort to the use of the club until the head has the audacity to show itself, and you have to look for the head to bob up, and if you keep a weather eye open you can see them bob.

"Very well, I slept with my weather eye open and I saw them bob, and this is what happened, that the large majority of the men whom you selected as representatives of the Democrats of Essex opposed all of the measures at the last session of the

[2] Wilson referred to the Smith-Nugent faction, comprised largely of the Essex County delegation in the legislature, which had opposed the Geran election bill and other reform measures and put up its own candidates under procedures described below. Since they had ignored the party platform, principles, and promises, Wilson put them in the bolting class and claimed that they were no longer entitled to be known as organization Democrats.

In order to open the way for all aspirants for office and to prevent the nomination of a single slate of candidates by the party bosses, the Geran law stipulated that nominations for the party primaries should be made by the petition of at least one hundred voters. Ordinarily, the names of all primary candidates for the same office were printed in alphabetical order under the several designations of the office to be voted for. However, candidates might by their own request be grouped together by means of a bracket under certain designations.

As has been said, the Smith-Nugent faction put up a slate of Assembly candidates within a "Regular Democratic" bracket. The anti-machine Democrats in Essex County had organized the Woodrow Wilson League of Essex County and were running a slate under their own designation.

The State House, Trenton

William Bayard Hale, Joseph Patrick Tumulty, and Wilson in the Governor's office, Trenton

Wilson, McKee Barclay, and Frank Parker Stockbridge

Wilson in Denver hotel

Rocky Mountain Princeton Club, Denver

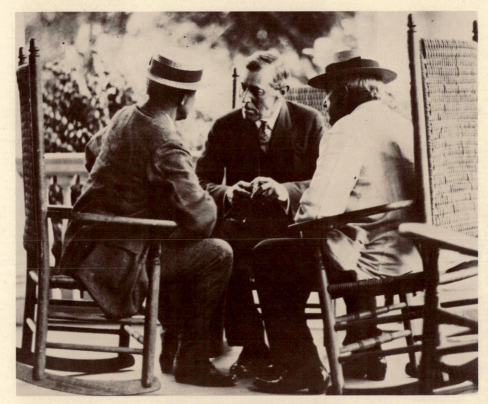

Wilson in conference at Sea Girt

The Governor's Cottage, Sea Girt

Commander-in-chief of the New Jersey National Guard at
Camp Wilson

Wilson in action

legislature which they had solemnly pledged themselves in the campaign to support.

"Only two of these gentlemen have been re-nominated by their friends,[3] and I think in this case their friends must have been their enemies. Those two men are Mr. Shalvoy and Mr. Bracken. They did not fulfil the solemn pledges in virtue of which you sent them to represent you at Trenton.

"There were four men in the Essex delegation who did. Three of these gentlemen have been renominated at the primary election,[4] at any rate, on your Assembly ticket.

"I mean Mr. Balentine, Mr. Boettner and Mr. Macksey, and the only man who has been renominated, and is understood to be supported by those who supported Mr. Shalvoy and Mr. Bracken, the only man who fulfilled his pledges, is a man about whose support by these gentlemen we entertain some very interesting questions.

"Senator Osborne is not opposed by the gentlemen who have supported that list upon which Mr. Bracken and Mr. Shalvoy appear. I wonder if the gentlemen who are nominally supporting him are really going to support him. Can they complain if I wonder? Have they sustained an enviable record for good faith in the past, and then am I not justified in questioning their good faith in the present?

"Did they display any good faith at all out in the open in the session of the Legislature at Trenton? And having destroyed my faith in them then, it is not yet re-established. I will have to have some pretty strong supporting evidence before I will believe that their promise actually is worth the paper it is written on.

"I do not judge men by what they say; I judge them by what they do. It is, as I said during the last campaign, a case of 'put up or shut up.'

"There is an interesting likeness in the action of men of this sort. It is none of my business, I suppose, what happens to the Republicans, but I have something to do about two Republican candidates in a neighboring county—I mean in Passaic County—two Republican candidates from Passaic County, Mr. Jackson and Mr. Leyden,[5] who honored themselves by supporting the measures which their party had promised to support, notwithstanding the measures which they supported were introduced in a Democratic House.

[3] He meant nominated by petition of the Regulars.
[4] Named in the next paragraph, they were in the Wilson League bracket.
[5] Arthur Phelps Jackson, manufacturer and member of the Passaic City Council, and Thomas R. Layden, an engineer employed by the Edison Electrical Co.

"Those two men are out for re-election at these primaries in Passaic; is it not an interesting coincidence that the corresponding Republican organization in Passaic should be doing or about to do the very same thing, namely, to wreak vengeance on the men who kept faith with the people?[6]

"Upon my word, I feel as if we were in the same boat together in saying what I have to say against the men who determine that politics shall be privately controlled, in the private interests, and that men who stand by the public interests shall not have a place in public life.

"That is the issue which will be before the Democrats of Essex County on the twenty-sixth of September. Ladies and gentlemen, if you don't want me for Governor, I give you my word I don't want to be Governor; but if you do want me for Governor and believe in decent politics, I am going to ask you to-night to stand by me—not by me as an individual, for the individual is neither here nor there.

"Tuesday of next week will be remembered in Essex County long after I am forgotten. The fortunes of the Democratic party in a large measure turn upon the fortunes of that Tuesday, because this is the point we have reached:

"Here are two leaderships offered you, the old and the new; the old leadership kept you for sixteen years in absolutely merited obscurity. The State of New Jersey would not trust the Democratic party during those sixteen years.

"Do you suppose that was an accident? Was the Republican party so admirable and formidable during those sixteen years as to make it natural that the voters of New Jersey should call for them?

"I could say some things that, while parliamentary, I am afraid would be very severe about the Republicans who ran the government of the State during those years. Do you suppose you could have left them there for life, seeing some of the things they did, if there had been anybody else to whom the people of the State felt they could turn?

"Essex County is not normally a Democratic county. Why did it go Democratic last time? In order to enjoy the leadership of men who are now trying to discredit the Democratic party? Certainly not. In order, if God were favorable, to escape that leadership.

"Very well; you escaped from it, and do you suppose now that the hog is going to return to his wallow? Do you suppose that the Republican voters of Essex County—a county in which there

6 Both were defeated by Republican regulars.

is perhaps the largest detachable, that is to say, the largest independent vote to be found anywhere in New Jersey? Do you suppose that the county of Essex is going to support those whom you turned away from you last fall?

"Now, I have nothing to say about the approval of my leadership; I have only to say what you can prove by the books—by the statute books—that we did in good faith what we promised to do. Perhaps you will say that you do not like some of the things we did. Very well, you ought not to have commanded us to do them.

"The Democratic platform last autumn was the most explicit platform, I suppose, that you ever heard from a State party; it promised to do definite things in definite ways, and you voted on the basis of that platform or else you didn't know what you were about.

"Now, that platform has been literally carried out at the last session of the Legislature. With what result? With the result that in the eye of the State not only, but in the eye of the United States, the Democratic party has been rehabilitated, with the result that New Jersey, from being at the tail end of the procession of those States that are new at reform, is now at the head of the procession, and every mail brings inquiries from belated States to know how it was done.

"There wasn't any trick about it; there wasn't any exercise of personal power about it; I didn't do it; you did it; I simply said at every turn, as my only argument: 'These are not private measures of my own, they are [not] things that I have a personal fancy for, although I believe in them; these are the things I was put in to have done, and I am not going back to those voting people of New Jersey until I have done everything honorable in my reach to do it.'

"Now, I have nothing to apologize for or to explain, because it was all done. We gave you more than we promised to give you." (A voice: "Yes, you did.")

"We gave you what at present you are prevented from availing yourselves of, namely, an act providing for commission form of government. You can't get it; the professional politicians will not let you have it; they are preventing you from getting it.

"But when the flood tide comes, these men will be the deepest drowned of any men who were ever turned down in an avalanche of votes. As soon as you make up your minds, in the first place as to the way you choose to vote, and in the second place to see your votes are counted, you are going to govern your cities in any way you choose to govern them. . . .

"These are the things that we stood for and are standing for, and these are the issues that are going to the jury—to the Democratic jury—on the 26th of September.

"Now, who is the jury going to find for? Is the jury going to find for the future or for the past? Is the jury going to find for hope or for retrogression and despair? Is the jury going to determine that men who have been trying to serve you shall be ordered to the rear, and that those who have betrayed you shall be put in charge again?

"If I know my own heart, ladies and gentlemen, I have no hard feelings against any man. I don't hate any man who hits me in the open, but if I can catch any man hitting me in the dark, I would not answer for the integrity of his anatomy after I got through with him. There will be no hard feelings; there will be no tempered gloss in the rough and tumble of politics provided the gloss verdict is rendered on the facts.

"I am here to try and represent to you the facts.

"I was saying at a meeting which I addressed earlier in the evening that I have listened to the prognostications of what is going to happen on Tuesday of next week and at the election. Do you know there is nothing in any of the predictions?

"You are going to use a ballot on Tuesday of next week, and on the seventh of November next, such as you have never used in New Jersey before. You know how easy it is for the managing politicians—they constitute a very small number—to work in an old style ballot; all they had to do was to put some responsible names at the top, and those names dragged all the rest of the ticket through, because you voted a ticket.

"You are not going to vote a ticket any more; you are going to vote a ballot, but not a ticket. You can't vote for anybody if you do not actually pick him out; if you don't put a mark opposite his name you don't vote for him. Therefore, inasmuch as you are going to pick and choose, nobody knows, and nobody can know, what your choice is going to be.

"There is only one way in which you can vote the ballot you are going to vote. The ballot permits the bracketing of certain names together. Now, there are going to be some brackets, and the only use of the bracket I know of is this, that you will know what company the man keeps.

"In one bracket you will see the name of Mr. Shalvoy and Mr. Bracken, and you will say to yourselves: 'Well, they went back on us once. Who are these other gentlemen in this bracket? We know what that bracket meant once; it meant that these men were not their own masters. Now, can it mean that this bracket means they are together with these other gentlemen associated with them?'

"I say that these men were not their own masters because I know it; I have been told so. I do not mean that Mr. Shalvoy and Mr. Bracken told me so, because they did not, but men associated with them in the last Legislature told me so. One of them one day came to me—I think I am not mistaken when I say that there were tears in his eyes—and said: 'Governor, I would to God I could stand by you, but I can't; they have got me.'

"Now, I don't want to search a man's heart by asking him what he means. But I knew what he meant. I do not know what the circumstances were in his case, but I have not been studying politics for thirty years to grow up an innocent child and not know what is going on. I know how votes are controlled.

"In former days men were foolish enough to go around with bills in their pockets and pay for votes. That is not the way money is used now, but money is used now in a different way. You can't get any money for legitimate purposes. What I mean by that is, if you are engaged in business and go to the Legislature, and we don't pay our legislators anything to live on, therefore they all have to be engaged in business of one sort or another.

"If you are a lawyer, and don't do what you are told, it may be, certain influential gentlemen get together and see that you don't have as many clients as you used to have; they will see that you will not have the same retainers on which you used to depend for the support of your family; they will see that certain rumors about your integrity are circulated, just as certain rumors, that no man dares make more than rumors, are now circulating about Senator Osborne. They circulate rumors that something is the matter with you, and if you are in business they say that you cannot renew your note at the bank, that you will have to go somewhere where they will renew your notes, somewhere where you are not known, and where you will have to put up extra gilt-edged collateral or you can't borrow any money at all.

"In other words, they put you out of business. That is the way they work it on you now. . . .

"Do you wonder that I sometimes say that I will go out and speak every name that I know and give it to you gentlemen as high as Heaven? God knows that self-government in this country and this State has many powerful names. But they shall not long remain concealed.

"It does not make any difference to me, so far as that is concerned, whether I stay in office or not. I know their names and I despise their power.

"And these gentlemen in the county of Essex who are trying to discredit the present administration are the men who are, hand and glove, closely allied and leagued with these other enemies of the public interests; they always have been.

"That is the reason they could never rehabilitate the Democratic party. They have always worked, as I dare say they still are working, with like minded gentlemen of the Republican party, who are going about in secret, doing the things that I have just said they were trying to do in Passaic County.

"I wish I could go further. I am under bond to mind my own business. There is a lot of other people's business that I would like to mind.

"But I want to say this, that there is an association in this county known as the Woodrow Wilson League of Essex County. I want you, my fellow citizens of Essex, to know that is [it] was against my protest that that name was taken, because no man is big enough to mark the purposes of a great party.

"Personally, I would a great deal rather had it called the Progressive Democratic League of Essex County, for that is what it is, and that is what I am going to call it whenever I refer to it.

"Now, the Progressive Democratic League of Essex County has not put up a ticket, but it has indorsed a list of candidates, and I want to say with regard to its indorsement that having carefully studied the personnel of the membership and committees of that association, and having dealt with members of its executive committee, I feel perfectly confident in saying that they have not indorsed any man for any venal purpose, and that they have tried to indorse the men they have indorsed because they believe they have, in so doing, indorsed true men upon whom they can rely to keep their pledges in the public interest.

"Are you going to discredit the progressive element that is now in control, when you know perfectly well that there is not any other progressive element that you can put in control? Is that good politics? Is that good sense?

"Are you, as Democrats, going to see to it that this element does not lose control of the Democratic party, or are you going to see to it that the reactionary element, the element of the opposition, is going to again be put in control of the Democratic party? Upon the settlement of that issue depends much [of] the settlement of the future political history of the United States.

"Essex is a great indepedendent county; Essex is not led by the nose; Essex can keep the professional politicians guessing as long as any county in the State; Essex is capable of making up its mind as to what it wants.

"I am here as a Democrat to plead for big politics as against little politics; politics based upon ideas instead of politics based upon persons. I would be abashed if I were standing here pleading for myself. I am pleading for the things I stand for. I stand here to-night in a great cause for the promotion of great principles. I stand for those who wear, as I do, the dignity of those principles temporarily."

Printed in the *Newark Evening News*, Sept. 19, 1911; some editorial headings omitted.

To John Maxwell Gordon[1]

Personal

My dear Mr. Gordon: [Sea Girt, N. J.] September 20, 1911.

I sent one letter to chase you in your travels, but evidently it did not get to you. I think, rather than risk it again, I will send a duplicate of this letter to you in care of the Brooklyn Eagle, for, by hook or by crook, I wish to have some assurance reach you of my very cordial appreciation of your generous friendship and interest. I shall await with the greatest interest, the result of your inquiries in different parts of the country. I have the strong feeling that, if the people desire it, I shall be a candidate, but if they do not, I do not wish to seek it.

You have been very thoughtful in sending me newspaper clippings, and I thank you very heartily.

Cordially yours,   Woodrow Wilson

TLS (Forbes Magazine Coll.).
[1] Special correspondent of the *Brooklyn Daily Eagle.*

To A. B. Lowe[1]

My dear Mr. Lowe: [Sea Girt, N. J.] September 20, 1911.

I have read your letter of September eighteenth[2] with a great deal of interest and with much appreciation of your candor in laying the whole case you speak of before me in detail.[3] I must say that settlement of such matters by conference and arbitration seems to me both just and reasonable. I shall take the liberty of sending your letter to our own Commissioner of Labor,[4] in the hope that he may find some way of cooperating with Mr.

Williams and Mr. Downey,[5] in behalf of an equitable method of settlement.   Cordially yours,   Woodrow Wilson

TCL (Governors' Files, Nj).

[1] Of Scranton, Pa., president of the International Brotherhood of Maintenance of Way Employees. He never divulged his given names.

[2] It is missing.

[3] A strike of trackmen on the Delaware, Lackawanna and Western Railroad for higher wages and improved working conditions, precipitated by the dismissal of a union leader for insubordination. When the company refused to submit the issues to arbitration, Lowe asked Wilson and presumably also Governor Dix to use their influence to persuade the company to agree to arbitration.

[4] Lewis T. Bryant of Atlantic City. He was also inspector general of the New Jersey National Guard.

[5] John Williams, New York State commissioner of labor, and P. J. Downey, deputy commissioner.

To Lewis T. Bryant

My dear General Bryant: [Sea Girt, N. J.] September 20, 1911

Here is a letter which explains itself. So far as this statement goes, it seems to me that the men are making what is clearly a just and reasonable demand, and that it is not in the interest either of good feeling or good government that the officials of the Lackawanna Company should maintain the position they have taken.

I have written to Mr. Lowe that I would send his letter to you with the suggestion that, if you could find any way in which to cooperate with Mr. Williams and Mr. Downey, of the New York Commission of Labor, you would be kind enough to do so. Perhaps, by communicating with Mr. Downey or Mr. Williams, on the ground that the Lackawanna system lies in part in New Jersey, you could assist materially in bringing more pressure to bear for just action in this important case.

Cordially and sincerely yours,   Woodrow Wilson

TCL (Governors' Files, Nj).

From William Frank McCombs

My dear Governor: New York September 20, 1911

I had a long talk with Mr. Untermyer yesterday. He expressed himself as being your friend and desirous of helping in any way possible. He stated that he gave out the Paris interview for the purpose of being of assistance. . . . The active enlistment of Mr. Untermyer in your behalf would be exceedingly valuable and I think an early conference between you and him is very desirable. He can tell you a lot of actual facts about the money trusts and other present day problems, which I think would be of service.

Won't you let me know as soon as it is convenient for you to see him. He expressed the opinion yesterday that it would be a good thing if, at some well selected time, you came out again with a vigorous statement against the recall of judges.

Jerry Sullivan enclosed a clipping from an Iowa newspaper which he gave out immediately upon his arrival there.[1] It is strongly in your interest and I am going to give it broad circulation.

Mr. Blake of Michigan[2] came in to see me a few days ago. We discussed a plan of immediate organization in your behalf there. In view of the strength of the men who now favor you in that state, I believe that something can be done immediately. My mind works toward the proposition now of taking as early steps as possible to get a national organization going, whose purpose is securing delegates. I think it essential that a majority of the delegates should go to the Convention absolutely instructed for you. Your opponents are struggling for uninstructed delegations. We have got to meet that by instruction. I am working along that line in several of the states and am paying particular attention to the states which hold primaries. I have some very interesting information from Maine today. William P. Thompson and Obadiah Gardner, former candidates for governor,[3] have expressed themselves as strongly for you. I am also informed that the larger portion of the Democratic voters are against Harmon and disposed to be for you.

I am very much gratified at the success of your meetings in Newark the other night. I think your manner of attack is absolutely correct. I don't believe you can go after the primary proposition too hard. I think it good tactics to take the same strong position and make the same vigorous speeches that you did last Fall. I had very interesting talks with Mr. Glass of Alabama[4] and Mr. Brown of Georgia,[5] and have made some suggestions which they are going to adopt.

I was sorry I did not see you the other day. Whenever you are at liberty, won't you let me know. There are a number of things which I should like to go over with you.

Yours sincerely,   W F. McCombs

TLS (Governors' Files, Nj).

1 In an interview in the *Des Moines Register and Leader*, Sept. 15, 1911, Sullivan declared that, after spending an afternoon recently with Wilson in Sea Girt, he was more than ever convinced that Wilson was one of the strongest men available for the presidential nomination in 1912. Clark was better known and probably more popular in Iowa, Sullivan admitted, but, he continued, "Let Governor Wilson show himself to Iowa and I think there would be a change." Wilson, Sullivan added, "is a great man—one of the greatest I have ever met. . . . He is so democratic, so progressive in ideas, so brilliant, such a champion of the 'under-dog'—why, he seems versed in every thing—politics, economics,

law and the equitable application of it. No wonder the people of New Jersey love him. He is a broad man, broad in every sense the word implies."

2 Aldrich Blake, chairman of the Democratic Club of Grand Rapids, Mich.

3 William Pitt Thompson, lawyer of Bangor, Me., Democratic candidate for governor in 1890 and for Congress in 1892; Obadiah Gardner of Rockland, Me., Democratic candidate for governor in 1908.

4 Wilson's schoolmate, Franklin Potts Glass, general manager of the *Montgomery*, Ala., *Advertiser*, and editor of the *Birmingham News*.

5 Edward Thomas Brown, lawyer of Atlanta, Mrs. Wilson's first cousin.

A Campaign Address in Jersey City, New Jersey

[[Sept. 21, 1911]]

Mr. Chairman and Fellow Citizens—It is with a sense of real privilege that I come back to this hall,[1] because this is one of the halls in which, it seems to me, I have received from the people of the State the strength which was necessary in the administration of their affairs. I have come here in response to what I believe to be a solemn obligation. I made many promises in the campaign a year ago, but I want you to know that I did not make any promise under the impulse of the moment. I promised always with deliberation. I promised always with the consciousness that it would be my bounden duty to redeem the promise. I promised that if you honored me with your votes and made me the Governor of this great commonwealth I would come back to you and tell you not only what I myself had done, but tell you what those associated with me had done in fulfillment of the obligations of the party platform.

It is not pleasant, ladies and gentlemen, to discriminate. It was not willingly that I went to Newark and came to Jersey City to point out to you the men who had redeemed the promises they made to you and the men who had not; and I want to say at the very outset that, while I discriminate between them in that respect, I do not wish you to understand that I discriminate between them in respect of any personal feeling that I may have toward them. I hope that you will hear no syllable of bitterness or of accusation from me. I shall try merely to speak of the facts with absolute candor and without fear that a statement of the facts can do more than strict and stern justice. Justice is not a sentimental thing; justice is not based upon personal consideration; justice does not discriminate between friend and enemy; justice speaks of the facts as they are and of the moral judgments which another generation might render concerning men whom they did not know.

1 St. Patrick's Hall.

Now, there were many obligations contracted in the last campaign and in the last session of the Legislature of New Jersey. Obligations, political obligations, have often been taken very lightly in this State, ladies and gentlemen, and in other parts of the country, but you will bear witness that it is true that neither the people of New Jersey nor the people of the United States intend any obligation to be taken lightly hereafter. We are done with deceit; we are done with trickery; we are out to see that the things that we believe in for the benefit of the country are carried out honestly, candidly, fearlessly and to the end.

The program of the Democratic party promulgated during the last campaign was one of the most definite programs that was ever written in a State platform. It was not written in rhetorical terms, as I reminded you the last time I was here;[2] it was not written so that you could put this interpretation or that interpretation upon it as you pleased; it was not written so that you could carry out the promises by this means or by that; it was written in such terms of detail that there was only one way to carry it out; and there was no man who did not stand by the leaders of the party in carrying out these pledges that can possibly explain his dereliction away. There is no exact answer for those who would escape responsibility.

Now, I find myself in a peculiar position with regard to the list of candidates upon the primary ticket for the Assembly. Ten of the twelve men who represented the county of Hudson in the last Legislature are upon this ticket. Those who seem to be associated with one another by the assistance of the long bracket[3] —I mean those who were in the last Assembly—are Mr. Thomas Griffin, Mr. Charles Simpson, Mr. Charles Egan, Mr. Thomas F. Martin, Mr. James Agnew, Mr. Thomas Donnelly and Mr. William Davidson. Every one of these men except one did what you expected him to do in the Assembly. That exception was Mr. Martin.

Now, perhaps, you expect me to ask you not to vote for Mr. Martin at the primary, but I have something particular to say about Mr. Martin. Mr. Martin never made any pretenses of any kind; he always stated with manly distinctness in public, in my presence, and out of it, just what he thought and just what he was going to do. There were some very strong reasons to doubt whether his immediate constituents—the constituents of his immediate neighborhood in the county—wanted him to do exactly

2 On January 5, 1911, when he spoke in favor of the senatorial candidacy of James E. Martine. His address is printed at that date in Vol. 22.
3 They were leaders in the faction of the party led by Eugene F. Kinkead.

what it was clear that the people of other parts of the county wanted him to do. Not only that, but after Mr. Martin had voted against Senator Martine and had opposed most of the many provisions of the Geran bill, he seemed to have discharged all of the duties that he thought he owed to his own special opinion and he turned around, in the most candid, straightforward and energetic way; he did some of the most important and beneficent legislation of the session. He was extremely useful and active in assisting in the passage of the Walsh bill for commission government, a bill the provisions of which you adopted, though you don't know it. He was extremely active and serviceable in passing those bills which have effected what seemed to be an indispensable reform for the administration of the school system. He displayed a public spirit and an energy which were, in my view, very admirable.

Now, I have this to say about Mr. Martin. Mr. Martin fought me, but he fought me like a man, and I have nothing to say.

The other gentlemen whose names I have read I earnestly hope will receive the support of the Democratic voters of this county on Tuesday next.

Now, there are two other gentlemen outside the brackett. Of Mr. [Peter H.] James, I have this to say: Mr. James stood by all the pledges of the Democratic party just as consistently as did these other gentlemen. I want to tell you the promise—the only promise that I made to these gentlemen and to Mr. James. They did not try to exact any promise of me—I don't mean to intimate that—but I did say to these gentlemen, "If you will stand by this great program of the party from the Senatorship through the whole business I will do all that I can to induce your fellow citizens to s[t]and by you, if you want to go back to the Assembly. All I can say to you to-night is that if you wish as Democrats on next Tuesday to express your approval of the present administration, you will vote for these men. In other words, I put myself frankly in the same boat with them and consign myself to your good judgment.

Now, Mr. [Cornelius] Ford did not vote for the popular candidate for Senator, he voted for a very admirable man, however, he voted for a man whom I personally greatly admire and entirely trust—I mean our distinguished fellow citizen, Mr. William Hughes. And with regard to the rest of the program Mr. Ford, so far as I know, is unimpeachable. It has been said about Mr. Ford that his interests are too much specialized and centered; that he does not really think of any legislation except that which is in the interest of the laboring man. Well, I might wish that he were interested in more things, but I cannot say that I can criticize him for being interested in the matter. I want to say that, whereas Mr. Ford and his associates in the great labor organizations of the State had independent preferences with regard to the provisions in the Employers' Liability and Workingmen's Compensation Act, they co-operated in the passage of the act that finally went through in a way which was wholly to their credit.[4] They were not working, so far as I discovered, for any private or partisan advantage; they were working for the thing that we all had at heart, namely, the true interests of the workingmen of this great commonwealth as before the courts of the commonwealth. Therefore I want very heartily to include Mr. Ford in the list.

Now, gentlemen, I have discharged my obligation and I do not want you to think that in saying that I am glad to get through with it. I would be glad to go over it. I do not care the toss of a penny for a man who won't go out in the open and fight for his friends, and I haven't got on my war paint to-night because I don't think it is necessary to have it on. I am talking to men in Hudson County who know what is necessary to do for the credit of the Democratic party next Tuesday, and I am simply pointing out to them what it seems to me is the best way they can show their approval of the present administration of the State and their hopes for the future.

I am very sorry that our most distinguished friend, Mr. Edward Kenny, was not renominated. It was by his own choice, of course, but we shall miss him sadly, for he was a wheelhorse. And I am bound to say that I am sorry that Mr. [James J.] McGrath is seeking renomination because Mr. McGrath did not live up to the obligation which he had assumed. I must say that. I must mention names. Politics, when it means the service of a great people, is not a milk and water business; it is a business of sterling purpose, and we must say these things in so many words.

Do you know what is going on in this State, ladies and gentlemen, and do you know where it is going on? There is this issue now involved: I want to say that last year was preliminary; you didn't know what was going to happen when you voted last year. Now you know what has happened. You said then that you wanted it to happen. Well, did you? (A voice: We certainly did.) If you meant what you said, then nobody can doubt what you will say next week. For it is up to you to say in so many words next week that these were the things that you believed in and

4 For a discussion of Ford's role, see WW to Mary A. H. Peck, April 9, 1911, n. 5, Vol. 22.

meant to stand by. Now, what was your decision? Your decision was that you were tired of and done with the private determination of public affairs; that you were done with having those things side-tracked behind closed doors by persons whom you could not discover, whose persons and activity you merely suspected, and were tired of having men nominated, persons whom they thought they could privately control; that you meant henceforth to seek your own objects and make your own choice and relegate everybody to private life, not only to obscurity, but to contempt, who stood in the way of the execution of your purposes. Now, what is happening in certain counties of this State? Men whom you fought, men whose methods you have utterly condemned, men whose methods have been a byword to the State and to the nation for years gone by are now seeking to defeat your purpose by discrediting your agents, men who pledged themselves in so many words to stand by programs which they are now trying to make the basis of discrediting those who carried them out. Their motive is a motive of personal revenge. They don't care anything for the interests of the people of the State, but they do care an infinite deal to get even with the persons who have made their private control of public affairs impossible. Now, this is not confined to one party. . . .

There is a very interesting county in the southern part of this State known as the County of Camden. There was in the last Legislature of this State a Senator—a Republican Senator from that county, who owned his own soul. He was one of the most useful members of the Senate of this State in promoting the passage of the very legislation to which I have referred—legislation to which both the Democratic and Republican parties were pledged. He owed it as his duty to his party, if his party meant what it said, though it didn't do it—to do the things that he did do.

And now are you reading the South Jersey papers? Do you ever see the Philadelphia Record, for example? Have you read the statements which Senator Bradley is putting forth, in which he is stating explicitly that he had a conference with Mr. David Baird and Mr. Thomas N. McCarter in which he was threatened with political death if he did not take orders from the Public Service Corporation? Have you read that? Mr. Bradley is a man who not only knows what he is talking about, but can be trusted to tell the truth. Now, how do you like that story? These gentlemen are perfectly non-partisan.

I do not mean to implicate the whole of the great Public Service Corporation in anything I may say. I do not know how many of the directors know of the things that are being done, but I do say that we have every evidence that the Public Service Corporation, through gentlemen who try to influence legislation, don't care whether they get it from Republicans or Democrats, and that we have every reason to believe that there are Republicans and Democrats who are willing to give them what they want. . . .

I have spoken of threatening. I want to make a clean breast of it. The only threat I ever uttered against anybody as I remember it, was in the form of an invitation to go down in the county and debate the thing with me. Now, that is not a very formidable threat. No man need to be afraid to go down if he was not afraid to look in the eyes of the audience he would face. It was not a question of eloquence; it was not a question of argument; it was a question of whether he would go and look those people in the face or not if he didn't do the things he promised he was willing to do—whether he would admit he got his place under false pretenses or not. For no man wants to go into a shop where he got money under false pretenses and face the shopkeeper again; and no man wants to face his constituents when he has said one thing before election and has done another thing after it. That is the only threat I ever remember to have uttered against anybody; the threat of in public exhibition to exhibit the goods in the shop window.

Now, what is involved; you have heard what is involved very eloquently stated by Mr. [Dudley Field] Malone. This is not a little piece of county business; this is not a little matter that confronts you next Tuesday; this is not a little matter which can end with next Tuesday and then be forgotten; it is a matter which affects the whole future of the Democratic party in this State and in some degree the future of the Democratic party in the nation.

I traveled last spring from one coast of this continent to the other and back again and there was one source of gratification to me during that journey, and that was that I found everywhere a manifest although not always clearly expressed surprise, that the people of New Jersey have turned progressive. The people of this country seemed to think that New Jersey was given over to the worship of and submission to the great corporations. Our reputation, I must say, was very bad, and I had everywhere to say "Why, the trouble has been that the people of New Jersey have never had a chance before; the trouble has been not with the people of New Jersey, but with the fact that every time they tried to get anything done they were cheated of it by men who promised to do for them."

The people of New Jersey have been keeping pace with the thought of the country; they have never looked behind, but they have been, again and again, deceived and all that you are witnessing now is their emancipation and their coming into their own. But suppose that the country should say that New Jersey had gone back to her idols; suppose that the country should say that New Jersey had no sooner realized the fruits of her progressive thinking than she turned against the uncommon taste and rejected those who had done the things that she had commanded them to do? Think of the chill that would go through that new nation if it were thought that New Jersey had lost heart. For you are not to mistake the fact, ladies and gentlemen, that the whole country now is buoyed up with the great spirit of progress, not only, but with the great spirit of sympathy. Men want to think that everywhere in the United States the same great cause of the sovereign people is loved by the rank and file of the voter. You do not want to check this handsome and noble thing; you want to say, as if with a great shout, that the armies of progress are abroad and are abroad in order that you may have your say to the end in New Jersey as they will everywhere else; because the achievements of the last Legislature in New Jersey are of the essence of the cause of the people. As I passed through Newark this afternoon a gentleman came aboard of the train who told me a very interesting piece of news. You know that sample ballots are mailed out to all voters on the polling lists. To-day it seems that there are five thousand sample ballots returned to the postoffice in Newark because the persons to whom they are addressed cannot be found. Some of them of course were wrongly addressed; the addresses of some of the voters may not have been known and they have been sent to the general delivery, but you cannot make enough subtraction of that kind from five thousand to reduce the thing very much. And some of the postmen themselves testified that a great many of these ballots were addressed to empty lots. Here you have one of the first intimations of what the Geran bill does for you. It advertises the old processes of politics. All you have to do is to go to the postoffice in Newark and take a photograph of those ballots and you have sort of a visible evidence of the men who did not exist or men who had gone off on a journey.

In the city of Orange already six hundred sample ballots have been returned. When you get the full figures of the returned ballots in New Jersey then you will know something of what the intention of the Geran bill was—namely, that real men should vote; that they should vote where they lived, and that their votes and only their votes should be counted.

Now that went along with the Corrupt Practices Act. I had a sudden pang yesterday; I was thinking of making a campaign contribution and I found that I had come within an ace of making it the wrong way and getting into jail. There is only one way you can make a campaign contribution now and that is through the managers who are designated as their agents by the candidates on the ticket. You cannot spend your own money independently and tell nobody about it unless you want to get into jail—of course you can do it then; you cannot go around using money in a private, indiscriminate way, but you have to use it in a particular way which will afterwards be described in sworn statements published in the newspapers. Therefore, if you combine an elimination of the voters that do not exist with an elimination of the voters whose votes were paid for by hard money, you begin to get down to the hard pan of American citizens.

I am interested—always interested—in finding out what the people really voted for. It is none of my business whether they voted the way I wanted them to vote or not. If they vote the way I do not want them to I may go home a very much disappointed man, but if I know that these were their real sentiments and their real wishes, I am not a man if I do not accept the thing like a sport.

I plead with you just now to fight for the gentlemen I have just named on the primary ticket and I told you that I wanted to know whether you approved of the present administration or not. But do you suppose, if you say on next Tuesday that you do not approve of it, that I am going to to [sic] respect you any less; do you suppose that I am going to sulk, do you suppose that I am going [to] throw up the game? How old do you take me to be? I am happy to say that when I was a little kid I did not leave the game when it went against me, and I despise any man who would. If you should vote the way I hope you won't, then I would be sure to come back and tell you that you were dead wrong and ask you to debate it out with me and prove that you were right, because you can go around very privately and nicely and have a wrong opinion, and that is very comfortable as long as you do not have to explain it. Now, all the discomfort I want to give anybody, if they vote the other way, is the discomfort of explaining, because we are entitled to a public explanation of the motives of the vote. Now, these gentlemen I have been speaking of in Passaic, Camden and Essex, are not going to be dragooned into any public explanation, because they have no idea of building the gallows and rigging the rope and getting on the scaffold and putting the noose around their own necks and falling off. They don't propose any such martyrdom as that; they don't propose to gibbet themselves. But it is not necessary, they will have a system.

Now you may think that I am simply asking you to support those who gave you what you wanted. But that is not the whole story. All over this country, gentlemen, the fight is for the primary. The fight is just as Mr. [John Joseph] Treacy said, to get rid of the middlemen—to say, "Here, we don't need anybody, and we don't want anybody to select the men who are going to run for office; we will do that for ourselves; we don't want anybody to manage these things for us; give us leave to manage them for ourselves, and we will get what we want; give us leave to put up just as many independent candidates as we choose; to those things which are our own, so give us leave to have direct access that we shall not have to depend in any particular upon private conferences by small groups of men anywhere.["] That is what the primary means. So that what you are fighting for, and what you fought for last autumn, was the right to choose for yourselves every officer that you voted for, including the members of the Senate of the United States.

A very interesting thing has happened in this country. We were very anxious last winter and this summer to see the Congress of the United States pass the bill which was the foundation for a constitutional amendment putting the election of United States Senators directly in the hands of the people. But we did not wait for that. In State after State steps have been taken to practically effect the same end. For example, in the State of Oregon they have gone so far as this: They have not the statement number one that we have; they have a very famous statement number one, which reads to this effect: "I pledge myself, if elected a member of the Legislature, to vote for the candidate for United States Senator who receives the largest number of votes at the polls." Observe that independence of party. Now, our statement number one is: "I pledge myself to vote for that man who receives the highest number of votes at the primary of my party." So that this interesting thing has happened in Oregon: That a Republican Legislature, in fulfillment of its pledges, has elected a Democratic United States Senator.[5] That is going the whole hog!

Now, this is the spirit that is abroad in this country. The peo-

[5] George Earle Chamberlain, elected for the term beginning March 4, 1909.

ple mean to have access to their own affairs and they do not intend to let any man withstand them.

If I had my way I would not let any man come before a national nominating convention except a man who had been ratified at the primaries of the people.

And so, all along the line, what we are fighting for is not wrapped up in particular reforms; it is not wrapped up in particular measures. We are for enthroning the sovereign people of this land again. . . .

I consider this a place of privilege. I consider any place a place of privilege where I am permitted to frankly state the cause that I am proud to represent, to men who are capable of understanding. I have found some of my comrades sometimes timorous and faint hearted and fearful of the result. I do not share their fear in the least. I believe that right is right and that there is a God in the heavens. I do not understand how any man can avert the complexities of public affairs or of any great business and live if he does not believe in the providence of God. There is no clew to the haze [maze] if he does not; there is no standard of right if he doesn't; there is no basis for his own spirit if there is not some great power to which it must be obedient. There may be an ebb and flow in the tide; there may be temporary reverses; but no man who has read the thrilling and moving pages of history and liberty can for a moment doubt what is happening in this country or what is going to happen.

Have men not read the history of liberty? Have men not seen how the human spirit has been marching from conquest to conquest? The happy circumstance of the time is that it is no longer necessary to spill precious human blood to accomplish the result, for we fight with ballots and not with bullets, we fight with the proud purpose of enlightening voters and not with the blind purpose of those who fight in the field, in the smoke, and confusion where they know not what they fight, but merely that they go from one gory record to another. And as I see the clouds lifting, as I see the sparkle that comes into the eyes of men that speak of liberty and look forward to hope, then I know that whether I live or die, whether I am approved or rejected, the cause of human liberty will go on and there will come a day when the great symbol that hangs on either side of me will stand once more for leadership of nations and the liberty of mankind.

Printed in the Jersey City *Jersey Journal*, Sept. 22, 1911.

From William Frank McCombs, with Enclosure

My dear Governor: New York September 21, 1911.

Enclosed herewith I am sending a letter from Mr. Louis Wiley of the Times. I am going to dine with him tomorrow or next day. When you get through with the primaries I want to bring him down. I hear you are making a perfectly splendid fight over there and I hope these alarmist fellows are not getting on your nerves. A guinea chicken makes more noise than a tiger.

Sincerely yours,   Wm. F. McCombs

E N C L O S U R E

Louis Wiley to William Frank McCombs

Dear Mr. McCombs: [New York] September 20, 1911

Acknowledging your courteous note of the 19th inst. I thank you for your enclosure from Gov. Wilson, which I am taking the liberty of sending to our Managing Esitor [Editor] for attention. We shall be very glad to have some specific statement from the Governor, and we hope he will watch our correspondence from Trenton and will report any mis-statement of fact.

Will you kindly let me know what evening you can dine with me?

With regards,   Very sincerely yours,   Louis Wiley

TLS (Governors' Files, Nj).

From Lewis T. Bryant

My dear Governor: Trenton, N. J., Sept. 22, 1911.

Since writing you yesterday relative to the controversy between the employees and the management of the Lackawanna system, I have been in telephonic communication with the New York Department of Labor. I have made definite arrangements for a personal interview with Mr. W[illiam]. H[aynes]. Truesdale, President of the Delaware & Lackawanna Railroad Co. at his office on Monday the 25th inst. at 3:30 P.M. This was the earliest sppointment [appointment] I could secure.

As suggested by you, I shall endeavor to co-operate with the New York Department of Labor in the matter.

Yours respectfully,   Lewis T Bryant

TLS (Governors' Files, Nj).

A News Report of Political Speeches in Orange and Newark, New Jersey

[Sept. 23, 1911]

WILSON FEARS OWN ELECTION WAS TAINTED

Asks Earnestly for Probe of Reason for Return of 11,000 Sample Ballots.

Governor Wilson believes the taint of crooked politics affected his own election, and he told two big audiences last night in this city and Orange that he wants the taint removed.

The crookedness, the Governor thinks, is shown in the return through the mails of 11,000 sample ballots in this city. He wants an investigation started, if it is possible, and the fraudulent registration traced to its source.

With the greatest earnestness he declared that the purification of the ballot was of more importance than the effect on his individual fortunes. His words were received with cheers.

Speaking in Orange upon the employers' liability law and the advantage that indemnity insurance companies have taken of it to raise their rates, the Governor gave an intimation that the State might be forced to go into the indemnity or workingmen's insurance business. His declaration was as follows:

"There are some gentlemen—some employers—who have refused to come under that act. I hope they will reconsider their action, for it is very ill-considered.

"There are a great many indemnity companies which have sought to discourage the whole business by raising their rates from 400 to 1,000 per cent., when the employers try to do what they must do—insure themselves against the risk.

"What are these indemnity companies doing? They are making it very likely that we shall have to do very much more radical things.

"I am not by any means sure that my judgment goes to the length of a State system of insurance, but these gentlemen can oblige us to establish one.

"If they want to go out of business they can go out of business, because the duty of the State is to see that justice is done—not to see that men make profits in their business. It is to see that that greatest of all principles, conservation, is studied and carried out —the conservation of human life and energy."

In commending the candidates on the Wilson League ticket for Assemblymen, the Governor mentioned by name Assemblymen Balentine, Boettner, Macksey and Mylod as men who had been faithful to their constituents in the Legislature last winter.

At the mention of each name the Governor was interrupted by applause. Mr. Mylod is not a candidate for renomination for Assembly, but is running for sheriff against John V. Diefenthaler, the choice of the Wilson League. Mr. Mylod and some of his friends, in their campaign automobile, went to both meetings.

At the Orange meeting, held in Columbus Hall, some over-enthusiastic friends hung a lot of Mylod posters about the hall. The friends were reproved for discourtesy to the Wilson League and the Mylod pictures were removed.

The Governor again referred to the fight that the Public Service Corporation is making against Senator Bradley in Camden County. He recalled the seance that President McCarter, of the company, and David Baird had with the Senator in the effort to have Bradley take the sting out of the public utilities bill last winter.

When speaking on the subject in Orange, the Governor went so far as to make a pun about the subsequent development. He said the whole scheme had been "Baird." At the Krueger gathering[1] he declared that the action had been one of disservice instead of service to the company.

At both meetings the Governor was heartily cheered as "the next President of the United States." The reference to this was made in Orange by Judge Daniel A. Dugan,[2] who took charge of the meeting as permanent chairman, after Frank A. O'Connor, of West Orange,[3] had opened it.

While the Governor was speaking in the Krueger Auditorium, Thomas A. Boyle, the Sixth Ward Democratic leader,[4] called for "Three cheers for the next President of the United States," and they were given. The Governor had to stop in the middle of a sentence. He smiled until he had a chance to resume his address.

There was no doubt about the friendliness of both audiences for the Governor. He was cheered when he entered both halls, his points brought out frequent applause, and enthusiasm for him broke out at the close of each address. In the Krueger Auditorium he had to submit to an informal reception.

The Governor arrived in Orange shortly after 5 o'clock and went to the Essex County Country Club as the guest of Stephen J. Meeker, of Orange,[5] who is a candidate for freeholder on the Wilson League ticket. At the dinner were twenty guests, candidates and officials of the Wilson League. . . .

Printed in the *Newark Evening News*, Sept. 23, 1911; some editorial headings omitted.

[1] In Newark.

[2] Daniel Aloysius Dugan, admitted to the New Jersey bar in 1900, who had earlier been a reporter for the *New York Herald* and New Jersey editor of the

Brooklyn Daily Eagle, the New York *World,* and the *New York Journal,* and publisher of the *Orange,* N. J., *Herald.* Wilson had appointed him judge of the district court of Orange.

3 Town Collector of Orange, 1904-13.

4 A saloon owner of Newark.

5 General manager of the Mt. Pleasant Cemetery Co. of Newark and a resident of Orange.

From William Frank McCombs

My dear Governor: New York September 23, 1911.

I spent last evening with Mr. Louis Wiley, Business Manager of the New York Times. He has agreed to print any of the facts concerning you that I furnish him. I regard this as a distinct advantage. While we were at dinner one of his friends, who did not know me, came over to the table and Wiley casually said to him: "What do you think of Woodrow Wilson?" The answer was: "He is a radical and his views are subject to change for political reasons." Without revealing my relation, I asked the gentleman in what respects he regarded you as radical. He said: "In a great many respects." Then I asked him to tell me what they were. He finally could not say anything except as to initiative and referendum and direct primaries. He left us in complete rout. Nevertheless he is a very intelligent man and his expressions were honestly made. He is the type of a very large number of people who honestly hold opinions against you not based upon proper facts. I asked him where he got his impressions that you were dangerous and politically unreliable. He said he had gotten them from what the New York newspapers said.

After he left I turned to Mr. Wiley and asked him if it was not fair that the New York newspapers make a thorough analysis of what you had done and what your fundamental positions were. I suggested that in view of your prominence in this country, it was the bounden duty of the great journalists to make a thorough study and analysis of you and to state the facts fairly. I told him that an analysis would show that your "dangerous radicalism" would boil down to one or two things, and then I told him what your real position was on initiative and referendum, as you expressed it at luncheon yesterday. Wiley agreed with me. Then we discussed the methods of doing this and finally considered the following: That the New York Times in its editorial column would ask you a series of questions, which would be formulated by yourself, with any assistance that the Times editors could give you; that before the propounding of these questions publicly ample time would be given for you to formulate your answers.[1] Mr.

Wiley stated that not only would the Times print these questions and answers, but that he would give them the broadest circulation throughout the country. After threshing it out thoroughly with him and revolving it in my own mind afterwards, I think the suggestion is well worth your consideration.

I asked Mr. Wiley whether it was impossible that the Times would support you henceforth. He replied distinctly "Not impossible." Next to [Adolph S.] Ochs, the owner, Wiley is the greatest influence on that paper and I know that Ochs lays great store by Wiley's judgment. I think I am justified in feeling that we will at least be treated with greatest friendliness.

Two or three days ago it occurred to me that inasmuch as you could not go to the Democratic Rally at Boston, it would be very well to have somebody there who would make a speech for you. Malone was the most available man I could think of. So I called up my friends in Boston and got them to invite Malone, telling them what he would speak about. They extended him an invitation. He left this morning to make the speech this afternoon. I am assured by my friends there that the remarks concerning you will be featured in the public press.

Yours sincerely,   Wm. F. McCombs

TLS (Governors' Files, Nj).
[1] Instead of posing these questions in an editorial, they were incorporated in the *New York Times* interview printed at Dec. 24, 1911.

From A. B. Lowe

My dear Sir: Scranton, Pa., Sept. 23, 1911.

I have received your welcome reply to my letter, asking for your good offices in the controversey between the officials of the Lackawanna Railway and their track employees. On behalf of a good body of men whose excellent deportment during this suspension of work shows the men to be of first-class character, I thank you, and will welcome the assistance of your Commissioner from whom I have received a telegram this morning and to whom I will give a full and detailed statement of the whole matter.

I can only repeat that any settlement fair to both parties to the controversy will be accepted by me on behalf of these employees, and the moment an agreement for a settlement is reached, that moment the strike will be called off, the safety of the road and its patrons will be again in the hands of competent track foremen and we will do our part to expedite a settlement.[1] You will be pleased to know that on the Cincinnati, Hamilton, Dayton where a similar rule and wage controversy led to a disagreement on the wages question, the matter has been mutually referred to arbitration and Mr. P. H. Morrissey, President of the Railroad Employees and Investors Association[2] has accepted the position of our arbitrator.

Again thanking you for your good offices, which I assure you are greatly appreciated, I am,

Yours sincerely,   A. B. Lowe

TLS (Governors' Files, Nj).

[1] On September 26, 1911, William Haynes Truesdale, president of the Lackawanna, rejected Bryant's suggestion that the strikers be permitted to go back to work, pending arbitration, and sent out strikebreakers soon afterward. Most of the strikers had given up the struggle by the first of October.

[2] Patrick Henry Morrissey, grandmaster of the Brotherhood of Railroad Trainmen.

To the Mayor of Newark, the Prosecutor of Pleas of Essex County, and the Sheriff of Essex County

My dear Sir: [Sea Girt, N. J., c. Sept. 24, 1911]

The enclosed papers explain themselves. They set forth very explicitly and with a good deal of detail the conditions of lawlessness and of scandalous public disregard of law and order in the City of Newark which are deeply demoralizing and disgraceful, and the evidence with which the recital is supported is direct, the evidence of eyewitnesses of scenes which meant, if they meant anything, that the police and civil authorities of the city not only connived at the lawlessness but in some instances countenanced it in person.

It may be that this evidence can be successfully combated, but it is so strong, so explicit, so direct, and so shocking that it is plainly my duty as governor of the state to act upon it and to call your attention to the absolute necessity of a searching investigation and thoroughgoing correction of these conditions if they exist. I have no means of enforcing this advice under the laws of the state except public opinion; but that is a very powerful force indeed in our time; and it is, perhaps, my duty also to remind you that (?)[1].

I would not have felt myself justified in taking the course I am now taking with regard to these very serious allegations had I not learned that your attention had already been called to these things and that absolutely no action whatever concerning them had been taken. I would be very much obliged to you indeed if you would be kind enough to let me know at your early convenience what course you expect to pursue with regard to them in view of this communication.

In the confidence that your action will be prompt and effective.

Very truly yours,   Woodrow Wilson

Transcript (WWshLS, WP, DLC).
1 Wilson's question mark.

To the Voters of New Jersey

[[Sept. 25, 1911]]

It is evident that the Geran election law, if properly executed by the election officers, will prevent the frauds which it is plain have been practised in the past. The return of over 11,000 official envelopes addressed to voters in Essex County alone, to say nothing of the many thousands in other counties, proves that frauds were perpetrated at the last election and presumably at the last primary.

It is plain also that those who planned and executed those frauds last year will endeavor to repeat them this year, and that an attempt will be made to vote upon the fraudulent names on last year's poll books at to-morrow's primaries, unless the election officers and other authorities prevent it.

There are two ways to prevent these frauds. The first is for the election officer to compel every voter who offers to vote at the primary to thereupon register for the ensuing general election. The second is for the prosecutor in each county to make preparation to gather evidence of every attempt to vote on these fraudulent names, in which work the police authorities of every city should co-operate.

There have been some opposing views expressed as to the intent of the new law with reference to registering for the general election. I have examined the laws carefully on this point and have consulted experienced lawyers and am clear that the intent of the Geran act is to prevent voting at the primaries upon last year's fraudulent names by compelling the intending voters to register for the ensuing general election and thereby answer the questions which no fraudulent voter can answer.

If there was any doubt on this point it is plain that every bona-fide voter would desire to so register on primary day, and thus save himself the trouble of coming to the registry place on another day. Any voter, therefore, who manifests a desire to vote at the primary without registering for the general election puts the election officers and the watchers on notice that he is at least a possible and very likely a probable fraudulent voter.

Every prosecutor should make careful preparation to gather evidence of false voting and of violating the law by the election officers. The new act imposes new duties on them with respect to these matters, and even without that each of them ought to regard it as an essential part of his duty to co-operate with all the other authorities in preventing frauds at primaries and election. False voting at primaries goes to the foundation of free government, and I give public notice that I will use the utmost power of my office to bring the full penalty of the law upon any person who fraudulently votes at to-morrow's primaries and upon any election officer and other public official who neglects any duty imposed upon him by law in this regard.

Printed in the *Newark Evening News*, Sept. 25, 1911.

From Andrew Jackson Montague

(PERSONAL)

My dear Governor: [Richmond, Va.] September 25, 1911.

Your letter of the 16th instant[1] is duly received. I am greatly interested in your nomination, for by it I see something more than a temporary victory for our party.

Harmon may be as easily elected as you but the Democratic party will not survive his administration. Your's would mean a long lease of supremacy. The people of America will not approve a Machine nomination and its inevitable administrative methods. You are believed to be against all of these, hence your strength and the confidence of the people in your patriotism and cleanliness of methods.

As to your inquiry. The Senators[2] have given no public expression. They are both of the gum-shoe type, and are so far reticent, though they may be at work stealthily for Marmon [Harmon]. Temperamentally, they are for the "Interest," but your popularity in Virginia may force them a little later on to be "original" Wilson men. However, you want their support, and your real friends in this State will help you gain them at any sacrifice short of dishonor.

I am advised that Mr. R. E. Byrd, Speaker of the House of Delegates is for you. He told a friend of mine so much. He is very close to the Senators. Has he written you? I am so advised. Therefore, I would suggest that you have Byrd sounded as to the attitude of the two Senators.

If you have in concrete form your expressions upon the Initiative and Referendum and Recall, kindly supply me with the same, as I would like to be wholly apprised of your views in order to meet such objections that are made to you as is asserted in this State. For example, that you favor the recall of judges. This is untrue I know, but I would like to have your attitude upon this point in some way particularly understood.

I hear you are to be in the City early in October, and if so, I hope for a chance to talk fully with you over the situation in this State. If you cannot come I may be able to see you on going or returning from New York about the 22nd of October, provided it is agreeable and convenient to you.

It occurs to me to suggest that if Alderman is for you, you can ascertain the standing of Senator Martin. Martin, however, is an old man now and I doubt if he takes a very active part. His chief lieutenant is Congressman Flood,[3] who has been a Harmon man, but who will change at Martin's request.

Sincerely yours,   [A. J. Montague]

CCL (A. J. Montague Papers, Vi).

[1] It is missing in the Montague Papers.

[2] Thomas S. Martin and Claude Swanson.

[3] Henry De La Warr ("Harry") Flood of Appomattox. He served in the House of Representatives from 1901 until his death on December 8, 1921.

From William Frank McCombs

My dear Governor: New York September 26th, 1911.

I am leaving for the South tonight to be gone until October 9th. On my way I shall drop in and see some of our friends in Chicago and St. Louis.

I have read the article in Munsey's magazine[1] and think it has exactly the right tone—especially what you say about not disturbing business. I find a great fear of you (of course unfounded) among business men. They feel that you are aiming at some sort of destruction. Their ideas are nebulous but, nevertheless, if they continue to hold them, in my judgment it will do you great harm. Of course, no candidate can win either a nomination or an election if business people are against him. By this I do not mean big business and bad business. I think it might be a desirable thing on some appropriate occasion in the East that you make a reassuring statement that you have no desire to disturb business but on the contrary you stand for business peace and prosperity. This talk against you is becoming more or less general. I know it is cruelly unjust and of course you are the only one who can correct it. I think it would be wise from now on to discuss nothing new and to stick to a few fundamental ideas. I think we are coming into a period of great disturbance. I believe that Mr. Taft has done himself incalculable harm by his recent drastic utterances[2] and Mr. Wickersham has added greatly to Mr. Taft's weakness by his recent foolhardiness.[3]

If I have any sort of intuition Taft is growing weaker every day and I further believe that the business men of the country will feel themselves forced to the Democratic party for safety. If anything comes up that I can do my office can communicate with me and I am always at your command.

Yours sincerely,   Wm. F. McCombs

TLS (Governors' Files, Nj).
    [1] It is printed at Oct. 1, 1911.
    [2] A reference to President Taft's speech in Peoria, Ill., on September 22, 1911, in which he said that the Supreme Court, in its recent decisions dissolving the oil and tobacco trusts, had decided what the Sherman Act meant, and that large corporations now had to obey the law and voluntarily reorganize in order to avoid prosecution.
    [3] Attorney General George Woodward Wickersham said on September 23 that the area of uncertainty about the Sherman Act had been greatly reduced by the "rule of reason" and that, in order to avoid forcible dissolution and its penalties, corporations under investigation might submit plans of reorganization to the Department of Justice, which would then approve or disapprove such plans.

A Statement on the Democratic Primary Election

[[Sept. 27, 1911]]

The returns, except in Essex County, are entirely satisfactory to the friends of progressive legislation among the Democrats.[1] The defeat of the progressive candidates in Essex County was expected and discounted beforehand, and represents a final effort from the Smith-Nugent machine to discredit the new regime in New Jersey.

Printed in the Trenton *True American*, Sept. 28, 1911.
    [1] In every other county, Wilson Democrats were victorious at the polls. In Essex, however, the Smith-Nugent candidates won a smashing victory, with every ward giving a majority to the Regulars. State Senator Harry V. Osborne was the only Wilson supporter nominated, and he had been endorsed by the Regulars.

To Andrew Jackson Montague

[Sea Girt, N.J.]

My dear Governor Montague: September 27, 1911.

Thank you sincerely for your letter of September twenty-fifth. It contained just the sort of information I most desired.

You can reassure my friends entirely upon the question of the initiative, referendum and recall. I shall try to have my only utterances about these matters mailed to you from New York. I have declared so explicitly and so repeatedly against the recall of judges that it is a mere piece of malicious mischief on somebody's part to hold me as representing the people [opposite]. The initiative and referendum are by no means a universal remedy. It depends upon the time and place and situation whether they should be pressed for acceptance or not. Our whole effort is to get legislative action which is responsive to the real judgment of public opinion; no one means is a panacea.

I am to be constnatly [constantly] on the go from now until the seventh of November, because I am accepting the orders of our State Committee and shall be stumping the State from end to end.

Pray let me know, however, when you come to New York so that if possible I may get in touch with you.

Cordially and sincerely yours,   Woodrow Wilson

TLS (A. J. Montague Papers, Vi).

A News Report of a Speech at the Laying of the Cornerstone of the Woodbury, New Jersey, High School

[Sept. 28, 1911]

LAYING THE CORNER STONE

Greeted by 1500 citizens of Gloucester County Governor Woodrow Wilson gripped the minds of his large audience present at the corner stone laying of the Woodbury High School.

It was a new and distinctly pleasing personality that told what education was and what it will do, and is doing. New ideas were presented and education shown to be a thing concrete and not abstract.

It was the largest gathering ever assembled, at one time, about the old walls of the new building to be. It might be called a distinct tribute to Woodrow Wilson, the man and educator, and not as the statesman or politician in its broadest sense. He was greeted not as the executive of a great State—indeed, he did not seem to be such, but as one who is making a pleasant visit, and he enjoyed his reception immensely, for it was so spontaneously given.

As he took the silver trowel and splashed the mortar about to seal the corner-stone, an irrepressible smile wrinkled his face, reminding him evidently of the joys of fifty years ago.

The corner-stone laid, he mounted the scaffolding, and with quiet eloquence began his address.

"This occasion reminds me somewhat of my former occupation. If a man did not know who he was yesterday, he would not know who he is to-day, or who he shall be tomorrow. In order to know ourself today we must have a knowledge of who and what we were yesterday. If we did not know anything of the past we could not progress toward the future. The education of the past or last generation must fit into this present generation as funnels interlap each other, in order to build up a substantial community or State. So the public school supplies this part of the work of bringing up the last generation to the present, and fitting the present generation to reach out beyond the knowledge thus attained, to a higher and broader usefulness as citizens without one generation becoming isolated from the other. Therefore we force our children to learn all we learned. We want to retain our own individuality in the rising generation so we cram this pill down their throats whether they want to swallow it or not. They profit by our mistakes, as we did by the mistakes of the preceding generation.

"If we know what happened in the past, we are better able to act in the future. Many things once regarded as true have been found to be untrue, and many things we now believe to be true will probably be found untrue in the future. It is only by a full knowledge of the past and present that we can lessen the number of mistakes. And men and communities alike learn by their mistakes.

"Every time the cornerstone of a new schoolhouse is laid it adds strength to our civilization, and civilization depends upon education. Following the dark ages there was a period known as the renaissance, when students began to grope for the knowledge of past ages, and immediately civilization began to advance. They had their eyes opened as is a baby's. A baby is a pagan. He knows nothing but what he sees, and he doesn't understand that. It is not until he begins to acquire language that he gets beyond paganism and begins his education.

"Every schoolhouse in New Jersey strengthens the state, and makes it a better state and a more important unit of the United States, and therefore it is that the state should take official cognizance of such events as this."

The program of the afternoon was under the direction of the American Mechanics. The Governor and Calvin N. Kendall, Commissioner of Public Instruction, were met at the 2.06 train by the American Mechanics, Board of Education, City Council, and the Moose Band. In parade formation, the body marched to the school building, when "America" was sung by the audience.

The new cornerstone was laid on top of the one laid three years ago, in the building destroyed by fire last December.

Printed in the Woodbury, N. J., *Gloucester County Democrat*, Sept. 28, 1911.

A News Report of a Speech Opening the Legislative Campaign of 1911

[Sept. 29, 1911]

GOVERNOR WILSON AT OCEAN CITY

Ocean City, New Jersey, Sept. 28.—This little city turned out fifteen hundred people tonight to welcome Governor Wilson. This being the first of the Governor's addresses in advocacy of the election of a Democratic Legislature this Fall, it attracted considerable interest. The Governor discussed the legislation enacted last Winter and suggested that if these measures met with the approval of the people of New Jersey they should elect men to the next Legislature who will continue the good work.

Judge Howard Carrow, of Camden County, also delivered an address along the same lines.

Printed in the Trenton *True American*, Sept. 29, 1911.

A News Report of Three Campaign Speeches in Cape May County, New Jersey

[Sept. 30, 1911]

WILSON SCENTS PRIMARY FRAUD

CAPE MAY, Sept. 30.—Coming into the southernmost county of the State, Governor Wilson met the citizens of this bail[i]wick at three meetings yesterday and gave to them an account of his work while in the Executive chair, as he had promised he would do.

The weather conditions were not propitious, but notwithstanding this the meetings were well attended and enthusiastic, as the Governor reported upon his stewardship and flayed the Republican and Democratic "machines" within the county.

Governor Wilson spoke first at Cape May Courthouse, where half the people seemed to have left their business and domestic cares to come out to hear their visitor. Early in the night he addressed an audience in Cape May, and then was whisked away by automobile to Wildwood.

One of the most significant points of the Governor's speech in this city was his reference to some information that appears to have come to him that, despite the corrupt practices act, there had been vote buying at the Cape May primaries Tuesday. It was stated that prior to the meeting the Governor had endeavored to get in communication with Prosecutor [Ernest W.] Lloyd, of this county, for what purpose is not known.

In the course of his speech, he said:

"I am told that some gentlemen hereabouts do not distinctly understand the provisions of the corrupt practises act, since 125 men who voted at the primaries last Tuesday have been told to come to a certain office Saturday night and get their money. If we can get a prosecutor who will prosecute and a grand jury that will indict, I think we can make some gentlemen who ignored that corrupt practises act very sorry.

"One of the sorrows that a Governor of this State has to bear is that in such cases he is powerless to do anything. It is time somebody had the power to right such wrongs.

"Cape May is growing up and is of age," continued the speaker. "It is made up of men of sturdy stock, of men able to take care of themselves. I haven't found any one who is not able to call the boss by name. I have not found any one who has not known that in Cape May County there have been two kinds of Democrats—'regular' Democrats and 'Bob Hand' Democrats.[1] There are men who once were Democrats, but who have become what they will be all their lives—members of the majority—no matter which side that may represent.

"You know what happened to Senator Bradley in Camden County,"[2] he said. "I want to say that I have been in close personal touch with Senator Bradley and I know he is one of the most honorable and capable of men. He stood for progressive legislation, for what the people had demanded, and he was punished for doing his duty. It only goes to show that the Republican organization, the machine in Camden County, doesn't mean to have men who do their duty."

"How about Smith?" shouted some one.

"We are not talking about back numbers," quickly retorted the Governor, "We are discussing issues." . . .

Printed in the *Newark Evening News*, Sept. 30, 1911; some editorial headings omitted.

[1] Democrats who collaborated with Robert Edmonds Hand, Republican leader of Cape May County, owner of oyster planting, lumbering, and general contracting enterprises, sheriff, 1892-97, assemblyman, 1897-98, and state senator, 1898-1903 and 1907-13.

[2] He had just been defeated for renomination by the Baird machine's candidate, William T. Read.

An Interview

[Oct. 1911]

WOODROW WILSON, PRESIDENTIAL POSSIBILITY

THE GOVERNOR OF NEW JERSEY AND HIS VIEWS ON THE PRESSING PROBLEMS OF THE DAY

By Isaac F. Marcosson

Less than two years ago, Woodrow Wilson was president of Princeton University, where, bulwarked by books, he fitted into an aloof and scholarly atmosphere. To-day he is Governor of New Jersey, boss wrecker of corrupt machines, and militant master of his party. To-morrow he may be the Democratic candidate for the Presidency of the United States. Here is a spectacle which any American, regardless of party affiliations, must view with interest and with a certain satisfaction that he lives in a country which can produce such a development within so brief a period. . . .

Ask Governor Wilson how this seemingly miraculous transformation has been achieved, and he will tell you that he was born a political animal.

"From my boyhood," he said to me, "I have aimed at political life. The reason I studied law was because, when I was a boy in the South, the law furnished the shortest path to public life. I gave it up, later, because I found I could not be an honest lawyer and a politician at the same time. At least, I did not know how to then. I tried the next best thing, which was studying politics. I went back to school, where I undertook to learn something of the facts of government. People think I was born a scholar; as a matter of fact, I was born a man of affairs."

There is an air of quiet and determined conviction about this spare, well-formed, gray-eyed man in whom the thinker and the doer meet so admirably. The face is long, the forehead high and smooth; the whole demeanor is that of some high-bred, well-controlled, but emphatic organization. The face shifts quickly from grave to gay, but there is always behind the bright, winning smile some evidence of hidden strength, latent determination, steadfast purpose. Governor Wilson's voice is clear, resonant, and distinct. Without effort he can reach the remote ends of a large auditorium. Keep in mind, however, the fact that he had been addressing audiences for twenty years before he began to arouse the Jersey voter from his lethargy in a stirring campaign that set a new mark for strenuosity.

When you go to see Governor Wilson at the State House in Trenton, two things impress you very strongly. One is the striking and convincing personality of the man; the other is the fact that the door of his office is wide open, so that "all who would might enter, and no one was denied." You can almost see him from the moment you step into the long conference-room hung with portraits of former Governors.

As you look across its stately stretch of space, you see a small chamber simply furnished in oak. Here, with ranks of law books behind him, this militant Governor sits at a real bar of the people. From the mantel on his left a bronze Washington in a sort of Roman toga and a metal Lincoln in a nondescript attire look down upon him. Through the windows in front of him he can see the tide of Trenton traffic moving up and down State Street. He has only to turn in his swivel chair to the left to see the shining Delaware fringed with green.

There is no "gum-shoeing" about Governor Wilson's office; no whispered and suspicious talk. Men who come there must speak their minds frankly and in the open. This is why the sound of the old order of things has ceased in the State House of New Jersey. Tuesday is "Governor's Day," when the executive office is a sort of forum for everybody. There is neither color line nor political bar to free speech with the head of the State.

I walked with Governor Wilson down State Street to a modest hotel, where we had luncheon. The humblest citizen of Trenton could not have been more unassuming. When people recognized him, he acknowledged their greeting with a dignified courtesy. At the restaurant he took a side table, and throughout the meal any special attention almost embarrassed him. I cite this instance merely to show one phase of the man, because a genuine sense of modesty seems to be ingrained in him. . . .

Later, I rode with Governor Wilson in his automobile from Trenton to Sea Girt, where the State troops were camped, and where the Governor's cottage—the New Jersey White House—is located. As we whirled through the country—and few parts of New Jersey are more beautiful than this—here and there a word of greeting was shouted at the Governor. In response there was always the same dignified courtesy—never anything of the "hale and hearty" manner which is so often affected by the politician.

On this trip we talked of the great problems that press down upon the mind of the country, and thus, as we sped toward the sea, there developed the interview which now follows.

No issue in the next Presidential campaign will be more important than the tariff. I asked Governor Wilson to define his position, and he replied:

"I believe in a tariff for revenue only, but I recognize the fact that our existing economic system has been built on the opposite theory. Any change in our scale of duties ought to be brought about by prudent and well-considered steps, and with statesman-like regard for every legitimate interest involved. We ought not to impair our industries or imperil the employment of our working people.

"Everybody will agree that if our tariff policy is indeed to be protective, and to seek the objects which it has always pretended to seek, it is perfectly legitimate that it should pay a very careful regard to the business interests of the country taken as a whole. But that is a very different matter from paying regard to the individual interests of particular undertakings and of particular groups of men. The long and short of the whole experience, as we now see it, is that our whole tariff legislation has degenerated from a policy of protection into a policy of patronage.

"The party which has stood most consistently for the so-called system of protection has derived not a little of its power from the support of the great business interests of the country. I do not mean the moral support merely. I mean that it has been supplied with immense sums of money for the conduct of its campaigns and the maintenance of its organization, and that, whether consciously or unconsciously, it has established a partnership with the manufacturing interests which has deprived it of its liberty of action in matters touching the tariff. It is bound by obligations, both tacit and explicit, to protect those interests which have been its most stalwart backers and supporters.

"It has again and again happened, therefore, to the scandal of the whole country, that items and clauses have been inserted into our tariff laws which were not even explained to the members of Congress, which were a matter of private arrangement between the representatives of certain great business interests and the members of the Ways and Means Committee of the House and the Finance Committee of the Senate. The Finance Committee of the Senate, in particular, during many years, was the stronghold of these special interests.

"I am not intimating direct corruption of any kind. I am speaking now only of that subtle corruption of the will to which I have already referred. The will dominant in the Finance Committee of the Senate has for many decades together been subservient to the dictates and to the interests of particular groups of men. Their interests have been served constantly, and often in defiance of the well-known opinions and purposes not only of the national administration, but of the members of the House as well, who struggled in vain against the dictates of the omnipotent leaders of the Senate. Here, displayed in its grossest form, was the intimate power of business over politics."

"What do you think about Canadian reciprocity?" I asked.

"I welcome reciprocity with Canada," replied Governor Wilson, "as a breach in the tariff wall."

Closely akin to the tariff is the great problem of real popular government, for today, as never before, the people are beginning to take the control of public office into their own hands. Oregon's precedent of drastic reform in this respect is spreading to other commonwealths, and the question of direct primaries, the initiative, the referendum, and the recall have a nation-wide interest and importance. Concerning them, Governor Wilson said:

"I believe emphatically in the direct primary. Every State in the Union should have it.

"I believe in direct and popular election of United States Senators. Such a law enforced in every State would prevent legislative control by special influence, and thus one of the greatest menaces to representative government would be removed.

"I believe, too, in the initiative and referendum, but I don't think it may be regarded as a general blanket remedy to apply with equal effect to every State. Each community has its own problems, and I believe that the initiative should be introduced in one State at a time to meet its peculiar needs and emergencies.

"If we felt that we had genuine representative government in our State Legislatures, no one would propose the initiative or referendum in America. They are being proposed now as a means of bringing our representatives back to the consciousness that what they are bound in duty and in mere policy to do is to represent the sovereign people whom they profess to serve, and not the private interests which creep into their counsels by way of machine orders and committee conferences. The most ardent and successful advocates of the initiative and referendum regard them as a sobering means of obtaining genuine representative action on the part of legislative bodies."

In the matter of the recall, the Governor makes some reservations, for he exempts the judiciary. Here are his views, which closely agree with those of President Taft, but which were expressed before the President wrote his forcible message vetoing the admission of Arizona to the Union because the judicial recall was embodied in the new State's constitution:

"The recall is a means of administrative control. If properly regulated and devised, it is a means of restoring to administrative officials what the initiative and referendum would restore to legislators—namely, a sense of direct responsibility to the people who choose them. The recall is going to be used—I feel safe in the prediction—against those who wilfully and dishonestly do the things which are contrary to the interests of their communities.

"The recall of judges is another matter. Judges are not law-makers. They are not administrators. Their duty is not to determine what the law shall be, but to determine what the law is. Their independence, their sense of dignity and of freedom, are of the first consequence to the stability of the State. To apply to them the principle of the recall is to set up the idea that determinations of what the law is must respond to popular impulse.

"It is sufficient that the people should have the power to change the law when they will. It is not necessary that they should directly influence, by threat of recall, those who merely interpret the law already established. The importance and desirability of the recall as a means of administrative control ought not to be obscured by drawing it into this other and very different field."

So far, we had discussed politics. Now we turned for the moment to a problem which lies very close to the whole American people—a problem which really should have no politics, and yet which has been closely identified with the policies of both of the great parties. I refer, of course, to the Sherman Anti-Trust Act, around which a fierce strife has raged for years.

I asked Governor Wilson to tell me his opinion of the Sherman Act, and he replied:

"I believe in the policy of the Sherman Act. At the same time, I believe that some combinations in the field of business and industry make for efficiency and economy, and stimulate rather than destroy competition. So soon as the object and the operation of the combination come to be a restraint, it is illegitimate, because it is opposed to the common interest."

"But what about the big corporations and their alliance with politics?" I asked the Governor.

"I am not hostile to corporations," he answered, "if corporations will prove that they are as much interested in the general welfare as we are. I am not opposed to anybody who is serving the public—who is giving them honest service, and at a reasonable rate, not with the primary idea of squeezing and exploiting them, but with the primary idea of serving them.

"America is willing to give abundant largess to anybody who will serve her, but she is very chary, if she can have her own way, of giving fortunes to anybody who imposes upon her. . . .

"The alliance of these men with politics is the most demoralizing thing that could possibly descend upon any country. And it has descended upon us." . . .

"What is the Democratic program as you see it?" was the next question.

"It is not difficult to answer that question," was the ready response. "The first item of that program is that the machinery of political control must be put into the hands of the people. That means, translated into concrete terms, direct primaries, a short ballot, and, wherever necessary, the initiative, the referendum, and the recall. These things are being desired and obtained, not by way of revolution, not even with a desire to effect such changes as will alter any fundamental thing in our governmental system, but for the purpose of recovering what seems to have been lost —the people's control of their own instruments, their right to exercise a free and constant choice in the management of their own affairs.

"Back of all reform lie the means of getting it. Back of the question what we want is the question how we are going to get it. The immediate thing we must do is to resume popular government."

We had sped swiftly across the country. Already the tang of the sea was in the air; our journey was near its end.

"One more question. What of the so-called 'new radicalism' of which you are the accredited leader?" I asked.

The Governor's face relaxed into a smile.

"All the people are radical," he said. "That is to say, the people are ready for any reasonable program that will get them the goods—the goods not being anybody's scalp, not anybody's ruin, not any damage to the honest business of the country, but the proper control of their own affairs. I will not permit without challenge the men who are holding back, the men who are afraid of the people, to appropriate to themselves the handsome word 'conservative.'

"I maintain that those of us who believe in the so-called radical program are intelligent conservatives. The distinction which I make is that time-old distinction between Liberals and Tories— between men who can move and men who are such Bourbons that they cannot forget anything and cannot learn anything.

"The so-called standpatter is a man who is fooling himself to the top of his bent. I suppose that a man on an ice-floe in the Arctic Ocean thinks he is standing still, but he is not. There is a great drift of the water under him. I suppose the so-called conservatives claim to be standing where their fathers stood. They are doing nothing of the kind, because the country is not where their fathers were. There is a great drift historically, a glacial movement, of which they are not aware.

"In a word, the so-called radicalism of our time is nothing else than the effort to release the powerful constructive energies of our time."

Most men—even the most astute politician trained to glib reply —would have quailed under such a continuous cross-examination; but Governor Wilson met every query with precise and ready response. Here was reflected his habit of thought. His mind thinks in one measure at a time, and he wants these measures to follow in sequence. He leaves nothing in the air, permits no doubt as to where he stands. Artistic finish marks his performances. Thus his political career has been a steady march of completed achievement.

One of his replies will give you an index to his mental procedure. I asked him for an expression of opinion about currency reform, and he said:

"My mind is to let on that subject."

In other words, he had not studied the subject sufficiently, and did not care to pronounce half-baked conclusions. . . .

You leave Woodrow Wilson with the feeling that you have rubbed up against the new kind of leadership in our public life. It is more than the mere domination of faction or party; it is the authority of high culture and the realization of a solemn responsibility.

Just as the programs of parties must henceforth be programs of enlightenment and readjustment, so must the processes of political change be processes of thought. The men to bring them about, whether Democrats or Republicans, must be men of broad mentality and large vision. To this task Governor Wilson brings a peculiar degree of fitness. He is still a teacher, only his school is the forum of a State; his textbooks are legislative bills; his pupils are the people who want good government.

Whatever may be the outcome of the approaching struggle that projects him before the whole nation as Presidential possibility, one thing is certain—the country is all the better for his participation in its politics.

Printed in *Munsey's Magazine*, XLVI (Oct. 1911), 3-13.

A Religious Address in Trenton, New Jersey[1]

[[Oct. 1, 1911]]

I take it for granted that the significance of a Sunday school lies in this circumstance: That it is an attempt to carry along the

[1] Delivered in the Second Regiment Armory before a Sunday School rally

religious education of the nation with the secular education of it. Almost all my life, I have been engaged in educational work. I have always had the same conception of it, from the beginning until now, namely, that education is a fundamental part of progress, that you can't make progress unless you tie one generation in with another. Any disconnection between one generation and another will be a break, and may be a fatal break in the continuity of progress. You can't make progress in disconnected groups, and, therefore, with each generation you have to take the younger people as they come on and supply them with those conditions of thought which have sustained the progress of the generations that have come before them. You have to see to it that the light that has been accumulated by scholars and sages and men of profound experience shall not be dissipated, because the next generation knows nothing of it.

There is a sense in which education may be said to be the memory of the race—recollecting its experiences, building upon the things that it has done, not forgetting its successes and always remembering its mistakes; throwing aside the things that have not borne the test of time and of thought and discovery, and going on to those things which are more and more sanctioned from generation to generation by what is known and thought and discovered in the world. You know that one of the experiences of the Christian Church has been that it from time to time has feared the effect of discovery and the effect of scientific thought —the effect of the thought based upon the mere phenomena of nature—upon the teachings derived from the Bible. It has turned out to be an idle fear, because there has [have] never been any fundamental discrepancies between the teachings of the Bible, which is God's written word, and the teachings of nature, which is God's cipher—which we make out more and more distinctly from generation to generation. Religious education is education in this very Word of God; not the Word of God written in nature, for that is the study of the schools on week-days, but the Word of God written in His Scriptures.

For my part, I am interested in Sunday School work only as a study of the Scriptures. The only significant book, the only book that can have any possible significance as a textbood [textbook] in the Sunday School is the Bible itself, and as we must train our children in the rest of the thought of the world, we must if we are to make progress as a nation ground each generation as it comes along in the established and tested moral judgments of the world.

---

of 6,000—"the flower," the Trenton *True American*, Oct. 2, 1911, said, of "Trenton's Christian citizenship."

When you think what this is—what all men in all ages have been in search of—the search for what is right to do and right to think and right to feel is not a search confined to Christian nations. It began long before the Bible began to have the pervasive and general influence that it has in the modern world. The great thinkers of the old so-called heathen nations thought along these profound lines of human morality—of the things that made human life pure, effective and happy. I take it that what every man and woman in the world is in search of, in the last analysis, is happiness, and that the trouble with the greater part of the world is the superficial view it takes of happiness. So many people waste so many years of their life in the pursuit of those things which they fancy will bring them satisfaction, but which bring them only repining and disgust. The search of the world is for peace of mind, happiness of relationship, the joy of living and of sharing the life of others.

All the great serious literature of the world has this as its burden and theme. If you go back to those wonderful old Greek tragedies you will find that they are an uncovering of the human heart and of human fate. I wonder if you ever saw a Greek tragedy put upon the stage. I suppose that if you should see it and hear its dialogues and its choruses in English translation, you would expect to hear something very remote from modern experience; and I dare say you would be astonished to find that their display, as it were, upon these ancient boards, was the familiar tragedy of life itself, known to you and to your parents and to your grandparents, and to all men, without distinction of race or place throughout the history of the world, because the Greek tragedies uncover more directly than any other production outside the Bible the inevitable moral consequences of everything that a man does.

You see in those tragedies a great network of action and motive, woven by the men and women themselves, in which they are more and more entangled, in which they are more and more entrapped if they don't know the weave and pattern with which it is put together, out of which only those who have the clearest vision of the soul emerge unspotted and triumphant. There, in moving picture, is displayed to you the fortunes of the human soul. Nowhere else, I take it, is the soul stripped so naked and bare as it is in the old tragedies of the Greeks. They saw the deep moral significance of the world, they saw that terrible interrogation point that is written after every movement of human conduct, and all that they sought in their plays was the answer to those questions which all the world has been trying to answer from the beginning.

And if you turn to the great plays of Shakespeare you will find that your delight in them is that they were not confined in their significance to the age of Shakespeare. The astonishing thing about Shakespeare's plays is that if you change the costume, if you change the historical circumstances displayed by the plot of the play, these might be your neighbors, these might be the men and women of today, the same variety, the same strength, the same weakness, the same pettiness, the same greatness, the same humor, the same tragedy, the same struggle to find the pathway, the same theme of life, the same harness of hatred in which men sometimes try to pull the inevitable load of circumstance.

If you turn to the works of Dante, the great Italian writer, to that extraordinary book of his which he denominated "The Divine Comedy," you will find the same thing. There is one thing in Dante which is, perhaps, to be found nowhere else. One of Dante's books—one of the divisions of his great work—is entitled "The Inferno"—in other words, it is entitled "Hell." It is a picture of the life of the damned, and the significant thing of that book is that Dante picks out characters living at the time that his book was written, and shows them already in hell, displaying, perhaps, for the first time in literature the significant fact that a man goes to hell of his own volition and of his own character, and gets there before he dies; that hell is the moral setting which he has made for his own life. It is the debauching and debasing of his own motives, it is the conscience that he lives and sleeps with, and he is tortured long before the day comes when he shall render his final account.

Is there no man present who can testify to that? Is there no man present who tosses uneasily on his bed at night because of the things that he remembers that he did in the daytime[?] Is there no man here who works feverishly during the day in order that he may forget what he did yesterday? Is there no man here who resorts to strong drink in order to forget? Is there nobody here who knows the impulse of plunging into that stream of forgetfulness that the ancients called the Stream of Lethe? You know what Dante meant when he depicted those still living as already caught in the tortures of iniquity; and so all great serious literature has this first or last as its theme: What was man born into the world for? What are the motives which will lift him along the highway? What are those that will drive him downward into the pit?

The beauty about the Bible is that it is the most wholesome, the most perfectly symmetrical, the least morbid picture of life and motives of men in the world. Almost every other book has a

lit[t]le streak of morbidness in it, but this book is wholesome and
sweet and natural and naif from cover to cover. Here are no
dull moralizings; here is the life of man set forth as it was simply
lived from generation to generation. I take it that the problem
which you would all study for the Sunday School is the biographies and the histories of the Old Testament and of the New. I
suppose that the Epistles of the New Testament are for the perusal
of those who are mature, because in the Epistles is set forth, as
it were, the philosopy of the whole thing, the thoughtful reflection based upon the providence of God and the revelation of His
Son. The Epistles constitute the theology of the Bible, and the
rest of it constitutes the experience of mankind in contact with
Divine Providence.

The reassuring thing about the Bible is that its biographies are
not like any other biographies that you know of. Take up almost
any biography outside of the Bible and the writer tries to make a
hero of the man he is writing about. No writer in the Bible tries
to make a hero out of mere human stuff. There isn't a character
of the Bible—there isn't a character even amongst those who are
picked out by the Bible itself, by the special representatives and
ambassadors of God—whose life is not displayed as full of faults
and shortcomings and natural slips from the way of virtue. It
were a matter of despair to those of us who have come after if
the Bible had represented these persons as unimpeachable in
character and unexceptionable in their conduct, because the
theme of the Bible, so far as it is a biography, is the theme of the
discovery of itself by the human soul, is the theme of the slow
"come on" which each man and woman may gain of himself or
herself under the guidance of the spirit of God.

After all, we fight not with flesh and blood, but with unseen
forces, most of which are within ourselves. The Bible says: "Let
no man say he was tempted of God, for God tempteth no man."
I am inclined to add: "Let no man say that he was tempted of
the devil," for the devil never comes into any man's life except
by his permission and invitation. Let each man say and realize
that his temptation is the suggestion of his own spirit, and then
let him know that the mastery he must seek is the mastery over
himself.

How often does the Bible eulogize the man who masters his own
passions! "Greater is he that ruleth himself than he that ruleth
a city," and the foundation of the mastery of cities and of States
and of nations is the mastery of one's self. Just so soon as the
man who tries to master human circumstance puts himself at the
front of it, then begins the day of his weakness, and the day of

his defeat. In every circumstance of life, for the child as well as for him who is grown, in every day and in every turn of every day, the question is: "Shall we rule our own spirits?" And here, set forth in such simple terms that the child may understand it, in the annals of the Holy Scripture are written the histories of men of every kind, whose glory was that they did master their own spirits, and through the whole thing lies what the Greek tragedies were never able to supply—the key, the thread to the labyrinth, the solution of the problem, the answer to the eternal question.

He alone can rule his own spirit who puts himself under the command of the spirit of God, revealed in His Son, Jesus Christ, our Savior. He is the captain of our souls; he is the man from whose suggestions and from whose life comes the light that guid-eth every man that ever came into the world. Ah, if we can make our Sunday Schools the blazing centers of that light, then indeed will the darkness of the world be dissipated. The happiness of seeing a great company of people like this gathered together in the interest of the Sunday School is the happiness of knowing that there are they who seek light and who know that the lamp from which their spirits can be kindled is the lamp that glows in the Word of God.

Every Sunday School should be a place where this great book is not only opened, is not only studied, is not only revered, but is drunk of as if it were a fountain of life, is used as if it were the only source of inspiration and of guidance. No great nation can ever survive its own temptations and its own follies that does not indoctrinate its children in the Word of God; so that as school master and as Governor I know that my feet must rest with the feet of my fellowmen upon this foundation, and upon this foundation only; for the righteousness of nations, like the righteousness of men, must take its source from these foundations of inspiration.

I am sorry for the men who do not read the Bible every day. I wonder why they deprive themselves of the strength and of the pleasure. It is one of the most singular books in the world, for every time you open it some old text that you have read a score of times suddenly beams with a new meaning. Evidently the mood and the thought of that day, bred by the circumstances that you cannot analyze, has suddenly thrown its light upon that page and upon that passage, and there springs out upon the page to you something that you never saw lie upon it before. There is no other book that I know of of which this is true; there is no other book that yields its meaning so personally, that seems to fit itself so intimately to the very spirit that is seeking its guidance. And so when we teach our children we must not teach them, I hope, dogmatically. We must not try to make them read the Scripture as we read it, but merely try to bring them into such contact with the Scripture that it will yield its meaning to their hearts and to their minds. Make it their companion, make it their familiar textbook, and the rest will take care of itself.

Who shall dare to guide another human spirit in the same path that he himself has trodden? Shall we not merely take those whom we teach to the road and say: "Here is the way of life. Walk ye on it; don't follow us; don't look to us as examples of the consequence of our teaching. Walk ye on it, and it will lead you to the City of Light."

There are great problems, ladies and gentlemen, before the American people. There are problems which will need purity of spirit and an integrity of purpose such as has never been called for before in the history of this country. I should be afraid to go forward if I did not believe that there lay at the foundation of all our schooling and of all our thought this incomparable and unimpeachable Word of God. If we cannot derive our strength thence, there is no source from which we can derive it, and so I would bid you go from this place, if I may, inspired once more with the feeling that the providence of God is the foundation of affairs, and that only those can guide, and only those can follow, who take this providence of God from the sources where it is authentically interpreted.

I congratulate you that you have a part in the development of the great Sunday School work. I sometimes wish very candidly, ladies and gentlemen, that there was more simple reading and interpretation of the Bible and fewer elaborated Sunday School lessons. I want to say very frankly that I never saw a Sunday School lesson that yielded the meaning of the text that it was trying to interpret. If you will only give these little people the pure bread itself you won't have to ask some inexpert chemical analyist [analyst] to tell them how the bread is made up. There is no man with insight enough to see how the bread of life is made, and I wish sometimes that we could strip off these superficial explanations and get down to those things that sustain our spirits. (Applause.)

Some of the songs that we sing are silly and meaningless. They have neither poetry or sense in them. Why can't we sing the old psalms? Why can't we take in paraphrase, if in no otherwise, those immortal verses which have sung the spirit of God through generation after generation? Why do we have to concoct silly rhymes of our own? I want to be very frank. Where is that ridiculous "Beautiful Isle of Somewhere"?[2] (Applause.)

Who has discovered it; who has charted it? Where is it? I don't want to float through vague seas like that. I know what the writer is trying to describe. I suppose he is trying to describe Heaven, not merely the Heaven to which we hope to go, but the Heaven we carry around with us, if we are in connection with the spirit of God; and that "Beautiful Isle of Somewhere" is here where we are standing, if we will appropriate the spirit of God. We don't have to go discover it. I must say that I want to enter my protest, if it be polite in the circumstances, against that sort of thing. We know where these things are. We know exactly where they can be discovered; the whole chart is laid out between the covers of the Holy Scripture, and any man who chooses can go upon that voyage with the knowledge that the haven is already discovered, the wind already abroad that will fill his sails and carry him happily into it, and the pilot on board under whose guidance he cannot go astray. I trust you will not regard it as bad taste for me to say this. I am not criticizing the program. I am simply illustrating my theme. I want to urge that we get down to hard pan again, that we regard the whole business of the Sunday School as the familiarizing of the children of the United States with the Word of God. (Applause.)

If you only made them read it again and again and again, and added no comment that they did not ask for, you would be doing an incomparable service for American morality and American progress. Thomas Carlisle used to say, skeptic though he was, in some fundamental respects, that the best thing that ever happened to him was that he was obliged to learn the Shorter Catechism when he was a small boy, and didn't understand it, so thoroughly that when he grew up it kept coming out like an infection. He got it in his memory so that he could never get it out again, and suddenly when he would come face to face with some situation sometime that tried his soul, those wonderful definitions of the Shorter Catechism would stare him in the face, and he would know where he was. You can't explain the Shorter Catechism to anybody under twenty-one successfully. Don't try to. Get it into their blood, and then it will come out sometime, and hold them like a monitor whom they cannot avoid, and similarly with the Word of God. Don't cheapen it with your poor explanations. Give it to them straight. It isn't too strong meat even for

2 Just sung, it was a popular hymn written in 1901 by Jessie Brown Pounds, with music by John Sylvester Fearis. It was first sung in 1901 at President McKinley's funeral by the Euterpean Quartette.

babes. It will set well on any stomach, no matter how tender. (Applause.)

Give it to them unadulterated, pure, unaltered, unexplained, uncheapened, and then see it work its wholesome work throughout the whole nature. It is very difficult, indeed, for a man or for a boy, who knows the Scripture, ever to get away from it. It haunts him like an old song. It follows him like the memory of his mother. It reminds him like the word of an old and revered teacher. It forms part of the warp and woof of his life.

I conceive my theme this afternoon, therefore, to be the exaltation of the Word of God as the only theme for study on this sacred day, when we call our children together to drink in the original fountains of human life. (Loud applause.)[3]

Printed in the Trenton *True American*, Oct. 2, 1911.
   [3] There is a WWhw outline of this address dated Oct. 1, 1911, in WP, DLC.

A News Report of Speeches at Toms River and Lakewood, New Jersey

[Oct. 2, 1911]

GIVES CREDIT TO LAWMAKERS

Governor Wilson Reviews Reform Legislation in Ocean County Stumping Tour.

LAKEWOOD, Oct. 2.—Governor Wilson finished the first week of his stumping tour here Saturday night, when he addressed a large massmeeting, reviewing his stewardship as the State's Chief Executive and placing all the credit for reform legislation on an "unbiased and free Legislature."

The Governor said that he had come to Lakewood primarily to speak in behalf of Assemblyman Harry Newman,[1] who is a candidate for re-election.

"I have known Mr. Newman well for a long time, as I used to lecture, if not instruct, him at Princeton," said the Governor, "and I have been interested in his career, which has given me solid satisfaction during the last session of the Legislature. We always knew just where he was. It was not necessary to be continually sending for him and asking him where he stood. He always made that plain. You don't know what a great satisfaction it is to be associated with men of that caliber. I don't have to tell you how well Mr. Newman represented Ocean County, not in a partizan way, but for all the people."

Before going to Lakewood the Governor addressed another large massmeeting at Toms River, presided over by Isaac W. Carmichael.[2]

"He has come to give an account of his stewardship, as he promised you he would if you elected him," said the chairman. "He has been faithful over a few things and we want to make him ruler over many things. It is my desire and the desire of every honest man to see him advanced to the Presidency of the United States. It is not necessary for me to introduce him; he has introduced himself by his acts."

"It is true," he said, "that I am here to give account of what has been done in the Legislature and I am also here to advocate the re-election of your Assemblyman, Mr. Newman," said the Governor. "Too much praise has been bestowed upon me for what was done by the last Legislature. To be sure, I did all I could to bring about the things for which we were pledged, but I would have been helpless if I had not been aided by the wide-awake members of that free Legislature."

The Governor told of the conditions of controlled government to which that system ultimately led and then the gradual awakening of the people to shake it off.

"I tell you that, since the second Tuesday of last January, that condition has not been going on in New Jersey," exclaimed the Governor, and the audience gave loud mark of approbation. That led him to a review of the work of the Legislature and the election of James E. Martine, the choice of the people as expressed at the primary polls, to the United States Senate.

"There were persons who tried to tell me that vote was a joke," he said, "Well, suppose it was, there will never be another such joke played in New Jersey."

Printed in the *Newark Evening News*, Oct. 2, 1911; one editorial heading omitted.
[1] Harry Ellsworth Newman, Princeton 1904, a lawyer of Lakewood.
[2] A lawyer of Toms River, N. J.

To William James Lee Bradley

My dear Senator: [Trenton, N. J.] October 3, 1911.

Allow me to acknowledge receipt of your letter of September thirtieth[1] about Dr. Paul Hamilton Markley.[2]

Let me say that no one deplored more heartily than I did the result of the Republican primaries in Camden County last Tuesday.

With sincere respect,

Cordially yours,   Woodrow Wilson

TLS (received from Marion Bradley Bothe).
[1] It is missing.
[2] Physician of Camden and an examiner for the state tuberculosis sanatorium. His letter is missing.

The New Jersey Democratic Platform of 1911[1]

[[Oct. 3, 1911]]

We, the Democrats of New Jersey, in convention assembled, indorse the able and brilliant administration of Governor Woodrow Wilson, and express our entire approval of the progressive legislation enacted during the winter of 1910-11.

In seeking again the suffrages of our fellow-citizens, we desire to pledge ourselves to the following program, which we believe to be based upon the principles of public service which we have successfully sought to put in operation in the series of important laws passed at the last session of the Legislature. We have succeeded in setting legislation free from private control and are able to act as we propose.

One—The successful administration of the criminal law of the State having again and again been defeated by the fact that the sheriffs of counties have been able to use and control grand juries for personal and political purposes, we favor a recasting of the law of the State so far as it affects the choice of grand juries and the supervision of the drawing of petit juries.[2]

Two—Both the administration of our system of taxation and that system itself demand immediate revision; we, therefore, favor such changes in our law in regard to these matters as will provide more satisfactory means of assessing and equalizing taxes and of readjusting our methods and rates of taxation.

Three—The present too lax methods of incorporation in our State having resulted in the creation of corporations both within and without the State is a way which does not safeguard the interests of the public, we favor such changes in our law as will throw the proper safeguards around the powers of the corporations henceforth to be created under it, and, wherever possible, around the further exercise of the powers of those already created, especially with regard to their power to issue securities not honestly based upon assets and actual business.

Four—We favor the immediate reorganization of the administration of the benevolent and correctional institutions of the State upon a plan similar to that by which the administration of the public school system of the State was reorganized at the last session of the Legislature.

Five—We favor the conservation by the State, for the benefit

[1] Wilson was chairman of the committee that wrote this platform. Its vocabulary, phrasing, and style indicate that it was largely his handiwork. There is a printed copy, with WWhw marginal notations, in WP, DLC.

[2] Under existing law, sheriffs selected grand juries. In counties controlled by political bosses, such as Atlantic, sheriffs often drew grand juries which would not return indictments for political corruption.

of all the people of the water rights and other natural resources still within the control of the State and the acquisition by the State for the purpose of conservation and common use of all the water rights and forest resources that may prudently and without extravagance be acquired; and the enactment of laws to prevent their control or exhaustion by private corporations, by individuals, or by local communities.

Six—In order to reduce the cost of litigation and to place the processes of our courts more readily at the disposal of persons of limited means, we favor the simplification of judicial procedure.

Seven—We favor the election of Assemblymen by districts, and the submission of a constitutional amendment for that purpose.[3]

Eight—We commend the action of the Democratic party in revising the rules of the Federal House of Representatives so as to facilitate the transaction of the public business without subjection to autocratic dictation or to committee tyranny, and we pledge ourselves to a revision of the rules of order of the Senate and General Assembly of the State of New Jersey so as to make them more conformable to the State Constitution, more fit to protect the people against the evils of slipshod law making and more apt to secure proper legislative provision for the general welfare. The conditions under which power is exercised are more important than the conditions under which power is gained, and the work which the Democratic party of this State has done and is doing to restore popular government will be incomplete unless accompanied by appropriate reforms in legislative methods. We authorize the chairman of this convention, as soon as possible after the election, to call a party caucus of members-elect of the Legislature that they may appoint a committee to study the subject and submit recommendations to the party caucus in advance of the legislative session.

Nine—We favor the enactment of laws with regard to the use of automobiles within the State, which will grant the same rights and privileges to the owners and drivers of machines from other States that are accorded the citizens of this State in the State from which said owners and drivers hold their licenses and which will tend to establish a proper reciprocity of responsibility as between the license granting authorities of the several States.

Ten—We favor the elimination of grade crossings and to that end the enactment of legislation giving the Public Utilities Com-

[3] Assemblymen were elected on a county-wide basis at this time.

mission power to compel the railroads to eliminate grade crossings where, in the judgment of the commission, such crossings are a menace to life.

Eleven—We favor further improvement and extension of the laws governing factory and workshop inspection for the purpose of better safeguarding the life and limbs of those engaged in the industries of the State.

Twelve—We call attention to the administration of State finances of last year as compared with the preceding year. The annual appropriation made by the Legislature for the year 1911 was $5,072,582.77. The total sum appropriated by the last Legislature for the year 1912 amounts to $5,468,217.90. The latter amount exceeds the former by $395,62[3]5.13. Included in the amount appropriated for the year 1912 is the sum of $250,000, required to return collateral inheritance taxes paid to the State under a law enacted by a Republican Legislature only recently declared unconstitutional, and $334,000 for new buildings and additions required for State charities and governmental purposes, so that the expenditures for State charitable and governmental purposes actually be less under the present administration than for the preceding year. A conservative estimate will show that on October 31, 1911, the end of the State's fiscal year, there will be in the State treasury a free balance of at least two million five hundred thousand dollars, a balance never equaled under Republican administration.

Thirteen—We favor safeguarding railway travel as far as possible, and therefore pledge ourselves to the passage of a law to accomplish the purpose contemplated in the "full crew bill," which failed to pass the last Republican Senate.[4]

Printed in the *Newark Evening News*, Oct. 4, 1911.

[4] This bill required railroad companies to employ an engineer, fireman, conductor, baggagemaster (except when no baggage was handled), brakeman, and flagman on express trains of five cars or more and an engineer, fireman, conductor, and two brakemen on freight trains.

A News Report of the New Jersey Democratic State Convention of 1911

[Oct. 4, 1911]

WILSON'S AIMS WELL-BACKED BY DEMOCRATS

Platform, Bristling with Reform Features, Adopted at Party's State Convention.

GOVERNOR HALTS BOOM

TRENTON, Oct. 4.—Several features besides the adoption of a platform made notable the first Democratic convention held under the election law of 1911, in Masonic Hall, here, yesterday afternoon.

One was an attempt by Assemblyman John J. Bracken, of Essex County, to retaliate on Governor Wilson for the latter's "labeling" of Mr. Bracken and Assemblyman Frank P. Shalvoy in one of his pre-primary speeches in Newark.

A second feature was the objection by Governor Wilson to the passage of a resolution indorsing the Governor for President. He protested that to do so would be against the spirit and legal power given by the Geran law.

The offer to indorse the Governor was in effect an answer to Mr. Bracken from the convention, but the Governor also spoke for himself.

The convention's action was taken as soon as Mr. Bracken had concluded speaking. Assemblyman Egan, of Hudson, rose, the spectators thinking he was going to take part in the Bracken-Wilson matter, and offered the resolution to indorse the Governor for nomination for President next year.

There was every indication that the resolution would be carried overwhelmingly, but the Governor himself moved that the resolution be laid on the table. Inclination was shown to override his veto, but the Executive's wishes were acceded to.

The second reply to Mr. Bracken was by the Governor himself. It was a flat declaration that "a retraction is out of the question." After the convention had adjourned, Mr. Bracken went to the Governor personally to ask for details of the reason why he had been "labeled" as an opponent of reform measures last winter. The Governor had said in his answer to Mr. Bracken during the convention that there were more ways of opposing measures than by voting against them, and repeated this to the member from Essex. This post-convention dialogue was brief.

The platform—formulated in an open session of the committee on resolutions and adopted without alteration—indorsed the administration of the Governor and demanded a revision of the laws controlling the powers of the sheriffs in selecting juries; a more satisfactory system of taxation; proper safeguarding of corporation powers, and especially of the issuance of securities; a reorganization in the administration of the State's benevolent and correctional institutions; conservation of water and other natural resources, and prevention of their exhaustion by either private corporations or local communities; simplification of judicial procedure; election of Assemblymen by districts; a revision of Assembly and Senate rules, to prevent slipshod lawmaking; automobile reciprocity; elimination of grade crossings and giving power to the Public Utilities Commission to compel their removal; a betterment of the condition of employes in workshops, and the passage of a law to require the railroads to maintain full crews on trains; all in addition to a boast about the showing of the State's finances after one year of Democratic administration.

An effort by the New Jersey Congressmen, made through John A. Matthews, one of the Essex candidates for Assembly, to have the convention practically instruct the Governor in the platform to call a special session of the Legislature to make a reapportionment of Congressional districts in the State, was twice lost.

The subject was first disposed of in the committee on resolutions when preparing the platform. It was brought up the second time on the floor in the form of a minority report. Both times Governor Wilson opposed it.

That the convention was with the Governor was apparent, both before it was called to order and at every stage of it. He was made chairman of the platform committee, and when he stood up on the floor to read the committee report was received with an enthusiastic outburst of applause and shouts, followed by "Three cheers for Governor Wilson, the next President of the United States," which were given with great gusto.

When the Governor read the reference to his administration in the preamble—after apologizing for having to do it—there was another outbreak of applause.

Again, following the introduction and reading of Mr. Egan's resolution, lively exhibitions of friendship were shown for the Governor. There was no doubt that it was a Wilson convention, except, possibly, for the Essex delegation.

The platform committee was scheduled to perform its work in half an hour—between 2 and 2:30 o'clock—but it was 4 o'clock instead when its session was concluded. As consideration of the platform was the principal business of the convention, if not its sole work under the Geran law, the convention had to wait for the committee, which was composed of one member from each county.

In the committee there was opportunity for full discussion of all matters brought forward, and there was nothing in the nature of a repression of expression.

The session was also marked by harmony. A compliment for Governor Wilson, given by John A. Matthews, Assembly candidate from Essex, evoked applause. While opposing a proposition by Charles O'C. Hennessy, Assembly candidate from Bergen, to declare for a constitutional convention, Mr. Matthews, addressing Governor Wilson, who was presiding, remarked:

"Governor, Essex stands by you in all the good work you have done in the administration, and in the quarrel Essex has had with you, the men of Essex thought they were right."

The harmony in the committee was not broken, even when the members defeated the suggestion to have the Governor call a special session of the Legislature to reapportion the Congressional districts, and when Mr. Matthews announced he would offer a minority plank in the convention.

When Senator Osborne, of Essex, the temporary chairman, called for the report of the committee on permanent organization, there was a surprise given which called out applause. This was the declaration by the committee that it would not recommend any persons for permanent chairman or secretary, because the convention was a Democratic one and all the members should be entitled to full recognition.

After this report was approved, Assemblyman Egan, of Hudson, nominated his county colleague, Assemblyman Thomas F. Martin, for permanent chairman. Senator Gebhardt named Senator Osborne, but the temporary chairman declined, and as no one else was proposed, Mr. Martin was chosen unanimously. William K. Devereux, secretary of the State Democratic committee, who was the temporary secretary of the convention, was retained as permanent secretary.

It was then the platform set forth elsewhere, was read by the Governor.

After the Executive had concluded reading, Mr. Matthews offered the Congressional reapportionment plank as a minority report, but failed to move its adoption.

Objection to the jury reform plank was made by Mr. Ford, who announced that he was speaking for the Hudson delegation. Senator Fielder, of Hudson, disputed this at once, and Assemblyman Donnelly did so later.

"Mr. Ford may be speaking for the Hudson Assembly delegation," said Senator Fielder, "but not for me. I believe there are evils in connection with the present jury system that should be remedied, and I believe that the means available now to abolish abuses are not sufficient."

Mr. Donnelly stated that he took the same position as Senator Fielder.

Mr. Matthews then returned to his minority report. Governor Wilson said he had understood Mr. Matthews would present the subject as a separate resolution because, as Mr. Matthews had framed and spoken for the idea, it would call for a special session of the Legislature prior to the election.

"Yes, that's so," answered Mr. Matthews, who showed no indication of altering his desire to have the subject in the platform.

"Well, it would be a queer kind of a platform," commented the Governor, referring to the point that the platform was a document promulgated for the election alone.

Mr. Matthews did not recede, but no motion to adopt the minority report was made and the platform went through as presented by the committee.

It was at this point that Mr. Bracken obtained the privilege of the floor and brought up his criticism of the Governor's speech in Newark.

"I wish," began Mr. Bracken, "to take exception to a statement made in Essex County on September 18—"

Senator Osborne here interrupted on a point of order that the matter with which Mr. Bracken was dealing had no reference to the work of the convention. Chairman Martin ruled out the point of order on the ground that Mr. Bracken had not completed his statement and also that the convention had given him the privileges of the floor.

"I am very much interested in the prelude of Mr. Bracken," said Governor Wilson, "and I hope that the gentlemen will be heard."

Mr. Bracken then read from the Newark Evening News the part of the text of Governor Wilson's speech of September 18, in which the Governor criticized him and Assemblyman Shalvoy for not adhering to their pledges of last year.

"The minutes of the House of Assembly failed to show," declared Mr. Bracken, "wherein we were against the matters to which we had pledged ourselves last fall. I would like to know where there is any record of such a failure on our part. I have gone through the minutes and cannot find any."

Assemblyman Egan, of Hudson, rose at once, before Governor Wilson could do so, and offered the following resolution:

"Resolved, That we, the members of the Democratic State convention, do hereby indorse the Hon. Woodrow Wilson for the Democratic nomination for President of the United States of America."

"I second the resolution most heartily," announced Assemblyman Ford.

With this came the outburst of applause and yells, the demonstration lasting almost a minute.

The Governor, smiling, rose to make his protest against the adoption of the resolution, and when he got the chance, said:

"Mr. Chairman, I need not say that I regard this proposed resolution as having been conceived in great generosity and that I would very greatly value the indorsement of a body of men like this. But, Mr. Chairman, I shall take the liberty—at the same time asking the pardon of the mover and seconder of this resolution in doing so—by moving that it be laid on the table.

"I do that, not out of any sense of modesty, for a man should be willing to receive so grateful an action on the part of a body of men like this, tendered in this way, but because I have a strong conviction, sir, that this action would be inconsistent with our recent legislation.

"The business of this convention is distinctly marked out by the primary and election law passed at the last session of the Legislature, which is confined, by that law, to the adoption of a platform, for our action as a body of Democrats in New Jersey.

"The law, moreover, provides for the expression of the preference of the people of New Jersey, not in convention assembled, but at their primaries, for the Presidential nomination.

"While I realize that this resolution may be taken as an expression of confidence by the gentlemen who vote for it, I nevertheless feel that we would be making a mistake to make this use of this convention, when we have provided so much more appropriate means of finding out the preference of the people with regard to national affairs.

"So I enter my earnest, but respectful, protest to this motion, and move that the resolution lie on the table, and I hope that motion will be seconded."

"The Governor is out of order," declared Chairman Martin.

"The motion to lay on the table has not been seconded," pointed out Mr. Egan. There was an apparent inclination to push the resolution through in spite of the Governor, until Senator Fielder rose to second the Governor and to advise that the Governor's desire be acceded to. Even at that there was opposition to the Governor's motion, so much so that when Chairman Martin called for a declaration, viva voce, he said he was in doubt, but after a bit of hesitation he formally declared the Governor's motion to lay on table carried.

Following this action, the Governor rose to a point of privilege and proceeded to answer Mr. Bracken.

"Mr. Bracken, one of the members of this convention from Essex County," the Executive stated, "has said something which,

perhaps, makes it proper that I should reply. Mr. Bracken cites
a statement which I made in a speech in Essex County on a day
which he remembers more precisely than I do. That is a matter
which, in courtesy to Mr. Bracken and Mr. Shalvoy, I do not
care to discuss upon this floor.

"I can only say that a retraction is out of the question, because
I was essentially right. I will merely ask the convention to remember that there are other ways of opposing measures besides
voting against them.

"I simply record my recollection of the action and attitude of
these two gentlemen with regard to some of the most important
transactions connected with the fulfilment of Democratic promises.

"I am very sorry, indeed, to have been obliged—but I call the
convention to witness that I have been obliged—to say this."

The tension was removed by a motion to adjourn. This was
at 4:35 o'clock. After the adjournment Mr. Shalvoy stated that
he had not known that Mr. Bracken intended to bring up the
subject of the Governor's criticism.

Printed in the *Newark Evening News*, Oct. 4, 1911; some editorial headings
omitted.

From Andrew Jackson Montague

My dear Mr. Wilson: [Richmond, Va.] October 4, 1911.
   Your letter of the 27th ultimo was duly received.

It appears to me that your strength is gradually gaining in
Virginia. The Machine in this State does not seem to be active
as yet, and unless it is quite early in the field, your popularity
will have gained such momentum that the Organization will follow in with it.

Have you heard from Mr. Byrd? He can advise you of the inner workings of the Virginia Organization and the exact status
of the Senators. I would advise however that you have his statements verified before giving too much confidence to them.

Dr. Denny, as you may know, has left Virginia to take the
Presidency of the University of Alabama. This is your gain. I
experience no regret in his departure, despite my personal regard
for him, because I do not think one should be a President of a
University who entertains his views upon politics.

Dr. Alderman can give you some information, though he is
too new in the State to understand the whole situation; but he
lives at Senator Martin's home[1] and might enlighten you upon
his attitude.

One of the Western states will select delegates to the National Convention in March or the early spring, I believe. It would be very well for you to secure this delegation. Harmon, I am sure, is making a tremendous effort to get this first voice of approval.

I will be in New York on the 26th instant, and if you or any of your friends wish to confer with me, a letter directed in care of Carnegie Foundation for Advancement of Teachings, No. 576 Fifth Avenue, will reach me; or better, advices here before my departure as to the convenience of yourself or your friends.

I trust the situation in New Jersey is satisfactory to you. And while you did right in objecting to endorsation of the Committee or Convention, as I learn from the morning's paper, yet as practical politics go, such endorsation would be helpful.

Yours sincerely,   [A. J. Montague]

CCL (A. J. Montague Papers, Vi).
1 That is, Charlottesville, Va.

A News Report of Campaign Speeches in Salem County, New Jersey

[Oct. 5, 1911]

WILSON SMITES G.O.P. PLANKS

SALEM, Oct. 5.—A spirited attack by Governor Woodrow Wilson upon the Republican "Board of Guardians"[1] and ridicule of the platform adopted Tuesday at the State Republican convention stirred many audiences on the Governor's speechmaking tour through Salem County yesterday.

"The Republican Platform," said Governor Wilson last night to a crowd that packed the local opera house and spread out into the street, "is one of these old-fashioned, smooth-bore brass-mounted affairs that goes off like a blunderbuss. I do not see the slightest difference between this platform that was adopted by the Republican convention yesterday and the Republican platforms that preceded it; it has the same boasting about things that never existed; it has the same claiming of credit for everything good that was done, it has the same promises put in such phrases that they can be read backward or forward and mean the same thing; just the kind of thing you have been familiar with and never did know the meaning of.["]

To an outdoor crowd at Elmer the Governor talked in much the same vein. He said: "The same old board of guardians got together and framed the Republican platform. Then the State

1 See H. E. Alexander to WW, Oct. 1, 1910, n. 2, Vol. 21.

convention swallowed the platform in its entirety. They produced one of the most verbose and preposterous documents I have read in a long time."

At Alloway, the Governor began to call the members of the Board of Guardians by name. He said: "As yet the managers of the Republican party don't seem to know that a new order of things is here. Former Governor Franklin Murphy, ex-Senator Kean, former Governor Stokes and Mr. Baird, of Camden, got together when a platform was to be drawn and determined what was to be done. None of them was a member of the convention. I tell you it is the same old board of guardians. These are the gentlemen who don't know that a new era has come."

At Pennsgrove the Executive declared, to the amusement of the crowd, that the character of the Republican platform made him think that its framers had put all the words in the dictionary in a grab-bag and pulled them out and strung them together as they came out.

"There are rays of light occasionally as an idea emerges now and then from the maze of words," he concluded.

The Governor seemed to find much solid delight in poking fun at the Republicans for asking for a rest before more new legislation is enacted. "We have carried out so many of the pledges made in our last year's platform," said the Governor, "that the Republicans in their platform say the State needs a rest.[2] I don't wonder that their stomachs are too weak to stand the kind of food we have been feeding them. Their statement that they are out of breath from passing so much legislation is practically an implication that they want to stand still a little while. They always have wanted to stand still; the same old standpat idea is still in their heads.

"If you paint a post white and want to keep it white, you must keep touching it up once in a while. So to-day, if things are to be kept right, you have got to be a radical, you have got to keep things jacked up to where they belong. And it puts the Republican leaders out of breath to jack things up."

At the meeting last night the Governor gave the knife another twist. He said: "So many of our platform pledges were carried

---

[2] "The nation is suffering from too much legislation. Fewer laws is a needed reform, and we pledge ourselves to this end. Laws should be enacted for the guidance and direction of the people, should be as few as possible and so clear in phraseology that every citizen can tell what they mean. Recent legislation has multiplied enactments so rapidly on so many subjects that the average citizen not only finds his almost every act subject to legal control, but is actually unable to familiarize himself with one law before another takes its place." The Republican platform of 1911, printed in *Manual of the Legislature of New Jersey* . . . *1912* (Trenton, N. J., 1912), pp. 168-73.

out that the poor breathless representatives of the Republican
party admitted that they were out of breath. They held up their
hands in protest and said, 'In God's name, let us go slow a while.'
I don't wonder. They had never been accustomed to such exercise. They had never in their time felt their blood quicken by
movement. They had experienced the unusual intoxication of
seeing something done. They had never intended while they
were in the saddle to let anything be done. They had intended to
let everything go its normal course, that everybody who then
had control of the affairs of State might sleep at night without
any apprehension that in the morning his control would be gone."

In all his speeches the Governor threw stiff uppercuts into the
Congressional aspirations of William J[ohn]. Browning, who has
been nominated by the Republicans as candidate for the place
left vacant by the death of Congressman [Henry Clay] Loudenslager.

"Look at the things which have been done recently by Congress," said the Governor at Elmer. "What has been done has
been accomplished through the efforts of the Democrats and
the Progressive Republicans. Is Mr. Browning likely to stand for
these things? Mr. Browning is already called the 'Frizzled Beef'
candidate because his nomination was cut and dried."

Later in the day Mr. Browning was characterized by the Governor as a "machine-made candidate," the Governor added [add-
ing] that the voters, when they knew who made him, would have
scruples about electing him. He said that Mr. Browning, personally, was probably a man of high character, but the question at
issue was whether he represented two or three men in Camden
or the people of his district as a whole. . . .

The Governor put in the entire afternoon and evening, urging
the voters of Salem County to support the Democratic candidates. Salem is looked upon as one of the three counties on
which the control of the Senate by one party or the other rests.
On that account, the itinerary of the Governor yesterday included open-air speeches at a half-dozen places, and an address
at the opera house here last night.

Governor Wilson had his crowd with him at the opera house
meeting last night. He spoke for forty minutes and completely
swayed his audience. There was rousing enthusiasm when some
of the earlier speakers praised the Governor's administration,
but the applause shook the house when the prediction was made
that he would be the next occupant of the White House. The
attendance at the meeting was so great that three hundred persons were turned away.

The afternoon's itinerary included stops at Elmer, Alloway, Woodstown, Pedricktown, Penn's Grove and Pennsville. At all these places he addressed street corner crowds of from one hundred to three hundred persons.

At Woodstown in addition to speaking on the village square he addressed a centennial gathering at the Baptist church. At nearly all the stops Thomas M. Ferrell, candidate for Congress,[3] spoke. Other candidates in the party were Rev. J[ohn]. Warren Davis, for Senator; John F. Ayres for sheriff, and Isaac S. Smick, for Assemblyman.[4]

Others in the party were County Chairman Clayton Batten, Charles Pancoast and Colonel D. Stewart Craven.[5]

One of the most significant of the Governor's utterances was his declaration last night that all Progressives, irrespective of party, must at the present time look to the Democratic party for their leaders, both in New Jersey and in the nation. He said:

"I believe that both parties have been singularly slow in waking up to the meaning of a new age, and what I want to call your attention to is that a larger proportion of the men now active in leading the Democratic party have waked up to the meaning of the new time and have waked up, too, to those who are leading the Republican party. The facts speak for themselves. The actual leaders of the Democratic party in the States which have put in a Democratic administration and in the nation at large, in Congress and out of Congress, are the Progressives in the Democratic ranks. Can we candid men gainsay that?

"Is it not true that the Progressive element of the Democratic party now dominates that party? Does not every man know that if the circumstances should change and the retrogressive element should get in control of the Democratic party that it would lose all possibility of success? That it would lose all the chances it apparently now has to lead the nation? The Democratic party realizes that, and the nation realizes it. Very well, what is true on the other side of the house? There are splendid men and splendid men by the score, among those who stand prominent in the leadership of the Republican party, who are just as progressive, just as clear-sighted as to the issues of the time as anybody on the Democratic side, but are they dominant in the

---

[3] Thomas Merrill Ferrell, who had earlier served in both houses of the legislature and, from 1883 to 1885, in the House of Representatives. He lost to Browning.

[4] All three were elected.

[5] Batten, of Lower Penns Neck, N. J., had been director of the Board of Freeholders of Salem County, 1905-1908. Pancoast was a retired hardware merchant and former councilman of Woodstown, N. J. Craven was a colonel in the New Jersey National Guard and had recently been appointed to the State Board of Education by Wilson.

councils of the Republican party? Answer that question frankly. Are they dominant in the councils of the Republican party in this State or in the nation?

"You know very well that they are not. They are practically without dominance and they are opposed by leaders, from the President of the United States down. And for the present everybody knows that neither now nor in the immediate future will they gain control. What is the moral of that? The moral is that the Progressives of this country at this time—I am not saying anything about the future, for I cannot foresee it—but the Progressives of this country, in New Jersey and out of it, at this time must look to the Democratic party for leaders.

"All that I can urge upon you is this: If you send Republicans to the State Legislature you have rebuked the present administration. If you send Democrats to the Legislature you have expressed your approval of it and your intention to support it. There is no escaping that[.] I can prove it by this: The Republican party, as it was led and as its plans were laid a year ago, was that a suitable party to accomplish for you the things that have been accomplished within the last nine months? That you showed by your own votes. Has it experienced any repentance? Have you observed anything changed in the leadership of the Republican party? Who picked out your Republican candidates in Salem County? The same old crowd.

"As some one was saying to-day, they are not only machine-made, but machine-finished. They may be very honorable and proper men. I have nothing against them personally. But you did not pick them out. There was a slate just as usual, and the slate was made up by the same persons that have always made up your slates. They may, if elected, have a lucid interval and break loose from this control, but I would say, from past experiences, that it is not likely, because a man does not ordinarily go back upon the men who made him."

Printed in the *Newark Evening News*, Oct. 5, 1911; some editorial headings omitted.

A Campaign Address in Woodbury, New Jersey[1]

[[Oct. 5, 1911]]

Mr. Chairman, Ladies and Gentlemen:

I am very glad that it is true that I am not a stranger in Woodbury. Indeed, some of you will remember that it was a very short

[1] Delivered in Green's Opera House. Wilson was introduced by Joseph J. Summerill.

time since I was here in Woodbury last. I came here only a few days ago to take part in the laying of the corner-stone of the new school building, and it is exactly one year to-night, I believe, since I came to solicit your suffrages for the office of Governor of the State.[2] Somehow, Woodbury is a place easy to become acquainted with. I found as I rode up the street this afternoon, coming in by automobile, that it had a very familiar and home-like look to me. Perhaps it has been in part by reason of my association with one of your fellow-citizens, with whom I have had the great pleasure of traveling in recent date. I mean Mr. Grosscup. I want to say that a tour personally conducted by Mr. Grosscup is a very agreeable affair; I have never been more kindly looked after, and I want to say also this, that as I have dealt with him from day to day, it has seemed to me that he had admirably in hand the work of the State Committee. I do not know how anyone could be a more effective or a more watchful Chairman. I suppose that it is sometimes in South Jersey difficult to manage a Democratic campaign. When I was here a few days ago to take part in the ceremonies connected with the laying of the corner-stone of the school, my theme was the sort of education which is necessary to connect one generation with another in all matters of schooling in a manner that will connect one generation with another as it comes along with the spirit of knowledge of the generation that preceded it. I was thinking to-night as I came to the hall, that in politics in recent years, and more particularly in recent months, we had been experiencing the teachings of the new school.

The school of politics is a very interesting school, because every school is made by the character of its pupils rather than by the character of its teachers. We used to notice at the University that every class that entered had a character of its own. It was not the character, so far as we could discover, given by a small group of men who happened to have the most noticeable capacity of the group, but in some subtle way we could never analyze. Each class had a distinct, an almost personal character. By the end of the Freshman year it was perfectly obvious what part that class was going to play in the life of the University; and I daresay, insensibly, almost, we adapted our instruction to this character. So with each generation. As a new generation comes on in politics it takes shape according to its needs; and the singular thing about changes of politics is that none are so blind to the changes that take place from day to day as some of the professional politicians. None are so blind as

2 His speech is printed at Oct. 5, 1910, Vol. 21.

those who will not see; none are so blind as those who insist upon forecasting the future by calculations of the past.

Many a man has been fooled, ridiculously fooled, for his forecast of what was going to happen in politics, notwithstanding that he had been steeped in experience in all his preceding political life; and that so soon as politics becomes a profession, the politician takes a professional point of view. I think that a lawyer also takes on a professional point of view, and presently, if he be not very careful, he will not be able to see things from a layman's point of view. I think that the doctor, too, does the same thing, and I am afraid also, that the minister does the same thing. The doctor, as he becomes more and more expert, seems to more and more regard us as curious pieces of mechanism, just as, I am afraid, some of the experimenters in University laboratories are more interested in cats as singularly good animals to dissect, than as domestic pets. And I think that some ministers are apt to take sort of professional care of us, as if he knew something about us that was extremely likely to be condemned, so that it sometimes creates strained relations between ourselves, and that makes a delightful proposition! And so with the politicians; a politician comes personally to regard us as voting machines upon which he can count, and some day he wakes up and finds that the machine did not work. He says to himself: "When I go to bed at night I fixed everything just right." All the workers are at work to see that the vote comes out, to get the vote out—*the* vote, not the votes—and with that consolidated body of co-operative opinion which he feels he has already salted down—he will make you accurate prediction that the vote tomorrow will be just so many on the one side and just so many on the other.

But there comes a day when the voter sits up and begins to take notice; when he lifts his eyes and sees that he has been imposed upon; when he makes another interesting discovery— that he has been acting according to label and not according to his real opinion; that he has not been doing any thinking at all. A man was saying to me the other day that a gentleman had boasted to him that he was so good a Democrat that he would vote for the devil if he was on the Democratic ticket, and my friend promptly said to him: "Well you may be a very good partisan but in that case you are a very bad citizen." But very often the partisan will, of a sudden, wake up and become a thoughtful citizen. Then all the calculations of the politicians go astray; then there comes a time such as came upon the eve of the Civil War, when a quiet, thoughtful man like Lincoln rises and smiles at the predictions of the politicians and says: "You men evidently have not been talking to the people of this country for a long time; you have been doing all the talking and have not done any listening. Suppose you listen for a little while, listen to the conversations on the street corners, to what men say to each other on the trains, notice the comment they make when they read certain things in the newspapers; find out if they have discovered the newspapers that lie to them and those that tell them the truth; see them disregard the editorial opinions of the lying sheets and pay attention only to the editorial opinions of those that give them the truth in the news columns and comment on the truth in their editorials.["] Listen for a while. Then you will have gone to school in the new school of politics; the school of rising opinion, and you will discover that America always renews her youth. She never goes stale for many decades together in her politics, and looking the facts in the face she insists upon having her politics, her legislation, she insists upon having the men best suited to the facts as they are. You know that we hear a great deal of talk nowadays about radicalism, and those are people who don't want anything. They are interested in distributing and using the word radicalism as a scarecrow to frighten people, and particularly to frighten men by telling them that if "you follow this man, he will lead you into untold woes." I will try to illustrate the radicalism of the present Democratic administration in New Jersey, and first of all, let us ask ourselves what it is that those who face these things candidly mean by radicalism.

You know that there is a very stirring and striking poem of Rudyard Kipling's[3]—I wish I could quote it, but I have not the verbal memory—in which he sets forth this idea: That there will come a time, perhaps in the next world when each man has a star to himself, or something of that kind, when he will not be bound by conventions, we won't care for old-fashioned criticisms and we will paint things as we see them for the god of things as they are. Now the modern radical is an apostle of things as they are. He insists upon seeing the actual facts of the modern world and declines to think in the formulas of the past age which do not fit the facts. That is a modern radical. There are a great many formulas being devised that do not fit the facts. We hear about the formulas of protection, for example. There is an hysterical passage in the Republican platform framed at Trenton day before yesterday—or rather adopted day before yesterday—it was framed a good deal before that—there is an hysterical passage in that platform about the assaults that

<hr />

3 "When Earth's Last Picture Is Painted," Stanza 3.

have been made upon the sacred doctrine and principles of protection,[4] but these gentlemen have not made inquiry as to who is being protected. I can point out to them—I can almost give them a list of the individuals—who are being protected by the present system of protection on the fingers of my hand. And that same list is a list of men taking advantage of that protection accorded a small minority of our fellow citizens in order to impose what prices they please upon the rest of us. As an apostle of things as they are I decline to be imposed upon by the word "protection." I decline to be imposed upon by thinking that has gone out of date, because it does not square with the actual circumstances of the times.

I want to bring my thinking up to the facts and not drag the facts back to my antiquated thinking. I want to protect American industries as much as anybody does, but I want to protect the rank and file of those who are engaged in it. And I am very much more interested in the prosperity of the nation as a whole than I am in the prosperity of small sections of the nation which will thereafter patronize the rest of us and give us such parts of the prosperity as they choose to share with us.

I decline, being a grown-up man with a mind of my own, to be imposed upon any longer, and therefore I am what is denominated a radical. I insist upon describing facts as they are, and I always take the liberty to laugh in the faces of those who do not know that the facts have changed since they were children and were imposed upon by their parents by what they were taught.

And so the radicalism of our new time is simply the symptom that I began speaking of. It is the coming on of a new generation with a life of its own, with problems of its own, that insists upon being led by men who deal with realities and not by men who deal with imaginary things. It is a day of renewed reality. We insist upon enjoying our institutions as they were meant to work and not our institutions as we have been fooled into supposing that they did work. We are told now that all of the new programs are assaults upon representative government, and we have heard

---

[4] After affirming that a protective tariff was essential to the nation's prosperity and the maintenance of high wages, the Republican platform continued: "We endorse the calm, judicial attitude of President Taft in the face of unreasonable clamor for hasty legislation and ill-advised remedies, and we approve his determination to apply business principles in the treatment of the problems of the day. The Democratic party of New Jersey, at its first opportunity in recent years, regardless of the interests of the industries of our State, sent to the United States Senate an avowed free trader. We call upon the friends of protection to prevent a repetition of this misfortune, and we remind them that the legislative election this fall will have a direct and important bearing upon New Jersey Senatorial representation in Congress."

recently some very eloquent tributes to representative government. I am entirely willing to join in those tributes provided I
can get it, but recently we have not had it, and therefore I am
just about as much interested in eulogies on representative government in the United States as I would be in eulogies on the
enjoyable life in the planet of Mars. It is beautiful in theory, but
does it work? Are the interests that you have been living under
in New Jersey—the institutions that you had prior to last Winter
—were they representative of you? Did you get the things that
you voted for? Were the promises of the platforms fulfilled for
you?

You know what happened. You had turned first to one party
and then to another. Now, I am not going to put myself in the
position of condemning one party and praising another party,
but I say that you had turned from one party to another, and
back again, and had not gotten what you voted for, and so long
as you don't get what you vote for, you never can have representative government.

Why didn't you get what you voted for? Simply because your
Legislatures were managed exactly as the Republican convention, which sat day before yesterday at Trenton, was managed.
The same gentlemen who managed the Legislature of New
Jersey and told it what it had to do and what it couldn't do,
prior to last winter, got together in the convention of the Republican party and told that convention what it could say and
what it could not say. I don't know what it did say, because
I don't understand that platform; it has so many words in it that
I can't find the meaning. There are high-sounding phrases written across those pages which may mean something, but I do
not, for the life of me, know what it is. It is a grand ambush
from which no sort of meaning may be had. And I want to call
the attention of the framers of that platform to a very interesting circumstance. They say, and very truly say, that we had
the assistance of the Republican Senate in carrying out the reform measures enacted by the last session of the Legislature;
and they have wreaked their vengeance upon all the men they
could get at who took part in voting for them. They tried to take
the credit from the Democrats by saying that those measures
originated and were chiefly framed in the Senate, and the men
who stood at the front in doing that in the Senate are the very
men they are now trying to repudiate. One of the men who did
the best service in that very particular, one of the men who gave
them a chance to do what they said they would do in their platform, was Senator Bradley, of Camden; and you know what

those very gentlemen who wrote that platform did to Senator Bradley; and you know that they did it to him because of the part he played in that legislation; they told him beforehand that they were going to do it to him, because of that legislation.

And then they take credit for the Corrupt Practices Act; they say that it was introduced by a Republican Senator. A Corrupt Practices Act was introduced by a Republican Senator;[5] another one was introduced by a Democratic Assemblyman,[6] and the final bill was neither of those bills; and the bill that was introduced by a Republican Senator lacked the essential features of the bill that was finally passed, and if it had not been for men like Senator Bradley, the Republican Senate would have passed a meaningless and worthless Corrupt Practices Act. I happen to know the inside history of these things, and these gentlemen cannot impose upon anyone who knows anything about that platform.

I want to be among the first to render respect and praise to those liberal-minded Republicans who did assist in these most important matters. But I want also to tell you that some of the gentlemen who voted for these things in the Senate voted for them because they did not dare to do anything else. They knew that contempt and rejection on the part of public opinion of the State awaited them if they did not, and that they would be put in the position of voting in the minority as against the Democrats in the Assembly, and the Republicans who were ready to stand by the program in its fullness.

Let us strip off all these pretenses and ask men to stand up and be candid, not only, but stand up and render an account of their proceedings; and let us see who is honestly for the people of New Jersey and who is not. The men who are honestly for the people of New Jersey are not confined to the Democratic ranks by any manner of means; but the men who are honestly for the people of New Jersey have not been allowed to have a controlling voice, as yet, in the councils of the Republican party. The men who want to hold things where they are, the men who want to obstruct these matters, the men who confess themselves confused and not contented with the actual movement of affairs in the last Legislature, are the men who are still dominant in the councils of the Republican party. Nothing ever shocked them so much as to see things done that the people had been promised.

I received letters during the past winter that had the most

5 John Dyneley Prince.
6 Charles E. S. Simpson.

extraordinary implication in them that letters could possibly have, though I daresay the writers were not aware of it. I received letters of extravagant gratitude for nothing more than having been an honest man. I had said that I would try to do certain things, and I did try to do them; and men fell upon my neck and said that there never had been such a leader before. There was something almost mortifying about it. I felt like replying "What would you have called me if I had not done these things?" I would have been worthy of nothing but your rejection and contempt, and I am certainly not worthy of your praise for having done what I said.

What a pass has it come to when people of a great State must be grateful to a man for being honest! The honesty, I dare say, was not so much the difference in character, for I am not silly enough, ladies and gentlemen, to suppose myself a very superior person! I am not silly enough to ascribe great moral qualities to myself. That is not my point. But I came into politics with a fresh eye, and these gentlemen have grown stale. As we used to say sometimes at the University of the foot-ball team, they are over-trained, and not being skilled in their ball game with regard to past experiences, I happen to see things as they are. That, I daresay, is exactly what happened, that a new generation had to use new men to do an old thing. Now, what did you do? Did you do anything very revolutionary? Is it revolutionary to make certain, if you want a thing, that you can have that thing? Is it revolutionary to make certain, if you only take a little pains, that you can put men in jail for using money corruptly in elections? Is it revolutionary to give a Public Utilities Commission power enough to see that you are not imposed upon by the public serving corporations, to give you some means of self-defence against them? Is it revolutionary to pass a bill, if you want to adopt a form of government which you can run yourselves, and give up one that you cannot for the life of you run yourselves? Is it revolutionary to pass a bill which provides that working men can really get compensation for injuries when forme[r]ly he could not get any? Are these things revolutionary? They sound to me like mere good government, and if good government is revolutionary, then I want to be put down as an out and out revolutionist. But so far as I am concerned, I regard these as the most conservative measures that have ever been enacted. If I have something radically wrong with me and a surgeon can cure me by the knife, I regard the knife as my salvation and as a conservative instrument. It would be rather revolutionary if he went so far as to expurge portions of my anatomy that were innocent of offence; but so long as he confines himself to removing those things without removing which I cannot live, then he is a conservator of conservators; he is conserving human life by saving human life. And I say these things that look radical are simply restoring life blood to the body politic; and that was done in the most conservative acts passed in New Jersey, for you had lost the liberty and the purity of the ballot.

I am not going to take the least stock, on the eve of the seventh of November next, in any predictions based upon the voting last November, because so many spooks voted last November that I do not know what the vote is going to be anyhow. Unless I could count the spooks as they moved about among the polling booths where they have been camping in such extraordinarily ghostly hosts, campaign after campaign, I could not for the life of me tell you what is going to happen. If you had an actual flesh and blood vote in the County of Camden, how many votes would there be? Not the same number there were last time. We haven't yet counted the votes down there; we haven't yet counted them in the way we did in Atlantic County; we have not been able to learn from the post-office in Camden how many sample ballots were returned. You know that a sample ballot returned ought to be an unusually revealing matter. In the single County of Essex, sixteen thousand sample ballots were returned unclaimed. Do you see what that means? In order to be perfectly fair, you must remember that in a great county like that, covered with cities, probably several thousand —let us say three thousand or four thousand—could be accounted for by death, removal and changes in addresses, but we cannot account for sixteen thousand in that way; and we have the testimony of the mail carriers up there that some of these sample ballots were addressed to vacant lots, and they would be addressed by the thirties and forties and fifties to lodging houses which never had lodged more than three or four persons. Therefore, we had at one time piled up in the post office in the city of Newark the names and addresses of our ghostly compatriots who used to vote in the County of Essex, but who now, thank God, have moved out. If there were not so secretive a postmaster in the City of Camden, we would have some interesting statistics for you from Camden, but the Camden post office is locked up tighter than ink. And then there were statistics almost as startling from Hudson County. So, that what I want to have you realize is that what we did last winter was to restore voting in New Jersey to actual citizens of New Jersey, which I consider a very conservative thing.

All of this, then, is what we did last Winter: to restore the institutions of which we hear such eulogies and to get back a really representative government, and what I have come here tonight to ask you is this: What judgment are you going to render in regard to these things on the 7th of November? Don't forget this, gentlemen. Do not let local prejudices and local considerations obscure for you the real thing that is at issue. There is only one way in which you can show your approval of the present administration of affairs in New Jersey, and that is to vote for Democratic candidates at the next election. And I say that without the least partisan feeling. I want to explain to you very carefully what I mean. I mean that the Democratic party in New Jersey is under the leadership of progressive men who mean to continue a policy like this, and I mean that we have no evidence as yet that the Republican party is under the leadership of men who mean the same thing. I ask you to ask yourself in all candor if that is not the simple truth? Where, except in the county of Hudson, have men of the same type that gave you that legislation and leadership won any kind of leadership in recent months in the Republican party? At the primaries in Hudson, the progressive Republicans, that is to say, the Republicans of the sort of radical conservatism that I have been trying to expound to you, won out. Everywhere else in the State of New Jersey they lost, and I call your attention to the fact that everywhere except in a single county the men who are ready to support the progressive policies of the Democratic party won in the primaries. There is a contrast of facts. But you are men enough to face the facts. I am not saying to you that the Republican party will not some day throw off the stupid leadership to which it is now submitting in the state of New Jersey—"stupid," in public affairs, is probably the most condemning word you can use. It means that they have not sense enough to see the signs of the times and the need of the State. I dare say—I confidently expect, indeed—that the time will come when the Republican voters, rank and file, who are not of that kind, will throw off that kind of leadership, but they have not done it yet; and in place after place, men pledged to follow that kind of leadership have been selected for office. Let me tell you a particular example—I know Mr. Kincaid[7] will dwell upon this later but he won't object to my anticipating some of it—of the nominee for

7 That is, Eugene F. Kinkead.

Congress in this district on the Republican side. They could not have found in this district a man more closely identified with the kind of politics that the Republican party is trying to get rid of than Mr. Browning. I mean Mr. Browning has been identified—I do not say in any way that casts a taint upon his character—but he was absolutely identified with what is known as Cannonism; he was one of the confidential associates and advisors of Speaker Cannon;[8] he was bred in that school and could not possibly think in the terms of any other school, and he is picked out as if what you might prefer was a fossil specimen. You have got to dig deep into the geological strata of politics to find men so thoroughly like Mr. Cannon as Mr. Browning. The judgment of America has buried Mr. Cannon so deep that he belongs to a previous geological age, and the idea of picking out a specimen of that kind to represent you in Congress is merely equivalent to asking you to turn around and go back a generation instead of keeping your faces forward and going forward a generation.

I want to say again that I am not impeaching the character of anybody concerned. That it [is] not it; but a man cannot represent us with good character unless he has got our good opinions. I do not care how excellent the character of an old fogy is. I do not reject him because he is bad, but because he has stopped thinking; the machinery in his head has stopped working; it needs to be wound up.

That is the only reason. I want suitable instruments for the life of the nation, and such persons with such opinions are not suitable instruments; they are no more suitable to lead than the stragglers in the rear of the procession; they cannot lead because they cannot catch up; they are permanently damaged; they are shop-worn. They are not put upon the counters or in the show windows as the display goods. They are kept in the background and sold at a bargain. And you know perfectly well that I say these things without any personal feeling. I had the pleasure of shaking hands with Mr. Browning at Mount Holly today, and I did so with a great deal of curiosity. I am merely trying to elucidate to you the undisputable fact that the men are not picked out for office by the leaders on that side who will serve your purpose. Have you got any purposes? Are you going to vote simply because a man is labeled this or that? Don't we want anything? Is voting just a means of exercise? Do you go to the polls without any opinions? Do you first empty your heads before you cast a ballot? If you don't go with some ideas in your

---

[8] Browning was chief clerk of the House of Representatives, 1895-1911.

head and then vote that idea by the nearest approximation you can get. All things are relative. I mean the nearest perfect. The man you vote for may not be exactly the article you want, but if he is the best you can get it is a great deal better to have him than one who is a great deal worse. I would say the same thing if I were a candidate. That is not the point. The point is not that any individual upon the present Democratic ticket perfectly represents the new ideas of the age. They may or may not; that is not the point. The question is relative. If you are going to vote either a Democratic or a Republican ticket, you will have to take what is, on the average, the better ticket, that is all. We have postponed the millenium and I don't know that even the Democratic party is in sight of it yet, but we are doing the best we can and I believe that you will all realize, when you go to the polls in November, that what you are doing is registering not a party vote but a set of individual opinions.

We have come to that age when a man does not elect himself by way of the label he has got on him. You say "I approve of this. I disapprove of that. This man will give me what I want and that man will not give me what I want so therefore I know perfectly well how I am going to vote." This time you have to vote for that individual—by "individual" I mean you cannot put your mark in one place—you cannot get anybody elected whom you do not individually pick out along with your fellow citizens, and if you put your mark in the wrong place, opposite the wrong name, you are going to make a fatal mistake. And even if you do what it is illegal to do, I wish now to inform you, take a cardboard with openings cut in it that will exactly match the spaces opposite the names somebody wants you to vote for, you will have to be careful not to slip the card or you may mark the wrong people. But I take it for granted that any man will be ashamed to stencil his vote, and my advice to you is if you do not know anything about a man, don't vote for him. Do not vote for anybody by label. Ask about the people. You can ask about them. The names have all been printed in the newspapers; ask about them and make up your mind whether you want them or not, then vote all over the ballot. All the names are there, Democratic, Republican, anybody who has got through the primaries or who has the necessary amount of signatures for an independent nomination after the primaries. There they are. Pick them out according to your preferences and knowledge and then you will exercise the genuine function of American voters. That is what I was ambitious to see done in the State of New Jersey and I know that is going to happen. And whether I agree with the results in November or not I am going to have the satisfaction of thinking that I had something to do with the rendering of those results genuine. I would great deal rather have a genuine vote against me than a fake vote for me.

There is a beautiful passage in one of the speeches of Lincoln to which my attention was drawn the other day. Again I must admit that I cannot quote it exactly; it was to this effect. He said: "It is not necessary that I should succeed but it is necessary that I should always stick to the man I think is right and never associate with the man I think is wrong."[9] Wasn't that like Lincoln?—a homely, frank, simplicity of morals. The question is, be true to your convictions. Act as you really think and fear no man. There was the stature of the man, measured up by his own symbols.

And so, ladies and gentlemen, I have come to plead with you for a frank judgment upon your own affairs and I have tried to point out to you, I hope without injustice to any man, the means you have of expressing that frank judgment. You cannot have an administration of any kind upon which you pass judgment before you vote. You did not pass judgment upon the present administration by the way you voted last November. That was a hope; that was an expectation; it was not a judgment. You did not know what was going to happen, and I dare say that you had grave doubts as to what was going to happen. I did not know what was going to happen. I simply knew that if anything happened there was going to be a lively time. That is all I knew. But what the outcome of the lively time was to be I did not know any more than the Irishman when he goes to the Donnybrook Fair. I simply knew if I was going to hit I was going to give myself the pleasure of hitting, but whether I should reduce order out of chaos I did not know at all. Neither did you. It was, as I have said several times, simply a sporting chance, and now the thing is over. The results of the election last November are before you and this time you utter your judgment. There is no conjecture about it. You know what happened; you know what was promised; you know what was done; you know how it was done. There has not been a secret movement made. The record is all kept, and if there is any of it that you do not know about you can find it out.

9 He was paraphrasing the following sentences of Lincoln's speech of October 16, 1854, at Peoria, Ill.: "Stand with anybody that stands RIGHT. Stand with him while he is right and PART with him when he goes wrong. Stand WITH the abolitionist in restoring the Missouri Compromise; and stand AGAINST him when he attempts to repeal the fugitive slave law." Roy P. Basler (ed.), *The Collected Works of Abraham Lincoln* (9 vols., New Brunswick, N. J., 1953), II, 273.

What is your judgment going to be? What are you going to say about it? What is going to be Gloucester's verdict?

Printed in the Woodbury, N. J., *Gloucester County Democrat*, Oct. 12, 1911, with a few corrections from the incomplete text in the *Newark Evening News*, Oct. 6, 1911.

From Daniel Moreau Barringer

Dear Woodrow,   Philadelphia, Pa. October 5, 1911.

Put this away among your other "clippings for reference" during your spare moments and when you have time read it carefully.[1] It is brief but it seems to me to be worthy of much concentrated thought and possibly to point the way for a solution of the problem of how best to deal with our big industrial combinations. I think Mr. Perkins is right when he indicates that they are the result of a great world-wide sociologic movement which cannot be checked; one which is as certain to go on as evolution. If this is true there is nothing to do except to see to it that these combinations are wisely controlled and regulated so that the laborer, the salaried man, the consumer and the investor are *all* protected. Mr. Perkins is a very able man and has given much thought to such subjects. It is interesting to note how he proposes to deal with a subject in which so many of his financial friends are vitally interested and that the method which he proposes would not at present find favor with any but the more enlightened and farseeing among them. We are gradually straightening out the banks and the railroads; why can we not, as Perkins points out, just as easily straighten out the great industrial combinations and exercise a sane and safe control over them, jailing their officers and directors if necessary for violations of the wise amendments of the Sherman Anti-Trust law yet to be made?

Don't take the trouble to answer this.

Affectionately,   D. M. Barringer

TLS (Governors' Files, Nj).

[1] The clipping is missing, but it was a report of George W. Perkins' speech of October 4, 1911, to the Detroit Board of Commerce suggesting the creation of a federal commission, modeled on the Interstate Commerce Commission, which should have close oversight over the finances and operations of large industrial enterprises. Perkins was perhaps deliberately vague about the powers of the proposed commission, but he did make it clear that he did not favor government ownership, management, or price fixing. *New York Times*, Oct. 5, 1911.

To Daniel Moreau Barringer

My dear Moreau: [Trenton, N. J.] October 6, 1911.

Thank you sincerely for your letter of October fifth with its enclosures. I value very much the things you send me and shall certainly keep them for perusal when I have time to put my brains on them.

I do not think from what I have seen of him that Mr. Perkins is a trustworthy guide for a clear thinker, but undoubtedly his experience makes it wise to pay attention to his suggestions out of which sometimes a great deal can be got.

Affectionately yours,   Woodrow Wilson

TLS (D. M. Barringer Papers, NjP).

A News Item

[Oct. 6, 1911]

Governor Has Amusing Experience With David Baird

WOODBURY, N. J., Oct. 6—The Governor had an amusing experience with David Baird, the South Jersey Republican leader, at the Mount Holly Fair in the afternoon. Baird had met the Governor once before, but had forgotten it. When one of the directors introduced the Governor to the South Jersey leader Baird did not recognize him, and said: "What did you say his name was?" "Why Governor Wilson," said the introducer. "Oh," said Baird, "glad to meet you Governor. I respect you as Governor."

The Governor also shook hands with Mr. Browning, whom he referred to in a speech as "the frizzled beef candidate" for Congress, and in answering his chiding the Governor said: "Oh, it's all in the game."

Printed in the *Trenton Evening Times*, Oct. 6, 1911; one editorial heading omitted.

A News Report of Two Campaign Addresses in Camden, New Jersey

[Oct. 7, 1911]

GOVERNOR IS FOR CHANGE IN PRIMARY LAW

Tells Camden Citizens He Favors Allowing Voter
to Keep Party Preference Secret.

URGES SHAKING OFF YOKE

CAMDEN, Oct. 7—Coming out strongly for a primary election at which it would not be necessary for a voter to make known his party preference, was one of the notable features of Governor Wilson's talks here, last night, to 4,000 voters, and with equal force he asked his hearers how long they intended to wear a yoke.

On the subject of the primary, the Governor said in part:

"There is a feature in the present election law that I have always dissented from and always shall dissent from; I mean the provision that makes it necessary for a man to declare when he goes into the primary polling place which party he is going to support. You know the result of that.

"No man in Camden County who was afraid of the machine in this county would venture to go into a primary polling place and ask for a Democratic ticket. You know he would not and you know there are score upon scores of our fellow-citizens who, either from personal or for any other reason, will not vote at the primaries upon those terms.

"Nobody knows what is going to happen at election; I don't and you don't. For one thing, real people are going to vote at that election, and nobody is going to know how those real people vote; and they are not going to vote for anybody that they do not pick out, for you are not going to vote tickets, you are going to vote for individuals. You cannot now insert a ticket in a man's mouth and say 'Now, swallow it, damn you!'

"You have got to make him take one name at a time—feed him—and if his stomach happens to turn on a particular name he is not going to swallow it. You cannot ram this thing down their throats, not if you exercise your manhood and independence.

"Here, gentlemen, is the opportunity for the emancipation of Camden County. Are you going to accept it?["]

After urging Camden voters to cast off the yoke of the boss, the Governor said:

"I hope that the seventh of November next will record the awakening and redemption of Camden County.

"I am as confident of the future of the nation as I am certain of what constitutes the warp and woof of American manhood. What I have come to ask you in Camden County is whether you are going to have a part in it or are going to keep Camden County hermetically sealed.

"It is my conviction that the people of Camden County have lived under a bad reputation, not because they are bad but because they were hopeless. Man after man has said to me, 'What is the use?' The first returns I turn to on election day shall be those of Camden County, for I know if Camden County redeems herself that a better day has not only dawned but that the sun has climbed to the zenith."

The Governor showed the first signs of fatigue last night since the opening of the campaign. He was entertained at dinner early in the evening by the Camden County Democratic leaders, and then made two speeches. The first was at the Temple Theater, where former Judge Howard Carrow presided. Next he went to the Broadway Theater, where former Judge John W. Wescott was chairman. Each theater was jammed to its capacity. . . .

At the Temple theater Governor Wilson plunged once into the subject of the redemption of Camden County. He said:

"I should feel very proud if I might lead Camden County out of her bondage. You know that when there is a movement in all the rest of the State to reclaim it from its political servitude, everybody says that Camden is hopeless. But when they say that Camden is hopeless and you ask them for the reason, they say there is an organization there that cannot be beaten.

"When you ask them for the details, they will tell you that every office-holder, every policeman, every fireman and every man that receives pay to enforce the laws of the city of Camden, is expected to get out and obey orders. I don't believe it, with regard to some of these men. If it be the truth, then it is time that Camden redeemed herself from her shame, and it is time that these men who take orders showed their manhood. But when people speak of this as a Bourbon county you want proof from the record that they are wrong.

"Now, what is a Bourbon? A Bourbon is defined to be a man who never learns anything and never forgets anything; never forgets the things that communities ought to turn their backs upon, and never learns the way by which to escape from a continual servitude. Now, is that going to be true of Camden County? Camden County, so far as is indicated from the Republican side, has not learned or forgotten a single thing." . . .

Printed in the *Newark Evening News*, Oct. 7, 1911.

A Campaign Address in Flemington, New Jersey[1]

[[Oct. 7, 1911]]

MR. CHAIRMAN,[2] Ladies and Gentlemen:

It is very delightful to find myself in Hunterdon county again, because, while we have persuaded the rest of the State to become

1 Delivered in the Flemington Opera House.
2 Adam O. Robbins, lawyer of Flemington, judge of the Court of Common Pleas of Hunterdon County, 1922-37.

Democratic, Hunterdon has always been Democratic. There is a delightful feeling for any Democrat who comes into Hunterdon county. It is true, as your Chairman has just said, that I am here in the fulfillment of a promise. We made a good many promises a year ago, and I felt for my part whenever I uttered a promise then that it was something that must lie on my conscience until it was fulfilled. The first of the promises, as he has said, that I made to you was that I would come back and report on what had been done, because I understand it to be my function to be the spokesman of the party during my term of office in respect to those things to which the people ought to hold the party responsible; and yet, at the same time, ladies and gentlemen, the past interests me only as an indication and earnest of the future. Our eyes are in front, not behind. We still experience and rehearse our past more as a guide to the future than anything else. I have never taken very much interest in those platforms, for example, so common in past years—so common still in the Republican party—which consist chiefly of rehearsing the glories of the past. I have almost felt in regard to them as I do with regard to some very insignificant person who boasts of his ancestors and yet does not do anything like his ancestors did; and when he is not like them and not doing such great things as they did, it is a disgrace to him to live in their history. The greater the past the greater your compulsion for looking forward to the future. Therefore, I do not see how any party or any individual can boast of the past without being very careful that the present shall correspond with it and the future improve on it. My interest in the Democratic party, therefore, is not merely an interest in its great annals, though we sometimes return, with a certain degree of hesitation to the remote past to which we as a party belong. It is very delightful to turn back to men like Thomas Jefferson; it is like turning back to the original fountains from which we derived our inspiration. But Thomas Jefferson was a leader of his own day, and our task is not merely translating what Jefferson did, but translating what Jefferson did in terms of our own; for we will not know Jefferson by merely quoting him and not being able to translate him. If we merely read his phrases and the principles upon which he lived and the terms in which those principles were uttered, we are like children in school, reading out of some old textbook that we don't understand; like a Greek scholar who understands Greek but cannot translate it into English. So that the present day language is a language of action and policy which was not the language of Thomas Jefferson, though we must try to square it with the spirit of Thomas Jefferson, but in the language of our own day and purpose, the interpretation of our own character.

What I am interested to speak of to-night is the future of the Democratic party; that is what we are met here to consider. I am going to take the liberty of reviewing the immediate past, not only by way of report, but for the purpose of illustrating what I anticipate for the future. But I take it that we are not here to-night merely for the purpose of reminiscence. You don't have political campaigns for the purpose of recollecting.

Men get together in order to do something, in order to concert something. The whole problem of politics is to keep men moving and to keep them moving in a definite direction.

The interest of this campaign, therefore, is summed up in this question: In which direction is the Democratic party headed? Where is it bound for? What is the future of the party? What do we wish to be the future of the party? For, ladies and gentlemen, we are not now engaged in securing triumph for the Democratic party merely that some of us may enjoy office; there is nothing in that. When men debase a party merely for the purpose of using it in their own behalf, that party, if it long submits, is on the road to decay and disgrace. The only excuse for a party is that it is a combination of men of like mind intending to do particular things for the interests of the community in which they live. That is almost the definition of a party, and, certainly it is the only excuse for a party.

Now what is the future of the Democratic party? We say that it has a very bright future; we talk with a great deal of confidence of the prospect of controlling the politics of this State not only, but the politics of the United States. On all hands we see predictions in the newspapers, in the speeches of hopeful orators, to the effect that the sky is rosy with the dawn of a new day for the Democratic party. That very prospect pleases, for it is certain that the confidence of the country is turning away from the Republican party and towards the Democratic party. If that is true, why is the country turning to the Democratic party? Merely out of disappointment with the Republican party and disgust for it? Merely by way of reaction? Are they turning to it simply because they cannot find anything better? Is it merely a negative reason? If it is something of that sort then there is nothing to interest an intelligent and ambitious man in the Democratic party. If we are merely a last resort, if the country is turning to us by way of reaction merely, then there is no future for the Democratic party. It must be that there is something that we are expected to do. It must be that there is something in our principles and in those things which we have shown ourselves capable of doing in which the country finds its hope for the solution of the great questions of its life.

Politics is no child's play. Politics does not concern the mere business of the platform; politics deals with the rights and ambitions of men. If the wrong policies are to be chosen, then you are going to suffer by the hundreds, by the thousands, by the helpless millions, and the men who conceive a policy a-wrong are going to be responsible for the sufferings of their fellow-men.

By the scale of states, by the scale of the whole continent, either you have to work some tremendous and colossal good, or you have got to work some colossal and tremendous evil. When you go to legislative halls and draft bills and pass bills, and when Governors and Presidents sign bills, they are ordering the lives of their fellow-men, they are saying either do thus or so, or either do not do thus or so. They are determining what men's lives shall be.

I would be very pleased not to have been distracted from what seems to me to be the business of the Democratic party. We have just begun, ladies and gentlemen; the great part of our road lies ahead of us and I want to impress upon you that that road is the road of life; it is not the road of ambition; it is not the mere road of the game of politics.

America is going to succeed as a republic, is going to succeed as a method of life only if somebody be found to lead us in the right paths, only if some party be combined for the purpose of leading us in the right path. What is the future, therefore, and what is expected of the Democratic party? You know, ladies and gentlemen, that this country is governed by the men whose votes cannot be anticipated. Did you ever think of that? And the people who determine elections are the people who vote as they please, whose votes cannot be counted on merely by guess in the one direction or the other because of the way they voted in the past. The people who rule this country, that is to say, who determine elections, are the people who vote now in this way and now in that, now for this public man and again for the other, according to their choice and judgment at the moment. And in the future of this country, in the immediate future, that party is going to rule the nation that can command this independent vote. That independent vote exists in both of the old parties, in both the Republican and Democratic parties. There is an enormous and growing element of the Republican party that is called the insurgent element of the Republican party because it refuses to be bound by the determinations of the older party leaders; it insists upon having a judgment of its own; it insists upon having a program of its own, and it will not take any stock in the men who do not profess to follow that program. Similarly, there is a section of the Democratic party that is independent. There is a section of the Democratic party that will not be led by the nose. There are millions of Democrats who insist that the only thing they will vote for is a program that will promise and effect a purpose. The party of the future, therefore, is the party that will draw these independent elements together to itself, and the hope of the Democratic party at this present moment rests upon that circumstance, for that is the fact, that the independent element of the Democratic party is in control of it, and the independent elements of the Republican party are not in control of it. Look at the circumstances; go over the roll of the men who were elected governors last autumn, the Democrats who were elected governors last autumn; go over the roll of men who constitute the majority in the House of the present Congress that has just completed a special session; go over the roll of the men who represent that majority in that Congress and look at the things they did; examine the recent national platforms of the Democratic party; look at the men whom the rank and file of the nation have insisted should be put up for office, and you will know to a point of certainty [that] the independent Democrats —I mean the progressive Democrats[—]are in control of the Democratic party.

Look on the other hand, at the Republican party, and you will see that the corresponding element in the Republican party is in the minority in that party and is not in control. Suppose, for example, that those Republicans who follow Senator La Follette, of Wisconsin, were in control of the councils of the Republican party. Don't you think that would change the prospects of the Democratic party a great deal? It is expected that President Taft represents a new age, but President Taft does not represent that section of his party. It is expected that that section of his party cannot control the next Republican convention.

It is expected that that section of his party cannot control the Republican convention, and, therefore, it is expected that because the corresponding section of the Democratic party will control the Democratic convention, the Democratic party will win the next Presidential election. Why? Because it will poll the usual Democratic vote? No; because the usual Democratic vote has not been big enough to elect a President. But because it is expected that it will poll the independent vote of both parties. That is the reason. The whole future of the Democratic party,

therefore, depends on its remaining under the control and guidance of its independent section. I am not imagining these things;
I am not saying that it is a vague idea of what I hope to see.
These are the things that are known to everybody who analyzes
the situation in this State or in the United States. Supposing
that there is a reactionary element in our party in this State, do
you suppose this State would put the progressive element in
power if it got control again? That element of the party had control for sixteen years and during those sixteen years we enjoyed
the distinction of being a minority party; and just as soon
as the progressive wave that is sweeping through this Nation
puts the progressive element in control, just so soon will the
party that puts the progressive element in control be in charge
of its affairs. The Democratic party holds its lease of power on
those terms and only upon those terms. The moral of my lesson,
therefore, and the point of my forecast for the future is this:
that the Democratic party is progressive.

Very well, that doesn't mean anything unless you know what
a progressive is. What is a progressive? Well, in the first place,
you can't make progress unless you know where you start from
and which way you want to go; you can't make progress unless
you get away from somewhere, can you? If you stay where you
are or where you were, you haven't made any progress, and
unless you know which way you are bound, you cannot make
any progress. You may wander all over the face of the earth,
but you cannot make any progress. I am going back to Princeton
to-night, but I couldn't get there starting out in the direction
towards Phillipsburg. If I should cross the Delaware and wander
all over the State of Pennsylvania, I wouldn't get to Princeton
to-night. So that we have to leave where we are and go in a definite direction in order to make any progress. In order to know
what has happened to the Democratic party, therefore, you
want to know the place it left. What did it leave? I wish the voters
of this State would reflect upon that; that is what I have come
to report about—about the place we left and how fast we left it.

We started at a place where the Democratic party was just
as much controlled by the special interests as the Republican
party was; that is where we started; that is where we were a
year ago. Those who controlled the action of the Democratic
party at that time were just as much under the thumb of the
special interests as those who controlled the Republican party,
and control it yet in New Jersey. The Republicans have not
changed a hair. If you want proof of it read the platform that
was adopted by the Republican convention held at Trenton last

Tuesday; it is one of the most verbose and preposterous platforms that was ever put forth—a regular old-fashioned brass-
mounted piece of imposition, and bearing every earmark of what
has been practiced by the same old crowd that tried to put it over
us a year ago. The Republicans haven't forgotten anything—I
mean the Republicans of New Jersey—and they haven't learned
anything. Well, what happened to the Democrats? What happened to the Democrats is written in the acts of the Legislature
of last winter; and some of it happened with the assistance of
the independent and intelligent Republicans, you will remember.
I would be ashamed if upon any occasion I forgot the meed of
praise which is due to the intelligent Republican Senators who
helped us carry out the program of last winter, for the Republicans were in the majority in the Senate; and the interesting
thing is that the Senators who helped us most in that contest
have lost caste with the party to which they belong. I know that
Senator Gebhart will bear me out that nobody acted with greater
independence than Senator Bradley, and you know what has
happened to Senator Bradley in Camden county; he has been
absolutely rejected by the Republican organization of Camden
county; they couldn't stand for that kind of a Senator, a man
who would not take orders and had a conscience and opinion
of his own. They are just where we were once upon a time, where
the Democratic party took orders from the special interests.
Thank God, we don't take orders from anybody any more. Our
first object, therefore, was to get disentangled from the net of
control that we were in, and what did we do to get there?

In the first place, we passed an election law which provides
that the votes that are cast shall be real votes cast by flesh and
blood persons. Then we provided a means of identification in
the process of registration. I have heard some men grumble at
the questions they have to answer. I heard one man say, "They
actually asked me where I lived, although I had been living at
the same place since I was a boy and they know where I lived."
Is there any harm in telling where you live? Do you mind everybody knowing where you live; do you mind it being written in
a book where you live? Because the purity of the ballot consists
of being able to put your finger on the voter, and if somebody
says he lives at a certain address you ought to be able to go there
and find him any day or hour, and if you can't find him you can
infer that some job has been put up. And then you know that
the law provides also that sample ballots shall be sent out to
the voters; and it happened that in the single county of Essex,
16,000 of these sample ballots were returned because the per-

sons addressed could not be found. Of course, several thousand of those may have been accounted for by death, removal, changes of address, and all that sort of thing, but 16,000 could not be accounted for in that way; and we know—we directly know—that a large number of them were addressed to vacant lots, and that there would be forty and fifty addressed to lodging houses in which no more than five or six had ever been known to lodge. Do you object to answering questions that will make those things impossible? We wanted to see to it that there was no vote that could be controlled except the vote of an actual person, and I am happy to believe that most of my fellow-citizens in New Jersey cannot be controlled.

You know how they used to forecast elections; they used to tell you beforehand exactly what the vote was going to be, and they could do it, because if they didn't have enough actual votes they could add as many fraudulent votes as they needed; and they got it down to a numerical nicety. That went on all over the State, and it went on largely because it was so easy to use money; therefore, we passed the Corrupt Practices Act, which makes it very dangerous and inconvenient to use money in a wrong way. You haven't seen the Corrupt Practices Act work yet; it is just getting its first breath. The interesting thing about the Corrupt Practices Act is that if you can prove corrupt practice, it isn't necessary even that you should put the men in jail, it defeats the office; in other words, you don't get the goods. That, to my mind, is the most important feature of all. By the corrupt use of money a man doesn't get the office; the office is vacated by the proof and you must begin all over again; the most effectual remedy you could possibly devise. You can use any amount of money you please if you use it for legitimate purposes, although there is a limit to the amount that individual candidates may contribute, but anybody else can contribute any amount that he wants to, as long as it is contributed for a right purpose. If you do the thing in the light, out in the open and for a legitimate purpose, you can spend all the money you can get hold of.

Now what constituted the old way of doing these things? The campaign contributions of the special interests; and the special interests paid it exactly the way a man does, as I understand, when he is betting on a horse race; he picks out a particular horse, a particular party to bet on, and puts most of his money on that; then he would get to thinking it over and, thinking that maybe that horse would not win, he hedged and put some money on another horse, or put it on the field as against the horse he originally bet on. In exactly the same way the old regime used

to contribute, generally to the Republican campaign fund, because the Republican party was in power and they wanted to
control the winning party. But they said, "Here, there may be an
accident and the Democratic party may win." Therefore they
contributed almost equally large sums to the Democratic campaign fund; and the result was that they had the two machines
harnessed together, and one would pull just as kindly as the
other in harness; they didn't harness together two horses that
were not accustomed to pulling with one another either; they
harnessed a pair that generally pulled together, and they could
be sure that they would be perfectly tractable under the whip.
And what was the whip? Certainly that if they were not quiet
and obedient there would be no more money forthcoming. Therefore, the old control consisted in being able to deliver, for money,
what was demanded for money, and they could deliver it under
the old fraudulent ways of voting that were possible; and the
object of the Corrupt Practices Act was to deliver the Democratic
party from that control. That was the sole object of the whole
thing.

But that was not enough; there were certain corporations
in this State that did what they pleased with the life of the State.
Did you never reflect what a trolley line, a gas company, an electric light company, a water company, or a steam railway company can do with a State or a community? It can make it or
unmake it. Don't you know that the prosperity and the commercial conditions of this town depend on the kind of train service you have? Don't you know that the town depends on the
kind and price of the power that can be supplied to it? Don't you
know that a great deal depends on the sort of light you get and
the price you pay for it? If these things are badly supplied, if
they cannot be got from the supply of them that you have, to
just such an extent your prosperity can be lifted or depressed,
just exactly like the quicksilver in the tube of a thermometer.
Railways have made cities and railways have also unmade cities; they have opened great districts for settlement and then left
them high and dry by changing their trunk line. You know what
is going to happen as soon as the trunk lines begin to turn on
their pivots, as it were, down to the Gulf of Mexico where the
great canal is to be opened, making a passage from sea to sea.
These things are the dynamics that change the life of whole
peoples. Now you cannot have these things administered according to the whim of those who are still the directors of them
and, therefore, to establish our equilibrium, in order that our
politics may not be dominated and our rights controlled by the

public serving corporations of New Jersey, we had to pass the act which gives adequate and complete powers to the Public Utilities Commission.

Now, notice what is going on. How these people are getting out of the rain. Unprecedented things are happening. There are certain parts of New Jersey where the gas companies are offering to reduce their rates. Did you ever hear of such a thing? They are offering to reduce their rates by that much for fear the Public Utilities Commission will make them reduce them by that much. They are getting under cover, and they are going to improve their business by supplying better light and transportation. They are going to make just as much money as ever, but they are going to serve us. We are actually in control of our own light, and it is going to turn out to be a great luxury.

Then we passed an act that is not quite comprehended yet and which New Jersey is not very fast in taking advantage of, but will some day take advantage of—I mean the Walsh act, which permitted any city in the State to simplify its form of government so it could understand it and control it. Our city governments are just so many intricate affairs in which you cannot chase anybody to cover, and the whole problem of city government consists in simplifying it so that the average voter can understand it and control it. So that the commission government act was another means offered to the citizens of New Jersey to control their own affairs and not be bossed and dominated and take orders from anybody.

The work of the last session, therefore, ladies and gentlemen, so far as the conspicuous and chief acts were concerned, consisted in establishing the freedom of the Democratic party and of both parties if they choose to exercise that freedom and act in response to public opinion and not in response to special interests.

That was emancipation, and you will find the unfinished business in the new platform of the Democratic party adopted last Tuesday. There we set out what we still have left to do and what we could not have done if we had not made this preparation. Do you suppose we could have organized the government of this State on an economical and efficient basis, as we promised to do, if we had not done these very things first? Don't you know that a political machine that is organized for control has to have an innumerable number of offices to give away? Now, you cannot organize the government of the State in a way to make it efficient and economical without abolishing a lot of offices, and under the old control you could not have abolished an office.

Now we are going to abolish some offices. There are innumerable unnecessary offices and commissions in the State of New Jersey. We cannot do the whole thing by process of sweeping change; that would probably be very dangerous. But we can take one thing at a time and correct the things that ought to be corrected.

I do not believe that the government of the State of New Jersey is corrupt in the administration of its affairs; I do not mean that I do not think it has been corrupt—there has been waste; a great deal has been spent that ought not to have been spent, and some people have got the benefit of it who need not have got the money, and I mean that instances of actual deliberate graft are not numerous, but it is exceedingly wasteful, exceedingly careless, and in some instances exceedingly inefficient. One of the most inefficient things being the administration of our system of taxation.

You will see, therefore, what I mean by saying that my review is merely by way of illustrating the conditions of our government, and what we hope to propose for the future of the Democratic party. The whole nation is now bent upon this purpose of reparation, upon this purpose of restoration; that government must be and will be restored to the people.

I know that that prospect sends a thrill along your faces as it does along mine. I do not find the least interest in serving those interests which I must find out in private conference. But when I get into my imagination great bodies of people whom I do not know, whom I never saw, who are living lives of all sorts, in the factory, on the farm, deep in the mines, doing things that I never even saw done, and conceive of myself as the trustee for these people, of the fundamental conditions of their lives, it quickens every pulse in my body. I am not excited by being any man's servant, to fetch and carry for him, but it does fill the imagination with a delightful vision to think of a whole people acting together for unselfish purposes, and serving the common interest [without] looking for individual gain so it has for that wholesome opinion the supporting of action which constitutes the greatness and life of a nation. And so the Democratic party has a future only in proportion as it realizes and lives up to this vision.

You know that progressives have been described as radicals, and there are men all over this country who are trying to scare the business men of this country by saying that the progressives are radical, by which they mean that they are fellows who will change everything—recklessly change everything—get things up by the root and replant them and take the chances of new water and new soil, regardless as to whether things will grow or not.

Most of them know that they are guilty of a cruel and unjustifiable misrepresentation in that. And some of them do not. They do not know what the spirit of the progressives is. Why, by the very description of the things I have been telling you, the spirit of the progressive is the spirit of common counsel for the common welfare. Nobody that is sane, nobody that is just, nobody that is respectable that I have taken counsel with proposes to injure business. Why, gentlemen, if we injured business, we would be injuring ourselves. We are part and parcel of the business and enterprise of the country and if that business and enterprise broke down, our own lives would break down, and those who are dear to us and dependent upon us would go without their daily bread. No sane man is engaged upon such an enterprise as that. All we are engaged upon is this: that little groups of men studying chiefly the enterprise[s] that they are interested in shall not constitute the only people that take counsel as to what the country is to do, but that they shall take the rest of us into their confidence; that they shall let us know what it is they are proposing; let us express an opinion about it; let us take part in it, and establish nothing but the ancient principles of justice in the things that are to be done.

Are we men to balk at that program? Will any man who claims that he has been trying to do justice refuse to bring every just man into council with him? The mission of the Democratic party at this moment is unparalleled in the history of America. I wonder how many Americans realize that America that once led the world is now behind the rest of the world in adjusting her affairs to the standards of justice. How many of you realize that? Do you know one of the reasons why reciprocity was rejected in Canada? Because a great many Canadians believed that it was just a stepping stone towards union with the United States, and they do not want to unite with the United States until the United States has caught up with them.

Canada is more progressive than the United States. Canada long ago learned how to successfully regulate its corporations, to prevent the watering of stock in corporate operations, to prevent unjust rates, to give the communities of Canada adequate protection against any such enterprises, and unsound enterprises. Canada adopted long ago a banking system and a currency system that is better than the banking and currency system of the United States, and while the United States has had panic after panic, partly because of its bad currency system, its unelastic currency system, Canada has had no panic. Canada does not have financial panics, and there is not any group of men in Canada that can bring on a panic, either.

When Mr. Gary, connected with the great steel corporation, went on the stand the other day before the Stanley Investigation Committee of Congress, he testified that there was a small group of men in New York who could bring on a panic if they wanted to. He said they never had and they were so patriotic they never would, but he admitted that they could.

There is no group of men in Canada who could bring on a panic in Canada. Now, when our little neighbor across the border—little in population, though of course not in area—with a population hardly larger than the State of New York, can claim that it has gone further and faster in setting an example for mankind as to how to set their affairs in order—isn't it time that America resumed her leadership of the nations?

When Americans were not entangled by the control of special interests they easily led the world, in industry not only, but in institutions, and we have a great deal of lost and neglected ground to catch up.

And what fills me with enthusiasm is that apparently in the immediate future it is the opportunity of the Democratic party to do this great thing for beloved America.

The last sentence of the preamble of the Democratic platform adopted Tuesday states the fact. It says, "We have freed ourselves from private control and are able to do what we promised to do." There never was a more pregnant sentence, if it is true, uttered in American history, and if it is true, it constitutes the glory of the Democratic party.

Free to do what? Free to realize the dreams of free men; free to carry out the promises of the ages to men who have been struggling through dark ways, to see the paths of light that lead to emancipation; that will relieve in some degree the burdens and anxieties of their lives; that will enable them to look for another new nation and not fear; not put their hands to their mouths and speak behind them for fear they will be overheard, not think that there is some ear near by that may betray them and deprive them of the bread that is in their mouths; that there will come a time when no man will feel that he is another man's bond servant, when we shall be free to think and free to act, for the glory of America, as we say, has changed vision.

It is a poor life into which nothing comes that does not forecast a better future.

I believe that the inspiration of most of the noble lives that have characterized the history of mankind has been that they saw a country to which they were heirs, and which they had not yet reached, which when they came to it would open up to them the freedom of the spirit that they had never known elsewhere. I believe that the visions of mankind are the source of their spiritual lives and it is within the choice of the Democratic party to renew the spiritual youth of America.

Printed in the Flemington, N. J., *Hunterdon County Democrat*, Oct. 10, 1911, with corrections and one addition from a FPS T transcript in WP, DLC.

From John Wesley Wescott

My dear Governor: Camden, N. J. October seventh, 1911.

Had you possessed all wisdom you could not have handled the situation in Camden County with more sagacity. I wish personally to thank you. Your speeches will produce an immense effect. Howard Cooper, one of our leading lawyers and a life-long Republican, just passed through my office and remarked, "Well, Judge, the Democrats are stirring things up." I replied, "We all want to have conditions improved." He replied, "You have a great Governor, and, if he isn't careful, he will make Democrats of everybody." This is a fair sample by which to interpret the significance of your work here.

I hope you are very well.

Sincerely yours,   John W. Wescott

TLS (Governors' Files, Nj).

To Mary Allen Hulbert Peck

Dearest Friend,   Princeton, New Jersey 8 Oct., 1911.

It seems an age since I saw you: those delightful hours at Sea Girt seem already months ago,—not only because I have missed you so much but also because I have been plunged again into a political campaign and each day seems itself a week long, so many tasks and such hard ones must be crowded into it! It is as hard and as absorbing as was the campaign a year ago. I have not had so much as a breathing spell until to-day,—for even last Sunday I had to come up from Sea Girt to Trenton to speak at a big Sunday School rally (so scrupulously do I take [c]are of myself! On Tuesday the family moved down to Princeton, and here we are ensconsed in as pretty and comfortable a little house as you would wish to see. (It is No. 25 Cleveland Lane, please note, and our telephone number is 98). It was built and is owned by a Mr. Parker Mann, an artist, many of whose pictures (quite indifferent affairs) are on the walls, and we are using his furniture, which is both pretty and comfortable. We were lucky to find such a place, and shall find content here, I am sure, even if it *is* next door to the Hibben's. Last night was only the second I have slept here,—the others were spent out "on the road." I have just come back (5 o'clock) from a walk (I slept till a quarter of one and dressed only in time for lunch) to see the changes in the old town. They are many, and all make the dear old place more beautiful; but my walk has left me sad,—all the more in need of a chat with you! For I am somehow made aware at every turn of how the University, for which I spent the best thoughts and aspirations and energies that were in me, has turned away from me, and of how full the place is of spiteful hostility to me. It is a dreadful thing to be hated by those whom you have loved and whom you have sought to serve unselfishly and without fear or favour! It sickens the heart and makes life very hard. I went about from familiar place to place with a lump in my throat, and would have felt better if I could have *cried.* But I did my duty, feared no man and no thing, and the event is in the hand of God! What a comfort, what a delight it is to think of you in the midst of such memories,—of your true heart and generous friendship and perfect comradeship! God bless you! All join me in affectionate messages,

Your devoted friend   Woodrow Wilson

ALS (WP, DLC).

To John Wesley Wescott

My dear Judge: [Trenton, N. J.] October 9, 1911.

Your letter cheers me very much. I rather thought I had not done particularly well in my speeches in Camden, for I was feeling very jaded and tired. It bouys me up that you should think to the contrary and I am grateful to you.

Cordially and faithfully yours,   Woodrow Wilson

TLS (J. W. Wescott Coll., NjP).

A Campaign Address in Trenton, New Jersey[1]

[[Oct. 9, 1911]]

Mr. Chairman,[2] Ladies and Gentlemen: This is my home county. I should deem it a great honor if I could win this county

1 Delivered in the Taylor Opera House.
2 Mayor Frederick William Donnelly.

to the support of government by the people. A year ago I was asking you for your suffrages for myself;[3] you did not vouchsafe them,[4] and I must say that if I had been in your place I would have entertained the doubts which probably you entertained. A year ago it was all promises, and you had been surfeited with promises. Why should you take one man's promise more than another's? Why should you believe either party when both parties had failed you? Some of your fellow-citizens were willing to take a sporting chance; you were not; you showed yourselves conservative in that regard. But while a year ago you heard promises, now it is my privilege to tell you of performances. The things that we promised we did; most all of the things that we promised we did; we didn't do more because the session was not long enough; and those that we did not have time to do we have put upon our program for the next session. But they can't go on, this unfinished business cannot be completed except by your support and permission. Last autumn you took a chance; this autumn you render a judgment.

Do you consider the government that you have had good and satisfactory, or do you not? That is what you will have to determine on the seventh of November. These gentlemen who are candidates for office this year, stand for something very definite, and they have, as you have heard, not been picked out by any machine whatever; they were picked out by the free processes of the primary, and you know who they are. I can personally tell you a great deal about some of them. I don't need to tell you about Dr. Madden,[5] for all Trenton knows him as a man who, in the office of Mayor, knew the right and had the courage to do it.

But I cannot tell you a great deal about the gentlemen who follow him. My one-time colleague at Princeton, Professor Ford[6] —Professor Ford has had an unusual experience in the field of politics. He was for a long time one of the most influential editors in the city of Pittsburg and a man who has observed politics in Pennsylvania knows a good deal of politics; a man who has influenced politics is a man whose influence is certainly a powerful factor. Not only that, but Professor Ford, as I can testify, has a mind which illuminates the processes of politics by casting upon them the light of truth; Professor Ford was

[3] His speech is printed at Oct. 3, 1910, Vol. 21.
[4] Actually, Wilson carried Mercer County in 1910. The official vote count was Wilson, 11,839, Lewis, 11,692. Gubernatorial candidates of the Socialist, National Prohibition, and Socialist Labor parties received 600, 152, and 92 votes, respectively.
[5] Ex-Mayor Madden was running for sheriff of Mercer County.
[6] Henry Jones Ford, Democratic candidate for the Assembly.

the first man in America to tell the natural history of the boss. He knows how bosses were made, and by the same token he knows how they can be unmade. He has been in at the birth and I expect to be with him when he is in at the death. I do not know so much about the other candidates, but I do know this, that I believe their professions, and have every reason to believe their professions, when they say they stand for a continuance of the business that we have had the privilege of beginning.

Now it is a comparatively easy matter, or should be, to demonstrate to the citizens of Trenton what took place last winter. This is the capital of the state; the Legislature sits here; the Governor's office is here. You know perfectly well that there has been a change of weather; you know perfectly well, if you know anything about the State House, that the lobbyist has gone out of business. You know that the whole aspect of affairs was altered last winter after the beginning of the session. We had an object lesson, a demonstration, at the outset which assisted us in carrying forward the business of the state amazingly; after that there was a look of discouragement and of astonishment upon the face of every gentlemen who, standing outside of the Legislature, had been in the habit of running each member, which was dear to the heart. The dejection of some men is the best symbol of the liberty of the people. I heard many an old fellow go away shaking his head and saying politics had changed. They reminded me of an undergraduate of Princeton who said that if we kept on with the reforms we were intending there that we would make it an educational institution, a thing very unusual in some colleges. These gentlemen began to realize that politics had changed, that it was not a question of whispering to a member here or there and drawing them out into the corridors and suggesting this, that and the other motive to them, and then going away and telling their employer the thing was all understood and fixed up. They knew the thing had to be debated in the open and it was a question of policies and not of favor, it was a question of serving the people and not private masters and effecting private understandings. You have been witnesses to this thing, you know that the character of the government of the state has been altered. Do you want it to go back to the old style, you men of Mercer, you men of Trenton who year after year have cast votes that promoted the old style—are you ready now to cast votes that will promote the new style? I think that from the action that you took in the case of commission government, that you are.

Do you realize that Trenton was not only the first large city in the state, but the first large city in the East to adopt this broader and direct form of government? Do you realize that Trenton was the pioneer in this part of the country in adopting a form of government which is redeeming cities all over the United States? I don't remember anything more satisfactory than the self-possessed way in which the citizens of Trenton made that decision for themselves not withstanding all the efforts that were made to control the votes after the usual fashion. And then there followed that, I dare say, very discriminating choice of the five men[7] out of the sixty-seven. There are going to be deep waters, for you don't change a city government easily. But the deep waters are pure waters; they are waters fit for men to struggle in, and the other shore is a happy shore.

I know what Trenton is going to do with its city government; it is going to establish here on the banks of the Delaware a model government for the rest of the state, and I take heart for the future in the evidence of the past. I believe Trenton is going to make a unique kind of government in the state, and that she will give confidence of that on the seventh of November next.

And then you had another shock in Trenton recently. I don't suppose many of you saw the Democratic convention that was held the other day in Masonic Temple, but probably you heard something about it. That convention, under the new law of the state, was made up of everybody that would have to do what he said.

You know the trouble with political conventions has been that all they had to do was to issue a platform which they did not have to carry out and then nominate somebody who would have to carry it out, just exactly as if they run your business, by holding a mass-meeting and determining how it should be run and then scuttling and letting somebody else run it. That was the old fashioned way of doing it—a lot of i[r]responsible members, party leaders getting together days and sometimes weeks before the convention got together, many of them not members of the convention at all, and they wrote the platform and then came down and imposed it upon this body that did not have to carry it out, and that swallowed it all the more readily because they did not have to digest it. But these gentlemen who sat in Masonic Hall the other day consisted of the Governor, of the holdover Democratic Senators, of the candidates for the vacant seats in the Senate, and of the candidates for Assembly. Every man in

---

[7] The newly elected city commissioners were Donnelly, J. Ridgway Fell, William F. Burk, George La Barre, and Edward W. Lee.

that room knew that he had to make good on the promises of that platform, and for the first time you had a convention in this state whose members meant business. And it was an absolutely free convention. Nothing was prepared for it beforehand; nothing was done for it behind closed doors. The whole public, so far as the accommodations of that committee room made it possible, were at liberty to come into the room where the committee on platform sat and where the platform was drawn.

I understand this was not the way with the Republican convention, as I am informed the same old crowd that used to draw the old-fashioned Republican platform drew this platform under the new-fashioned law and told them from the outside what the managers who would not have to fulfill these promises desired the convention to promise. I do not know that it was the same old crowd, but I have been reading choice pieces of literature for a great many years, and the story was extremely familiar. If they did not write it, they ought to have seen to it that somebody wrote it who did not use that style. It had the same sort of fatuous boastfulness about it; it had the same sort of cloudy vagueness about it; it had the same sort of claiming everything in sight. Why, the preamble of that platform claims that the Republican party made the American people moral.[8] I knew that the Republican party was rattled, but I did not know that it had lost its mind. The Republican party, that was born only sixty years ago, it, as I understand the implications of this platform, created the liberties of America. It was like a student I once had, who said that Christianity was introduced into Britain fifty-four years before the birth of Christ. I dare say these gentlemen discovered America, but I think that after they have found themselves, after they have left these ways of vagueness and come down to hard pan, they will find that the citizens of New Jersey are not quite so easily imposed upon. For these gentlemen have been saying these things for sixteen years and have done none of them. That is the record; that is not the utterance of a Democrat opposed to them; it is the fact. They have been saying these things again and again and again, and again and again and again they have fooled you; they have taken you in; you have been subject to their necromances; you have not examined anything except what they have said. Then you have clearly gone about

---

[8] It read: "The Republicans of New Jersey, speaking through their candidates, declare their allegiance to the principles of the Republican party, whose policies and whose administration of affairs have made this nation first among all the countries in material prosperity, in the high standard of wages, in the universality of education, in morality and in the promulgation of peace among all nations."

your business and failed to notice that there was nothing that they did. And so it seems to us that what we are going to decide on the 7th of November is simply this: Do you want the old style politics or do you want the new style?

What was accomplished at the last session of the Legislature? What was it that we promised you, and did? Well, in the first place, we promised you that we would disentangle the politics of the state from the special business interests of the state. That is the fundamental thing. If things had gone on as they were going on nine months ago, business in this state and in this country would have come to a period of peril and danger from which it might not have recovered in a generation, because what the people of this country were realizing was that they were being deceived, that they were being put upon, that they were being used and controlled, and that it had come to such a pass that there was no visible means by which they could recover the use and management of their own government.

The foundation of business—the only safe foundation of business—is public confidence, and big business had lost the confidence of the public. It was absolutely necessary for some business, as well as for some politics, that politics and business should be divorced and that something should be had, that nothing could be done in a free country that was not done by men save in a plain and free understanding. Well, what was [it] necessary to do? First, it was necessary to see to it that the people had direct possession of their own government processions [processes]. That is the reason why we passed the Geran act—the primary and elections bill. That bill does not establish free government; it gives you the chance to have it. If you don't use the new instrumentalities you cannot have it. Legislation does not make you free; you make yourselves free. Nobody can give you control of your government; they [the] only thing that can bind is that you get it by your own effort and the object of the Geran act was to give you the right to select those who were going to be elected to office. The whole control of politics hitherto has lain in the selection of candidates. Elections have been dumb shows so long as little coteries of politicians could select the candidates. If you will let me select the men you are going to vote for I am perfectly willing to stand behind the scenes and let you vote for them; and if you will let me, unobserved, and uncriticised, while I have the understanding with the other men of the other parties who have named the other men, then I am a partner in a nice little game which will get you going and get you coming. And this is exactly what was going on in New Jer-

sey nine months ago; the candidates were selected by groups
of men sitting in private, whom you had not asked to select men
for you, whom you had not authorized to take any part in their
selection, and they were subsidized and supported by the contributions of great corporations on the tacit and sometimes explicit understanding that they were to govern their puppets in
such a way that these interests would be served in such a way
as they wanted them to be served. That was the old story of politics, and it worked; it worked again and again and again, and
you were helpless in the presence of it. That was the reason we
were anxious to give you an election law by which you could
pick out candidates for yourselves. You may have picked well
or you may have picked ill. That is not my business; that is your
business. But you are free to pick, and that is the business of
government; and having picked, you are free to elect; you are
not now taking a slate from one set of party managers or a slate
from another set of party managers; you are picking out the
men. On the ballot on the seventh of November next you will
find all of the names that were picked out in the two primaries,
the Democratic primary and the Republican primary, and in
that booth, all by yourself, you will be at liberty to pick and
choose among those candidates without respect to anything but
their personal qualifications and the pledges they have made
and that you believe; you are free to make up your own Legislatures; you are free to fill the office of sheriff in your county;
you are free to fill all the offices that are to be filled at that election according to your individual selection. That was the only
way to break the grip of the old machine.

And there went along with that the Corrupt Practices act,
which made the use of money very dangerous indeed, and had
one feature to which I would like to call the attention of all candidates, that any tainted use of money vacates the office. It is
not a matter of paying a penalty, it is not a matter of going to
jail; you don't get what you pay for. Just as certainly as you pay
for it you don't get it. Do you understand? It is the reversal of
the law of trade. In trade you get what you pay for; in this instance you get what you don't pay for. And, furthermore, it
means, not only that you don't get the office, but that you may reflect failure to get the office in jail, just the best place for reflection upon such subjects that I know of. Another peculiarity of
this interesting law is this: that if certain things go on and are
not taken notice of by the Prosecutor of the Pleas, it constitutes
a misdemeanor on the part of the Prosecutor of the Pleas, and
he may go to jail. It is the most persuasive piece of legisla-

tion that I know of; and that is because we know that elections in this state had been controlled by money. We know it. We read with astonishment and with vociferous condemnation what went on in Adams County, Ohio, where practically everybody came into court and admitted that they had bribed or given a bribe. But have you read of the investigations in Atlantic County?[9] Have you read of some of the things that took place in Hudson County? Have you ever heard of what took place at every election in Camden County? Do you suppose that Adams County, Ohio, has no parallel in New Jersey? They pleaded in Adams County, Ohio, that they did not realize how heinous it was because it had become the custom in Ohio. I have to admit with a blush of shame that there have been communities not so far removed as Ohio where this acceptance and giving of money in elections had become a habit, and I have known of very responsible men say: "Well, what are you going to do about it? Both sides do it." Shame upon any such community that rules [lives] under such conditions and not go to the very limit to abolish them.

There is another feature about the election law that I want to call your attention to; you have to register in person and some of you have not registered yet. If you do not register on the 24th of October you cannot vote at all, and if you have any drop of patriotism in you, if you care a pepper-corn for the county of Mercer and the State of New Jersey, you will go and register, if you have not registered before.

And the reason that you have to go and register is that a great many people who did not consist of flesh and blood have been in the habit of voting in New Jersey. You have got to go and be looked over by the election officers to make sure you are a real person, and it is characteristic of a real person that he has a name, that he has a residence, that he knows how old he is, and that generally he can sign his name and sign it twice the same way; and, therefore, you will be asked certain questions which are not impertinent, but which are means of identification and

---

[9] He referred to the indictment of the Republican boss of Atlantic County, Louis Kuehnle, for fraud and violations of the corrupt practices act. Kuehnle had juggled city contracts, stuffed ballot boxes, bought votes, and stolen elections, but could not be brought to justice because he controlled Enoch L. Johnson, the sheriff, who had the power to select grand juries. When Wilson appointed Samuel Kalisch as the new associate justice of the Supreme Court for the Atlantic County circuit, Kalisch circumvented the sheriff by introducing the British practice of having court-appointed elisors, rather than the sheriff, draw grand jurors. They had no qualms about indicting Kuehnle and his mayoralty candidate, Harry Bacharach, and exposing the operations of the Kuehnle machine. Link, *The Road to the White House*, pp. 292-93, and the Trenton *True American*, Aug. 16, 1911.

which are asked you in order that unrealities, imaginary persons, imported persons, persons that vote again and again under different names may not settle elections in the State of New Jersey any more.

Gentlemen, elections have been settled by voters of that kind in New Jersey. Campaign managers have sent word to headquarters to ask how many votes were needed, and when told, have supplied that exact number of votes. Anybody who knows the least about the inside of politics knows that was a common practice in some parts of this state—they delivered just as many votes as they thought were needed. You cannot do that with flesh and blood voters, and I want to call your attention everywhere to the interesting experience we have had with the first workings of this new election law. You know we sent out sample ballots for the primaries, and in one county in this state 16,000 sample ballots were returned because the persons could not be found to whom they were addressed. You must always remember that in a populate[d] county like the county of Essex, of which I am speaking, there would be several thousand changes from natural causes, from deaths, from removals from the county, from changes of addresses, but it stands to reason that you could not account for 16,000 in that way, and we have the direct testimony of mail carriers who handled that mail that a great many of these ballots were addressed to vacant lots, and others would be addressed by the twenty-five and thirty and forty and fifty to lodging houses which never had lodged more than four or five persons. And in one of those houses there lodged the clerk of the city itself, from whose office these envelopes had gone out. I don't need to tell you what that means. That means that spooks voted in the county of Essex. Real persons cannot lodge six deep in a lodging house; they have to be made of unreal and ghostly stuff and impersonated by persons of nondescript appearance from poll to poll on the day of voting. So that at one fell stroke the veil was torn from the practice that had gone on in that great county, full of independent voters, full of men of thought and energy, full of men who would scorn to do a dishonest thing; that the franchises were practically stolen from them because their votes were overwhelmed by a false registration.

It seems to me that this kind of registration is meant and will succeed in restoring to the people of New Jersey their control over their own affairs.

And there was another thing that we did which falls in the same class, although it is not ordinarily discussed in this class. The Public Utilities act went a very long way toward restoring the government of this state to the people. The government of New Jersey was once regulated by the Public Service Corporation. The government of New Jersey now regulates the Public Service Corporation—a very wholesome change, which is not only for the benefit of the people of New Jersey, but I take leave to tell the directors of the Public Service Corporation is for the benefit of the Public Service Corporation itself. When we see the inside of that business and have the testimony of disinterested persons that it is properly and thoroughly and individually conducted, we will cease to be suspicious of it and will be glad to pay its rates, because it renders us indispensable service. If it is good service honestly based there is not an honest man in the state of New Jersey who will quarrel with rates that are charged, but we insist upon knowing the inside, because these gentlemen control our lives. Don't you know that control can order the whole life of a community? Don't you know that a trolley company can order the whole life of a community? Don't you know that a power company can control the industrial development of a community? Don't you know a telephone company can put a man out of business. Just let them insist upon some rule which, because you were forgetful, and thinking more of your business than their interest, you ignored and let them take the telephones out of your business house, and they will almost stop your business, and they have not hesitated to do it, and have no[t] hesitated to make all sorts of discriminations in the use of telephones, and to give some telephones to men who use a great many at rates that many a poor man could have paid, at the cost to the poor man of putting upon him a rate that he could not pay.

These public service corporations, I repeat, control our lives, our industrial lives. Railways make cities. Railways unmake cities. I have seen, myself, in my lifetime, a city die because it was sidetracked by a change in the trunk line of a great railway. It was killed at the pleasure of a board of railway directors. And that sort of thing has gone on all over the United States.

We were a lavish and reckless people at one time; we gave all sorts of powers and subsidies to the railways, and it was worth while, because we needed a quick and miscellaneous development, but there came a time when that period was over and it was necessary to look to it that these creatures of ours did not dominate our lives, and I want to report to you that in cities where laws like our present laws have been enforced long enough to test them there is not a railway man or a man connected with an electric light or gas company or water company who would on any condition consent to seeing the laws changed, because everywhere they have been for the benefit of the corporations that were regulated. I would not stand before any audience and advocate a law which I did not think was fair all around. All I am insisting upon with regard to it at first is that if all the benefits stand on one side and all the burdens on the other it is perfectly fair, and indeed, necessary, to distribute the benefit along with the burden. Therefore, the emancipation of the state of New Jersey from machine control dates from the new election laws and the Public Utility act.

Then there was added an act to which Mr. Donnelly was referring, the commission government act—the act which enabled you to destroy the ambushes of cities and create some plain plan upon which you can govern yourselves. You may not at first succeed, but you have the means of succeeding, and in the long run you will succeed.

I do not know what Mercer County is going to do on the seventh of November, gentlemen, but I know what the American people are going to do. Mercer County can be in the procession or fall out of it as it pleases. That is Mercer County's concern and the procession won't stop if you fall out. If you have not got a weather eye, that is not going to change the weather. If you can't see the signs of the times you will some day, belated, perceive them, for what is abroad in this country is something that has never failed of triumphant conquest or the support of the American people. Did you ever reflect what that has meant in the history of the world? It was that spirit which brought hope out of despair, for not until this spirit brooded upon this young continent and begat a nation did the peoples of the world see the highways of hope, not until America showed that great peoples, ungoverned by little coteries of selected men, could govern and direct their own affairs, did the rest of the world take heart to be free. You know that it was the American Revolution that bred the French Revolution; you know that it was the French Revolution that showed the lurid dawn of the liberties of Europe. You know that the fires and blood of that terrible time marked the end of an old regime which could never thereafter return, when people should be trodden upon like slaves and not admitted into the councils of their own affairs, and that slow fire though it was, spread from country to country until every old and rotten and discredited thing was consumed and its ashes used only to fertilize the ground upon which it had stood.

This winnowing spirit of the American people that blows where it listeth, that comes like a great breath out of a great heart, this spirit that is pure of eye, pure of heart, that is evidence of the longings and strifes and aspirations and visions of men everywhere, has now awakened from a sleep for a long generation in America; this spirit has simply allowed itself to be lulled to sleep by all sorts of narcotics, chiefly the opium of successful business, but now it has shaken itself free from sleep, and woe unto the man that withstands it, woe unto the party that withstands it; woe unto the man that does not understand it and take into his lungs the fine afflatus that it will supply him for the purification and elevation of his life.

We have come upon a new age, we have come upon a new age in which America again shakes herself like a [great] and powerful creature, and says to the whole world, "We have for a little while gone astray; we had forgotten our destiny in the world; we had forgotten that it was our business to see that men were not ruled but rulers; and we chide ourselves with having forgotten, but the vision has come back to us; it will lead us on. There is no limit to the lands of achievement which we may reach in following it."

Printed in the *Trenton Evening Times*, Oct. 10, 1911.

From Henry Burling Thompson

Dear Wilson: [Greenville P. O., Del.] October 9th, 1911.

I have been trying in vain to seek an interview with you, but shall have to let this letter tell the story.

My friend, Willard Saulsbury, who is the Delaware member of the Democratic National Committee, and also a member of the Executive Committee of that same body,[1] is anxious to meet you; and I should think it might be to your interest if you could grant him an interview at an early date.

Mr. Saulsbury has been a prominent leader in the party for a number of years, and was probably the most potent factor in his party during the Addicks' fight.[2] He is a strong party man,—believing in party methods,—robust, but no hypocrite.

He is not identified with the Rail Road wing of the Democratic party of this State, but, on the other hand, has been fought very bitterly by them.

He was a sound money Democrat in the first Bryan campaign, but I should consider him an anti-corporation Democrat.

From my personal experience with Mr. Saulsbury, I have always had reason to believe he kept his word.

           Yours very sincerely,   Henry B Thompson

TLS (Thompson Letterpress Books, NjP).

[1] Lawyer of Wilmington, Del., in the firm of Saulsbury, Morris and Rodney, and director of the Equitable Guarantee and Trust Co. and the Union National Bank of Wilmington. Long active in Delaware politics, he was United States senator from 1913 to 1919.

[2] He referred to the long and successful struggle to prevent John Edward Addicks, Republican boss of Delaware, 1894-1906, from winning a seat in the United States Senate.

To Walter Hines Page

My dear Page: [Trenton, N. J.] October 10, 1911.

You are absolutely right about publishing the frank statement with regard to the money,[1] and the only reason it has not been done sooner is that McCombs has been away and I did not like to authorize the things in his absence. He will be back presently and we will then get together and have a full conference about it, laying out not only what is to be done now but what is to be done hereafter in regard to this and similar matters.[2]

I heartily appreciate your kind thought of these things and subscribe myself,

Very heartily and gratefully yours, Woodrow Wilson

TLS (W. H. Page Papers, MH).

[1] Page's letter, to which this was a reply, is missing.

[2] In a statement in the *New York Times*, Dec. 31, 1911, McCombs declared that none of the contributions to the Wilson campaign fund had come from Wall Street or big business, or any quarter that might have an ulterior motive; that no contribution had been for more than $5,000; and that a scrupulous record of every contribution and expenditure was being kept. However, he added, he could not make the names of contributors public without their permission.

A News Report of Campaign Speeches in New Brunswick and Perth Amboy, New Jersey

[Oct. 11, 1911]

WILSON TALKS ON "MOB RULE"

NEW BRUNSWICK, Oct. 11.—In his address here last night Governor Wilson paid his respects to the men in high position in the United States who have recently had much to say about "mob rule." . . . In his speech at Perth Amboy the Governor took up the work of the Public Utilities Commission, and defended it against those who have criticized it as slow and ineffective. . . .

At the theatre here the Governor found an audience that completely filled the building, but the auditorium at Perth Amboy was crowded to suffocation. The aisles were jammed and the wall of people extended half way down the outside stairways.

The audience at New Brunswick numbered about 1,500 and at Perth Amboy about 2,200. . . .

At New Brunswick the Governor was the first speaker and found his audience in a quiet, sober mood. But when he reached Perth Amboy he found that Congressman Eugene F. Kinkead had waked things up and that the great throng was in lively humor. Particularly was this true of the Woodrow Wilson League that occupied a solid block of seats on the main floor.

At Perth Amboy the Governor had a rap for some of the rules of the Public Service Corporation. He said:

"I moved a short time ago, to a new house in Princeton, that is, the house was new to me. There was an electric meter in the house and I wanted to turn on the lights, but a representative of the company came and insisted on taking the meter out. He told me that if I wanted light I would have to go down to the office and pay $5 and arrange for a new meter. So far as I could find out there was nothing wrong with the old meter; it was simply one of the company's rules.

"It wasn't until it was discovered that it was the family of the Governor of the State with whom the company was dealing that there came a change of attitude. If they hadn't found they were dealing with the family of the Governor we would have had no light that night. There were no gas fixtures in the house and we had no candles.

"I want to say that I have the utmost contempt for a company that would give favor to the Governor over any other family in the State. I refuse to accept favors given through fear of the Governor's office.

"The thing which I object to is this rule. We would have suffered merely the inconvenience of being without light for one night. But these people have played by their rules with the fundamental rights of the people. They haven't a right to a single penny except for service and the people have a right to demand that service be afforded them under reasonable rules."

The work of the Public Utilities Commission under the new law came in for the Governor's commendation. He said:

"Some people have complained—some people in Middlesex County have complained[—]of the slow movement of the Public Utilities Commission. I have had people come into my office and bang the table with their fists and say 'These people have got to do something right away.' And I said, 'Whether it is just or not, whether they know what they are about or not?' 'Oh, well, it is obvious, too,' was the reply, 'that things cannot run in ruts.' 'I dare say,' was my reply, 'but is it obvious where the wrong is

and how it is to be righted? Is it not obvious that if these gentlemen hasten and make false steps that the courts will step in?'

"These gentlemen are doing things so that when they put their
foot down it will be put down to stay and nobody will venture
to request them to move it, and so every time they have put their
foot down everybody has gotten out of the way so as not to be
stepped on; and they are going with a very slow tread, but a
very sure tread.

"Have you not noticed the very extraordinary signs of the
times? Have you not read in the newspapers that the gas companies are offerling [offering] to reduce their rates? Did you ever
hear of any such thing before in your life, and don't you see
what it means? It means the development of their weather eye.
They are so afraid that they may be obliged to bring the price
of gas down to what it should be—let us say, eighty cents—that
they offer to reduce it to ninety cents and bind you by a contract
to the Public Service Corporation, which you have to respect, so
that they cannot bring it down to eighty cents very soon. Isn't
it a very interesting game, but isn't it a sign of the times? They
know they will have to get under cover, and, therefore, they are
making the cover as comfortable as possible for themselves.

"I do not say this in the least spirit of vindictiveness, nor am
I trying to make fun of these people; they are acting exactly as
persons would act in the presence of unknown forces, and what
I want them to know is that the forces they are in the presence
of are the forces of justice and nothing else; that no man need
fear the Public Utilities Commission except the man who fears
justice. But justice, as these gentlemen have not too often reflected, has two sides to it. There are two parties to a just settlement, and no ex parte, one-sided judgment can be just. The
great litigant, that great inclusive party, which is the community
itself, has never until now been in court; now it is admitted as
a party to the suit, and the justice which is to be dispensed will
be a justice so many-sided that it will accommodate itself to the
interests of communities as well as the interests of those who
are the managers of great bodies of capital."

There was a note of impatience in Governor Wilson's words
as he took up criticisms he had heard that the Democrats were
"backing down" on their legislative program of the last session
of the Legislature because they had not specifically promised in
their platform to maintain the laws enacted last year.

"A gentleman told me to-night," he said, "that a Progressive
Republican, so-called, had expressed his disappointment in the
Democratic platform, because we do not State in the preamble

of our platform that we are going to stand by the legislation of the last session. What does he take us for? What does he suppose we passed that legislation for? Does he suppose that we were going to ask for the approval of it in our platform? Do you suppose that we are going back to Trenton to upset these reforms? It just shows the state of mind of these gentlemen. Some men have to promise to be rational; they have to undertake by a written bond to be honest. We are not of that kind; we will try to be honest without bail."

It appeared when former President Austin Scott, of Rutgers, began at the New Brunswick meeting the speech which was to introduce the Governor, that there might be a clash over the initiative and referendum. Dr. Scott declared that he did not believe in the initiative and referendum, and that years ago he was confirmed in his views favoring representative government by reading Woodrow Wilson's book, "The State."

After a brief preface Governor Wilson took up the subject of initiative and referendum by way of reply. He said:

"Dr. Scott said that he did not believe in the initiative and referendum. I do. But in the same breath in which I avow that belief I want to point out to you what they are for. They are not to supplant representative government; they are to recover it; they are not necessary where you can recover it without their use; they are necessary where you cannot recover it without them. If special interests for private control is [are] so thoroughly established in the State that you cannot by the existing instrumentalities recover control to the people you must, by one means or another, recover it. Nothing must be allowed to stand in the way of a government of your own affairs by your own opinions."

There was another reminder of Governor Wilson's passage at arms with other Governors at the recent Governors' conference at Spring Lake over the subject of popular government, in what he said last night about mob rule. Referring to the fact that men in high positions in American life had recently talked much about "mob rule", the Governor went on:

"Men have spoken—men who live by the suffrage of their fellow-citizens have allowed themselves to speak[—]as if those judgments were based upon impulse, founded on passion, not the rational judgments of a thoughtful body of men. But we must have bodies of men acting, it might be, in a spirit of prejudice, or it might be the passion of the mob.

"What is a mob? No rational conception of the mob conceives it otherwise than a body of persons moved by the same passion in the same place, not stopping for any sort of discussion, not stopping to reflect what the consequences of their action will be, and rushing to one end under a common impulse. Do you think that a great body of men scattered as wide as a State, scattered as wide as a nation, would have come together in rooms like this to listen to rational men, and then have gone out and plunged into the spirit of the mob in depositing their ballots—does that look to you like a mob? Is there any possible justification in speaking of such action as the action of a mob? And you will never speak of it as such, except when you are disappointed in the way they vote. A mob, according to the definition of these gentlemen, is a body of voters that votes against them. I have known occasions when personally I disagreed with the judgment of the major part of my fellow-citizens; I have known it a great many times, because this country has been going Republican an unreasonable number of times, and I believe that every time you put in a Republican President or Republican Governor you have been mistaken.

"But it does not mean to me that they were acting in the spirit of the mob. It meant that I had to sit down and possess my soul in patience because I was a member of the minority; that is all it meant. And I want to register my conviction that the judgments of the people, in the long run, are the judgments of soberness and of truth. I want to utter my entire dissent from the uneasiness, the distrust, the innuendo, toward the people, which has filled the utterances of some men who occupy high office in this nation, and I want to say that the distrust of the voter, so far as that distrust is justified, is based upon the fact that our institutions have been so manipulated that the real judgments of public opinion have not been uttered.

" 'By the people' insinuates that we mean that population of our fellow-citizens who are least qualified to judge upon public affairs. Now, of course, some men are less qualified to judge of our public affairs than others. An English writer once said: 'If you have a man on a ledger and knock something off his wages every time he stops adding up you cannot expect him to have intelligent views about the Antipodes.' He hasn't time to think over anything for himself, and of course his vote is not going to be as intelligent as the man with the instinct and opportunity to discuss affairs with his neighbor. But it seems to me that when we speak of the people we mean the less reflecting portion of the people. As a matter of fact, we mean the warp and woof of communities; we mean those bodies of men, including all sorts and conditions that make up the modern life of cities and countrysides and quiet villages; we mean those men and women whose lifeblood throbs steadily through the day's task; we mean those who are in contact with the conditions of life in this country in all their variety.

"We certainly do not mean any particular class, and I want to say this, after association during the previous part of my life with the intellectual classes of our community, that I consider them more ignorant of the general conditions of life in this country than the men who have enjoyed less advantages, from an intellectual point of view, because the atmosphere of books is not the atmosphere of life; nations do not live in libraries. Nations live in the shop, on the farm, in the mines, and you can find that sort of a people only in these places. If you confine yourself to the reading of books, therefore, you will not know human life, because it is one of those things which is known only by contact—just as the fabled strength of old Greek heroes used to come from contact with mother earth, so the strength of the thinking mind in politics comes in contact with the great mother body of the people as a whole. And it is upon these foundations that we are seeking to establish government again."

Printed in the *Newark Evening News*, Oct. 11, 1911; some editorial headings omitted.

A News Report of Four Campaign Speeches in Monmouth County, New Jersey

[Oct. 12, 1911]

WILSON HOLDS NATION'S ILLS DUE TO TAFT

RED BANK, Oct. 12.—Governor Woodrow Wilson laid the fault for the present business depression and lack of confidence squarely at the door of the Taft administration in a speech here last night.

The Governor declared that the vacillation of the President and his advisers in dealing with the regulation of big business, the announcement by the President of a certain policy one day and its retraction the next, has produced an uncertainty in the commercial world that has made capital fearful.

Governor Wilson followed up this line of thought with a statement at Freehold that he did not much blame the Canadians for refusing reciprocity if their reason was a disinclination to become annexed to the United States.

"Canada declined to have commercial relations with us," he said. "Why should they fear union with us? Because they are vastly ahead of us in things that make for orderly life and steady business. We have staggered from panic to panic, while their banking system, their financial system and their corporation system are on a stable basis that we have not known or reached. America is behindhand."

Four big audiences, aggregating fully 4,000 persons, heard the Governor in Monmouth County. He spoke at Asbury Park, Long Branch, Red Bank and Freehold. Thoroughly exhausted after his strenuous day he started for Princeton from Freehold late last night in a big limousine. The Democrats of the county were jubilant over the wave of interest which swept through the county as the Governor proceeded on his tour from one point to the other.

When Governor Wilson began here his arraignment of the Taft administration for its policy—or lack of policy—in regulating business, he spoke with the utmost care and with the utmost seriousness. At few times in his political life in New Jersey has he thrown the vigor and fire into a speech that he put into his words upon this subject.

With only a few introductory remarks, he said:

"I am sick of professions. I am sick of reminiscences. Nothing will sit upon my stomach except action. And this country is sick of professions.

"What is the matter with the business of this country at the present time? Men continually say in my ear that business is not in a satisfactory condition in this country. They point out this undertaking and that undertaking and the other that is running at half force as if waiting for something.

"Is there a business man in my hearing who does not know that the trouble with business now is uncertainty? You d[o] not know what is going to happen to-morrow. Why don't you know? Because the men who are in authority tell you one thing to-day and another to-morrow; because the President of the United States, his Attorney-General, all those associated with him give out one utterance one day and then the next day take it back and apologize for it.

"You have heard the President speak about the execution of the anti-trust law. You have heard the Attorney-General quoted with regard to that. Do you know what either of them is going to do? Does anybody know? Do they themselves know what they are going to do? What evidence have you that you know what they are going to do? They have everybody guessing, their friends included, and you cannot conduct sound business upon a test of guessing. You have got to know what the morrow is going to bring forth.

"A friend of mine was quoting to me to-day a remark he had heard in New York. Some impatient business man said: 'If they are going to send somebody to jail why don't they get to work and send them to jail and let us get through with it. We are not objecting to sending them to jail; we are objecting to not knowing whether they are going to jail or not.' And this country is backing and filling, backing and filling, under an administration which never defines what it is going to do.

"I say, therefore, that the only thing that this country should insist upon is that affairs should be taken charge of by some persons with definite opinions and absolute unconquerable resolution and then say what they are going to do and then do it. You want them first to say what they are going to do, because you want to know whether they are wise and sound men or not, and after you determine that they are trustworthy and their object is to cure and set aright the ills that we are suffering from, that they are not vindictive, that they are not revolutionary, that they intend to apply the principles of justice to the affairs of business and of politics, then you are going to get behind them with the irresistible might of the American people and you are going to say: 'In God's name, do this sublime work of justice and we will follow you and support you.'

"You know what the programs of justice are. Why, gentlemen, upon what does business subsist? Do you know what a panic is? I mean a panic in the money market. It is merely a state of mind. To-day, let us say, there is confidence. To-morrow there is a panic. Is there any less wealth in the country to-morrow than there is to-day? Is there any less money to-morrow than there was to-day? What has changed? Nothing except the state of mind of the persons involved. To-day they were willing to lend money and to-morrow they are not willing to lend it; they call in their notes, they won't renew notes; they get their hands on every bit of cash they can lay them on, and the difference is that they have lost confidence in the processes of business for the time being. That is a panic.

"Now that illustrates the whole situation in business with regard to public opinion. Unless business is sustained by the confidence of the public that it is just; that it is founded upon necessity; that it rests upon fair dealing; that there be fair competition; that everybody has an equal show—you know what is going to happen. There is going to be universal restlessness, suspicions, envy, malice, a gathering force of passion which sooner or later will tear at the very roots of the whole structure and destroy it.

"What is justice, then, in politics and in the field of business?

Here are the remedies we propose in order to reproduce confidence. That is the object of every bill that I am interested in. I want to see the policies of the party that I belong to shaped not to the temporary, but to the permanent interests of business in this country. You know that what we did last winter in Trenton was merely meant to give us a chance to go on and do these things. The new election law did not re-establish confidence in business; the corrupt practises act did not touch the foundations of business; the public utilities act, giving the Public Utilities Commission power to regulate the business of public service corporations, only paved the way for re-establishing confidence in these corporations; it did not itself re-establish that confidence. It merely made us free to see that these undertakings were in right and just relations to the communities which they served. That is all that it did."

The Governor's first speech in Monmouth was at the Casino at Asbury Park at 2:30 o'clock in the afternoon. It was feared that the unusual hour would keep down the crowd, but when the Governor entered the big seaside hall he found an audience of a thousand waiting to cheer him. The gathering was one of the finest he has addressed during the campaign and time and again a wave of spontaneous applause swept through the hall. Dr. R[eginald]. S. Bennett, the Democratic candidate for Mayor, presided.

The Governor again trained his guns on the platform adopted by the Republicans last week. He ridiculed the Republicans forever proclaiming themselves as the followers of Lincoln. He said:

"What I am interested in knowing is this, that having for a long period forgotten the principles of the party, having drifted further away from the principles of the immortal Lincoln, having lost the advantage to the great body of the people that amounted to genius, having forgotten all that, what I want to know is are they going to turn about again and take up the principle, the simple inspiration with which they started?

"I am not interested in the circumstance that Abraham Lincoln should have represented the Republican party, unless I can be assured that if Lincoln were living now he would belong to the Republican party.

"Do you suppose that Abraham Lincoln would have had anything to do with the Republican party either in this State or in this nation during the last two decades? Do you suppose that the great men who was [were] associated with Lincoln would recognize the party formed in order to effect the liberation of men from the bondage of ownership when the industrious effort in recent decades has been to establish another kind of industrial ownership? Don't let these men prate to us of the immortal example of Lincoln until they show that they are ready to follow it; then we will admit that they are of the lineage, otherwise we must proclaim that they are not."

It was here that the Governor openly charged that the Republican Senator (Senator Prince, of Passaic), who introduced the corrupt practises act in the Senate at the last session of the Legislature, deliberately left out of the bill certain paragraphs, the omission of which from the bill would have made the act, if enacted, a mere joke so far as efficiency was concerned.

"The Republicans are now bragging that the corrupt practises act was theirs. Let them take what credit for it they want. They are bragging about the stand they took on other progressive legislation. Let them be careful how they brag about the things for supporting which they are now rejecting Senator Bradley, of Camden. Let's have done with this hocus-pocus. I am not here to indict the Republican party, but I am indicting the managers of the Republican party. Their platform is as full of hypocrisies as of bombast."

Having finished at Asbury Park, the Governor was whisked in a motor to Long Branch. He was met on the outskirts of the municipality by a band and escorted through the business streets to the Lyceum, where he spoke to nearly a thousand persons. Long Branch is a Democratic community, and applause was continuous.

Governor Wilson here discussed the duties of the Progressive Republicans in the present campaign.

"Everywhere I go," he said, "I am seeking to convert Republicans. I am seeking to convert them not away from what ought to be the intentions of their own party, but to the impulses which really ought to underlie the principles of both parties when they are true to their vows.

"What is a sane man going to do on November 7? I am not going to ask him to look as far ahead as 1912? The Republican party has no intention at present of putting itself under the leadership of the progressive element of the party.

"What is a Progressive Republican going to do on election day if he is not to stultify himself? He is going to vote the Democrat ticket. I challenge any Republican to think out any other conclusion—unless he is a standpatter. If he's a standpatter he is welcome to his views. I've never found a standpatter who reasoned. My good father used to say that you couldn't reason out of a man what wasn't in him.

"We have got the Democratic standpatters pocketed; they are stalled on side-tracks and the switches are blocked. I don't know what their cargo is, but it is not going to be unloaded just yet."

When the Governor began to speak at Red Bank he found more than a thousand persons in the theatre. Daniel H. Applegate[1] presided. Other speakers were Assistant Corporation Counsel Dudley Field Malone, of New York City, and Congressman Eugene F. Kinkead, of Jersey City. After this meeting the Governor was taken in an auto over slippery, muddy roads to Freehold, where another big crowd was waiting.

Printed in the *Newark Evening News*, Oct. 12, 1911; some editorial headings omitted.
[1] Lawyer of Red Bank, N. J.

A News Report of a Campaign Speech in Princeton

[Oct. 13, 1911]

WILSON AGAIN HITS AT TAFT'S VACILLATION

PRINCETON, Oct. 13.—An enthusiastic massmeeting of Princeton students at Alexander Hall here last night heard Governor Wilson renew his attack on the shifting policy of the Taft administration in its regulation of big business.

But the Governor went a step farther last night and began to analyze the real faults with the business situation, and to propose remedies. Because of the indication it gave as to the Governor's probable attitude toward the business interests of the country, the speech was one of the most important of the campaign.

Governor Wilson attacked the Sherman anti-trust law for its looseness in defining both offenses and penalties. Then, too, there was another word by the Governor on the subject of money monopoly. As a side issue, Governor Wilson called former United States Senator James Smith Jr. and former United States Senator John Kean partners in an effort to deliver the State into the hands of the special interests.

"You can't conduct business on guesswork," the Governor said, "and there has been nothing but guesswork for the last decade. We need something definite; we need some analysis of the situation that will show us what we ought to do. When the thing is done we shall have the feeling that something has been not wrecked, but reconstructed.

"First of all, we want some definitions. We want a law for our business that will give an absolutely clear definition of what is illegal and what is legal. We want an absolute definition of what is going to be done if the law is violated.

"To-day a person who violates the law doesn't know which of the things possible under the law is going to happen to him. He doesn't know whether he is to be indicted and sent to jail or whether action is to be brought for the dissolution of his business—he doesn't know just what awaits him if he violates the law. It may be any one of several things. Under the present law he is in the position that he doesn't know what the offense is and he doesn't know what the penalty is to be.

"One of the fundamental things to remember is that there are legitimate corporations and illegitimate corporations. The one is intended to aid business, the other is intended as a monopoly in restraint of trade and does exercise monopoly. It is that thing the country has made up its mind it is not going to stand.

"There are many things outside the field of law to-day that should be brought within the field of law. For instance, if A, B, C and D are directors of a certain bank, and then of corporations that use that bank, and of other banks and other corporations, and there is a certain personnel running through business after business, it is right for us to ask what these gentlemen are lo[o]king for. Are all our business affairs to be tied up in a small community of interest? Are we going to have a small body of men running things no matter where we move? We should inquire how far we may disentangle without upsetting business these too much entangled affairs. When we have settled these matters we shall find business fairer, cleaner, more energetic—because stimulated by competition, more in the confidence of the people—because stimulated by conformity to law. I would be ashamed of myself if I favored legislation aimed to injure legitimate business."

The student body gave their former president a great reception. Just after 8 o'clock the thumping of the student band— two bass drums and a pair of cymbals vociferously wielded— woke the campus to life. Soon the student parade was on. From one dormitory to another the singing, cheering line marched, getting new recruits all along the line. At every stop there was a rousing "locomotive" for the Governor.

Once inside Alexander Hall, the students were as decorous as if at a prayer-meeting. True, they did whistle some old Princeton airs, but such things are in order any time in a college gathering.

At just 8:30 the Governor marched out on the platform, accompanied by Head Coach "Bill" Roper and a group of county candidates. Immediately there was a din of enthusiastic applause. The Governor had no cause to feel anything but elation at his reception. It was his first political speech at Princeton since his election.

Head Coach Roper acted as chairman and made a little speech challenging any one to show that the Democrats had not "made good" in New Jersey during the past year. N. N. Arnold, 1911,[1] told the students how to register and vote. . . .

Printed in the *Newark Evening News*, Oct. 13, 1911; some editorial headings omitted.
[1] Nezza Nevello Arnold of Dillsburg, Pa.

To Charles F. Herr[1]

My Dear Sir: [Trenton, N. J., c. Oct. 13, 1911]

Allow me to acknowledge the receipt of your letter of October 10th,[2] and to express my warm appreciation of the desire of the campaign committee of the Essex County Democratic Association[3] that I should be present and address the mass meeting which the committee is planning to hold in the new auditorium in Newark in behalf of the candidates nominated on the Democratic ticket in Essex County, and also for the compliment that the committee has paid me in leaving to me the choice of the date.

While I warmly appreciate this action on the part of the committee, I feel that the best interests of the party would not be served by my participating in the meeting and, therefore, feel constrained to decline.

[Sincerely yours,   Woodrow Wilson]

Printed in the *Trenton Evening Times*, Oct. 14, 1911.
[1] Lawyer of Newark.
[2] It is missing.
[3] The Smith-Nugent Regulars.

A News Report of Campaign Speeches in Hackensack and Ridgewood, New Jersey

[Oct. 14, 1911]
KEEP AWAY "GUARDIANS," SAYS WILSON

If They Again Secure Control He will Take a Long Vacation.

HACKENSACK, Oct. 14.—A vigorous plea that the Board of Guardians be kept out of the State house at Trenton for another year was made to two big audiences of commuter voters in Bergen County by Governor Woodrow Wilson last night.

At Trinity Hall here and at the theatre in Ridgewood the Governor was greeted by crowds so appreciative that he warmed up to making two of the happiest speeches of the campaign. The listeners laughed and applauded in rapid alternation.

Without going very deeply into any subject, the Governor skimmed over the history of the past nine months in New Jersey and asked for the continued co-operation of the voters of Bergen County in keeping the State in its present political status.

"I never enjoyed inactivity," said the Governor, "and if the Legislature next year is going to work for those for whom it formerly worked, I shall not enjoy cooling my heels in the Governor's office. If the Board of Guardians comes back to the State house I am going on a long vacation."

The commuters gave close attention as Governor Wilson touched upon the work being done by the Board of Public Utility Commissioners. He urged that they have patience in waiting for the completion of the board's work on the subject of commutation rates.

"I know in some communities like Hackensack, which is a commuter community to a great extent, that a great deal of impatience has been felt at the slowness with which the Public Utilities Commission used its new powers, but you will notice that the commission is doing this very sensible thing, it is waiting to see where it can put its foot down on solid ground so firmly that when the foot is down no one can ever make it move the foot, and that, to my mind, is a great deal better than hasty and ill-considered action.

"For example, its recent order does not as yet offer you any relief; it merely commands the various railways to sell tickets to such points as you desire them to sell tickets to; it forbids them to oblige you to buy a through ticket to New York, provided you do not want to buy a through ticket to New York; it obliges them to serve you as you desire to be served in that matter, and then directs them to submit to it, the commission, the rates that they are going to charge for these new tickets. Then will come a time when it will determine whether those are reasonable rates or not,[1] but the first step was to determine that they must readjust their practises in respect to the termini they put upon their tickets. . . .

"There was another measure that we passed with the same object in view, though apparently public opinion is very slowly coming up to that measure. I mean the Walsh act, the object of which is to give the cities of this State the right to adopt a commission form of government. That was an enabling act, to enable cities to take charge of their own affairs when they got ready. If they are not ready, of course, that is nobody's business, but as long as that act stands there, whenever you get ready you can govern your[s]elves. I dare say they are too busy; they are like the god Baal, they are asleep and are gone on the shelf, or are engaged in other business, but when they wake up or come back or adjourn their other business for a little while, then they can take up their own affairs. . . .

Turning then to the subject of reform, Governor Wilson declared that its object was not to impress upon the public the private views of a few national men, but rather to uncover the common interest by means of the common judgment. He continued:

"And gentlemen say, business men in particular—most of you are business men; I daresay you go in and out from the great metropolis and are engaged in this, that and the other business —that all this reform that is in the air is disturbing business.

"Is it going to disturb business to get back on a constitutional and honest basis? Are you willing to stand for that business? Is it going to hurt business to restore confidence? What is the basis of prosperity? The basis of prosperity is co-operative; the basis of business and prosperity is confidence; the basis of prosperity is a new figure and spirit in the social body. If you depress the working classes, for example, make them hopeless and resentful, and give them the feeling that they are not getting their just dues, do you suppose that they are going to be the producing class they were; do you suppose the wealth is going to be produced as it would be if they felt they were partners in the thing, justly treated, honorably dealt with, generously paid?" . . .

Printed in the *Newark Evening News*, Oct. 14, 1911; some editorial headings omitted.
  [1] In its decision of October 27, 1911, the Board of Public Utility Commissioners disapproved of the commuter rate increases recently applied for by the Pennsylvania Railroad, the Reading, the Erie, the Susquehanna, the New Jersey Central, and the Lehigh Valley Railroad.

A News Report of Three Campaign Speeches in Morristown, Dover, and Madison, New Jersey

[Oct. 16, 1911]

WILSON SAYS REFORMS NOW UP TO VOTERS
ONLY ONE PROGRESSIVE PARTY

MORRISTOWN, Oct. 16.—Governor Wilson, in his speeches here and at Dover and Madison, Saturday, made a special appeal for the election of a Democratic Legislature that would continue the policies of last winter. He told his audiences that if they wanted a progressive government the only party they could vote for with the expectation of getting it was the Democratic party. At the coming election, he said, the people would have their first opportunity of expressing their judgment upon recent events in this State and he, personally, was very anxious to know whether they wanted to support or reject the present administration. . . .

Referring to the light registration in Morris County, the Governor said:

"Now I am informed, if I may say so parenthetically, that there has been a very light registration in Morris County. Being flesh and blood persons, don't you want to vote? You cannot vote unless you register. Are you indifferent? Don't you care how affairs go in New Jersey? Don't you want to have a voice in them? Nobody else can register for you; you must go and register for yourself. Do you object to registering? It will take a little trouble; you have to be at the polls in order to register, but do you object to being looked at and identified?

"I think I understand why the registration thus far has been light. There was an early registration day, which came before a great many of you got back from your vacations, or before it attracted your attention. Then the next registration day was primary day, and I know what happened on primary day. I am sorry to say that this is one feature of the act that I don't care for, namely, that a man cannot vote at the primaries without declaring which party he is going to act with.

"There are thousands of voters in this State, I have reason to believe, that did not vote at the primaries because they did not make that discovery. They either resented that invasion of what ought to be their own affair, or they wanted to hold themselves free at the next primary to act as they pleased, and it was a little awkward to go to the voting place and not vote, but simply register, because they were doing a very singular thing; they were declining to perform their duty as a voter at the same time they were performing the act of registration, which would entitle them to vote at the election, and the primary is just as imperative upon you as a voter as the election itself. I hope that this is true, and that on October 24, which is a week from next Tuesday, every man who is entitled to register who has not registered will register. Because by what other means are we to know what is the judgment of New Jersey, for we must know what the judgment of New Jersey is, or we cannot go on; and what I want to impress upon you is that the seventh of November is the first op[p]ortunity you will have of expressing your judgment upon recent events in this State. I personally very much want to know what you think about the present administration; I very much want to know whether you want to support it or reject it; it is very important that I should know, and, therefore, I want to call your attention to the fact that a year ago I was merely asking you to take a chance. You took the chance. You did not know what I would do; I did not know what I could do; I simply knew what I would try to do."

At Dover the Governor said that the issue was squarely up to the people this year as to whether they wanted progressive legislation and an administration in the executive branch of the State government for all the people or whether they preferred to go back to the old way. If they wished to have carried out the reforms already started it would be necessary to elect members of the Legislature who were in sympathy with progress, as a reform administration in the executive branch was only possible when supported by a reform Legislature.

He said that in twenty out of the twenty-one counties the Democrats had nominated men for the Assembly and Senate who were favorable to political progressiveness, and it was simply for the voters to see that they are registered and go to the polls on November 7 and elect the men who can be depended upon to represent the people, rather than the political machine.

"The whole issue is," he declared, "do you want reform government or do you wish to go back to the old way of doing things. If you want progressive legislation you must elect progressive legislators. If you want reactionary statecraft you should elect reactionary candidates."

At Madison he spoke upon the same lines.

"The main fight in this and future campaigns," he said, "will be between a Republican party, which has rejected progressive measures, and the Democratic power [party] dominated by its progressive element—call them radicals if you will. With the same Republican leaders standing for the same corrupt conditions as before, it is the duty of every member of that party to repudiate it. The Democratic party is the only one now that will give you a voice in the affairs of your State. If you don't vote to return a Democratic Legislature on November 7 you lied when you voted for me last fall. We have only removed the handicaps from our path so we can work out our plans. You must elect Democratic legislators to sustain the stand you took last election."

Printed in the *Newark Evening News*, Oct. 16, 1911.

An Interview

[Oct. 16, 1911]

WILSON'S VIEWS ON FURTHER IMPROVING ELECTION SYSTEM

. . . "I believe in evolution, not revolution."

That statement needs elucidation. The Governor fully explained it when visited in the executive offices by a [Newark Evening] News man seeking information. Some of the history of last winter's legislative doings—doings outside of the chambers of the lawmaking bodies—had to be recounted.

Governor Wilson desired an absolutely open primary. He wanted the voters to be given the privilege of casting a ballot for any aspirant for nomination they desired, regardless of party designation. He gave his views to the drafters of the Geran law. They told him that a bill giving such a privilege would be revolutionary in character. They said the voters of New Jersey were conservative and would not stand for such a rapid radical change from prevailing conditions.

The Governor expressed a belief that this was a mistaken view. Then came the declaration—which proved to be founded on fact—that the majority of the members of the Legislature could not be prevailed upon to pass a measure with such a radical provision.

The Governor was forced to bow to the will of the majority. He did so reluctantly, but he was not at all discouraged. He saw in the Geran bill a step in advance in the program to take from the bosses and special interests the control of party machines and the choice of candidates.

"The Geran law is progressive," he said in effect. "It is a move ahead. We'll take this step and then later we will be strong enough to take another step and perhaps two or three."

The weakness of the separate primary boxes provision was demonstrated in the recent primaries. Governor Wilson has been thinking how best to strengthen this weak place. He is more than ever convinced of the correctness of his position of last winter. The problem, however, is to devise a plan that will mean substantial betterment, that will not be considered revolutionary, and that will receive the approval of the legislators.

"There is a sort of half-step that could be taken," said the Governor, "that some people think might be advisable. I wouldn't so consider it except on the principle that it would be as far in advance as we would be permitted to go by a majority of the lawmakers. This would be to make the party test for primary voting not the question as to how the would-be voter voted at the primaries the year before, but how he voted at the previous general election.

"Thousands of voters frequently vote in a party box at the primaries and then vote for the candidates of the opposite party at the subsequent election. Their original intention has been changed as a result of enlightenment that has come to them during the progress of the campaign between the primary and the election. They may have become converted from Republicanism to Democracy, or from Democracy to Republicanism, and they want the right to cast their votes at the primaries in accordance with their new political beliefs.

"This opportunity is denied them now, with the result that thousands of voters failed to take part in the primaries recently held. A change of this kind in the law would still compel primary voters to declare their party allegiance, and I object to that. Still, if we can secure nothing more than such a change, I would favor that change."

There might be a chance, the Governor thinks, to take a full step in advance instead of a half-step. If that chance should offer he would be found favoring as strongly as possible—and that would mean something approaching a compelling power— the adoption of the system prevailing in Wisconsin.

"You know how the law works out there," said the Governor. "There is only one box used at a primary. When a voter enters the polling place he is given a pad containing ballots for all parties entitled to participate in the primaries. There may be Republican, Democratic, Prohibition and Socialist ballots in the pad. The voter goes into the booth, detaches from the pad the party ballot he desires to cast, marks it, and then deposits it in the general ballot-box.

"The ballots remaining in the pad are folded, returned to the election officers and deposited in a separate receptacle. At the close of the voting the ballots are sorted according to parties and counted just as we count here in New Jersey. No voter in Wisconsin is required to state his party affiliation, and no member of the election board can discover for which party the voters cast his ballot. The adoption of this plan by New Jersey would wipe out one of the most objectionable features of the Geran law."

Yet Governor Wilson, when he favored such a law, knew there was a strong objection to the Wisconsin plan—a very practical objection. There was no need to point out this fact to him.

"There would be an opportunity under this plan," he admitted, "for the voters of one party to help nominate weak candidates on the opposition party ticket. Suppose there should be no contest of any consequence for the Republican nominations, and there should be a strenuous fight for the Democratic nominations. Then the Republican voters could be swung over to cast Democratic primary ballots and bring about nominations that would tend to render easy the defeat of the Democratic ticket. I've heard that claim, and there is something to it. It would even be possible for the two party bosses to get together, where one boss had a walkover, and arrange for the nomination of the other boss's favorite by a non-partizan combination in the primaries. I do not believe, however, that such a thing would happen often. In my estimation it could only happen in one of the 'dead' times we call 'off years,' when no vital principle is at stake."

In spite of his belief that the fears expressed by opponents of the Wisconsin system were groundless, Governor Wilson was still willing to discuss the step he considered necessary if a test should prove that his view was a mistaken one.

When it was suggested to the Governor that the preferential ballot might solve the whole difficulty and accomplish the ends desired, his face beamed.

"Do you know," he retorted, "that the preferential ballot was put into use in Princeton some years ago? The men of the senior class devised the plan for the election of their class officers. It worked like a charm. Before the preferential ballot can be adopted here, however, there must be a course of instruction. Every politician would tell you that preferential voting would create a maze out of which the great majority of voters would be unable to find their way on election day.

"This is in spite of the fact that the voters of the State of Washington have made use of the system in their primaries since 1907; that Grand Junction, Col., and Spokane, Wash., have tried it out in municipal elections, and that it has been adopted as one of the provisions of the Cambridge, Mass., charter, which is to be submitted to the voters at the coming general election.

"If we had the short ballot," Governor Wilson continued, "preferential voting might be used to consolidate both the primary and the election.

"That is the way it is done in Grand Junction and Spokane. The names of all the candidates nominated by petition are placed on a blank ballot. Then each voter is given the opportunity to designate his first, second and third choice for the candidates running for each office. He puts a cross in the first column opposite the name of the man he prefers to have elected. In the second column he puts a cross opposite the name of his favorite in case his first choice is not chosen by a majority of the voters. Then in the third column he designates by a cross the candidate he would prefer if neither his first nor second choice receive a first choice majority. The will of the voters is then determined by the count of the ballots.

"If no one candidate receives a majority as first choice, the votes cast as second choice are added to the first choice totals. If still no candidate has a majority of first and second choice votes, then the third choice votes are added to the first and second choice totals and the majority candidate is declared the winner."

The fact was called to the attention of the Governor that this system had worked without a hitch wherever it had been tried, and that the people were enthusiastic over the cutting out of one of the contests at the polls each year. With the primary and the election consolidated, the cost of the struggle to the taxpayers is reduced one-half.

"As I said before," Governor Wilson replied, "we need the short ballot before the plan will work well here. You must remember, however, that there were only five offices to be filled from these ninety-two aspirants. Suppose there had been twenty or more offices to be filled, as is the case here at a general election.

"The blanket ballot, then, would be of immense size. There would be so many running for office in each group that the voters would be apt to become confused. We need to safeguard against any such confusion. Election laws should be drawn not only to safeguard the honesty of the election, but also for the purpose of making it easy for the voters to record their individual will. The Geran law provides such a plan that will work well at the election, I believe. At least that is the intent of the law.

"There may come a time when the short ballot principle will be established, and then such a device as preferential voting will become desirable. It might even be incorporated now in the Walsh law for commission government with good effect. In a municipal election, with only five offices to be filled, there is no good reason why the preferential vote should not be used, thus doing away with the primary entirely."

In the Governor's estimation, however, the time is not ripe for any recasting of the Geran law. There has been no election under the provisions of that act as yet. The test of the primary feature of the law has demonstrated some defects that need remedying. November 7 next may make other faults glaringly apparent. But evolution rather than revolution is desirable. In fact, such a procedure is the only way in which progressive laws may be made effective.

Printed in the *Newark Evening News*, Oct. 16, 1911.

From Edward Mandell House[1]

New York City.

My dear Governor Wilson: October 16th, 1911.

We have so many mutual friends that I feel that I need no introduction to you.

I have been so earnestly advocating your nomination for President both in Texas and elsewhere that in a way my friends look to me for information concerning you. I have a letter this morning from Senator Culberson[2] in which he says:

"There is a good deal of talk now as to Governor Wilson's attitude to the Party in the past and it is not doing him any good. A member of Congress told me a few days ago that it is being circulated that Governor Wilson refused to support Bryan in 1896, 1900 and 1908 and even voted against Parker in 1904. This is a very important matter and ought to be cleared up at once. I take it for granted that he voted against Bryan in 1896 on the money question as did Harmon but the other cases I doubt. I cannot believe the story yet it ought as I have said be no longer left open. The report is being circulated in this state on very plausible authority and will do him harm if untrue and is not promptly corrected. I would like to know the real truth and at first hand."[3]

I do not like to intrude upon as busy a man as I know you to be but in this instance it seems to me important that the facts be known from you.

I would appreciate your sending me a line in regard to the matter so that I may inform Senator Culberson and our friends in Texas generally before you make your speech at Dallas on the 28th.   Faithfully yours,   [E. M. House]

CCL (E. M. House Papers, CtY).

[1] Born in Houston, Tex., on July 26, 1858, he was at this time living in Austin and New York. From 1880 to 1892, House was primarily engaged in managing the fortune derived from his father's cotton plantations and trade. Between 1892 and 1902 he served as campaign manager for and adviser to four Texas governors—James Stephen Hogg, Charles Allen Culberson, Joseph Draper Sayers, and Samuel Willis Tucker Lanham. Moderately progressive in political philosophy, House was influential in the enactment of reform measures relating to railroads, voting procedures, and municipal government. He withdrew from active participation in Texas politics in 1902 and spent several years studying political, social, and economic conditions in the United States and Europe. After the Democratic landslide of 1910, he decided to enter the national political

arena; in 1911 he joined the movement for Wilson's nomination. His contribution to Wilson's preconvention campaign consisted of a small donation and occasional advice. However, he would soon play an important role as Wilson's confidant and chief adviser on foreign policy during his presidency.

² Attorney General of Texas, 1890-1894; governor, 1894-98; United States senator, 1899-1923.

³ C. A. Culberson to E. M. House, Oct. 13, 1911, ALS (E. M. House Papers, CtY).

From Isaac Henry Lionberger

My dear Doctor: St. Louis, Mo. October 16, 1911.

Relying on your magnanimity, I venture to inform you of a significant change in the opinions of many of your friends. A year ago we followed you with enthusiasm; today many of us are perplexed, and hesitate. The doctrines and measures which are now associated with your name have aroused a vague fear of your future conduct. We trust you implicitly, knowing your sincerity and courage; and because we trust you, realize that you will follow where your convictions lead, regardless of the consequences. You have changed your mind with respect to the Initiative and Referendum, and we think we understand why. No honest man can confront the evils necessarily involved in machine politics without searching for some remedy; yet we think the remedy you now advocate worse than the disease. We have believed that a democracy is best governed by representatives. A legislature may be instructed, its regulated procedure admits of its enlightenment by argument, its committees hear evidence and act advisedly. The people must rely upon the newspapers, and the newspapers depend upon circulation, that is, popularity. "Uttering brawling judgments unashamed on all things all day long," they revel in what is sensational and injurious; they are prone to attack, inclined to innovation, thrive on novelty; goodness is not praised by them, nor any excellent thing.¹ Conspicuosity has supplanted reputation. Wise men, just men are not discovered; they lack a platform and an occasion. Public measures are discussed ex parte always. There is no one to oppose what is popular. The people are always for a time deceived, they never understand; the issues are not argued. Men like you rarely lead. They lack opportunity or eloquence. For these and many like reasons we prefer representative government.

We oppose nomination by primaries, because machines act in concert while disinterested men do not. In our experience none but machine candidates can win at the primaries. A convention allows of attack, of compromise, of some good. If one party goes wrong it is always possible to trade with the other—votes for good men. The primary law rests upon the assumption that the people will know whom to support, that there are in every community men of known capacity and virtue and that among many candidates those will be preferred who are best fitted for office. We think otherwise.

Pardon me for stating such simple things. I seek to vindicate our sincerity and not to instruct you. You, hating the sordid, cynical and unscrupulous character of the men who construct and conduct machines, advocate reforms which we have tried and found futile. You, perceiving the wrongs which result from the present industrial system, propose corrections which involve the intrusion of the State into private affairs. We cannot think an office confers wisdom, and we know officers may be corrupted. We do not think one man should bear another's burdens. If I, who have one thousand dollars, must pay another five thousand for an injury resulting from his own neglect, the ruin falls on the innocent, and enterprise is discouraged.

We think the Democratic party now stands for conservatism, and that you incline to radicalism. We wish the restoration of the old beliefs and the triumph of the old doctrines: equality, economy, non-intervention in private affairs, local government and local responsibilities, preservation of the states, constitutional limitations, little government as distinguished from much government, taxation for revenue and not for oppression nor protection nor any other object.

These views I know you share and yet you have become associated with others in which we lack confidence. I beg you to forgive my frankness. I have admired you too much to deceive you. Many Princeton men and many local Democrats of influence have expressed to me what I convey to you. I wish to serve you and through you the principles which have become dear to me. I had hoped that some time, on some conspicuous occasion, you would make a great speech upon the National issues and dissociate yourself from the local experiments and the local animosities which now alarm your friends, and in that hope I have ventured upon a letter which otherwise would be unpardonable.

Believe me to be,

Very sincerely yours,   I H Lionberger

TLS (Governors' Files, Nj).

¹ Alfred Lord Tennyson, *The Idylls of the King*, "Merlin and Vivien," lines 663-64.

A News Report of a Campaign Speech in Paterson,
New Jersey

[Oct. 17, 1911]

TABASCO IN WILSON TALK AT PATERSON

Tells Passaic Voters in Plain Words that They Haven't
Waked Up Yet.

PATERSON, Oct. 17.—The greatest crowd Governor Woodrow
Wilson has addressed at one meeting since the opening of the
present campaign heard him excoriate Republican "machine"
methods at the opera house here last night.

Every one of the 1,800 seats in the theatre was filled. In addition the people were jammed in a solid mass wherever there
was standing room. The stairways were packed and the crowd
extended out through the lobby to the sidewalk. Several hundred
persons failed to get into the hall.

The Governor did more plain speaking in Passaic than in any
county he has yet visited. Bluntly and forcefully, and at times
with undisguised sarcasm, he asked the voters of Passaic County
if they were as content to do nothing as they seemed to have
been; if, while all the world was going forward, they were satisfied to let things go as they had been going.

"To my mind it is incredible," said Governor Wilson. "One of
the most prosperous, one of the most industrious, one of the
most enlightened counties of this State, if you take it man by
man, has nevertheless been perfectly willing to do no thinking
at all in the field of politics."

The Governor said he could find an explanation for such a
course in Paterson which he called an excellently governed city.

"It may be that you are so selfishly content that things are
going well that you don't care how things go outside of Paterson.

"Is it possible that Paterson is so complacent about her own
affairs that she does not care anything about the State of New
Jersey. Because you are at present following the least progressive leadership in the State of New Jersey.

"I am not passing any judgment at all upon the character of
the gentlemen concerned; some of them I know and personally
esteem, but they will not allow their minds to move a single inch
forward in the sphere of political thought or political action and
they take the chance to rebuke any one who does move forward
in those fields."

The Governor's tones took on added severity as he discussed
the part that money had played in the politics of Passaic County
in the past.

"Every man here who knows anything knows the part that money used to play in the elections of Passaic County," he said.

Then even more vehemently he added, "I have not come here to sprinkle rose water, gentlemen. I know just about as much of the general procedure in Passaic County as it is necessary to know, and I know that there were times when that party won that had the most money to spend. I am free to say that there were times when if the Democrats had the money they won, and if the Republicans had the money they won."

A ripple of laughter spread through the theatre at this thrust.

"You laugh," continued Governor Wilson. "Are you really amused? Is it really anything to you that Passaic County should have that reputation? Is it really a matter of indifference to you? Don't you care? Aren't you in the least bit ashamed, and aren't you willing, now that it is made an extremely hazardous thing to use money in politics, to bring Passaic into the front again as one of the counties that thinks and acts and achieves?"

Contrasting the Democratic record of the last nine months with the Republican record, Governor Wilson held the G.O.P. method of doing things up to ridicule.

"I assert that they made promise after promise, and invariably failed to fulfill the promises, if inconsistent with certain vested interests in this State. They did the little things; they did the little things on the side, but they did not do the main things. They promised to give you a public utilities commission, with power, but they did not do it.

"They promised to correct this, that and the other abuse, but they did not do it. They fooled you again and again at the elections, and, if you are in love with being fooled, why go on—in God's name, go on. Nobody will do anything but pity you; nobody, I hope, in the State of New Jersey, will follow your example.

"Wake up! Get a move on you! What are you waiting for? Are you waiting for the millennium? Do you see any signs of it? Have you seen any Republican who looked as if he had the millennium in his eye? I don't mean any Republican voter, but I mean any Republican leader. Would you take his note of hand for the delivery of the millennium?

"I sometimes suspect that the Republican party is in the condition of a certain elephant I heard of some time ago, that had been standing in the same place for a long while, and finally when they took the chains off of him you could not convince that elephant that he was free.

"If you were to offer him the most tempting morsel, just beyond the reach of his snout, if he could not reach it standing still he would let it alone. So far as I know he has not discovered yet that he was free."

There was a burst of applause as the Governor suddenly made an appeal for Passaic County's support in the work of regenerating New Jersey. He said:

"What I want to arouse you to is the consciousness that New Jersey is on the eve of a new era in her politics; is awakening to the reality of independent voting, of pure voting; voting according to conviction and not according to particular and private interests; and that it is of the utmost consequence that a county famed for its intelligence and industry, like the county of Passaic, should take a foremost part in this new development.

"I have come here to summon you to exercise your free sovereign right as Americans and to assist in redeeming the State of New Jersey from her old order. By redeeming the State of New Jersey I do not mean supporting me. I am not going to redeem the State of New Jersey. But, maybe I may say it for myself, that I am merely an honest man, that is all. I merely try to do what I say I am going to do; and I would be absolutely useless to the State of New Jersey if it were not fortunately the case that I have been associated with some scores of other honest men who meant to do what they said.". . .

Printed in the *Newark Evening News*, Oct. 17, 1911; some editorial headings omitted.

Walter Measday to Edward Mandell House

My dear Sir: [Trenton, N. J.] October 17, 1911.

Governor Wilson has asked me to acknowledge the receipt of your letter. The story that Governor Wilson refused to support Bryan in 1896, and 1900, and 1908, and even voted against Parker in 1904 has been industriously circulated for several months past, and on several occasions has been denied. The fact of the matter is, Governor Wilson has consistently voted the Democratic ticket.

The Governor is now engaged on a tour of the State in the interests of the Democratic moninees [nominees], and so is absent from Trenton, but I will see that he gets your letter immediately.   Yours very truly,   Walter Measday.

TLS (E. M. House Papers, CtY).

A News Report of Two Campaign Speeches in
Sussex County, New Jersey

[Oct. 18, 1911]

DEMOCRACY PROGRESSIVE, SAYS WILSON

Again Appeals for the Support of Independent Republican Voters.

NEWTON, Oct. 18.—That the day has gone by when a Progressive Republican may vote the Republican ticket merely for loyalty to a party fetish was the strong new declaration in Goverernor Woodrow Wilson's speech here last night.

"I must say," said the Governor, "that I doubt the discretion, even if I may not say I doubt the sanity, of a Progressive Republican, at any rate in the State of New Jersey, who does not vote the Democratic ticket.

"I can only conjecture that he wants to throw his vote away, that he wants to run all the risks of not getting what he wants, and that at the bottom of it all must lie the feeling that what he really wants it [is] to have people in office who are called Republican, no matter what happens in the field of legislation and politics.

"Have we come to that? Have we made a party such a fetish that we have to have it whether we get the things we ought to have or not?"

Governor Wilson declared that for this year at least—he would make no predicitions about what will happen next year—there is no place for the progressives of all the parties to go except to the Democratic party.

"When I talk with a Progressive Republican," said he, "I cannot see any difference between his opinions and mine, and I wonder why in the world he calls himself a Republican; why in the world he doesn't get into the game.

"The distinction is so artificial, the distinction is so picayune why these grown-up men who absolutely agree with each other insist on voting against each other. When they are engaged in the same enterprise, want the same things, by the same means, why in the name of heaven shouldn't they co-operate?"

Governor Wilson made it clear, however, that he realized that the "machine" element in the Democratic party was not dead and that it was struggling eagerly for restoration to power.

"There are men still active in the Democratic party," he said, "who would, if they could, break us down to the old miasmic levels where everything unwholesome prevails." . . .

The Governor addressed two meetings in Sussex County last night. First he spoke to a large though very quiet gathering in

Hornbeck's hall, Sussex. Here Samuel S. Vandruff, the Republican Mayor, paid him the unusual tribute of presiding at the meeting. By way of explanation Mayor Vandruff said that not as a partizan, but as a citizen and an official of Sussex he desired to extend a welcome to the Governor. The Boy Scouts acted as an escort from the hotel to the hall.

The meeting at Newton was held in the auditorium at the High School. The hall was filled to its capacity and every inch of standing room was taken. Here, too, the audience was an extremely quiet one. Fully representative of the best people of Newton and vicinity, it gave the Governor a hearing that was so earnest and respectful that apparently every one forgot to applaud.

Martin Rosenkrans, of the class of '67 at Princeton,[1] presided, and, with the simple dignity of the old school, made an introductory speech for the Governor that ranks among the gems of the campaign. In closing his brief tribute to the Governor, he said:

"He is a scholar, a teacher, a lawyer, an historian, an orator and a leader in intellectual force of all the Governors of all the States of our country."

Though Sussex is overwhelmingly Democratic year after year, a fear has taken hold of some of the leaders that Assemblyman Charles A. Meyer, candidate for the fourth term, may go down to defeat. There is some sentiment against him because of a feeling in some quarters that he ought to have retired this year. The grangers of the county have shown a disposition, too, to support his opponent, Thomas De Kay, who is at the head of the county grange. Most of the Democratic leaders say Meyer will go back with the same old Democratic plurality but Meyer himself is not sanguine.[2]

Last night the Governor strongly urged Mr. Meyer's election. He said:

"I want to tell you that after close association with Mr. Meyer I can assure you of his steady devotion to the principles of the Democratic party and to the programs of its platform. I can report to you that when the members of our party in the Legislature had reached the critical stage in their proceedings Mr. Meyer was one of the men that they picked out as a member of the committee that was to steer the councils of the party.

"I want to report that in the matters which were local, as well as general, which particularly concern the interests of Sussex County, he was vigilant and diligent and watchful. These things I know. And therefore you would be without excuse, if you want to support the present administration, if you rejected a man who has absolutely supported the administration as your representative."

The theme that ran all through the Governor's address in the evening was that of the choice of party to be made by the independent voters. He called the Republicans claim that they were the party of Lincoln "rank hypocrisy."

"I know which party Lincoln would have belonged to if he had been living now—I mean if Lincoln had been living in the year 1911—I am not going into past politics; that is a closed book. I am not saying that the Democratic party has always had an unsmirched record or lived up to its pledges in the State of New Jersey, for I know it has not." . . .

Printed in the *Newark Evening News*, Oct. 18, 1911; some editorial headings omitted.
1 Lawyer of Newton.
2 He was re-elected.

To Edward Mandell House

My dear Mr. House: [Trenton, N. J.] Oct. 18, 1911.

It is very provoking how lies frame themselves and run current and I despair of keeping up with them, but I am none the less thankful to you for your referring to me the question contained in your letter of October 16.

The facts are that I voted for Palmer and Buckner in 1896, but I have never supported at any time a Republican ticket. I do not consider myself as supporting a non-Democratic ticket when I voted for Palmer and Buckner. My difference with Mr. Bryan was over the money question.

I appreciate the courtesy and fairness of Senator Culberson in making careful inquiry of you of the truth of the reports.

With warmest regards, believe me
              Sincerely yours,   Woodrow Wilson   M.

TLS (E. M. House Papers, CtY).

A News Report of a Campaign Speech in Phillipsburg, New Jersey

[Oct. 19, 1911]

WILSON JABS OLD REGIME

Warren County Gives Governor Warm Reception Under Adverse Conditions.

PHILLIPSBURG, Oct. 19.—The warmth of Warren County's greeting to Governor Woodrow Wilson yesterday and last night showed that county in the front rank of those that are loyal to the Governor.

The rain was falling fast when Governor Wilson reached Hackettstown yesterday morning, and because of the Governor's physical exhaustion it was deemed unwise for him to make the long auto trip through the county that had been arranged. . . .

The day reached its climax in the evening, when after addressing a crowded house at Washington, Governor Wilson came to Phillipsburg and delivered an address to an audience that gave him rousing approval. . . .

In a general way Governor Wilson discussed the proposition last night that the people must control big business and not big business the people.

He took several heavy whacks at the "Board of Guardians." "If you go through the leaders of these who have controlled the Republican party you will find first one and then another connected with the special interests of the State in such a way that it is unreasonable to expect them to disentangle and separate themselves.

"It is not necessary to imply that they are dishonest men, for I do not believe with regard to them that the real point of the thing is any kind of pecuniary dishonesty but there is something just as dangerous to the State as pecuniary dishonesty and that is an utter inability to think in terms of the common people."

Referring to the election of Joseph Hoff as chairman of the Republican county committee in Ocean County,[1] Governor Wilson asked "Can you imagine anything more grossly insulting to the intelligence of the people of New Jersey than what has happ[e]ned in Ocean County, where the man who is under indictment for trying to cheat the people of their suffrages is again preferred to leadership in the Republican organization of that great county? If the thing were not true it would be incredible."

As an example of what leadership independent of corporation control is able to do for the people, Governor Wilson pointed out the bill which passed last year after having failed in other years, providing for semi-monthly payment of railroad employes.[2] This is a railroad community and the Governor's remark touched a popular chord. He also received applause when he announced that the Democratic party was pledged to the enactment of a full crew bill.

"A few years ago," said the Governor, "you could not have passed such a bill through the Legislature, now we are free to pass any act of justice of which we are convinced. The whole question is whether we are convinced or not, not whether we are controlled or not." . . .

Printed in the *Newark Evening News*, Oct. 19, 1911.
1 Businessman and member of the township council of Lakewood, N. J. In 1910 he had managed the campaign of Thomas Alfred Mathis, Republican state senator, in his bid for re-election against the Democrat, George Clark Low. Low won by a majority of eighty-one, and Mathis asked for a recount. Discrepancies soon appeared in the ballots of the second district of Lakewood. The grand jury of Ocean County indicted Hoff on March 30, 1911, charging him with removing ballots from the box of the second district and substituting others. Low won the recount. The indictment against Hoff was eventually dismissed; he continued to play an important role in the Republican party in New Jersey.
2 *Laws of New Jersey, 1911*, Chapter 371, pp. 767-68.

A News Report of Eight Campaign Speeches in Union County, New Jersey

[Oct. 20, 1911]

UNION COUNTY HEARS WILSON

Has an Arduous Day's Work

PLAINFIELD, Oct. 20.—Eight audiences paid hearty tribute to Governor Wilson in his tour through Union County yesterday and last night.

At [Westfield,] Elizabeth, Roselle, Rahway, Garwood, Plainfield, Cranford and Summit he got a warm welcome. . . .

The Governor put in the most strenuous day of the campaign. He left Easton, Pa., at 11 o'clock yesterday morning, and from his arrival in Westfield an hour after until after 10 o'clock last night he was dashing from one point to another in the county, making various speeches for the success of the Democratic ticket in the county.

If the size and enthusiasm of audiences might be taken as indicative of the probable outcome of an election, the Democrats in Union County would be justified in regarding their success as probable. Though it rained almost constantly through the day, the crowds at all the points were big. All the county leaders expressed themselves as astonished at the great interest shown in politics in an off-year. . . .

The Governor in his speeches last night made a fresh attack on the Republican platform. This time he leveled his lance at the plank in the Republican platform pledging abolition of grade crossings. He said:

"This year, as last, the terms of the Democratic platform are much more explicit than the terms of the Republican platform. There is one matter I wish to use as an illustration because I know that it interests you. Take the matter of the abolition of grade crossings. The Republican platform pledges the party to abolish all grade crossings at the expense of the railways. I wonder if the men who drew up that platform knew how many grade crossings there are in the State of New Jersey, all through the extended rural districts of this commonwealth. And do they for one moment want you to believe that they are going to undertake to abolish all the grade crossings in this State, and at once, at the expense of the railways? You know they are not; you know they cannot have intended to do so; you know that they have had close alliances in the past with the railway companies, and you have every reason to suspect that they made these big promises, these important promises, with the knowledge that they could not be carried out.

"In the first place, it would not be fair to carry it out. If you undertook to abolish at once all the grade crossings in the State you would propose something which was financially impossible for the railways and, therefore, if enforced, very unfair. I do not hold any brief for the railways, but I do hold a brief for justice; I do hold a brief for what is fair, and I want to call your attention to the plank that corresponds with that in the Democratic platform. It proposes to do a perfectly feasible thing, to put into the hands of the Public Utilities Commission the right to abolish every railway crossing which it is immediately imperative should be abolished for the safety of human life. That is perfectly feasible; that is a workable plank, and the other is not. Moreover, it is put upon this footing of fairness: that a semi-judicial tribune can act upon it with full knowledge and hearing of the facts. The Public Utilities Commission has to determine which grade crossings are to go at once.

"Now, I know some of you are concerned as to who is going to pay for this. The Public Utilities Commission has no power, and so far as the men in my councils are concerned there is no purpose to give it the power to impose expenses upon any municipality. Those who try to deceive you in this matter are proposing something that the Democratic platform does not propose. It does not propose to give the Public Utilities Commission the right to saddle these expenses upon the communities affected. It proposes something that must be done. We took it for granted that the expense to the railways must be limited to what the railways are immediately financially able to do."

Printed in *Newark Evening News*, Oct. 20, 1911.

From Edward Mandell House, with Enclosure

My dear Governor Wilson: New York. October 20th, 1911.

Your letter to me of October 18th supplemented by your verbal message to Mr. McCombs is very clear and will destroy one line of attack.

I enclose you a copy of the telegram I sent Senator Culberson this morning.

Mr. McCombs, and perhaps Mr. McAdoo, will dine with me Monday and among other things I want particularly to discus[s] with them the feasibility of asking the people when they select delegates to the next National Convention to also pass upon the question of majority rule.

It h[a]s come to me that the opposition to your nomination is determined to invoke the two thirds rule in order to defeat you.

We had this issue in Texas in 1894 when I was in charge of Senator Culberson's campaign for Governor and by having the people express their wishes we abrogated the undemocratic two thirds rule and nominated him on the first ballot.

I do not want to move in this matter without your approval or that of your advisers but I am strongly of the opinion that it should be done.   Faithfully yours,   [E. M. House]

CCL (E. M. House Papers, CtY).

E N C L O S U R E

Edward Mandell House to Charles Allen Culberson

[New York, Oct. 20, 1911].

Governor Wilson informs me that he voted for Palmer and Buckner in 1896 and later for both Mr. Bryan and Judge Parker and that he never at any time supported a Republican ticket. The friends of Governor Wilson would appreciate your giving wide publicity to this statement.   E. M. House

T telegram (E. M. House Papers, CtY).

A News Report of a Day's Campaigning in Somerset County, New Jersey
[Oct. 21, 1911]

NEW JERSEY'S REPUTATION IS NOW AT STAKE

Governor Wilson Declares Election Will Show Whether or Not State Wants Reform.

SOMERVILLE, Oct. 21.—Returning to this place last night, after a long, hard day of campaigning in an auto through the mud and rain in Somerset County, Governor Woodrow Wilson thrilled an audience with an address likely to become one of the classics of his political career.

The Governor declared that New Jersey is at the parting of the ways in her political affairs, that on November 7 she is to decide whether she is to maintain her fight for political freedom or is to sink back to servile subjection to the Board of Guardians. . . .

All over Somerset County Governor Wilson received a warm welcome. There were eleven stops on his itinerary, and the eleven autos in the touring party had to make fast time to keep up to the schedule. At many points the school children were drawn up in a body, waving flags and singing songs, when the Governor arrived.

At Bernardsville Governor Wilson spoke in the open air in the square at noon. The whole town closed up and went to hear him.

It is related that at this place State Chairman Edward E. Gross-cup, who travels with the Governor, made use of the stop to change his collar. Taking off his soiled collar in the hotel, he pitched it out of a window in disgust when he saw it was bespattered with mud. But he hunted through his grip for another in vain. Finally, turning up his coat collar, he sallied forth to purchase another. But this was equally in vain, for every business man in the place was out on the square hearing the Governor.

Governor Wilson remarked when he learned of the incident that it was just as well that the State chairman "wear no man's collar."

In his address here, Governor Wilson said in part:

"I have come here upon a very serious errand, and I fully realize the responsibility of that errand. I have been doing what I am told is a very unusual thing—in a year when a Governor is not to be elected, in a year called an off year, I have been going through every county in the State and arguing the questions at issue.

"I am not seriously disturbed by the statement that this is unusual, for I have recently been accustomed to doing unusual things; and the reason that it was necessary for me to do unusual things was that unusual measures were necessary to put at least one of the machines out of business, and to substitute for machine management of parties their management by public discussion. If it be unusual to appear before my fellow-citizens and summon them to a consideration of the public affairs of the State, then I hope I may have the happy fortune of having inaugurated a new practise.

"I have come here because it seems to me that the State of

New Jersey is at the parting of the ways. You are to determine on November 7 next which way you are going in the conduct of your affairs. You determined a year ago in which direction you hoped you might be led. You now know in which direction you were led and must determine whether you are satisfied to pursue that direction or not. This is, therefore, the parting of the ways.

"A good many unusual things have happened recently in the politics of New Jersey. The usual thing was for the parties to make promises and repeat promises, and repeat them again; to spend the intervals in explaining why they did not carry them out, and always to fail to give the real reason why they did not carry them out. Underneath the surface, in quiet offices, in private places of consultation, gentlemen met who had not been elected to be the representatives of the people, and decided what the representatives of the people were to be allowed to do and what they were not to be allowed to do. We knew the names of these gentlemen; we knew the names of them not only in the ranks of the Republican party, but also in the ranks of the Democratic party; and we knew that, whether they called themselves Republicans or Democrats, they were in close and confidential relationships with each other.

"I am not going to mince matters in stating facts. The fact was that we had neither Republican management nor Democratic management; we simply had private management in the interests of special groups of undertakings. Then a change took place. There came a time when the Democratic party, as it happened—let me say as it happened so as not to claim special credit for anybody—when the Democratic party had tried an experiment. They tried this experiment of substituting public discussion and public leadership for private management.

"Observe that I am not saying that some of the gentlemen who had managed the Democratic party knew that they were about to try that experiment. They did not. They knew the man they had nominated for Governor said that they were about to try that experiment, but I am informed that they had heard other candidates for Governor say the same thing, and they thought that this person had simply caught the echo of the usual thing, that he had learned out of books, no doubt, certainly not out of practise, that [what] it was habitual to say on the stump; that, in other words, he was a quick imitator of the old methods of the play. I cannot otherwise understand their ardor in his support. He told them in private as well as in public, that he meant what he said. He told them with brutal frankness that he meant what he said, but he could not make them believe it. And so he was chosen, and inasmuch as he and his colleagues running with him all meant what they said, the new order was instituted; a new experiment was tried—an unusual practise in New Jersey politics began. Those unusual practises were the practises of openness, the practises of con[s]tant frank appeal to public opinion, the practises of putting everything upon a basis of discussion. The practise of leaving every door open, so that the State might be audience and spectator of its own affairs.

"Now it happened that this change in the politics of New Jersey coincided with a similar change throughout the country. New Jersey need not blame herself upon having been peculiar in the private management of her politics. Politics had been managed everywhere with this careful privacy and secludedness; politics had almost everywhere been determined by the size and course of campaign contributions. There was nothing novel in it. New Jersey had not discovered it—it was known in Pennsylvania; it had been heard of in New York. Men everywhere had had intimations from day to day that this was the way in which politics was played, and even upon the national scale there had been rumors that money was at the bottom of politics.

"But just at the time that New Jersey shook herself awake and repudiated these things it happened that most of the rest of the country had also set up in the light of the new morning and began to notice what was going on and to determine that that day that thing should stop.

"You see, therefore, that it was a time of extraordinary opportunity for parties. If I may so express it, there were two parties that were candidates to be beforehand in leading the people in these new paths and availing themselves of these new opportunities, and the circumstance which interests me as a Democrat is that the Democrats almost everywhere got in first, because the year 1910 did not mark a Democratic victory in New Jersey merely, as you know. It marked an extraordinary series of Democratic victories from one end of this country to the other, and this interesting circumstance was disclosed, that every State that elected a Democratic Governor elected a new kind of a Democratic Governor—elected a progressive, elected a man who had the zest of the new age and the new principles in his build."

Governor Wilson said that the same thing happened in a few States where the Republican party was enjoying new leadership, citing California and New Hampshire as instances; but, he said, fortunately for the Democratic party, there were a good many more Democratic than Republican Governors of that kind.

The Democratic party in all parts of the country, he claimed, responded to the new impulse, but it was not so with the Republican party. The change in New Jersey, he said, was most noticeable because it was least expected, and the country is now watching New Jersey and will decide from the result of the election on November 7 next whether the change was accidental or intentional.

In his opinion, the Governor said, "the reason these things occurred—I don't know just how to state it without seeming to claim credit which I do not wish to claim and which I have no consciousness of deserving—but if I may speak of it impersonally, as if it did not concern myself, let me say, I believe these things occurred in New Jersey as they occurred in New Hampshire, because a man with fresh eyes, not connected with the old order, not connected with the old processes, not caught in the old entanglements, was put at the front of affairs."

The Governor then referred to the defeat of Senator Bradley for renomination as proving the insincerity of the Republican leaders, and declared that the turning point in the political history of our times in New Jersey is to be November 7 next. "Then you are to determine which men you think genuine; then you are to determine which processes you think genuine; then you are to determine whether you want to continue to live under the new regime, or do not wish to continue under the new regime.

"And gentlemen," said the Governor in conclusion, "what is the field of excitement? What are you dealing with? You are dealing with the concerns of men. Do you deem it of no consequence that the great body of our fellow-men are struggling so from day to day that they do not know how it is going to be possible, with the present prices, to buy enough to wear and eat and keep them warm? Do you know that our affairs are characterized by a gathering complexity which must be reduced to a simplicity by one process or another? Do you realize that in playing with politics you are playing with the only means discovered among men by which they may introduce justice into their affairs? Do you realize that you are dealing with the very stuff and fiber of life in American liberty? Do you realize that you are illustrating when you go to the polls the feasibility of the hope of self-government among modern men? Don't you know what you are doing? You are weaving American life. Men's lives must follow along this fiber; men's lives must depend upon the wholesomeness of what you make.

"Men's hopes must ebb and flow as you play with them or keep pace with them. You can make a quicksand of your politics and who will be engulfed if you do? Your fellow-men, the free men of a great nation. Men will find themselves sinking in despair, and the very hope of life choked out of them as they sink."

Governor Wilson left the Queen City Hotel at Plainfield at 10 o'clock yesterday morning. The local party was headed by Assemblyman George M. La Monte, candidate for Senator. A. M. Beekman, candidate for the Assembly, was also a member of the party.[1] Chief of Police Bellis, of Somerville,[2] acted as guide.

The Governor spoke first to a crowd on the sidewalk in North Plainfield and then went on to the Somerset School, where he spoke to the pupils in front of the school. He told them not to imagine that athletics and fun was all there was to going to school, and added that when they grew up doing the double trapeze with their business partners would not be their chief business in life.

At the Watchung School the Governor found the children drawn up at the roadside waving flags and singing "My Jersey Land." There were short stops at Liberty Corners and Mt. Bethel, and a speech by Mr. Malone to 300 persons at Basking Ridge. At Bernardsville the party stopped for luncheon.

In the afternoon the Governor found the school children and a big crowd of citizens awaiting his coming at Gladstone. At Bedminster there was another stop. Tunis Melick, the "Mayor of Pluckemin," was on hand with a warm greeting at the general store in Pluckemin. At Raritan and East Millstone there were other outdoor audiences. A big crowd gathered outside the hotel at Bound Brook where the Governor ate supper. Mr. Malone made a speech.

The audience which greeted the Governor here was of a fine, representative character. Business men rubbed elbows with laborers and the balconies were filled with women. At every opportunity they showed their enthusiasm for the Governor. Daniel H. Beekman presided.[3] The Senatorial and Assembly candidates preceded the Governor in speaking, and Mr. Malone and Eckard P. Budd, of Mt. Holly,[4] followed. After the meeting the Governor went to Princeton. He took with him a great mass of flowers that had been presented to him, one bouquet at a time, along the day's march.

Somerset is regarded as one of the doubtful counties this year. The Republicans assert they will have no trouble electing their

[1] Azariah M. Beekman, lawyer of Somerville, who was running against William De La Roche Anderson, a real estate dealer and insurance agent and Mayor of Watchung. Beekman lost in 1911 but ran again and won in 1912.

[2] Lewis A. Bellis, a blacksmith.

[3] A lawyer of Bound Brook.

[4] Eckard Payson Budd, Princeton 1882, lawyer, for many years Burlington County's representative on the Democratic State Committee.

legislative candidates, but the Democrats are equally confident. The Democrats are certain that their Assembly candidate will be elected, and say that they will have to fight only for the Senatorial candidate's election. They admit the strength of William W. Smalley, Mr. La Monte's opponent, but are preparing to make an assault on his legislative record which they expect will bring about his defeat.[5]

There has been considerable fear in Democratic circles that Samuel S. Swackhammer, who was defeated for the nomination by Mr. La Monte, was preparing to run for Senator as an independent. But Mr. Swackhammer in an interview this morning authorized the News to state that he had no intention whatever of becoming a candidate.

Mr. Swackhammer was not a member of the Governor's party yesterday, but Governor Wilson made a call on him while in Plainfield.

Printed in the *Newark Evening News*, Oct. 21, 1911; some editorial headings omitted.
[5] La Monte also lost to his Republican opponent.

A News Report

[Oct. 23, 1911]

MY MISTAKE, SAYS WILSON

Admits His Error in Criticizing Grade Crossing Plank.

CRANFORD, Oct. 23.—In a letter to Carlton B. Pierce, Republican candidate for Senator from Union County, Governor Wilson admits that in his speech at Elizabeth on the nineteenth he was in error in his criticism of the grade crossing plank in the Republican State platform.

In his Elizabeth address Governor Wilson claimed that the plank called for the immediate abolition of all grade crossings, which, he declared, was both impossible and unfair.

Mr. Pierce, who was the author of the grade crossing plank to which the Governor referred, called the latter's attention to his error in the following letter:

"My Dear Governor—As the author of the grade crossing plank adopted by the Republican State convention and one who recognizes you would not intentionally misstate an adversary's position, I beg to call your attention to the plank and your Elizabeth speech of the nineteenth inst., and respectfully ask that you make the appropriate correction.

"The plank reads: 'We favor the elimination of grade crossings at railroad expense, the work to be done gradually, in the order of necessity, and to proceed as rapidly as the expense involved will permit.'

"Your speech, as reported in the Elizabeth Journal, Times and Newark News, says:

" 'The Republican platform pledges the party to abolish all grade crossings at the expense of the railways. I wonder if the men who drew up that platform knew how many grade crossings there are in the State of New Jersey, all through the extended rural districts of this commonwealth. And do they for one moment want you to believe that they are going to undertake to abolish all the grade crossings in this State, and at once, at the expense of the railways?

" 'You know they are not; you know they cannot have intended to do so; you know their close alliance in the past with the railway companies, and you have reason to suspect that they made these big promises, these important promises, with the knowledge that they could not be carried out. In the first place, it would not be fair to carry them out. We are supposed to be arrayed, as they are supposed to be arrayed, against corporate interests, and if you undertook to abolish at once all the grade crossings in the State you would propose something which was financially impossible for the railways, and therefore if enforced very unfair.'

" 'I do not hold any brief for the railways, but I do hold a brief for justice; I do hold a brief for what is fair, and I want to call your attention to the plank that corresponds with that in the Democratic platform. It proposes to do a perfectly feasible thing, to put into the hands of the Public Utilities Commission the right to abolish every railway crossing which it is immediately imperative should be abolished for the safety of human life. That is perfectly feasible; that is a workable plank and the other is not.'

"Your speech reads the words 'at once' into the Republican plank—changing the meaning—and then proceeds to demolish the structure erected.

"The Republican plank was drawn with care, to provide a gradual elimination, with due regard to the expense involved.

"As the grade crossing issue is important in Elizabeth, and many have doubtless been misled as to the facts by the speech, may I rely on your courtesy to give an authoritative correction? I am, yours very truly,

"Carlton B. Pierce.

"Cranford, Oct. 21, 1911."

To this Governor Wilson replied as follows:

"My Dear Mr. Pierce—I, of course, did not intend to read into the plank of your platform which concerns grade crossings any words it did not contain. I regret having made the mistake. I spoke from an imperfect recollection of the language, and should have refreshed my memory.   Very truly yours,

"Woodrow Wilson."

Printed in the *Newark Evening News*, Oct. 23, 1911; one editorial heading omitted.

From John Franklin Shafroth

Denver Colo, Oct 23, '11

The Woodrow Wilson Democratic Club, formed tonight from the free and fighting membership of the party is the first step in a state wide organization for the promotion of your presidential candidacy and the triumphs of those great principles so ably presented and championed by you. It is in enthusiasm and confidence that we send this telegram of support and congratulation Governor John F. Shafroth   Ex-Senator T. M. Patterson, Ex-Gov G. S. Thomas, Judge Ben B. Lindsay, Mrs Dora Phelps Buell, Edw J. Eating, Henry J Arnold, Geo E. Hosmer, and Geo Creel.[1]

T telegram (Governors' Files, Nj).

[1] Not hitherto identified: Dora Phelps (Mrs. William J.) Buell of Denver, "silver-tongued girl orator of the West," an early president of the Colorado Equal Suffrage Association and leader in the fight which culminated in the triumph of woman's suffrage in Colorado; Edward Keating, editor of the Denver *Rocky Mountain News*, 1906-11, president of the Colorado State Board of Land Commissioners, 1911-13, and congressman, 1913-19; Henry J. Arnold, real estate businessman of Denver, at this time city assessor; George E. Hosmer, publisher of the Fort Morgan, Col., *Herald*; and George Creel, muckracking author, editor of the *Denver Post*, 1909-10, and of the *Rocky Mountain News*, 1911-13, chairman of the Committee on Public Information, 1917-19.

To John Franklin Shafroth

[Trenton, N. J. c. Oct. 23, 1911]

I cannot tell you how deeply I appreciate the message sent me from the Woodrow Wilson Club formed October twenty-third. It puts me in heart to have such friends and such generous support. Allow me to send my warmest greetings and a message of genuine gratitude to you and to the other gentlemen concerned.

Woodrow Wilson.

T telegram (Governors' Files, Nj).

To Isaac Henry Lionberger

Personal.

My dear Mr. Lionberger: [Trenton, N. J.] October 23, 1911.

I have been going from one part of New Jersey to another on campaign, because we every year elect the whole of our Assembly and three-thirds [one third] of our Senate, and so did not see your letter of October sixteenth until to-day. It is much too important a letter to answer off hand and I am going to give myself the pleasure of replying later. In the meantime, may I not express my very sincere appreciation of your candor and say that it increases my appreciation of the value of your friendship. Many things look to me now as they did not look to me before I was in close contact with the interior of our politics. I wish that I might have an opportunity of saying to you orally what it will be so difficult to tell you in a letter.

Cordially and faithfully yours,   Woodrow Wilson

TLS (I. H. Lionberger Papers, MoSHi).

To Cleveland Hoadley Dodge

My dear Cleve: [Trenton, N. J.] October 24, 1911.

Your letter of the twenty-first has filled me with complicating emotions.[1] I dare not protest against the step you are contemplating, because your life is too valuable to be sacrificed, even to the institution we love so deeply, and yet it makes me very sad indeed to think of the withdrawal of your splendid influence and of the subtraction of the power which you add to things that are religious and of good report. I can only pray God that some turn of Providence may put the old place in a way to be redeemed very soon.

What you write me about the Presidency is certainly reassuring as far as it goes. It would have been a real misfortune to the place had Hibbens succeeded in gaining the Presidency.

I shall be in the midst of our campaign here until the seventh of November and after that engagements hold me until the tenth. I certainly hope that I may have a chance to get at you in New York when you move down from Riverdale.

In haste, with deep affection,

Faithfully yours,   Woodrow Wilson

TLS (WC, NjP).

[1] It is missing, but in it Dodge told him that he had written a letter resigning from the Princeton Board of Trustees and intended to send it at once. His

letter, C. H. Dodge to the Board of Trustees of Princeton University, Oct. 21, 1911, ALS (UA, NjP), said simply that he was resigning on the advice of his physician. The letter is reproduced in "Minutes of the Trustees of Princeton University, April 1908-June 1913," bound minute book (UA, NjP), minutes for the meeting of Oct. 26, 1911.

To Edward Mandell House

My dear Colonel House: [Trenton, N. J.] October 24, 1911.

Thank you sincerely for your letter of the twentieth.

I feel very strongly that the two-third's rule is a most un-Democratic regulation and puts us at a particular disadvantage as compared with the Republicans, whose arrangements respond more readily to the opinion of their party than ours can do in the circumstances.

I feel that there would be a certain impropriety in my urging a change because it would be so manifestly in my interest, but certainly any change of the sort would have my entire sympathy and approval, if it could be brough[t] about, and I think would commend itself to the judgment of the whole country.

With warm regards,

Sincerely yours,   Woodrow Wilson

TLS (E. M. House Papers, CtY).

An Address in Madison, Wisconsin, on Community Centers[1]

[[Oct. 25, 1911]]

I do not feel that I have deserved the honor of standing here upon this occasion to make what has been courteously called the principal address, because five months ago I did not know anything about this movement. I have taken no active part in it, and I am not going to assume, as those who have preceded me have assumed, that you know what the movement is. I want, if for no other purpose than to clarify my own thinking, to state as briefly as possible, what the movement is.

The object of the movement is to make the schoolhouse the civic center of the community, at any rate in such communities as are supplied with no other place of common resort.

[1] Delivered in the gymnasium of the University of Wisconsin to the first national conference on civic and social center development. Louis E. Reber, dean of the extension division, presided. Duncan McGregor, secretary to Governor Francis E. McGovern, delivered the address of greeting, and President Charles R. Van Hise gave a welcoming address on behalf of the university. Josiah Strong, president of the Social Center Association of America, spoke briefly.

It is obvious that the schoolhouse is in most communities used only during certain hours of the day, those hours when the rest of the community is busily engaged in bread-winning work. It occurred to the gentlemen who started this movement that inasmuch as the schoolhouses belonged to the community it was perfectly legitimate that the community should use them for its own entertainment and schooling when the young people were not occupying them. And that, therefore, it would be a good idea to have there all sorts of gatherings, for social purposes, for purposes of entertainment, for purposes of conference, for any legitimate thing that might bring neighbors and friends together in the schoolhouses. That, I understand it, in its simplest terms is the civic center movement—that the schoolhouses might be made a place of meeting—in short, where by meeting each other the people of a community might know each other, and by knowing each other might concert a common life, a common action.

The study of the civic center is the study of the spontaneous life of communities. What you do is to open the schoolhouse and light it in the evening and say: "Here is a place where you are welcome to come and do anything that it occurs to you to do."

And the interesting thing about this movement is that a great many things have occurred to people to do in the schoolhouse, things social, things educational, things political,—for one of the reasons why politics took on a new complexion in the city in which this movement originated[2] was that the people who could go into the schoolhouses at night knew what was going on in that city and insisted upon talking about it, and the minute they began talking about it, many things became impossible, for there are scores of things that must be put a stop to in our politics that will stop the moment they are talked of where men will listen. The treatment for bad politics is exactly the modern treatment for tuberculosis—it is exposure to the open air.

Now you have to begin at the root of the matter in order to understand what it is you intend to serve by this movement. You intend to serve the life of communities, the life that is there, the life that you cannot create, the life to which you can only give release and opportunity; and wherein does that life consist? That is the question that interests me. There can be no life in a community so long as its parts are segregated and separated. It is just as if you separated the organs of the human body and then expected them to produce life. You must open wide the channels

[2] Rochester, N. Y., in 1907-1908. See Edward J. Ward, "The Rochester Movement," *The Independent*, LXVII (Oct. 14, 1909), 860-861.

of sympathy and communication between them, you must make channels for the tides of life; if you clog them anywhere, if you stop them anywhere, why then the processes of disease set in, which are the processes of misunderstanding, which are the disconnections between the spiritual impulses of different sections of men.

The very definition of community is a body of men who have things in common, who are conscious that they have things in common, who judge those common things from a single point of view, namely, the point of view of general interest. Such a thing as a community is unthinkable, therefore, unless you have close communication; there must be a vital inter-relationship of parts, there must be a fusion, there must be a coördination, there must be a free intercourse, there must be such a contact as will constitute union itself before you will have the true course of the wholesome blood throughout the body.

Therefore, when you analyze some of our communities you will see just how necessary it is to get their parts together. Take some of our great cities for example. Do you not realize by common gossip even, the absolute disconnection of what we call their residential sections from the rest of the city? Isn't it singular that while human beings live all over a city, we pick out a part, a place where there are luxurious and well-appointed houses, and call that the residential section? As if nobody else lived anywhere in that city. That is the place where the most disconnected part and in some instances the most useless part of the community lives. There men do not know their next-door neighbors; there men do not want to know their next-door neighbors; there is no bond of sympathy; there is no bond of knowledge or common acquaintanceship.

I am not speaking of these things to impeach a class, for I know of no just way in which to impeach a class.

It is necessary that such portions of the community should be linked with the other portions; it is necessary that simple means should be found by which by an interchange of points of view we may get together, for the whole process of modern life, the whole process of modern politics, is a process by which we must exclude misunderstandings, exclude hostilities, exclude deadly rivalries, make men understand other men's interests, bring all men into common counsel, and so discover what is the common interest.

That is the problem of modern life which is so specialized that it is almost devitalized, so disconnected that the tides of life will not flow.

My interest in this movement, as it has been described to me, has been touched with enthusiasm because I see in it a channel for the restoration of the unity of communities. Because I am told that things have already happened which bear promise of this very thing.

I was told what is said to be a typical story of a very fine lady, a woman of very fine natural parts, but very fastidious, whose automobile happened to be stalled one night in front of an open schoolhouse where a meeting was going on over which her seamstress was presiding. She was induced by some acquaintances of hers whom she saw going into the building, to go in, and was at first filled with disdain; she didn't like the looks of some of the people, there was too much mixture of the sort she didn't care to associate with—an employe of her own was presiding—but she was obliged to stay a little while, it was the most comfortable place to stay while her automobile was repaired, and before she could get away she had been touched with the generous contagion of the place. Here were people of all sorts talking about things that were interesting, that revealed to her things that she had never dreamed of before with regard to the vital common interests of persons whom she had always thought unlike herself, so that the community of the human heart was revealed to her, the singleness of human life.

Now if this thing does that, it is worth any effort to promote it. If it will do that, it is the means by which we shall create communities. And nothing else will produce liberty—you cannot have liberty where men do not want the same liberty, you cannot have it where they are not in sympathy with one another, you cannot have it where they do not understand one another, you cannot have it when they are not seeking common things by common means, you simply cannot have it; we must study the means by which these things are produced.

In the first place, don't you see that you produce communities by creating common feeling? I know that a great emphasis is put upon the mind, in our day, and as a university man I should perhaps not challenge the supremacy of the intellect, but I have never been convinced that mind was really monarch in our day, or in any day that I have yet read of, or, if it is monarch, it is one of the modern monarchs that rules and reigns but does not govern.

What really controls our action is feeling. We are governed by the passions and the most that we can manage by all our social and political endeavors is that the handsome passions shall be in the majority—the passion of sympathy, the passion of justice, the passion of fair dealing, the passion of unselfishness, (if it may be elevated into a passion). If you can once see that a working majority is obtained for the handsome passions, for the feelings that draw us together, rather than for the feelings that separate us, then you have laid the foundation of a community and a free government and, therefore, if you can do nothing else in the community center than draw men together so that they will have common feeling, you will have set forward the cause of civilization and the cause of human freedom.

As a basis of the common feeling you must have a mutual comprehension. The fundamental truth in modern life, as I analyze it, is a profound ignorance. I am not one of those who challenge the promoters of special interests on the ground that they are malevolent, that they are bad men; I challenge their leadership on the ground that they are ignorant men, that when you have absorbed yourself in a particular business through half your life, you have no other point of view than the point of view of that business and that, therefore, you are disqualified by ignorance from giving counsel as to the common interests.

A witty English writer once said: "If you chain a man's head to a ledger and knock off something from his wages every time he stops adding up, you can't expect him to have enlightened views about the antipodes." Simply, if you immerse a man in a given undertaking, no matter how big that undertaking is, and keep him immersed for half a life time, you can't expect him to see any horizon, you can't expect him to see human life steadily or see it whole.

I once made this statement that a university was intended to make young people just as unlike their fathers as possible. By which I do not mean anything disrespectful to their fathers, but merely this, by the time a man is old enough to have children in college, his point of view is apt to have become so specialized that they would better be taken away from him and put in a place where their views of life will be regeneralized and they will be disconnected from the family and connected with the world. That, I understand to be the function of education, of the liberal education.

Now a kind of liberal education must underlie every wholesome political and social process, the kind of liberal education which connects a man's feeling and his comprehension with the general run of mankind, which disconnects him from the special interests and marries his thought to the common interests of great communities and of great cities and of great states and of great nations, and, if possible, with that brotherhood of man that transcends the boundaries of nations themselves.

Those are the horizons to my mind of this social center movement, that they are going to unite the feelings and clarify the comprehension of communities, of bodies of men who draw together in conference.

I would like to ask if this is not the experience of every person here who has ever acted in any conference of any kind. Did you ever go out of a conference with exactly the same views with which you went in? If you did, I am sorry for you, you must be thought-tight. For my part I can testify that I never carried a scheme into a conference without having it profoundly modified by the criticism of the other men in the conference and without recognizing when I came out that the product of the common council bestowed upon it was very much superior to any private thought that might have been used for its development. The processes of attrition, the contributions to consensus of minds, the compromises of thought create those general movements which are the streams of tendency and the streams of development.

And so it seems to me that what is going to be produced by this movement,—not all at once, by slow and tedious stages, no doubt, but nevertheless very certainly in the end,—is in the first place a release of common forces now undiscovered, now somewhere banked up, and now somewhere unavailable, the removal of barriers to the common understanding, the opening of mind to mind, the clarification of the air and the release in that clarified air of forces that can live in it, and just so certainly as you release those forces you make easier the fundamental problem of modern society, which is the problem of accommodating the various interests in modern society to one another.

I used to teach my classes in the university that liberty was a matter of adjustment and I was accustomed to illustrate it in this way; when you have perfectly assembled the parts of a great steam engine, for example, then when it runs, you say that it runs free; that means that the adjustment is so perfect that the friction is reduced to a minimum, doesn't it, and the minute you twist any part out of alignment, the minute you lose adjustment, then there is a buckling up and the whole thing is rigid and useless. Now to my mind, that is the image of human liberty; the individual is free in proportion to his perfect accommodation to the whole, or to put it the other way, in proportion to the perfect adjustment of the whole to his life and interests.

Take another illustration; you are sailing a boat, when do you say that she is running free, when you have thrown her up into the wind? No, not at all. Every stick and stitch in her shivers and you say she is in irons; nature has grasped her and says: "You cannot go that way"; but let her fall off, let the sheet fill and see her run like a bird skimming the waters. Why is she free? Because she has adjusted herself to the great force of nature that is brewed with the breath of the wind. She is free in proportion as she is adjusted, as she is obedient, and so men are free in society in proportion as their interests are accommodated to one another, and that is the problem of liberty.

Liberty as now expressed is unsatisfactory in this country and in other countries because there has not been a satisfactory adjustment and you cannot readjust the parts until you analyze them. Very well, we have analyzed them. Now this movement is intended to contribute to an effort to assemble them, bring them together, let them look one another in the face, let them reckon with one another and then they will coöperate and not before.

You cannot bring adjustment into play until you have got the consent of the parts to act together, and then when you have got the adjustment, when you have discovered and released those forces and they have accommodated themselves to each other, you have that control which is the sovereignty of the people.

There is no sovereignty of the people if the several sections of the people be at loggerheads with one another; sovereignty comes with coöperation, sovereignty comes with mutual protection, sovereignty comes with the quick pulses of sympathy, sovereignty comes by a common impulse.

You say and all men say that great political changes are impending in this country. Why do you say so? Because everywhere you go you find men expressing the same judgment, alive to the same circumstances, determined to solve the problems by acting together no matter what older bonds they may break, no matter what former prepossessions they may throw off, determined to get together and do the thing.

And so you know that changes are impending because what was a body of scattered sentiment is now becoming a concentrated force, and so with sympathy and understanding comes control, for, in place of this control of enlightened and sovereign opinions, we have had in the field of politics as elsewhere, the reign of management, and management is compounded of these two things, secrecy plus concentration.

You cannot manage a nation, you cannot manage the people

of a state, you cannot manage a great population, you can manage only some central force; what you do, therefore, if you want to manage in politics or anywhere else is to choose a great single force or single group of forces, and then find some man or men sagacious and secretive enough to manage the business without being discovered. And that has been done for a generation in the United States.

Now, the schoolhouse among other things is going to break that up. Is it not significant that this thing is being erected upon the foundation originally laid in America, where we saw from the first that the schoolhouse and the church were to be the pillars of the Republic? Is it not significant that as if by instinct we return to those sources of liberty undefiled which we find in the common meeting place, in the place owned by everybody, in the place where nobody can be excluded, in the place to which everybody comes as by right?

And so what we are doing is simply to open what was shut, to let the light come in upon places that were dark, to substitute for locked doors, open doors, for it does not make any difference how many or how few come in provided anybody who chooses may come in. So as soon as you have established that principle, you have openings, and those doors are open as if they were the flood gates of life.

I do not wonder that men are exhibiting an increased confidence in the judgments of the people, because wherever you give the people a chance such as this movement has given them in the schoolhouse, they avail themselves of it. This is not a false people, this is not a people guided by blind impulses, this is a people who want to think, who want to think right, whose feelings are based upon justice, whose instincts are for fairness and for the light.

So what I see in this movement is a recovery of the constructive and creative genius of the American people, because the American people as a people are so far different from others in being able to produce new things, to create new things out of old.

I have often thought that we overlook the fact that the real sources of strength in the community come from the bottom. Do you find society renewing itself from the top? Don't you find society renewing itself from the ranks of unknown men? Do you look to the leading families to go on leading you? Do you look to the ranks of the men already established in authority to contribute sons to lead the next generation? They may, sometimes they do, but you can't count on them; and what you are constantly depending on is the rise out of the ranks of unknown men, the discovery of men whom you had passed by, the sudden disclosure of capacity you had not dreamed of, the emergence of somebody from some place of which you had thought the least, of some man unanointed from on high, to do the thing that the generation calls for. Who would have looked to see Lincoln save a nation? Who that knew Lincoln when he was a lad and a youth and a young man—but all the while there was springing up in him as if he were connected with the very soil itself, the sap of a nation, the vision of a great people, a sympathy so ingrained and intimate with the common run of men that he was like the People impersonated, sublimated, touched with genius. And it is to such sources that we must always look.

No man can calculate the courses of genius, no man can foretell the leadership of nations. And so we must see to it that the bottom is left open, we must see to it that the soil of the common feeling of the common consciousness is always fertile and unclogged, for there can be no fruit unless the roots touch the rich sources of life.

And it seems to me that the schoolhouses dotted here, there, and everywhere, over the great expanse of this nation, will some day prove to be the roots of that great tree of liberty which shall spread for the sustenance and protection of all mankind.

Printed in *Bulletin of the University of Wisconsin*, Serial No. 470 (Madison, Wisc., 1911), pp. 3-15.

A Luncheon Address in Madison to the Democratic League of Wisconsin[1]

[[Oct. 26, 1911]]

The whole country recognizes that Wisconsin has led the way in bringing about reforms the country desired.

For the first time in America, recent years have disclosed the conditions most favorable to serious debate, to the very thorough consideration with perfect candor, of questions which may divide parties simply because they classify opinions, but which do not constitute the ground work of passionate party differences: and when I try to sum up for myself in a single phrase, what it is we are all interested in, it seems to me that I cannot better express it than by saying that we are interested in establishing a people's government in America.

[1] Delivered in the university gymnasium before an audience that included progressives of both parties, members of the university faculty, justices of the state supreme court, and various state officials. John A. Aylward presided and introduced Wilson.

But that phrase does not mean anything unless we know what we mean when we use the words "the people," and I believe that the fundamental difficulty in America is that these words have different meanings in different minds. When I ask myself what I mean by the "people," I can candidly answer that I mean "everybody"; but when I ask myself what the representatives of "special interests" mean when they say "the people," I am aware that they don't include themselves!

By Republicans, speaking, of course, of the majority of the party, I understand a person who really believes that the persons best qualified to judge the true interests of the country are those who have the largest material stake in the country, and that a genuine Republican, at any rate of the historical variety, believes that government is in essence a sort of trusteeship, that it is necessary that certain persons more deeply versed in the larger kinds of business should, in an industrial and commercial nation, be the trustees of the rest; that so soon as you establish their prosperity upon the lines suggested by their management, you have done something which may be handed on to the rest of the country, and that the people are those who share the prosperity of the trustees.

I should not like to misrepresent the leaders of that great party. My despair of them is that they seem really to believe those things. If they didn't really believe it, if they were merely putting up a bluff, then I should have more respect for their intelligence and some hope for their conversion. But they seem really to believe the incredible, really to credit the things which are incredible, which are known to be incredible by everybody who has read history, even superficially.

And so I deem a Democrat to be a man who utterly dissents from that belief, and who, when he speaks of the people, includes everybody, even including the special interests. We are more gracious than they. They do not include us. We do include them. We are perfectly willing that they should take part in the common counsel which is to disclose the common interests, but they are not willing that we should take part.

And so, when I speak and think of the people's government, I am thinking of the government in which we are all included as vital partners and the purposes of which cannot be determined except by genuine common counsel. When we look at our political difficulties we will find that they, most of them, come by the circumspection of the field of confidence.

Government has been conducted in the United States, not only in the nation, but in the States and in the city, by "middlemen" to whom have gone most of the profits as often happens with middlemen; I mean those who have arranged what should be undertaken and have privately determined how the matter should be controlled, by determining the nominations. That is no people's government.

There are men who have been engaged in this kind of thing who are, so far as I can see, honorable men, honest men. I mean men who really believe that if their interests are safeguarded the interest of the community are promoted; there are men connected with this system who do not believe it safe to submit public questions to the general judgment. Those are the men whom you hear going about the country speaking of the people with distrust, making the incredible comparison between the people and a mob, speaking about mobocracy, as if that were a synonymous term with government by the people, evidently supposing that outside of their own circles nothing but passion, nothing but prejudice, nothing but irresponsible impulse governs, and that only within their little circle is there circumspection, is there knowledge, is there the precaution and prevision which are necessary for the prudent and successful conduct of public affairs.

I am perfectly willing to believe them honest, if they will permit me to believe them ignorant. But if they insist upon my believing that they understand the situation as it is, then they must forgive me for my believing them deeply dishonest. I do not see any escape from that logical quandary. Now what we are engaged in in this country is nothing more or less than this breaking up of the business of the middlemen, carrying the government directly to the judgment of the people.

You have to apply only one test to see how the middleman can be put out of business. He could not conduct his business in public; it is inconceivable that he should be willing to let everybody know the grounds upon which he acts and the agreements by which he binds himself, either the explicit or the implicit agreements, and if what he does is not susceptible to exposure to the public view, then what he does is not consistent with the public interest.

I would test any man's public purpose by his willingness to state it, and having heard some of these gentlemen state their public purposes and having been accustomed to hearing the English language used, I know that they are talking through their hats and I have conceived it my business in public life to translate into plain English just what they mean. They mean that they don't want you to invade those private areas of judgment by which they determine what their interest is and what the government shall do; they are not willing to play the game in public.

I believe that the impressions of radicalism which these gentlemen get from some of us is merely the shock at hearing the truth. It is just as if they said: "Yes, yes, of course, that is so, but don't say it so loud. You shock the air when you say these things out loud; of course if you will only shut up we will privately condemn it, but don't stand up and talk about it."

And yet it seems to me that the only way to come to a common understanding is by standing up and talking about it, and the radicalism lies in the statement of the fact, not in the proposal of the remedies.

I understand, just as you understand, that we can go at a too rapid or radical pace in remedying the things which are wrong, because the structure of society is made of a very delicate fiber. Interests, whether these gentlemen will admit it or not, are so interlaced that you cannot deal with one at a time without dealing with all of them; we are so bound together in common causes of life that if you detach one part of it impression thrills through every part, and every sane man understands, therefore, that you have got to touch the body politic with the nice art of the prudent physician, but what would you say of the physician who was so prudent that he did not get to the bottom of the diagnosis?

The diagnosis is radical, but the cure is remedial; the cure is conservative. I do not, for my part, think that the remedies applied should be applied upon a great theoretical scale; nobody is wise enough to have the absolute "by the wool"; nobody is big enough, nobody comprehends in his single brain, no group of men comprehend in their common conference all the interests involved in the great nation. You have to take item by item and symptom by symptom; you have got to remedy one thing at a time, but you must do it, not upon a principle of hostility, but upon a principle of reconciliation.

What I wish that I could proclaim with a voice loud enough for the whole country to hear it is this: These gentlemen who represent the special interests are now suffering from the circumstance that the country does not trust them, and what we are trying to bring about is such a change of circumstances that they will go into the common conference, and, being understood, will begin to be trusted, and there shall be reconciliation and reunion.

But that cannot happen so long as they regard the people with suspicion, so long as they think the people are going to make inroads of conquest upon them; that cannot happen so long as they divide themselves from the people in thought.

What are the people to the great business interests of this country? Why, they are the very soul out of which they spring, the very soul from which they draw sustenance and existence. Without the capacity of these people, without their common interests, without their impulses and genius there could be no great structure of material wealth in this country. You are trading upon the capacity of your fellow-men, you are drawing upon their very life, and unless you reconcile your interests to their interests, that life will begin to ebb away from you, the very foundations of your structure will become quicksand, and the whole structure will crack and crumble.

Is it not a work of patriotism and piety to bring about such an understanding as will constitute a reconciliation? Is it not the duty of statesmanship, and is not that the object of popular government?

The object of popular government is not to array class against class; the object of popular government is not to put things in the hands of the thoughtless and heedless; the object of popular government is to bring everybody into the noble game of establishing the fortune of every man in the world. So it seems to me that the appearance of radicalism which is worn by some modern programs, at any rate in the hearts of those who are afraid, is due to the fact that they are looking fearfully upon a thing which they do not comprehend, and which when they once comprehend they will be glad to embrace.

I cannot imagine a man of large imagination, a constructive genius, characteristic of some very great business men, who would not, if he once let his mind yield to this view, turn to it with a new enthusiasm, see his own business in more majestic proportions and know that in serving the nation he was building up his own fortune. And men who stand in the way stand not only in their own light but in the light of all mankind.

And so the reason that I for one desire popular government is because I believe it is the only basis sufficiently secure and sufficiently broad for modern civilization and because I believe that it is the only atmosphere which we can breathe with stimulation to the lungs and the only air that is pure, the only air that for long sustains life, the only air that quickens the blood for all the great enterprises of modern complicated society. It is a privilege to take part in public life in a day when such thoughts brood over a whole nation. There is an infinite exhilaration in feeling that men everywhere are returning to that attitude, that mind which characterized America at the very outset, when she set up institutions which were destined to be a model to the world.

Now the great problem in politics is expressed in the very familiar words of "Get together." There are artificial lines involved; the real division in politics is between Liberals and Tories; the great division is between those who see the things that ought to be done and are ready to do them, and those who do not see them and therefore do not do them, or, seeing them, are unwilling to attempt them. The cleavages of politics are now beginning to gape just there between those who will and those who will not, between those who move and those who stand pat. And we have got to recognize that the men with life in them, with purpose in them, with resolution in them, and with knowledge, must get together, and they have been getting together with the result of considerable confusion.

I do not recognize any great difference between my own principles and the principles of the Progressive Republicans I talk with. I understand that the two kinds have got sadly mixed in Wisconsin, that the Progressive Republicans have had to make certain drafts on Democratic ranks in Wisconsin to carry their measures through and win their elections; that means the labels they are wearing are so that you have to examine them inside instead of outside, to see what they really are.

And now I propose that we match our insides and get together; we all know the program, the items that are perfectly well known; we don't have to debate what we want, we only have to debate how we are going to get them. Politics to my mind, now is simply a question of co-ordination of forces, a putting aside of affectations of condition and recognizing genuine agreements of opinion, of looking each other squarely in the eye and say[ing] "We agree with each other and we will clasp hands on the proposition and act together."

Now we know our point of departure and we are sick and tired of the things that have been put upon us, we are going to turn our backs upon them, and we want to turn our backs upon them with our faces in such a direction that our goal is certain. We can have one standard, we are not going to listen to anything that is not certified to us as based upon a general understanding of the common interest. And we are going to insist upon drawing everybody into the common interest whether they want to be drawn in or not and we are going to serve the very men who are opposing us only we are going to serve them better than they know how to serve themselves.

I know you share with me a passionate conviction of the seriousness of the situation in America. We have come to a parting of the ways, to choose the wrong way would be fatal. We cannot postpone the day of adjustment, because if we postpone it we may come to such a point of passion that it cannot be justly effected. We must undertake it now while we are calm and when we can come to a fair settlement. We must not wait until things become so complicated and hopeless that we shall undertake unwise and hasty remedies. And therefore I say that the point of choice is now, that it cannot be postponed, and the whole country must determine on which side it is going to stand. It must not allow personal consideration, personal prepossession, to stand in the way of a clear vision of duty.[2]

Printed in the *Newark Evening News*, Oct. 27, 1911, the opening sentence from the partial text in the Madison *Wisconsin State Journal*, Oct. 26, 1911.

[2] There is a WWhw outline of this address, dated Oct. 26, 1911, in WP, DLC.

A Religious Address in Dallas, Texas[1]

[[Oct. 28, 1911]]

Cordial as your reception to me has been, I find myself abashed in such a gathering as this, at being to any extent its center. In no way have I earned a right to speak for the millions of English-speaking people who are celebrating the three hundredth anniversary of the translation of the Bible into their common tongue, nor will I undertake to expound the good old book to you today. I rise merely as one from the ranks of the common men to speak of this great book, which seems to me to contain the fountain of life.

I have chosen to speak to you on "Life and the Bible." These two are connected in very intimate and singular fashion. For the Bible is revealed to us, not in any abstract form, but in concrete experiences of men like you and me, men not lifted suddenly to an undeserved sainthood, but men slowly ascending through this life from one correction of error to another correction of error. Gradually, steadily, they have struggled to square themselves to the line of the Scriptures, not to any creed, but to the immortal examples.

It seems to me, if we had the New Testament alone, and had had the example of Christ suddenly revealed to us, they would

[1] A news report of this affair is printed at Oct. 29, 1911.

have been robbed largely of their efficacy. Jesus came, as the Scriptures themselves say, in the fullness of time, after mankind had gone through the long struggle typified in the characters and the history of the Old Testament. He had not come as if unbidden. He did not come unheralded. The world had been struggling toward him. Then he stepped out as one who should say "I am He"; one who would illustrate what mankind was striving for in all the dim history of the past. The Old Testament is a manual of life, and needs to have the light of the New Testament thrown upon it to bring out its wonderful teachings. The theologian must look to the New Testament for his suggestion of doctrine. But man must look to the Old Testament for his example of life, so far as the example is the human example.

The Old Testament contains no eulogies of men and no sophistications or theories. Men are shown as men with all their errors and all their heroic triumphs, and it says: "This is the way in which men struggled toward the light," and we find couched in their experiences the experiences we ourselves have. So also when we go to the catalogue of "saints" in the New Testament, we find [men] sinful as you and I, men who climbed to saintliness with tears of repentance, and mortification for transgressions. There would be no consolation in the Scriptures, for me at any rate, if it were not an interpretation of such men as I have known. We can consort with the kind of "saints" we find in the Old Testament, but with the ideal saints I would feel very much out of place. The men in the Old Testament are the kind I know, of the kind who struggle round about me, who slowly approximate to that yet impossible example revealed in the Lord Jesus.

The sources of life are spiritual, and the essences are from the soul. Only the immortal parts of man contain the elements of life. These elements represent both sides of the picture. For I have reason to believe, yea, to fear, that the bad in man is as immortal as the good, at least as far as mortal life is concerned. And when these bad influences get a hold upon you, you can drag down whole generations into the pit. The pages of the Old Testament thunder the immortality of evil,—at least on earth. It shows life as a grand tragedy, the struggle between the influences of good and bad.

Nor is the Bible alone in this drama of the spirit. The Greek drama thrills with it. We derive too little of the benefit to be obtained in the great lessons of the Greek tragedies. They lose much in translation as to their forcefulness, but not as to their truth. They are the pictures of the inevitable consequences of moral choices. In them, sin produces its progeny of ugliness, and virtue produces its children of light. In the unraveling of their skeins, there is revelation of truth. In their stories none escape the consequences of his action, none is let off. None ought to be let off from the consequences of his action.

I recall that when I was associated first with the discipline of a university I had a silly tendency of the heart to excuse those upon whom would fall the effects of their breaking of the college rules. Often I begged them off before the faculty. But I have never found that those thus excused have come forward with that showing of appreciation which might reasonably have been expected. And I made up my mind that it is better that a man shall lie in the bed he has made. Only be sure that he has made the bed. Students have come to me and begged that the rules shall not be enforced upon them, pleading that we would break a mother's heart. But I have as often called to their attention that the thing which will break the mother's heart is that the boy should have done such a thing, and that it is he who has broken her heart.

Sooner or later there comes back upon men the inevitable consequences of their own doings. Life is a dramatic contest between the bad and the good. I do not subscribe to that teaching which has been rather common, that it is mind which has full control of the affairs of men. Often have I seen the mind reign, but never have I seen it govern. What man really follows is his passions. The best we can hope to accomplish, in individual or political life, is to keep the handsome passions in the majority. Men make their revolutions, and accomplish their reforms, not by the intellectual reasoning and mental control, but by going straight at the evils of which they complain and sweeping them away.

Wonderful is the effect of concerted action between the handsome passions. They operate in the open, and it is easy to anticipate the next move they will make.

The ugly passions, on the other hand, are difficult to come at; for they operate under cover, and their purposes are not easy to discern. It is a common thing for us to cloak our purposes when they are improper, striving to make men see them as the things we say they are, masquerading them in clothes we put upon them. What a depth of concealment there is from our consciences when we deploy thus upon ourselves!

The interesting thing, however, that makes the contest less unequal, is that the bad passions always lead to their own confusion. You have to have a good memory to keep on lying. I recall the cynical advice given by a politician to his son, "Don't worry about the lies people tell on you. They'll take care of themselves. But when you hear me denying something you may know it's so." Bad passions eat into themselves as acids do. They will be evident in the faces of the persons who harbor them. Their ear-marks are evident in those who are made timid and afraid. Many of those who have ruled the world for a while have not kept faith, for they had no faith to keep, and after a while they bring about their own destruction.

Nor is it enough to say that truth is mighty and will prevail. The handsome passions will not triumph if you sit back and say, "Truth will triumph." They must be encouraged. You must put on truth as if it were war paint. You must draw and use it as if it were a sword. You must everywhere and all the time force the fighting, if the handsome passions are to be in the majority. If they simmer, if they sleep, the "machine"—of course the bad passions always have a "machine"—is going to get in its work.

But it is the lesson of the Scripture that men—every-day men, wholesome men—are capable of embodying truth in themselves; that imperfect men, sinful men, are able, by the grace of God, more and more, to square themselves with the splendors they entertain.

There are those who argue that truth is known because it is beautiful; that beauty is the best antiseptic against evil; that it is because truth is perfectly expressed that it is immortal. There are those who say that the best literature endures because it is thought perfectly expressed. But better than that, it is necessary that great literature shall be true. All great literature has its truth. The only difference between literature and the Bible is that the Bible is the complete interpretation of truth, and sup-plies for that interpretation a universal language. It does not seem to be Jewish; it does not seem to be a part of a national literature that is not our own, but to have the warp and woof of our own experiences, national and personal. There are in the characters of the Bible, the same integrations and disintegrations, the same growth in beauty where men obey God, and the same destruction, for the destruction does come when they deny God.

On the campus at Princeton a delightful old gentleman told me one day that he had discovered the microbe of hyper-Cal-vinism.

"Gracious; I hope you haven't it about you," I said to him.

He replied that it was in the title chapter of a book that he had at home. I have forgotten the words of this title, but he said that it confounded the will of God with right, denying that there is such a thing as absolute right and wrong, teaching that God, in the beginning, might have ordered right what he ordered to be wrong, and might have called wrong, what he did call right. To such a person it is inconceivable that God has absolute immutability, and that truth is unchangeable.

Now there is something very striking in the criticism of my friend, because the Bible does not display men as right merely because they have obeyed the Ten Commandments. But it displays the triumphs of men who have tried to approximate what God has revealed as right. The Bible has its pictures of right and wrong, showing what men must live for, or die; for they shall surely die, as they did die, when wrong is done.

Dante in his "Inferno" did not hesitate to put into that inferno gentlemen who were high in the public life of his day; men who, though they were living, were truly in that place of torment, as far as their own consciences were concerned. I have met gentlemen, and you know gentlemen, who are in torment. Their faces and their words show it. It is not necessary that they should go to a place already arranged for them. We have seen men who had made all the necessary arrangements themselves.

Man gropes about for the light until he conforms, in some measure, to the right, whether he has ever read the revelation or not. I take it that we would have discovered the standard, as it is revealed to us in the Old Testament. But we could never have found the plan of salvation except by revelation. The golden rule of living was spoken by Socrates. His teaching differed from the Christian only because he never saw the Christ nor had the vision of love that can release the spirit even at the end when the law of evil has worked its way among the members of the body.

That is the reason that the New Testament had to be added to the Old. The Old Testament shows what we could have found out in time. The New Testament discovered to us what we could not have found out for ourselves. We could not have found such a person as Christ. We could not have invented such a person. We could not have put the words into the mouth of any living creature. And yet there was nothing, so far as I can see, that was original in the teachings of the Christ. Christ merely put into exquisitely perfect form what our spirits at once recognize to be true. Here was something that no man could gainsay, and coming from those lips, no man could refrain from worshiping.

And so, the simple thing that I came to say today is this: The Bible is not something to turn aside to; the Bible is not something to which to resort for religious instruction and comfort; the Bible is not something to associate merely with churches and sermons. It stands right in the center, in the market place, of our life, and there bubbles with the water of life. It is, itself, the fountain; it is, itself, the inexhaustible fountain. Only those who have learned from it, and only those who have drunk of those waters, can be refreshed for the longer journey.[2]

Printed in the *Bible Society Record*, LXIX (April 1924), 58-60, with corrections from the text in the *Dallas Morning News*, Oct. 29, 1911.

[2] There is a WWhw outline of this address, with the composition date of Oct. 27, 1911, in WP, DLC.

An Address in Dallas at the Texas State Fair[1]

[[Oct. 28, 1911]]

My Fellow-Citizens—It is with a very profound feeling, the privilege, that I find myself facing this great company of my fellow-citizens of Texas. I realize as I stand here from how many quarters of your imperial domain you have come. I realize what it means to face a body of men who represent the thought and vigor of the great State of Texas, because Texas is recognized from one end of this country to the other as one of the States which has led in the progressive movement of our times. (Cheers.)

It has showed the way for the establishment of commission government in our cities: the way out of chaos into self-government. It was the leadership of Texas that showed us the way in which to regulate railways by railway commissions. It was Texas that first began to regulate the bond issue of public service corporations.

I wish that some of the gentlemen who played a leading part in these great movements were still living in order that I might pay them my tribute of respect and admiration. I wish that Governor Hogg[2] (tremendous applause) and Senator Reagan[3] were

[1] Delivered in the State Fair Coliseum before an audience of about 7,500 persons. Senator Charles A. Culberson introduced him as a Virginian imbued with "the fundamental principles of free government of his native State"; a Southerner who in his work in the North had demonstrated a broad Americanism; a great governor who had driven the forces of corruption from power; and a Christian and Democrat who stood "unreservedly and bravely, though probably somewhat in advance as to some methods, with the Democratic party on the vital issues of the hour." *Dallas Morning News*, Oct. 29, 1911.

[2] James Stephen Hogg, district attorney of the seventh judicial district of Texas, 1881-85; attorney general, 1887-91; governor, 1891-95. As governor he helped to establish a state railroad commission, recovered for the state some 2,000,000 acres of land held by railroads, and obtained the passage of legislation to prevent the establishment of landholding companies, the watering of railroad securities, and the indiscriminate issuance of municipal securities. Returning to the practice of law in Austin after 1895, he continued to support progressive reforms until his death on March 3, 1906.

[3] John Henninger Reagan, Postmaster General of the Confederacy, 1861-65;

still here to lend the vigor of their intelligence and undaunted courage to the progress of our times. (Cheers.) I am happy that Judge Terrell of Austin[4] is still living and I wish I might confer with him to-day in person my feeling of obligation for the example he set us in his activity in Texas.

And so I feel that it is a particular and vital thing to be permitted to come and speak in Texas, because there is some progressive language that would not be understood anywhere else except in Texas. I like to know before I begin that I am speaking language to which you are yourselves accustomed, and the singular thing about Texas is that she has always known her own mind and always found the means of expressing it. (Laughter.) Some other States have known their own mind. New Jersey has long known her own mind but she only recently found a way to express it. (Laughter.)

There is this interesting vitality in Texas that there is always pouring in upon you a renewal of the original elements of which the State was made. You never settle to any bad habits in Texas. You are always drawing fresh strength, young strength, original strength, out of the rest of the Union to build up your empire and rejuvenate the life of Texas. It seems to me that nowhere else in the United States is the variety and vitality and self-renewal of her life so admirably expressed as it is in this great Commonwealth.

And so it is proper for me to discuss here the great question of how the States are to express the freedom of the people, because it seems to me, ladies and gentlemen, that the liberty of the people must be expressed in their home government before it is expressed in their National Government; that the National Government will be vital in proportion as the States are vital; that the central Government will reign in proportion as the citizens control their own affairs at home.

There will be no invidious reflections in what I shall say about State Government because you have generally been able to control your own State Government. And two years ago one of the most prominent public men in the United States delivered an address before a Pennsylvania society in Philadelphia in which he questioned whether it would not be necessary for the Federal

congressman, 1875-87; United States senator, 1887-91; joint author of the bill to establish the Interstate Commerce Commission; member of the Texas Railroad Commission, 1891-1903.

4 Alexander Watkins Terrell, state district court judge, 1857-62; state senator, 1876-84; member of the state house of representatives, 1891-92; Minister to Turkey, 1893-97. Author of the law establishing the Texas Railroad Commission.

Government to take over some of the powers that have been exercised by the States, not because those powers had been wrongly exercised by the States, not because the States had acted in a way that was detrimental to the public, but because they had not acted at all—because the Governments of the States were refraining from using the great powers which had been put at their disposal from the first in the organization of our National Government.[5]

And since that speech, you will bear me witness—though I think not because of that—an entirely different aspect has been put upon affairs. States have been one by one reasserting their powers and exercising them in response to public opinion of the people and in accordance with the public interest of their people. There has been witnessed in our day a rejuvenation of the powers of the States. What is the matter? Why do not the States exercise their great power? It was not because the people of the States did not know what it was necessary to do, it was not because the people of the States did not take part in the exercise of suffrage, it was not because the States did not choose representatives pledged to do the things which were for the common interest, but it was because election after election was followed by sessions of Legislatures in which nothing was done in response to the public interest. Men began to realize that there was interposed between them and the Legislature a power somewhere concealed with which they could not reckon; that there was something hidden somewhere that prevented the Legislatures of this country from representing the people they were elected to represent.

I have again and again been told that those who advocated some of the more radical changes now proposed in our program were expressing a hostility to representative government. I want you to look this Nation over and ask if in recent years in most of our States whether we have had representative government. (Cheers.) Everything that I can personally do, everything that may turn out to be necessary in this country will be done for the purpose of recovering our governments and making them representative. (Applause.) . . .

So that what renders this a critical age in American politics is nothing more nor less than this: That we have changed our political methods at the very same time that we are changing our life itself. It is a very serious thing. In Texas, I dare say,

[5] He referred to Theodore Roosevelt's speech before the Union League Club of Philadelphia on January 30, 1905, in which he made precisely this point. See T. Roosevelt, *The Roosevelt Policy* (2 vols., New York, 1908), I, 240-242.

you have political instrumentalities, but in most of the Union satisfactory instrumentalities do not exist. It is not necessary to create the means at the very time you are debating the measure. There never was a time, therefore, when more clear-headed, sure-footed, thoughtful and moderate statesmanship was necessary than at the present moment. There is an enormous problem to solve and imperfect instruments with which to solve it. It is very dangerous, indeed, to swap horses in the middle of the stream, and we are doing something very like that.

We are swapping horses right in the middle of the stream. We have got to be mighty sure that we are getting on a good horse, and we have got to be mighty sure that we know how to make the escape without falling in the river, because all the while this great river of economic tendency, this great river of public discontent, this great body of flooding waters, representing the National feeling, is running stronger and stronger under our very feet. We need all of the circumspection, all of the wisdom, all the good sense, all the hard moderation that we can command. There was a long time when it did not seem to make much difference. For several generations in this country we could simply open the gates and say: Here are our boundless resources; here are things that must be done and done quickly. Here is a great population for which food and work must be found and we ask anybody to come at any price and help us. That is what we did with the railroads. . . .

During that time it was not necessary for the Legislatures to do anything in particular, or to understand anything in particular. It was the grand open aid to free exploitation. But that age has gone by and now we have found what we intended to be instruments are masters. (Applause.) Now we find that combinations which were necessary to begin the business have got such a grip upon it that we can not even break in as partners. We don't want to break in in any other way. We don't want to break up the prosperity of this country. We don't want to put men out of business who have devoted extraordinary genius to the development of our material prosperity, but we do want them to understand that they are partners with us, and we can't afford to belong to them. (Applause.) That is what they do not understand. . . .

I do not believe any man understands the interest of the country who is not struggling in the midst of its current. The man who has made—the man who has reached the point of master, the man who has great financial power within his grasp, does not know what the struggle of life is, and therefore he does not know what the life of the country is. But so far as nine-tenths of us are concerned our life is made up of struggle, desperation, endeavor and failing hope. And so if I want a jury to tell me what the condition of the country is I would not make it up from the captains of industry, not because they do not understand their own business, but because, if I may judge from my conversations with them, they do not understand anything else.

Men of genius, extraordinary accomplishments; some of them, men of wonderful achievement, but could not see the horizon if they were to raise their eyes. They do not know what the most of their fellowmen are doing; they don't see the foundations of their own business. They do not realize that there could not be a secure business constructed if it rests upon quicksand, and that it is resting upon quicksand if it rests upon a sense of injustice.

So let us who believe in the people and rely upon the people's judgment understand prosperity better, and we do understand it better than the men who are now leading it. I challenge any man engaged in a big business to describe what the rest of his fellowmen will recognize as a true description of the state of the public mind in America, and the state of the general life in America. They know nothing of it. When those gentlemen make speeches—when some of their representatives standing high in the Republican party make speeches about the people, note the tone in which they speak. They do not include themselves. When they use the word people they are thinking of us but not of themselves.

I don't know what they call themselves, but they do not call themselves the people. I suppose they think that here are a group of us that really know what is what, and then there are all the rest of you, and all the rest of you are the people. Now I claim to be a part of the people. (Tremendous cheering.) And I make the modest suggestion that they are themselves also parts of the people. What we want is to cease being wards and become partners; not that we want them to take us into their partnership. We need to take them into partnership, the business is ours. We support it, we constitute it. Our efforts and our brain are the warp and woof of it, and we mean to show them that we are more generous than they. We mean to show them that we recognize the part that they are playing and just as soon as they are willing to come into the common council by which the common interests shall be determined, we are glad to have them come, for we are not engaged upon any such iniquitious projects as setting class against class.

Most of human men, human spirits, can not make way in that direction. There is nothing but confusion, nothing but hostility, nothing but hopelessness if you set class against class, if you stir up jealousy or speak unjustly even of those who do you unjust[ly]. The thing to do is to be fair all around. The thing is to propose programs which will include everybody and the interests of everybody; of the minority as well as the majority. . . .

I have been very much interested in a document which I read on the way down here. I made some statements in a speech in Pennsylvania about the control that certain moneyed men exercised in this country, and some newspapers jumped on me with both feet and said he is an academic person who is talking about what he does not understand. And yesterday I read a brief submitted in the name of the United States Government which contained the exact allegations that I put into my speech.[6] I am sorry that the representatives of the United States in a great lawsuit should be so ignorant and so academic. I am interested to find out that they knew as much as I knew, because they had appeared to be ignorant of the whole thing.

What gives appearance of radicalism to modern politics is simply this—that document submitted to the Circuit Court of the United States in Trenton sounds very radical. Why, because of the facts it set forth, but it is not radical in the remedies it proposes, as far as I can discover. The remedy is the mere enforcement of the existing law. If that is radical now, it was radical before.

And what gives the appearance of radicalism to modern politics is that we insist upon stating the facts as they are. Now the facts are very extraordinary. It does not follow that we are going to follow radical remedies. We have got to apply remedies but they need not be radical. For example, take the course of the Democratic majority in the last House of Representatives. If you take the whole tariff and begin to change it, then you practically affect every business in the United States, but if you do what those sensible gentlemen did, take one schedule at a time which has been thoroughly sifted and the facts which are thoroughly known and legislate about that schedule, then that was

6 He referred to United States v. United States Steel Corporation et al., a brief filed by the Justice Department in the federal circuit court in Trenton on October 26, 1911. The government charged that United States Steel had been created in 1901 for the purpose of monopolizing the steel market and that it had violated and was still violating the Sherman Act by various monopolistic practices. More to Wilson's point, the brief described in detail, with accompanying documents, the interlocking directorates and other devices that J. Pierpont Morgan (named as a defendant) used to monopolize credit. *New York Times*, Oct. 27, 1911.

not radical.[7] It is not radical to try the one demonstrated thing at a time and settle that. I think it would not break up politics, but on the contrary reduce it to a new order. If you adopt the very pleasing principle said to be observed by the Donnybrook Fair, of striking each and every head you see—the Donnybrook Fair seems to have cleared the air in many a community.

Now, of course I am playful in using that illustration, but what I mean seriously in saying this is for you to take one thing at a time, then you can avoid radicalism. Radicalism is abstract. Radicalism follows huge programs that no man is wise enough to make. Radicalism tries to run the whole gamut of change at once, and that no prudent man would desire.

We will have to make up our minds that we are going to be as radical as possible in telling the things that we know, and then having established them beyond doubt we can get together and change as much of them as we think wise. . . .

And so, ladies and gentlemen, I have played with the subject, but I have tried to lay before you what seems to be to me the problem and the opportunity of the moment. We can not afford to do anything more in politics in which we do not take the whole people into our confidence. (Applause.) We can not afford to arrange anything more privately. We can not afford to do anything less than what we should have done all along, namely, to draw all of the hearts of the American people into the enterprise of reform. America is a generous people. America loves freedom, but does not mean to obtain it by unfairness, and I believe that nothing is so hopeful as the present temper of America, absolutely wide awake, but perfectly self-possessed. I see in the audiences I meet from time to time in this country men who have been oblivious to the wishes of those who want free government but who are ready to unlock themselves in their own affairs, so that the American people may show the world that she has not lost her political genius, that she does not wander in the maze of helplessness, without resources, but that we come with principles united; for she knows, what is more, how to bind herself together in the great enterprise of restoring the integrity of government and freedom of mankind; that though she has kept her eyes closed for a season she has again opened them to find in response to which America was born visions of a day when the government shall look fair and pleasant to all men, because all men should know that under her

---

[7] The Democrats passed bills greatly lowering the duties on cotton textiles (Schedule I), on wool and woolens (Schedule K), and farm products (Schedule G). They also adopted a farmers' free list. All these bills were either vetoed by President Taft or lost in conference committee.

banners there march those who are free, resourceful and full of confident hope; those who have seen and shall accomplish the freedom of the human race.[8]

Printed in the *Dallas Morning News*, Oct. 29, 1911.
[8] There is a brief WWhw and WWsh outlined of this address, dated Oct. 28, 1911, in WP, DLC.

A News Report of a Strenuous Day in Dallas and Fort Worth, Texas

[Oct. 29, 1911]

GOV. WILSON GIVEN ROUSING RECEPTION

LEADERS OF POLITICAL FACTIONS MEET HERE TO GREET NEW JERSEY MAN.

The visit here yesterday of Gov. Woodrow Wilson of New Jersey, who traveled from that distant State to Texas in response to an invitation to meet and address his friends and supporters from all over the State at Woodrow Wilson Day at the Fair, inspired one of the most extraordinary gatherings of political leaders ever seen in Texas. . . .

Gov. Wilson, accompanied by his secretary, Walter Measday, and E[dward]. D. S. Underhill of the Newark Evening News, reached Dallas yesterday morning at 9:10 o'clock over the Katy.[1] The Governor spoke upon the subject: "Life and the Bible," at the First Baptist Church at 10:30, to an audience of 5,000 people. At 12:30 he was the guest of honor at a luncheon at the Oriental Hotel, where he spoke briefly, and at 3:30 he delivered an address at the State Fair Coliseum. Last night at 6:30 Gov. Wilson went to Fort Worth, on a special interurban car, accompanied by a reception committee from Fort Worth, and in that city he spoke last night. . . .

Delegations from Muskogee and other Oklahoma towns met Gov. Wilson on the way to Dallas and sought to have him arrange to make a speech in that and other Oklahoma cities. These invitations, however, force of circumstances made it necessary for him to decline.

The reception given the distinguished visitor upon his arrival yesterday morning, and all during his stay here, was unusually cordial. As he stepped from the train at the Katy station, Gov. Colquitt[2] of Texas was the first to shake his hand; then came Senator Charles A. Culberson, and if anybody else got ahead of

[1] The Missouri, Kansas and Texas Railway.
[2] Oscar Branch Colquitt, state senator, 1895-99; state railroad commissioner, 1903-11; governor, 1911-15.

Patrick O'Keefe—who was throwing up his hat and doing his best to give the Princeton yell[3]—it wasn't apparent. Relk & Harris' Band began to play, the Princeton men present burst into their college yell, the several hundred citizens gathered there cheered, and everyone crowded forward to meet the visitor.

After greetings were exchanged Gov. Wilson entered a carriage, in which, besides himself, were seated Gov. Colquitt, Senator Culberson and John C. Robertson,[4] president of the Dallas County Woodrow Wilson Club. In the next carriage rode Mayor W. M. Holland and City Commissioners Henderson, Nelms, Lee and Bartlett.[5] Murrell L. Buckner,[6] chairman of the arrangement committee; Thomas B. Love, president of the State Woodrow Wilson Association, and the scores of prominent men gathered to receive Gov. Wilson rode in other carriages. These formed a procession, behind which marched many men afoot, and which proceeded to Main street, and on to the Oriental Hotel.

The streets were lined with crowds all the way. Office buildings and all windows along the streets were filled with people, who added their cheers to those on the sidewalks. When the hotel was reached a solid mass of people filled the lobby and was packed out upon the sidewalks and to the car tracks. Cheers and applause met Gov. Wilson's arrival, and, smiling, bowing and shaking hands, he made his way through the crowd and to the desk. Gov. O. B. Colquitt stood by his side as he registered and received the key to his room. Then the crowd began to demand a speech. "Wilson! Wilson! Speech! Speech!" the people insisted.

On the stairway landing Gov. Wilson and his party halted, and Gov. Colquitt introduced the New Jersey Chief Executive. Smilingly surveying the crowd until the applause subsided, Gov. Wilson, in pleasing manner, expressed his very great delight at finding himself in Dallas, adding that he had for a long time planned to visit Texas. He related a humorous story of a man who had told his father that instead of railroads they traveled on parallels of latitude in Texas. Gov. Wilson said that he had

---

[3] O'Keefe was assistant to the Mayor of Dallas and frequently served as sergeant-at-arms at local and state Democratic conventions.

[4] John Charles Robertson, lawyer of Dallas.

[5] William M. Holland, judge of the Dallas County Court, 1907-10, Mayor of Dallas, 1911-15; Walter T. Henderson, city auditor, 1908-11, commissioner of finance and revenue, 1911-15; Richard Runnells Nelms, water commissioner, 1911-15; Jubal Early Lee, commissioner of streets, elected in 1911; and Frederick W. Bartlett, police and fire commissioner, 1911-13.

[6] A real estate and insurance broker of Dallas. He managed the gubernatorial campaign of Oscar Branch Colquitt in 1906, was secretary of the state Democratic executive committee, 1910-1911, and served on Governor Colquitt's staff, 1911-13.

been denied the unique experience of traveling on parallels of latitude in Texas, but it gave him great pleasure to be in the State, just the same. He thanked the people who were so generous in their greeting, saying he felt at home here, having been born in the South and not having to have things explained to him here. This reference brought applause, and a minute later, as Gov. Wilson concluded, it being necessary for him to prepare to go to the First Baptist Church for his morning address, the band began to play "Dixie," and the cheering became intense.

Every moment of Gov. Wilson's time here was fully occupied. Crowds waited about the hotel, at the church and Coliseum wherever he appeared to shake his hands. He had scarcely a moment for rest. Because of these conditions he did not care to discuss in an interview any public questions other than those considered in his speech, but before leaving for Fort Worth last night expressed to newspaper men his favorable impression of Dallas, of the State Fair and of his sincere appreciation of the reception given him.

"No, I did not find a larger and busier city, a more prosperous and up-to-date section than I had expected here," he said in answer to a question. "Because, you see, although this is my first visit to Dallas and to Texas, I had expected much."

As the saying is, Gov. Wilson "takes a good picture." His appearance is almost exactly like the portraits of him with which almost everyone is now familiar. He wore a light tan felt hat yesterday, a dark overcoat and dark blue suit. Tall, wiry of build, yet without an indication of angularity, his appearance gives first an impression of an abundant store of energy. His handshake is firm and magnetic. His glance is piercing, but calm and kindly. His face is that of a student, but of a man of initiative, of action. He leaves the general impression of a man who can not be other than a leader.

Gov. Wilson's style of delivery is also characteristic. He speaks with the greatest fluency, never pausing for an expression, always, indeed, seeming to use the specific word. His gestures are always calm, but each seems to carry emphasis. His voice is always well modulated. He never seems to speak with effort, to shout, to exert himself, yet there is a convincingness about his utterance that could not come from much gesticulation or loud tone.

At the luncheon at the Oriental at 12:30 o'clock yesterday . . . Gov. Wilson received assurances from Congressman Henry,[7]

---

[7] Robert Lee Henry of Waco, Democratic congressman from 1897 to 1917.

former Gov. Campbell[8] and Cone Johnson,[9] in their speeches, that they were for him, and that they believed the people of Texas would support him.

Judge Cato Sells of Cleburne, who presided as toastmaster, introduced Gov. Wilson to those present with a high tribute and as "our honored guest, whom we all hope will be the next President of the United States."

Gov. Wilson, with the relation of an anecdote and in a slightly humorous vein, expostulated against the heaping of too many honors upon him in his introduction to the assembly.

Expressing his sincere pleasure at being present, Gov. Wilson said his only regret was that his meeting with these citizens became one of "touch and go." He had met so many men here during this day in Dallas whom he would like to know better, more closely. He had met men of whom he had heard, progressive men, men who represented all the better things in public and political life.

He told of the changes which had come over political affairs within the last ten years. Whereas, formerly political meetings were almost altogether partisan, and audiences came together in that spirit purely, to whoop it up for somebody, and with their minds already made up as to their course, whether the speakers' arguments held water or not, conditions were now changed. He now found audiences made up of all elements, of leaders of al[l] parties. Men today were ready to hear matters discussed upon their merits. They were ready to vote for men and measures, instead of blindly for parties.

He gave in substance his views expressed in his speech at the Coliseum with regard to there being little difference between some men who called themselves Republicans and himself, saying the Democratic party, by following the course of wisdom, could secure much of this progressive Republican vote.

It was in this connection that he declared his belief in the certain success of the Democratic party next year, because of the demand of the people for government by a progressive party, and because this could only be secured through the Democratic party.

He took occasion to refer to the editorial policy of New York newspapers, and declared that because of the lack of reliability

[8] Thomas Mitchell Campbell of Palestine, Governor of Texas, 1907-11. He helped to obtain passage of measures to strengthen the antitrust laws, to regulate lobbying and public utilities, for the abolition of the convict-lease system, and for pure food.

[9] Lawyer of Tyler, Tex.; a leading Wilson supporter at the Democratic national convention of 1912; Solicitor of the State Department, 1914-17.

of such utterances there was now no one who was really influenced by what any New York newspaper said editorially.

In elaborating upon his contention that big business is concerned only in its particular interests and not in the welfare of the people, Gov. Wilson cited the Aldrich monetary plan as an example.

"Aldrich's outfit went to Germany and brought back their proposition, which embraces the banking system of Germany," he said. "They did not take into consideration that conditions here are different nor that the system there is unsatisfactory. It would not be acceptable to the bankers themselves if they understood it." . . .

Immediately after the luncheon preparations were made for the trip to the grounds. The same carriage parade formation was observed that prevailed coming from the station in the morning. Upon reaching the Coliseum those in the Governor's party took seats upon the stage, and after the preliminary exercises Gov. Wilson spoke, as reported in full elsewhere in these columns.

At the conclusion of his speech Gov. Wilson was driven about the fair grounds, but this trip was necessarily of a hurried nature. He returned to the Oriental in time to get a few minutes' rest before proceeding to Fort Worth on the special interurban car, with the Fort Worth reception committee, which came over to escort him.

Printed in the *Dallas Morning News*, Oct. 29, 1911.

A News Report of a Religious Address in Dallas, Texas

[Oct. 29, 1911]

GOV. WILSON SPEAKS AT BAPTIST CHURCH

DELIVERS ADDRESS ON "LIFE AND THE BIBLE"
AT TERCENTENARY CELEBRATION.

Bishops, statesmen and laymen united in the exercises at the First Baptist Church yesterday morning when, with Gov. Woodrow Wilson of New Jersey as the chief speaker, there was celebration of the 300th anniversary of the translating of the Bible into the English tongue. Men who had come hundreds of miles from five States in the Southwest heard an expression of the need of intimacy between life and the Bible, as the Christian statesman and scholar portrayed the lesson. The attendance is said to have been about 5,000.

The exercises, under the direction of the American Bible Society, began at 10:30 o'clock. For about twenty minutes before that time, Gov. Wilson, in the parlors of the church, had met first the pastors of the city, the members of the Men and Religion Forward Movement[1] committee of one hundred and the Bible Society executive committee. Afterward he met as many others as could pass before him until the time for his address. His impression upon the people was pleasing and when he began to speak upon his chosen theme, there was ready and frequent response in applause to the homely truths beautifully expressed.

Bishop E. R. Hendrix of Kansas City, of the college of bishops in the Methodist Episcopal Church, South, and president of the Federation of Christian Churches of America,[2] presided. Dr. William M[adison]. Anderson, pastor of the First Presbyterian Church, delivered the invocatory prayer. Bishop Collins Denny[3] of Nashville, Tenn., led in the recital of the Apostles' Creed. Dr. Robert Stewart Hyer, president of the Southern Methodist University at Dallas, led in responsive reading of Psalm XIX, "The heavens declare the glory of God."

The prayer was said by Dr. George W. Ray, pastor of the First Congregational Church, Fort Worth. Dr. S[amuel]. P[almer]. Brooks, president of Baylor University, Waco, presented Dr. Wilson.

At the conclusion of the address and the closing song, Rev. James Thornton Lodge, rector of the Church of the Incarnation, Episcopal, pronounced the benediction. Bishop Alexander C[harles]. Garrett,[4] who was to have had part in the program, was unavoidably absent. . . .

Printed in the *Dallas Morning News*, Oct. 29, 1911; two editorial headings omitted.

[1] A Protestant ecumenical movement.

[2] The Rev. Dr. Eugene Russell Hendrix, president of the Federal Council of Churches of Christ in America and prolific author.

[3] Princeton 1876; professor of mental and moral philosophy, Vanderbilt University, 1891-1910; elected bishop of the Methodist Episcopal Church, South, in 1910.

[4] Bishop of the Episcopal Diocese of Dallas.

A News Report of an Address in Fort Worth, Texas

[Oct. 29, 1911]

WILSON PRAISES TEXAS FOR COMMISSION FORM

Given Pronounced Ovation in Fort Worth.

Fort Worth, Tex., Oct. 28.—An enthusiastic reception was accorded Hon. Woodrow Wilson, Governor of New Jersey, when he spoke here tonight. He was acclaimed as the Democratic chief of the Nation and the next President of the United States, and his speech was applauded vigorously. When he entered the hall he was given an ovation, and when he closed his address many pressed forward to shake his hand. Gov. Wilson complimented Texas and Galveston, which established the commission form of government for cities, which plan, in time, he said, would become known as the "American" form, and declaring Texas had been foremost in regulating railroads and corporations and other States owed her a debt of gratitude.

Gov. Wilson's speech was clear and forcible and interspersed with anecdotes which provoked laughter and illustrated his argument. The hour for the reunited Democratic party to serve the country, he said, had come. By the action of the minority[1] in Congress the people of the country are now saying that the Democrats had at last forgotten how to blunder. He predicted a great victory at the next National election.

An audience of about 1,000 people awaited the arrival of Gov. Woodrow Wilson at the City Hall auditorium. The decorations of the interior consisted of flags, bunting, potted palms, streamers and cut flowers, which almost concealed the walls and railing surrounding the rostrum. Above the speaker's stand were several streamers bearing the words, "Woodrow Wilson and United Democracy," "Woodrow Wilson, the Representative American," and above the front entrance of the City Hall was a placard containing the words "Woodrow Wilson, 1912." . . .

At 8:40 o'clock when Gov. Wilson entered the hall escorted by Judge William McLean,[2] Col. R. M. Wynne, State Railroad Commissioner Williams,[3] former State Insurance Commissioner T. B. Love, Rev. William Caldwell[4] and others, he was greeted with an ovation which lasted until the party was seated on the rostrum. . . .

A second ovation was given Gov. Wilson, who smiled blandly as he was presented to the audience. He said he was exceeding glad to be in Fort Worth. . . .

Printed in the *Dallas Morning News*, Oct. 29, 1911; some editorial headings omitted.

[1] He referred, curiously, to the Democrats. They controlled the House of Representatives. The Republicans technically controlled the Senate, but insurgent Republicans usually cooperated with the Democratic minority to form a majority.

[2] William Pinkney McLean, lawyer of Fort Worth; state legislator, 1861 and 1869; congressman, 1873-75; judge of the fifth judicial district, 1884; member of the state railroad commission, 1891-93.

[3] William D. Williams, city attorney of Fort Worth, 1897-1903; state legislator, 1903-1907; Mayor of Fort Worth, 1909; state railroad commissioner, 1909-16.

[4] Pastor of the First Presbyterian Church of Fort Worth, 1904-15.

From William Garrott Brown[1]

My dear Governor Wilson: Asheville, N. C., Oct. 30, 1911.

I am extremely loath to write to a man so admirably occupied as you are. But I have been wanting to write for more than a year, and I trust my reason for writing now will keep this letter from seeming impertinent.

As an editorial writer for Harper's weekly I have had the keenest pleasure in following Colonel Harvey's lead and helping to do what we could to support your fight in New Jersey and to get the country interested. An invalid these five years, working after [Robert Louis] Stevenson's fashion, in bed, I thank you heartily for much of the happiness I have recently found in my work. You have been a godsend to all of us who take our political writing seriously. I have also had a chance to help a little in other ways: at Lakewood[2] in 1909-10—Newman[3] was offish at first, but I believe he finally came around—in this state, and in Alabama, through influential friends and kinsmen. I think, by the way, you will find some of Oscar Underwood's most active supporters[4] anything but hostile to you. With Senator Johnston[5] working for Harmon and the anti-Bryan feeling making against you, there was fear of the outcome if only your name and Harmon's were to be considered.

Please don't misunderstand; this is merely to indicate the strong, even aggressive good-will in which I write, and to explain my deep concern about your stand on a particular question.

You have, I think, declared that monetary reform, the improvement of our financial system, is really our biggest public question. I fancy you will also agree that our trained economists have long felt our present system to be the worst reproach of all to our government and our public men.

Feeling that way, I turned from fighting Aldrich's tariff bill as hard as I could—that particular subject had been turned over to me entirely—and set to work to find out just what he and his monetary commission were doing and driving at. I got into cor-

[1] Historian and journalist, born and educated in Alabama; lecturer in American history, Harvard University, 1901-1902; sometime editorial writer for *Harper's Weekly* since 1908. Afflicted with tuberculosis, the cause of his death in 1913, he was at this time in St. Joseph's Sanitarium in Asheville, N. C.

[2] A resort town on Lake Carasaljo in Ocean County, N. J.

[3] That is, Harry Ellsworth Newman.

[4] The Underwood presidential campaign had recently begun as a favorite son movement in Alabama under the leadership of Tyler Goodwin, chairman of the state Democratic executive committee, and Senator John H. Bankhead. See Arthur S. Link, "The Underwood Presidential Movement of 1912," *Journal of Southern History*, XI (May 1945), 230-245.

[5] Joseph Forney Johnston of Birmingham, Governor of Alabama, 1896-1900, United States senator, 1907-13.

respondence with A. P. Andrew, who was then with Aldrich in the West, and he wired me to meet them both in New York, but as I was unwell Andrew came to me at Lakewood and we went over the matter very candidly indeed, not shirking in the least the question of Aldrich's disinterestedness and the country's fear that great selfish interests would control any establishment that might be set up. I arranged to have the commission send me proofs of all its publications, and gave them much study as they successively appeared. Later, I went to Washington and talked with Aldrich, who met my inquiries with unexpected frankness and directness—for instance, he told me just what had been J. P. Morgan's attitude, quoting his words; as I suspected, Morgan had shown instinctive hostility to the idea of a central bank. As Aldrich put it: "They think they can do it all themselves." I examined the commission's material and methods, have since watched its every step, and have studied the comments from all quarters.

My conclusions are: (1) that the commission's investigations have been thorough and pertinent, covering our own and the world's experience better than was ever done before; (2) that the two dangers, control by special interests and political control, have been steadily kept in mind, with intent to guard against them; (3) that the necessity of adapting any plan proposed to our own usages and our existing machinery, copying nothing outright, has been also steadily felt; and (4) that Aldrich is so completely bent on giving his name to a sound financial system, sound enough and scientific enough to last for ages, that we can safely disregard the not unnatural fear of his being the agent of selfish interests, certainly to the extent of considering the commission's proposals on their merits. Studying with this preparation the plan and its recent modifications, I believe it has the features essential to a sound system, that it is by far the best plan yet offered, and that it is infinitely preferable, *particularly in respect of the two dangers we all have had in mind,*[6] to our present system.

The OUTLOOK recently reported you as saying that you had not yet studied the plan or the subject fully enough to give a positive judgment.[7] I give you mine in the hope that you will treat it simply as the report of a man who has looked into the

[6] That is, control by the special interests, especially concentration of money power in Wall Street, and complete political control.
[7] He referred to Wilson's statement in the interview printed at Aug. 26, 1911: "I have not given sufficient study to the question. As it is the greatest question before the country to-day, it requires a great deal of consideration and involves wise and sound economic planning."

matter carefully and whom you may perhaps think at least sincere and fairly competent to study such a question intelligently. But I give it also, after reading a report of your Texas speech, in the earnest hope that you may decide to look into the matter more thoroughly for yourself before committing yourself any further in regard to it.

I fear I cannot make clear to you how much concern I really feel about the relation of this question to your leadership. I give you my word that from the very start of your political career I have been troubled with precisely this anxiety, and I believe I now speak for thousands of sincere men to whom your rise and your party's renascence have seemed to offer their first chance in many years—their first opportunity to take the aggressive for their political faith and ideals. In Cleveland's day, our hopes were wrecked by the free-silver blunder, and we feel that the party's greatest weakness and danger is still its proneness to go wrong on questions of finance. There is not a Democrat in Congress of proved competence to deal with such questions, and the country is full of men ready to appeal to prejudice and ignorance, to class and section, when such questions come up. Such questions are the severest test of a democracy. It is therefore peculiarly the duty of the country's trained minds to master them, and peculiarly incumbent upon the trained minds of the party to guard it against its most fatal weakness, against repeating its worst blunder, and thus give the country a chance to deal with its hardest problem dispassionately.

And never before was the party so amenable to warnings, so ready to be advised rather than run away with.

It is my deliberate judgment that you can at this moment do more in this matter for sound ideas and wise action than any other American—more than Taft or any other Republican, for it is clear that neither Republican faction can govern—and more than any other Democrat. I mean *now*—not soon. Without rising a step higher, you are in a position to keep your party from going wrong—or to set it wrong, hopelessly, irretrievably. As the leader of the Democratic Progressives, you can speak for caution and fairness, for a dispassionate and open-minded treatment of the whole issue, more effectively than any other Democratic leader except, possibly, Bryan—who of course will not. I believe, too, that that is precisely the wisest thing you could do, the best thing to win your support where you most need it, the best thing to win confidence for the party in quarters where it is distrusted. But I urge it rather as a duty, and freely confess I would urge it even if I thought it impolitic. It is your *courage*, Governor, that has made you really our leader. Your brilliant campaign, your eloquence and parts, would have won only our admiration if you had not proved yourself a fighter of the kind that, as Grant put it, fights his battles *through*. Do not, then, spare the patience and care and candor to master this money question and make us sure of your fairness and soundness on it—frankly, your reported speeches seem to me not only dangerous but unfair and unworthy of you—and let us follow you with the devotion we have so long held ready for a leader we could trust. Don't, we beg of you,—I will be old-fashioned and *implore* you—don't throw away what Cleveland kept, what Roosevelt lost—the confidence of men of your class. Don't, with Roosevelt's fall before you, take his view as to what kind of public opinion you should most consult. Don't underestimate the amount and the power of the quiet intelligence and independence to be found all over the country, which is far abler to sustain sound statesmanship than our public men suppose, which is making concessions to ignorance more and more unnecessary, which is working steadily such a tremendous decline of mere partisanship, which is at this moment anxiously studying the quality, and measuring the hope, of your stirring leadership.

And don't, I beg, do as Taft did recently, after inviting my advice about his Southern policy[8]—pat *me* on the back with a compliment, and disregard my advice. Take no account of me whatever, dismiss me as an annoying meddler, tell Colonel Harvey to make his young men stop bothering you, but consider what I have urged, deal with this troublesome issue as bravely and candidly as you did with machine-rule in New Jersey, and I will still be

Sincerely and confidently yours,

William Garrott Brown

P.S. I have no doubt Andrew would gladly accept a chance to go over the matter with you, and I will, if you like, undertake to arrange an interview. And can you not also talk it over with men like Seligman, of Columbia,[9] who have looked into it as carefully as I have, and far more competent.

Sincerely yours,   W. G. B.

TLS (Governors' Files, Nj).

[8] About this, see n. 2 to the notes for an address printed at Jan. 25, 1909, Vol. 19.

[9] Edwin Robert Anderson Seligman, McVickar Professor of Economics at Columbia, an old friend of Wilson.

A News Report of a Speech in Little Rock, Arkansas

[Oct. 31, 1911]

ARKANSAS IN WILSON LINE

ST. LOUIS, Oct. 31.—There is every evidence that Governor Woodrow Wilson is as popular in Arkansas as in Texas. The enthusiasm shown by the Democrats in the Lone Star State was paralleled wherever the Governor stopped in Arkansas on his homeward trip.

While on his way to Texas the Governor accepted an invitation to speak from the train at Little Rock. The scheduled time was 8:10 P.M., but when the Iron Mountain's, mistakenly-named "Cannon Ball Express," neared Little Rock, the train was more than three hours behind schedule. At each station, however, there was a telegram assuring Governor Wilson that though hundreds of persons had gone home a substantial audience was awaiting him.

The reception took on an atmosphere of extreme significance. At Benton a reception committee of a dozen of the leading citizens of Little Rock got on the Governor's train. There was immediately an enthusiastic promise that Arkansas would give almost unanimous support to Governor Wilson.

In this party were Secretary of State Earl W[illiam]. Hodges, State Treasurer J[ohn]. W[esley]. Crockett (a grandson of the famous "Davy" Crockett), State Superintendent of Education George W. [B.] Cook, State Senator Lee Miles and J. A. Harrod, president of the Wilson Club of Little Rock.

United States Senator [James Paul] Clark[e] started out with the party, but was taken with an attack of vertigo and had to return to his home after reaching Benton. Senator Clark is reckoned among the Wilson supporters.

United States Senator "Jeff" Davis[1] is also lined up with the Wilson forces. In an interview last week he declared in characteristic fashion that "a man who was not for Governor Wilson was a fool."

Arriving at Little Rock, the Governor was heartily welcomed by Mayor Charles E. Taylor, Democratic State Chairman [Rufus Franklin] Milwee and State Auditor John R. Job[e]. He was escorted quickly upstairs to the street level platform, where, mounted on a box, he was introduced by Judge George L. Basham, a wealthy planter.

The Governor made a stirring speech, declaring that the people of America are getting ready to take back to themselves their lost liberties.

Considerable amusement was expressed by the Wilson leaders over the fact that importance had been attached outside the State to a statement made a few days ago by National Committeeman Guy B. Tucker that he was for Harmon. As an indication of Tucker's real position in Arkansas it was pointed out that at the last election he was easily defeated for secretary of State.

The Wilson leaders are planning to petition the State central committee that at the State primaries, to be held in March, the names of all the Presidential candidates be placed on the ballot in order that the voters may thus give instructions to their delegation to the national convention. If this course is followed, they say, Wilson will sweep the State. The candidacy of Champ Clark is not regarded seriously and the Arkansans believe that when the time comes he will not be a candidate.[2]

Printed in the *Newark Evening News*, Oct. 31, 1911; some editorial headings omitted.
[1] Jeff Davis was his real name.
[2] An optimistic prediction. The state Democratic convention, on June 5, 1912, instructed the state's delegation to the national convention to vote for Clark.

To John Wesley Wescott

My dear Judge Westcott: [Trenton, N. J.] October 31, 1911.

I have read your letter of October twenty-fifth,[1] which came during my absence, with concern and distress. I need not assure you that absolutely nothing was in my mind or purpose which questioned your loyalty or your absolute devotion to the cause for one moment, or the loyalty and devotion of any one of the gentlemen who were present that afternoon.

I hope that you will not allow yourself to be distressed by things that are said and done by persons evidently determined to produce mischief by one process or another. They are apparently as indifferent to my reputation as to yours, for I certainly would not be guilty of anything such as they have ascribed to me. I knew all along the attitude of all of you. I did not question for a moment, but I felt it my duty as the leader of the party to have a conference in which I assured myself by personal contact with everybody concerned that everything was being done that could possibly be done to secure the success of the ticket in Camden, where there seems to me more than a fighting chance that we should win out.

I cannot tell you how personal intricacies and misrepresentations and jealousies of politics sometimes distress me. My only comfort is that my own thought is clear, my own motives disengaged from this turmoil of petty things. I know that you have been temporarily annoyed, but I know that you have a big soul like most of the men I have been dealing with in the group you refer to, and that you will not allow these things to ruffle more than the surface of your mind. You and I understand one another perfectly and I pray God there may never be anything to alter the absolute confidence we feel in one another.

Cordially and faithfully yours,   Woodrow Wilson

TLS (J. W. Wescott Coll., NjP).
  1 It is missing.

A News Report

[Nov. 1, 1911]

GOVERNOR'S SCRUPLES SILENCED BY ACTION OF TEXAS PREACHERS

The spectacle of New Jersey's Governor perched on a stool in a quick lunchroom in the depot at Texarkana eating "ham and" with gusto, gave gaping residents of that village much amusement while Governor Woodrow Wilson was en route from Dallas to St. Louis last Sunday.

The Governor made this particular part of his trip over the Iron Mountain road on an express called the "Cannon Ball." The train left Dallas at 8:40 A.M. and persistently lost time all the way. A diner was to have been attached to the train at Texarkana, but instead, the conductor walked through the train, scratching his head in a dazed sort of a way and announced that the diner had failed to show up and that passengers would be allowed twenty minutes for supper.

On the way to Texarkana Governor Wilson did some Sunday campaigning that was not down on the program. When the train rolled into Longview, Tex., the Governor was enjoying a quiet snooze in his drawing-room. When the train stopped cheers could be heard outside, and then Mayor G. A. Bodenheim, who used to be a Congressman,1 entered the car and asked the Governor to speak. The Governor, with sleep still in his eyes and with rumpled hair, started out.

On the platform, he found 300 enthusiastic Texans, who needed no urging to join in the proposal of Mayor Bodenheim that there be three cheers for the next President of the United States.

When he got back on the train the Governor expressed some doubts as to the propriety of making political speeches on Sunday. His scruples disappeared, however, when, at Marshall, the next stop, he was called on for a speech by another big audience, headed by Rev. C. C. Kramer, rector of Trinity Episcopal Church, and Rev. Dr. [William Thomas] Tardy, of the Baptist church.

The two clergymen told the Governor, with a show of pride, that they had "got up" the reception. There were lusty shouts, led by the ministers, when the "next President" formula of introduction was again used.

At Texarkana Governor Wilson took enough time from his meal period to make a little speech to the crowd gathered there.

"I am opposed to the phrase 'square deal,'" he said, "because it seems to imply that there is some one person or some one interest that has the right to deal out the cards. As a matter of fact, we do our own dealing and the cards must all be face up on the table."

At Marshall a railway mail clerk handed Governor Wilson a slip of paper, reading as follows: "Forty-one postal clerks on this line stand: Wilson, 39; Harmon, 2."

Printed in the *Newark Evening News*, Nov. 1, 1911.
1 Bodenheim was never in Congress.

To Joseph Hodges Choate

My dear Mr. Choate: [Trenton, N. J.] November 1, 1911.

I am of course deeply interested in what you tell me of the plans of the National Citizens Committee with regard to stimulating interest in the general arbitration treaties with France and Great Brittain,[1] and wish with all my heart that the season during which they have planned to have mass meetings were one in which I was at liberty to co-operate. Unhappily I am absolutely tied by the leg by engagements which I cannot honorably withdraw from. I can only express my deep appreciation that you should have thought of me in this connection and should have taken for granted my deep interest in the movement.

Cordially and sincerely yours,   Woodrow Wilson

TLS (J. H. Choate Papers, DLC).
1 About these treaties, see A. Carnegie to WW, March 21, 1911, n. 1, Vol. 22.

A News Report of a Campaign Speech at Glassboro, New Jersey

[Nov. 1, 1911]

GOVERNOR HITS SHERMAN VISIT

Browning Also Target for Wilson in Speech To-day
at Glassboro.

GLASSBORO, Nov. 1.—Governor Wilson, the first Governor who has spoken in Glassboro in more than 100 years, held the Republican leaders of the First Congregational [Congressional] District up to scorn in an address at the auditorium here this afternoon.

The Governor attacked the Republicans for their failure to see the kind of speakers they are securing to speak for their candidate, William J. Browning.

Particularly the Governor ridiculed the Republicans for bringing into the campaign Vice-President James S. Sherman. He said:

"If I were the manager of the Republican campaign in this district I would honestly suggest that someone else be sent for to support Mr. Browning. If they saw anything of the signs of the times they would at least make believe that they wanted to be progressive Republicans, but I don't suppose they could get a Progressive to come down here and speak for Mr. Browning.

["]Mr. Browning could not make himself look like a Progressive if he tried, so they have to send for the most notorious standpatter in the United States.

"I understand they have sent for Mr. Sherman, Vice-President of the United States. He is a stand pattern of stand patterns. He is the model they keep in their shop. He is the thing they trim by when they make standpat candidates.

"They are doing the same thing that fools some of us again and again. They are fooling us about protection. The kind of protection they stand for lines the pockets of a little group of men and doesn't distribute itself among the people.

"The American people have waked up. They are not going to kindergarten any more. I understand that a certain suit of clothes has been prepared for exhibition in this district. It is to cost—well, let's say $2.50. I'd like them to conduct an exhibition of working men to the place where such suits can be bought for $2.50.

"I'd like to say to them that this kindergarten business of appearing in a suit of clothes isn't going to fool anybody. Every workman knows that these people have not distributed their gains except as they have been forced to, step by step, through the unions.

"We know who these gentlemen have been working for. Let us have done with pretense. The jig is up. The game is called."

Printed in the *Newark Evening News*, Nov. 1, 1911; one editorial heading omitted.

A News Report of a Campaign Address
in Atlantic City, New Jersey

[Nov. 2, 1911]

GOVERNOR LASHES THE PLUNDERERS OF COUNTY

Terrific Arraignment Of The Band
That Controls The Community

HANDFUL OF CROOKS GOVERN

In tones that trembled at times with indignation and words that stung like a whip lash, Governor Wilson, in one of the most masterly orastorial [oratorical] efforts of his career, paid his respects last night at the Apollo Theatre to what he termed the "plunderers" who have held control of the government of Atlantic City and County for so many years.

Before him as he arose to administer the castigation so well deserved, stretched a sea of faces that filled the theatre from pit to dome, and the thunderous applause that greeted his many telling points could be accepted only as positive proof that his hearers were entirely in accord with the sentiments he expressed, and that they had at length become aroused to the gravity of the situation and were ready to apply the remedy suggested by their Chief Executive.

It was in every way the most remarkable gathering ever held in the resort. In the vast throng that had gathered, there were some who hoped that the Governor would "cut loose" and handle the local situation without gloves.[1]

That he would from his opening sentence, however, place the "Machine" leaders and their henchmen on the grill and cause them to twist in torture over the heat of his burning eloquence, was as unexpected as it was pleasing to those interested in the cause of good government, and even those who came with idle curiosity hung on his every word from the time he commenced his powerful arraignment of the deplorable conditions existing here, until he concluded with a peroration that brought his hearers, cheering madly, to their feet.

Governor Wilson had arrived in the city late yesterday afternoon, and with the members of his party went direct from the station to the Hotel Traymore, where he was the guest of

[1] The mayoralty candidate of the Republican Kuehnle machine, Harry Bacharach, was opposed by Daniel S. White, a Republican running on a fusion ticket of reform Republicans and Democrats. Vying for the office of sheriff were Robert H. Ingersoll, Republican, and William B. Loudenslager, a Democrat on the fusion ticket. For the Assembly seats, Carlton Godfrey and Emerson Richards, Republicans, opposed Joseph Thompson and John T. French, Democrats and fusionists.

Daniel S. White, Fusion candidate for mayor. He entered the theatre shortly after 8 o'clock and from the time he entered the door until he had taken his seat on the stage he was given a continual ovation, the vast audience arising en-mas[s]e and cheering madly. Mr. White entered a moment later, and he, too, was given a rousing reception. Little time was lost in the preliminaries, Louis A. Repetto, the chairman of the Democratic County Committee, introducing William B. Loudenslager, Fusion candidate for Sheriff, as chairman of the meeting.

Governor Wilson was the second speaker, following Dudley Guild Malone, assistant Corporation Counsel of New York City, who has been touring the country with the Governor. There was an enthusiastic outburst from the audience as the Governor uttered his opening words.

"Mr. Chairman[2] and Fellow Citizens: What do you think of the government of Atlantic City?

(Voices) "Rotten!"

"I don't want you to tell us out loud. You might be indicted. Men have not dared to avow their real opinion in Atlantic County; men have known what awaited them in their business, in their personal relationship, if they dared avow the things they really thought.

"As I have stood here tonight and looked into your faces I have wondered how it feels to live under a reign of terror. How does it feel? How does your selfrespect fare in the circumstances? Atlantic City is famous all over the United States and over a greater part of the world for its charm and for its shame. A city with unequaled natural advantages; the Mecca of those who seek pleasure; a place of resort for all those who seek companionable hours with kindred spirits like yourselves; a place to which all the continent comes and of which all the continent thinks with condescension and with pity because you have submitted—you have not done the thing; you have stood cowed and submissive and seen the thing done.

"You are my fellow-countrymen; you are men like myself; you are men like other men in New Jersey. Why is it that here, and here only, men like yourselves have permitted such things to exist for a single twelve-month? I have come to challenge you to self-consciousness. Have you been asleep? Have you not known it? Have you not felt the shame of it?

"Mr. Malone said, more truly perhaps than he realized, that this is not a partisan meeting. This is not a partisan contest, for we do not fight against parties. The men who have done these

<hr />

2 Loudenslager.

things in New Jersey are not partisans, they are not Republicans; those who have co-operated with them and called themselves by another name are not Democrats. They are nothing except lawless plunderers. They know that they have no party claims to your sup[p]ort; they know that the only hold they have upon you is the hold of self-interest so far as they have been able to tie you to themselves, and to fear, so far as they have been able to put you in awe of them.

"Who are supporting the candidates of these gentlemen? Who are supporting the opponents of the candidates put up by these gentlemen? You don't need me to come and tell you what all New Jersey knows. Who are the gamblers supporting? (A Voice: Harry Bacharach) Whom do the men support who are living by the daily bread of the commonwealth of New Jersey? They are supporting the candidates proposed by this gang, that is all. Neither party except the party of those who seek to line their own pockets and increase their own power.

"Partisan indeed! I have come here to summon you to support the men whom honest and independent men are sup[p]orting. I do not have to point them out to you. You know them: and you also know that there are some among you who do not dare say that you are supporting them.

"I have privately tested many a gentleman in New Jersey by suggesting that he be requested to sit on the platform, and I have made up my mind not to consort with or call myself a fellow-partisan to any man who is afraid of anybody. My utter and ultimate and final contempt is for the public coward. And yet I check myself in the very impulse of contempt because I know how some of my fellow-citizens are situated. I know perfectly well that if they exercise the least degree of political independence in a legitimate undertaking they may have the bread and butter taken out of the mouths of those whom they love, and who are dependent upon them. I do not blame these men; I do not know how my heart could stand the strain of that temptation.

"I can only thank God that I have never been in such a situation as to be subjected to it. But I do know this; that my chief interest in the new form of voting is that it has set these men at liberty. They are now able to choose whom they will support, and no man shall know what their choice was.

"For the first time in the history of New Jersey in our day, the men of Atlantic County, great and humble, of high degree and of low degree, are free. How will you exercise your freedom? No man can challenge your right to go into the polling places and pick out whom you will vote for upon a ballot which any free man might rejoice to vote, where he will exercise his absolute independence and call himself his own master once more.

"I tell you, my fellow-countrymen, if there is nothing else in my political career, I shall always be just a little happier because I had some part in establishing this freedom for my fellow-citizens of New Jersey.

"I now can look, not as I used to look upon some humble fellow-citizen going to the polls, with sympathy, but with an honorable feeling of comradeship that a man feels for everybody else, of the man looking everybody in the eye, keeping his own counsels and going and expressing his own judgement, which lies nearer to his heart not only, but nearer to the life of the community in which he lives; a man who can serve his country in the fear only of God.

"That is the reason why I asked you what you think of the government of Atlantic County, and I invite you to tell me on the seventh of November—not tonight; there are policemen at the door, and they would lay their hands on me if they dared, because I have come here and told you what you know, but, perhaps, would not like to stand on this stage and say it. It is not a question of party politics, it is a question of emancipation from everything that is disgraceful and rotten.

"Now what I want to point out to you is that the processes by which the opponents of these gentlemen have been nominated for office have been free processes and not closed processes. The comrades of these gentlemen, for they have comrades elsewhere, have all done the same thing; they have chosen their tickets, as usual, in private, whereas their opponents have chosen their ticket in public; where you have this choice to make—are you going to follow leaders that are free, or are you going to follow leaders that are bound to special interests?

"There are leaders in New Jersey who are free. To my mind it doesn't make any difference whether you call yourselves Democrats or Republicans; the question is whether you call yourselves free or enslaved, whether you are trying to the best of your ability to serve yourselves, or whether you are serving somebody else, some master whom you dare not fight. Some of your candidates have made the assertion, I am told, that if they are elected—I state this merely by way of illustration—that if they are elected contracts will be freely awarded in open competition. They will be, will they? How have they been awarded hitherto? Do these gentlemen not know the meaning of the English language? Do they not know that by that very promise they are convicting themselves? Who have ruled you but these gentlemen? And they are promising you in fact that they will not hereafter put up jobs on you; that if you will only endorse them once more, they will come out and do what it was always their sworn duty to do. A more open—perhaps I ought to say a more unconscious—confession of Judgment I have yet to hear. They who have been governing you will in the future make the awarding of contracts an honest, open competition. I do not need to be told how they have awarded contracts in the past, but I am surprised to be told it by their own lips. How unconsciously they involve themselves; how inevitable it is that whenever they make you a promise they also make you a confession.

"And so, from day to day, by the mouths of the men themselves, you are hearing such arguments as ought to convince these who hitherto have been deaf to reason, that there is only one way to emancipate Atlantic City and Atlantic County, and that is to take a clean slate and begin all over.

"And you have to, ladies and gentlemen. You have fine people, you have people of unimpeachable life, you have men of honor, you have men of established reputation, you have men of big and honorable business, you have men of pure private life crowding the streets of Atlantic City and the country visitas [vistas] of Atlantic County, all of them walking like driven sheep under the grip of the management of a little group of men from whose domination they could escape with but the slightest assertion of independence. A handful of men against a population. A body of crooks against a great self-respecting population! The thing is incredible! If it wasn't so I wouldn't believe it.

"I remember when, years ago, somebody described to me the conditions of Atlantic City and of Atlantic County, I refused to believe it, because they have existed for a great many years, but the accumulation of evidence, the insight I have had of the inside local politics of this State, the evidence of legislative committees, the evidence that comes up whether you have asked for it or not, has overwhelmed all my incredulity, and I am sorry to have to admit what I used to consider an impossibility.

"A great many things that we find out to be true, that we can prove, are incredible, and I believe that all that it is necessary to do is to awaken you to the fact that it is intrinsically incredible and fundamentally impossible to have you put an end to it by the very silent and peaceful method of your voting at the polls. No bloodshed; no disorder; simply insisting upon it, that the law be enforced as it is, and then letting the results speak for themselves on the morning after election. And the law must be enforced. I stand here not merely as the titular leader of the Democratic party in New Jersey, but as the Governor of the Commonwealth, and say that by every means in my power I shall see to it that every public officer is held to his duty.

"One of the painful things about being Governor of New Jersey is that when you become Governor you are made to take a solemn oath to see that the laws of the State are enforced, and that then you find that you have not been given the adequate means of carrying out the promise. But there is one means which I possess and shall use to the uttermost. I can find out about things and I can proclaim them from the housetops. Any gentleman who is a candidate to have his name gibbetted knows how to apply.

"This is as solemn a business as grown men could be concerned in, it is the business of caring for the integrity of the community and the people. A man who would spare words about such a matter does not know how deep his duty lies. A man who would spare action in such a matter does not know what tribute his conscience will exact of him when he goes to his last reckoning, because men of high ideals do not figure in politics for the temporary satisfaction of office. They know that there is a last reckoning, with themselves, even if they don't believe in another world; a last reckoning with themselves which is the most terrible ordeal of fire that a man can risk. And I say, because I am Governor of the State, as well as one of those who are attempting to guide a great party, that nothing must be omitted which will see to it that our politics are cleared of those who debauch them.

"And the truth is a terrible whip. Only draw the whip from under your coat and see the dogs slink! There is nothing more terrible than an accusing conscience. There is nothing more formidable than an argument hurled at men who know that it is true, and all that we need in the State of New Jersey is the men to say what they know, and tell the truth as they have learned it, and always square what they do with what they know.

"It is a high ideal, but it is the ideal to which the human race has been struggling by painful stages ever since liberty was first proclaimed to a hopeful world. They are standards which America once set up and established once and forever in the field of political life; they are standards by which American communities are judged and honored or dishonored; they are standards by which American communities can contribute their part to the making of an immortal character. No man need be proud of being an American because America is rich. There have be[e]n many rich nations in the world, ladies and gentlemen; there have been nations much richer than the United States in proportion to the standards of their times; there have been nations that dominated the known civilized world at the very moment when they were at such a stage of decay that in after ages honorable men blushed as they wrote their epitaphs. Honorable men read these records of physical triumph as the deepest condemnation that could be uttered against people who use their power, not for humanity and not for justice, but merely for the exercise of sovereignty over their fellow men.

"America was established to do away with the sovereignty of wealth—not to do away with wealth, because nations subsist upon that, as their sustenance, but to do away with the selfish use of wealth; to do away with that thing which lies at the heart of your whole problem in Atlantic City. For what word is the centre of your disease? The word is the word 'contract.' The centre of your disease is that your taxes are used to enrich those who may or may not have rendered you the service they contracted to render you. You are not exploited for any kind of glory, you are exploited for the money there is in it. The least of all motives is the motive of government amongst honorable men in thriving American communities. And so America is selling her heritage for a mess of pottage. All the world is turning to America and saying: 'Is it true that you have come to such a pass that you let men rule you for the sake of the profit there is in it? Is it true that you let men rule you in behalf of special interests which are not your interests but only theirs? Is it possible that the boasts uttered so proudly in the time of setting up of your great republic have given away to these confessions? Is it possible that men may rule you and not love you; that men may rule you as those who would consume you and not as those who would serve you; have the standards of your life come to that?[']

"Ah, gentlemen, do not leave this hall thinking the issues of Atlantic County are merely the issues of Atlantic County. Do not forget that you are Americans; do not forget that America's character is in your ke[e]ping; do not forget that the vindication of American institutions is in your keeping; do not forget that every time you vote you pull down or exalt the name of a great country. Let these things fill your minds as with a sort of divine afflatus, so that you may go out transformed from the image of those who slink about in fear to keep out of trouble into the image of those who carry themselves erect, and come what may, men will die facing their God as honest men.

"I could not exaggerate the feeling of solemnity with which I face an audience like this. You do not constitute the voters of Atlantic County; you are only a fraction of them, but you represent them, and in speaking to you I am speaking to men who are the only men, they and those whom they represent, who can emancipate this great and beautiful county from the conditions under which she has lived. You are the men who are responsible; you are the men whose happiness will be affected; you are the men whose honor is involved, and I have come to you as the Governor of the State to challenge you to show what sort of Jerseymen you are.

"The rest of New Jersey is throwing off the yoke, not the yoke of party, but the yoke of those who misuse the name of party; not the yoke of party principle, but the yoke of those who exploit parties for their own interests. The rest of New Jersey is throwing off the yoke. Will you bend your necks to it? Will you not see to it—men of all sorts and creeds and colors—will you not see to it that you tie yourselves to the sum total of American manhood? For what I am asking you to do is something which you tan [can] take or leave. I know the choice that the rest of New Jersey is going to make—almost all of the rest of New Jersey—and I know the choice that the rest of Amerisa [America] is going to make. Will you come into the procession, or won't you?

(Voices from various parts of the hall: "Yes, yes, yes.")[3]

"We will miss you sadly if you don't come, for you are good fellows, but the procession will go on just the same. We will say, 'too bad; old Atlantic did not fall in, but we cannot stop the proceedings on her account.'

"She will come in some day when she gets a little older, when she spends a little more money for nothing; when she has humbled herself a little more before those who are plundering her; then some day she will wake up and wonder why she was such a fool to sleep so long.

"For the stuff is in you. The question is whether you are going to say at this time or some other time. It will come. It is rising in you. I remember once saying of a college sophomome [sophomore] that the sap of manhood was rising in him but it had not

[3] All the regular Republican candidates were victorious, but Republican majorities were greatly reduced from earlier years. For example, in the previous shrievalty election—that of 1908—the Republican received 8,838 votes to the Democrat's 4,473. In the race in 1911, Ingersoll received 7,412 votes to Loudenslager's 5,340. In the Assembly election of 1910, the Republican candidate won 10,313, the Democrat, 4,745. In the Assembly race of 1911, Godfrey's vote was 7,383, Richards', 6,681; Thompson received 4,835 votes, French, 4,556. In the mayoralty race, Bacharach received 4,958 votes, White, 3,671.

yet reached his head. Now it may be that Atlantic County is in a soporific condition, but the sap is rising in you, and some day it will get to your head.

"I hope that that day will be soon; I hope that it will fully have reached your head and flooded your intelligence by the seventh of November.

"I did not come here to make a partisan speech. The Democratic party is ready to lead you in a house-cleaning. The Democratic party is ready and is free to do the things that ought to be done for New Jersey, while apparently, to judge by the leaders to which it submits, the Republican party is not free and is not ready, and, therefore, for the time being, without any boasting of the past or predicting for the future, I say that the Democratic party can 'do the trick' for you. But that is not partisan, for I am willing to admit that that may be temporary. Those are the circumstances, and everybody familiar with the facts knows that those are the circumstances; therefore, I am acquitted of all partisan intention in coming here; I am acquitted of everything except the performance of what I regarded as my bounden duty when I came and solicited your suffrages a year ago[.] You did not give them to me in any very great abundance (A Voice: 'We didn't have the chance')—but I came and solicited them, and many of you honored me by voting for me; and I promised those who voted for me, as I promised those who did not vote for me, that I would come back here and tell you what I thought of your own affairs; because that is my instrument of warfare—what I know and what I can say; and, therefore, I have fulfilled my duty with as much frankness and simplicity as I could gather; but I would not fulfill it and be seated without once more trying to put before your minds a vision of what it is that we are engaged in.

"Gentlemen, life—physical life—is not of much consequences; it does not last long; we are all presently to go out of this fitful and feverish game of life; we are mere items; we are one generation in a long line of generations that stretches away back of us and can be seen in ghostly outline down the slopes of the future; we are mere items in regaining the universal history of the Republic. But I would like to be part of an item that shone with a little glory, with a little luminance.

(A voice: "You will.")

"I would like men in future generations to say 'That was a generation that settled the interests of America, a generation that sought to serve them, that had a vision of them, that did what it could in the time allotted it, to set forth that great battle against wrong which must be waged until the day of judgment.['] I would like to know that we could never be accused of letting American liberty slip back a single pace. I would like it to be said of us in the days to come, 'They took their turn in the great movement of human liberty, they set the signs and signals; they set the channels of the great army of free men a little forward toward that day of full fruition when men shall look each other in the face and recognize each other as brothers and as equals.[']"

Printed in the *Atlantic City Review*, Nov. 2, 1911; one editorial heading omitted.

A News Report of Four Campaign Speeches in South Jersey

[Nov. 3, 1911]

WILSON QUOTES SUGAR SENATOR

How Trust Was Rewarded for Liberal Contributions
to Party Funds.

MILLVILLE, Nov. 3.—Governor Woodrow Wilson told here last night of a certain former Democratic United States Senator from New Jersey,[1] who had confided to the Governor his views on the obligation a politician is under to the men who furnish his campaign funds.

The Governor was telling how the new corrupt practises act will eliminate corrupt money from New Jersey politics. He went on:

"Why, a certain Democrat, who was once the United States Senator from New Jersey, once told me without any apparent appearance of shame that he had collected funds for the national Democratic committee, and that a large portion of these funds came from a central group of men connected with the Sugar Trust.

"He said he had felt it to be the duty under the circumstances to see that not a cent more of duty was placed on sugar."

That a great political awakening is taking place in South Jersey took on new manifestation yesterday all along the Governor's itinerary. At Pleasantville, in Atlantic County, and in Vineland, Bridgeton and Millville, in Cumberland County, the Governor talked to large and enthusiastic audiences. In Cumberland, as in all the other counties of the State, the meetings resolved them-

[1] James Smith, Jr.

selves into pandemonium when some one suggested that Governor Wilson be the next President of the United States

The Governor reached Pleasantville at 11:30 in the morning. There was a band at the station waiting for him. Also there was a group of boys and a group of girls. Each group carried a large American flag, and joined in the procession which escorted Governor Wilson to the moving picture theatre. The theatre was crowded, and old-time politicians declared they had never seen such an outpouring of citizens for a political meeting at such an unusual hour. Rev. E[dward]. J. [A.] Wells, of the Wesley Methodist Church, presided.

By a strange coincidence, when the meeting was at its height, the village firebell, which is located just across the street from the theatre, began to ring a merry tune. A few children, thinking it was the school bell, left the theatre, but the meeting was almost undisturbed. A few minutes later the firebell sent out another round of wild peals. This also failed to break up the meeting.

Inquiry after the meeting brought out the information that there was a fire "way out in the country." But the citizens of Pleasantville merely shook their heads and declared that the ringing of the firebell and the holding of Democratic campaign meetings had occurred at identically the same moment too many times to fool anybody.

The Governor in his address pointed out that he had no power under the State law to remove a prosecutor or a sheriff who refuses to do his duty.

"You have arranged things so in the State of New Jersey," he said, "that no one can save you but yourselves. I don't know that I am sorry. Nothing takes strength so from a people as to be taken care of. It is for you people to say whether you want to continue to live under the kind of government you have in Atlantic County. You have to live under it; I don't, thank God. I'd probably get indicted in a week if I did."

Rev. Mr. Wells made a few comments on the county's politics and referred to the grand juries of the past as the "quarterly meeting of the perjury society."

At Vineland, at 3:30 in the afternoon, the Governor spoke to another packed house. The meeting was held in Mystic Chain Hall. In the front rows sat a score of veterans from the Soldiers' Home.

Almost at the outset, Governor Wilson addressed these veterans with reference to an article that appeared in the Republican papers of Camden several weeks ago, setting forth that the Governor, on a recent visit to the Soldiers' Home, had insulted the veterans by ignoring them.[2]

"I am particularly complimented," he said, "by the presence of the venerable soldiers to my right. After my visit here a few months ago a slander was circulated about it. It was said—and nothing could have distressed me more—that I had been discourteous in some way to the old soldiers of the Union when I visited the Old Soldiers' Home here.

"I am sure everyone that was there will exonerate me from that charge. I usually do not take any notice of a lie, for a lie dies of its own disease, and if these gentlemen had not been present I would not have referred to the matter. I refer to it for the sake of giving myself the pleasure of paying the tribute which I, as a Southerner, can pay to the soldiers of the Union.

"I know, as well as any man living knows, that this emblem upon which my hand rests (the flag), is the emblem of the Union, not only, but of its happiness. All men upon whichever side of the struggle they may have been engaged now recognize that the happy issue of the contest was an issue of Divine Providence, saving to the nation its noble history. I would be the last one to lose respect and veneration for those who fought for their country to save it."

The Governor expressed the opinion that the next Legislature would be Democratic.

"I believe we are going to have a safe Democratic majority in both houses," he said. "I believe this, because the Democrats have done the things they promised. The Republicans could have done these things any time in the past sixteen years, but they failed to do them. Had they done them they might have remained at the head of the State government for the next generation.

"What Cumberland does will make no difference with the general result. We shall win without her. But when I pick up the returns next Wednesday morning I hope that I will find that old Cumberland has said, 'Go ahead.' "[3]

At Bridgeton, in the evening, the theatre contained what the manager of the house described as the greatest crowd that it had

[2] "Why Did Governor Wilson Snub the Old Soldiers and Their Wives?" Camden *Daily Courier*, Oct. 5, 1911, alleged that Wilson, during his visit to Vineland on August 25, 1911, alighted from his automobile without acknowledging the presence of the veterans who were lined up in military order to greet him. Moreover, the story went on, when asked to speak to the veterans, Wilson replied that he had nothing to say to them. Finally, the article implied that Wilson's actions stemmed from his southern origins and urged those who wore the blue and their kin to vote against men like Wilson in November.

[3] In the Assembly race, Albert R. McAllister of Bridgeton, Republican, won over J. Howard Vail of Millville, Democrat. Harry J. Garrison, Democrat, was elected sheriff over the Republican, Joshua Cassaboom.

ever contained. Many persons failed to get in. The front seats and the boxes were occupied by women. County Chairman George Ebner[4] presided.

"I am here to talk to you about the Assembly," said Governor Wilson. "I do not conceive it to be any of the Governor's business to go around and advocate the election of local officials, though I am very proud of the appointment I made of sheriff in this county. But, as Governor, I am here to suggest that I do not enjoy playing the game by myself, and I want to know if you men of Cumberland are going to take part in leaving me high and dry.

"Here you have the captain of the team; the team has played the game, and won the game. Now, do you want to shelve the captain, and have him sit on the players' bench, and let another team, without any captain, play it? Do you want them to go in and decide the new game should go back to the old rules? They will go back to the old rules, for the managers of the team, the umpires and everybody concerned with the business, could not play the game if they tried."

From Bridgeton the Governor was hurried in an auto through the cold night to Millville. Here there was the same old story—a crowded theatre and an enthusiastic audience. Mark Branin[5] was in the chair. Eckard P. Budd spoke until the Governor's arrival.

Printed in the *Newark Evening News*, Nov. 3, 1911; some editorial headings omitted.

[4] A lawyer of Bridgeton.
[5] A glass blower of Millville.

A News Report

[Nov. 4, 1911]

WILSON VISITS OLD SOLDIERS

Governor Woodrow Wilson paid a visit to the Soldiers' Home, at Kearny, yesterday afternoon, just in time to take part in the ceremony of lowering the colors, as the sun went down.

The Governor was the first Chief Executive of the State who has visited the home during his term of office. The old veterans seemed to appreciate his visit and when the hour for lowering the colors came, every man in the home who was able to get there was standing in the ranks, drawn up before the home of the commandant, General E. Burd Grubb.

There was a deep impressiveness in the scene as the bugler slowly sounded the tattoo and the colors came down. With uncovered heads, Governor Wilson, General Grubb, the veterans and every visitor paid their tribute to Old Glory.

While the men stood there, Governor Wilson, with his head still bared, made a speech to the veterans. He spoke but a minute or two, telling how glorious was the lot of those who had fought to establish a more stable union and who had lived to see the fruits of their efforts.

"I am glad to stand here," the Governor said, "with my hat off to those who had so great a part in giving added structural strength to our nation."

Governor Wilson and his party spent a half hour going through the various departments of the home. Several of the veterans were presented to him. Just after the flag ceremony the veterans gave three rousing cheers for the Governor, and again in the dining-room there were three cheers.

Among those present were Mayor Louis M. Brock, Councilman James J[oseph]. McAteer, Town Clerk William B[orland]. Ross, Street Commissioner John Durkin and William F. Davis, of Kearny,[1] Speaker Edward Kenny, of East Newark, and Police Justice Edward J. Branegan, of Harrison.

Members of the board of managers of the home in attendance were General Joseph W. Brensinger and Colonel Henry H. Allers.[2]

Printed in the *Newark Evening News*, Nov. 4, 1911; two editorial headings omitted.

[1] Kearny city directories list him as a "collector."

[2] Brensinger was an employee of Henry R. Worthington Co. of Kearny, manufacturers of steam pumps, water meters, and air compressors; Allers was a physician who practiced in Harrison, N. J., and lived in Kearny.

A News Report of Three Campaign Speeches in Hudson County

[Nov. 4, 1911]

GOV. WILSON ON PUBLIC PLUNDERERS WHO ARE DEMOCRATIC ROGUES

SPOKE AT THREE WELL ATTENDED MEETINGS

Entering St. Patrick's Hall last night, Gov. Wilson was cordially greeted by more than a thousand persons who had come to hear his arguments for the Democratic candidates for Assembly and for county and city offices, but as he proceeded the audience turned a cold ear to him and he was unable to arouse anything but sporadic enthusiasm during the remainder of the evening. The Governor very quickly caught the temper of his hearers and devoted himself to urging reasons why Republicans should vote the Democratic ticket rather than their own.

It was easily observed that a majority of those in the hall were disappointed. The Governor mentioned only Mayor Wittpenn by name, said nothing directly about the candidates for the Assembly,[1] and his only argument for the other candidates on the ticket appeared to be that in turning out Democrats the voters would be merely installing Republicans in their places, and his point was that the Democrats, being united, would be in a position to accomplish more than would the Republicans.

But the Governor did not forget that his audience have become acquainted during the past year with some facts concerning the methods of certain gentlemen who are now the reputed leaders of the Democracy in this county,[2] and he frankly said that the mere calling of a man by an honorable name was no badge of his principles.

"I have known some gentlemen," he said, "who called themselves Democrats, who are neither Democrats nor Republicans. They were simply public plunderers, stalking behind the ambush of a great party name; talking great principles and dragging them in the mire. Would you vote for such men because they call themselves Democrats when you knew they were rogues?"

There was something like a warming up when the Governor gave this opinion and there was a nearer approach to sympathy yith [with] his remarks when he said:

"Now go home and ask yourselves before you go to bed, 'I am not a Republican, nor am I a Democrat, but what kind of a thinking citizen of Hudson County am I? What do I want to do for Hudson County and the State of New Jersey? How am I going to do it? Where am I going to find the instrumentalities to do it? Where on that ballot can I put the marks that will do the business?' That is what you are here to decide, and I congratulate you upon the circumstance that you can make a real decision on that ballot. You don't have to swallow anything whole."

"What do you want to use them for?" asked the Governor, continuing his remarks on the men whose names appear on the ballot. "If you are an honest man you want to use them in the

[1] The Democratic (and successful) candidates were Thomas F. A. Griffin, Charles E. S. Simpson, Charles M. Egan, Thomas Francis Martin, James C. Agnew, Thomas M. Donnelly, Cornelius Ford, William Stewart Davidson, Peter H. James, Joseph M. Branegan, Philip Steuerwald, and George F. Brensinger. Their Republican opponents were William D. Ives, Edward A. Ransom, Jr., Charles C. James, John D. Pierson, John H. Cooper, Henry F. Haese, George H. Jones, Harry I. Lefferts, Walter E. Morris, George C. Mohr, John E. McArthur, and John H. Paul.

[2] James Hennessey of Jersey City, Democratic county chairman, Patrick R. Griffin of Hoboken, John McMahon of North Hudson, Sheriff James J. Kelly, and Michael J. Fagan, city clerk of Jersey City. Known as the "Big Five," they had assumed a tenuous leadership of the Hudson County Democracy after the death of Robert Davis.

service of the community you live in. And that is the only legitimate purpose you can have, and if you don't choose them for
that purpose they are going to stick in your throat because there
is going to be a little something lodged in the aesophagus of your
conscience which you can't cough up." . . .

Following his speech in this city the Governor went to Hoboken and talked to a large audience in Public School No. 9.
Archibald Alexander presided at this meeting and launched a
Gubernatorial boom for State Senator Fielder. The latter said
that he wasn't a candidate for any office, but said he did not
wish to be understood as one who would not take a nomination
for Governor if it came his way. The Governor came in while
Senator Fielder was speaking. As in Jersey City he mentioned
none of the candidates who are on the Democratic ticket and
although many of these were present and prepared to speak, the
audience, as in Jersey City, for the greater part went home as
soon as the Governor had finished. Later he spoke in Public
School No. 3 in Weehawken.

In opening at St. Patrick's Gov. Wilson referred to his former
visits to this hall and said he detected a change in this particular
audience and remarked that he hoped the coolness of his hearers
was probably indicative of a determination already made with
respect to what they intended to do on election day. Those who attended the Martine meeting early in the year[3] when the "marked,
labeled and remembered" phrase was used, agreed with the Governor that there was a difference in the meeting. He compared
his audience with those in South Jersey and incidentally gave
an interesting sidelight on the political situation there.

Coming to the ticket in Jersey City and Hudson County the
Governor said that all contests within the party had been decided
at the primary and he paid a tribute to Mayor Wittpenn and expressed confidence in his election. He said:

"The very distinguished gentleman, for instance, who has been
nominated on the Democratic ticket for the office of Mayor stands
before you with his candor, with his honesty, with his straight-
forward methods in politics more clearly displayed than ever.
He has made criticisms like a man, he has insisted that frauds be
looked into, he has done those things which we would have expected him to do, and now we are more confident than ever of
the character of the man we are going to support.

"What would you suggest that a Democratic Mayor would do
that Mayor Wittpenn has not done, and is not likely to do? What
program will you map out for him?"

[3] See Wilson's address printed at Jan. 5, 1911, Vol. 22.

The Governor said the contest for Assembly nominations had resulted satisfactorily to him. He then described the conditions in the Republican party and averred that no good could be accomplished by electing Republicans, whether Progressives or not. The Democrats alone, he said, have a definite program of reform and they alone are, in his opinion, able and worthy to carry it out. He said no Republican could expect to accomplish any purpose by putting the government of the State in the hands of his party. He declared that the result would be merely negative, that Democrats would be turned out for Republicans. He wanted to know if any one thought more could be accomplished by an honest Republican than by an honest Democrat.

The Governor said he was interested in the lineup as shown on the face of the tickets of the principal parties. He declared that the Democrats are all progressives, but the Republicans as a whole are solidly opposed to the progressives in their party. . . .

The Governor then appealed to the progressive Republicans to vote for the Democratic candidates so that those of progressive tendencies in both parties may be solidified. He said the Democrats of this county do not need the votes of Republicans, because he understood the ticket would win without them, but he wanted them to be with the Democrats for the sake of the whole State. He said the party should be an instrumentality to be used for good government and should not be a body of men getting together to get a lot of offices and to fool their fellow citizens into helping them get them. He asked the Republicans to show him where they had an organization that could accomplish anything for the good of the State. He said he had no use for those who are loyal to a mere name. He wanted thought behind every vote, he said. He asked the voter to take every name of every candidate and to consider first what principles of good government that candidate stands for.

"I believe in the principles of the Democratic party down in my heart," he continued, "but I want to see men whose minds, when they are held up to those standards, reflect them like the perfect surface of a pure mirror. Then I will say, 'This man is a genuine Defocrat [Democrat].'"

The Governor concluded with a description of what he conceives to be the present state of politics in this country and predicted a realignment of forces, with the progressives in both parties on one side and the standpatters on the other.

Printed in the Jersey City *Jersey Journal*, Nov. 4, 1911; one editorial heading omitted.

To the Editor of the *Newark Evening News*

Sir: [Trenton, N. J.] November 5, 1911.

May I not, on the eve of the election, express, through the News, my deep interest in the return of Senator Harry V. Osborne to the State Senate? I would not take this liberty did I not feel that his return is of the utmost consequence for the maintenance of what has already been accomplished and for the continuance of the policies of the past ten months.

I venture to make this appeal to the voters of Essex because I feel sure that they desire progressive policies and because I know that they can promote them most effectually by the re-election of Senator Osborne. I am sure that they will understand that I do this from a sense of public duty and not merely out of admiration and friendship for Mr. Osborne.

Sincerely yours,   Woodrow Wilson.

Printed in the *Newark Evening News*, Nov. 5, 1911.

A News Report of Three Campaign Speeches in Burlington County, New Jersey

[Nov. 6, 1911]

BURLINGTON HEARS GOVERNOR TALK

Democrats Forget Factional Differences
in Their Welcome to Mr. Wilson.

BURLINGTON, New Jersey, Nov. 5.—Governor Wilson addressed three Burlington County audiences yesterday. Incidentally he took occasion again to place himself on record as opposed to the recall of judges. Beside speaking in this city, the Governor addressed large gatherings at Mount Holly and Moorestown.

Burlington County gave Mr. Wilson a royal welcome. There was an automobile parade through a chain of towns, with well known party leaders apparently forgetting all their personal and factional difference in the general desire to make the Governor's visit a success. At the three meetings which the Governor addressed, allusions to the Governor's possible nomination for President next year evoked applause.

At the Moorestown meeting Congressman Kinkead, who was the first speaker, made an appeal for support for the Governor, who, he declared, had carried out the pledges he had made in his campaign for election. He reviewed what had been accomplished during the first year of the Governor's administration.

At Mount Holly a big crowd assembled in the quaint old court house. The Governor, referring to his recent trip to the west, said he had found little difference between Wisconsin and Texas, though the one was Republican and the other Democratic. In both, he asserted, the people were aroused and deeply interested in the processes going forward for the return of the government to the people. He paid a warm tribute to Senator Robert M. La Follette. He called attention to the character of the candidates named by the Democrats of this county, and said that "while the Republican candidates might be men fully as good, they are not a part of the organized team pledged to do the things you want."

The Governor went back to Princeton last night, and will make his last speech of the campaign at North Plainfield tomorrow night.

Printed in the Trenton *True American*, Nov. 6, 1911; one editorial heading omitted.

A News Report of Two Campaign Speeches in Somerset County, New Jersey

[Nov. 7, 1911]

Wilson Closes Campaign With High Confidence

With Somerset county as the scene of his final efforts, Governor Wilson last night brought his wonderful campaign for Democratic victory to a close at two tremendously enthusiastic meetings in Bound Brook and North Plainfield. Although the Governor refuses to pose as a prophet, it is known that he is quite confident of the result today.

The first meeting last night was in Bound Brook. Arrangements for it had only been completed early yesterday morning, and announcement that it would be held was not spread until 10 o'clock, yet, despite a heavy downpour the hall which would comfortably seat 300 persons was crowded with nearly twice that number, and yet other hundreds were unable to gain entrance.

When Governor Wilson arose to speak he received an ovation. There was that in the demeanor of those in the audience that showed their respect, affection and belief in the man who had rescued the State from the ignom[in]y it had suffered as a trust-ruled commonwealth under successive Republican administrations through a long series of years.

Governor Wilson once more set forth, with that clarity of expression all his own, the dominant issue of the campaign—"Shall the People Rule?"—as they have ruled since his advent to office. Quoting an editorial from the Newark Evening News, he said it was representative government alone that was on trial before the people.

But his special mission last night was to speak for Messrs. LaMonte and Beekman, the Democratic candidates for Senator and Assembly[man] respectively. Mr. LaMonte was unfortunately absent, having been called to Northampton, Mass., because of the serious illness of his daughter, Miss Isabella LaMonte, but Mr. Beekman was present.

Governor Wilson described Mr. LaMonte's valuable services in the last legislature as assemblyman, and assailed the record of Mr. Smalley,[1] his opponent. Speaking from the record he showed that Smalley had consistently opposed bills designed to give rate-making and other necessary powers to the Public Utilities Commission, and had also opposed other measures designed in the public interest.

In North Plainfield, where opposition to the Democratic ticket has shown more strength than elsewhere in the county, he found another big audience awaiting him. Mr. LaMonte had been criticised for his failure to vote for a sewage bill which North Plainfield folk wanted passed. The bill had passed and had been vetoed by the Governor, who showed conclusively last night that Mr. LaMonte had only done his duty, and that he, the Governor, had vetoed the measure because it was against the established policy of the State.

The meeting at an end, Governor Wilson returned to his home in Princeton, where he will vote today, and where he will await the decision of the electorate of the State. He was asked to make some forecast of the result, but refused to say more than he had said publicly—that he was confident that the voters would not reverse their judgment of last year.

Thus ended, perhaps, the most extraordinary campaign ever participated in by a Governor of New Jersey. In five weeks of constant speaking he had visited every county but one in the State. He had spoken an average of about four times a day, had everywhere been received with enthusiasm, and on all occasions, except one, had faced audiences that filled auditoriums to overflowing. His appeal had been simple, yet the more effective because of its very simplicity. "You elected us because we promised to do certain things you wanted done," he had said. "Well, we have kept our promise to you; are you going to keep your faith with us?"

Arrangements have been made by Democratic State Chairman Edward E. Grosscup to keep the headquarters open all today and this evening, and to collect returns from all parts of the State. It is not expected, however, that the full results will be known until very late. From information supplied to him by the various county chairmen and from independent sources, Chairman Grosscup is serenely certain of Democratic success.

Printed in the Trenton *True American*, Nov. 7, 1911; some editorial headings omitted.

    1 William W. Smalley of Bound Brook, Republican assemblyman, 1907-10. He defeated La Monte.

To William Garrott Brown

My dear Mr. Brown: [Trenton, N. J.] November 7, 1911.

I am genuinely indebted to you for your letter of October thirtieth, which has made a great impression upon me.

I want to begin by saying frankly that I know perfectly well that I went off half cocked about the Aldrich matter. I so thoroughly distrust him that it was incredible to me that anything bearing his signature could be other than a scheme to put us more completely in the hands from whose domination we are trying to escape. After further inquiry, I am ready to accept your conclusions, so far as I believe, that the "commission's investigations have been thorough and pertinent, and that they have kept in mind the danger of political control and the necessity of adapting any plan proposed for our usages and our existing machinery." What I am [not] convinced of is that they have succeeded in proposing a plan which would avoid the danger of control by a dominating group of financiers.

The greatest embarrassment of my political career has been that active duties seem to deprive me absolutely of time for careful investigation. I seem almost obliged to form conclusions from impressions instead of from study, but I intend to go more thoroughly into this matter before saying anything about it, and I heartily agree with you that this, the most fundamental question of all, must be approached with caution and fearlessness and receive dispassionate and open-minded treatment. I wish that I had more knowledge, more thorough acquaintance, with the matters involved. All that I can promise you is sincere study. I wish that I could promise you a constructive ability.

My own feeling as a "politician" is that it is wisest not to frame definite proposals upon this matter while the power of the Democratic party is inchoate. If it should become real and be based upon majorities in Congress, then the opportunity will rise for a fearless stand regardless of incompetent critics and thoughtless opinion. I wonder what your own view is with regard to the strategy of the matter. To inject a definite scheme now into political discussion would seem to me to divert the country from principle to details.

It distresses me that you have to speak of yourself as an invalid. I hope that you are taking the best care of yourself and that you will be spared for many years to give counsel to us all.

Cordially and sincerely yours, Woodrow Wilson

TCL (W. G. Brown Papers, NcD).

From John Miller Turpin Finney

My Dear Governor: Baltimore, November 7 11

You may possibly have heard that the Presidency of Princeton has been offered to me, as I understand it, by a unanimous vote of the Committee. I have also been assured that this offer will be confirmed by a unanimous vote of the Board of Trustees. May I bother you long enough to ask, if you care to, to write to me frankly just what you think of my qualifications, rather lack of qualifications, for the position, knowing it and what it means, as you well do? I will keep as absolutely confidential what you write, if you desire me to do so.

Appreciating any light you may give me on the subject and with the sincere regret that if it seems best that I should accept the Presidency, your mantle should fall on so unworthy shoulders,

Believe me, Sincerely yours, J M. T. Finney.

TLS (WP, DLC).

To John Miller Turpin Finney

My dear Doctor Finney: [Trenton, N. J.] November 8, 1911.

I am glad to have confirmed by your letter of the seventh what had reached me as a mere rumor, too good to be true.

I do not know how the suggestion that you accept the presidency of Princeton will strike you, from the point of view of your professional engagements and ambitions, but my own earnest hope is that you will see your way to accept.

Of course, you have had no experience which directly prepares you for a service of that sort, but I know so well what your views and principles are in the field of education and I am so sure that both in character and temperament, as well as in judgment, you are highly qualified for this particular position, that I feel warranted in urging you to serve the University in this conspicuous way in her hour of perplexity and need.

I need not tell you of my own cordial personal feeling and genuine admiration. I must speak now chiefly of Princeton. If the Board is willing to concentrate upon you, it is a most happy solution of the present difficult situation and I, for one, as a Princeton man, would be delighted to have an opportunity to stand by you in restoring the tone of administration in the University we all love.[1]

Cordially and faithfully yours,   Woodrow Wilson

TLS (J. M. T. Finney Coll., NjP).
[1] Finney did not accept the presidency.

A Statement on the New Jersey Election of 1911

[Nov. 8, 1911]

I, of course, deeply regret the loss of the House by my party through the loss of Essex and the failure to gain the Senate;[1] but I look forward with great interest to the next session as affording an opportunity to the Republican leaders to fulfil the very explicit pledges of their platform. If they do that the session should be productive of legislation of considerable importance and benefit to the State, and I shall earnestly hope for their cooperation in reforms planned in the interest of the whole State, which we are all sworn to serve.

Printed in the *Newark Evening News*, Nov. 8, 1911.
[1] The Republicans won thirty-seven of the sixty Assembly and five of the eight Senate seats contested. Thus, a Democratic majority of twenty-four in the Assembly of 1911 became a Republican majority of fourteen in 1912. The Republicans lost one seat in the Senate but still controlled it, eleven to ten. On the other hand, fifteen out of the seventeen sheriffs elected in 1911 were Democrats; a total of 160,184 persons voted for Democratic legislative candidates, while their Republican opponents were supported by 157,081; and Democrats made huge inroads in traditional Republican South Jersey. The Democratic loss of both houses of the legislature was directly attributable to the failure of the Smith-Nugent machine to get out the Democratic voters in Essex County. In 1910 the average of votes for assemblymen there had been 35,577 Republican and 40,516 Democratic; in 1911 it was 30,648 Republican and 23,360 Democratic. The result was the defeat of State Senator Harry V. Osborne and the previously all-Democratic delegation. State of New Jersey, *Annual Returns of the General Election of 1911* (Trenton, N. J., 1912), p. 59; *Newark Evening News*, Nov. 8, 1911; Trenton *True American*, Nov. 18, 1911; and Link, *Road to the White House*, pp. 294-96.

A Thanksgiving Proclamation

[[Nov. 8, 1911]]

Another year has passed; we have enjoyed peace at home and abroad; our fields have yielded their generous increase in response to our labor; our business enterprises have gone forward, if without unusual increase, at least without crisis and without untoward check or hindrance; and our State has won credit among her neighbors for thoughtful and well-considered reform. For these things and for all the manifold blessings of life; for days of greater and greater enlightenment and a hopeful betterment of the conditions of civilization, for knowledge of what is true and right; for all things that make for righteousness and purity and increase of confidence we owe devout and heartfelt thanks to Almighty God, to whose providence we owe all that sustains and brightens our life, whether as individuals, as communities or as a nation.

Therefore, I, Woodrow Wilson, Governor of the State of New Jersey, do designate Thursday, the thirtieth day of November, instant, as a day to be observed for general Thanksgiving and prayer, and recommend that upon that day all business ceases and that the people gather in their respective churches and other places of public worship, or in private at their homes, to make fitting acknowledgment to Almighty God of his unbounded benefactions to us as nation, State and individuals.

Given under my hand and seal, at the executive chamber, in the city of Trenton, this ninth day of November,[1] in the year of our Lord, one thousand nine hundred and eleven, and of the independence of the United States the one hundred and thirty-sixth.

Woodrow Wilson.

Printed in the *Newark Evening News*, Nov. 9, 1911.
[1] It was actually given to the press on November 8.

From Eckard Payson Budd

Dear Governor: Mount Holly, N. J., Nov. 8th, 1911.

I am very sorry that I cannot write and congratulate you upon the election of both a Democratic House of Assembly and a Democratic Senate.

I feel, however, that I can write and congratulate you upon the magnificent campaign you made.

We came so near electing democratic senators in several counties that it seemed a shame we could not have concentrated our votes on some one senator and gotten the other one, which would have given us a majority of the senate.

I feel that the election is a strong endorsement of you and your administration. Had you been running your majority, in my judgment, would have been greater than it was a year ago.

A great many local conditions arose, which made it impossible to impress upon the voters the true situation. In Union County, for example, the stupidity of the democrats in nominating all of their ticket from the City of Elizabeth, could not help but cause the citizens of other places in the county to feel that such a slight had been put upon their locality that they would vote against the candidate of their party.

The narrow majority by which the republicans won Camden and Gloucester also shows that the campaign you made aroused the people in a way they have never been aroused before, and was a practical vindication of you and your administration.

Personally I desire to express my deep appreciation of the great consideration shown me by yourself during the campaign. I am more than glad to have been associated with you in the movement to purify politics and to rescue our state from the grip of selfish politicians, who for so many years have delivered her bound and gagged to the special interests.

As the result of my association with you I feel that I return to the practice of my profession with higher aims, nobler aspirations and loftier impulses.

Trusting that when I write again it may be to congratulate you on your elevation to the highest office in the gift of the people, I remain,   Very sincerely yours,   Eckard P. Budd

TLS (Governors' Files, Nj).

To Charles Henry Grasty

My dear Mr. Grasty: [Trenton, N. J.] November 10, 1911.

Thank you for your generous letter of November ninth.[1] I think the results in New Jersey mean simply this, (indeed upon an analysis I am sure that they do) that wherever the influence of James Smith, Jr., could be made effective, it was exercised to defeat the Democratic Assembly candidates. There was trading all over the State in which Assemblymen were traded off for the Sheriffs. Fifteen Democratic sheriffs having been elected out of seventeen to be voted for. From what I can gather this will cause a very serious reaction even among machine politicians against Mr. Smith, because it is obviously a bad game to deprive your own party of power in order to accomplish a personal revenge.

I am hoping to come down to Baltimore the first week in December[2] and shall look forward to seeing you then.

Cordially and faithfully yours,   Woodrow Wilson

TLS (RSB Coll., DLC).
[1] C. H. Grasty to WW, Nov. 9, 1911, CCL (RSB Coll., DLC).
[2] News reports of Wilson's addresses in Baltimore are printed at Dec. 6, 1911.

To William Gibbs McAdoo

Personal.

My dear Mr. McAdoo: [Trenton, N. J.] November 10, 1911.

I am very much interested to learn through Mr. [Hooper] Alexander that you are gracious enought to want any suggestions I may have with regard to the address you are going to make in Atlanta. It always seems to me absurd for me to make suggestions to you, because you are so easily a master of what you try to do.

The only thing that occurs to me is this. In every one of my speeches in which I have put forth what seemed radical doctrine, I have accompanied the radical exposition with a statement of the absolute necessity that we should be careful; that we should remember the delicate tissue of the economic body politic; that we should recognize our task not as one of hostility to any interest but as one of accommodation and readjustment, so that what we seek is the interest of all, of the capitalists as well as of those whom capital had too nearly got in its own power. I think you will find this plan of ideas in every address I have made.

Newton at 42 Broadway, I am sure can supply you with abundant extracts to prove this and I am sure he will be glad to do so.

Again let me say how generous I think it is that you should undertake missions of this sort.

In haste,

Cordially and sincerely yours,   Woodrow Wilson

TLS (WP, DLC).

From William Garrott Brown

My dear Governor Wilson,   Asheville, N. C., Nov. 10, 1911

I cannot wait for a stenographer to write my thanks for your letter. It brings me more than I dared hope for from my first letter. You could not have answered more honestly and courageously. I am very happy over it. Of course you have been too driven to study out such questions carefully, and that was precisely why I was so uneasy.

I agree with you entirely as to the "strategy" of the matter. It would be unwise even if it were not useless to attempt to commit the Democratic party to any definite scheme until power and responsibility shall come to it. The great thing is to keep the discussion non-partisan—as it has been so far. If we can only keep the Democrats from committing themselves either for or against anything we shall render both the party and the movement for reform an incalculable service. It is just there that your own power seems to me so important.

After writing to you, I dropped a line to A. Piatt Andrew, and in his reply he agrees with me as to your ability to help or hurt the movement. He is, it appears, not only a Princeton man but your sincere admirer, particularly in the matter of your academic ideals, and is ready and eager to come to Princeton or Trenton and go over the plan with you. He says he believes he can tell the purpose and meaning of every comma in it, and I strongly suspect it is quite as much his as Aldrich's. A line to him—A. P. Andrew, Assistant Secretary of the Treasury, Washington,—will put him at your service, and I can think of no more expeditious way to make your enquiry, though of course you will wish to use other means to get at the truth. As to the danger of control by "the interests"—your stenographer makes you say you are satisfied on this point, but I feel sure you said the contrary—Andrew can at least explain why the commission hopes its safe-guards will be sufficient.

Just one other suggestion: I trust you will not feel like saying *anything* on this subject for some little time, not even anything by way of modifying earlier utterances. It might be thought to be prompted by the election results. Those, while measurably unfortunate, do not strike me as disastrous. All depends on the sincerity of your friends, and if they respond man-fashion the seeming reverse may prove good fortune. I have just sent word to Colonel Harvey that if he weakens—which he won't—I shall be on his back if I have to hire the *Outlook* to do it with! And I am writing to my nephew, who is Secretary of State in Alabama,[1] for fuller reports of the situation there.

It is going to be a year of extraordinary possibilities in politics —how remarkably world-wide are these agitations!—and I feel almost as fortunate in looking on and commenting as you are in having a big rôle. It's noble business, for all the pettiness and meanness there is in it.

Cordially yours,   William Garrott Brown

ALS (Governors' Files, Nj).
¹ Cyrus Billingslea Brown of Montgomery, Ala.

From Isaac Henry Lionberger

My dear Doctor: St. Louis, Mo. November 13, 1911.

I heartily regret that I put you to the trouble of answering a letter which as I now perceive must have tended to exasperate a man tried by many annoyances. I sought personal relief, and was not mindful of your comfort. Pardon my indiscretion. You think an expedient curative, and I that the disease must be outgrown.

Will you be good enough, in justice to myself, to accept my assurance that however radically we may differ upon so important a matter, I still cherish for you the sincerest regard and will ever have the most implicit confidence in the disinterested patriotism of your motives.

Very sincerely yours,   I H Lionberger

TLS (Governors' Files, Nj).

Two News Reports of a Visit to Charlottesville, Virginia

[Nov. 15, 1911]

GOV. WILSON AT UNIVERSITY

Unheralded and unannounced Woodrow Wilson, governor of New Jersey and probably the next president of the United States, on his way South for a rest, stopped off here yesterday afternoon for a brief visit to the University of Virginia, where he was once a student.

Dropping into town without having told anyone of his intention to visit the University, Governor Wilson was in the city several hours before it became known that he was here. He passed the Fayerweather gymnasium just as the football squad was filing out, followed the players down on the field, and was an interested spectator throughout the workout. He was first recognized by Mr. W. Christie Benet, of Columbia, S. C., who is here to assist in preparing the team for the annual game with Georgetown on Saturday. The Governor inquired as to the team's record, and congratulated Head Coach Yancey on his success as a coach.

Leaving Lambeth Field about dark, Gov. Wilson dropped in to pay his respects to President Alderman. Last night he was the guest of his old college mate, Prof. Richard Heath Dabney, dean of the graduate department. Today he dined with President Alderman, and later in the evening will leave for Staunton, the place of his birth. After a brief stay in the valley city, he will go direct to St. Augustine, Fla., for quiet and rest.

Gov. Wilson was a student at the University of Virginia for two sessions—'79-'80 and '80-'81—a matriculate in the law department. He did not complete his last year in college, being compelled to withdraw about Christmas on account of ill health.

Printed in the Charlottesville, Va., *Daily Progress*, Nov. 15, 1911.

❖

[Nov. 16, 1911]

WILSON HITS STANDPATTER

Woodrow Wilson, governor of New Jersey, a possible Democratic candidate for the presidency of the United States, and an alumnus of the University of Virginia, spoke to the students of his Alma Mater last evening, and in particular to the members of the student Woodrow Wilson Club and the members of the Jefferson Literary Society, of which organization he was president 30 years ago, and at which time he won the medal for oratory.

When he was introduced by Mr. D. H. Ramsey[1] as "the next President of the United States," Governor Wilson said that he felt like the woman, who, in the side show of a circus, seeing a man apparently reading a newspaper through an inch of pine board, declared, 'This is no place for me.' He stated that he was speaking very unexpectedly, but like any other American citizen he must be prepared to make a few remarks. . . .

After the address, as well as at the time he appeared on the rostrum of Cabell Hall, the distinguished visitor was cheered loudly and for several minutes each time. At the close he shook hands and was introduced to each of the several hundred students present.

Printed in the Charlottesville, Va., *Daily Progress*, Nov. 16, 1911.
    [1] Darley Hiden Ramsay, senior at the University of Virginia. He was a newspaper editor in Asheville, N. C., for many years.

To Richard Heath Dabney

My dear Heath, Staunton, Va., 16 Nov., '11

We did not have a chance when I was with you to have our talk out about the initiative, referendum, and recall; it may be worth while, therefore, in view of the importance of the subject, for me to summarize somewhat more formally what I said to you in scraps.

In the first place, with regard to my own state of mind. I surrendered to the facts, as every candid man must. My whole prepossession—my whole reasoning—was against these things. But when I came into contact with candid, honest, public spirited men who could speak (with regard, for example, to Oregon) from personal observation and experience, they floored me flat with their narration of what had actually happened. I found in the men who had advocated these things, who had put them into operation, and who had accomplished things by them, not critics or opponents of representative government, but men who were eager to restore it where it had been lost, and who had taken, successfully taken, these means to recover for the people, what they had unquestionably lost, control of their own affairs.

In short, they were not trying to change our institutions. The initiative, referendum, and recall were in their eyes (as they are in mine) merely *a means to an end,*—that end being the restoration of the control of public opinion. Where opinion already controls, where there is now actual, genuine representative government, as I believe there is in Virginia and in the South in general, they are not necessary. Each State must judge for itself. I do not see how it could be *made* a subject of national policy. The people will, in my opinion, demand these measures only where they are manifestly necessary to take legislation and the control of administrative action away from special, hopelessly entrenched interests. They are no general or universal panaceas!

The recall of judges I am absolutely against, and always have been. It is a remedy for a symptom, not for a disease,—the disease being *the control of the system* by influences which general opinion has ceased to control.

It interested me very much to find that even in Oregon literally *no* one thought of these new methods of action as a *substitute* for representative institutions, but only as a means of stimulation and control. They are as devoted to the idea of our representative institutions as we are—and are bent upon realizing those ideas in practice. That is their conscious object.

As for the recall, it is seldom used, outside the municipalities.

I do not remember an instance of its use on a State officer. It is merely "a gun behind the door."

Faithfully Yours,   Woodrow Wilson

ALS (Wilson-Dabney Corr., ViU).

From Edward Mandell House

My dear Governor Wilson: New York. November 18th, 1911.

I have been with Mr. Bryan a good part of the morning and I am pleased to tell you that I think you will have his support.

The fact that you did not vote for him in '96 was on his mind but I offered an explanation which seemed to be satisfactory.

My main effort was in alienating him from Champ Clark and I believe I was successful there.

He sent you several messages which he asked me to deliver to you in person which I shall be glad to do sometime when you are in New York provided you return before I go South around December first.

I have been keeping in close touch with the Harmon situation and it seems to me that he is practically out of the race. They are as you know centering upon Underwood but I feel that there will be no [more] difficulty in dislodging him than Harmon if your speech upon the tariff has the effect which I believe it will.

I am inclined to congratulate you and felicitate with the Party over your nomination which I am sure will come provided no mistake is made between now and the Convention.

Faithfully yours,   [E. M. House]

CCL (E. M. House Papers, CtY).

A News Report of a Visit to Augusta, Georgia

[Nov. 19, 1911]

GOVERNOR WOODROW WILSON SPENT YESTERDAY
IN HOME OF BOYHOOD

Governor Woodrow Wilson arrived in Augusta yesterday morning at 11:35 o'clock on the Southeastern Limited of the Southern Railway. He was welcomed by a committee of citizens, taken for a motor drive around the city, and then to the Albion Hotel where he is staying during his visit. During the afternoon, he went for a leisurely stroll to visit some of the scenes of his boyhood days and returned to his hotel and held an informal reception in the parlors from 6 until 7 o'clock. He dined at the home of Bowdre

Phinizy, editor of The Augusta Herald and former Princeton student[1] and afterwards joined a box party at the Grand theater to see Ty. Cobb in the College Widow.[2] He will attend services at the First Presbyterian church this morning, lunch with Dr. and Mrs. Joseph R. Sevier[3] afterwards and will leave for Savannah at 9:40 o'clock tonight. From Savannah he will go to St. Augustine, Fla.

When Governor Wilson stepped from the New York sleeper, at the Union station, he was greeted by a committee of citizens among whom were . . . Rev. Joseph R. Sevier, pastor of the First Presbyterian church and Mrs. Sevier. . . .

Dr. and Mrs. Sevier now occupy the manse in which the governor resided as a boy, when his father was pastor of the church. When they greeted the governor, Dr. Sevier invited him to be their guest there during his visit. "Yes," said Mrs. Sevier, joining heartily in the invitation, "we want you to come back home." But expressing his appreciation for the pretty compliment and thoughtful hospitality regretted he could not accept the invitation.

After a few minutes spent in an exchange of pleasantries and good wishes, the distinguished guest was escorted to an automobile waiting outside and was driven around the city for about two hours. . . . During the drive they visited the hill as well as almost every other section of Augusta and the Governor recognized many of the places in passing. He expressed himself as having enjoyed the drive thoroughly. From the time of his arrival at the hotel until the hour for luncheon, he spent in resting and receiving a few callers.

After dinner, he went for a walk. He said he wanted to go alone and look over the city and visit the places he has not seen for many years and note the changes that have taken place since the time he went away as a 14-year-old lad.

At six o'clock, he returned to his hotel and for an hour received a large number of citizens who called to shake his hand and extend their good wishes for his future success. Among those who came were several who were the friends of other days. Dr. T. R. Wright[4] who was a member of the famous baseball team of their boyhood known as the "Lightfoots."[5] Governor Wilson played on this team and recalled the fact to Dr. Wright as soon as he came

[1] Princeton 1892.

[2] Tyrus Raymond Cobb, the famous baseball player, was a native of Georgia. The play, first produced in 1904, was George Ade's *The College Widow*, a highly successful comedy of college life and football.

[3] Joseph Ramsey Sevier and Edith Rogers Love Sevier.

[4] Thomas R. Wright, physician and president of Margaret Wright Hospital.

[5] About the Lightfoot Club, see n. 1 to the item from a Wilson notebook printed at July 1, 1874, Vol. 1.

to shake hands with his former playmate. Numerous little personal instances of this kind were cropping up during the day. The guests were presented to the governor as they arrived, by Mr. Phinizy and Mr. Hook.[6]

An interesting feature at this reception, was the introduction of Ty. Cobb to the other distinguished son of Augusta. "How do you do, Mr. Cobb?" exclaimed Governor Wilson as soon as he heard the name and the two shook hands warmly. "I had the pleasure of meeting you in Atlanta last year Governor," said Ty. "Yes," answered the governor, "and I hope I will meet you often again." Ty then told him of the victory of Princeton over Yale in the football game earlier in the afternoon[7] and the former Princeton president was much pleased and said so.

A few minutes after the last caller had departed, Governor Wilson went to the home of Mr. Phinizy and dined quietly with his friend of earlier Princeton days, when the host was a student and the guest his teacher.

From the home of Mr. Phinizy, they went to the Grand theater to see Ty Cobb's debut as an actor in "The College Widow." A box party, of which Governor Wilson was the guest of honor, had been arranged by a number of his admirers.

Governor Wilson is taking a vacation. He is traveling as quietly as possible and is trying to secure rest from the arduous duties of his office and the unceasing demand upon his time. He has no plans except that he is on his way to St. Augustine, where he hopes to find complete rest and recuperation.

He will not discuss public matters or politics. When asked for an interview by a reporter for The Chronicle, he would not consent to talk, except upon subjects that did not pertain to official affairs. The short talk with him was more of a conversation than an interview. He was asked about the changes that have taken place since he knew Augusta, and he fell into a reminiscent moment and began to recall the places he had seen during the drive of the forenoon and the walk of the afternoon that he remembered. He has not been in Augusta since 1885, when he spent the greater part of the day here on his wedding trip, after his marriage in Savannah. That is the only time he has visited Augusta since his father moved with his family to Columbia, in 1870. He recognized many places during the day, around which clustered memories of his happy days here. The church, the manse, St. Patrick's church and school buildings, the older factories and many of the larger places and institutions, he

6 Edward B. Hook, city sheriff and assistant assessor of Augusta.
7 By the score of 6 to 3.

found much the same as he remembered them. Among other places that seemed to stir memories most was the home on the Hill now occupied by Joseph S. Reynolds.[8] It was there his aunt, Mrs. Bones,[9] resided and where he frequently played with other boys of his age. Governor Wilson enjoyed seeing a number of his former associates, but few of them were the friends who played with him as a boy. Those can be counted on the fingers of his two hands, but there are others whose acquaintance he has made since that time, some of them at Princeton and some elsewhere.

When Governor Wilson leaves Augusta tonight for a season of well-earned rest in St. Augustine, his friends and admirers in this city will feel that he has again caught step and touched elbows with the people of his old home and will wish him "Good bye, good luck to you."

Printed in the *Augusta*, Ga., *Chronicle*, Nov. 19, 1911; three editorial headings omitted.
  [8] Lawyer, solicitor general of the Augusta Circuit Court.
  [9] Marion Woodrow (Mrs. James W.) Bones.

To Ellen Axson Wilson

My precious one,   Augusta, Ga., 19 Nov., 1911

Don't be surprised to see me follow this letter soon! I am having a good time, full of interest and pleasure,—but with no *rest* in it at all. I am not left to myself at all. Publicity (my own dear, pet Publicity) has closed about me like a prison. I am freer at home than anywhere else,—and *you* are there, my pet, my darling. I think I will come back and put my vacation into taking you to the theatre.

I am perfectly well,—and, strangely enough, do not feel fagged. I am snatching a moment before going to Church,—father's old church. Even there I am to be made a public man of! But what I am most *conscious* of being is

Your own   Woodrow

Deep love to all.

ALS (WC, NjP).

A News Report of a Day in Augusta

[Nov. 20, 1911]

GOV. WILSON LEFT LAST NIGHT

Governor Woodrow Wilson, after a day and a half spent among the scenes and friends of his boyhood in this city, left last night for Savannah and from there will go to St. Augustine for a few days of recuperation. Yesterday morning, he attended services at the First Presbyterian church, where as a boy he sat under the spiritual guidance of his father, the lamented Dr. Robert Wilson, at that time the pastor of the church. He afterward dined quietly with the present pastor, Dr. Joseph R. Sevier and Mrs. Sevier at the manse that was for 14 years his home. Later, he motored out to Summerville and spent the afternoon at "Tanglewood Hall," the home of Mr. and Mrs. Eugene E. Verdery[1] and Mrs. Verdery's mother, Mrs. Anne McKinne Winter.[2] The home of Mrs. Winter and that of the Wilson's were near each other and there was a warm friendship between the families during Dr. Wilson's pastorate here. Mrs. Winter was then a member of his congregation and is now the oldest living member of that church. During the visit of Governor Wilson at the Verdery home a number of the neighbors dropped in and an informal hour was spent.

Just before the morning hour for divine worship, R. Roy Goodwin,[3] called at the Albion hotel and joining Governor Wilson, escorted him to the church. Immediately upon entering the edifice, the governor observed and commented on the changes that had been made in the interior arrangement since he saw it last. The balconies that once were on both sides of the church have been removed and the pews that in those days stood in straight, orderly rows have given place to the more modern plan of semicircular arrangement. He was shown to a pew well toward the front of the church and from this seat he listened intently to the sermon by Rev. C. O. Jones,[4] one of the visiting ministers in attendance upon the Methodist conference who was filling the pulpit for the morning.

At the conclusion of the services many of the congregation, probably 200 in number, pressed forward and shook him warmly by the hand.

After his return from his visit to the Hill, he went to his hotel and rested for a while. He left at 9:40 o'clock for Savannah amid the good byes and good wishes of a number of his friends who had gathered at the station to bid him farewell.

Printed in the *Augusta*, [Ga.] *Chronicle*, Nov. 20, 1911.

[1] Eugene F. Verdery and Annie Winter Verdery. He was a cotton manufacturer of Augusta.

[2] Widow of George W. Winter.

[3] Managing director and first vice-president of the Augusta Chamber of Commerce.

[4] The Rev. Charles Octavius Jones, pastor of Grace Methodist Church, Atlanta.

A News Report of a Visit to Savannah, Georgia

[Nov. 20, 1911]

GOV. WILSON WAS VISITOR IN CITY TODAY

This morning at half after eight o'clock Gov. Woodrow Wilson arrived from Augusta by the Central Railway. He was met at the station by Mr. Benjamin Palmer Axson, his relative,[1] and by Mr. Pleasant A. Stovall, who had been his school mate in Augusta.[2]

Gov. Wilson was placed in one of Sawyer's Packards and whirled down to Thunderbolt,[3] where he was given a breakfast at Bannon Lodge. He was joined by a few friends, Judge George T. Cann, Col. A. R. Lawton, Congressman Charles G. Edwards, Mr. W. W. Osborne, and Mr. Joseph F. Gray.[4] After breakfast Gov. Wilson rode through Bonaventure,[5] and back home along Estill avenue, admiring the improvements of Chatham Crescent and Ardsley Park. Returning to the city he rode slowly by the Independent Presbyterian Church, where he was married 26 years ago to a granddaughter of the late Dr. Axson, at that time pastor of the church. He was carried by the Presbyterian Manse and took great interest in viewing the place which of all spots in Savannah is probably dearest to him. He was carried up and down Liberty and Oglethorpe avenue, along Broughton and finally out to the Central Railroad and Ocean Steamship terminals and shown the large cotton shipments waiting to be compressed and shipped.

Finally he visited the cotton exchange where he was received by President Paul T. Haskell and introduced to a large number of members who dropped in to pay their respects. He was carried to the balcony of the Exchange and given the view of the river with its shipping which, by the way, he was very anxious to see.

From the Exchange he rode to the offices of the Morning News and of The Savannah Press and was introduced to many of the officials and workers of those papers. Mr. E. N. Hancock, of The News,[6] had joined the party at the Cotton Exchange. He was introduced as a former Jersey man and was cordially greeted by the governor.

Governor Wilson then walked up Drayton street and was shown through the beautiful building of the Citizens and Southern Bank and from there went to the Court House, where Judge Cann presented him to Judge Charlton,[7] who adjourned court for a few minutes in honor of the visiting governor. Solicitor General Hartridge[8] and all the county officers of Chatham were brought up and presented with most of their deputies and assistants. Judge Henry McAlpin,[9] the ordinary, was a Princeton man and had known Gov. Wilson before. Other Princeton men who met him were Messrs. Fred C. Wiley[10] and Fred T. Saussy.[11] Several New Jersey citizens greeted him from time to time, among them Mr. J. M. Hartfelder,[12] who met him in front of The Press office.

Capt. W[illiam]. G. Austin, chief of police, was introduced to the governor, and asked him if he would like to drive around the course in one of the racing machines, which at that time were practicing. Gov. Wilson, however, excused himself. He had met Ty Cobb in Augusta and was afraid that with even this automobile experience he might not be able quite to get in his class. The red flags warned the governor's party this morning not to ride over the race course.

After leaving the Court House Gov. Wilson went to the home of Mr. Palmer Axson, on the corner of Hall and Barnard streets, and was given luncheon. He left this afternoon at half past three for the North on the Atlantic Coast Line train. Gov. Wilson came South this time for the purpose of going to Florida. He had just been through a strenuous campaign and contemplated a short vacation. He received a telegram, however, which made it necessary to return home immediately. He said that Savannah in this beautiful sunshiny day really made Florida unnecessary. He regretted very much that he could not stay longer. . . .

Printed in the *Savannah Press*, Nov. 20, 1911; three editorial headings omitted.

[1] First cousin of Mrs. Wilson and an accountant with Charles Neville Audit Co.

[2] They were schoolmates at Joseph T. Derry's school in Augusta.

[3] A suburb of Savannah.

[4] George Turner Cann, lawyer of Savannah and former judge of the superior court, eastern judicial circuit of Georgia; Alexander Rudolf Lawton, lawyer of Savannah and president of the Central of Georgia Railway Co., son of Mrs. Wilson's friend, General Alexander Robert Lawton; Charles Gordon Edwards, congressman since 1907; William W. Osborne, lawyer and president of the Exchange Bank; and Joseph Francis Gray, state railroad commissioner and vice-president and secretary of the Savannah Chamber of Commerce.

[5] Colonial plantation on the Wilmington River, at this time owned by the City of Savannah and used as a cemetery.

[6] Elmer N. Hancock, editor of the Savannah *Morning News*.

[7] Walter Glasco Charlton, judge of the superior court, eastern judicial circuit of Georgia.

[8] Walter Charlton Hartridge, lawyer and solicitor general of the same court.

[9] Henry McAlpin, Princeton 1881, judge of the court of ordinary (probate) of Chatham County.

[10] Albert Wylly, Wilson's classmate, in the real estate business in Savannah, county commissioner of Chatham County.

[11] Frederick Tupper Saussy, Princeton 1896, lawyer of Savannah.

[12] Unidentified.

To Mary Allen Hulbert Peck

Dearest Friend,   [New York] Wed, the 22nd [Nov. 1911].

Ellen and I are in town. I have three tickets for the theatre this evening, and I am coming (at about 6.15) to take you to dine with us at the Hotel Astor at 6.30 this evening. May I not count on you? I shall be here on time, waiting in the parlor. How I wish I could see you now, instead of writing!

As always   Your devoted friend,   W.W.

ALS (WP, DLC).

To John Sayles[1]

My dear Mr. Sayles: [Trenton, N. J.] November 27, 1911.

Very few of the letters I have recently received have given me so much pleasure as yours of November twenty-second,[2] containing the resolution of the Democratic Society of Western New York, favoring my candidacy for the presidential nomination. I know how much weight attaches to the opinion of the Democrats of Western New York, and I consider myself very much honored by the generous resolution which the Society was kind enough to pass. Will you not express to all concerned my sense of obligation and appreciation.

Sincerely yours,   Woodrow Wilson

TLS (WP, DLC).
[1] Lawyer of Buffalo, N. Y.; private secretary of Mayor Louis P. Fuhrmann of Buffalo; founder and president of the Democratic Society of Western New York.
[2] It is missing.

To Henry St. George Tucker

My dear Mr. Tucker: [Trenton, N. J.] November 29, 1911.

You are very thoughtful and generous and I appreciate sincerely your letter of November twnety [twenty]-seventh with its enclosure.[1]

I should certainly feel very much mortified if my native State should not find a way to support me, and I am very grateful to my friends there.

I was distressed to learn through one of my Secretaries that you had to go to the Hospital for an operation. I hope that it was very slight and that you have suffered no great inconvenience from it.

Cordially and faithfully yours,   Woodrow Wilson

TLS (Tucker Family Papers, NcU).
[1] It is missing.

To Mary Allen Hulbert Peck

Dearest Friend   [Trenton, N. J.] 1 Dec., 1911.

I grieve to think how useless I shall be as a correspondent! I have hoped each day to write—have been prevented—and now here I am at the last moment with a sick headache, in my office, after one of the most exacting days I have ever had!

But, after all, there is nothing to tell. I would love to wander on from sentence to sentence indulging the delightful impression that I was having a leisurely chat with you but I would not be *saying* anything. This letter—like all the others I write you—is sent only to convey a message,—only to tell you how we have missed you, and yet how happy we are that you have got away from the work that was taking all the spring out of you and making you *ill*, and that you are in dear Bermuda, where you can loaf and invite your soul. Please do it and come back with freshness and vigour radiant in you, to all who wait for you as does

Your devoted friend, Woodrow Wilson

Love to all

ALS (WP, DLC).

From Edward Mandell House

Dear Governor Wilson: New York. December 1st, 1911.

I have a telegram from Doctor Houston[1] saying that he will be very pleased to dine with us here on the evening of Thursday December 7th at seven o'clock.[2]

I am anticipating a delightful and profitable evening.

Sincerely yours, [E. M. House]

TCL (E. M. House Papers, CtY).

[1] David Franklin Houston, Chancellor of Washington University; Secretary of Agriculture and Secretary of the Treasury in the Wilson administration.

[2] Houston later recalled that he and Wilson talked mainly about the tariff and currency problems. He also remembered a discussion of Wilson's meeting with George Harvey and Henry Watterson earlier in the day on December 7, 1911, about which see WW to G. B. M. Harvey, Dec. 21, 1911, n. 1. See David F. Houston, *Eight Years with Wilson's Cabinet, 1913 to 1920* (2 vols., Garden City, N. Y., 1926), I, 18-20.

From Oswald Garrison Villard

My dear Governor: [New York] December 1, 1911.

I am sending you herewith a copy of Congressman Redfield's[1] admirable speech on the tariff delivered last summer.[2] It is by all odds the freshest and broadest representation of the subject that has been made for some time, and comes with all the more force since Redfield is a manufacturer and knows whereof he speaks. Probably with your busy campaign you did not see it and it has occurred to me if you are thinking of speaking on the tariff before long it might be of value to you.

May I not see you before long? I am keeping in close touch with you though you may not know it, as I am having weekly conferences with McAdoo and McCombs, and trying to be of some help to them.

Faithfully yours,   [Oswald Garrison Villard]

TCL (O. G. Villard Papers, MH).

1 William Cox Redfield, manufacturer and businessman, congressman from New York, 1911-13; Secretary of Commerce, 1913-19.

2 His speech in the House of Representatives on June 12, 1911, is printed in *Cong. Record*, 62nd Cong., 1st sess., pp. 1939-48. He discussed the comparative costs of production in various industries in the United States and abroad, arguing that many American manufacturers could and did compete successfully in foreign markets and hence that in many instances a high protective tariff was unnecessary. Redfield later claimed that over a million copies of his speech were printed and circulated by the Democratic National Committee during the presidential campaign of 1912. William C. Redfield, *With Congress and Cabinet* (Garden City, N. Y., 1924), pp. 13-14

A News Report of a Memorial Address

[Dec. 4, 1911]

WILSON URGES UNSELFISHNESS

TWO ROADS IN LIFE, HE SAYS

ASBURY PARK, Dec. 4.—Urging the virtues of unselfishness and of brotherhood, Governor Wilson yesterday addressed the Elks Lodge at its memorial service in the Savoy Theatre. The theatre was crowded and the Governor was cordially greeted.

In opening, Governor Wilson said:

"I suppose that an occasion like this would be without significance if we did not believe in the immortality of the human soul. Why should we sit here and render this tribute of respect and sorrow to men who are gone, if, indeed, they are merely turned to dust; if their spirits have no further life, and if their lives, once lived, are ended and have no further meaning for us?

"The whole basis of a benevolent organization like this is the basis of organized society itself. You are but a little group, illustrating the purposes of social and political organization. You are a political state, in small. Political societies are not organized for the benefit of anybody in particular. They are organized for the common benefit, upon the principle that one man's rights stand upon a perfect equality with another man's rights.

"The man who does not see an ordered course in the development of human society does not see the standard to which he must conform his own individual actions.

"God is in His heaven; the world is not ruled by chance; it is not ruled by whim; it is not ruled by the whim of any single generation.

"There are only two roads in life,—the road of selfishness and the road of unselfishness.

"But it is not possible to walk both roads with any degree of consistency. And the sooner a man chooses to walk the road he is going to walk upon, the sooner he will know what life is and what lies before him.

"We have a very false conception of heaven, I venture to think.

"If you woke suddenly out of an iniquitous transaction into heaven, how would you feel? I have no means of penetrating the inscrutable decrees of Providence, but I shrewdly suspect that if a man got into heaven so late there must be a place for novices, where they will be introduced into unaccustomed practises.

"But the point I want to make is that heaven and hell have begun with you already.

"Many men are laboring in something very much like hell, while they are living in a veritable hell, striving to get away from the torture of their own conscience. On the other hand, many men have begun to have their eyes brightened with a light which must surely shine out of heaven, because they have squared their accounts with their conscience and have accommodated themselves to the nobler laws of life.

"I believe one of the ways—one of the most significant ways —in which America has shown her spirit is by the multiplication of orders like your own. Nowhere else in the world do men draw together as they do in this land of ours; nowhere else have so many orders of this kind been originated. Of nowhere else is it true that this kind of thing flows as if from a great eternal spring of human unselfishness and of human brotherhood. Every order like this that celebrates a memorial service like this connects itself—whether it is conscious of it or not—with all the old forces of American life, the vital forces of American life.

"Let every man examine his own heart; let him ask himself, is he a loyal son of America; does he think of his fellow men as America thinks of them; does he conceive his purposes as America expected him to conceive them?

"America expects every man to do his duty!

"And this is the whole duty of man—to 'fear God and to keep His commandments.' "[1]

Printed in the *Newark Evening News*, Dec. 4, 1911.
[1] There is a WWhw outline of this address, dated Dec. 3, 1911, in WP, DLC.

To Richard Heath Dabney

My dear Heath: [Trenton, N. J.] December 4, 1911.

I certainly owe you a very humble apology. I ought at once to have told you that my plan for going to St. Augustine miscarried. I found that the big hotels there were not open, and moreover I was getting no vacation at all, but only running into new engagements. I therefore came home as straight as I could come. I hope that you will forgive me for not writing sooner. The trouble is that I found so many things waiting for me here that I became at once absorbed.

Your letters reforwarded to me from St. Augustine have reached me and I am going to give them my very careful attention. Two other notes have also reached me here.[1] I am just about to go off to Baltimore but shall digest them on the way and let you hear from me at the end of the week. I sincerely hope it will be possible for me to meet the wishes of the Messrs. Bryan[2] by going to Richmond.

I do not know any reason why you should not publish the letter I wrote you and which you showed Mr. Bryan,[3] but if you think that it could be put in better form for publication, pray send it to me with such suggestions as may occur to you and I will be glad to put it in shape.[4]

In haste, with warm affection and renewed apologies,
Faithfully yours, Woodrow Wilson

TLS (Wilson-Dabney Corr., ViU).
[1] They are missing.
[2] George Bryan, attorney of Richmond, schoolmate of Wilson's at Charles H. Barnwell's school in Columbia, S. C., and Davidson College, at this time secretary of the Woodrow Wilson Club of Richmond; John Stewart Bryan, publisher of the Richmond *Times-Dispatch* and the Richmond *News Leader*. The two Bryans were not related.
[3] John Stewart Bryan.
[4] See WW to R. H. Dabney, Dec. 11, 1911.

To Edward Mandell House

My dear Mr. House: [Trenton, N. J.] December 4, 1911.

Thank you sincerely for your note. I shall look forward with genuine pleasure to dining with you and meeting Dr. Houston at 7 o'clock on the seventh.

Cordially and sincerely yours, Woodrow Wilson

TLS (E. M. House Papers, CtY).

A News Report About Wilson's Application for a Carnegie Pension

[Dec. 5, 1911]

WOODROW WILSON SOUGHT A PENSION

Carnegie Foundation Considered and Denied His Request.

NEVER HAD ANOTHER LIKE IT

And Really, You Know, With His Youth and
His Prospects It Didn't Seem—

When Woodrow Wilson left his students of Princeton to other hands a year ago this fall and accepted the possibility of becoming the Chief Executive of New Jersey he wrote to the Carnegie Foundation for the Advancement of Teaching and asked to be pensioned.[1] At that time he was 53 years old. He was relinquishing a place to which an emolument of $8,000 a year was attached and moving toward an office that paid $10,000. The shadow of a $50,000 job[2] was already being cast before him by some of his more enthusiastic friends.

Gov. Wilson's communication asked something for which the trustees in a broad construction of their powers had the permission of the fund's donor. But the way in which his request was worded gave them every reason to believe that he considered a pension to be the inevitable result of the twenty-five years of service as a teacher of the young which he had barely completed. He was informed that it was not automatic and that no such pension had ever been granted, for very possibly, the reason that this was the first request of the kind that the trustees had received in the four years of the foundation's life.

When this was explained to the retiring President of Princeton he received the added information that if he considered his claim well enough founded to apply formally the matter would come before the executive committee, which meets in the intervals between the full board's annual gatherings.

The formal application followed. It was considered by the executive committee. The merits of the case were discussed and the application was denied.

This action was not made public at the time because the board doesn't disclose the names of its unsuccessful applicants. . . .

The ground on which Gov. Wilson based his claim was purely financial. It will be recalled that the Governor was then 53 years old and that he was the author of several textbooks used in the colleges year after year throughout the country, and that his "History of the American People" was more or less prominent at that time in the book advertisement pages of the magazines.

There has been some discussion of this act of Gov. Wilson's among the few persons who have become acquainted with the facts. It has been known by a number of men who are not members of the board of trustees or of the executive committee. . . .

At a dinner in this city recently one of the trustees gave his opinion of the reasons underlying Dr. Governor Wilson's request.

"There was considerable public discussion about the time of Gov. Wilson's nomination," said he, "about the injection of an academically trained mind into politics. Undoubtedly some of this came under the Governor's notice. It appears that he was convinced that when he left the work to which he had devoted most of his energies and went into the business of uplifting the moral condition of politics of New Jersey he was entitled to some compensation. It would have been something of an asset to have the indorsement of such a body of men as the Carnegie Foundation; morally for the good of its effort upon the minds of voters, and financially for the good of a campaign fund."

The qualification upon which his application hinged, as the Governor apparently saw it, was his term of service. . . .

After his election as Governor he resigned from the board in these words:

"I have severed my connection with Princeton University and have given up teaching, after twenty-five years of service, to enter public life.

"I feel that in such circumstances I should tender to you my resignation. I do so with genuine reluctance and only out of a sense of duty.

"I wish to express my sense of the privilege I have enjoyed in having been permitted to share in the administration of this great and beneficent trust, and wish also to congratulate the founder and the board on the great good it has accomplished."

Printed in the New York *Sun*, Dec. 5, 1911.

¹ About Wilson's application for a Carnegie pension, see WW to H. S. Pritchett, Nov. 11, 1910, n. 1, Vol. 22. A New York *Sun* reporter had wind of Wilson's application at least as early as December 29, 1910; see H. S. Pritchett to WW, Dec. 29, 1910, Vol. 22.

² The presidency.

A Statement About His Application for a Carnegie Retirement Allowance

[[Dec. 5, 1911]]

The Carnegie Foundation for the Advancement of Teaching is not a plan for old age pensions, but for the granting of retiring allowances on the ground of length and quality of service. Before I was elected Governor of New Jersey, when I had just entered the uncertain field of politics, I applied to the Foundation for a retiring allowance, to which I understood myself to be entitled, under the rules adopted by its trustees.

I have no private means to depend upon. A man who goes into politics bound by the principles of honor puts his family and all who may be dependent upon him for support at the mercy of any incalculable turn of the wheel of fortune, and I felt entirely justified in seeking to provide against such risks, particularly when I was applying for what I supposed myself to be entitled to by right of long service as a teacher under the rules of the Foundation and not by favor.

I understood that upon the receipt of my application the executive committee of the trustees of the Foundation restricted the interpretation of their rule and declined to grant the allowance. Why the matter should have come up again now I do not know. I have had nothing to do with it since the early autumn of 1910. I have not renewed the application.

Printed in the *Newark Evening News*, Dec. 6, 1911.

From Edwin A. Newman[1]

My dear Sir: Washington, D. C. December 5, 1911.

On the eighth of January, 1912, Jackson Day, a banquet will be held at the Raleigh Hotel, in Washington, D. C., under the auspices of the Democratic National Committee, the Democratic Congressional Committee and the Democracy of the District of Columbia, in commemoration of that great Democrat, Andrew Jackson, and the day he made memorable in American history.

At a meeting of the general Banquet Committee, held at the Shoreham Hotel, Monday evening, December 4th, 1911, you were chosen as one of the speakers to address the assembled Democrats and the country on that occasion.

Hon. Norman E. Mack and Hon. James T. Lloyd[2] have appointed sub-committees of five gentlemen from the Democratic National and Democratic Congressional Committees to co-operate with a large Committee of local Democrats to arrange for the banquet, and celebration, and recognizing you as one of the great leaders of our party, we sincerely and earnestly desire your presence at that time. It has not yet been decided whether toasts will be assigned to the respective speakers, or to allow each speaker to select the topic he will speak upon. We will be pleased to have you say in your acceptance what subject you would prefer to have assigned to you.

The National Committee meets in this city January 8th, and the banquet will be to an extent in their honor also. It will be the Presidential year; the eyes of the Nation will be upon the Democracy that night; Congress will be in session, and history will be made.

We will not take no for an answer.[3] Again assuring you that we will be highly honored by your early acceptance, I have the honor to be,

Yours most respectfully,   Edwin A. Newman

TLS (Governors' Files, Nj).
[1] In the real estate business in Washington and member of the Democratic National Committee for the District of Columbia.
[2] James Tilghman Lloyd, Democratic congressman from Missouri.
[3] Wilson's address is printed at Jan. 8, 1912, Vol. 24.

A News Report of a Day in Baltimore

[Dec. 6, 1911]

GOV. WILSON SEES DANGER IN CITIES

Offers Commission Government as a Remedy.

Gov. Woodrow Wilson, of New Jersey, closed in Baltimore last night what had been a busy and strenuous day, with a speech in the Lyric, in which he depicted the evils in municipal government and in which he put forth the commission form of government. Incidentally he made onslaughts on crooked and corrupt political "machines" and "bosses."

Governor Wilson will today return to Trenton. If he possibly can he will return on Friday and at[t]end the gathering of Governors in this city.[1]

He began the day yesterday with a ride in an automobile, through the city and suburbs.

Shortly after the noon hour he went to the Emerson Hotel, where he had been invited to be a guest of personal friends and political admirers. In the parlors of The Emerson he held an informal reception, at which he met many Princeton alumni with whom he had been associated while a student at Princeton University and later while president of that institution. He also met many of his former fellow-students at Johns Hopkins University in this city. He was also introduced to several Democratic politicians.

With Senator Blair Lee, who was his college mate at Princeton, Governor Wilson led the way into the dining-room of the hotel. Others at the table were: Governor Crothers,[2] Dr. John M. T. Finney, who recently declined the presidency of Princeton University as Dr. Wilson's successor: Gen. Clinton L. Riggs,[3] W. L. Wilson, Dr. C. W. Mitchell, Dr. Hiram Woods, W. M. Meesday, Governor Wilson's secretary; Edgar Allan Poe, George Stewart Brown,[4] Sylvan Hayes Lauchheimer,[5] R. Brent Keyser,[6] B. Howell Griswold, Jr.,[7] C. C. Homer, Sr.,[8] and J. Y. Brattan.[9] Most of the gentlemen at the lunch table were Princeton alumni. The affair, however, was designed to be a gathering of gentlemen interested in the future political welfare of the Governor of New Jersey, though not a word of politics was spoken. Plenty of good wishes were tendered to the Governor.

After the lunch Mr. W. H. Fehsenfeld[10] conveyed Governor Wilson and party to the new Fifth Regiment Armory, where the Governor of New Jersey and the Governor of Maryland inspected the horticultural exhibits and then ascended the platform, where the Governor of Maryland introduced the Governor of New Jersey to the audience. He spoke for over half an hour. His speech was devoted largely to the praise of the South since its rejuvenation from the war between the states.

After his speech in the Armory Governor Wilson was conveyed to one of the local hospitals where he called upon Mr. Edwin R. Webster, of Belair,[11] who recently underwent an operation at the hands of Dr. Finney.

Governor Wilson returned to the home of Mr. and Mrs. W. M. Ellicott,[12] whose guest he was during his stay in Baltimore, where dinner was served, a few friends of Mr. and Mrs. Ellicott being present.

The climax of Governor Wilson's visit to Baltimore was his speech in the evening in the Lyric, where a large auditnce [audience] greeted him.

Printed in the *Baltimore American*, Dec. 6, 1911; some editorial headings omitted.

[1] In fact, he did not attend. The governors of Idaho, Minnesota, Montana, Nevada, North Dakota, Oregon, South Dakota, and Wyoming, together with the lieutenant governor of Colorado and a special representative of the governor of Washington, were on a tour of the country to exhibit samples and promote the sale of the agricultural and mineral products of their states. They arrived in Baltimore on December 8, the same day that the governors of Alabama, Mississippi, Missouri, South Carolina, and Virginia met there with officials of numerous railroads to discuss the best means of promoting "desirable" immigration to the South. Governor Harmon also was passing through Baltimore on his return from a speaking engagement in Atlanta. Baltimore officials and civic leaders arranged an elaborate program of entertainment for the visitors. Baltimore *Sun*, Dec. 8 and 9, 1911; *New York Times*, Nov. 28 and 29, Dec. 1, 9, and 10, 1911.

[2] Austin Lane Crothers, Governor of Maryland, 1908-12.

[3] Clinton Levering Riggs, Princeton 1887; graduate student in political economy, Johns Hopkins, 1887-88; adjutant general of Maryland, 1904-1908; at

this time president of the Riggs Building Co. Wilson appointed him as commissioner to the Philippines in 1913.

4 Johns Hopkins 1893, lawyer of Baltimore.

5 Johns Hopkins 1890; graduate student in history, 1890-1891, lawyer of Baltimore.

6 Robert Brent Keyser, associated for many years with and president (1905-10) of the Baltimore Copper Smelting and Rolling Co.; president of the Hopkins board of trustees since 1903.

7 Benjamin Howell Griswold, Jr., Johns Hopkins 1894, elected trustee in 1911; partner in the Baltimore banking firm of Alexander Brown and Sons.

8 Charles Christopher Homer, president of the Second National Bank of Baltimore.

9 Joseph Yancey Brattan, Princeton 1883, editor of the Baltimore *American*.

10 William Henry Fehsenfeld, president of two petroleum companies of Baltimore and vice-president of the Fehsenfeld Cigar Company.

11 James Edwin Webster, Wilson's classmate at Princeton.

12 William Miller Ellicott and Elizabeth Tabor King Ellicott. He was an architect of Baltimore.

A News Report of an Address in Baltimore[1]

[Dec. 6, 1911]

LOOKS TO SOUTH

Wilson Urges Farmers To Organize in School Houses And Churches.

Governor Wilson's speech at the Fifth Regiment Armory yesterday afternoon was a thoughtful discussion of the problems of Southern development and his hearers listened with the closest attention.

In spite of the difficulty of speaking in so large a hall and one in which people were constantly moving about he spoke without apparent effort and was heard by all who gathered to listen to his speech. He was frequently applauded. . . .

Governor Wilson was introduced by Governor Crothers, whose reference to him as New Jersey's "great Governor" was heartily applauded.

In opening his address Governor Wilson referred to the invitations that had been given him to return to Baltimore on Friday, "when the town will be full of Governors."

"I have told them," he continued, "that I don't care particularly about meeting Governors, but that I did care particularly about meeting the representative citizens of the State. We are Governors because of you, and you do not exercise your functions because of us. It is a great deal more vital to deal with you than to deal with them. (Applause.)

"They are like the fruits that I see displayed about me upon these tables. They are the crop. (Laughter.) We are very much more interested in those fundamental processes of the soil and

1 To the Maryland Week Celebration and Horticultural Exhibition.

of culture that produce the crop, the thought of the people, their consciousness of right, their knowledge of the conditions under which they live—a knowledge which, if the politician does not share it, he cannot lead and cannot serve. (Applause.) We are dealing with the stuff of affairs when we deal with the rank and file of citizenship. Moreover, I wanted to see country people in Baltimore. (Laughter.)

"I have been a great deal in Baltimore first and last during my life, and Baltimore is like a great many other cities. It needs fertilization and refreshment from the country. (Applause.) I have felt in recent years that the South was in some respects the newest part of the United States. Baltimore is interesting to the country, is interesting to the world, because it is the gate to the South, one of the gates to that great coun[t]ry whose development through a whole generation or more has been arrested and held back. And the South is now coming into a consciousness of the sort of vitality that has been laid up in her all these years.

"Now, I believe she is about once more to assert every kind of energy she possesses and to play a great role under the guidance of what is not old in the South, namely, her immemorial principles. Here is an unexhausted reservoir of the pure waters of the ancient political and social principles in America, from which the country can now draw, and, if it please, be refreshed. (Applause.) We speak of the South, and we speak truly of it, as the most conservative section of America. The South is the place where, more than any other, men look back to old-established principles so as to square what they now do with those principles. She has the sort of reverence and living memory for deeds that are gone, for deeds that constitute a long-past achievement, and she wishes to see her present and her future squared with that.

"Very well, then; what is the South interested in? The South is not interested in change, but it is interested in renewal[.] And in order that there shall be renewal it is necessary that she should be deeply and constantly interested in knowledge. If the South is not merely to consume her own products, farm by farm, she must go to school to the great masters of science; she must be interested in the consumption by youngsters and old men of the great stores of knowledge which have been laid up in the modern world with regard to agricultural and other processes with which we have flattered ourselves we are familiar. I am not an expert in this knowledge. I merely sit at the feet of those who tell me that I must believe, because I have not enough knowledge to contradict.

"I rejoice in conferences of this sort, but you must do something more. If I may be permitted to say so, the farmers of this country must organize themselves for various purposes, and there are two places where I would suggest that they organize —in the country schoolhouses and in the country churches.

"I am not one of those who believe that the entire use of religion is reserved for the next world. (Applause.) I hear it quoted from Scripture that Christ came into the world for the salvation of the world, for the transformation of human life, and I believe that if the country pastors of this country were to make themselves the centres of conferences in everything that concerned the life of the people about them and insisted that the church was a perfectly suitable place to discuss any honest piece of business they would begin a very important part of the revivi[fi]cation of church life and religion in America. (Applause.) Every problem of our modern life, social and political, ladies and gentlemen, is a problem of co-operation. It is a problem of bringing everybody into the game.

"I hear some gentlemen now upon the political forum speak of the people in such terms as make it evident that they do not include themselves. They are debating what we, some little especially equipped coterie, are to do for the people. There is an unmistakable tone of condescension in it. Now, I have no conception of the people that does not include those gentlemen and everybody else. (Applause.) I am more generous than they; they do not invite me into partnership, but I am ready and willing to invite them. They are part of the people, and, until they realize it, they cannot serve the people. You cannot serve anybody by standing outside of them and determining what is good for them. They are not children; they are not your wards; they are not people for whom you are privileged to do the thinking; they are people with whose minds and purposes you must match and harness your own. And then you will assure their strength and they will assure yours.

"Now when the farmers come together, not for the purpose of squeezing out an indispensable middle man, but for the purpose of seeing that they are themselves not squeezed out (applause), then business will begin to be transacted on the farm. When they begin to co-operate so that the small farmer can handle his products just as advantageously as the big farmer can, because he is in co-operation with him, when they begin to co-operate so that they shall all know from a common source of information which they themselves have established where the best markets are, where such and such prices prevail, how they can best ship their goods and deliver them, then they will

deal with the railroads, for example, upon a very different footing from the footing upon which the small producer now deals
with them, and they can make everybody realize that the farmer
is a collective term and not an individual term, that the farmers
know what they are about and all know what they are about.

"Then it will begin to dawn upon certain gentlemen who have
not yet perceived it that their interest is common with the interest of the producer and that the lessons of our country are not
mere lessons of commerce and of manufacture, but that they
are lessons which go back to the original processes of production also, and that the sources of prosperity are the sources of
nature herself and of the men who deal with nature herself.
These are the things that you ought to think about and ought to
get together and think about.

"And so it seems to me that what the South is now interested
in is not only knowledge but opportunity. You want personal opportunity and you want financial opportunity. Therefore, although you may not know it, you have a deeper interest than
almost anybody else in seeing to it that the financial system of
this country is not controlled in any particular place. (Applause.)
The opportunity for achievement, the freedom for investment,
the opportunity of individual and independent action must be
kept absolutely open because the South has not yet achieved her
economical development, and unless that door stands open she
cannot achieve it."[2]

Printed in the Baltimore *Sun*, Dec. 6, 1911; some editorial headings omitted.
   [2] There are two WWhw outlines of this address, one dated Dec. 2, 1911, in
WP, DLC.

A News Report of an Address in Baltimore
on Behalf of Commission Government

[Dec. 6, 1911]

AWAKE! HE SAYS

Woodrow Wilson Analyzes Faults In American City Government.

Proclaiming that there is nothing in city government which
should be kept secret from the public and pointing out that publicity which attends commission rule is the reason why, in his
opinion, that is the kind American cities should adopt, Gov.
Woodrow Wilson, of New Jersey, held under the spell of his
oratorical power at the Lyric last night one of the most representative audiences gathered in Baltimore for many years.

Regarded today as one of the big men of the nation, Mr. Wilson's coming drew a large audience, many of which were probably not in favor of the commission plan of city government. Some had to stand and on the stage were many prominent persons and members of the Women's Good Government Committee, under whose auspices the meeting was held. . . .[1]

In his speech at the Lyric last night Governor Wilson said:

"I am afraid that the disguise which my friend, George Gaither,[2] has thrown around me is very transparent. I must thank him for his kindness when I remember that he is a Republican and that he was a sophomore while I was a freshman at Princeton.

"I remember my presence in this hall several years ago. It was an occasion when your citizens met to protest against municipal conditions which do not seem to be much improved. On that occasion the protest was against the administration of public affairs by Republicans, who, so soon as in power, proceeded to imitate their Democratic predecessors. Among the speakers was Hon. Theodore Roosevelt, then police commissioner of New York.[3]

"The hopes of America have been disappointed in American city government. There was a time—you do not have to be very old to remember it—when there was a universal complacency in America about our success in matters of political organization. No American anywhere would admit that anywhere in the

[1] This meeting was an episode in a long struggle by Baltimore reformers to achieve a basic revision of the city's charter. In September 1909, Mayor John Barry Mahool appointed a Charter Revision Commission composed of well-known civic leaders and reformers. After considerable debate over the advisability of adopting the commission form of government, it decided instead to propose a new charter increasing the powers of the existing Board of Estimates and replacing the bicameral city council with a unicameral council of fourteen members with broad investigatory powers. The proposed charter also called for the merit system in the city's civil service and for increased home rule powers in the areas of taxation of corporations, public health, and recreation. However, the proposed charter was opposed by the Democratic majority on the existing city council, and the Democrats in the Maryland General Assembly tabled the charter bill in March 1910.

A revised charter bill was submitted to the General Assembly in 1912. The major changes by the Charter Revision Commission and a citizens' Committee of Fifty were provisions for nonpartisan primaries and elections and for the recall of elected officials. This time the General Assembly did pass the charter bill, but only after eliminating the nonpartisan and recall provisions and increasing the size of the council to twenty-six members. Because of these changes, the Charter Revision Commission persuaded Governor Goldsborough to veto the measure. No substantial revision of the Baltimore city charter occurred until 1918. See James B. Crooks, *Politics & Progress: The Rise of Urban Progressivism in Baltimore, 1895-1911* (Baton Rouge, La., 1968), pp. 102-107, and John A. Lapps (ed.), "Current Municipal Legislation," *National Municipal Review*, 1 (July 1912), 465.

[2] George Riggs Gaither, Princeton 1878, lawyer of Baltimore, unsuccessful Republican candidate for Governor of Maryland in 1907, and a leader in the charter reform movement.

[3] This and the preceding paragraph from the partial text in the *Baltimore American*, Dec. 6, 1911.

world there were to be found governments organized more successfully than they were organized in America.

"But we have got over that complacency. We have had to admit the fact that most of the well-governed cities of this world are on the other side of the water and that most of the worst governed cities of the civilized world are on this side of the water.

"There must be some reason for that. We do not abate in the least our pride in the political capacity of America. We do not for one moment indict our own characters or suspect that we desire to debase our Government. We know that the impulse of freedom beats just as strongly in America now as it ever beat before. We have made some mistake, some fundamental, organic blunder.

"We cannot purposely have gone astray. We must somewhere have missed the road that leads to the goal which we all desire to reach, and now we are beating about in the jungle to find again where the open road lies, because we all admit that in the field of municipal government there is a scene of universal confusion, there is exhibited the most wasteful expense, and that something, not public opinion, controls the government of our cities and prevents our controlling it. I do not know; I have no personal or intimate knowledge of what has been going on in the city of Baltimore. I could venture a guess, because there are so many examples that I do know of that I know what the violent probabilities are with regard to Baltimore. (Laughter.)

"I understand that you have just had a committee of fifty, which has agreed to recommend a charter. The remarkable thing to my mind about that achievement is that a committee of fifty agreed. (Laughter and applause.) I do not know anything about the charter, but I should like to see a charter upon which 50 active-minded men have agreed. (Laughter.) And so you are seeking through the instrumentality of your most active citizens for the solution of the matter for which a solution is everywhere being sought. We do not have to lay the foundations of this discussion. We do not have to prove that something is the matter. We only have to explain, if we can, why something is the matter and what it is that has gone amiss.

"I take it that the problem that we have set ourselves is the problem of responsibility. We want governments which respond to public opinion and we have not been able to get them. The explanation you can hang on your wall if you choose, if you will only take the pains to buy a copy of that old cartoon by 'Tom' Nast, which represented the Tweed Ring in New York as an actual circle of men, each with his thumb to his neighbor, the title of the picture being ' 'Twan't Me.'

"What I wish to explain tonight is that we have invented or stumbled upon a ' 'Twan't Me' system of government and that what we are in search of is a ' 'tis you' system of government. (Applause.) We cannot fix responsibility because responsibility depends upon certain things. It depends upon obviousness in the processes of government. It depends upon intelligibility in the methods of government. It depends upon openness in the councils of governments. Unless the thing is obvious the eye of the general public is not going to perceive it. Unless it is intelligible the eye of the general public cannot perceive it. Unless it is open there is nothing to be seen.

"I think one of the most distressing things in the world, at any rate to me, in whom a large share of the boy still remains, is to go to a four-ring circus and try to watch it. (Laughter.) I want to see everything that happens in every ring and the consequence is that I do not see all of anything that happens in any of them, and I sometimes have thought to myself in such a place that I was trying to do exactly what the American people try to do in their city government. They try not only to watch four rings, but 20 rings, and they do not see any of the private tricks; they do not see any of those sleight-of-hand performances which are at the bottom of the whole deceiving business.

"You know that the art of deceit upon the stage, where all sorts of sleight of hand is attempted, is the art of distracting the attention of the audience to something that does not constitute the trick; that men who are engaged in that business understand the human eye better than they understand anything else, and they know how to make the human eye wander at the right time.

"Some gentlemen connected with political machines are past-masters in that. (Applause.) They distract your attention to a perfectly irrelevant matter just at the right point, and you do not see what is done.

"Next morning the transaction is complete and irrevocable: the contract is let and nobody can get into the competition. What we have to ask ourselves, therefore, is this: Do we prefer to hunt in a jungle, or would we rather hunt in the open? Do we like political hide and seek?

"I am for burning down the jungle (applause) and then letting the beast take his chance. (Applause.)

"I heard a gentleman today—this is none of my business, and I bring it in parenthetically (laughter)—I heard a gentleman say today that he did not want to see a commission government in Baltimore, because he knew certain gentlemen who had an organization that could capture all of the commissioners. I said to him, What better fun do you want? Let them have them. It is all in the open, and you will have the best sport of your life to see them perform. (Applause.)

"Give me the harness and the whip and I do not care what team you supply me with; just get in the commanding position, put curb-bits in their mouths, hold the reins—and I think American opinion knows how to hold them—and have the whip, and if they do not keep to the road I am a poor prophet. (Applause.)

"Centre responsibility, make it unmistakable, and it is almost a matter of indifference who has the offices provided only they have the instinct of self-preservation. (Laughter and applause.)

"We want to unify in order to control. I do not understand the reason of those persons who say that unification, centralization, is un-democratic. I do not know a thing which is un-democratic, except that which prevents the people from controlling. (Applause.) And I stand for the proposition that anything that secures control by public opinion is fundamentally and radically democratic. (Applause.) I do not have to argue that. It is too obvious. As a friend of mine said, 'I am not arguing with you; I am telling you.' (Laughter.)

"In order to get control you must get unity. I would, if I could, speak with entire reverence of our system of checks and balances in American government, but with due apologies I cannot. Because, leaving aside the greater sphere of government, the government of the States and the government of the nation, nothing has so played into the hands of corruption in our State governments as the attempt to establish in them a set of checks and balances, offsetting authorities against one another.

"That means that you set up a series of co-equal departments intending to check one another, intended to foil one another's purposes, intended to see to it that nothing can be done which all of them do not agree upon.

"After you have set up this series of independent authorities, what have you done? Why, if you will pardon me for what will seem a pedantic digression and which may prove a little interesting, I will say that you have constructed a government on the Newtonian theory of the universe.

"Now, the universe, as I understand it—which is very imperfectly—is a mechanical contrivance, and each part of it is intended to stay where it is and mind its own business. I understand that there would be deep mischief if it did not. (Laughter.)

"And the writers in the Federalist and all of the expounders of the checks and balances of the American system think in the terms of the Newtonian universe. They speak of the centripital and centrifugal forces and of the powers of gravitation which hold the various bodies in their proper orbits and spheres.

"Now we have no orbit and spheres; we talk about woman's sphere and man's sphere, but we are talking nonsense most of the time. (Applause.)

"What we have to realize is that we and our Government are organisms, and there is only one law by which an organism can live, and that is the law pointed out not by Newton, on a mechanical analogy, but by Darwin on the analogies of living beings.

"Our governments do not work that way. The parts do cooperate; if they did not, there would not be any government.

"But what makes them co-operate? A power outside of them—namely the political machine. I agree with Mr. Gaither that the machine is, in one sense, an essentially un-American thing, inasmuch as it is in many of its aspects a secret and despotic thing, but I cannot agree with him that it was not a natural growth of American politics. We have got to have the machine under present conditions or go out of business.

"I do not mean that we have got to have a corrupt machine, but we have got to have a machine, an outside organization, an organization outside of this complicated piece of machinery whose single command shall bring order out of chaos, whose united will shall unify and control the governments we have set up.

"The American boss is one of the most characteristic and inevitable fruits of American politics. You cannot put him out of business, as your governments are at present organized. You can get disgusted with a particular boss; you can put him out of business; you can see to it that some one more honest or more in accord with your principles takes his place, but whatever the kind of boss, there will be a boss. That is the reason why we have a special political organization and machinery in this country which exists nowhere else. Nowhere else has it been made absolutely necessary that it should exist.

"You have this problem, therefore. Are you going to boss your governments or are you going to make it necessary that somebody else should boss them? They have got to be superintended, they have got to be given a unity and co-ordination of purpose, and the choice is with you as to the source from which these forces will come, because we know that we do not stop with the machine. What troubles us is not that the machine controls the action of our government so much as that we see shadowy shapes behind the machine.

"It is very expensive, our way of controlling government. The machine has to have money; where is it going to get it? It must come from men who want to be sure that they will get something for their money. They say, 'Certainly, if you will see to it that our interests are promoted, or at least safeguarded, you can have the money, otherwise you cannot.' And the goods are delivered upon those terms.

"If the machine did not have to spend any money, if the machine did not have a great deal of money, if the machine was merely a volunteering of certain men with the capacity to do it to control our government, I for my part could look on with a certain degree of indifference, if not complacence.

"But when I know that these men are in the pay of those who are working for their own profit and special interests and who do not care a peppercorn for the general interest of society, I know then that the most dangerous oligarchy that could be possibly set up has been set up in the United States.

"How do you explain that there is no politics as between machines? (Applause.) How do you explain the fact that men give money both to the Democratic and to the Republican machines? And money is assured between the two machines, all going back to that absolutely true but cynical remark attributed to a politician in New York city, who said, 'There ain't no politics in politics.' (Laughter and applause.)

"Machines are not divided by a principle, they are divided by opportunity. (Applause.) I want you to distinguish, as I try sharply to distinguish in my own thoughts, between the machine and party organization. They are absolutely different things[.] (Applause.)

"A machine is a little coterie of capable and designing men who are using the party organization for their own purposes; no man should be ignorant or stupid or unjust enough to bring into condemnation the legitimate organization of our great parties, but every man should be intelligent enough to know that those organizations constantly stand in danger of being controlled by the machine and that the machine in its turn is controlled and employed by those who do not appear upon the political forum at all. That is the beast and there is the jungle.

"Now, what are we going to do about it? I am not here to advocate anything in particular for Baltimore. I am afraid that I have a reputation of not very scrupulously minding my own business, but I want to observe at any rate the forms of minding it.

(Laughter.) So, if you will permit me, I will say a few words about commission government. (Applause.)

"Some 100 cities in the United States have adopted commission government, and no city that has ever adopted it, so far as I know, has gone back to the old form of government. (Applause.)

"But before I speak of that I want to call your attention to an interesting circumstance. Why is it that Americans follow with so much interest the actions and fortunes of the English Government? I believe it is because the English Government is the simplest and most democratic government in the world. England is governed by a committee in the House of Commons. That is all that the English Ministry is. That is commission government, and we watch it from this distance because it is so obvious and easy to understand.

"Take another example. One of the best governed cities in the world by common consent of the students of that matter is the city of Glasgow, in Scotland. The city of Glasgow is governed by a single assembly, consisting of 32 members. There are 32 districts in the city of Glasgow, each district electing one member of this central body.

"Nobody in Glasgow ever gets a chance to vote for more than one person so far as his city government is concerned. That body of 32 divides itself up into as many committees as there are departments of the city government. Each committee has entire charge of that department, under responsibility, of course, to the party as a whole.

"Every morning in the Glasgow Herald you can read what the body as whole did and what each committee did. You can follow your own man as if with an index finger, and he can never get away from you. You have your attention concentrated upon your man, and it breeds a self-consciousness in him (laughter), which is very wholesome for the maintenance of his morals. (Laughter and applause.)

"Now the city of Glasgow has one of the simplest governments in the world, and one of the best governments in the world, and the city of Glasgow undertakes things that you would not dare allow your own city government to undertake, and it undertakes them without suspicion even of graft or bargain.

"Are the Scots more honest than we? I don't think so. They are shrewder than we in some respects, but I do not think they are more honest. There is no more patriotic and civic interest in the city of Glasgow than there is in the city of Baltimore, but the city of Glasgow owns its own government, and you do not. (Applause.)

"You say, if that is the principle, why not do what several American cities have tried, to concentrate all your power in one man—the Mayor? For the good reason that very often a single man has too many ambitions to serve and a single man does not debate things with himself out loud. (Applause and laughter.)

"But, make it five men or six men, or a dozen men, and unite them in authority. They can not do anything without doing it together. They won't combine to serve the interests of any one of them, and when they do combine they combine after a debate, at which you have been the audience.

"Publicity added to shared authority, to authority which is unified without being put in one person, is the key to the simplification of government. A single man can hold his own counsel, but I have yet to meet the man in this country who can hold his own counsel under the aggravation of debate.

"All you have to do is to say things about him. All you have to do is to tread upon some tender toe. All you have to do is to seem to be about to carry a motion which he does not want carried, and you have drawn his fire, and the minute you have drawn his fire you expose his motives and have exposed him.

"If you could get each of your public officials to stand upon this public stage upon some occasion and explain his own actions, you do not have to sit there and keep explaining very long to get at the whole of his mind. Particularly is that so if he does not know how to talk.

"Very well, then, you must have a debating government, and therefore you must have more than one man, but the government must be concentrated in a set of men, so that there can be no doubt who issued the orders, and above everything else it must be specified and established that everything done shall be done in public (applause); that nothing voted behind closed doors shall have the validity of laws (applause); that no record of what is done shall be withheld from the general public inspection. (Applause.) You have got to establish the principle and back it with severe penalties that there is nothing connected with the government of a city which can conceivably be made private.

"Everything should be done with open doors and everything be accessible to everybody."

Governor Wilson referred to the Walsh law in New Jersey, which provides for the commission plan, and a non partisan primary.

"No parties," he said, "are recognized. Anybody who can get a certain number of signatures to his name, can have his name put upon the ticket at those primaries. Then, at the primaries, if there are to be five Commissioners, every voter votes for 10, and out of those nominated five are chosen. There are no party designations, no description of the candidates, nothing but the name.

"Men are not elected by pluralities, but are elected by majorities. Necessarily, if one man of two is elected, he must be elected by a majority, a majority of those who vote, and under the New Jersey plan, when we adopt or vote for the adoption of the Commission plan of government, at least 30 per cent. of the voters of the city must vote in the affirmative in order to adopt it. So, we have tried to avoid the domination or undesirable activities of minorities, and to make everything operative by the majority of votes.

"You will say, Is there nothing more to commission government? There is nothing more. That is the beauty of it. There doesn't have to be anything more. We say to these five gentlemen who are elected in New Jersey, 'The way the government under you is constituted is nothing to us. The number of people that are employed by you is nothing to us—at present. The way you organize or reorganize your departments is your business, but we are going to hold you responsible for every bit of it, and if it does not work out, then we are going to try somebody else until we find somebody who knows how to make it work.'

"Some cities in New Jersey were not fortunate in their choice of Commissioners, but as soon as those commissions got to work it was shown which cities were unfortunate, and there is the recall. (Applause.) Under our system of commission government there is a very great advantage in having an opportunity to identify your undesirable commission.

"I have heard men say, 'Do you think that a government so concentrated and simple as that would be desirable in a great city with a great teeming population?'

"I don't know the point of that question. What has the number of people got to do with it? (Applause.) Is a government less safe when it is watched by a million eyes than when it is watched by a thousand eyes? Is the miscellaneous makeup of the government merely another way of saying that those men will be looked at from every point of interest and those men will be watched more than in a community where the number of eyes is not so great?

"I don't know what the size of the city has to do with it, except that it will be a much more severe test. You will have to try to get big men, and if that don't succeed, you must try again until you have got the biggest men that you have got, and then think of the distinction which will come to a city which is governed by its best men. (Applause.)

"I am saying this—I want to repeat it—in all earnestness by way of illustration. It would not be permissible or excusable for me to say what is right for Baltimore, because I don't know. It would have been once, because I lived here once. (Applause.)

"It may be that you deeply enjoy the kind of government that you have, and, if so, I might, upon inquiry, marvel at your taste, but I could not quarrel with your judgment, because it is your funeral and not mine. (Applause.)

"I am expounding a thing, ladies and gentlemen, which extends into all conditions of American life. The thing we are looking for in city government, we are looking for in every kind of government in America. The ways of finding it are not the same, but the quest is the same. We are seeking for responsible action, in response not to special interests or to parts of the opinion, but to the whole opinion of the nation. We are seeking to embody it in the judgment of common men.

"The human race is not to be saved by a remnant; the human race is not to be saved by a few instructed persons, but it is to be saved by the consciences and purposes of common men. (Applause.) If you cannot carry the instinct of the common man with you, then you have done nothing to increase the forces or to enhance the hopes of the nation.

"Ah! ladies and gentlemen, you cannot touch gove[r]nment at any point without touching the very springs of life. Government is not something set apart. Government is part of our lives. Government sets conditions 'round about our lives. Government affords us opportunities to spend and be spent in the interests of our fellow-men.

"And, so, in studying the interests of Baltimore, you are studying the interests of Maryland—you are studying the interests of America—you are trying to get yourself the standards which, as they spread from community to community, will call men's thoughts back to those fundamental things for which we live.

"We do not live for material success. Not one of us has ever been satisfied for a single moment by material success. We live in order that our spirits may be serene. We live in order that days may come in which, when the work is over, we look our fellow-men in the eyes with unfaltering gaze, when we shall come to the brink of the grave and go down into its depths, knowing that we, at least, have done our little parts to see that men are elevated to the uplands of vision and unselfish achievement." (Long continued applause.)[4]

Printed in the Baltimore *Sun*, Dec. 6, 1911; some editorial headings omitted.
    [4] There is a WWhw and WWsh outline of this address, with the composition date of Dec. 2, 1911, in WP, DLC.

From Edward Ingle

Dear Wilson: Baltimore, Md., Dec. 6, 1911.

When I wish to emphasize my unswerving belief in your integrity I am obliged to disregard the titles of honor and distinction that are justly yours and to think of you as of the time of our association at the Johns Hopkins, nearly thirty years ago. I could not get to hear you yesterday when you were in Baltimore, though I should have liked to tell you face to face my opinion of the attempt to belittle you in connection with the Carnegie Pension Board.[1] So I am writing.

I feel confident that the dominating influences in that board would never have had the chance to reveal their real character, in making public an application from you for a retiring pension, had you been acquainted with the purpose of that Carnegie benefaction. Such knowledge on your part would have barred you from making the application. The Carnegie benefactions, like the benefactions of Rockefeller, are a species of social insurance, an attempt to avert the righteous judgment of a re-awakened common sense of the American people. The intent is not to promote a healthy development of honest opinion and ethical conduct, but to dam—better still, damn—courageous truth at its source. The Woodrow Wilsons of the land naturally do not commend themselves to the Carnegies and Rockefellers.

Sincerely yours,   [Edward Ingle]

CCL (E. Ingle Papers, MdHi).
    [1] About these criticisms, see Link, *Road to the White House*, pp. 348-52.

A News Report and An Address in New York Protesting Russian Discrimination Against American Jews

[Dec. 7, 1911]

BREAK WITH RUSSIA NOW, 5,000 VOICES CRY

A great meeting was held in Carnegie Hall last night to protest against the discrimination of the Russian Government in recognizing passports issued to American citizens.[1] The pent-up feelings of a great body of American people who have suffered the effects of this discrimination through forty years of protest found expression in a gathering which has rarely been equalled here for earnestness, well-contained indignation, and enthusiasm.

Carnegie Hall, seating about 4,500 persons, was filled to its last square foot of space long before the meeting began. In the two great tiers of boxes were gathered many prominent men of the city with their families. The audience was representative of New York. All classes and creeds were there.

Dozens of prominent men c[a]me acress [across] States to join in this protest, which was not made on behalf of Jewish citizens, or on behalf of the Catholic clergy, or on behalf of some of the Protestant clergy, bunt [but] it was many times declared, on behalf of American citizens, individually and as a whole, against a condition which has existen [existed] since 1832, and against which this country has vainly protested against for forty years.

On the stage were some of the most prominent men of the country, both as speakers and participants in the purpose and spirit of the meeting. Among the speakers were ex-Ambassador Andrew D[ickson]. White, President of the National Citizens' Committee, under whose auspices the meeting was held, and for three years the representative of this country at the Czar's court; Speaker Champ Clark, United States Senator James A. O'Gorman, Gov. Woodrow Wilson of New Jersey, who was repeatedly hailed from the galleries as the next President; Bishop David H[ummell]. Greer, President [Jacob Gould] Schu[r]man of Cornell University, William R. Hearst, Congressman William Sulzer, Chairman of the House Committee on Foreign Relations; ex-Congressman Herbert Parsons, Congressman William A. [Musgrave] Calder, ex-Congressman William S[tiles]. Bennet, and Congressman Henry [Mayer] Goldfogle. . . .

Gov. Wilson was evidently a favorite. Cheers started at the mention of his name, and calls of "our next President" came from the eyrie places in the top of the great room. The Governor straightened his tall form perceptibly at the sound, and he smiled broadly while he waved down the cries—gently waving them down, it should be said. Gov. Wilson said:

Mr. Chairman[2] and gentlemen, the object of this meeting is not agitation, it is the statement of a plain case in such terms as may serve to arrest the attention of the Nation with regard

---

[1] About this matter, see WW to H. Bernstein, July 6, 1911, n. 2.

[2] William G. McAdoo, chairman of the executive committee of the National Citizens' Committee.

to a matter which is of no mere local importance, which does not merely affect the rights and essential privileges of our Jewish fellow citizens as freemen and Americans, but which touches the dignity of our Government and the maintenance of those rights of manhood which that Government was set up to vindicate.

The facts are these: For some eighty years a treaty has existed between this country and Russia in which it is explicitly covenanted and agreed that the inhabitants of the two nations shall have the liberty of entering any part of the territory of either that is open to foreign commerce; that they shall be at liberty to sojourn and reside in all parts whatsoever of the territory thus opened to commerce, in order to attend to their affairs; and that they shall enjoy the same security and protection as inhabitants of the country in which they are sojourning, on condition, of course, that they submit to the laws and ordinances there prevailing, and particularly to the regulations there in force concerning commerce. For some forty years the obligations of this treaty have been disregarded by Russia in respect of our Jewish fellow citizens. Our Government has protested, but has never gone beyond protest. After forty years of mere correspondence the Russian Government naturally does not expect the matter to be carried beyond protest to action, and so continues to act as it pleases in this matter, in the confidence that our Government does not seriously mean to include our Jewish fellow citizens among those upon whose rights it will insist.

It is not necessary to conjecture the reasons. The treaty thus disregarded by Russia is a treaty of commerce and navigation. Its main object is trade, the sort of economic intercourse between the two nations that will promote the material interests of both. Important commercial and industrial relations have been established under it. Large American undertakings, we are informed, would be put in serious peril were those relations broken off. We must concede something, even at the expense of a certain number of our fellow citizens, in order not to risk a loss greater than the object sought would seem to justify.

I for one do not fear any loss. The economic relations of two great nations are not based upon sentiment; they are based upon interest. It is safe to say that in this instance they are not based upon mutual respect, for Russia cannot respect us when she sees us for forty years together preferring our interests to our rights. Whatever our feeling may be with regard to Russia, whatever our respect for her statesmen or our sympathy with the great future in store for her people, she would certainly be justified in acting upon the expectation that we would follow our calculations of expediency rather than our convictions of right and justice. Only once or twice, it would seem, has she ever thought our Government in earnest. Should she ever deem it in earnest, respect would take the place of covert indifference and the treaty would be lived up to. If it was ever advantageous to her, it is doubly and trebly advantageous now, and her advantage would be her guide, as has been ours, in the maintenance of a treaty of trade and navigation.

If the Russian Government has felt through all these years that it could ignore the protest of American ministers and Secretaries of State, it has been because the American Government spoke for special interests or from some special point of view and not for the American people. It is the fact that the attention of the American people has now been drawn to this matter that is altering the whole aspect of it.

We are a practical people. Like the rest of the world we establish our trade relations upon grounds of interest, not sentiment. The feeling of the American people toward the people of Russia has always been one of deep sympathy, and I believe of ready comprehension, and we have dealt with their Government in frankness and honor, wherever it appears that the interests of both nations could be served. We have not held off from cordial intercourse or withheld our respect because her political polity was so sharply contrasted with ours. Our desire is to be her friend and to make our relations with her closer and closer.

But there lies a principle back of our life. America is not a mere body of traders; it is a body of free men. Our greatness is built upon our freedom—is moral, not material. We have a great ardor for gain; but we have a deep passion for the rights of man. Principles lie back of our action. America would be inconceivable without them. These principles are not incompatible with great material prosperity. On the contrary, unless we are deeply mistaken, they are indispensable to it. We are not willing to have prosperity, however, if our fellow citizens must suffer contempt for it, or lose the rights that belong to every American in order that we may enjoy it. The price is too great.

Here is a great body of our Jewish fellow citizens, from whom have sprung men of genius in every walk of our varied life, men who have become part of the very stuff of America, who have conceived its ideals with singular clearness and led its enterprise with spirit and sagacity. They are playing a particularly conspicuous part in building up of the very prosperity of which our Government has so great a stake in its dealings with the Russian

Government with regard to the rights of men. They are not Jews in America; they are American citizens. In this great matter with which we deal to-night, we speak for them as for representatives and champions of principles which underlie the very structure of our Government. They have suddenly become representatives of us all. By our action for them shall be tested our sincerity, our genuineness, the reality of principle among us.

I am glad this question has been thus brought into the open. There is here a greater stake than any other upon which we could set our hearts. Here is the final test of our ability to square our policies with our principles. We may now enjoy the exhilaration of matching our professions with handsome performance. We are not here to express our sympathy with our Jewish fellow citizens, but to make evident our sense of identity with them. This is not their cause; it is America's. It is the cause of all who love justice and do right.

The means by which the wrongs we complain of may be set right are plain. There is no hostility in what we do toward the Russian Government. No man who takes counsel of principle will have in his thought anything but purposes of peace. There need be for us in this great matter no touch of anger. But the conquests of peace are based upon mutual respect. The plain fact of the matter is that for some forty years we have observed the obligations of our treaty with Russia and she has not. That can go on no longer. So soon as Russia fully understands that it can go on no longer, that we must, with whatever regret, break off the intercourse between our people and our merchants, once the agreements upon which it is based can be observed in letter and in spirit, the air will clear. There is every reason why our intercourse should be maintained and extended, but it cannot be upon such terms as at present. If the explicit provisions of our present agreement cannot be maintained, we must reconsider the matter in the light of the altered circumstances and see upon what terms, if any, of mutual honor our intercourse may be reestablished. We have advantages to offer her merchants, her mine owners, her manufacturers, which her Government will not despise. We are not suppliants. We come with gifts in our hands. Her statesmen see as clearly as ours. An intolerable situation will be remedied just as soon as Russia is convinced that for us it is indeed intolerable.[3]

Printed in the *New York Times*, Dec. 7, 1911; some editorial headings omitted; the text of Wilson's address from *Cong. Record*, 62nd Cong., 2nd sess., Vol. 48, Appendix, pp. 497-98, with corrections from the partial text in the *New York Times*, Dec. 7, 1911 and from the WWsh draft, dated Jan. 6, 1911, in WP, DLC.

[3] There is a WWhw outline of this address, dated Dec. 6, 1911, in WP, DLC.

From William Gibbs McAdoo

PERSONAL.

Dear Governor: [New York] December 8, 1911.

I know you will be gratified to learn that your speech at the meeting Wednesday evening made a great impression, and everyone with whom I have talked says that you carried off the chief honors of the occasion. This is decidedly my own opinion. I am glad you came. You not only rendered great service to the Cause, but to yourself as well.

By the way, Mrs. Harriman tells me that she and Mrs. Alexander are going to invite you to dinner on the evening of January 2nd, following your talk to the Colony Club.[1] I hope you will accept this invitation, as they contemplate having as their guests some people whom I would be very glad to have you know. Won't you give this careful consideration?

Mr. Morgenthau[2] told me yesterday that Mr. Filene,[3] of Boston (a very prominent merchant over there and one who stands high and who is an admirer of yours) feels hurt because he sent you an invitation some weeks ago to speak in Boston on one of several occasions which he suggested in his letter, and that he has never had a reply. I told him I felt sure you could not have received the letter. He is going to send another invitation. Before you decline it, I wish you would let me speak to you about it. Meantime, I think it would be well for you to do nothing in the matter.

I am going to Washington on Saturday, and shall make it a point to get in touch with my old friend "Bob" Taylor, Senator from Tennessee.

I enclose a letter from Mr. Algernon T. Sweeney,[4] of Newark. I do not know him very well and am not prepared to make a definite recommendation, but I should be very glad if you will give what he says consideration.

Yours very sincerely,   W G McAdoo

TLS (LPC, W. G. McAdoo Papers, DLC).
[1] A New York women's social club organized on December 7, 1903. The Editors have not found any news report of this talk.
[2] Henry Morgenthau, lawyer and president of the Henry Morgenthau Co., a real estate firm of New York. Morgenthau soon became a large contributor to Wilson's preconvention campaign fund and, after the nomination, chairman of the Democratic finance committee for the presidential campaign of 1912. He was Ambassador to Turkey, 1913-16.
[3] Edward Albert Filene, partner in William Filene's Sons Co., a large department store of Boston.
[4] Algernon Thomas Sweeney, lawyer of Newark. He was seeking appointment as juvenile judge of Newark.

From Thomas Bell Love

Dallas, Texas,

My Dear Governor Wilson: December 8th, 1911.

My correspondence with all portions of the State indicates that the Wilson sentiment is overwhelming in the State, and in most sections is practically unanimous. While this is true there seems to be a lethargy in politics which prevents as much headway being made in formal organization as I would like, but I do not think there can be any mistake about the overwhelming sentiment, or any doubt that the sentiment will find expression in the selection of the Texas delegation to the National Convention.

After much deliberation, I am fully persuaded that a full and striking declaration of your views upon the tariff question is the thing which the Wilson movement most needs at this time. The campaign is going to be fought out on the tariff question, and while the people are not especially interested in the schedule details, they are very much interested in knowing the tariff lines upon which the battle of 1912 is to be fought out.

I am sure you will appreciate the spirit in which this suggestion is made. Its importance impresses me so strongly that I cannot forbear to make it.

With kind regards, I am

Very truly yours,   Thomas B. Love.

TCL (T. B. Love Papers, Dallas Hist. Soc.).

To Oswald Garrison Villard

Personal.

My dear Mr. Villard: Trenton, N. J. December 9, 1911.

It was very thoughtful and kind of you to send me Redfield's speech, and I am sincerely obliged to you. Indeed, I do know that you are keeping in close touch with me and it gives me a feeling of reassurance and strength. I know through McCombs how much you are doing and with how sincere and thoughtful a friendship.

Perhaps I shall be a little freer for the next week or two to move and shall try to look you up in New York.

Cordially and faithfully yours,   Woodrow Wilson

TLS (O. G. Villard Papers, MH).

To Mary Allen Hulbert Peck

Dearest Friend,   Princeton, New Jersey 10 Dec., 1911

Apparently nothing in the way of forethought or planning will nowadays yield me leisure to write you such a letter as I *want* to write. I find that I have to fight (and take firm command of myself) to keep the circumstances of my days from getting on my nerves,—the constant pursuit of me by persons of all kinds and stations, and, above all, the way in which publicity is beginning to beat upon me,—not my own kind of publicity, the publicity of public affairs, but the kind the sensational newspapers insist upon, the publicity of private affairs. Everywhere it it [*sic*] is beginning to be perceived that the likelihood of my being nominated is very great and must be taken seriously,—and it *is* beginning to be taken very seriously, by certain big business interests in N. Y., who know that I could not be managed to their mind, and by everybody who, like Hearst, for personal reasons,[1] wants to see me beaten. They are looking high and low for some means by which to discredit me, personally if not politically. Just at this moment (in spite of a perfectly frank statement by me of all the facts) they are trying to make me seem ridiculous and discredited because I applied to the Carnegie Foundation for a retiring allowance,—and may, by lying misrepresentations, partially succeed—with the people who always want an honorable man brought down to their level. Next they will turn to something else upon which to put a false colour. All these things are in the long run futile. They discredit only those who do them. But for a little while they are very trying. They make me feel as if I were, in a sense, set about by vindictive men, determined to destroy my character, by fair means or foul. The war upon me, from this on, is to be heartless, relentless. For I am greatly feared. Every illegitimate force instinctively dreads the possibility of my becoming President. They know that I am "on to them" and that I can neither be fooled nor bought. I try, and for the most part succeed, to keep my soul serene amidst it all, but it is an unhappy thing to be so hated and hounded.

We are all perfectly well. Nellie is just about to leave for Mexico, to spend some six weeks there with friends. Her apartment in Phila. was burned out last week, but fortunately she was here, getting ready. Her room mate had a narrow escape, and the people in the next apartment were burned!

I am so sorry to hear that Mrs. Allen does not gain her strength more rapidly. Give her warmest messages from me—and Allen also. All join me in affectionate regards.

Your devoted friend,   Woodrow Wilson

ALS (WP, DLC).

¹ Several friends of Wilson later testified that, during the summer and autumn of 1911, he rejected out of hand several offers of friendship and assistance from William Randolph Hearst, going so far as curtly to refuse a dinner invitation to meet Hearst and, perhaps on this occasion, saying "Tell Mr. Hearst to go to hell." Frank P. Stockbridge, "How Woodrow Wilson Won His Nomination," *Current History*, xx (July 1924), 570, and Link, *Road to the White House*, p. 382.

To Richard Heath Dabney

My dear Heath: Trenton, N. J. December 11, 1911.

This is literally the first opportunity I have had to answer your letter of December sixth.¹ I think that you yourself suggest just the sentence to add to my Staunton letter now, as follows: "Before the experiments in Oregon, there had been no American facts to floor me with. I had been going altogether upon my theoretical conclusions as to how far the facts in Switzerland would fit conditions in the United States." I think that will, by implication at any rate, set the matter through my former opinion in its proper light.² I have an inveterate disinclination to explain things away.

I appreciate more than I can say all that you are doing and send this note as a hasty message of thanks.

Affectionately yours, Woodrow Wilson

TLS (Wilson-Dabney Corr., ViU).

¹ This letter is missing.

² Wilson's letter to Dabney of Nov. 16, 1911, was printed verbatim in the Richmond *Times-Dispatch*, Dec. 18, 1911. It was prefaced by a letter from Dabney to the Editor, dated Dec. 13, 1911, in which Dabney included in quotation marks the two sentences in Wilson's letter to him of Dec. 11.

In his own letter, Dabney asked why Virginia, the birthplace of seven Presidents, was thus far so lukewarm to the candidacy of another native son. "Virginians," he explained, "are a conservative people, and a considerable number of them have been led astray by wholly erroneous statements to the effect that Woodrow Wilson is a radical demagogue, who is either insincere in character or intellectually too vacillating to be trusted as a political guide. This notion—supremely absurd to those who really know the man—is based chiefly upon the fact that, after disapproving for some years, in his Princeton lectures, of the initiative, referendum and recall, he has now expressed a qualified approval of those measures." Dabney insisted that this approval was very qualified indeed. He referred to his thirty-two-year friendship with Wilson as evidence of his fitness to judge Wilson's character and then wrote, "with the coolest deliberation, and with the utmost earnestness," that Washington himself was not more incapable than Wilson of "even the faintest insincerity, either in private or in public life."

The *Times-Dispatch* responded with an editorial printed on the same page of its issue of Dec. 18, 1911. About this editorial, see J. G. Pollard to WW, Dec. 19, 1911, n. 1.

To Andrew Carnegie

My dear Mr. Carnegie: Trenton, N. J. December 11, 1911.

Allow me to acknowledge the receipt of your letter of December eighth,[1] and to say that I am perfectly willing that the letter I wrote you about the peace union banquet should be publicly read.[2] I should like to endorse the movement for peace in every possible way.

Cordially and sincerely yours,   Woodrow Wilson

TLS (A. Carnegie Papers, DLC).
   [1] Carnegie's letter is missing.
   [2] Wilson's letter is also missing. He referred to the mass meeting in support of the ratification of the arbitration treaties with Britain and France held in Carnegie Hall on December 12, 1911, about which see A. Carnegie to WW, March 21, 1911, n. 4, Vol. 22. Carnegie could neither make a speech nor read Wilson's letter due to the uproar created by partisans of Germany.

To Edward Ingle

My dear Ingall: Trenton, N. J. December 11, 1911.

I think you are a little hard on the Carnegie Foundation; but I, nonetheless, appreciate your generous friendship and thank you heartily for your letter. I am very sorry, indeed, that I did not have a chance to see you when I was in Baltimore.

Yours very cordially,   Woodrow Wilson

TLS (E. Ingle Papers, MdHi).

From Charles Sumner Moore[1]

Personal

My dear Governor: Atlantic City, N. J. December 13th, 1911.

Mr. Archer[2] is doing splendidly in the work of preparing the indictments for trial on the 18th inst. I do not see how the defendants are going to escape conviction, although there is one matter that is troubling me. I cannot set it forth in a letter, however.

My father-in-law[3] spent Saturday and Sunday with us, and I gather from his remarks that our enemies in Washington are trying to make considerable capital out of the Carnegie Pension Fund incident. While in the main I agree with your position to absolutely ignore personal attacks that are made upon you and your candidacy for the Presidency, still it is just by such little things as the Carnegie incident that the special privilege "Bunch" hope to prevent your nomination. I did not see the newspaper accounts of this matter, and if there were any accounts of the same that correctly set forth the facts regarding your position, I will thank you to point me to them. If the latter be impossible, might I have a few words from you in explanation that I can use when I stop over in Washington during the holidays. My notion is to give them a body blow every time now that they show their hand.

There is another matter that I think we need to give considerable thought and attention to during the coming months, and that is the question of the platform that is to be adopted by the Democratic National Convention. I note that Mr. Bryan is taking the position that the Sherman Anti Trust law is all right as it stands with the addition thereto of his theory of the 50% limitation upon monopoly.[4] In my humble opinion, that will never work. Neither do I think we ought to adopt Mr. Underwood's idea that the Sherman Anti Trust law itself is good enough. It seems to me that we must take the position that the big combinations of capital are here to stay and the only possible remedy for adequate relief is government regulation and strict control.

I have felt for some time that Roosevelt will be the next Republican nominee. There are many reasons why I think this will happen. I will discuss them with you when I see you again. He will be no mean antagonist, and we will have to be up and doing, shaping our policy and program if we hope to defeat him.

Perhaps you have already worked out in your own mind a program or a set of fundamental principles that will deal adequately with the great trust problem in this country. It seems to me, however, that the time has gone by when it can be dealt with along the old theory of free competition, which was so long the attitude of the Democratic party toward it.

I am, as ever,

Very sincerely yours, Charles S. Moore

TLS (Governors' Files, Nj).

[1] Lawyer of Atlantic City. He had served as foreman of the elisor-drawn grand jury which indicted Kuehnle and many others connected with his organization.

[2] Franklin Morse Archer, Princeton 1894, lawyer of Camden, associated with the Attorney General and Assistant Attorney General of New Jersey in the trials of the leading defendants in the Atlantic City corruption trials. It was Kuehnle himself who came to trial on December 18, 1911. Four days later, he was convicted of criminal conflict of interest in connection with the awarding of a city contract.

[3] Benjamin Ryan Tillman, senator from South Carolina. Moore had married Margaret Malona Tillman on April 26, 1911.

[4] Moore referred to an idea advanced as early as 1899 by Bryan but stated most clearly in the Democratic platform of 1908. That plank proposed limiting any single corporation to 50 per cent of the product of any given industry.

To Thomas Davies Jones, with Enclosure

My dear Mr. Jones: Trenton, N. J. December 15, 1911.

The enclosed letter affords one amongst a great many evidences that I have that certain Princeton men are planning to cooperate actively with those who are trying to discredit me in politics. Among other things, as you doubtless have heard, there is said to be a letter of Mr. Cleveland's springing out of the graduate school controversy which they are intending, at the effective moment, to print and by which they hope to damage me. It has occurred to me that such members of the Board as yourself, McCormick, McIlvaine, Jacobus, Sheldon and Garrett ought to know of what is in contemplation in order that if you choose, in your generosity to do it, you might be ready in a joint statement which would effectively meet all the counts of the indictment they evidently intend to bring against me. I think the country at large already pretty well understands the situation with regard to Princeton, but such a joint statement would have overwhelming force.

If I am proposing too much, please rebuke me. I do not feel that I ought to let myself be defenceless on any side, and I know how absolutely I can count on the men of the Board who stood by me so splendidly and whom I greatly respect and admire.

With warmest regards to your brother and to all,
Cordially and faithfully yours,   Woodrow Wilson

TLS (Mineral Point, Wisc., Public Library).

E N C L O S U R E

From Henry G. Steinson[1]

Dear Sir: Chicago Dec. 14, 1911.

About a year ago, I said to a friend of mine that Woodrow Wilson would be heard of for the next presidency.

The prediction has come true: that is, your name for the democratic nomination has been much in the papers.

Some time ago, I was a month in Atlanta, Georgia. The Southern papers were then full of your name.

I have been saying to my acquaintances and others that I would vote for you and that I hoped they would do so, too.

Recently, I met here a business man from Newark, your state. He is a large manufacturer. I said to him, inasmuch as he was from the same state, that he would be voting for you. After a moment's hesitation, he said he could not! I asked him for his reasons.

He said you were *unreliable*! This certainly was a shock to me. For being a countryman of Witherspoon, I have ever taken an interest in all things, Princeton.

I asked him for instances. He said there had been trouble between you and the Board, that it had charged you with reviewing or annotating a book and that you had denied doing such.[2] The book was produced. It had your pencil marks on the margin!

Anything else, I asked? He said that at Board meetings and such like that you would agree to a thing and then disagree with it or repudiate it next day.

He said, too, that the Board let you down easy by accepting your resignation instead of demanding it.

Verily, this would look like unreliable. I don't feel like giving you up on my friend's statements. Though an honorable and upright man, he may be mistaken and have wrong information.

If there is any truth in his accusations, it would seem to me inadvisable for you to have yourself put forward as the democratic candidate.

I asked him why there was no mention of such accusations in the papers. He said these and others would be published in due time, and that they were, in the meantime, being collected and put in shape for publication when the time should come, and that it should be necessary to down you.

Yours very truly,   H. Steinson.

TCL (Mineral Point, Wisc., Public Library).
  [1] Secretary of the American Envelope Co. of Chicago.
  [2] See particularly the Editorial Note, "Wilson at the Meeting of the Board of Trustees on January 13, 1910," Vol. 20.

From Edward Mandell House

Austin, Texas.
My dear Governor Wilson: December 15th, 1911.

I have been having some spirited correspondence with William Garrett Brown concerning your attitude on the Aldrich plan.[1]

He is very insistent that you study the measure at once and announce yourself either for it or at least in favor of a non-partisan consideration of it.

There are many reasons why I think it well for you not to do this at this time but they are of such a nature that I prefer not giving them to Mr. Brown so my replies to him are something in the line of a subterfuge.

I tell him that your views are perfectly sound and that your friends should be content with this assurance and let you decide as to the proper time to make them public.

Mr. Brown also tells me that he thinks North Carolina should be handled by Mr. Page's brothers[2] rather than by Walter Page himself.

This is a more delicate matter but I take it that your relations with him are such that it can be arranged, provided Mr. Brown is correct in his views.

I am glad to tell you that our affairs here are in good shape. I shall have a few of the leaders in conference next week so that we may outline a more complete organization.

I have not forgotten your request in regard to Louisiana and I shall take that up immediately and advise Mr. McCombs.

With kind regards and best wishes, I am,

Faithfully yours,   [E. M. House]

TCL (E. M. House Papers, CtY).
    [1] W. G. Brown to E. M. House, Dec. 5 and 9, 1911, ALS (E. M. House Papers, CtY); E. M. House to W. G. Brown, Dec. 2, 14 [and 17], 1911, TLS (W. G. Brown Papers, NcD).
    [2] Robert Newton Page, congressman from North Carolina, 1903-17, and Frank Page, businessman of Moore County, N. C.

To Mary Allen Hulbert Peck

Dearest Friend,   Princeton, New Jersey 17 Dec., 1911

I wonder if I missed one of your letters? The spare little note I received the other day had written between all its lines that you had been ill,—that some sort of collapse (such as I had feared those last days, as I saw you work and saw the colour go out of your face and the elasticity out of every movement) came after you got to "Glencove"[1] and the strain was over. You always speak so bravely and put everything off with so easy a pleasantry, when you do not wish those to whom you speak or write to be anxious, that I do not know what to think or hope or fear. *Please* let me know just how you are and how you are faring. I cannot escape anxiety, otherwise. I must not guess. I must know.

Things go as usual with us. My darling Nellie has gone to Mexico, to climb to that noble table-land of Chihuahua (wa)(wa), lifted six or eight thousand feet above the sea, where there are splendid solemn pine forests as well as deep mines, and ranches where there is tonic enough in the air to give zest to every moment afoot or on horseback,—and be with congenial friends for six or eight weeks. I miss my dear little chum sorely, and feel it quite intolerable for her to be away at Christmas time. There has not been time yet to hear from her after her arrival. Letters take five days. The rest of us are well and things go with a sweet serenity with us. The Smith's[2] are delightful to live with,—as we knew they would be; and Nellie[3] has none of the cares of house keeping.

Politics shows daily signs of hastening to its quadrennial crisis, and my enemies are opening fire on me with guns of every calibre. I must hold constant conferences now with political friends of every rank and kind, but the details are too many and too complicated to write into a letter when one has only a cramped hand to hold the pen with. I will tell you of anything of consequence. It is generally interesting, but sometimes palls a bit on me,—forever talking about myself. There is nothing either novel or exciting in the theme. I shall be glad when the time comes to discuss *questions*. So far as I can judge, everything is going very well. It now looks very much as if Roosevelt, not Taft, would get (or, rather, take) the Republican nomination. *That* would make the campaign worth while. Just because there is nothing nowadays in my programme of day by day, my letters must, I fear, be very dull. It is not interesting,—though it may be satisfactory,—to report that I am well,—and yet that is all there is to report,— except, what you must know, that I miss my absent friend sorely, envy the people who are about her in Bermuda, and wish that I could convert our letters into real talk,—the talk that stimulates me more delightfully than any other. But I shall try to be content if only I can learn that you are well. All join me in warmest messages.

Your devoted friend,   Woodrow Wilson

ALS (WP, DLC).
[1] Mrs. Peck's house in West Paget, Bermuda.
[2] Lucy Marshall Smith and Mary Randolph Smith of New Orleans had come for an extended visit.
[3] Mrs. Wilson.

From Charles G. Heifner

Personal.

Dear Governor: Seattle, Wash., December 18, 1911

When I returned home a week ago I found your kind favor of the 27th ultimo, for which I thank you very much. Because I believe you best typify the kind of a man who is needed today to lead the Democratic party and to carry into execution its principles, I am for you for the Democratic candidate for President of the United States. I find sincere gratification and pleasure in

supporting a man whom I believe is destined, not only to be our
party nominee, but the next President of the United States.

We organized a large and enthusiastic Wilson Club here in
Seattle last Friday evening and steps have been taken for a meeting on January 8th of the Democrats all over the State of Washington to organize a Wilson League for the entire state. I do not
think I am mistaken when I say that the State of Washington
will send fourteen delegates to the National Convention, who
will use every honorable means to secure your nomination.

With kind regards, and wishing you the compliments of the
season, I am   Sincerely yours,   C. G. Heifner

TLS (Governors' Files, Nj).

From Thomas Davies Jones

My dear Governor: [Chicago] December 19th, 1911.

I have your letter of the 15th instant enclosing letter of Mr.
Steinson to you, which I return to you herewith.

You can, of course, safely count upon your old friends on the
Board to do anything which may be found to be possible to contradict any false statements that may be made with regard to
your conduct as president of the University. When you speak of
being ready in a joint statement to meet the counts of an indictment against you, you probably do not mean the actual preparation of such a joint statement, as I do not see how we could frame
a statement which would meet counts of an indictment until we
know what those counts are going to be. I shall be glad to co-
operate very promptly with others of your friends as soon as
those counts have taken any tangible shape. You are in better
position to judge than I am as to the probability of their formu-
lating any such counts in the near future. I myself very much
doubt whether they will formulate any charges unless and until
you shall be nominated for the presidency. Even then I have
my doubts whether these charges will actually be made in a
form which calls for contradiction. I rather doubt whether any
of the Princeton men would be willing to drag the University
into a public controversy, and think that any charges that will
be made will be by way of insinuations, and by irresponsible
newspaper paragraphs, which you can well afford to disregard.

As to any letter of Mr. Clevelands which they may have, it will
have to speak for itself when it is published, and the chances of
its containing any personal reflections upon you are so remote
as to be negligible.

The other matter you mention, namely the controversy in the Board over West's book on the Graduate School is more definite, and if any attack is made, I should guess that it will be on this ground. The statement has been made quite persistently that West has in his possession a copy of the proofs of his book annotated in your hand writing. I think the statement first appeared in the "Alumni Weekly" under the authority of Jesse Lynch Williams. We could not, of course, deny the existence of any such proofs, and I do not suppose that you could go any further than to say that you have no recollection whatever of having revised any such proofs. If they should charge you with having stated to the Board that you wrote the introduction to the book before you had read the book itself (presumably after conversations with West as to what it would contain) that statement could not be denied, nor is it, in my judgment, seriously damaging. I felt at the moment you made the statement that it would have been much better for you to say that you had learned a whole lot from observation of West in action since you wrote that introduction, and that you had been driven to a modification of your own views. But I cannot take a very serious view of that matter, and if any references are made to it in public, I think it would be very easy to commit the blunder of giving to the incident an exaggerated importance by entering into controversy over it. I am not a politician nor the son of a politician, but I feel sure that it would require more damaging statements than I think your enemies will make to draw me into any public controversy over the matter, and that if I were actually forced into controversy I would waste very little time on the defensive, but would boldly charge that the hostility to you in connection with your administration of the affairs of the University arose out of your determination to stamp out what you believed to be exclusive privileges which had begun to show themselves in the University, and which threatened injurious consequences to the University. The whole pack would then "give tongue" on this new and larger issue, in which the public would be with you, and such relatively insignificant matters as the West book would be lost sight of.

Faithfully yours,   [Thomas D. Jones]

CCL (Mineral Point, Wisc., Public Library).

From David Benton Jones

My dear Governor Wilson: Chicago December 19th, 1911.

My brother has shown me the letter which you enclosed to him, and his reply.

I shall regard it as almost a fortunate thing for you (and for Princeton in the long run) if that brainless gang down at Princeton were to re-open the Princeton controversy in such a way as to enable you to make a full statement of the reasons why you left the University. They never could have voted you out of the presidency, and they know it, consequently your withdrawal was based upon the fact that while they could not vote you out, they could probably have, in one way or another, defeated the social reorganization of the University which would make it worth your while retaining the presidency of the institution.

It would, I think, be an incomparable opportunity for you, and would be exactly in line with what large masses of the people already feel about you. I am sure you will excuse me for saying that when you were elected to the presidency of Princeton you were somewhat mediaevally inclined in the cause of education, but that you very soon saw that in education, as well as in politics, we had passed into another time, and that if one could not be in a conservative sense a progressive, one would have to be a reactionary. Your progress was much faster than some of your faculty, and threatened the only side of University life which appealed to the New York and Philadelphia contingent. You have frankly stated that you had become more of a progressive in politics after a deeper examination into the situation than you were some years ago. This is exactly what happened on the educational side, and knowing your power of statement, as I said before, I almost hope they will reopen the controversy.

Numerically the Princeton alumni would in any event be divided politically, as well as upon the local issues developed at Princeton, or rather in the New York Club, hence you will practically have nothing to gain or lose from the small Princeton contingent, and in my judgment you will have everything to gain by a full statement of the situation which in the long run cannot help benefiting Princeton as well. Your enemies there are so fatuous and foolish,—so utterly lacking in thinking power, that you and your friends can be perfectly serene and abide the event.

I agree with my brother that it is highly improbable that any formal statement will be made. West, of course, would be willing to wreck Princeton to gratify his hate, but a man so wanting in character and in academic standing as Dean West, is powerless to harm when the Princeton social set ceases to be the constituency to which he must appeal.

We are here naturally watching the development with a great deal of interest, and so far as I am able to work the thing out, the signs are increasingly favorable. Once you are nominated, if that should come to pass, Princeton would form such a very tiny little bubble that no one would know of its having been blown at all, unless you took advantage of the opportunity, which I always hoped would come, of making a public statement of the conditions as they really are.

Very sincerely yours, David B. Jones.

Dodge's resignation is a capital background for any reopening that may take place and others may follow if it doesn't soon mend.

TLS (WP, DLC).

From John Garland Pollard

My Dear Mr. Wilson: [Richmond, Va.] Dec. 19, 1911.

Mr. Dabney has doubtless sent you a copy of the enclosed clipping from the Times-Dispatch of Dec. 18th, giving editorial based upon your letter of Nov. 16th, 1911, written to Mr. Dabney.[1] I am writing you concerning the matter because I have become convinced that your interests in Virginia demand that more vigorous steps be taken at once to organize the state.

I wrote you last summer on the subject, and you referred me to Mr. McComb, who invited me to come to New York to see him. I called on him during the month of September and discussed the situation. He feared that inasmuch as Ex Governor Montague, H. St. George Tucker, Congressman W. A. Jones, as well as myself and other known friends in Virginia, belong to what is known as the Anti-Machine Faction, it would be unwise for the movement to eminate from us. So far as I have been able to learn, none of the leaders of the Machine Faction in Virginia have declared for you.

I am fully satisfied, however, that the rank and file of the Democrats of this state are heartily in favor of your nomination for the Presidency. All that is needed is wise and vigorous leadership and prompt action. I think the machine leaders recognize that the people of Virginia are with you, and I think I see signs of an effort to take the state from you by delivering our delegation first to Underwood, on the ground that he is a southern man; and then when Underwood is dropped, to deliver our vote to Harmon. I was talking with Ex Governor Montague a few days ago about the situation, and he thinks we are making a mistake to hold back any longer as we have been heretofore, fearing lest the advocacy of your claims by representatives of a faction might injure you. He does not think that any of the leaders of the Machine forces can be relied on to organize the state for you.

I would write direct to Mr. McComb on this subject, but I am informed that he does not bear the same relation to your candidacy as formerly. I am interested in your nomination chiefly because I believe in the principles you advocate; at the same time I am particularly anxious to see your native state give you her hearty support.

Yours very truly,   [John Garland Pollard]

CCL (J. G. Pollard Papers, ViW).

1 This long lead editorial, "Woodrow Wilson and Virginia," praised Wilson for his opposition to the recall of judges and further pointed out that he had spoken out against that measure in California, "where the recall of judges was almost being made a test of patriotism." What did concern Virginians, and concerned them very deeply, was "the mental processes that led Governor Wilson to change his mind almost overnight on the value of the initiative and referendum." It was only fair to admit that until the recent experiments in Oregon, the initiative and referendum had been used liberally only in Switzerland. Based on the Swiss experience, Wilson had opposed these measures. However, after going to Oregon and viewing the political scene there firsthand and with an open mind, he had become convinced that the initiative and referendum were methods which could be used to re-establish a political atmosphere in which representative government could flourish in its original vigor. Both Wilson and the Oregon leaders regarded the initiative and referendum as "temporary expedients for bridging the gulf between a brokendown and a restored government by representatives." It was the "clearly unfounded" belief that Wilson had suddenly abandoned representative government for government by "the untrained and unskilled body of voters at large" that had "disheartened and chilled the ardor of his friends in Virginia." However, even in Virginia, the idea of a referendum did not necessarily carry the implication of wild radicalism. Many voters and legislators had demanded a state-wide vote on state-wide prohibition. Such persons obviously thought that representative government had ceased to represent—precisely what the voters of Oregon had concluded. Moreover, Wilson had no desire to impose the initiative and referendum on any state that did not want it. The *Times-Dispatch*, the editorial continued, agreed completely with Wilson on this point, concluding:

"Finally, we are glad to say that we fully adopt Dr. Dabney's statement that Governor Wilson's attitude, as stated by himself, involves no reflection on his fixity of purpose or clearness of vision. The position of Governor Wilson on all public matters is a matter of profound concern to his native State, to the Democratic party and to the whole country, and his letter on the initiative, referendum and recall will clear up many doubts and quiet many misgivings on the part of his friends and fellow-citizens in Virginia."

From William Gibbs McAdoo

PERSONAL AND CONFIDENTIAL.

Dear Governor: [New York] December 20, 1911.

McCombs has written you about the Joline letter,1 about which I talked to you on the telephone a few nights ago. I hope you have a copy of it. I am looking forward to seeing you on Tuesday.

Hoping that the New Year will bring you the supreme honor

now "threatening you," and for which your character and attainments eminently qualify you, I am, with best wishes,

Very sincerely yours,   W G McAdoo

TLS (LPC, W. G. McAdoo Papers, DLC).
¹ WW to A. H. Joline, April 29, 1907, Vol. 17, in which Wilson had expressed the wish that something could be done, "at once dignified and effective, to knock Mr. Bryan once for all into a cocked hat!" The New York *Sun* published a garbled version of this letter on January 7, 1912; with Joline's permission, it and other newspapers published an accurate version on the following day, just before the Jackson Day Dinner in Washington, where Wilson, Bryan, and other Democratic leaders were to speak. For an account of this affair and its repercussions, see Link, *Road to the White House*, pp. 352-55.

To George Brinton McClellan Harvey

Personal

My dear Colonel,   University Club [New York] 21 Dec., 1911

Every day I am confirmed in the judgement that my mind is a one-track road, and can run only one train of thought at a time! A long time after that interview with you and Marse Henry at the Manhattan Club it came over me that when (at the close of the interview) you asked me that question about the *Weekly*, I answered it simply as a matter of fact, and of business, and said never a word of my sincere gratitude to you for all your generous support, or of my hope that it might be continued. Forgive me, and forget my manners!¹

Faithfully Yours,   Woodrow Wilson

ALS (WP, DLC).
¹ Wilson, Harvey, and Henry Watterson had discussed the preconvention campaign in the latter's apartment in the Manhattan Club on December 7. Watterson suggested that Thomas Fortune Ryan, Virginia-born New York financier, was eager to contribute to Wilson's campaign fund. Wilson rejected the suggestion out of hand. Near the end of the meeting, Harvey asked Wilson whether his support was embarrassing his campaign; when Harvey insisted upon an answer, Wilson replied that some of his friends were saying that the Colonel's support was not doing him any good in the West. Harvey replied that he would have "to put on the soft pedal." The conferees parted, Wilson thought, in perfect friendship.
This was the origin of the famous Harvey-Wilson-Watterson affair—an attempt by Harvey to wreck Wilson's presidential chances—about which there will be many documents in this and the next volume. For the whole episode, see Link, *Road to the White House*, pp. 359-78.

To Thomas Davies Jones

My dear Mr. Jones: [Trenton, N. J.] December 22, 1911.

As always you have a better judgment and a better poise than I have and it is delightful to be steadied and reassured by your letter of December nineteenth.

Of course I had no thought of the preparation of a statement beforehand without knowing what was to be answered, but it gives me a feeling of strength that you should know of the possibility of what may happen and of what it may be necessary to do.

Your advice as to what it would be wise to say is most acceptable and I shall be glad to be guided by it as much as possible.

With grateful appreciation,

Sincerely yours,   Woodrow Wilson

TLS (Mineral Point, Wisc., Public Library).

To Edward Mandell House

My dear Mr. House: [Trenton, N. J.] December 22, 1911.

I need not tell you that I value your letter of December fifteenth. You are certainly handling Mr. William Garrett Brown in exactly the right way. He has the impatience of a man who is not entirely well, but the man has a very noble nature and we should try in every way to convince him that we are not out of sympathy with him.

His advice about handling affairs in North Carolina is very interesting, and I hope that it can be taken up with Mr. Walter Page himself.

We are interested just now in our conferences in New York, in the means of creating an actual organized movement throughout the south, and I should value very greatly your suggestion in that now pressing matter. I do not think that there is any time to be lost during the next few months in view of the activities of the forces arrayed against us.

With warmest regards,

Cordially yours,   Woodrow Wilson

TLS (E. M. House Papers, CtY).

To Richard Heath Dabney

My dear Heath: [Trenton, N. J.] December 22, 1911.

You are certainly doing yeoman's service and I thank you with all my heart. The publication of the letter and its effect seem to have been a capital stroke and I am glad that you have written to Mr. McCombs, for Duke's idea[1] is certainly an excellent one. I think that Mr. Bryan's editorial in the Times-Dispatch is as much as could have been expected of him in the circumstances.

Affectionately and gratefully yours,   Woodrow Wilson

TLS (Wilson-Dabney Corr., ViU).
1 Richard Thomas Walker Duke, Jr., lawyer and author of Charlottesville. His idea was undoubtedly to give Wilson's letter to Dabney the widest possible circulation.

To John Garland Pollard

My dear Mr. Pollard: [Trenton, N. J.] December 22, 1911.

Your letter of December nineteenth puts me in your debt. The judgments it expresses are my own and you may be sure that I will profit by the advice and suggestion it contains. I cannot too highly appreciate this evidence of your friendship.

Cordially and sincerely yours,   Woodrow Wilson

TLS (J. G. Pollard Papers, ViW).

From Daniel Moreau Barringer

PERSONAL

Dear Woodrow,   Philadelphia, Pa. December 22, 1911.

My eye fell upon the enclosed this morning.[1] If this Mr. Untermyer is sincere, and until we have reason to believe differently we should credit him with being sincere, he sees the danger clearly as you and I do and seems to be unremitting in his efforts to make other people see it. It seems to me that Aldrich with incredible ingenuity, if it was done intentionally, has framed a bill, which I see by this morning's paper the President has approved, which will greatly facilitate the formation of this money trust. When we remember Aldrich's training it is difficult to see how he could or would prepare any other kind of a bill.

I feel with you that this is the root of the whole evil and the most dangerous possibility with which we are confronted today. It would be impossible for me to tell you how deeply I feel on this subject and I do most sincerely hope, since you feel as I do, that you will be given the opportunity to put your heel on the head of this rattlesnake. Do you know Untermyer and have you ever had a talk with him on the subject? It might possibly be mutually helpful. . . .

Wishing you and yours a Merry Christmas and that the New Year will bring to you something which we all wish for, I am,

Cordially yours,   D. M. Barringer

TLS (Governors' Files, Nj).
1 It is missing but was a clipping about a letter from Samuel Untermyer to Representative Charles Augustus Lindbergh of Minnesota, which Lindbergh made public on December 21, 1911. On December 4, the first day of the new

session, Lindbergh had introduced a resolution calling for a congressional investigation of the "money trust." Untermyer wrote his letter to support the resolution
when it appeared that it would be buried by the House Rules Committee.

"We shall never be able to solve the trust or tariff or currency questions,"
Untermyer wrote, "until we have been made to realize that this is the greatest
and most difficult problem of them all—and the one that underlies the others.

"Those who suppose that it is to some extent at least a figment of the imagination created or encouraged by the demagogues know nothing of the dangers of
the situation. It is not only the greatest peril that confronts the country, but
it is sadly underestimated.

"By reason of its potency no new enterprise is possible which competes with
any existing enterprise which is under the protection of any of the great
interests. Until this question is understood nothing substantial will ever be accomplished toward solving our vexatious economic problems." *New York Times*,
Dec. 22, 1911.

To Mary Allen Hulbert Peck

Dearest Friend,   Princeton, New Jersey 24 Dec., 1911.

There's nothing for it but to write on Sundays, whether they
are near the Bermudian's sailing days or not. Sundays are the
only days that contain any time I can call my own.

Your last letter cheered me greatly.[1] It was not only in itself
delightful, but showed such evident signs of reviving spirits and
returning strength that my anxiety about you was very much
relieved indeed. The rest and the quiet are beginning to tell and
you are beginning to be yourself again. I can now think of you
as I prefer always to think of you in Bermuda (it is most natural
for me, by the way, to think of you there: it was there I found
you and it is there, as it will always seem to me, that you have
your most suitable environment, of bright waters and sweet,
cheerful, interesting countrysides) as surrounded by everything
that makes for cheerfulness and peace and quiet human interest.
It is a country—God bless it!—where there is time for friendship
and neighbourly cheer and unhurried intercourse and long talks
that disclose the deeper interests and genuine preferences both
of the mind and of the heart. I revolt against these hurried days
in which tasks trip upon one another's heels, when every affair
moves breathlessly, and all thinking must be done on the run,
all feeling cut short or shunted on one side. In Bermuda you
have a chance to flower and be natural and follow your own
thought! I envy you, but rejoice that you are there. I could wish
that you might always be there. I do not wonder that you suffer
under the unpleasant publicity that is for a little while ahead of
you; for I know how sensitive you are.[2] But it will soon be over,
and can disclose nothing of which you need be ashamed. Everything keeps to its usual pace with us. I am well; discuss politics
till I am sick of them and heartily wish I had never been thought

of for the presidential nomination. But the day's work brings back the zest, and I do not allow the talk to master me in any way. I know that I speak for all of our little household when I send to you all the warmest and most affectionate greetings of the season. I hope you thought the little trifle pretty that I sent the other day by registered mail. I am perfectly well, go through my days happily, and am serene in the thought that you are in a sort of haven.

Your devoted friend   Woodrow Wilson

ALS (WP, DLC).

[1] Mary A. H. Peck to WW, Dec. 15, 1911, ALS (WP, DLC).

[2] "While I thought myself quite prepared and fortified for the inevitable publicity of the divorce," Mrs. Peck wrote in her letter, "I found it gave me a shock to see myself figuring large on the front page of the 'Times' of Dec. 9th and in the sensational legal page of the 'Herald' of the same date. As there will be more—and worse[—]publicity, I am trying to further blunt my sensibilities."

An article, with the dateline of Pittsfield, Mass., December 8, appeared on the first page of the New York Times, Dec. 9, 1911, under the headline "WIFE SUES THOMAS D. PECK. Charges Woolen Manufacturer with Desertion, and Asks Alimony." It described the circumstances of the suit and said that Peck was living in Warrenton, N. C., where he had established woolen and cotton mills. A similar brief article appeared on page five of the New York Herald, Dec. 9, 1911.

Two Interviews

[Dec. 24, 1911]

PROGRESSIVE DEMOCRACY IS REMEDY FOR EVILS OF TARIFF AND

TRUSTS, SAYS WOODROW WILSON

A quizzical smile stole over the intellectual features of Woodrow Wilson, Governor of New Jersey, as he leaned back in his chair and repeated the question:

"What is a Progressive Democrat?"

The former President of Princeton University paused for a moment, unhooked his eye-glasses from a little gold catch on his vest and, holding them in his hand to emphasize his reply, said:

"I can best answer that question by first trying to define a Republican. I do not mean a progressive Republican—for a progressive Republican is only a Republican in a way to become a Democrat—but an orthodox Republican, still dominated by the older standards of his party.

"An orthodox Republican is a man who really believes that the Government of the country ought to be a sort of trusteeship; that those who have the biggest material stake in its industrial affairs should be the trustees, and that all policy should be made to conform to their judgment and interest, in the expectation that, as trustees, they will hand on to those whom their enterprise controls a fair and reasonable share of the prosperity of business.

"Now, a Progressive Democrat is a man who sees, what ought to be patent to everybody, that these self-constituted trustees have been both blind and selfish; that a dangerous and iniquitable system of business has been built up and that changes must be effected which will square the commercial and industrial methods of the country with the general interest, the interest of the people at large, as understood by the people themselves and not by special coteries. When the representatives of 'big business' think of the people, they do not include themselves."

Gov. Wilson was speaking in low, well-modulated tones. His voice has a particular charm, even in ordinary conversation; it is admirably pitched and has retained more than a trace of Southern softness. His diction reminds one forcibly of Sir Henry Irving's. Classic is the only word that describes it.

Forestalling the next question, Gov. Wilson continued:

"What policies characterize progressive Democracy? All those policies whose object is to wrest government from the control of special groups of men, and restore it to the control of the general opinion of the country. All the policies that re-establish the connection between representatives and the people. All well-considered measures that will tend to re-establish general opportunity and freedom of enterprise."

The good-natured but rather cold-blooded face grew stern, almost grim, and with an evident realization of the difficulties to be overcome, the Governor went on:

"It will need wide, common counsel to work such policies out. No one class or group of men can work them out alone. The man of affairs and the politician must come into conference with the student and the ardent reformer."

"Do you not think that there is everywhere manifest a very great discontent with existing conditions?" was the next question.

"Most assuredly. It is discontent with the trusteeship and its results."

A humorous twinkle in the Governor's eye and the most genial of smiles relieved the bluntness of the answer. Gov. Wilson's expression changes quickly. A moment before it had been grim, now is was beaming.

"Well, Governor, is the discontent greater in the West than in the East?"

"I do not think so. The difference seems to me to be that in the West a clear perception of the real facts of the situation and a conviction of the need of intelligent change has penetrated all classes; while in the East, those who are at the top of our industrial system stand stubborn and unconvinced."

"What do you think of the increase in the Socialist vote?"

"I cannot give my own impression about it better than by quoting what a Socialist acquaintance of mine in Nebraska said to me last May when I passed through Nebraska on my way westward. At Wymore, while the train lingered some fifteen minutes, I had the pleasure of talking with the very frank and intelligent young Mayor of the town.[1] He is a Socialist. When I asked him how he interpreted the vote by which he had been elected, he said, 'Why, I think, sir, that it was about twenty per cent. Socialist and eighty per cent. protest.'

"There is a rapidly growing body of voters who are utterly disgusted with those who have controlled political affairs, because they have seemed unable or unwilling to do anything to meet and correct the evident situation of things."

From Governor Wilson's manner there could be no doubt that he has abundant confidence in his own ability to "meet and correct" the existing evils. So the next question was:

"Is the demand of business men to be 'let alone' reasonable in the circumstances?"

Gov. Wilson toyed for a moment with a pencil on the desk, and said:

"The demand does not come from the rank and file; it comes from those who have created the very conditions we wish to correct. They wish—so far as I can make their programme out—to have the Government accept the consequences of what they have done, legalize them, and assume control of them, without the least effort at correction.

"There is nothing the matter with the mass of business in this country. It is as sound as it ever was. No change contemplated need touch ordinary business men at all, except to set them free of some of the trammels and disadvantages under which they now labor. The very object in view is to set business free—free from the control of the few—and then let it alone to follow its own right laws.

"It is not for those who have created the mischief to cry out to be let alone. They are thinking of themselves, not of the country. Legitimate processes of business will never be interfered with by legislation. If business, as now embarrassed, were let alone, it

---

[1] As has been noted earlier, he was Edward E. Mauck.

would be let alone to continue upon a basis upon which business can never safely rest—the basis of universal distrust and suspicion."

With more feeling than he had previously displayed, Gov. Wilson sat up in his chair, raised his hands in a gesture of demonstration and, speaking in the low, emphatic voice of the well-trained lecturer, asked a series of earnest questions:

"Who are the business men of the country? Are not the farmers business men? Are not the small traders business men? Is not the sub-contractor a business man as well as the contractor-in-chief; the man who is building up enterprise as well as the man who has built it up? Is not the man whose credit is small and 'on the make' a business man as well as the man whose credit is unlimited and established? Is not every employer of labor, every purchaser of material and every master of any enterprise, big or little, and every man in a profession, a business man?

"These smaller men, who constitute the body of the nation, so far as business is concerned, do not want to be let alone. They want to be set free of artificial trammels, of high prices, and of the restricted opportunities that have been created by our tariff-walled system of privilege."

Gov. Wilson's scholarly features were lighted up with enthusiasm. He is not—at first sight—a man of very commanding personality. His geniality wins immediate sympathy, but his individuality is cloaked by a very unostentatious manner and democratic bearing. He is not an inspired genius who proceeds to force his views upon those surrounding him; on the contrary, his mind is of a very formative character and his opinions are slowly and gradually evolved as the results of investigations and experience. He is a man who does nothing hastily.

"The very antithesis of Roosevelt" is perhaps the most accurate and concise description that can be given of Woodrow Wilson. It is true both mentally and physically. Gov. Wilson is a man who ponders long and carefully before he acts, he is modest and unassuming to a degree, and he is accurate in his speech and truthful in his statements. Also he means what he says.

Physically, the Governor of New Jersey is a tall, spare man, one might almost call him lean. He has long limbs, a long neck and a very long, narrow, big-boned face, with a high forehead and long, square jaw. The ears are somewhat overnormal in size, with very small lobes and are large and well rounded at the top. They are set high up on the sides of the head, and this, with the prominent cheek bones and aggressive chin, give the jaw an appearance of great length.

The face is a pleasing one. Very refined but not exactly handsome, and yet it is hard to tell why. The eyebrows are beautifully arched and the mouth is uncommonly well shaped for a man. It is sensitive but firm. The eyes are blue gray, and although generally very kindly, at times take on a hard, piercing expression. The tip of the nose is most mobile, and twitches whenever the Governor lays emphasis on a word.

Gov. Wilson's reference to "our tariff-walled system of privilege" suggested the question:

"What is to be the greatest issue of the coming campaign?" There was no hesitation in Gov. Wilson's answer:

"The tariff, of course. It must be so by its very nature. No frank mind can doubt that the great systems of special privilege and monopolistic advantage that have been built up have been built up upon the foundation of the tariff. The tariff question is at the heart of every other economic question we have to deal with, and until we have dealt with that properly we can deal with nothing in a way that will be satisfactory and lasting."

Gov. Wilson is for a "tariff for revenue only," first, last and all the time. He believes that tariff revision is the most pressing need of the country, and that the people are right in their determination to settle this question unequivocally at the coming election. In reply to a question as to what value he attaches to President Taft's Tariff Board,[2] Gov. Wilson said:

"So far the Tariff Board has served chiefly as an excuse for delay in doing things which it was obviously fair and necessary to do. It may serve a very useful purpose in supplying information. At least it will so soon as it is given authority to obtain authentic information. At present it cannot command it. It can only ask for it. No one need supply it with facts who does not wish to.

"All economists agree that there can never be any such thing as an expert tariff board. There is no expert in the business of the entire country. There can be no such thing as an expert in the general readjustment of the tariff schedules.

"In the somewhat rough and ready and experimental readjustments that it will be necessary to make, the judgment of an experienced committee of Congress is as good a guide as the judgment of a professional board. The question is then one of statesmanship.

"Since it is a question of statesmanship, the principle to be followed is that in a country of developed commerce and industry

2 About this short-lived board, see Frank W. Taussig, *The Tariff History of the United States*, 7th edn. (New York and London, 1923), pp. 403-405, 423-24.

the only legitimate object of duties on imports is revenue for the support of the Government. We have under our Federal system a great many governments to support. Direct taxes must, for the most part, be left to the individual States. The Government at Washington must depend chiefly on indirect taxes.

"But a great system of industry has, as a matter of fact, been built up on the basis of a protective tariff, and the question of statesmanship ahead of us is one of fairness and good judgment. It is a question of expediency in the large sense of that word. Where shall we bring our tariff duties to a revenue basis at once? Where must we go slowly and ease the process off by well-considered, gradual measures of reduction?

"The economic life of the nation is a very delicate, very sensitive fabric. We are all business men, as I have just been pointing out. What affects the business of the country affects all of us. Whatever changes may be made must be made in the interest of all; must be thoughtfully considered and carefully squared with actual circumstances.

"With regard to some schedules it is already abundantly evident what it is just and necessary to do. Congress in the special session showed that it understood which they were and how they ought to be dealt with. The President did not seem to understand either the spirit and purpose of Congress or the temper and opinion of the country."

"But, Governor, it is being urged that the interests of the East and West are divergent as to the tariff. Do you think that is so?"

"No; the interests of the East and the West do not seem to me to be divergent in any important matter of national policy."

"What effect has the tariff had on wages?" Gov. Wilson was next asked.

"Very little, directly. When wages have risen they have generally risen more in response to the demand of organized labor than from any other cause. The men who have chiefly profited by the tariff have not many of them voluntarily shared its benefits with their workmen. The workingmen of the country have been grossly deceived about this matter from the first. But, fortunately for the country, their eyes are being opened now to the real facts and to the real forces that are at work."

A pile of reports of investigating committees, and of the Department of Commerce and Labor, on the Governor's desk was evidence of the interest he takes in the so-called "trust problem." It suggested the next line of questioning.

"How are the trusts to be dealt with?"

"The tariff lies at the bottom of much of the trust question.

That is the reason why the tariff question is the central and dominating question. It is behind the shelter of the tariff wall that the trusts have been able to build up a system by which they have limited opportunity and all but shut the door upon independent enterprise."

"Will the reduction of the tariff schedules by which the greatest trusts thrive virtually solve the trust question, then?"

"By no means. It will do a vast deal to cut away the artificial advantages upon which the trusts depend for establishing monopoly; but there is something beyond that. Looked at from the side of business organization, the trusts are chiefly a means of economy and efficiency. It is from that side that they are so vigorously and persuasively defended by their advocates and by many thoughtful students of modern economic effort. But along with their efficient organization goes a tremendous power and they have used that power to throttle competition and establish virtual monopoly in every market that they have coveted."

"Do you think, Governor, that competition can be re-established by law?"

"It is not necessary to answer that question until we have done what the law certainly can do. The methods by which the greater trusts have driven competitors out of business are well known. So are also the methods by which those who have financed them have seen to it that those who tried to establish rival enterprises were prevented from doing so. There are lawyers available who can describe these methods with abundant precision in statutes. Those methods can be made criminal offenses and the monopolistic use of trusts can be stopped by the punishment of every person who tries to make such use of their power.

"Guilt is always personal and we shall never get at the root of these things by changing merely the size and organization of the business corporations. The offenses they have been committing against freedom of opportunity and of enterprise are well known and can be put a stop to. It is not a question of their size but of their acts. These have been brought out in detail by the inquiries of half a dozen committees and many legal contests."

Gov. Wilson had looked at his watch, and rising asked his interviewer to walk with him to his street car. On the way he answered two more questions in terse, epigrammatic form.

"Do you think, Governor, that the direct primary and direct nominations will eliminate the 'boss'?"

"Nothing will eliminate the 'boss' but such a simplification of the processes of government as will enable public opinion to control it without the intervention of the elaborate organization at present needed to take care of nominations and to keep the various parts of government from working at loggerheads with one another, as a result of their lack of internal unity. But the direct primary and direct nominations do afford the people an opportunity to override the 'boss' or thrust him aside when they choose to do so. They are indispensable instruments of reform. They will at least create honest and open political managers. The 'boss' is a gumshoe political manager."

"What of publicity, Governor? Is it the salvation of the Republic?"

"There is, of course, no single, sovereign remedy for anything; but publicity certainly acts upon crooked projects like the fresh and open air upon tuberculosis; it is a great antiseptic against the germs of some of the worst political methods. Government that is kept constantly in the open is very apt to be honest and healthy government."

And then waiting at a windy street corner for a car which was to take him back to his Princ[e]ton home, Gov. Wilson suddenly revealed his second self. There are two Gov. Wilsons, just as there used to be two Presidents of Princeton. Away from the executive chamber, as he used to do when away from the classroom, Governor Wilson relaxes. The extremely scholarly and painstaking polite public man gave way to a gleeful companion with a most wonderful fund of human interest stories, and a passion for nonsense rhymes. It is extremely doubtful whether the former President of Princeton is more familiar with the classics than he is with that most fascinating branch of literature, the detective story. For nearly twenty minutes—till his car came—he discussed the weaknesses of the most famous Sherlock Holmes stories in a way that made one suspect him of sometimes writing detective stories himself.[3]

Printed in the New York *World*, Dec. 24, 1911; many editorial headings omitted.
    [3] There is a WWsh draft of the questions and answers contained in this interview, dated Dec. 11, 1911, in WP, DLC.

❖

WOODROW WILSON TALKS ON BIG PUBLIC QUESTIONS

In a towering skyscraper on lower Broadway there has been in operation for many months a well-equipped plant to further the Presidential aspirations of Dr. Woodrow Wilson, the scholarly and militant Governor of New Jersey.

It is the proud boast of its manager that not a laudatory Wilson line has ever originated with the willing workers in his establishment. It is merely a clearing house for the dissemination of pro-Wilson "sentiment" as voiced in editorial page or in news colum[n]s throughout the United States.

For all that, this work of holding up a mirror in which people in one part of the country may perceive what people in other parts think of Woodrow Wilson as a candidate for the Presidential nomination has rendered the Wilson headquarters one of the busiest places in one of the busiest sections of America's busiest thoroughfare.

Of all the men whose names have been mentioned in connection with the Democratic nomination for President next year the most widely discussed is Gov. Woodrow Wilson of New Jersey. He has piqued the people's curiosity until everybody is anxious to know all there is to know about him. Thus he has become a National figure. He has taken hold of the imagination of the people, too, in a manner no other man has in recent years, with the exception of Theodore Roosevelt and, possibly, William J. Bryan after he made his famous speech at the Chicago convention in 1896.

The writer of this article has been swinging the circle of Democratic aspirants for White House honors recently. In his journeyings he has learned, of necessity, what is on the minds of Democrats in the sections he traversed. On railroad trains, in hotel lobbies, on street corners, even in the inner sanctum of men of large affairs, there was more talk of Woodrow Wilson than there was of either Harmon, Underwood or Champ Clark, not to mention the smaller fry that would like to call the White House their home. With some modification, providing for the immediate home localities of the several other candidates, the man in the street is "cussing" or discussing Woodrow Wilson when his thoughts turn to 1912 and its National contest.

But from the lips of both friend and foe of Woodrow Wilson his name comes, coupled with questions. The people of the United States are off on a guessing contest, and Woodrow Wilson is the conundrum.

Nearly all the Democrats with whom I talked—even those who have their misgivings regarding his availability as the Presidential nominee of his party—have somewhere in their hearts a warm spot for Woodrow Wilson. Those who have come in contact with Gov. Wilson have fallen easy prey to the personal attractiveness there is about the man. Those who have merely heard him speak have been captivated by the scholarly charm of his more deliberate public utterances. Nor was there disclosed any widespread grudge against Gov. Wilson for the manner in which he has been "cutting up" during the turbulent twelve months he has held the centre of the political stage in the once boss-ridden State of New Jersey.

Woodrow Wilson is loved, too, after the vague fashion Theodore Roosevelt was loved—as a heroic figure and a man familiar with the art of making things move. The two men, however, are much different in their personal make-up. Where the frank impulsiveness of "Teddy," given vent on the public platform, has caused upheavals, the more deliberate utterances of Gov. Wilson, at least, have been tempered with all the scholar's fine caution. And yet he is feared, and very much as Col. Roosevelt is feared.

It is a fact that the utmost uncertainty with regard to his ultimate attitude on the leading questions of this Democratic day exists among Democrats with whom this writer has discussed Gov. Wilson as a Presidential possibility.

What would he do if by chance he were to become the next President of the United States? Would there be another four years of unrest and agitation? These and similar questions are asked by thoughtful Democrats everywhere.

With Democrats of a conservative turn of mind the prospect of "Woodrow Wilson, President of the United States," conjures up disquieting thoughts of a Big Stick unloaded with the Wilson baggage at the White House doors. The more radical Democrats are raising questions regarding his radicalism.

It cannot be denied that in a large measure Gov. Wilson himself is responsible for the Nation-wide guessing bee that is in progress six months before the Democratic National Convention. The radicals remember that he was known as a conservative and taught conservative doctrine to the college youth before he entered public life. They also remember that he obtained his nomination for Governor of New Jersey with the bosses' aid. The conservatives are not harboring any resentment against Gov. Wilson for what he did to the bosses after he had been elected. But they cannot forget the tumult he created while he did it, and some of his recent speeches.

Gov. Wilson only added to the perplexities besetting Democrats who are seeking to determine his exact status when, in the course of his New Jersey campaign, he proclaimed himself "a conservative with a move on," and followed it up by attempting to render in precise language his definition of the apt terms progressive and stand-patter.

The stand-patter, as Gov. Wilson defines him, is a man who

has stopped and cannot be started. A progressive is a man who has started and cannot be stopped.

A conservative Democrat, discussing these definitions with the writer, remarked on the difficulty brilliant men encountered in withstanding the frequently recurring temptation to make epigram and commented in a somewhat caustic vein on the dangers of applying the theory of perpetual motion in politics and in public life. He said it reminded him very strongly of that homely outburst which has assailed the pale moon and the silvery stars more frequently than it has been heard in sober daylight: "We don't know where we're going, but we're on our way."

In due time the writer journeyed to the State House at Trenton, New Jersey's capital, and the scene of Gov. Wilson's most recent activities, as well as his widely heralded victories over the bosses.

Gov. Wilson is not given to the habit of preparing important public utterances between two railroad stations. When I opened negotiations for an interview, stating broadly his attitude on the leading questions of the day and how the principles of Democracy might be successfully applied to their solution, he smiled wanly.

"I am a very busy man," he explained. "And, moreover, I fear that I am not much good at turning corners quickly. Furthermore, questions having reference to public policy I feel should be answered only after the utmost thought and deliberation."

The outcome of it was that with a few questions submitted in writing as a basis, Gov. Wilson during the two weeks that followed, in stray moments of leisure snatched from a multiplicity of exacting duties, and, I fear, from periods that he should have given to rest or recreation, prepared the interview as given below.

Some of the questions submitted, Gov. Wilson did not answer directly. Among these was one which had regard to the application of a tariff for revenue only, one framed to elicit his views on the plan for Federal incorporation and supervision of stock concerns engaged in inter-State commerce, and another, again, sounding him on the Aldrich currency plan and related subjects.

In regard to Federal incorporation Gov. Wilson in earlier utterances has made it clear that he does not favor the plan. In regard to the Aldrich currency plan, he pronounced it a matter properly the subject of a treatise, and not to be sandwiched in between other questions within the space of a newspaper interview. The Governor intimated that he might have something to say regarding the Aldrich plan in some of his public speeches in the near future.

Gov. Wilson does not believe that Democracy holds any panacea for all the evils that beset the time.

"The question of how we should wisely deal with the present difficulties and confusions of policy is a very comprehensive one, indeed," said Gov. Wilson. "No man knows enough to answer it, of course. But one thing is plain, and that is that we must begin by dismissing from our minds the idea that there is any one general specific or cure-all that will clear the situation. We must go step by step, under the guidance of judgment and good sense. We must move, moreover, by common counsel. No one group of men, no one class of men, can wisely determine the policy of a nation. The conclusions of the student must be corrected by the experiences of the politician and the man of affairs. There is no one programme of politics that will suit the whole country. Fortunately, we can no longer speak of 'sections' in this country or of sectional divisions of interest and sentiment, but there has not ceased to be a great diversity of conditions both in politics and economic development, and we ought to congratulate ourselves that we have our flexible system of State and Federal Governments, by which we can adapt our policies to the places where they are to be tried out, and so conform to the actual diversity of circumstance."

Gov. Wilson is an out-and-out advocate of "State rights," though his interpretation of the term does not wholly agree with its generally accepted meaning.

"I put the emphasis on the duties of the States rather than on their 'rights,'" said the Governor. "There is no longer any hostility to the Federal Government in the idea of 'State rights' nor any sense of rivalry, but only the thought that there is a fortunate liberty and variety in our methods of co-operation and an unrestricted opportunity to meet a great variety of local conditions by a corresponding variety of measures. There is no legislative strait-jacket for our life, but a most serviceable elasticity. The central question of statesmanship with us is always when to do different things in different parts of the country and when to insist on having the same thing done everywhere."

"Where can you nowadays draw the line between the field of the Federal Government and the field of the States?" Gov. Wilson was asked.

"It is a little more difficult to draw it now than it was a couple of generations ago, but it is plain enough, after all," said the Governor. "The Constitution draws it on broad and obvious principles. For example, nobody doubts, I suppose, that it is the Governments of the States, not the Federal Government, that must determine the ultimate basis and character of Government among us. They determine all questions of suffrage. They plan all matters of nomination and election, like the system of primaries and direct nomination. It is within their choice to adopt or reject the initiative, the referendum, and the recall as a means of controlling their affairs by public opinion. In short, it is their function to determine the scope and method of democracy among us, and they are under no compulsion to determine those things in the same way. They are the nurseries of popular Government, and they may, within certain broad constitutional limits, give it such form as they prefer."

When Gov. Wilson first appeared as an advocate of the initiative and referendum, and of the recall, as well, except in the case of men holding judiciary office, his public utterances gave rise to considerable astonishment. They were tempered with few, if any, qualifying statements, in the first place, and, in the second place, they contrasted sharply with the views he had expressed in his lectures and in his writings. In his book, "The State," he condemned the system as an utter failure.

In those speeches the Governor pointed to the Oregon plan of direct legislation as a distinct success from a popular point of view, and a pattern for other States to follow. The speeches were made shortly after Gov. Wilson had received a visit from William S. U'Ren, the "Blacksmith Reformer" of Oregon. It was taken for granted everywhere that the Governor had gone back on representative government and become a convert to this exaggerated form of Simon-Pure U'Ren Democracy.

The writer is in a position to state with exactitude and authority the views of Gov. Wilson on the subject. Gov. Wilson is a firm believer in representative government in the accepted sense of the term. He believes that the proper ends of government can be best attained in a republic only through the party system, if only pure and effective leadership is provided for and placed so that there can be no question of divided responsibility. He does not believe that direct legislation is practicable and desirable as a general proposition. The initiative, the referendum and the recall he regards merely as measures to be resorted to only in an emergency—as a scourge and a deterrent to promote righteousness among public officials and political bosses. He does not look upon them as involving a National question.

"It is a National question only in the sense that it is of universal interest and that public men everywhere are seeking for or trying to avoid the means by which public opinion may be made supreme in public affairs," said Gov. Wilson. "Our Constitutions have time out of mind committed us to representative government, and I have not found any thoughtful man anywhere who wanted to get rid of it. But in some States representative government has come to exist only in name. Legislatures not only, but the entire organization of the government, have become subject to the control of political machines, which are themselves, in turn, known to be subsidized and used by special business interests. In those States the people have insisted, or will insist, upon bringing their governments back under their own control by means of direct legislation, the referendum, and, if necessary, the recall.

"Witness the result of the recent vote in California and the vote for a Constitutional Convention to determine these matters in Ohio. The leaders of opinion in those States do not intend to substitute direct for representative action in legislation, but they do mean to control their own affairs independently of special interests, even if they employ these new means only by way of admonition, only as the 'gun behind the door.'

"In other States there is, fortunately, no serious question of the representative character of the existing Legislatures. The political organization of parties has not been transformed into the sort of 'machine' which has proved so sinister a power elsewhere. Those States may never resort to the new measures because they may never need them. It may be that the example of such things elsewhere will put such fear of God and respect for liberty into the hearts of their politicians that they will never be obliged seriously to debate them."

The Governor added that it was self-evident that the initiative[,] referendum, and the recall should not be catalogued as a National question.

"We have not altered our system of government simply because we have all come to think about these things at the same time," he remarked.

I took the Governor to task for his apparent change of front on the question.

"In theory," he quickly replied, "these things are all wrong. In practice they have worked well. But when I lectured and wrote against the initiative and referendum the system had not been put to a practical test anywhere in this country."

Turning to National questions, Gov. Wilson said that the main question was the tariff.

"Approach that in the right way and with something like statesmanlike judgment and sagacity," said the Governor, "and you have cleared the way for the successful treatment of almost every other question of great consequence that now confronts us, except the currency question, and perhaps even that will be set forward if we can once throw off the provincialism bred in us by our exclusive tariff policy."

"Don't you think it would be a good thing to take the tariff out of politics?"

"That might be, but it would be hopeless to try to do it as long as the protective tariff forms the basis for special interest and there is a militant Democracy in the field to comfort [confront] special interest and contend for equal opportunities for all."

"Then you include the trust question among those which the proper treatment of the tariff would help you solve?"

"Most assuredly. The tariff underlies the trusts."

"But is that the whole of the trust question?"

"Of course not. Combinations in restraint of trade will be more difficult when the tariff has been transformed into a revenue measure instead of a means of creating artificial advantages for particular groups of producers, but they will, of course, still be possible and will still be attempted."

"Do you think that war should be made on the combinations?"

"I do not think that 'war' should be made on anything; our problem is one of equitable readjustment. I do not understand that the policy of our law was ever directed against combinations as such, or against their mere size, but only against combinations in restraint of trade. Combination has proved an extremely successful means of economy and efficiency, but restraint of trade is another matter and affects the healthful operation of our whole economic system."

"But how are you to distinguish between the combinations which restrain trade and those which do not?"

"By their operations and effects, by what they do, by the method and result of their operations. A score of searching investigations have recently disclosed with perfect clearness just what is done by the managers of great combinations to throttle competition and monopolize markets. Those who once denied all wrongdoing on the part of the trusts and defended them without qualification against all criticism, now admit—their very officers included—that they have been guilty of inexcusable wrongs in the restraint of free opportunity and the smothering of rival enterprise. The acts and processes to which they have testified should be made criminal offenses and put a sharp stop to. That is the only way to throw the gates open to fresh talent and independent capital."

"But to go back to the tariff, how should that be dealt with?"

"With common sense and judgment like the rest. The Democratic leaders in Congress have already shown that they know how to deal with it, schedule by schedule, acting where the facts and interests affected are known and the occasion for reduction plain and admitted."

"But what of the business interests of the country in the meantime?"

"There are no separate and distinguishable business interests in a matter like this or in any other matter of general economic policy. The whole country depends upon its business. Where will you draw the line between those who are business men and those who are not, between those whom business affects and those whom it does not affect?

"No one who cares for the welfare of the country as a whole can overlook or do an intentional disservice to its business men, for they are, in a sense, all of us. The process of tariff revision, like everything else we have to undertake, must be a process of readjustment, not revolutionary, but carried carefully forward upon a definite principle. That principle is a tariff for revenue. The weight and arrangement of the taxes levied under it must be determined, as all taxes should be, by the economic interests of the whole community."

Gov. Wilson is a warm believer in reciprocity, not only with Canada, but with other countries.

"I greatly regret that the voters of Canada rejected reciprocity," said the Governor. "But it was only part of a policy. We have strangely neglected our trade with our neighbors both to the north and to the south of us. I was interested in reciprocity with Canada as the beginning of a new outlook and policy which should reawaken our trade. Among other things that the tariff has done has been to destroy our merchant marine. Our navigation laws have, of course, contributed to the same end, but they are simply part of the tariff policy—part of our determination to prevent Americans, if possible, from buying anything anywhere except in America. Calling ourselves a commercial and industrial Nation, we have so hampered all our foreign commerce that it has existed only in spite of huge artificial difficulties, and the most enterprising people in the world have forfeited their initiative in foreign markets by deliberately giving up the carrying trade of the world. We shall grow rich some day when we really learn how, when we cease preying upon our own people by putting them in a hothouse, where they sweat as much as they profit, and turn our eyes to genuine enterprise and free effort again throughout the world."

"Do you expect much help from the Tariff Board in settling the tariff question?"

"A great deal of help might come from it if it were not put upon a false quest. It is seeking differences in cost of production upon the fatuous principle of the last Republican platform. Differences between whom? Between the manufacturers of this country and the manufacturers of foreign countries? Which of our manufacturers are to be taken as the standard? Is there the same cost of production for the most efficient of them and the least efficient in any line of industry? Is there the same cost of production for any one of them at different times? Are the inefficient to be protected along with the efficient? If not, where is the line to be drawn? Who shall be left out in the cold? And are the most efficient as efficient as they might be if they had to meet foreign competition and had no tariff wall to lie snug behind? The board is looking for what no man can find. It may furnish us with much valuable information and may be worth keeping for that, but it cannot do what it was set to do. So far, it has been made a mere excuse for doing nothing."

Gov. Wilson has been reported as being in favor of incorporating a local option plank in the Democratic National platform. The Governor's detractors have declared this a piece of political sharp practice undertaken for the purpose of creating an issue on which to fight Gov. Harmon of Ohio, his most formidable rival for the Presidential nomination. When Gov. Wilson's attention was called to this report he laughed most heartily.

"I had never heard of that before," he said. "I am in favor of local option—yes—because I am in favor of the greatest degree of home rule in local government. But I am utterly opposed to having it incorporated in any party platform. It cuts up parties in the most hopeless fashion. It blurs party lines and forces itself to the front as a topic for discussion to the exclusion of all other issues whenever it figures as an issue in a party campaign."

Gov. Wilson laughed again when his attention was called to the fact that the words "new" and "modern" had been somewhat overworked in his public speeches. The fact naturally led up to the question if he recognized a "new" and an "old" democracy and drew a distinction between them.

"No," said Gov. Wilson, "in its essence democracy must always remain the same. Jefferson laid down the principle when he defined it as the enemy of special privilege and the opener of the door of opportunity and enterprise to all on equal terms. Democracy must always mean just that. But we live in a new world to-day, we deal with new conditions and a new society, and the party that cannot adjust itself to new conditions has outlived its usefulness."

"Can you see any indication of a breaking up of party lines—

of a readjustment along the Old World lines, where liberals are opposed to conservatives, radicals to reactionaries?" Gov. Wilson was asked.

"I cannot in the Democratic Party," was the reply. "In our party the progressive element is in control, and that element is in complete harmony with the original tendencies of Democracy, as the word has been understood from the beginning. In the Republican Party the situation is very different. While there is a large progressive element in the Republican Party to-day, that element is compelled to work at cross purposes with the party leaders. The Republican Party in the Nation is controlled by the reactionary forces."

When Gov. Wilson made his campaign in New Jersey a little more than a year ago, much was made of it when he said on the stump that he was willing to be the "un-Constitutional Governor of New Jersey."

This sally from Woodrow Wilson was prompted by the attitude proclaimed by his opponent, who declared in his speeches that he intended to be a "Constitutional" Governor, who, after recommending legislation to the lawmakers, would keep his hands off and let them dispose of it in the fashion they saw fit.

"My utterances have been misunderstood," said Gov. Wilson when this question was broached. "There was an 'if' which the newspapers evidently left out of their accounts. I said that if my opponent was correct in his definition of a Constitutional Governor—and I did not believe then and do not believe now that he was—then I was ready to become an un-Constitutional Governor. I have not only respect but real affection for the Constitution. But most of our State Constitutions and certainly the Constitution of New Jersey, give the Governor the right to recommend legislation to the law-making body, and also vest in him the veto power. Now, wouldn't that imply that he is permitted to take an active interest in what the law makers are doing in the intermediary stage? I certainly contend that it does, and I regard it as quite proper for a Governor to go to the people direct and advocate by every fair argument the passage of the laws he has recommended when the legislators show unwillingness to comply with his recommendations. That, to my mind, does not involve any disregard for the well-known principle of American government, under which a sharp line is drawn between the functions of the executive, legislative and judiciary branches."

Some one has said that the way to perfection leads through frequent changes of mind. Such changes certainly indicate an open mind and a receptive intellect, even though some are inclined to regard them as indicative of a fatuous faculty for forming judgments too hastily and for rendering decisions before all the evidence is in.

In connection with this the apparently studied restraint of Gov. Wilson's utterances to-day and his evident caution must be regarded as very significant. His silence, too, on many topics which he has discussed for publication in the past is as eloquent, to say the least, as anything that he has said.

Take his refusal to discuss the Aldrich currency plan, for instance, not to revert to his modified views on the initiative and referendum and the recall. In his public speeches in the New Jersey campaign a year ago and last Summer Gov. Wilson freely denounced the "money power" and the "money trust."

"The great monopoly in this country is the money monopoly," he was quoted as saying in one of his speeches. "So long as that exists our old variety and freedom and individual energy of development are out of the question. A great industrial Nation is controlled by its system of credit. Our system of credit is concentrated. The growth of the Nation, therefore, and all our activities are in the hands of a few men who, even if their acts be honest and intended for the public interest, are necessarily concentrated upon the great undertakings in which their own money is involved, who necessarily, by very reason of their own limitations, chill and destroy genuine economic freedom. This is the greatest economic question of all, and to this statesmen must address themselves with an earnest determination to serve the long future and the true liberties of men."

An interviewer who called on Gov. Wilson last Summer took up this portion of his speech for the purpose of sounding him further on the subject. Here is the result set forth by that writer in his article, published last August:

"I referred to this part of the Governor's speech and asked him if he would go more into detail regarding this reform.

" 'I have not given sufficient study to the question,' he replied. 'As it is the greatest question before the country to-day, it requires a great deal of consideration, and involves wise and sound economic planning.'

" 'But Mr. Aldrich and the lame ducks of the Monetary Commission have presented a plan of currency reform.'

" 'I am afraid that any measure of that character bearing Mr. Aldrich's name,' replied Mr. Wilson, 'must have been drawn in the office of the few men who, through the present system of concentrated capital, control the banking and industrial activities of the country.' "

Much interest is being displayed just now with regard to the probable attitude of Gov. Wilson toward "big business." In part it is reflected through the interview he has given to the Sunday Times. Gov. Wilson is not an enemy of "big business" as such. His whole endeavor to the extent that he has been in a position to put his principles into practice has been to break up the corrupt combination between "big business" and big bosses in politics, as a means of shattering the control of lawmaking bodies by the corporations and compel the latter to live strictly within the laws enacted for the benefit of the greatest number.

Gov. Wilson once made his attitude on this subject very clear when he described unlawful corporations as "joy riders."

"I have no objection to the ordinary automobile properly handled by a man of conscience, who is also a gentleman," said Gov. Wilson on that occasion. "Many of the people I see handling automobiles handle them as if they had neither conscience nor manners. I have no objection to the size and beauty and power of the automobile. I am interested, however, in the size and conscience of the men who handle them, and what I object to is that some of these corporation men take joy rides in their corporations.

"You know what men do when they take a joy ride. They sometimes have the time of their lives, and sometimes, fortunately, the last time of their lives. Now, these wretched things are taking joy rides in which they don't kill the people that are riding in them, but they kill the people they run over."

While in some quarters Gov. Wilson has been regarded as a man of extreme and dangerously radical views, his harshest critics are found in the radical camp of his party. There one finds those who look back over many pages of Wilson history, and who, taking due notice of his earlier teachings, as well as of his most recent sponsors in public life, are ready to place upon him the brand of insincerity. They imagine behind the publicly spoken words which have aroused such popular plaudits a set of cruel fangs and under the proverbial sheep's clothing of the reformer the gray pelt that any one who wishes to get along in public life must conceal behind a carefully selected mask, attractive to the greatest possible number of men with votes.

There is nothing in the public record of Gov. Wilson to justify this lack of faith in his sincerity. He has shown himself so far neither a hypocrite nor a man who has sought to carry water on both shoulders. His twelve months as Governor of New Jersey certainly have been characterized by the utmost candor, the utmost fearlessness, contempt for any degrading compromise, and a due regard for the welfare of the people.

Men may differ in their views as to his wisdom and fitness. Anybody who knows Gov. Wilson at all could never for a moment doubt his absolute integrity and his desire to do justice between man and man, or between the corporations and the people.

Gov. Wilson's first step in seeking to bring about an improvement in the relations between the people and the corporations would be to conciliate, to adjudicate, to readjust. He would constitute himself the whole board of arbitration, perhaps. Should the corporations fail to respond to that treatment, Woodrow Wilson, LL.D., would promptly assume the functions of an M.D. and make them take their medicine, even if the treatment should happen to be heroic enough to kill where it did not cure. But Dr. Wilson has great faith in the efficacy of the milder mode of dealing with "big business."

When Dr. Woodrow Wilson came to the front as the Democratic nominee for Governor, the political stage in New Jersey had been fully set for the coming of such a man. The State was still tightly clutched in the grasp of the political bosses. They acted as the middlemen for the corporations, seeking special favors from those who by virtue of their official positions had such favors to give. The Republicans happened to be in power. They controlled both houses of the Legislature and all the public offices worth having. John Franklin Fort was Governor. He was a Republican, but not the bosses' man. He had worked manfully to bring about some well-needed reforms in his State, and had patterned his administration somewhat on the lines of the Hughes administration in New York. But he had only a handful of followers in the Republican majority of the lawmaking body. They were the butts of jeers and coarse jokes whenever they made a speech, and they were easily snowed under when the roll was called and the vote taken on legislative measures.

There existed in New Jersey, as there did in New York, a corrupt coalition between the bosses of the two big political parties, based on a division of spoils. Only a few months before, Trenton, New Jersey's capital, had witnessed its "night of shame" when the bosses' proxies in the New Jersey Legislature, on the evening when that body adjourned sine die, celebrated their short-lived triumph over decency by a wild Saturnalia in the very halls where the lawmaking body met.

Gov. Wilson frequently told the voters during the Gubernatorial campaign that he could never understand how he got the nomination. His chief sponsor in the Democratic State Convention was former United States Senator James Smith, Jr., the old-time Democratic boss of New Jersey. Without his aid Woodrow

Wilson could not have been nominated. It is a surmisal merely, but it seems safe to assume that the Democratic bosses of New Jersey when they nominated Woodrow Wilson were exactly in the position of the Republican bosses in New York when they brought about the nomination of Hughes in 1906. They needed a respectable figurehead and they trusted to fate and earlier experiences that they would be able to manage him after he once had been elected.

Political history will relate in the future how the Democratic bosses of New Jersey played a bad joke on themselves when they placed Woodrow Wilson, the Princeton schoolmaster, in a position of political power, just as the Hughes experiment in New York will be regarded by future generations as "a good one on the Republican bosses." . . .[1]

It is on a "Governor's Day" that Woodrow Wilson is seen to his best advantage. There is at no time any trace of exaggerated official dignity about him, but on Governor's Day any one stepping into the Executive Chamber in the State House at Trenton is apt to meet Woodrow Wilson the man rather than Woodrow Wilson the Governor.

All parts and conditions of men and women with grievances, with suggestions, with supplications, drop in on the Governor on his Tuesday at home. The door to the Governor's inner sanctum has always been wide open during official hours ever since he first took his seat in the Governor's chair. Every morning as he enters his private office he kicks a wedge under the door to make sure that it will remain not ajar but opened wide.

On these days there is a constant stream of visitors. From 10 in the morning until 5 at night the flow is unbroken. The Governor receives one, talks with him, dismisses him, and then very much after the fashion of a doctor in his office hours appears in the door to the anteroom, looks about, and calls out, "Next."

There is only one break in the long day. That is the luncheon hour. Then the Governor adjourns to a bare basement room in the State House, where "Sam" Gordon, the colored doorkeeper, who for thirty-seven years, under both Republican and Democratic administrations has held his job, provides a plain luncheon for the Governor and any member of his official family or any visitor who cares to partake.

The Governor is the life of these luncheon parties. On the day I visited Trenton, State Banking Commissioner Vivian Lewis, his defeated Republican opponent for Gubernatorial honors, occu-

[1] Here follows a review of the New Jersey senatorial fight of 1910-1911 and of Wilson's accomplishments as governor.

pied the seat on the Governor's right and seemed to enjoy the funny stories the Governor told as much as any one about the table. The Governor's guest on the occasion was Britton D. Evans of "brainstorm" fame. Dr. Evans is head of the New Jersey State Asylum for the Insane, and had come to visit the Governor on official business. At table they got into a controversy over the qualities of conscience. Dr. Evans maintained that men might change their conscience with changing moods, very much as they changed their minds on their clothes. He had observed it among his insane wards. The Governor, on the other hand, maintained that the standards of conscience were immutable, until the subject was changed and darkey stories began to flow from Gov. Wilson, who is a Southerner by birth.

Whether Gov. Wilson's name will go before the Democratic National Convention for the Presidential nomination will depend in a measure on what progress he makes with the Republican Legislature during the next four months. The Republican lawmakers are meeting in caucus at Trenton almost weekly, deliberating on a legislative programme of their own, which they are preparing to pass and then adjourn quickly sine die, ignoring the Governor's recommendations. If this programme is carried out New Jersey is likely to witness a fight picturesque enough to engross the attention of the Nation, for Gov. Woodrow Wilson has very definite views regarding what the next Legislature of his State should do.

Democratic bosses whom Gov. Wilson has antagonized, too, are lying in wait for him in the dark alleys of New Jersey politics, armed with all the bludgeons and blackjacks of bossdom. They are bent on preventing him having the support of the New Jersey delegation to the National Convention, hoping thus to bring about his undoing as a candidate for the Presidential nomination. But Gov. Wilson's friends pin their faith to a section of the Geran election law which provides that where 1,000 Democratic voters make petition the party shall be permitted to designate its preference for the Presidency at the primaries in May. Gov. Wilson is content to leave his fate with the rank and file of his party.[2]

Printed in the *New York Times*, Dec. 24, 1911; one editorial heading omitted.

[2] There is a WWsh draft of the questions and answers contained in this interview, dated Dec. 1911, in WP, DLC. These two interviews were widely distributed in 1912 under the title, *Two Notable Articles About Woodrow Wilson* (n.p., n.d.).

To Edward Mandell House

My dear Mr. House: [Trenton, N. J.] December 26, 1911.

Thank you sincerely for your letter of December fifteenth. I am very much obliged to you for dealing with Mr. William Garrott Brown so tactfully. You took exactly the right position with it. I note what he says about handling North Carolina and shall try to deal with that as carefully as possible.

We are just now anxious to have the best possible advice and assistance in having actual organization undertaken throughout the South such as will result in looking aafter the delegates from the several States. It seems to us, and I am sure it must seem to you, that the time for definite action has come.

I hope that you all had a very happy Christmas; may you have a very happy New Year indeed.

Gratefully yours,   Woodrow Wilson

TLS (E. M. House Papers, CtY).

From Frances B. Denton[1]

Dear Sir: [Austin, Tex.] December 26th, 1911.

I am sorry to tell you that Mr. House is still quite sick with an attack of malaria.

He bids me say that his last letter to you was written when he had a high fever.

He is some better today and hopes that within a short time to be able to answer your kind letter of December 22nd.

Very truly yours,   [Frances B. Denton]

CCL (E. M. House Papers, CtY).
[1] Colonel House's confidential secretary for many years.

To George Brinton McClellan Harvey

Personal.

My dear Colonel: [Trenton, N. J.] December 27, 1911.

The boys of the Press Club of Princeton University are very anxious to find out if they might venture to hope that you will come down and make them a little address this winter. They were abashed at the idea of approaching you directly and I am glad to act as their sponsor.

May I say to them that you are approachable on this subject?[1]

Cordially and faithfully yours,   Woodrow Wilson

TLS (WP, DLC).
[1] Harvey did not speak to the Press Club during the rest of the academic year.

To Richard Heath Dabney

My dear Heath: [Trenton, N. J.] December 27, 1911.

Your letter of the twenty-first[1] came in due course of mail and I have read it with growing appreciation of what you are doing and of the value of what you are telling me from time to time.

Apparently it would be literally impossible for me to make a series of speeches in Virginia, as Mr. Harris[2] so kindly suggests, though I hope it might be possible some time during the legislative session to make one. I do not know what to say about your suggestion that the Legislature of the State invite me. You are in a better position to judge of the wisdom of that than I am.[3]

The impression of your letter with mine appended seems to have been excellent and the men at my headquarters in New York are planning to send out a great lot of them through the South.

In haste,   Faithfully yours,   Woodrow Wilson

TLS (Wilson-Dabney Corr., ViU).
  [1] It is missing.
  [2] Unidentified.
  [3] Wilson spoke to the legislature of Virginia and the Richmond Common Council on Feb. 1, 1912. His address is printed at that date in Vol. 24.

To Daniel Moreau Barringer

My dear Moreau: [Trenton, N. J.] December 28, 1911.

I myself have not the least doubt but that Mr. Untermeyer is sincere and in earnest. I have not had an opportunity to talk with him about the great subject he has tackled but I am seeking an early opportunity.

I feel more and more as the days go by the central importance of that great question.

Cordially and faithfully yours,   Woodrow Wilson

TLS (D. M. Barringer Papers, NjP).

From Frances B. Denton

Strictly Confidential.

My dear Sir: [Austin, Tex.] December 30th, 1911.

Mr. House asks me to quote the following from a letter he has just received from Mr. W. J. Bryan.[1] Mr. House is still in bed but thinks it important for this information to reach you at once.

"Am anxious to get back and find out more of the political situation. I shall attend the Washington banquet on the 8th of

January and will have a chance to learn how things are shaping up.

I am glad Governor Wilson recognizes that he has the opposition of Morgan and the rest of Wall Street. If he is nominated it must be by the Progressive Democrats and the more progressive he is the better.

The Washington banquet will give him a good chance to speak out against the trusts and the Aldrich Currency scheme."

Very truly yours,   [Frances B. Denton]

CCL (E. M. House Papers, CtY).
¹ W. J. Bryan to E. M. House, Dec. 17, 1911, ALS (E. M. House Papers, CtY).

From William Frank McCombs

STRICTLY CONFIDENTIAL:

My dear Governor: New York December 30, 1911.

I have a letter from Mr. Villard and one from E[lijah]. Prentice [Prentiss] Bailey to him. Mr. Bailey is the editor of the Utica Observer. Yesterday I had luncheon with Mr. Villard. The question of a letter of yours to Mr. Joline concerning Mr. Bryan was brought up. It was decided that Mr. Villard's confidential man would go to Mr. Joline and find out if such a letter was in existence and what it was. It seems that Mr. Joline made a speech during one of Bryan's campaigns against Bryan. He says he communicated that speech after printing to you. The last paragraph of your reply, Mr. Joline says, reads somewhat as follows: "I wish that some means at once effective and dignified might be found for putting William J. Bryan out of the party once and for all." Mr. Joline also says that he would not give this letter out for publication because he and you, while still friendly, have had discussion on a number of points over the management of Princeton University, and that you defeated him in the race for trusteeship for Princeton; further if he gave out the letter it might be considered an act of resentment. He offers to let Mr. Villard see the letter himself some night at his house. A very troublesome fact is that he has given it to a reporter on Hearst's papers, with the understanding that it would not be published without his permission. Of course it will be and undoubtedly it will be forwarded to Mr. Bryan himself.

As to the Cleveland letter, Nicholas Murray Butler, Dr. Elisha J. Edwards,¹ Ex-Post Master Thomas L. James² and Dr. Joseph B. Bryant³ are persons who Mr. Bailey discreetly says might give the facts. The words supposed to be used in the letter are "lacks intellectual integrity." Mr. Villard will run these things down and may take the matter up with you. He has not asked me not to say anything to you about it. If he consults you it might be well not to advert to this letter. I think the information should be gotten to you as soon as possible and therefore I am sending this letter.　　　　　　　　　　Yours sincerely, Wm. F. McCombs

TLS (WP, DLC).

[1] Elisha Jay Edwards, a free-lance journalist of New York with an honorary doctor's degree from Seton Hall College. He had scored a journalistic scoop by publishing in the Philadelphia *Press*, August 29, 1893, an account of the removal of a portion of Cleveland's jaw, less than two months after the operation.

[2] Thomas Lemuel James, Postmaster General in Garfield's cabinet; at this time president of the Lincoln National Bank of New York.

[3] Joseph Decatur Bryant, surgeon, long-time personal friend and physician of Cleveland and his family, who had performed the operation.

To Mary Allen Hulbert Peck

Dearest Friend,

Princeton, New Jersey
New Year's Eve., 1911

A Happy, happy New Year! I know that it begins with anxiety and the mortifications of the proceedings you have to go through with; but beyond that lies complete release,—free years in which you can live a life such as you have never been able to lead since you first married: a life which you can fill with a realization of your own ideals (the ideals I know to be natural and dear to you) of friendship and service, and thoughts that are not shut up to a round of unpalateable duties which take the very heart out of you! I rejoice to think of the way in which your life is to flower anew—and you are to be brought back to youth and poise and elasticity again,—nothing any longer to dread, only what and whom you choose to fill it with, and make it satisfy what you have never had a chance to satisfy, while you felt like a spirit in a cage. What made you open your friendship to me was that I at once penetrated the case-hardening you had superficially hid yourself in and discovered what you had all along been,—the idealist and lover of true and pure and simple things. A happy, happy New Year! You will be ten years younger on New Year's Eve, 1912!

What the year will bring forth for *me* who can tell? The political scene changes almost every week, as the elements in it alter. For my own part, you know how I feel about it all, so far as it concerns me personally, and how my mind is safe against surprise, taking nothing for granted until it has actually happened. A year from now I may be as free as you,—still Governor of New Jersey, but with no larger obligations saddled upon me and the prospect of choosing a life of my own when my term is up. Or, I *may* be in for something much harder and more taxing! Either way, there is nothing for my thought to do but to hold steady on the present opportunity and please itself with the present duty.

We have had a happy holiday season,—except for my darling Nellie's absence in Mexico. She is having a delightful time, by the way, in a very novel kind of community (Chihuahua) and is enjoying it with all her characteristic zest. Her letters are vivid and charming and give us a sense of having seen it all. But, ah! how we miss her! Our circle has been complete, otherwise, and last Thursday and Friday I had the great treat of having my brother from Tennessee with me. I had not seen him for two years.

All join me in most affectionate messages to you all and warmest greetings for the new Year. You may be sure that my thought follows you in every minutest affair of your life.

Your devoted friend   Woodrow Wilson

ALS (WP, DLC).

A News Report of a Speech to New Jersey Mayors in Hoboken, New Jersey

[Jan. 3, 1912]

JERSEY CITIES WAKING UP

THEIR MAYORS MEET TO TALK OF GOVERNMENTAL REFORMS.

Gov. Woodrow Wilson and the Mayors and representatives of a score of New Jersey municipalities[1] helped to-day to launch a movement which bids fair to open a new era in the administration of the cities of the State. Together with a number of other men, city attorneys and heads of boards of trade, they met in conference at the residence of Mrs. Caroline B. Alexander, Castle Point, Hoboken, with the general purpose of discussing the need for better charters for their several towns. But wholly aside from the question of charter planning, which was the chief topic of the day, there was evident a pronounced trend toward more enlightened city government, with a leaning on the part of most of the speakers toward the adoption in one form or another of the commission plan.

The conference was called by the new Mayor of Hoboken, Martin Cooke, and the president of the Hoboken Board of Trade, C. H. C. Jagels,[2] in whose efforts Mrs. Alexander and her sister-in-law, Mrs. Robert L. Stevens,[3] coöperated enthusiastically. Indeed, one of the most interesting features of the movement was the importance assumed in it by a number of women. They were just as much to the fore as any of the men present, although they did not speak. . . .

Jagels introduced Gov. Wilson as chairman of the conference, and the Governor began by remarking that he had not known that he was down for an address.

"Indeed," he said, "I have come here to be instructed in the necessities of municipal charters, and I do not pretend to tell you anything which you do not know. Still, I can say that it seems to me that nobody should be more interested in the whole subject of municipal charters than the Mayors of the cities of the State, and I am more than glad to notice that you take such an active interest in this movement. City officers often go into office with high intentions and ideals, only to find themselves hopelessly embarrassed by the restrictions of their charter. It is this subject that we have before us, and we cannot discuss it too thoroughly.

"We are entering upon a period of remarkable business efficiency all over the country, and it seems to me that we should make every effort to introduce this particular kind of efficiency into government, as well as into commerce, and most particularly, into city government. City government should not be political, except in the ordinary sense of the word—I mean, except in the sense that any political administration is political. But at any rate it should not be a party government. Yet almost nowhere in this country do we find an example of sound success in the introduction of business ideas and principles of efficiency into the government of municipalities.

"Think of that! We have a higher business efficiency in America than in any other country in the world; but it is entirely a business efficiency of commerce. It is found only in the business field; it is not shown in government. True, we hear of many scientific systems of graft, but when do we hear of a scientific system of city government? In place of that, we are forced to admit that we are in the humiliating position of knowing that every other country in the world of our own rank has a better system of city government. We ought to change this, and I do not hesitate to say that if every man in this room went at the situation with a determination to change it we should do so.

"We all know what we want, but we don't know how to get it. Team-work is the secret of it, I think. Let us adopt it. Last winter I did not sign a number of bills that were passed by the Legislature, because I thought that they restricted the independence of municipalities, and I disapprove of governing municipalities from Trenton. I believe that people should be allowed to work out their own salvation. They should be allowed to draw up their own charters, make their own alterations in them, say what exact form of city government they want.

"And that brings me to another point—sooner or later, we are going to find that the only satisfactory way to secure results is to govern people out in the open. No detail of city business should be kept secret. Every man should be able to inquire at his City Hall, with the foreknowledge that his queries will be answered. He has a right to know. Governments are servants of the public, and servants cannot object to answering questions. And yet, notwithstanding this obvious truism, there are city councils that hold secret sessions, and I say that they are an offence to good government. The only excuse for such a course is when discussions of appointments to public office are in order, and it is conceivable in such situations, when the character and fitness of men are being canvassed, that fairness to them should dictate secrecy. But even this argument is not conclusive.

"After all, our law is that a candidate for office cannot resent any review of his record. He should first determine for himself whether a public review of his record will prove embarrassing to him. If his record will not support the full glare of the spotlight, then he should not seek office, for the place for the officeholder to stand is full in the spotlight's glare. It may not be pleasant, but it is part of his job. A man without the stomach for it ought to retire.

"Now, in conclusion, gentlemen, I think we ought to determine, here, how we can get efficiency of government and compactness of organization. Efficiency is the most important of the two, though, involving, as it does, perfect coördination, economy of administration, and all the other requisites of systematic government. I can't advise you on this. All I can do is to listen, for I have never held a city office. I am here to learn as much as any of you."

Printed in the New York *Evening Post*, Jan. 3, 1912; some editorial headings omitted.

1 The mayors present included those of Atlantic City, East Orange, Hackensack, Harrison, Hoboken, Jersey City, New Brunswick, Paterson, Summit, Trenton, West Hoboken, and West New York. There were some fifty additional representatives from these and other cities and towns, while William Harvey Allen and Henry Bruère, both directors of the Bureau of Municipal Research of New York, attended.

2 Claus Henry Carl Jagels.

3 Mary Stuart Whitney Stevens, widow of Robert Livingston Stevens.

An Address on the Tariff to the National Democratic Club of New York

[Jan. 3, 1912]

Mr. President[1] and Members of the National Democratic Club:

It is with real pleasure that I find myself here again and realize as I look about me that these are familiar surroundings, for it has always been with unfailing cordiality that you have welcomed me, and I have always had the feeling that this was a place where it was worth while to say something, if one had anything to say.

I want to begin by congratulating the club upon the program of action which it has formed under the leadership of its intelligent officers. It is very delightful that a club should see at the outset of a campaign just the most effectual way of conducting that campaign. A campaign can be conducted only by the intelligent and earnest cooperation of men. There is a singular difference, into the psychology of which I will not try to enter, between a campaign for tariff reform initiated by a professedly reform society and a campaign for tariff reform initiated by a professedly political association, for a political organization is known to exist in order to transact business. It does not exist merely for the purpose of discussing abstract ideas. You realize that when a club like this argues about tariff reform, that's the basis of a constructive program, not merely the basis of exposition. You are not merely going to send lecturers around the country, but are going to debate the affairs of the nation with the idea of getting a sufficient number of fellow citizens to stand with you; for, in spite of what some gentlemen have stated to the contrary, I am absolutely in favor of organization, but it depends upon what the organization is for. It depends upon how the organization is controlled. If the organization is privately owned, then I am not for it, because I don't propose being owned myself; but if the organization is intended for the cooperation of men of like minds, in order to accomplish a common purpose and to advance the fortunes of a party which means to serve the nation, then I am for it. You judge an organization by the way in which it is controlled and the objects to which it devotes itself. If it devotes itself to public objects, then every man must believe in it; if it does not, then honest men must withdraw from it—and so I congratulate you upon having the true spirit of organization —an organization which is not meant merely to associate your-

[1] Thomas Frederick Donnelly, justice of the City Court of New York and president of the National Democratic Club.

selves together, but to associate yourselves together for a common purpose, a national purpose, a purpose which has for its object legislation to affect the conditions of the whole country. There is something that stirs the red blood in a man when a program of that sort is adopted.

I deem it an honor, therefore, to be associated with such men at the beginning of this campaign; and to have been asked to speak first,[2] is a particular honor, as if I could in some degree voice the purposes you have formed. If I do so, it will be simply because I have had a lifelong conviction that a very great degree of wrong has been done this country by the way in which the policy of protection has been applied to its affairs. I am not going into a general discussion of the theory of protection, because, according to a very classical phrase, it is not a theory but a condition which confronts us, a condition of the country, a condition of affairs, an organization of our economic system to our business system which has risen out of a special policy, a special set of circumstances. One of the peculiarities of the tariff question is that it never seems to be settled; it is constantly recurrent, and there must be something very subtle to anybody who has studied history, in coming upon our old familiar friend in this question which has come up in every generation to vex and perplex the American nation again and again and again. You know it is one of the complaints of our business men that it is never settled; that Congress will not let it alone; will never let business live on any fixed schedule of duties. Now, that is generally said to be true because there is an uneasy set of persons called politicians who must have some means by which to stir up trouble and create unfavorable opinion. The first thing I want to call to your attention—a thing that has caused a great deal of discussion up to the present time—is this: it is not the politicians who have started this business. If you want to take business out of politics, business ought voluntarily to get out of politics. The reason business is in politics now is that it has thrust itself in by going upon every occasion to Washington and insisting upon getting all that it can get from Congress. Politicians have not put the question of the tariff into politics. Business men have put the question of the tariff into politics, and there have been circumstances and situations in our politics of which they were all aware even when they could not be proven. At least one great political party has long been controlled by business interests. Why has the Republican party habitually been associated with the policy of high tar-

2 The other speakers were Francis Burton Harrison and William C. Redfield, both congressmen from New York.

iffs? Because the Republican party consisted of a number of gentlemen of a practical turn of mind, who could prove to you the economic necessity of the tariff? Not at all, but because the bills of the Republican party were paid by business men who wanted a high tariff. Now, suppose we put the shoe on the other foot, and invite the gentlemen who want business let alone to let politics alone. I for my part agree to withdraw from troubling business if business will withdraw from troubling politics. I want to know who first steps in and troubles the waters of the pool? We don't go in first, we are chased out of the pool; we are not allowed to get in first. And so I want to shift the burden of responsibility at the very beginning. Is it the politicians who rush to the hearings of the Ways and Means Committee when this question is going to be touched? Not at all. It is the gentlemen who want the tariff schedules arranged according to their interests who later state "it is just like you politicians, you never let business alone." I am not jesting; this is the true state of affairs, and I suggest a little reciprocity in "letting alone." I suggest that somebody else take the medicine they try to administer to us. Are they ready to make the bargain? They are not ready to make the bargain yet. They say, "We don't want the trouble of having to fix this up every time with the Ways and Means Committee. It worries us. We cannot calculate on to-morrow, because we do not know who are going to be members of the Ways and Means Committee. We do not know when it will happen that some men may get on that committee who know we are hampering them, and when that happens, the game is going to get awkward."

Now, having shifted the responsibility, we are going to discuss the tariff question. We are to discuss it with the purpose of taking the tariff question out of politics. The only way to settle it is for the good of the country and not for the good of anybody in particular. Link it with special interests; let special interests have the chief interest in it, and you cannot settle it and take it out of politics. But once apply the rule of general interest and you have taken it out of politics. The minute you make it a tariff for revenue you have taken it out of politics. Then you have got something to stand on. I am not saying that you must do this thing offhand, without considering all the vested interests that have been built up. That's a different proposition. How you are going to do it is a different question. I am now discussing the idea you must hold in view when undertaking it. Well, then, let us realize that there is another reason we are taking up the tariff question again. The tariff question is not now what it was a generation ago. It is not the same question. We are not agitating the old question. We are taking up a question, old in one sense, but which must be dealt with under circumstances so radically different that it is now a different question. There was a great deal to be said for the policy of protection. I was going to say a generation ago—but a generation and a half or two generations ago the men in favor of it defended it with the greatest success. They said:

"It does not matter how high a tariff wall you build around the country, because here is a great continent with almost inexhaustible resources, in which initiative will build up a great many enterprises of a great many kinds and a great many enterprises of the same kind and prices will be kept down by competition.["] One of the things the people do not realize is that we have exhibited one of the biggest experiments in business that has ever been set up. There was once free trade within the whole area of this great country, free trade between innumerable competitors, and it was reasonable to expect then, as the earlier advocates of of protection did expect, as great men later constantly believed it was reasonable to expect, that prices would be kept down by internal competition. But I don't have to argue with you. Prices are not kept down by internal competition. I don't have to point out to you gentlemen, noticing that the tariff wall was kept high and there was a snug covering behind it, that the beneficiaries consulted with one another and said: "Now, is it really necessary that we should cut one another's throats? These gentlemen in Washington will build this wall as high as we want it built. Let's get together. If the law is too watchful, let us have an understanding. We are men of honor. We will keep our word of honor. We can form an arrangement by which we can determine, to a very considerable extent, at any rate, the price of the raw material. We can, if we will, control the sources of the raw materials, by means *ad libitum*. We can buy mines we do not intend to use for a generation and keep them in our side pockets, and so we can cut out any automatic regulation of this kind, instead of having a price schedule that is not our own and in open competition with the market."

Don't you realize, in short, that the great combinations of modern business have made the old theory of protection absolutely antiquated? It is a preposterous theory. It is very beautiful as theory, but it doesn't work. If it worked, I would have some respect for it, but it is moribund. It has forgot how to work. It is stiff in the joints. And so I say we are not arguing with those who were not revered when alive, but, having died, are very much revered. You know Dean Swift's cynical translation of the

old latin, "When scoundrels die let all bemoan them." There is
a great pity that encaseth the dead, but even the dead, if they
were to come back to life, would not say that the theory of protection is what it was once. It has lost all signs of vitality and
youth.

Then there is another circumstance. This country was once
in a process of development which has peculiarly come to an end.
When Mr. Redfield came in this evening, the first thing I said
to him was that I would not be here if I hadn't looked at his
speeches. I primed myself on Mr. Redfield's speeches. If he recognizes these points, he must forgive me.

I really thought of some of them myself. I leave it to him to
pick out which is his. But one of the things which has impressed
me jibes in with what I have often thought about the sharp turning point that occurred in the year 1898, after the Spanish War.
This marks the end of an epoch for America. It marks the end
of a domestic epoch. After the Spanish War was over we joined
the company of nations for the first time—at least for the first
time since the very beginning when we were very, very young—
a child of the nations, having recently been the colony of a great
trading nation. Without wealth we had many other things—a
merchant marine, which we have carefully destroyed. Our flag,
though a new flag, was on many seas. Our carrying trade was
that of a nation young in its nationality, from whose coasts came
men who could invade the seas, who could build any kind of
craft, who knew the trading laws and trading ports of the round
globe. But we invited this generation to forget all this and said:
"We are going to shut ourselves in until we have formed this
garden of our own." We have developed that, and an interesting
thing has happened, and if I am right in my facts the dealers
in grain tell me that we are reaching the point when we won't
export grain, when we will need practically all the grain for our
own consumption, and some men may live to see that day unless
we do something for our farms. Now, the consequence is we will
have no surplus grain to supply the world with at the time we
reach the stage where we have a great deal of surplus manufac-
tured product, and the whole thing has turned up by reason of
this extraordinary condition.

Do you realize the extent of the audacity of the men who created the protective system? They said, "We are going to see to
it that nothing is done for the farmers,"—who at that time were
producing the wealth of the nation "and that everything is done
for the men who have not yet produced any wealth at all," and
by this process of favoritism and subsidizing of one kind or an-

other, direct or indirect, we have altered the natural plans of life in this country.

How does it happen that when immigrants come to this country from agricultural regions they do not go to the farms, but are caught in the meshes of our cities? For the same reason that the boys of the plow of our country have been turned away from the farms and into the factories. All the life blood of the country is being drained from the farms into the factories. A great many of the morbid conditions of our society are due to this same excessive fostering of one side of national life at the expense of the other. The alterations and economic balance of our life, the artificial stimulation, have destroyed that poise and balance which have been created by this protective policy. And now see what a point we have reached. We have stimulated it so much that we have not a large enough market or the means of disposing of the surplus product. This nation calls itself a trading nation, and has the knowledge of other manufacturing nations as to foreign markets, but whenever you have to ship any goods you have to ship them under some other flag than the flag of the United States. How did it happen that we destroyed our own merchant marine and were associated with the policy by which we taxed the stuff out of which ships were built? We could not build them, and so, as if by deliberation, we deprived ourselves of the carrying trade of the world, which, if we had kept on our original plan, we might have had almost to the exclusion of other nations.

It is a very rare treat, and possibly more delightful because it is so rare, in foreign waters, to see the stars and stripes on a great ship. I never realized what the stars and stripes meant to me emotionally until one day in Plymouth Harbor I saw a ship sweep past me with the stars and stripes at her gaff. It was an exceptionally rare sight, and I have never seen it since. I will remember that flag to my dying day. It was a rare specimen, an isolated testimonial to the spirit of a great national policy. And now we are getting very much interested in foreign markets, but the foreign markets are not particularly interested in us. We have not been very polite, we have not encouraged the intercourse with foreign markets that we might have encouraged, and have obstructed the influence of foreign competition. So these circumstances make the tariff question a new question, our internal arrangements and new combinations of business on one side and on the other our external necessities and the need to give scope to our energy which is now pent up and confined within our own borders. And yet the standpat Republican leaders remain unenlightened, uninformed, absolutely blind and stubborn! They don't know anything has happened. I wish I remembered some non-sense rhymes I once knew, the only nonsense I ever talked. I would apply them to these gentlemen who talk in the same phrases that were used thirty, forty, and fifty years ago; who quote the eminent statesmen of those days, supposing they are talking about the same things then talked about, whereas they cannot find those things anywhere within their range. Now, one of the things they say is that they are the guardians of prosperity, and that nothing but the protective system can bring us prosperity, and when you press them to define prosperity they will define it in terms of the bulk of business. One of their most delightful expositions of patriotic purpose is we must have new industries; if we have not got them we must acquire them at any cost. Professor Taussig calls attention to the fact that in the debate in the Senate on the Aldrich Bill, Mr. Aldrich said, in defense of a duty of 50 per cent. on some article, that he was just as willing to pay 300, 400, or 500 per cent., provided he could thereby bring that industry to this country.[3] Mr. Aldrich's idea of prosperity is to get as many industries as possible established in this country at any price. Who pays the price, I would like to know? The consumer, of course; but, rather, the price is distributed in the readjustments of the whole economic system. It is impossible to find who pays it. If you could, you might make him mad. But the trouble is you cannot convince anybody in particular that they are paying it. But we, let us say in general terms, we are paying 50, 100, 200, or 300 per cent. in order that some gentlemen may set up and make a profit in some business that ought not to be set up in America, because America does not offer the ideal conditions. And that is prosperity! I understand prosperity to be the abundant, intelligent, economic development of resources possessed by the country itself. That is prosperity. It is using the plow, engines, mills, and water powers of this country just as you would use your own intellectual and physical resources. My prosperity consists in the best possible development of my powers. It does not consist in my loading my back with borrowed plumage that I have to pay something for and wear with an unaccustomed awkwardness. That is not prosperity. And by the same token they say you are making business, therefore you are making employment, and we must assume, we must still assume, that the American workingman is so ignorant, so unintelligent, as to suppose they are doing it for his sake. I'd

[3] Frank W. Taussig, Henry Lee Professor of Economics at Harvard, in *The Tariff History of the United States*, 5th edn. (New York and London, 1910), pp. 364-65, n. 1, and "The Tariff and the Tariff Commission," *Atlantic Monthly*, cvi (Dec. 1910), 722, n. 1.

like to know how he ever got into the game? I'd like to know
how many gentlemen voluntarily share the profits of production with their workingmen? I know how the workingmen got
their share—they got it by saying that they would not work until
they did. That's the way they ever got it. They tell you, gentlemen,
that you cut up the pie very well, but we are not going to supply
the pie any more unless we have a piece of it. And I don't blame
them. It's a grab game, anyhow. That's exactly what their manufacturers were doing—going down to Washington and saying,
"If you don't give us these things, who is going to pay the campaign expenses this year?" They were on strike, they were combined on strike. Now, it was only treating them with their own
medicine when their workingmen said, "We, too, can play at that
game. We are on strike. How much are we going to get?" And
the only reason they did not get it is they did not have the resources to stay out. That's the reason the heart of America really
sympathizes with the combinations of labor; that's the only way
they are going to prosper in what is a selfish game.

Now, what is really the source of wages? Here I want to say
explicitly that I sit at the feet of men like Mr. Redfield, who pay
wages, who have handled the matter, and who know what they
are talking about. Though the political economists say the same
things, they don't say them in the terms of specific instance the
way these gentlemen say them. Wages come from the intelligence and energy of the workingmen, made effective by the
presence of natural resources and their management by efficient managers. That's where wages come from. For example,
we talk about American laborers competing with the pauper
labor of Europe. I heard that only last night, and I thought I was
in a dream; it sounded medieval. Haven't you known a machine
that cost $500 to compete successfully with a machine that cost
$50? That did the same work? Haven't you known instances
where it was profitable, economically profitable, to pay $500
rather than $50 for a machine, because the machine did so much
more and better work, that the $500 machine was cheaper than
the $50 machine? Isn't that true? Do we protect expensive
American machinery against European pauper machinery? What
do Englishmen, Frenchmen, and Germans—not Germans now,
because they have put their unmatched studiousness on to this
job—but what do Englishmen and some continental countries do?
They send for Americans as experts to tell them how they can
make more out of their industrial plants, and what they are told
in almost every instance is that they will have to get American
machinery, and that means that they have to put their pauper

machinery on the junk heap. Isn't the analogy perfect? I don't see any fault in it. If they imported American machines and American laborers they would also have to import the superintendents who know how to organize labor. The high cost of production is, almost in every instance, due not to high wages, but to the loss and waste in respect of bad management, poor machinery, or locating your whole plant in such a way that it is not in proximity to railroads and the other things necessary to the markets of the country. If you put your factory in, in the right way, organize it right, put right machinery in, and then get the highest priced labor, you will find that you will make your profits; because in proportion as you improve the economic efficiency of your business, your profits will be greater. You need more intelligent laborers, and you cannot get them except at a higher price. To my mind that's rudimentary, but there are gentlemen who have never heard of it. There are manufacturers upon whom that idea has never dawned, and they may not believe it. I give their intelligence the benefit of the doubt. They will tell you that the American manufacturer has to be protected because he has to pay his laborers so much, and they will tell the laborer that protection is going to increase his wages, and now the laborer is finding out that they do not increase his wages, and that there is something the matter with the working of the machinery.

That leads me to the most beautiful theory of all—the theory of the cost of production. It took the Republican party a long time to be absolutely frank in disclosing their ignorance of political economy. They were not perfectly frank until the last campaign, and then they said they wanted to proportion protection —proportion the rate of duty—to the difference in the cost of production between American factories and the factories with which they had come into competition abroad. I wonder if those gentlemen wrote that plank with a straight face? I don't see how it was possible unless they employed someone who didn't know anything about it. The difference between whom? You say between the foreign manufacturer and the domestic manufacturer. Which foreign manufacturer and which domestic manufacturer? Where is your standard in the difference in cost of production? Suppose you wanted to find differences that, as the Tariff Commission suggests, are average differences? An average is a variable thing. It might accidentally hit somebody, but I doubt whether it would hit many of us. If reduced it might not hit persons over forty years of age, and if you are going to protect men under forty, what would the poor devils do over forty?

They are in more need of protection than the others. The men under forty years of age can take care of themselves, and if you are really going to do the fatherly and generous thing you purpose in the theory of protection, you will take care of the least efficient. They are the ones who need looking after. If you reduce it to an average then you leave out the most helpless of the lot—the men who don't know how to organize their business, who don't know how to use their expensive laborers, who don't know how to use or assemble their expensive machinery or utilize the markets in an intelligent fashion. They are the men toward whom I feel a considerable degree of generosity, and if I was a protectionist I would go the limit and protect the least efficient; and frankly I do not see where you are going to succeed on any other basis. If you protect the least efficient you are going to protect absolutely everybody, and you have reached the ultimate goal of that kind of government—a government that is taking care of everybody and everybody is assured a reasonable profit. Isn't that a very *reductio ad absurdum?* Otherwise, let us see. We are going to protect the most efficient who know how to do business and who use their resources when needed, to regulate it. You will protect only the trusts, that is to say, if their own account of the matter is to be accepted, because the trusts are defended by great combinations to bring about the high degree of efficiency caused by protection. I don't believe it. I believe there is a point in combination beyond which the economy is lost and there is a very great loss and waste. It is like the law of diminishing returns in agriculture. Up to a certain point an addition of fertilizers, an addition of workingmen, and additional work on the farm will bring increasing returns, but you reach a limit where you have got too much fertilizer on it and too many men. Then your returns begin to diminish, and there is the same law in industrial combinations. Then let us see: We are going to take those industrial combinations which have reached that highest point of efficiency and protect only them. They are the only fellows who can afford to sell anywhere in the world. Why be benevolent to the self-supporting? It is like reserving your charity and conferring it only on millionaires. These are the gentlemen who know how to run the world, and do run a considerable part of it—and they are going to be protected! Turn any way you please, gentlemen, it is a will o' the wisp.

Nobody deserves more sympathy than the honest gentlemen who construe the tariff question, because they are put upon this impossible quest to find the cost of production. There is not the same cost of production between any two factories unless they absolutely match each other. Then, there is not the same cost of production in the several parts of the same combination. Now you notice how the combinations meet that matter of the cost of production. Let us see: Where there are twenty mills or factories and a combination is effected they put those various properties into the combination at, let us say, a reasonable figure; that is not generally so, but we will admit it. They then put them in at the real figure of their value. I won't go on to the next step because that is painful. They then double the whole business with a lot of manipulation, which is a delicate matter, but suppose they went no further than that and put them in at what they are really worth? Then they shut up five or six of them, because, compared with the rest, they are operated at a loss and put out stocks and bonds on the face of those shut up, as well as on the basis of the other fourteen, and we go on paying interest on what it cost to shut those six up. They have eliminated those five or six, but so far as the consumer is concerned, they go on as ghostly mills that work while you sleep and you keep paying the price.

Now, the nation could just as well afford to do that as what it is doing now. I would rather have the credit of American efficiency, shut up the inefficient factories, and continue to pay out of the public treasury a reasonable profit. I say I'd rather do that than go on letting the inefficient work and go on assuring them a reasonable profit. The newly discovered ground is quicksand, and I advise the Republican party to move off before it disappears. They will certainly be engulfed if they stand on that theory long enough. This cost of production has no stability anywhere in it. It is a constant flux and, as Mr. Redfield has somewhere said, a disgrace to any concern if it is not a constantly changed quantity. The cost of production ought to be constantly reduced in a business that is making profit. It ought not to stand in the same place for two of twelve months.

Now, what is the conclusion of the whole matter? There are three conclusions. In the first place, we have been doing this thing at a tremendous economic disturbance, artificially changing our whole plans of society, and I fear we will go on doing it at an enormous waste. Has this country really husbanded and used its resources properly? Hasn't it used them in a way disgracefully wasteful? Haven't we stopped working a mine the minute it began to be difficult to work? Haven't we stopped using them the minute our native virgin properties seemed difficult to manipulate? Haven't we left scrap heaps everywhere? Haven't we left off taking care of our forests, the splendid trees, ripping and tearing everywhere we have gone? Hasn't our progress been marked by scenes of devastation? Nothing looked to, nothing saved, nothing utilized to the utmost, though we did not have to utilize it to the utmost. The government has made everybody pay this bill of wastefulness, and we have even gone to the extent of paying bills of the next generations. Don't you know the combinations bought up mines they do not intend to use while we are still alive, and we are paying the interest on what it cost them to buy those mines which the next generation is going to use? Isn't there an enormous economic waste when every generation must not alone pay its own bills, but the next generation's bills? The whole thing is an extravagant mirage of philanthropy, and this economic waste has bred in us something that is contrary to our trade genius: a sort of indulgence of loosness, a method of imperfection.

In the second place, we have got ourselves in the habit of legislating for the few instead of for the many on an interesting theory that I am very fond of explaining:

The theory of the Republican party has been, if a few prosper, all will be given a share of their prosperity; if you make the great captains of industry rich, they will make the country rich. It isn't so, but we have been foolish enough to believe it sometimes. We have been foolish enough to settle national elections on the belief that it was so. We believed that factories would be shut up and some thousands of poor devils sent out of employment and that symptoms of distress would be established, when there was no genuine necessity for distress at all. Oh, the greed of these men, the indulgence, the eternal indulgence of selfishness! They will say you have paid the bills for us and for our fathers, and you have got to pay them again or we will know the reason why. I don't feel any bitterness about this, gentlemen; all that is buried; but it is the fact that we should have been so put upon, that we should have been so innocent as to believe the incredible— which we could demonstrate as untrue, if we only took the pains and looked into the facts—what the consumers knew to be untrue at the very time they were patiently casting Republican ballots and made believe they thought it wise; this putting the advantages of legislation in the hands of the few at the constant sacrifice of the many; and the dream of America has been reversed, to a government for the privileged few and not for the many.

There is a quotation which we have been applauding nearly every Fourth of July, as I remember, but which we have not believed since I can remember. We have applied that quotation from the Virginia Bill of Rights and from one of Washington's addresses, in which he lays it down as a fundamental conception of American affairs that when the people deem their government is not serving their interests they have a right to resume it into their own hands. Haven't you heard that before and haven't you applied it? Well, do you believe it? America has not acted upon that in my lifetime. That belief is merely intended to be engraved in golden letters upon some tablet of our memories and enshrined as a fragrant recollection.

Now, there is another thing that this has done—and I am ashamed to see how long I have spoken—it has reversed all our natural conceptions of government. The worst feature of protection is the demoralization of our political ideas. We have based government upon patronage and privilege instead of upon justice and equality. That's the cancer that eats at the hearts of all.

Now, what are we going to do? Are we going to turn revolutionists? Are we going to act as free traders? I wish I might hope that our grandchildren could indulge in free trade, but I am afraid even they cannot, because they have to pay the bills of the Federal Government. We have a Federal system of government, and it is wise, it is good housekeeping, it is good management to leave direct taxes, for the most part, to the State governments, because they have current bills to pay. It is likely that for an indefinite period we shall have to pay our national bills by duties collected at the ports. Though I am not for drastic changes, yet I wish I saw some ultimate escape from it. At present I do not. Therefore, what we have to ask ourselves is not the principle upon which we are to act, for that is plain. We are to act upon the fundamental principle of the Democratic party, not free trade, but tariff for revenue, and we have got to approach that by such avenues, by such stages, and at such a pace as will be consistent with the stability and safety of the business of the country. Fortunately, there are some things that are plain. The very wide-awake gentlemen who constitute the Democratic majority in the lower house of Congress saw the opening in the line and carried the ball through. They saw the schedules upon which it was safe to act, and unanimously agreed that it was safe and wise to act now, which they did; and now they may have to act again to the same effect, because all excuses, so far as I can see, for any co-operation are swept away. Many excuses were offered. The cover of the Tariff bill was an excellent cover while it lasted, but the Tariff Board has uncovered the defense, and now there are certain schedules upon which our minds are fixed, with a sufficient illumination of the facts and conditions to enable us to act upon them. We can act upon them, and, feeling our way prudently here and there, not like doctrinaires, but like practical and prudent men, we can by prudent stages bring this tariff down to our children on a proper tariff basis. That's a plain program. It is a practical man's program. It is not a theoretical program; it is not a program based upon a desire to get even with anyone; it is not a program based upon patience that special privilege has exhausted; it is merely an open-minded, prudent, statesmanlike course of action.

I congratulate you, gentlemen, upon undertaking this campaign of education, not of agitation; of demonstration, not of abuse; a campaign where the facts will be more eloquent than figures of speech, and where back of the whole thing will lie that natural impulse of public service upon which alone a permanent national policy can be founded.[4]

Printed in the *Cong. Record*, 62d Cong., 2nd sess., Vol. 48, pp. 4748-52; with minor corrections from the texts in *The Tariff Address by Governor Woodrow Wilson . . . January 3, 1912* (New York, 1912), and the *New York Times*, Jan. 4, 1912.

[4] There is a WWhw and WWsh outline of this address, dated Dec. 21, 1911, in WP, DLC.

To Samuel Huston Thompson, Jr.

My dear Thompson: [Trenton, N. J.] January 4, 1912.

I shall be most happy to put my name in the history[1] and am complimented that you should wish it.

I know only too well how many splits and cross-splits there are in the forces in Colorado and am holding my breath as to the consequences, but feel, at this distance, quite unable to thread the labyrinth by my own judgment. I am very happy, as I need not tell you, to have you so patiently stand ready to do whatever it is possible for you to do.

You speak[2] of the financial strain. Fortunately, it has not been very great. The amount of money expended up to this time is comparatively small and I believe that it will be possible for us to get such funds as are necessary without going very far afield. So many Princeton men in particular stand ready to help, who are apparently able to. I, nonetheless, appreciate your suggestion that assistance might be had in your part of the country, and want to thank you very much for the generous suggestion which it may be necessary to recur to later.

With warmest regards,

Cordially yours,   Woodrow Wilson

TLS (S. H. Thompson, Jr., Papers, DLC).

[1] That is, he would be glad to autograph Thompson's copy of *A History of the American People*.

[2] Thompson's letter is missing.

To Daniel Moreau Barringer

My dear Moreau: [Trenton, N. J.] January 4, 1912.

Your letters about the control into which our economic system is falling interested me very deeply and you may be sure that I agree with every word of them. This is only a line to thank you very warmly for your letter of December thirty-first[1] and to wish you all the best things of the New Year.

Cordially and faithfully yours,   Woodrow Wilson

TLS (D. M. Barringer Papers, NjP).
  [1] It is missing.

To Alexander Jeffrey McKelway

My dear Mr. McKelway: [Trenton, N. J.] January 4, 1912.

I need not tell you how deep my interest is in the work of the National Child Labor Committee, because we have so often talked about it, but unhappily I am bound by engagements from the 25th to 27th of January, as indeed throughout the month, I am sorry to say, and can only reply to your interesting letter[1] that it is a great disappointment to me that I cannot be of assistance this time.   Cordially yours,   Woodrow Wilson

TLS (A. J. McKelway Papers, DLC).
  [1] It is missing.

To Edward Mandell House

My dear Mr. House: [Trenton, N. J.] January 4, 1912.

I am very much distressed to learn through Mr. [Miss] Denton that you have been real ill, and I hope with all my heart that before this reaches you, you will be out of your room and free from discomfort. You were looking so particularly well and fit when you left New York that I must believe that this is the part of the country to which you belong. It would be immensely comfortable to have you at hand for frequent conference. Pray, take care of yourself and be sure to get strong again.

I very much appreciate the quotation from Mr. Bryan's letter, contained in Mr. Denton's favor of December thirtieth.

Allow me to extend to you the warmest greetings of the season.

Cordially and sincerely yours,   Woodrow Wilson

TLS (E. M. House Papers, CtY).

From George Brinton McClellan Harvey

Personal.

My dear Gov. Wilson: New York. January 4. 1912.

Replying to your note from the University Club, I think it should go without saying that no purely personal issue could arise between you and me. Whatever anybody else may surmise, you surely must know that, in trying to arouse and further your political aspirations during the past few years, I have been actuated solely by the belief that I was rendering a distinct public service.

The real point at the time of our interview was, as you aptly put it, one simply "of fact and of business," and when you stated the fact to be that my support was hurting your candidacy, and that you were experiencing difficulty in finding a way to counteract its harmful effect, the only thing possible for me to do, in simple fairness to you no less than in consideration of my own self-respect, was to relieve you of your embarrassment, so far as it lay within my power to do so, by ceasing to advocate your nomination.

That, I think, was fully understood between us at the time and, acting accordingly, I took down your name from the head of the *Weekly*'s editorial page some days before your letter was written.[1] That seems to be all there is of it.

Whatever little hurt I may have felt as a consequence of the unexpected peremptoriness of your attitude toward me is, of course, wholly eliminated by your gracious words.

Very truly yours,   George Harvey

Printed in the New York *Evening Post*, Jan. 30, 1912.

[1] Harvey had printed "FOR PRESIDENT WOODROW WILSON" beneath the masthead of *Harper's Weekly* in the issue of November 11, 1911. The last issue in which the slogan appeared was that of December 9, 1911.

From Charles Spalding Thomas

Personal

My dear Governor: Denver, Colorado January 4th, 1912.

Some of our mountain friends who reside in the mining regions of the State, and who have a vivid recollection of the campaign of 1896, have taken it upon themselves to attack Governor Harmon because of his bitter hostility to bimetalism, and his constant support while Attorney General of the United States of the old Palmer and Buckner Gold Democratic ticket. The silver question is still a sore point with people out here, and particularly with mine-owners and miners where directly affected by the ultimate demonetization of the white metal. Hence it is not surprising that this echo of the past has been sounded.

By way of retaliation some of Harmon's partisans have asserted that you were active in writing articles upon the money question during the same period, and that you also supported Palmer and Buckner. As a result, I have been appealed to upon the subject, which is my excuse and apology, if any be necessary, for calling the matter to your attention. If the statement concerning yourself be well founded, of course we should not hesitate to say so, and let Governor Harmon's friends offset the fact as fully as they desire against the corresponding charge of the anti-Harmon people. If, on the other hand, the statement is not well founded, there is no reason why that fact should not be known here as well. Of course I know personally that nearly all prominent members of the party in the Eastern States in 1896 were in sympathy with President Cleveland's views upon the money question. I do not recall, however, having seen any articles from your pen upon the subject during that period when I sought to keep myself fully informed as to every phase of the discussion in so far as the current magazines were concerned.

I need not add that any reply to this letter will be regarded as absolutely confidential, and I will use the information conveyed as discreetly as possible. I have already suggested that no further agitation of the subject be indulged in for the present, and I indulge the hope that such will be the case.

Very sincerely yours,   C S Thomas

TLS (Governors' Files, Nj).

To Richard Heath Dabney

My dear Heath: [Trenton, N. J.] January 5, 1912.

In the midst of my daily rush I can only turn to thank you for your letters and for their enclosures.[1] Your kindness is certainly unlimited.

I have just received an answer to a letter[2] from Archie Patterson[3] about speaking in Richmond. I have no place into which I could put such an engagement this side of the middle of February, but I have written to express my willingess to come then if it can be arranged.

The information contained in your letters stands me in good stead and I am deeply grateful.

In haste,

Always faithfully yours,   Woodrow Wilson

TLS (Wilson-Dabney Corr., ViU).

¹ They are missing.

² It is missing.

³ Archibald Williams Patterson, Richmond lawyer and fellow student at the University of Virginia.

From Mary Allen Hulbert Peck

Paget West, Bermuda. Jan 5th 1912.

It is a wild night. The wind which has been blowing hard all day has risen to a gale, and now, at full tide, tears the crests from the waves that roll in and dash themselves on the rocks below the drawing room windows, and carries them hissing away across the lawn to the little boat house. The moon shows fitfully and when this whole little inlet is flooded with light it's a wondrously beautiful, wild scene. I love it! If you were only here to see it, how it would rejoice your soul, much better than the stormy sea of politics. Not the reward however, of duty well done, just a little dimming of the waters bright blue in the morning from depths disturbed, some sea weed on the shore, and a walk or two. Like my life, isn't it? Only there was nothing ever beautifully dramatic in that. By day this seems a large and beautiful country, but at night, in a storm one sees it with the mind's eye, as on the map, such a tiny dot.

Your letter came today with its good wishes. Because *you* say so, I feel I *may* again be "brought back to youth and poise and elasticity," to the last two, perhaps, to the first, alas, never, and I would not care to be. To be again anything that I once was of eager joyous life savors of miracles, for I'm fighting *desperately* this numbing grey cloud that seems closing round me. It is not that I dread the coming final step so much, for I have nerved myself to that, but I am tired and I thought I would be rested by this. I fancy it is because I have been robbed, or defrauded myself, of the natural rounding out of a woman's life, and am conscious that woman is not meant to be, and I am not capable of being both Father & Mother. Isn't that funny? Worse than a "bloomin' heerumphridite." I love it when I get all tangled up in trying to express my feelings, even if I laugh alone. The winds are certainly "howling at all hours," and it does not seem from the roar and hiss and boom and shriek now that they could ever be uplifted like sleeping flowers, unless they were passion flowers. The house shudders in the blast and the matting is ballooning so it makes one giddy to walk on it. . . .

I was reading a foolish short story in Munsey's last week,[1] in which there was a paragraph that convinced me, if I had not been before, that you were really known to fame. The young married lady who played opposite the heroine is asked who her political favorites are. She replies, T. Roosevelt and Woodrow Wilson. Upon being asked *why*, says, "Roosevelt is so lovely about children, and there is something about W.W.'s forehead that reminds me of Frank!" Apropos of T.R. is it to be Roosevelt and Beveridge? with B. as Vice Pres. or are they mentioning him for the first place? I once met him, and was deeply impressed by his conceit and insincerity. Even at a small dinner he was posing and playing to the gallery.

Mother's condition saddens me although she seems better the last day or two, but I must stand by now every hour until the end. Old age is *tragic*, and I can't *bear* to see her getting ready, as she is in so many little ways, for the long journey. When she goes and Allen marries, I shall be alone indeed, and, how busy I am crossing my distant bridges.

It's an imposition to write as I do, to a dear friend, whose heart needs rest, but here are nearly eight sodden pages. Bless you! I don't know what I would do without you for a handkerchief to weep in. You will have to be as stiff with starch as the handkerchiefs our laundress sends home. *They* stand alone, too. There is nothing to write. I am still reported engaged to the Govr.[2] and now that I can be *Lady* K. my ambitions are gratified so the world says.

I had a little service all to myself on your birthday. May you have many *many* happy ones. I even enjoyed reading your biography,[3] and knowing more of what you were doing before I knew you. We have kept step curiously, and Mr. Hulbert was in Rome [Ga.] when you were there with your dear sweetheart. I wrote Mrs. Wilson last week asking her to come down here, thinking she might need and like the change. We are very quiet but would love to have her. It is definitely decided that I go up in April. Goodnight dearest friend,   God bless you,   M.A.

ALS (WP, DLC).

   [1] Margaret Busbee Shipp, "Reciprocity," *Munsey's Magazine*, XLVI (Jan. 1912), 497-500.

   [2] Frederick Walter Kitchener.

   [3] She was reading William Bayard Hale's biography being serialized in *World's Work*.

A News Report

[Jan. 6, 1912]

HARVEY AND WILSON HAVE NO QUARREL
GOVERNOR'S DENIAL

Reports of a break in the friendly relations heretofore existing between Governor Wilson and Colonel George Harvey, editor of Harper's Weekly, were categorically denied by the Governor yesterday. After reading a dispatch published yesterday to the effect that because of this break Col. Harvey's magazine had withdrawn its support of the Governor as a Presidential candidate, Governor Wilson made the following statement:

"My attention has, of course, been drawn to the fact that the last two numbers of Harper's Weekly have made no mention of my name, but this is certainly not due to any breach of any kind between Colonel Harvey and myself."

Authoritative denial was also made yesterday of another story circulated to the effect that Governor Wilson had written Colonel Harvey a letter intimating that the latter's advocacy of his candidacy was in reality injuring rather than aiding the Governor's candidacy, and suggesting that a less active manifestation of interest upon the part of Colonel Harvey would be acceptable.

If any such intimation was conveyed to Colonel Harvey, it was said yesterday, it did not come from Governor Wilson, and was not sanctioned by him. One view of the situation taken here is that Colonel Harvey has been told that his extreme solicitation on behalf of the Governor was open to a misconstruction, and that he had thereupon decided upon his own volition to not thrust himself conspicuously in the foreground as a champion of the Governor.

Printed in the Trenton *True American*, Jan. 6, 1912; one editorial heading omitted.

ADDENDA

To Charles Franklin Thwing

My dear Sir,   Baltimore, Md., 26 February, 1895

Your letter of February 22[1] has been forwarded to me here. Its contents of course surprise me; but I have no hesitation at all in releasing you from your engagement with me.[2] It causes me no inconvenience.

I regret to learn that your plans for the course of lectures have miscarried.   Very truly Yours,   Woodrow Wilson

ALS Printed in *Letters of the Presidents of the United States of America: Reproduced from the Collection of Don Belding* (Los Angeles, 1952).
  [1] See EAW to WW, Feb. 25, 1895, n. 2, Vol. 9.
  [2] About this, see WW to EAW, Feb. 25, 1895, n. 1, *ibid.*

To Ellen Axson Wilson

My own darling,   [Chicago] Saturday [March 14, 1908].

I am sure you understand why I have not written; and yet I do not believe that anybody who is not here can imagine the rush. I am perfectly well, perfectly comfortable, and have had a jolly good time. This evening I go up to Madison; Monday afternoon I start for N. Y.

I have sent to the University for your letters, but none had come. I am uneasy, but suppose it means nothing to be alarmed at. Your sweet face fairly haunts me: I love you more and more passionately every moment of my life, it seems to me—I want to get back to you, for all the good time I'm having, more than I ever did before!   Your own   Woodrow

ALS (WC, NjP).

To Joseph R. Wilson, Jr.

My dear Brother: [Trenton, N. J.] March 31, 1911.

I am delighted to hear of your promotion on the staff of the Banner. I take it for granted that the new position is one that you really wanted or you would not have accepted it, and I have not the least misgivings as to your success in it.

As to my coming down to address the Legislature, it begins to look as if that would be impossible. I have tied myself up for the whole of April, and in May I am to undertake a trip to the far West which will occupy the whole month.

I dare say you know as much of what is going on here as what I could tell you in the limits of a letter. It is intensely engrossing work and I hardly have time to think of any one but those who are pressing about me, with regard to one matter or another in connection with public business, but I keep very well in spite of the fatigue of my days and think very, very often of the dear ones in Nashville.

All at home join me in warmest love.

Affectionately yours,   Woodrow Wilson

TLS (received from Jessie McElroy Junkin).

To Verner R. Lovell[1]

Personal.

My dear Mr. Mayor: [Trenton, N. J.] November 7, 1911.

Thank you sincerely for your letter of October thirty-first. It is certainly most gracious of you to consult me with regard to what my wishes are in respect of the action of the delegates from North Dakota, in case Governor Burke[2] is an approved and successful candidate for the nomination on the Democratic ticket.

I do not feel that at this distance I can give you advice that is worth having. I should suppose that an "aggressive campaign" made in my behalf might seem an attempt to set Governor Burke aside, and I have carefully refrained from encouraging aggressive action in states which had candidates of their own. I can only say, therefore, what goes without saying, namely, that I should be deeply complimented if I might receive the support of the delegation from North Dakota, in case they were free to turn to me.

Cordially and sincerely yours,   Woodrow Wilson

TLS (received from Roland Dille).
   [1] Lawyer, long active in Democratic politics in North Dakota, Mayor of Fargo, 1911-12.
   [2] John Burke, Governor of North Dakota, 1907-13.

INDEX

NOTE ON THE INDEX

THE alphabetically arranged analytical table of contents at the front of the volume eliminates duplication, in both contents and index, of references to certain documents, such as letters. Letters are listed in the contents alphabetically by name, and chronologically within each name by page. The subject matter of all letters is, of course, indexed. The Editorial Notes and Wilson's writings are listed in the contents chronologically by page. In addition, the subject matter of both categories is indexed. The index covers all references to books and articles mentioned in text or notes. Footnotes are indexed. Page references to footnotes which place a comma between the page number and "n" cite both text and footnote, thus: "624,n3." On the other hand, absence of the comma indicates reference to the footnote only, thus: "55n2"—the page number denoting where the footnote appears. The letter "n" without a following digit signifies an unnumbered descriptive-location note.

An asterisk before an index reference designates identification or other particular information. Re-identification and repetitive annotation have been minimized to encourage use of these starred references. Where the identification appears in an earlier volume, it is indicated thus: "1:*212,n3." Therefore a page reference standing without a preceding volume number is invariably a reference to the present volume. The index supplies the fullest known forms of names, and, for the Wilson and Axson families, relationships as far down as cousins. Persons referred to in the text by nicknames or shortened forms of names can be identified by reference to entries for these forms of the names.

INDEX

WOODROW WILSON

APPEARANCE

FAMILY LIFE AND DOMESTIC AFFAIRS

GOVERNOR OF NEW JERSEY

HEALTH

INTERVIEWS

OPINIONS AND COMMENTS

POLITICAL CAREER